Mastering ROS 2 for Robotics Programming

Fourth Edition

Design, build, simulate, and prototype complex robots using the Robot Operating System 2

Lentin Joseph

Jonathan Cacace

Mastering ROS 2 for Robotics Programming
Fourth Edition

Portfolio Director: Rohit Rajkumar
Relationship Lead: Kaustubh Manglurkar
Project Manager: Sandip Tadge
Content Engineer: Anuradha Vishwas Joglekar
Technical Editor: Tejas Vijay Mhasvekar
Copy Editor: Safis Editing
Indexer: Rekha Nair
Proofreader: Anuradha Vishwas Joglekar
Production Designer: Prashant Ghare
Marketing Owner: Nivedita Pandey
Growth Lead: Namita Velgekar

First edition: December 2015
Second edition: February 2018
Third edition: October 2021
Fourth edition: July 2025

Production reference: 1270625

Published by Packt Publishing Ltd.
Grosvenor House
11 St Paul's Square
Birmingham
B3 1RB, UK.

ISBN 978-1-83620-901-0

www.packtpub.com

I sincerely thank my wife, Aleena Johny, for her constant support and encouragement. My son, Elon, has been a true inspiration and a source of great joy. I am grateful to my parents, Jancy Joseph and C.G. Joseph, for their unwavering guidance and blessings. I also thank all my friends for their continued support throughout this journey.

– Lentin Joseph

To my family, my friends, and all the people I've met along the way. A special mention to my love, V.M.

– Jonathan Cacace

Contributors

About the authors

Lentin Joseph is an accomplished Indian roboticist, author, entrepreneur, and educator with over a decade of expertise in robotics software development, machine vision, and artificial intelligence. He is the founder and CTO of RUNTIME Robotics Pvt Ltd, an Indian company focused on R&D in robotics software development and artificial intelligence. He also runs robocademy.com, an online platform for robotics education. With strong proficiency in ROS, OpenCV, and PCL, Lentin has authored 10 widely acclaimed books on robotics, including *Learning Robotics Using Python* and *Mastering ROS for Robotics Programming*. He holds a bachelor's degree in Electronics and Communication Engineering from FISAT and a master's in Robotics and Automation from Amrita University. During his studies, he developed a gesture- and speech-interactive social robot that gained media attention. Lentin has also conducted research at Carnegie Mellon University's Robotics Institute, delivered a TEDx talk, and actively contributes to robotics education through workshops, blogs, and training programs.

I want to thank the people who have been close to me and supported me, especially my wife Aleena Johny, my son Elon, and my parents Jancy Joseph and C.G. Joseph.

Jonathan Cacace was born in Naples, Italy, on 13 December 1987. He earned a Bachelor's and Masters of Science in Computer Science from the University of Naples Federico II. He then joined the university's PhD program, earning the title of Philosophiae Doctor in Automation and Computer Engineering in 2016. During his research career, he had the opportunity to participate in and lead various applied research projects focused on robotics, funded by the European Union. This allowed him to explore several areas of robotics, ranging from robot manipulation to navigation.

After completing his PhD, he continued his scientific research and work in applied robotics, contributing to more than 50 scientific publications in leading robotics conferences and scientific journals. He also worked as a private consultant for several startups across Europe. From 2019 to 2023. He worked as an assistant professor at the University of Naples, where he taught two courses: Laboratory of Robotics and Mobile Robotics. During this time, he mentored many undergraduate students in the field of Robotics and Computer Engineering. He was also invited to speak at an international robotics workshop held at one of Europe's most prestigious research centers and universities.

Currently, Jonathan works as a senior researcher in the field of Cognitive Robotics and Human-Robot Interaction at Eurecat - Centre Tecnològic de Catalunya in Barcelona.

About the reviewers

Tobit Flatscher received his B.Sc. and M.Sc. degrees (with distinction) in mechanical and computational engineering from the Graz University of Technology, Austria. He has 6 years of experience in programming and debugging robots using ROS. Tobit began his career as a research associate at Fraunhofer Italia, contributing to applied research projects, primarily for North Italian industrial clients. Since 2023, he has worked as a robotics software engineer at the Oxford Robotics Institute (ORI), University of Oxford, where he supports the academic research within the Dynamic Robot Systems Perception (DRS-P) group with his technical expertise. Before transitioning to robotics, Tobit developed simulation codes for computational fluid mechanics using the lattice-Boltzmann method at Graz University of Technology. In his spare time, he enjoys working on his personal robotic projects and hiking, particularly in the mountains surrounding his hometown in the Italian Dolomites.

Baslin James is a project engineer at the Advanced Manufacturing Research Centre (AMRC) in Sheffield, UK. With a strong background in robotics, he previously worked as a robotics researcher at the University of Sheffield. His experience includes leading-edge projects such as MediTel, robot-assisted dressing in medical robotics and digital twins for industrial processes. He brings expertise in C++, Python, ROS, embedded systems, and MATLAB, with a focus on applied robotics in both industrial and healthcare domains.

Table of Contents

Chapter 2: Getting Started with ROS 2 Programming   31

Chapter 4: Working with Robot 3D Modeling in ROS 2   119

Chapter 5: Simulating Robots in a Realistic Environment 177

Part 2: ROS 2 Applications: Navigation, Manipulation, and Control   215

Chapter 6: Controlling Robots Using the ros2_control Package   217

Part 3: Advanced Applications and Machine Learning   367

Chapter 11: Aerial Robotics and ROS 2   369

Chapter 12: Designing and Programming a DIY Mobile Robot from Scratch   397

Chapter 13: Testing, Continuous Integration, and Continuous Deployment with ROS 2   419

Preface

ROS 2, the **Robot Operating System 2**, is a major milestone in robotics software development. More than just a tool, it is a modular, open-source ecosystem designed to support the creation of scalable, distributed, and intelligent robotic systems. Its adoption has grown rapidly across sectors—from startups developing autonomous robots, to aerospace and manufacturing companies, to leading research institutions—thanks to its strong community, robust architecture, and a rich set of tools that streamline the development of complex robotics applications. *Mastering ROS 2 for Robotics Programming* is a comprehensive guide designed for developers and roboticists who want to go beyond the basics and learn how to leverage the full capabilities of ROS 2. Whether you're building mobile robots, manipulators, drones, or hybrid systems, this book will provide you with the knowledge and practical skills needed to develop and integrate advanced robotic behaviors using ROS 2.

We will begin by introducing the ROS 2 architecture and programming model, guiding you through setting up your development environment and creating your first nodes using C++. From there, we will cover key ROS 2 concepts—topics, services, actions, parameters, and launch systems—providing real-world examples along the way. As we move forward, you'll learn how to:

- Build 3D models of robots and use them with simulators like Gazebo to test behavior in realistic environments
- Implement robot control systems with the `ros2_control` framework
- Develop behavior trees for task planning using the `BehaviorTree.CPP` library
- Use **ROS 2 Navigation Stack (Nav2)** to enable autonomous movement
- Apply robot manipulation with MoveIt 2 for grasping and motion planning
- Incorporate sensor data and vision systems into perception pipelines
- Work with aerial robots using ROS 2 interfaces and control systems

Advanced chapters will introduce you to modern practices, such as writing tests, setting up continuous integration and deployment pipelines for ROS 2 packages, and using cloud-native tools to build robust robotics software. You'll also explore how to interface ROS 2 with artificial intelligence, including:

- Task planning using large language models
- Training reinforcement learning agents with ROS 2 environments
- Creating custom visualization and simulation plugins for more interactive development

Additionally, you will learn how to connect motors with ROS 2 nodes using Raspberry Pi boards.

This book is filled with practical examples helping you improve programming ROS 2 applications. The code examples in the book are based on ROS 2's jazzy, the latest long-term-support distributions and compatible with widely used robot platforms. We hope this book becomes a valuable companion in your own robotics journey and helps you to truly master ROS 2.

Let's get started!

Who this book is for

This book is intended for robotic software developers and IT professionals who have a foundational understanding of robotics and ROS programming. Readers should be familiar with Ubuntu Linux and command-line tools, have basic experience with C++, and have the foundational knowledge of robotics concepts to fully benefit from the content.

What this book covers

Chapter 1, Introduction to ROS 2, introduces the **Robot Operating System 2 (ROS 2)**, its architecture, communication mechanisms, and its advantages over ROS 1. It sets the foundation for developing modern, distributed robotic systems.

Chapter 2, Getting Started with ROS 2 Programming, walks you through setting up a ROS 2 development environment on Ubuntu, creating and building packages, and writing basic publisher and subscriber nodes in C++.

Chapter 3, Implementing ROS 2 Concepts, dives into core ROS 2 functionalities, such as services, actions, parameters, and lifecycle nodes, demonstrating how to build modular and maintainable robotic software.

Chapter 4, Working with Robot 3D Modeling in ROS 2, explains how to create 3D robot models using URDF and Xacro, including sensor and actuator integration, and how to visualize the models using RViz.

Chapter 5, Simulating Robots in a Realistic Environment, shows how to set up robot simulations using Gazebo, Webots, and Nvidia Omniverse, integrating ROS 2 interfaces for testing robot behavior in virtual environments.

Chapter 6, Controlling Robots Using the ros2_control Package, explores how to configure and use the ros2_control framework to manage hardware interfaces and controllers for differential, wheeled, and articulated robots.

Chapter 7, Implementing ROS 2 Applications Using BehaviorTree.CPP, introduces the BehaviorTree.CPP library and explains how to create flexible and reactive decision-making logic for robotic tasks.

Chapter 8, ROS 2 Navigation Stack: Nav2, covers the setup and configuration of the **ROS 2 Navigation Stack (Nav2)**, including map building, localization, path planning, and obstacle avoidance for mobile robots.

Chapter 9, Robot Manipulation Using MoveIt 2, provides a practical guide to using MoveIt 2 for robot arm planning, motion execution, collision checking, and integration with perception systems.

Chapter 10, Working with ROS 2 and Perception Stack, introduces tools and libraries for integrating cameras and depth sensors with ROS 2, processing sensor data, and using it for object detection and scene understanding.

Chapter 11, Aerial Robotics and ROS 2, explores the integration of ROS 2 with aerial robot platforms such as drones, including flight control, localization, and sensor integration.

Chapter 12, Designing and Programming a DIY Mobile Robot from Scratch, explains how to build and interface with ROS 2 and Nav 2, a cheap Do It Yourself robot, using a Raspberry pi board and eclectic motors and micro controllers.

Chapter 13, Testing, Continuous Integration, and Continuous Deployment with ROS 2, presents best practices for testing ROS 2 packages, setting up CI pipelines, and deploying software updates reliably in robotic systems.

Chapter 14, Interfacing Large Language Models with ROS 2, explores how to integrate LLMs with ROS 2 for high-level task planning, command interpretation, and natural language interfaces.

Chapter 15, ROS 2 and Deep Reinforcement Learning, introduces deep reinforcement learning concepts and demonstrates how to train and evaluate policies for robot control using ROS 2 environments.

Chapter 16, Implementing ROS 2 Visualization and Simulation Plugins, covers how to extend RViz and simulation tools with custom plugins to support visualization and interaction with specialized robot components and data.

To get the most out of this book

Before diving into the content, it's important to clarify the foundational knowledge and tools that will help you make the most of this book. This book assumes that you have a basic understanding of C++ and are comfortable working in a Linux environment, particularly Ubuntu, as many of the examples and tools are designed and tested on this platform. You do not need to be an expert, but familiarity with command-line usage and package management.

As for hardware requirements, a **standard computer** is enough for most chapters, though in a few cases, having a **GPU-enabled system with an NVIDIA card** is suggested but not required. Finally, standard webcams and depth sensors are used in the computer vision chapter.

Download the example code files

The code bundle for the book is hosted on GitHub at `https://github.com/PacktPublishing/Mastering-ROS-2-for-Robotics-Programming`. We also have other code bundles from our rich catalog of books and videos available at `https://github.com/PacktPublishing`. Check them out!

Download the color images

We also provide a PDF file that has color images of the screenshots/diagrams used in this book. You can download it here: `https://packt.link/gbp/9781836209010`.

This book contains some wide screenshots. These have been captured to provide readers with an overview of the entire console. As a result, the text on these images may appear small at 100% zoom. Kindly refer to color images in the graphics bundle above for better comprehension.

Conventions used

There are a number of text conventions used throughout this book.

`CodeInText`: Indicates code words in text, folder names, filenames, file extensions, pathnames, dummy URLs or user command input. Here is an example: "After enabling the `universe` repository, let's add the `ROS 2 GPG` key and `apt sources list` "

A block of code is set as follows:

```
<inertia ixx="${mass / 12.0 * (width*width + height1*height1)}" ixy="0.0"
ixz="0.0"
        iyy="${mass / 12.0 * (height1*height1 + width*width)}" iyz="0.0"
```

Any command-line input or output is written as follows:

```
colcon build --symlink-install
```

Bold: Indicates a new term, an important word, or words that you see on the screen. For instance, words in menus or dialog boxes appear in the text like this. For example: "In a few seconds, the calibration will be ready, and the **COMMIT** button will be enabled."

Warnings or important notes appear like this.

Tips and tricks appear like this.

Get in touch

Feedback from our readers is always welcome.

General feedback: Email feedback@packtpub.com and mention the book's title in the subject of your message. If you have questions about any aspect of this book, please email us at questions@ packtpub.com.

Errata: Although we have taken every care to ensure the accuracy of our content, mistakes do happen. If you have found a mistake in this book, we would be grateful if you reported this to us. Please visit http://www.packtpub.com/submit-errata, click **Submit Errata**, and fill in the form.

Piracy: If you come across any illegal copies of our works in any form on the internet, we would be grateful if you would provide us with the location address or website name. Please contact us at copyright@packtpub.com with a link to the material.

If you are interested in becoming an author: If there is a topic that you have expertise in and you are interested in either writing or contributing to a book, please visit http://authors.packtpub. com/.

Join our community on Discord

Join our community's Discord space for discussions with the authors and other readers: `https://packt.link/embeddedsystems`

Share your thoughts

Once you've read *Mastering ROS 2 for Robotics Programming, Fourth Edition*, we'd love to hear your thoughts! Scan the QR code below to go straight to the Amazon review page for this book and share your feedback.

`https://packt.link/r/1836209010`

Your review is important to us and the tech community and will help us make sure we're delivering excellent quality content.

Download a free PDF copy of this book

Thanks for purchasing this book!

Do you like to read on the go but are unable to carry your print books everywhere?

Is your eBook purchase not compatible with the device of your choice?

Don't worry, now with every Packt book you get a DRM-free PDF version of that book at no cost.

Read anywhere, any place, on any device. Search, copy, and paste code from your favorite technical books directly into your application.

The perks don't stop there, you can get exclusive access to discounts, newsletters, and great free content in your inbox daily.

Follow these simple steps to get the benefits:

1. Scan the QR code or visit the link below:

https://packt.link/free-ebook/9781836209010

2. Submit your proof of purchase.
3. That's it! We'll send your free PDF and other benefits to your email directly.

Part 1

ROS 2 Programming and Simulation

This part provides a practical introduction to ROS 2, covering essential programming concepts, 3D robot modeling, and simulation in realistic environments. It lays the groundwork for developing and testing robotic applications using modern ROS 2 tools and workflows.

This part includes the following chapters:

- *Chapter 1, Introduction to ROS 2*
- *Chapter 2, Getting Started with ROS 2 Programming*
- *Chapter 3, Implementing ROS 2 Concepts*
- *Chapter 4, Working with Robot 3D Modeling in ROS 2*
- *Chapter 5, Simulating Robots in a Realistic Environment*

1

Introduction to ROS 2

You might see robots doing tasks like picking and placing objects or moving objects from one point to another. These tasks look simple to us, but they are difficult to accomplish with robots. We humans are powered by a very flexible body and an intelligent brain. However, robots still struggle with limited hardware capabilities and intelligence, which are limited by the instructions we provide in the form of software. It may take years to achieve human-like intelligence and capabilities in robots. As you may know, robots have three main sections: sensors, actuators, and a computer. The computer acts as the brain of the robot, and that is where we load different software applications to perform different tasks. The development of software for robots plays an important role in making the robot intelligent and adaptable for different use cases.

In this chapter, we are going to focus on the **Robot Operating System (ROS)**, a popular software framework for programming robots efficiently. The ROS framework is widely used in academia and industry to model, simulate, and develop different robotics applications. This is an introductory chapter that gives you a general overview of this framework. This chapter will be useful for people who already know ROS and those who are just starting with ROS as well.

In this chapter, we're going to cover the following main topics:

- ROS as a framework for robotics
- Important features of ROS
- Comparison of ROS 1 and ROS 2
- Communication stack in ROS 2
- DDS vendors in ROS 2

Understanding ROS as a robotics framework

Developing complex robotics applications from scratch can be a tedious task. Even if we develop it, if our software is not modular and not reusable by others, the same process must be repeated by others, which is like *reinventing the wheel*. This situation applies not only to robotics but also to other technology domains. That's why we come across a lot of software frameworks and libraries. These frameworks have ready-made functions or an **Application Programming Interface (API)** of commonly used algorithms that can be integrated into our program to help us quickly develop our applications.

In robotics software development, we have several software frameworks to create robot applications quickly. One of the popular frameworks available is ROS. Using ROS, we can quickly develop robotics applications by reusing existing code that other developers have already developed. Before jumping into the details, we will start by addressing the question: What is ROS?

What is ROS?

Contrary to what the name might suggest, ROS is not a real **Operating System (OS)** like Windows, Linux, and macOS. It has some OS-like functionalities, but it is not a real OS. ROS is an open-source framework designed to develop robot software applications. It provides a set of robot-specific libraries, software tools, and implementation of the robot's high-level capabilities.

ROS provides robot software in packages, and developers can create and reuse existing packages. Each package can contain the implementation of different algorithms, datasets, robot configuration files, robot models, etc.

There are two main versions of ROS: **ROS 1** and **ROS 2**. ROS 1 is a legacy version, and ROS 2 is the latest one. ROS 1 is fully supported on Linux-based OSs, while ROS 2 is compatible with Windows, Linux, and macOS. This book is completely focused on ROS 2. *Figure 1.1* shows the logo of the ROS framework.

Figure 1.1: ROS logo

The official ROS website can be found at [1]. Open Robotics [2] develops and maintains the ROS project. They work with the global ROS community of developers, academic researchers, and industry professionals to accelerate ROS package development. Using ROS, we can develop almost all the software components of a robot.

Important features of ROS

Here is a list of important features of ROS:

- **Inter-Process Communication (IPC) Infrastructure**: Programming robots simply means creating different applications in the robot computer to accomplish different tasks. The computer might have some OS like Ubuntu/Linux installed. The robot's sensors and actuators are connected to this computer via USB or other interfaces. We may have to write multiple ROS programs, also called ROS nodes, in the OS to acquire and process data from sensors and send control commands to the actuator. Developing a single program that handles all the tasks of the robot will not be a good idea for programming a robot because it adds more complexity to the program and makes debugging difficult. That is where ROS comes into the picture. The ROS libraries provide different APIs to communicate between these programs, which are running on OS. In that way, we can run multiple ROS nodes in the OS that communicate with each other to accomplish the entire robot's operations. This IPC infrastructure is the most important feature of ROS 1 and ROS 2. The IPC infrastructure in ROS 2 differs from that in ROS 1. ROS 2 uses the latest and most reliable software components for communication, which will improve the robot's overall performance.

- **Reusability and Modularity**: The software developed by others can easily be reused in our applications. This is one of the most useful features of ROS because it avoids *reinventing the wheel* and saves development time. The ROS packages are designed to be modular and there are more than 10,000 packages in ROS contributed by Open Robotics and the ROS community. Each package serves one or more purposes. We can reuse any of these packages in our robot software stack and significantly reduce the development time. For example, if we need to combine a list of laser scans from the robot, we can use the `laser_scan_merger` [3] package and integrate it into our robot application.

- **Open-Source License**: ROS 1 and ROS 2 software mainly comes with a **Berkeley Software Distribution (BSD)** 3-Clause license; with this license, we can modify and redistribute our robotics application for commercial purposes. The BSD licensing enables a high degree of flexibility. Not all packages come with a BSD 3-Clause license; some packages are the **Apache 2.0 License**, the **MIT License**, or the **Lesser General Public License (LGPL)**, depending on the contributions from different developers and the specific requirements of the software components. It's always a good idea to check the individual package licenses for specific details.

- **Tools and Libraries**: ROS comes with a set of software tools. What are ROS tools? ROS tools help developers visualize different types of sensor data sent and received by ROS nodes. Another important use case is debugging, as multiple ROS programs/nodes may communicate with each other and there can be different issues in the communications. These issues can be debugged using ROS tools. The ROS libraries are designed for specific purposes. The **client libraries** in ROS help the ROS nodes to communicate with each other. We can use the **rclcpp library** to write ROS 2 C++ nodes and **rclpy** for Python nodes. Libraries like **TF (Transformation)** in ROS help developers keep the transformation of each link and joint of the robot. There are multiple libraries in ROS, which will accelerate the robot software development time. We will see some examples of ROS tools in the next section.

- **Hardware Abstraction**: A ROS driver for a robot is a set of nodes that help developers interact with different hardware components like actuators, sensors, or an embedded platform. ROS provides a hardware abstraction, which means that if hardware components change, developers can easily integrate them into the robot. ROS provides a standard interface for developing hardware drivers, so replacing robot components becomes easier.

- **Ready-to-Use Robot Capabilities**: This is the main reason why ROS has become highly popular. ROS provides a ready-to-use template for the implementation of high-level tasks like autonomous navigation, manipulation, and perception. Developers can use this template for their robots and customize it for their applications.

- **Cross-Platform Support**: Mostly, the OS in robots is powered by Linux-based distros like Ubuntu, but any OS, like Windows, macOS, Android, etc, can be used. Cross-platform support is an important feature in ROS in which developers can create ROS packages and deploy them on multiple OS platforms. ROS 1 was mainly supported for Linux distributions like Ubuntu, whereas ROS 2 supports Ubuntu Linux, Windows 10, and macOS.

- **Middleware Independence**: One of the core components of ROS is the communication middleware. So, what is the communication middleware for? We already discussed that ROS provides APIs to communicate between different nodes. Underlying the API is a communication layer, which facilitates communication. The middleware is the intermediate layer that exists between the user applications and the OS. In ROS 1, there was only one fixed middleware for communication, but in ROS 2, that changed. In ROS 2, we have a pluggable middleware infrastructure like Data Distribution Service (DDS) or **Zero Overhead Network Protocol** (Zenoh). We can change the middleware based on the application we are dealing with. We will look at DDS in more detail in the upcoming section. Some examples of DDS are Fast DDS, Cyclone DDS, and RTI Connext.

- **Community and Ecosystem**: Compared to other robotics software frameworks, the ROS community is huge. Most of the packages in ROS are contributed to and maintained by developers across the globe. These packages can be reused and reduce overall development time. There are not only packages but also forums and blogs to support new ROS developers. ROSCon [4] is the annual event where the community meets to share innovations in the ROS framework.

- **Testing and Simulation:** ROS comes with a testing framework and simulation tools to validate the robot application before deployment. Multiple robot simulators, such as Gazebo, Webots, and Isaac Sim, support ROS 1 and ROS 2.

- **Production-Ready Framework**: One of the most asked questions when developing robot applications with ROS is whether they are production ready. ROS 1 was designed for robotic research applications. However, this is not the case for ROS 2. It is designed to be used in production. It uses much-improved architecture compared to ROS 1, and we can use ROS 2 in many use cases, such as the automation industry, healthcare, autonomous vehicles, etc.

We have seen some of the important features of ROS. Now, let's have a look at the ROS equation.

ROS equation

The ROS equation depicts the important components within the ROS framework. The important elements of ROS are shown in *Figure 1.2.*

Figure 1.2: ROS equation (source: Open Robotics [5] | https://www.ros.org/imgs/ros-equation. png)

The important components of ROS 1 and ROS 2 are as follows:

- **Plumbing**: The term *plumbing* refers to IPC, which is facilitated by ROS communication middleware. In ROS 1, the communication between nodes uses TCPROS (a TCP-based protocol), whereas in ROS 2, it uses DDS.

- **Tools:** There are GUI tools and command-line tools in ROS. The main examples of GUI tools in ROS are the **ROS Visualizer (RViz)** [6] and **rqt** [7]. These tools can be used to visualize the data exchange between ROS nodes and for debugging communication between nodes. The command-line tools can be invoked from the Linux shell.

- **Capabilities**: The important capabilities of ROS are *navigation, manipulation*, and *perception*. In ROS 2, the robot navigation is implemented as an open-source project called **Nav2** [*8*], and the robot manipulation is implemented as an open-source project called **MoveIt** [*9*]. The perception stack in ROS has tight integration with popular perception libraries like **OpenCV** [*10*], **Point Cloud Library (PCL)** [*11*], BT.CPP [*4*], and **Open3D** [*12*].

- **Community**: ROS has a big, active, open-source community. There is a list of community-contributed packages and libraries in ROS [*13*], which includes **Nav2** and **MoveIt 2**. There is a ROS community engagement platform hosted on Discourse [*14*]. We can get the latest updates here. Also, there is Robotics Stack Exchange website to solve your ROS issues [*15*]. There is ROS Discord for real-time communication [*16*]. This strong community is the backbone of the ROS framework.

The following section details the ROS project development time, giving insight into its evolution.

ROS development timeline

So far, we have reviewed the main features of ROS and the ROS equation. Now, let's have a quick look at ROS evolution. When did this project start, and what is the latest version of ROS?

- **2007**: ROS development began in 2007 at the Stanford Artificial Intelligence Laboratory and was later continued and significantly expanded by Willow Garage. [*17*].

- **2008**: An early version of ROS (0.4, Mango Tango) is released by Willow Garage.

- **2010**: The first official ROS 1.0 distribution of ROS, Box Turtle, is released. In the same year, ROS C Turtle is released.

- **2011**: ROS Diamondback and Electric Emys are released.

- **2012**: ROS Fuerte and Groovy are released.

- **2013**: ROS Hydro Medusa is released, which includes major updates to packages and documentation.

- **2014**: ROS Indigo is released. After Hydro, ROS began to be developed and maintained by the Open Source Robotics Foundation (OSRF). Their first release was Indigo.

- **2015**: ROS Jade Turtle is released.

- **2016**: ROS Kinetic Kame is released.

- **2017**: ROS Lunar Loggerhead is released; in the same year, the first ROS 2 distribution is released: ROS Ardent Apalone. ROS 2 is a separate project from the legacy ROS 1, with many components redesigned and reimplemented to address ROS 1's limitations.

- **2018**: ROS 1.0 Melodic Morenia and ROS 2 Bouncy Bolson are released.

- **2019**: ROS 2 Dashing and Eloquent are released.
- **2020**: ROS 1.0 Noetic Ninjemys and ROS 2 Foxy Fitzroy are released. ROS 1.0 Noetic Ninjemys is the final distribution of ROS 1.0. It will be supported until 2025.
- **2021**: ROS 2.0 Galactic is released.
- **2022**: ROS 2.0 Humble Hawksbill is released.
- **2023**: ROS 2.0 Iron Irwini is released.
- **2024**: ROS 2.0 Jazzy Jalisco is released. The End of Life (EOL) of this distribution is 2029. This is the distribution we are using in this book.
- **2025**: ROS 2.0 Kilted Kaiju is released.

Here is a link to the ROS 1 distribution [*18*] and the ROS 2 distribution [*19*].

Now that you have an overview of the ROS framework, let's compare its two versions.

Comparing ROS 1 and ROS 2 architecture

In this section, we will examine the fundamental architectural changes of ROS 1 and ROS 2 and the important reasons why the ROS 2 project started. *Figure 1.3* shows the architecture of ROS 1 and ROS 2.

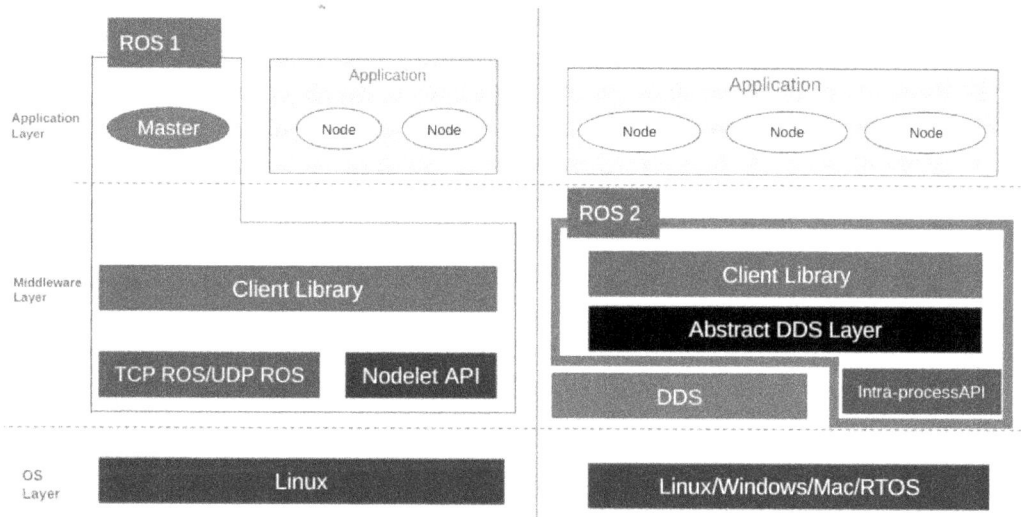

Figure 1.3: ROS 1 and ROS 2 architecture comparison

As you can see in *Figure 1.3*, there are three main layers in both of the architectures. They are:

- **OS Layer**
- **Middleware Layer**
- **Application Layer**

Let's take a look at each layer in detail.

OS layer

On the left, you can see the architecture of ROS 1, and on the right, ROS 2. The bottom layer is the OS layer. As you know, ROS is a software framework that can be installed on an OS. ROS 1 is mainly compatible with Ubuntu/Linux, whereas ROS 2 is compatible with Linux, Windows, macOS, RTOS, etc.

Middleware layer

The next layer is the middleware layer, which constitutes the main ROS components. If you look at the ROS 1 architecture, it has the core middleware components like TCP ROS/UDP ROS and the Nodelet API. The middleware layer of ROS 1 is custom-built and distributed along with ROS. In ROS 2, the communication middleware is DDS. DDS is a protocol implemented in different libraries by different vendors. ROS 2 developers use these implementations. DDS is already used to develop production-grade IPC-based software for autonomous robots, aerospace, and defense. ROS 2 is built upon DDS implementations. Examples of popular DDS implementations are Fast DDS, Cyclone DDS, and RTI Connext [20].

In the ROS 1 middleware layer, we can see the **Nodelet API** section, which is used for implementing intra-process communication in ROS nodes. Intra-process communication differs from inter-process communication. In intra-process communication, data is exchanged between different parts of a single process, like threads, modules, etc., by sharing memory space. It allows fast and efficient data transfer, whereas IPC is data exchange between different processes. Nodelet in ROS 1 offers significant performance benefits, such as zero-copy data transfer, reduced CPU load from avoiding serialization, lower memory usage by preventing data duplication, and faster, low-latency communication that improves throughput for high-frequency data like images or point clouds.

The **client libraries** in ROS 1 and ROS 2 provide APIs for communicating between different nodes in ROS. The nodes can be implemented in different programming languages, such as C++, Python, Java, etc. There are separate client libraries for each programming language. For example, `roscpp` is a client library for C++, and `rospy` is a client library for Python in ROS 1, whereas `rclcpp` and `rclpy` are the client libraries of C++ and Python in ROS 2. In ROS 2, all client libraries are built on top of the **ROS Client Library** (**RCL**), a core client library in ROS 2. The RCL implements **ROS** 2 concepts and other programming languages can use this API and wrap it and use. It avoids the need to build client libraries from scratch, making the development of client libraries easier and more efficient.

Like the Nodelet API in ROS 1, there is an intra-process API in ROS 2, which has the same purpose. In ROS 2, there is a new layer connecting DDS and client libraries, called the abstract DDS layer or ROS Middleware (RMW). This layer is not only for DDS but also applicable to other communication protocols like Eclipse Zenoh. This layer decouples the ROS 2 core libraries from DDS and other protocols. This design enables us to change the DDS at any time. In short, the abstract DDS layer acts as an interface between the ROS 2 API and various DDS or other middleware implementations. This design approach in ROS 2 gives developers more flexibility and modularity.

Application layer

The application layer is where developers can create different robotic applications by using ROS APIs in the client library. We can write different ROS nodes that can communicate with each other. If you look at the ROS 1 architecture, you will find a node called master in the application layer. The master node comes with ROS 1 installation, and it is basically a broker program. With the help of this broker program, ROS 1 nodes can discover other nodes and communicate with each other. So, we must run the master node in the OS before starting any ROS 1 node. If the master node fails to run, it will affect the complete ROS 1 application running on the robot. This is a major issue, and it was fixed in ROS 2.

If you check on the ROS 2 side, there is no master node, but the nodes can communicate as well. This is a major change in ROS 2, which uses DDS as middleware. In ROS 2, developers can write nodes, and nodes can make discoveries using DDS and start communication.

Feature comparison between ROS 1 and ROS 2

Here is an important feature comparison between ROS 1 and ROS 2.

Features	ROS 1	ROS 2
Communication Middleware	Custom TCP-based communication middleware. The master node is for node registration and lookup, which can be a single point of failure.	Use DDS and communication protocols like Zenoh.
Real-Time	Not designed for real-time processing, but it can be tweaked with significant effort.	We can make real-time applications with a bit of tweaking and effort.
Security	Lack of built-in security features, less suitable for sensitive or critical applications.	Built-in security features through DDS security, which offers authentication, encryption, and access control, make it suitable for industrial and commercial applications.
Modularity and Scalability	Highly modular and compatible with multiple programming languages.	Enhanced modularity, compatibility with multiple programming languages, and more flexibility for different development needs.
Platform Support	Primary support in Linux-based OS.	Multiple OS support like Windows, Linux, and macOS.
Community and Ecosystem	Vast and established community with extensive libraries and tools. Widely used in academic research.	Rapidly growing community. Community shifting from ROS 1 to ROS 2 because of the architectural drawbacks of ROS 1.

Table 1.1: Comparison between ROS 1 and ROS 2

Next, let's understand why we should migrate from ROS 1 to ROS 2.

Why should you migrate from ROS 1 to ROS 2?

In this section, we will discuss the important reasons for migrating to ROS 2 from ROS 1. Here, we will not discuss the technical aspects of it but, more generally, why it is better to migrate to ROS 2.

Here are the important points to note:

- ROS 1 Noetic Ninjemys will reach EOL in 2025. After EOL, we will not have new features, bug fixes, or security updates for the ROS 1 packages. There will not be any ROS 1 versions after this; ROS 1 Noetic is the final official distribution of ROS 1. The primary OS supporting ROS 1 Noetic is Ubuntu 20.04, which is also going to EOL in 2025, so there won't be any OS updates as well. After 2025, we will only have ROS 2 distributions.

- ROS 2 can be used in any robotic application, including research and commercial applications. ROS 1 is mainly designed for academic and research use. If you plan to prototype and commercialize a robot, ROS 2 is a good choice because of its enhanced security, robustness, and the ability to orchestrate complex robotics tasks.

- When comparing the features, ROS 2 leads all the way. If you consider the security, real-time, **Quality of Service (QoS)**, and scalability aspects of ROS 2, it is far better than ROS 1.

- ROS 1 was platform-specific and mainly compatible with the Linux OS. There are ROS 1 ported versions for Windows and macOS, but they are not stable and maintained. On the other hand, ROS 2 is cross-platform, which makes it ideal for robot application development on Windows and macOS platforms.

- If you are already a ROS 1 developer, the learning curve to migrate to ROS 2 is very low. The communication concepts are the same, but changes are mainly at the API level. We must replace ROS 1 nodes with ROS 2 APIs. This can take some time, but the migration is relatively easy compared to a beginner in ROS 2 because of the common concepts in both. There are new complex concepts in ROS 2 that can take more time to understand, but generally, ROS 1 knowledge will help you to get started with ROS 2 and start developing.

We have discussed why we need to migrate from ROS 1 to ROS 2. Now, let's explore the core concepts of ROS 2.

Diving into DDS in ROS 2

In this section, we discuss more details about ROS 2's core module, **DDS**, which works as the communication middleware for ROS 2, as shown in *Figure 1.3*.

What is DDS?

DDS [*21*] is a standard from the **Object Management Group (OMG)** [*22*] that was established in 2004 for standard publisher/subscriber communication. It is mainly used in mission-critical applications like air traffic control and management, financial trading, and complex telemetry systems. DDS enables scalable, real-time, dependable, and high-performance data exchange between the publisher and subscriber.

The OMG is a global, open-membership, non-profit consortium responsible for creating and maintaining a number of standards in technical and business domains.

Publisher/subscriber communication involves sending and receiving data. The publisher sends data, and the subscriber listens to and receives it.

The DDS standard mainly came into existence when a group of companies developed their middleware solution. These companies needed their applications to be interoperable and compatible with other middleware.

DDS has various use cases, like:

- **Aerospace and Defense**: Used in command-and-control systems and also for real-time communication in **UAV** (short for **unmanned aerial vehicle**).
- **Healthcare**: Used in patient monitoring systems, health information systems, etc.
- **Transportation**: Autonomous vehicle and railway signaling and control systems.
- **Finance**: High-frequency trading systems and market data distribution.
- **Robotics**: Autonomous robots and industrial robots.

There are many such use cases for DDS. The following link shows which organizations use DDS in their products: `https://www.dds-foundation.org/who-is-using-dds-2/`.

Components DDS standard

Figure 1.4 shows a block diagram of different components of DDS.

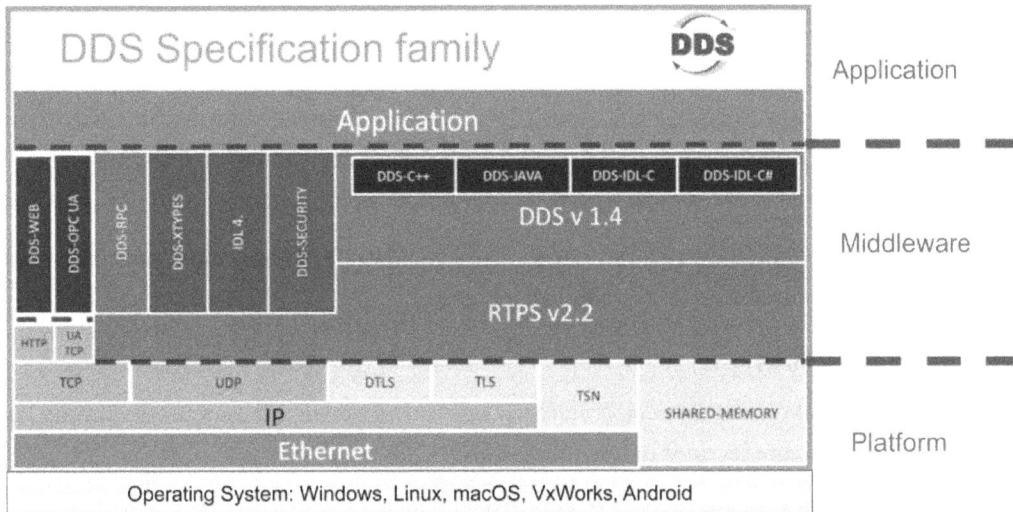

Figure 1.4: Components of the DDS standard (source: RTI | https://www.rti.com/products/dds-standard)

We can see three main layers: platform, middleware, and application. The following are explanations of each layer.

Platform layer

This is the bottom layer in the DDS standard diagram. It consists of the OS, network protocols, and network interfaces like Ethernet. We must install the DDS implementation in an OS and configure the network protocol and interface to make it work. We can say that the platform layer is the foundation for DDS to work. Here is a brief idea of other components in the platform layer:

- **Internet Protocol (IP)**: This is the set of network layer protocols or rules for routing data to reach the correct destination [23].

- **Transport Protocols**: This is the layer just above the IP layer, which helps applications communicate with each other without directly interacting with the IP layer. DDS uses different types of transport protocols in different scenarios.

- **Transmission Control Protocol (TCP)**: DDS uses TCP in situations where reliable communication and ordered message delivery is essential.

- **User Datagram Protocol (UDP)**: DDS uses UDP for minimal latency applications and real-time systems, such as those in robotics, aerospace, and defense. It is often preferred when the timely delivery of the message is more important than reliability.
- **Transport Layer Security (TLS)**: This is for secure TCP communication.
- **Time Sensitive Networking (TSN)**: This is for real-time communication.
- **Shared Memory**: This is for high-speed data transfer within the same machine. It is useful when the DDS participants (publisher and subscriber) are running on the same machine, and allows lower latency and higher throughput.

The next layer is the middleware layer, which consists of DDS standard implementations. We will discuss a few components of the middleware layer.

Middleware layer

This layer consists of *core DDS protocols and their implementation* in different programming languages. Here are the core sections in the middleware:

- **Real-Time Publish-Subscribe (RTPS)**: This is the bottom layer in DDS, which ensures interoperability or compatibility across other DDS implementations over the network by using standard protocols. RTPS is part of this standard. This protocol is mainly designed for real-time systems, which can be used for critical applications like robotics, defense systems, etc.
- **DDS**: This layer manages the distribution of data using the publish/subscribe method. This layer ensures the publishers who send the data and subscribers who receive the data can communicate in a decoupled manner. Here are the key features of DDS:
  - **Data-Centric Publish/Subscribe Model**: As we mentioned above, DDS uses a publish/subscribe communication model, which decouples the publisher and subscribers. This model allows flexible and scalable data distribution.
  - **QoS Policies**: DDS provides many QoS policies that can be easily configured, thereby configuring the behavior of data exchange. Using QoS policies in DDS, we can control the reliability, durability, latency, and resource usage of communication.
  - **Interoperability**: DDS is designed to be platform-independent, allowing us to use it with different OSs and hardware platforms. The APIs provided by DDS implementations are standardized, ensuring interoperability between different DDS implementations and facilitating integration with current systems.

- **Real-Time Communication**: DDS is optimized for real-time communication by providing low-latency and high-throughput data exchange. It also delivers deterministic data delivery, which makes it suitable for time-critical applications.

- **Scalability**: DDS supports the dynamic discovery of publisher and subscriber nodes, meaning publishers can connect to subscribers automatically and find each other without any configuration. DDS offers scalability because it can accommodate large-scale systems with numerous participants (publishers and subscribers).

- **Security**: DDS comes with built-in security features such as authentication, encryption, and access control to protect and secure communication.

- **Language-Specific Implementations**: The publisher and subscriber of DDS can be from any programming language, such as C++, Java, Python, etc. The DDS layer provides supported APIs in these languages for implementing publishers and subscribers. In Figure 1.4, you can see that DDS-C++, DDS-JAVA, etc. provide support to these programming languages. You can also find DDS-IDL-C and DDS-IDL-C#; IDL stands for Interface Definition Language. This helps to define different data types and interfaces for communication between participants. DDS-IDL-C implements an API in C with IDL to define data types for communication.

- **Addition DDS Specifications**: These are additional specifications of DDS that go hand in hand with the DDS standard:

    - **DDS-WEB**: Integrating web technologies into DDS.

    - **DDS-OPC UA**: Compatibility with OPC Unified Architecture, which is a machine-to-machine communication protocol.

    - **DDS-RPC**: This enables remote procedure call support in DDS.

    - **DDS-XTYPES**: This extends to complex data modeling.

    - **IDL 4**: This is the version of IDL used in this DDS architecture, which defines data types.

    - **DDS-Security**: This is a set of specifications for ensuring secure data exchange and access control.

In the next section, we can see the application layers in the DDS.

Application layer

This is where user applications come in. We can use the APIs for different programming languages in DDS to create our own publisher and subscriber programs for different applications.

How DDS works?

In this section, we will examine how DDS works and how the user applications communicate with each other. The following are some of the key concepts we must understand before proceeding.

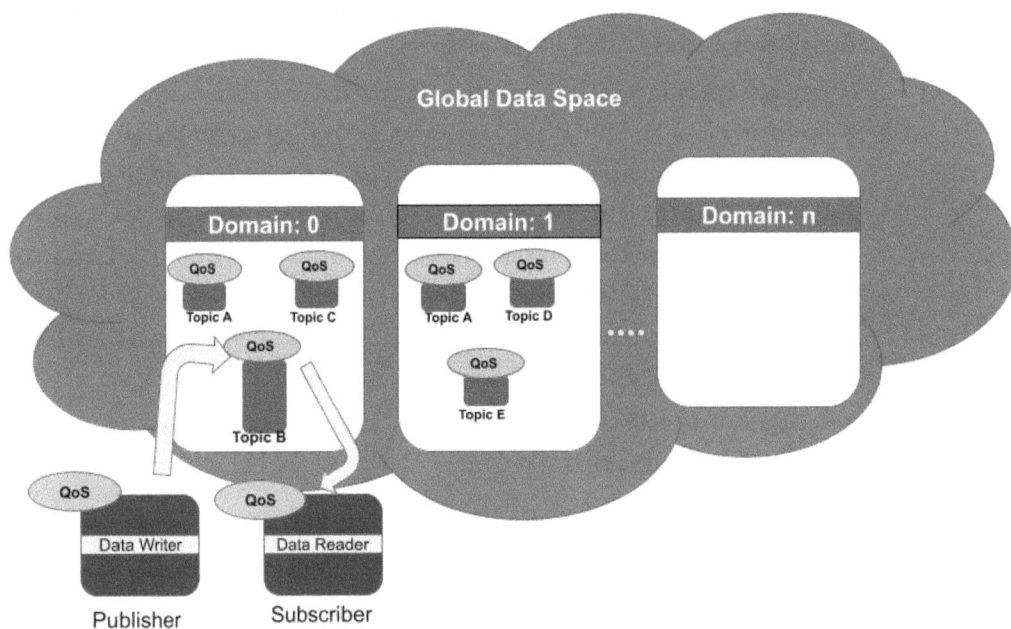

Figure 1.5: DDS global data space

Figure 1.5 shows various concepts in the DDS architecture. The first concept we will be discussing is Global Data Space (GDS):

- **GDS:** In DDS, the GDS refers to the virtual shared memory or network where all data exchange between participants (nodes) occurs. This will act like a shared data pool that is accessible to all DDS participants regardless of their location. The GDS is data-centric, meaning it prioritizes the data itself over the applications that use it. This also ensures that the data publishing/subscribing will be decoupled from the application logic.

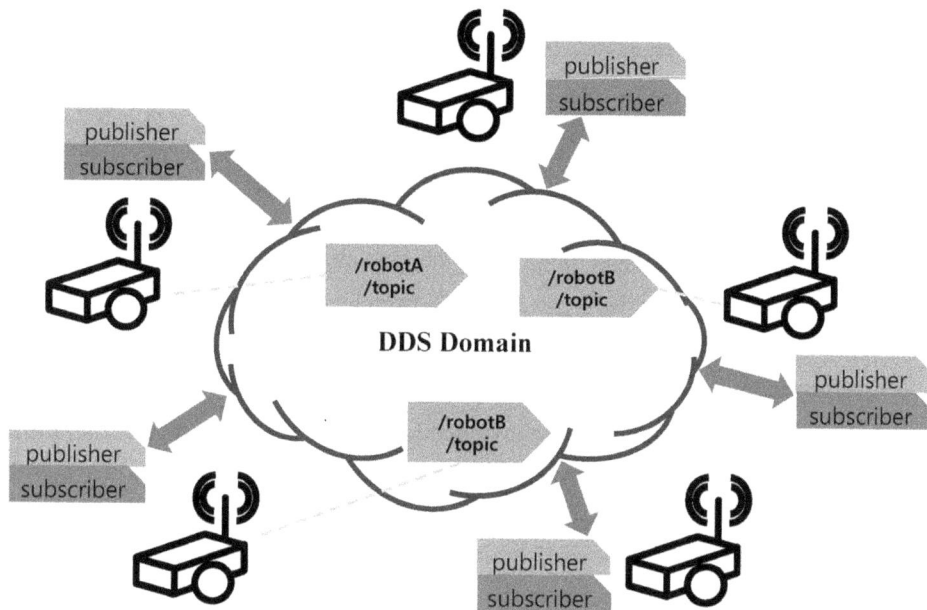

Figure 1.6: Example of DDS domain and publisher/subscriber nodes (source: Research-Gate [24] | https://www.researchgate.net/figure/Data-sharing-in-the-global-data-space-in-DDS_fig2_358142403)

- **Domains**: A domain in DDS is a logical partition in the GDS. It creates a boundary within which the exchange of data takes place. There can be multiple domains in a GDS. The participants inside the domain can discover each other and easily communicate, but they will be isolated from other domains. Based on the application need, domains help scale, secure, and separate data spaces. In *Figure 1.6*, we can see an illustration of domains. Multiple robots are communicating on different topics inside the domain.

- **Topics**: As you can see in *Figure 1.5*, each domain contains topics. Topics are a named data bus or channel that acts as a bridge between publishers and subscribers. Each topic has a name, a data type, and a set of **QoS** policies. The data can be published and subscribed using the topic name and it can stream data that is already defined. No other data types can be published through the same topic name. QoS policies ensure data is transmitted reliably within the given parameters. The data type of topics is defined using the IDL format. We will see more about IDL in the next chapter. The publisher and subscriber should agree on this format for exchanging data. Domains can have multiple topics, and there can be many publishers and many subscribers for a single topic.

- **Publishers and Subscribers**: Applications that use DDS for communication are commonly called domain participants. Applications that send data to a topic are called publishers, and applications that receive data from a topic are called subscribers. Domain participants can be publishers, subscribers, or both. A publisher contains multiple data writers, and a subscriber can have multiple data readers.

- **Data Writers and Data Readers**: The data writers are components in DDS responsible for writing data on a specific topic. They act as the source of data for a topic, whereas data readers are responsible for reading data from a specific topic. Data writers and readers can be configured using QoS policies to specify the behaviour of data publishing and data subscribing.

- **QoS**: QoS policies define the behavior of data exchange. We can define the QoS for a topic, publisher, subscriber, data reader, or data writer. These QoS policies help define how the data is being transported. We can assign QoS policies for individual components, or we can assign a set of QoS policies, which are called QoS profiles. We will discuss QoS in more detail in the DDS feature list in the next chapter.

We have discussed how DDS works and seen its important components. In the next section, we can see an example workflow of publish-subscribe using DDS.

Exploring a workflow for sending and receiving data using DDS

Now that you understand the basic terminology of DDS, let's start exploring a workflow for sending and receiving data using DDS. Here is an example of a *temperature value getting published and subscribed using DDS*.

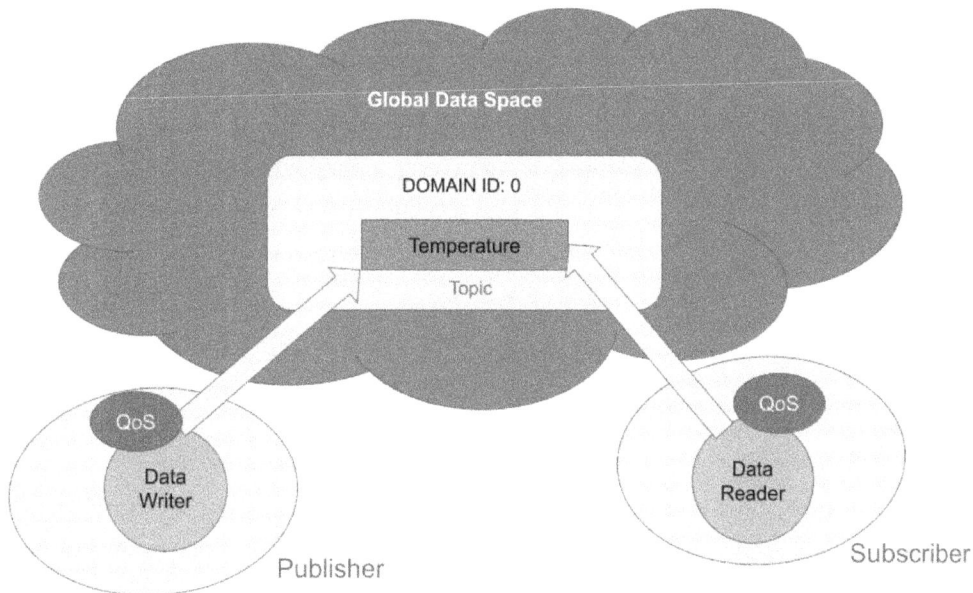

Figure 1.7: DDS topic-based communication example

Let's delve into the workflow:

1. **Defining the Topic:** The first step is to define a topic for a specific application. For example, if we want to send the temperature of a robot body, we can define a topic called *Temperature* and have a data structure with fields like temperature values, timestamps, and sensor ID.

2. **Creating a Publisher:** In the next step, we can create the publisher node, which can read the sensor data and send it through the topic named *Temperature*. Before publishing the topic, it is mandatory to configure the domain ID. Using the domain ID, the publisher can understand in which domain it is going to publish the topic. Let's set the domain ID to 0 here. After setting the domain ID, define the QoS policies for reliable delivery. After the QoS policies, set up the data writer for the *Temperature* topic. After this, keep on publishing the temperature data.

3. **Creating a Subscriber:** On the subscriber side, we must set the domain ID first and then the QoS settings. After those settings, we can define a data reader for the *Temperature* topic. Use the data reader to receive the temperature data and do the rest of the processing.

We have seen an example pub-sub workflow using DDS; now, we can see a list of popular DDS vendors and their features.

List of DDS vendors

There are commercial DDS vendors and free and open-source vendors. Most commercially available DDS vendors offer enhanced performance, better control, advanced security, support, and certification. Open-source DDS is adapting more to research and education and is being used more in robotics because of ROS 2 integration. Commercial DDS vendors are preferred primarily in mission-critical sectors like defense, aerospace, and medicine. It is also used where more stability, certification, and long-term support are needed.

Here is a list of different implementations of DDS standards by different organizations

- **Real-Time Innovations (RTI)** [25]:

    - **Name of DDS:** Connext DDS [26].
    - **Description**: Widely used DDS implementation, best known for its high performance and scalability. It supports a wide range of applications from embedded devices to the cloud.
    - **Core Features**: It provides different tools for design, monitoring, and analysis, great documentation and support, and interoperability with other DDS implementations.

- ADLINK Technology [27]:

    - **Name of DDS: Vortex OpenSplice** [28].
    - **Description:** Known for its high performance, reliability, and extensive features like QoS, real-time data propagation, and integration with other DDS implementations. It is widely used in aerospace, defense, industrial automation, etc.
    - **Core Features**: High availability and reliability, support for various programming languages and OSs, extensive QoS.

- Eclipse Foundation [29]:

    - **Name of DDS:** Eclipse Cyclone DDS [30].
    - **Description**: This is an open-source DDS implementation under the Eclipse Foundation, mainly designed for IoT and edge computing applications.
    - **Core Features**: It is lightweight and efficient, supports multiple OS platforms, and development is driven by the community.

- **Twin Oaks Computing** [*31*]:

  - **Name of DDS: CoreDX DDS** [*32*].

  - **Description:** This product is suitable for a small-footprint, high-performance DDS implementation, which is suitable for embedded and real-time systems.

  - **Core Features**: It has a small memory footprint, high throughput, and low latency. It supports safety-critical and real-time systems and is interoperable with other DDS implementations. A light version, CoreDX DDS Lite, is available.

- eProsima [*33*]:

  - **Name of DDS**: Fast DDS (formerly Fast RTPS) [*34*].

  - **Description:** It is an open-source DDS implementation better known for efficiency and performance.

  - **Core Features:** High performance and low latency, open source and community-supported, customizable QoS setting, integration with other protocols via integration service.

- **Object Computing, Inc. (OCI)** [*35*]:

  - **Name of DDS:** Open DDS [*36*]

  - **Description**: An open-source DDS implementation for high performance and data distribution.

  - **Core Features**: Open-source and community-driven, customizable QoS settings, interoperability with other DDS implementations, comprehensive DDS features, extensive documentation and support

- Zettascale [*37*]:

  - **Name of DDS**: Cyclone DDS [*38*].

  - **Description**: It is an open-source DDS implementation that is designed for reliability and scalability in real-time distributed systems.

  - **Core Features**: Open-source and community-driven, comprehensive QoS settings, suitable for small-footprint and high-performance applications, high throughput and low latency, interoperability with other DDS implementations.

We have discussed DDS and its vendors in detail. Now, it's time to explore the different layers built on top of it.

Dissecting some important ROS 2 layers

We have gone through the basics of DDS and explored its different features. In this section, we are going to explore the layers in ROS 2 that work on top of DDS. We can start with a detailed discussion of the **RMW abstraction** layer, which is one of the important layers connecting DDS to the ROS 2 framework.

RMW layer (ROS middleware abstraction interface)

Figure 1.8 shows a detailed architecture of the ROS 2 framework with all its layers.

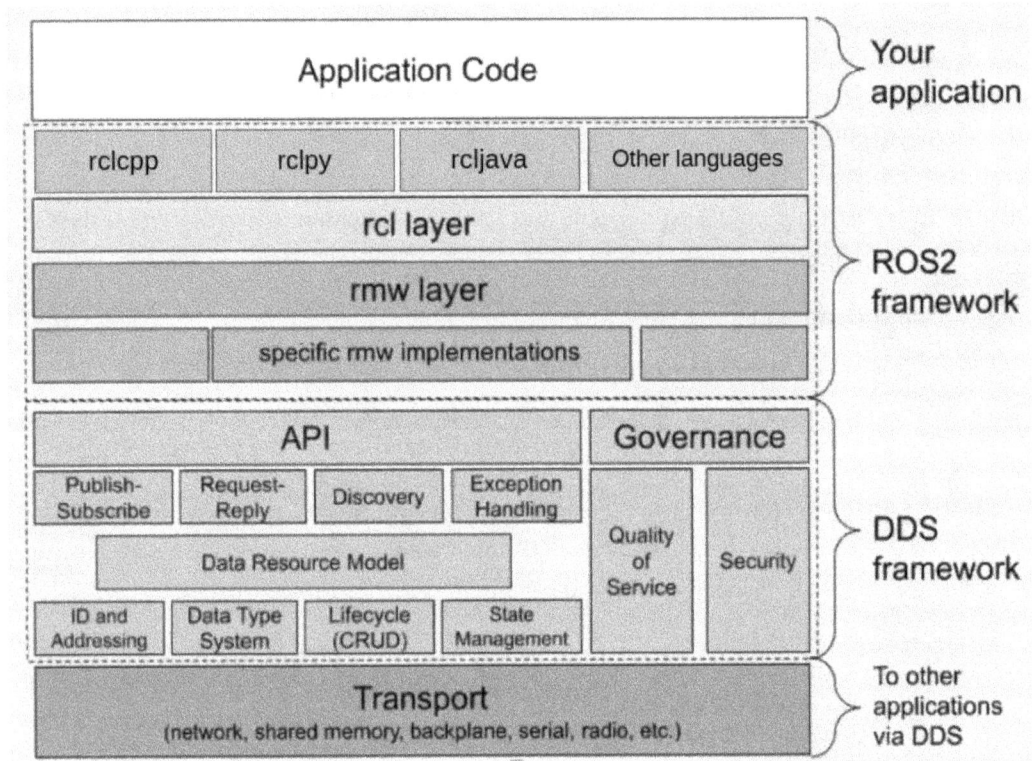

*Figure 1.8: ROS 2 detailed architecture (source: RTI | https://www.slideshare.net/slideshow/
deep-dive-into-the-opc-ua-dds-gateway-specification/99648467)*

We already discussed the DDS framework in *Figure 1.2*. We learned that DDS has an application layer or APIs that we can use to build our own apps. This is where ROS becomes relevant. The ROS 2 framework is built on top of the DDS API layer. If you take a look at *Figure 1.8*, you can see that after the DDS framework layer comes the ROS 2 framework.

There are different implementations of DDS, like Cyclone DDS, Fast DDS, etc. ROS 2 has interoperability between different DDS, so the ROS 2 nodes should work with any DDS. The RMW layer is the important layer in ROS 2, which enables communication between different ROS 2 nodes, which are independent of underlying middleware (e.g., DDS implementation). It offers flexibility and interoperability and abstracts the communication details of DDS. There are different RMW implementations in ROS 2 for each middleware. We are using DDS by default, but in the future, there may be different RMW implementations for other non-DDS middleware as well.

Here are some popular RMW implementations that support different DDS vendors:

- **rmw_fastrtps_cpp**: This implementation uses eProsima Fast DDS (formerly **Fast RTPS**) as the underlying DDS middleware. It is designed for high performance and ease of use. It is used in low-latency and high-throughput applications.

- **rmw_cyclonedds_cpp:** This implementation uses Eclipse Cyclone DDS, which is mainly used in resource-constrained environments like embedded systems and IoT devices.

- **rmw_connextdds_cpp:** This implementation uses RTI Connext, a commercial DDS solution known for its robustness and extensive features. It is used in mission-critical applications.

- **rmw_opensplice_cpp:** This implementation uses ADLINK's OpenSplice DDS, which offers high scalability and real-time capabilities.

- **rmw_zenoh**: This is the RMW for ROS 2 that uses **Zenoh** as the middleware. Zenoh [*39*] is a lightweight publisher/subscriber protocol that helps different devices and systems to talk to each other, share data, and perform computation efficiently. Zenoh is not DDS, but another protocol that can work as middleware for ROS 2. Zenoh shows comparable performance to DDS in certain scenarios, particularly in bandwidth-constrained environments. The choice of Zenoh or DDS is dependent on specific requirements like network condition, data criticality, and system scalability. This page provides a performance comparison between different publisher/subscriber frameworks available: [*40*]. The benchmark concludes that Zenoh is the best choice for industrial, IoT, robotics, and automotive applications. Open Robotics selected Zenoh as an alternate middleware to DDS for ROS 2. It may become a popular choice among developers in the future.

- **rmw_email**: There is even an RMW called rmw_email. It contains a middleware that can send and receive strings over email and has an RMW implementation that allows ROS 2 to use the middleware to exchange messages [*44*].

We have seen different RMW implementations that connect DDS to the ROS 2 framework, but on top of the RMW implementation, we can see an RCL layer. This layer provides ROS core APIs for writing ROS 2 applications.

> **Note**
>
> We will see the practical implementation of Zenoh as an RMW in *Chapter 3*.

RCL layer and client libraries

RCL [*41*] is an important layer connecting ROS client libraries (like **rclcpp** for C++, **rclpy** for Python, and **rclc** for C) and the underlying RMW layer. The client libraries are for writing ROS nodes in a specific programming language. The primary client libraries in ROS 2 are rclpp, rclpy, and rclc. There are community-maintained client libraries like Node.js, Rust, Dart, and C# [*42*].

RCL is written in pure C. It provides stable APIs for the client libraries without needing to interact with the lower-level DDS APIs. The C-based API can be wrapped inside different programming languages and extend the ROS 2 programming support to other languages.

ROS 2 application layer

This is the layer where all the ROS 2 nodes and packages come in. A ROS 2 package is a software module that can contain ROS 2 nodes, configuration, data, etc. In the application layer, we can see that many existing packages, tools, and robot capabilities, like navigation, manipulation, and perception stack, have been implemented.

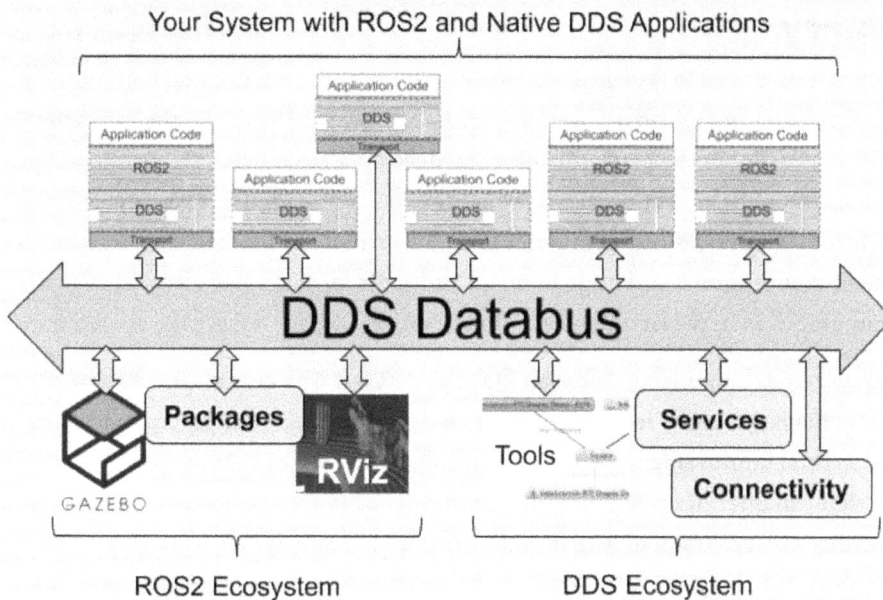

Figure 1.9: ROS 2 DDS connection diagram (source: RTI | https://www.rti.com/products/dds-standard)

Figure 1.9 illustrates how DDS connects different modules of ROS 2, like tools, simulators, and capabilities.

In theory, ROS 2 developers can focus entirely on the application layer without worrying much about the underlying DDS implementation. However, in practice, deploying ROS 2 in large-scale networks often requires significant debugging, unlike ROS 1. This has led to a growing interest in alternatives like Zenoh, which was selected last year as an alternative ROS 2 middleware [43].

We have now looked at most of the important aspects of ROS 2 architecture and have gone over the details of DDS, which is the core of ROS 2.

Summary

This chapter introduced ROS 2, a very popular framework for the development of robotic applications. The chapter provided an overview of the role played by ROS in the provision of modularity and reusability in the platform, allowing developers to quickly create and adapt robotic applications through the reutilization of existing code. It provided an overview of key elements of ROS, including inter-process communication infrastructure, hardware abstraction, licensing under open-source terms, and huge libraries and tools for tasks like visualization, debugging, and communication between different parts of a robot.

It also drew some comparisons between ROS 1 and ROS 2. The latter is more robust because of DDS, has enhanced security features, and is cross-platform compatible. It provides insight into the architectural improvements in ROS 2, focusing on the use of DDS as a communication middleware that can offer flexibility and high performance in real-time applications. The chapter also described the evolution of ROS from the Stanford AI Lab, where it was first introduced, to the very latest version, ROS 2 Kilted Kaiju, and discussed migration from ROS 1 to ROS 2. We then went into the details of DDS, the components that compose it, and how it is integrated with ROS 2 to enable scalable and efficient communication in robotic applications.

This chapter provided a foundation for following along with later chapters. In the next chapter, we will discuss the installation of ROS 2 and its detailed concepts.

References

- [1] https://www.ros.org/
- [2] https://www.openrobotics.org/
- [3] https://www.openrobotics.org/
- [4] https://roscon.ros.org/
- [5] https://www.openrobotics.org/
- [6] https://github.com/ros2/rviz
- [7] https://github.com/ros-visualization/rqt
- [8] https://nav2.org/
- [9] https://moveit.picknik.ai/
- [10] https://opencv.org/
- [11] https://pointclouds.org/
- [12] https://www.open3d.org/

- [13] https://www.ros.org/blog/community/
- [14] https://discourse.ros.org/
- [15] https://robotics.stackexchange.com/
- [16] https://www.ros.org/blog/discord/
- [17] https://www.linkedin.com/company/willow-garage/
- [18] https://wiki.ros.org/Distributions
- [19] https://docs.ros.org/en/jazzy/Releases.html
- [20] https://docs.ros.org/en/jazzy/Installation/DDS-Implementations.html
- [21] https://www.dds-foundation.org/
- [22] https://www.omg.org/
- [23] https://www.cloudflare.com/en-gb/learning/network-layer/internet-protocol/
- [24] https://www.researchgate.net/
- [25] https://www.rti.com/en/
- [26] https://www.rti.com/products
- [27] https://www.adlinktech.com/en/data-distribution-service
- [28] https://www.adlinktech.com/en/vortex-opensplice-data-distribution-service
- [29] https://www.eclipse.org/
- [30] https://projects.eclipse.org/projects/iot.cyclonedds
- [31] https://www.twinoakscomputing.com/
- [32] https://www.twinoakscomputing.com/coredx
- [33] https://www.eprosima.com/
- [34] https://fast-dds.docs.eprosima.com/en/stable/
- [35] https://objectcomputing.com/
- [36] https://objectcomputing.com/platforms/opendds
- [37] https://www.zettascale.tech/
- [38] https://cyclonedds.io/
- [39] https://zenoh.io/
- [40] https://zenoh.io/blog/2023-03-21-zenoh-vs-mqtt-kafka-dds/
- [41] https://github.com/ros2/rcl/

- [42] https://docs.ros.org/en/jazzy/Concepts/Basic/About-Client-Libraries.html
- [43] https://newsroom.eclipse.org/eclipse-newsletter/2023/october/eclipse-zenoh-selected-alternate-ros-2-middleware
- [44] https://github.com/christophebedard/rmw_email
- [45] https://www.behaviortree.dev/

2

Getting Started with ROS 2 Programming

In the previous chapter, we discussed the fundamentals of the ROS framework and its important features. We made a detailed comparison between ROS 1 and ROS 2 architecture and discussed why we must migrate from ROS 1 to ROS 2. We also saw the work of DDS, which is the core part of ROS 2. We listed popular DDS vendors and different layers of ROS 2, which connect to ROS 2 and DDS. I hope that the chapter provided an overview of ROS 2 architecture and its relevance in robotics software.

This chapter will give you a practical overview of how to quickly set up ROS 2 on Ubuntu 24.04 on any computer and start working on it. We will explore multiple ways to set up ROS 2 on our computers. After setting up ROS 2, we will start familiarizing ourselves with its basics. Then, we will start discussing ROS 2 concepts using its tools, packages, workspace, and Turtlesim, a 2D simulator that can be used to learn about ROS 2 concepts. Ultimately, we will see a detailed discussion of ROS 2 client libraries, which help developers write ROS 2-based applications in multiple programming languages. After understanding the ROS 2 client libraries, we will learn how to start developing robot software using ROS 2.

Here are the main topics we are going to discuss:

- Mastering ROS 2 installation
- Mastering ROS 2 tools and concepts with Turtlesim

Technical requirements

To follow this chapter, it is better to have a computer/embedded board (e.g., Raspberry Pi, Jetson board, etc.) with **Ubuntu 24.04 LTS** installed or any other Ubuntu version. If you don't have Ubuntu on your machine, make sure you have **Windows 11/10** or **macOS**.

The reference materials for this chapter can be found in the `Chapter02` folder of the following GitHub repository: `https://github.com/PacktPublishing/Mastering-ROS-2-for-Robotics-Programming/tree/main/Chapter02`.

Mastering ROS 2 installation

When you read this section's title, you may wonder what we must master to install software on a computer. I think you will get clarity after going through this section completely.

Most robots' computers run on a Linux distribution, most commonly Ubuntu. The robot computers were chosen based on the robotic application requirements. They can be industrial PCs with x86_64 architecture or ARM64-based compute modules such as Jetson Orin or Raspberry Pi.

As you know, we will deploy the robot application on the robot computer. However, robot software development will mostly happen on a developer workstation or laptop, which can be loaded with Windows, Ubuntu, or macOS.

Can ROS 2 be installed on all platforms? Yes. It is possible with the help of tools such as Docker, VirtualBox, VMware, UTM, and so on. Let's explore different ways of installing ROS 2 on a robot and in our development machine.

Installing Ubuntu 24.04 LTS and ROS 2 Jazzy

As you have already seen in *Chapter 1*, this book mainly focuses on ROS 2 Jazzy, which is primarily compatible with **Ubuntu 24.04 LTS** (**LTS** stands for **Long-Term Support**) [1]. ROS 2 Jazzy will not install on any Ubuntu version other than 24.04. So, let's explore how to set up Ubuntu 24.04 in our development machine and the robot.

Installing Ubuntu 24.04 LTS

There are multiple ways to set up Ubuntu 24.04 on a computer. Here are some references to get started with Ubuntu 24.04 installation for setting up ROS 2 Jazzy:

- **Setting up Ubuntu in the development workstation (x86_64/ARM64 architecture):**

    - *Installing Ubuntu in dual boot*: Suppose you have a development workstation with an Intel or AMD processor with an x86_64 architecture-based processor. In that case, you can download the official ISO image from the Ubuntu website, flash it into a thumb drive, and install it on your real machine with Windows or another OS. If you already have another operating system, such as Windows, on your machine, you can do a dual-boot installation by following these instructions [2]. Make sure you are opting for a manual installation from the instructions. The manual installation will allow us to format the desired partition on the drive. Installing Ubuntu on a real machine will perform better than any other virtualization method because it works without other software layers.

        If you use macOS on Apple Silicon, you can check out **UTM** [3], which is easy virtualization software for installing Ubuntu 24.04 on a Mac with an M1 series chipset. This software allows us to install the complete desktop version of Ubuntu and work with it without rebooting the machine. Switching between multiple virtual OS installations and the host OS, which can be Windows or macOS, is straightforward.

    - *Installing Ubuntu on VirtualBox/VMware/UTM/WSL 2*: Installing Ubuntu on a real machine is sometimes risky for beginners. Due to mistakes, it can sometimes crash the OS and not boot after that.

        If you are comfortable working with another OS such as Windows 10/11 or macOS, you can install Ubuntu virtually on these operating systems. Software such as VirtualBox and VMware can be installed on these operating systems, and Ubuntu can be installed using this software. These types of software are called virtualization software. You can download VirtualBox from reference [4], and you can download VMware from [5]. VirtualBox is free to download and use, and VMware Workstation is free for personal use, but not for commercial applications. The detailed instructions on installing Ubuntu 24.04 on VirtualBox can be found in reference [6], and the detailed instructions to set up Ubuntu 24.04 in VMware can be found in [7].

If you use macOS on Apple Silicon, you can check out UTM [8], an easy virtualization software that can install Ubuntu 24.04 on macOS with the M1 series chipset. This software allows us to install the complete desktop version of Ubuntu and work with it without rebooting the machine. Switching between multiple virtual OS installations and the host OS, which can be Windows or macOS, is straightforward.

Windows 10/11 comes with **Windows Subsystem for Linux (WSL)**, an additional feature in Windows that allows developers to run Linux environments such as Ubuntu without the need for separate virtual machines. Here is the reference to set Ubuntu 24.04 LTS in Windows WSL 2: [9]. WSL 2 is good for learning and experimenting with Ubuntu without having a dual-boot setup.

- *Installing Ubuntu on Docker*: Docker [10] is an **operating system-level virtualization** platform. The main difference between virtualization software, such as VirtualBox, and Docker is that VMS virtualizes a complete OS. In contrast, Docker containers virtualize the application layer on top of the host OS. It uses a containerization concept, which can isolate the application and its dependencies in portable and lightweight units called containers. The containers share the host OS kernel. We need a host OS such as Ubuntu, Windows, or macOS to install Docker.

  Docker is comparatively lightweight and ideal for ROS 2 application deployment in robots. Many Docker images are hosted publicly in Docker Hub [11]. Docker images are files that contain all the libraries and dependencies, and containers are the running instances of an image. Using the Docker CLI, we can download, manage, and run different Docker images.

  The upcoming section will discuss Docker setup because it is a useful technology for deploying ROS 2-based robotic applications. It will also show how to deploy a robot application efficiently using Docker.

- **Setting up Ubuntu in your robot:** Most robots have x86_64 or ARM64-based boards such as Raspberry Pi, Jetson Orin, or an industrial PC with an Intel or AMD processor. We can install Ubuntu on these machines. If we have an x86_64 machine, the installation procedure is straightforward; you can follow the above instructions. However, if we have embedded boards such as Raspberry Pi or Jetson series boards, the instructions are different. Ubuntu is customized for these boards, and we can see some references for installing Ubuntu on these boards. The setup instructions for setting Ubuntu 24.04 in Raspberry Pi 5 can be found in reference [12], and you can find a reference for Ubuntu installation in Jetson boards here: [13].

We have seen different references for installing Ubuntu 24.04 LTS in robots and our development workstation. Now, let's see how we can install ROS 2 Jazzy on Ubuntu.

Installing ROS 2 Jazzy on Ubuntu 24.04 LTS

This section provides detailed instructions for installing ROS 2 Jazzy on Ubuntu 24.04 LTS. This instruction will work on x86_64 and ARM64 machines.

To make the installation easy, you can also find a shell script to automate this installation and uninstallation procedure. You can find the script `ros2_install_jazzy.sh` in the `Chapter02` folder for installing ROS 2 Jazzy and `ros2_uninstall_jazzy.sh` for uninstalling the same.

You can run the following commands inside the `Chapter02` folder for installing ROS 2 Jazzy with an automated shell script:

```
chmod +x ros2_install_jazzy.sh
./ros2_install_jazzy.sh
```

Here is the command for uninstalling ROS 2 Jazzy in the future:

```
chmod +x ros2_uninstall_jazzy.sh
./ros2_uninstall_jazzy.sh
```

Here is the official link for installing ROS 2 Jazzy in Ubuntu, RHEL, and Windows 10: [*14*]. The recommended OS for installing ROS 2 Jazzy is Ubuntu 24.04 Noble Numbat. For easy setup, it is recommended that you install via the Debian package manager.

The following section explains the different steps in the ROS 2 Jazzy installation, which are mentioned in the installation script.

Setting the locale of your system

It is important to set the language and character encoding in Ubuntu before installing ROS 2. This is because DDS uses **UTF-8** (short for **Unicode Transformation Format-8 bit**) as the character encoding of IDL type string. To check the UTF-8 encoding of Ubuntu 24.04, you can use the `locale` command in Ubuntu. The `locale` command in Ubuntu 24.04 (and other Linux distributions) is used to display and set the system's locale information, which defines how data such as dates, times, numbers, currency, and text are formatted and displayed based on regional and language preferences. During installation, the Ubuntu locale is automatically generated based on the language preference we provide.

Here are the steps for setting the locale in your machine:

1. Open a new terminal in Ubuntu and execute the following command to check your Ubuntu's current locale:

    ```
    locale
    ```

    You will get the following output as the first line if the UTF-8 is properly set:

    ```
    LANG=en_US.UTF-8
    ................
    ................
    ```

    If it is already set, you don't have to execute the following command, otherwise, you have to execute the command to set the encoding.

2. This command will update the list of Ubuntu packages from the server and install the `locales` command if it is not installed already:

    ```
    sudo apt update && sudo apt install locales
    ```

3. The following command ensures that both the basic en_US and en_US.UTF-8 locales are generated and available for use on your system:

    ```
    sudo locale-gen en_US en_US.UTF-8
    ```

4. After generating locales, we can set the system-wide locale using the following command:

    ```
    sudo update-locale LC_ALL=en_US.UTF-8 LANG=en_US.UTF-8
    export LANG=en_US.UTF-8
    ```

5. We are done with configuring the locale now; you can verify the settings by executing the `locale` command again:

    ```
    locale  # verify settings
    ```

After setting the locale in your machine, the next step is to configure Ubuntu repositories. In Ubuntu, there are many software packages available to download. Some packages are free, and some packages are not. The packages are distributed in four main repositories, as follows:

*   `main`: This is supported by Canonical, which is the creator and maintainer of Ubuntu. The packages available in the `main` repo will be free and open-source software.

*   `universe`: This repository has community-maintained free and open-source software.

- `restricted`: This repository contains proprietary drivers or firmware that are not open source, but are still freely redistributable. These are typically essential for enabling specific hardware functionality.

- `multiverse`: This repository contains software restricted by copyright, licensing, or legal issues, and may not be freely usable in all regions or for all purposes.

ROS 2 Jazzy packages are in the Ubuntu `universe` repository, so we have to enable the `universe` repository first.

Enabling the repository in Ubuntu

Ubuntu provides software tools to manage and configure software sources or repositories. These tools help to add or remove third-party software repositories, manage **GNU Privacy Guard** (**GPG**) keys [15] for those repositories, and configure the systems' software sources. We have to install `software-properties-common` first to enable the `universe` repository.

We can install the `software-properties-common` package to get those tools to manage any repository in Ubuntu:

```
sudo apt install software-properties-common
```

After installing this package, we will get a command-line tool called `add-apt-repository`. This command allows us to easily add/remove repositories or **Personal Package Archives** (**PPAs**). A PPA is like a personal software store where developers upload their software [16].

Here is how we use `add-apt-repository` to enable the `universe` repository:

```
sudo add-apt-repository universe
```

After enabling the `universe` repository, let's add the ROS 2 GPG key and `apt sources list`.

Adding the ROS 2 Jazzy GPG key and apt sources list

GPG keys are like digital locks used to keep software safe. They are used to verify the authenticity and integrity of downloaded packages. They ensure that when you download software (such as from a PPA), it's really from the person or company that made it and hasn't been changed by anyone else.

The source list is a system file in Ubuntu that contains information about the software repositories (sources) that our system can use to download and install packages using the apt package manager. This file tells Ubuntu to look for software updates and new software. The location of the sources list file is in `/etc/apt/sources.list`.

ROS 2 provides a package called ros2-apt-source, which can provide keys and apt source configuration for the various ROS repositories. Installing this package will configure ROS 2 repositories
in our system. The repository configuration will be updated automatically when new packages
are released to the ROS repositories. We use a software tool called curl to download this package
and save it into a specific path.

The following command will update the Ubuntu package list from the repository and install curl.
When it does the updating, it will include the universe repository package list as well:

```
sudo apt update && sudo apt install curl -y
```

After installing curl, we can download the latest version of ros2-apt-source package. The following command fetches the latest version of the ROS APT source configuration.

```
export ROS_APT_SOURCE_VERSION=$(curl -s https://api.github.com/repos/ros-
infrastructure/ros-apt-source/releases/latest | grep -F "tag_name" | awk
-F" '{print $4}')
```

After fetching the latest version, we can download ros2-apt-sources using the curl command.

```
curl -L -o /tmp/ros2-apt-source.deb "https://github.com/ros-
infrastructure/ros-apt-source/releases/download/${ROS_APT_SOURCE_VERSION}/
ros2-apt-source_${ROS_APT_SOURCE_VERSION}.$(. /etc/os-release && echo
$VERSION_CODENAME)_all.deb"
```

Now we can install the ros2-apt-source using the following command

```
sudo apt install /tmp/ros2-apt-source.deb
```

We are now done with saving the ROS 2 Jazzy GPG keys and apt sources list. In the next section,
we will see how to install the ROS 2 development tools.

Installing development tools

Installing development tools in ROS 2 helps automatically format code written in C++/Python,
analyze potential errors or inefficiencies before compiling or running, provide build tools/scripts
to set up and build ROS 2 packages, and finally, provide tools for identifying bugs and running
unit tests on ROS code.

The following command installs these tools in Ubuntu 24.04:

```
sudo apt update && sudo apt install ros-dev-tools
```

After installing ROS development tools, let's install ROS 2 Jazzy.

Installing ROS 2 Jazzy

The first step before installing ROS 2 Jazzy packages is to update the list of packages and upgrade the packages that have already been installed. The following commands will update the latest ROS 2 packages and upgrade all the Ubuntu packages so our Ubuntu will be up to date with the currently installed packages:

```
sudo apt update
sudo apt upgrade
```

After doing the update and upgrade operations, you can finally install ROS 2 Jazzy. There are two options: ros-jazzy-desktop installation or ros-jazzy-base installation. If we need most of the features in ROS 2, go with the desktop installation, which is the recommended method. If you only need the core communication libraries, you can go with the ros-jazzy-base installation. It will not have any GUI tools and contains mainly communication libraries, message packages, and command-line tools.

Here is the command to install both methods. You can choose one among these:

- **Desktop installation:**

```
sudo apt install ros-jazzy-desktop
```

- **ROS-Base installation:**

```
sudo apt install ros-jazzy-ros-base
```

The installation of the desktop version of ROS 2 will take longer, depending on the internet speed and PC specification. The ROS-Base version will be installed much faster and it is more preferred in embedded boards.

Congratulations, you are done with the ROS 2 Jazzy installation. So, is it completely done? *No.* To start working with ROS 2 commands and tools, it is important to source the environment by executing the following command:

```
source /opt/ros/jazzy/setup.bash
```

The sourcing of this file makes the ROS 2 tools and packages visible in the current terminal. This command is very important because, without it, ROS 2 commands will not be visible to users.

Here is an easy way to source this line every time we open a new terminal. This will be the best way to start learning and experimenting with ROS 2:

```
echo "source /opt/ros/jazzy/setup.bash" >> /home/$USER/.bashrc
```

This will write source /opt/ros/jazzy/setup.bash to the ~/.bashrc file, which is the configuration file of the Linux terminal. This script will execute whenever a new terminal is created, so we don't have to execute the ROS 2 source command every time we open a new terminal.

Now we have completed all the steps in the installation of ROS 2 Jazzy in Ubuntu 24.04, we can run a test to ensure the ROS 2 environment is set up properly:

1. Open the terminal application in Ubuntu and add one more tab.

2. In the first tab, run this command:

```
ros2 run demo_nodes_cpp talker
```

3. In the second tab run this command:

```
ros2 run demo_nodes_py listener
```

The following image shows the output of the test if everything is configured correctly.

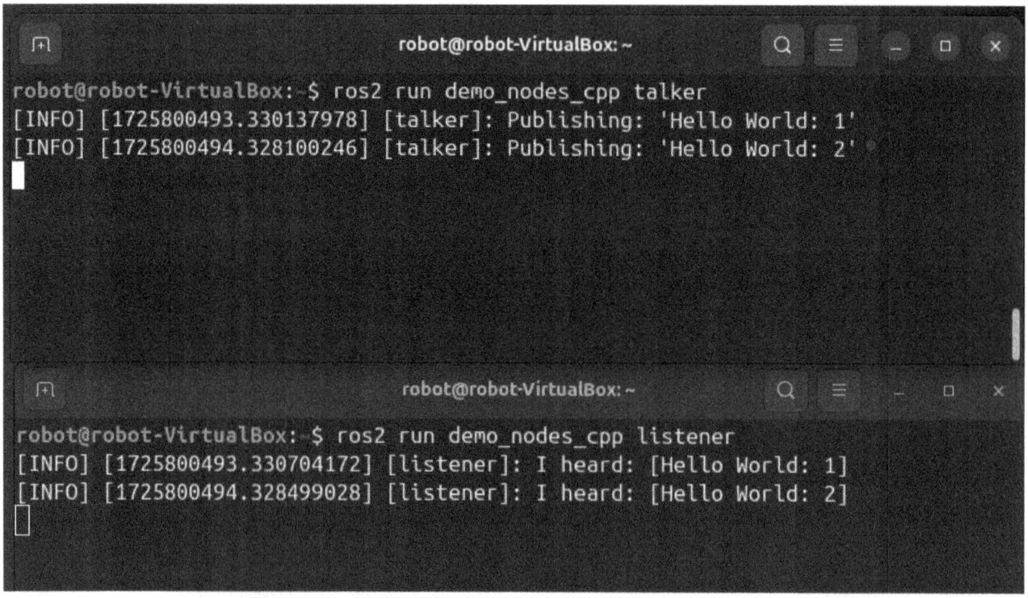

Figure 2.1: ROS 2 talker and listener demo

The above example is simply a publisher/subscriber demo using ROS 2. If this is working fine, it means the installation and configuration are working. If it is not working or if you are getting errors, make sure the sourcing of ROS 2 is correct. You can press *Ctrl + C* to cancel each of the running nodes.

In this section, we discussed the installation of ROS 2 Jazzy in Ubuntu 24.04 LTS. Now let's explore how we can set up ROS 2 Jazzy in other OSs such as Windows and macOS, mainly for development.

Installing ROS 2 Jazzy on Windows 11/10

We can install ROS 2 Jazzy on Windows in multiple ways. Here are the main methods we can follow:

- **Installing ROS 2 Jazzy in VirtualBox/VMware:** We have already discussed installing Ubuntu 24.04 LTS on virtualization software such as VirtualBox. To install ROS 2 Jazzy on it, we can follow the same instructions we have discussed for Ubuntu 24.04 LTS. This is very easy to set up and safe for experimenting with ROS 2 as well. Even if the guest OS crashes, it will not affect the main host OS, which is Windows here.

- **Installing ROS 2 Jazzy in WSL 2:** WSL is a feature in Windows 10/11 that allows the running of a Linux environment on a Windows machine without the need for a virtual machine or dual-boot setup. Here is the official tutorial on how to enable WSL on Windows: [17]. The first version was WSL 1, and the latest is WSL 2. WSL 2 has more features than WSL 1. Using WSL 2, we can install new versions of Ubuntu, such as Ubuntu 24.04 and 22.04. The same installation instructions for ROS 2 Jazzy in Ubuntu 24.04 LTS can be followed to install ROS 2 Jazzy on WSL 2. It is not only command-line-based but can also visualize GUI tools. There is also easy file sharing between Windows and WSL 2.

- **Installing ROS 2 Jazzy in Windows 10 (without any virtualization):** We can install ROS 2 Jazzy natively on Windows 10 but not on Windows 11. This method does not use WSL, but everything runs natively without any layers. The setup instructions are tedious and time-consuming, but if we really want to integrate ROS 2 with any Windows-native application, this is the path to go. Here is the reference for installing ROS 2 Jazzy on Windows 10: [18].

We have explored methods to set up ROS 2 Jazzy on Windows 10/11; now we can discuss methods to install ROS 2 Jazzy natively or virtually on macOS.

Installing ROS 2 Jazzy on macOS

We can install ROS 2 Jazzy on macOS in multiple ways. Here are the main methods we can follow:

- **Installing ROS 2 Jazzy in VirtualBox/VMware/UTM:** If you are using a Mac with an Intel processor, you can install VirtualBox and VMware and install Ubuntu 24.04 LTS and ROS 2 Jazzy on it. If you are using a Mac with an Apple silicon chipset such as M1/M2/M3, you can use VMware or UTM [19] to install Ubuntu 24.04 LTS.

- **Installing ROS 2 Jazzy on macOS (source code)**: If you are interested in running ROS 2 code natively on macOS without any virtualization, then this is the way to go. You can download and build the source code and run it using the following procedure: [20]. These steps are a bit complex, but if your application really needs native support, it's better to follow this approach.

- **Installing ROS 2 Jazzy on Mac (dual boot)**: In this option, we are not installing on macOS, but we are performing dual boot. We can install Ubuntu 24.04 LTS along with macOS on an Intel-based Mac directly using a USB flash drive [21]. You can follow the ROS 2 Jazzy installation instructions thereafter. If you are using an Apple Silicon-based machine, it's better to check Ubuntu Asahi [22]. This is a community project porting Asahi Linux to Ubuntu, which aims for stability and full-featured installation with Apple silicon hardware.

We have seen setting-up instructions and references for ROS 2 Jazzy on Windows, Linux, and MacOS. Here is another method for setting up ROS 2 Jazzy quickly on all operating systems.

Installing ROS 2 Jazzy in Docker

Docker [23] is an open-source technology that helps software developers quickly develop and deploy Windows, Linux, and macOS applications. Docker is also widely used in robotics software development and deployment. The main advantage of using Docker is that we can quickly develop and deploy your ROS-based application in any ROS distribution and Linux distribution. Even if your host OS is Ubuntu 20.04, you can develop ROS 2 applications in ROS 2 Jazzy (which uses Ubuntu 24.04) using Docker. It will help to build and test your ROS 2 application in different ROS 2 distributions. The only requirement is to install Docker software on these operating systems. Docker is one important technology we use in this book. We will discuss Docker in more detail in this section.

Docker is a software tool to create, deploy, and run applications using a technology called containers. Each container in Docker has a lightweight instance of the software environment to run our application. The environment has code, libraries, and dependencies. This helps containers work in different environments. Each container has no separate OS, like the VM we have seen before. The containers work alongside the host Linux kernel and create an abstraction to run different environments. So, like a VM, we do not have to install a full OS to run an application. Before diving into Docker, let us see how to install it on Ubuntu 24.04 LTS as the host machine.

The official installation of Docker is on their website [24]. In this book, we have added an automatic script to do the same. It will install Docker in Ubuntu 24.04 as well as the **NVIDIA Container Toolkit** [25]. The NVIDIA Container Toolkit enables users to build and run GPU-accelerated containers that will work alongside Docker.

Installing Docker and the NVIDIA Container Toolkit

Follow these steps to install Docker and the NVIDIA Container Toolkit:

1. Open the book's GitHub repository and navigate to Chapter02 | ros2_jazzy_docker/
    docker_setup_scripts. You can find setup_docker_ubuntu.sh there. You can run this
    script by opening a terminal inside this folder:

    ```
    chmod +x setup_docker_ubuntu.sh
    ./setup_docker_ubuntu.sh
    ```

    This script helps install all the dependencies of Docker. If you have an NVIDIA graphics
    card and driver installed properly, it will install the NVIDIA Container Toolkit, which gives
    the container graphics acceleration.

2. If everything is installed properly, you can check that Docker is running in the background
    using the following command:

    ```
    systemctl status docker
    ```

    You will get the following output if everything is properly set up:

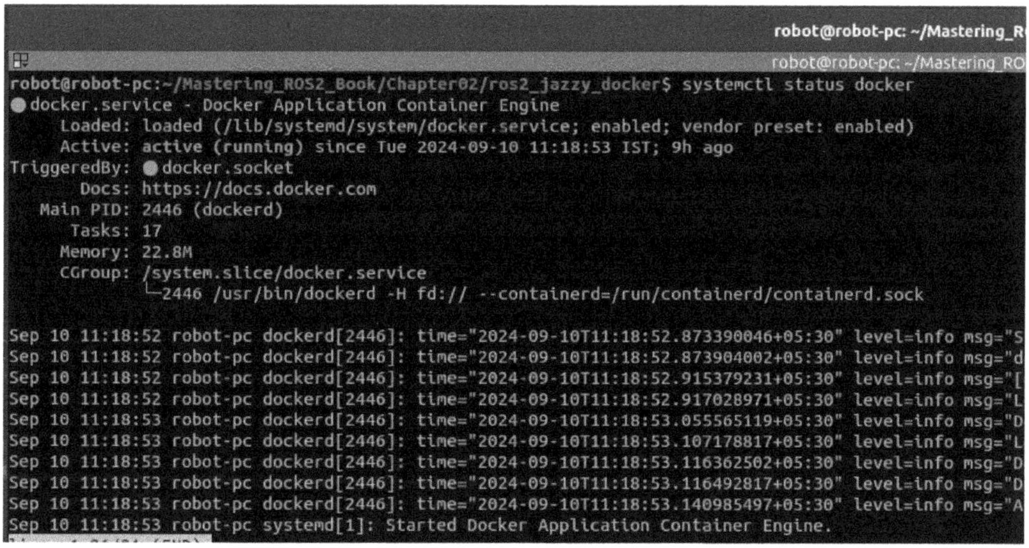

Figure 2.2: Checking Docker status

3. If the Docker status is active, then you can check the docker command in the terminal to make sure everything is okay:

```
docker info
```

You will get the following output. This is all the system details of Docker:

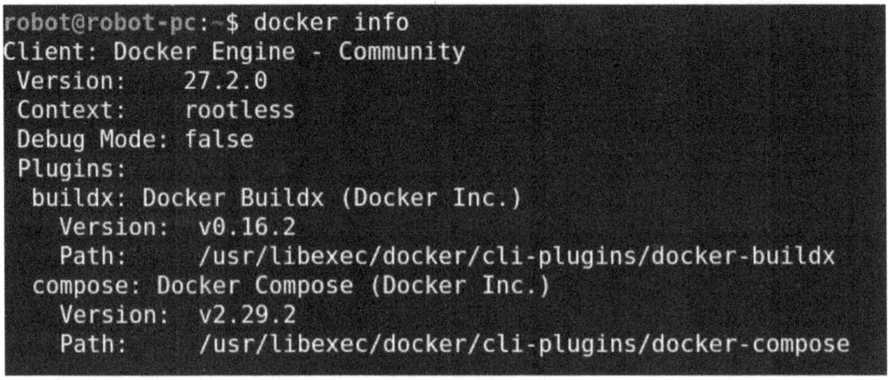

```
robot@robot-pc:~$ docker info
Client: Docker Engine - Community
 Version:    27.2.0
 Context:    rootless
 Debug Mode: false
 Plugins:
  buildx: Docker Buildx (Docker Inc.)
    Version:  v0.16.2
    Path:     /usr/libexec/docker/cli-plugins/docker-buildx
  compose: Docker Compose (Docker Inc.)
    Version:  v2.29.2
    Path:     /usr/libexec/docker/cli-plugins/docker-compose
```

Figure 2.3: Checking Docker information

After making sure everything is okay on our PC, we can start working in ROS 2 Jazzy using Docker and discuss the underlying concepts of Docker along the way.

Running Docker with ROS 2 Jazzy

We must perform a few steps before starting to work with ROS 2 Jazzy on Ubuntu 24.04 LTS. The steps are elaborated on in the following subsections.

Step 1: Pulling the base image and building a custom Docker image

The first step to getting started with Docker is pulling a base image from Docker Hub or another source. Let's first understand what Docker and base images are.

Docker images are files that contain all the application code, dependencies, and runtime environment. We can say that Docker images are templates for creating a Docker container. A **base image** is the base Docker image we are using to build our Docker image. For example, we can take the ROS 2 Jazzy Docker image as a base image, and using that, you can create your image with all dependencies.

Docker Hub [26] provides developers with free access to public Docker images and allows them to upload their own Docker images. These Docker images allow developers to use them as a base image and create containers out of them.

After installing Docker on your machine, you can directly pull the Docker image of ROS 2 Jazzy from Docker Hub. Open Robotics publishes all the ROS 1 and 2 Docker images in their account [27]. You can pull any image from their account.

The following command helps to pull the base image of Jazzy from Docker Hub. This will take you directly into the ROS 2 Jazzy environment without installing anything:

```
docker pull osrf/ros:jazzy-desktop-full
```

After entering this command, you can see the image is getting downloaded, and it will take some time based on the internet speed. Once everything is downloaded, you will have the base image of ROS 2 Jazzy. The next step is to create a container using this image. As we already discussed, Docker images are like templates for the container, so once a container gets started, we will get the ROS 2 Jazzy environment inside it. We mostly work inside the container using a shell because most base images have a lightweight environment, which does not include a desktop environment as we see in Ubuntu 24.04 LTS.

After getting Jazzy's Docker image, we can start creating a container out of it. The following section discusses the steps.

Step 2: Creating a container out of the ROS 2 Jazzy image

To create a container, you can use the following command:

```
docker run -it --name master_ros2 osrf/ros:jazzy-desktop-full bash
```

After running this command in your terminal, you will be able to see a new terminal with a different user, which might be a root user, like the following:

```
root@eafa922c9072:/#
```

This line is the shell of the ROS 2 Jazzy container with the name master_ros2. If you check the command above, you can see that we use the docker run command to create a container. We must add the image name; we can also mention the container name using the --name argument. The --it argument in Docker helps interact with the container by providing text commands through the bash shell. The bash shell tells the Docker container to run the bash command once it starts. So, this command creates a Docker container with an interactive bash shell with a container name of master_ros2. The container's name is optional here. If you do not include a name for the container, it will randomly assign a name. It will be better to put a name so we can start, stop, and delete this container easily.

After creating the container from the image, you will get a ROS 2 Jazzy environment where you can do anything. Your progress will be lost if you delete the container. The changes you make in the container are cached, so you can start and stop the container without losing data. Only rebuilding it will cause you to lose any data that is not mounted on the host system.

You can perform the following test to make sure ROS 2 Jazzy is working correctly.

Execute the sample publisher node in ROS 2, which publishes a Hello World string. This must execute in the Docker terminal:

```
root@eafa922c9072:/# ros2 run demo_nodes_cpp talker
```

If you get a message such as the following, it means it is good to go:

```
[INFO] [1726068567.949579583] [talker]: Publishing: 'Hello World: 1'
[INFO] [1726068568.949567985] [talker]: Publishing: 'Hello World: 2'
[INFO] [1726068569.949575774] [talker]: Publishing: 'Hello World: 3'
```

Now, we can run the next command to subscribe to this message. To run a new shell in Docker, you can follow the next section.

Step 3: Running a new command in the ROS 2 Jazzy container

After creating a container and accessing the shell, we executed the publisher program in ROS 2, and we can see it is working. Now, how do you access another terminal of this container and run the subscriber code? That is where docker exec commands come in. The docker exec commands help us run another program or command in the same container. So, take a new terminal in your host OS and execute the following command to get access to the container terminal:

```
docker exec -it master_ros2 bash
This command attaches a new shell to the running container. Now, you can
source the ROS 2 Jazzy environment using the following command. This
command makes the ROS 2 tools visible in the current terminal.
root@eafa922c9072:/# source /opt/ros/jazzy/setup.bash
```

After sourcing this command, you can run the listener node:

```
root@eafa922c9072:/# ros2 run demo_nodes_cpp listener
```

You will get the following output if everything is working well:

```
[INFO] [1726069883.429240302] [listener]: I heard: [Hello World: 3]
[INFO] [1726069884.429221835] [listener]: I heard: [Hello World: 4]
[INFO] [1726069885.429212317] [listener]: I heard: [Hello World: 5]
```

Press *Ctrl* + *C* to terminate each running node and press *Ctrl* + *D* to exit from the shell. After exiting the shell, the container may still be running in the background. You can stop the container using the command in the next section.

Step 4: Starting, stopping, and removing the container

Here is the command to stop the running container:

```
docker stop master_ros2
```

If you want to find the status of all containers in your computer, use:

```
docker ps -a
```

This will show all the existing containers and their status, such as whether it is stopped or running. After stopping the container, if you want to start it again, you can use the docker start command with the container name:

```
docker start master_ros2
```

After starting the container, you can attach a shell using the docker exec command and access the container's shell:

```
docker exec -it master_ros2 bash
```

So, once you create a container, you do not need to create it again unless you have any changes in the Docker image. You can simply start and stop the container whenever you want.

If you want to remove the current container, you can use the docker rm command. Make sure you stop the container before you delete it:

```
docker stop master_ros2
docker rm master_ros2
```

After deleting the container, you must create a new one using the docker run command again to create a container.

We have explored the basic commands in Docker. Here is a reference to a Docker command cheat sheet that you can use for learning more commands: [28]. Now, let us discuss another important concept in Docker, called a Dockerfile.

Dockerfile for ROS 2 Jazzy

A Dockerfile is a text file containing instructions used to build a custom Docker image. It defines how the custom Docker image should be built. So, why do we need to build a custom Docker image? Imagine you have developed some robot software using ROS 2; running this software requires some dependencies to be installed. The ROS 2 Jazzy base image we used earlier may not have all the dependencies installed. In this scenario, we can write a Dockerfile by putting ROS 2 Jazzy as the base image and adding the dependencies and environment to create a new custom Docker image. The Dockerfile helps us create custom Docker images with dependency packages for running the application. It is similar to a recipe, like a set of instructions for producing an image. We can write the Dockerfile using Dockerfile-specific instructions and build this file using the docker build command.

Here is what a basic ROS 2 Jazzy Dockerfile looks like:

```
#Base Image
FROM osrf/ros:jazzy-desktop-full

#Update and upgrade Ubuntu package and install pip
RUN apt update && apt upgrade -y
RUN apt install -y python3-pip

#Execute command, bash when it create the container
CMD ["/bin/bash"]
```

You can switch to the Chapter02 | ros2_jazzy_docker/docker_basics folder and find this file as a Dockerfile. The name *Dockerfile* is the default name of all Dockerfiles, but you can name it as you prefer, such as Dockerfile.basic, Dockerfile.master_ros2, and so on if you want to keep multiple Dockerfiles for different applications. During the Docker image building, you can mention this Dockerfile name, and it will build the corresponding Dockerfile.

Let's first build the custom Docker image and then explore how the Dockerfile works.

Here is the command used to build a Dockerfile and create a custom image. Open a terminal from the same folder where the Dockerfile is placed and execute this command:

```
docker build -f Dockerfile -t test_ros2:v0.1 .
```

This command reads the Dockerfile, which is mentioned with the -f argument, and -t to mention the image name and its tag. The tag is optional, but it is better to put a tag on each image to identify the version if there are any changes in the Dockerfile. You can find a dot (.) at the end, which refers to the current directory. The Dockerfile will now look for files to copy to the container with respect to this directory.

After a successful build, you can be able to find messages like this in the terminal:

```
[+] Building 0.0s (7/7) FINISHED
 => [internal] load build definition from Dockerfile
 => => transferring dockerfile: 272B
 => [internal] load metadata for docker.io/osrf/ros:jazzy-desktop-full
 => [internal] load .dockerignore
 => => transferring context: 2B
 => [1/3] FROM docker.io/osrf/ros:jazzy-desktop-full
 => CACHED [2/3] RUN apt update && apt upgrade -y
 => CACHED [3/3] RUN apt install -y python3-pip
 => exporting to image
 => => exporting layers
 => => writing image sha256:7f8d1636c4adaf6a64d36291dbc3eeae9c3bd251549
 => => naming to docker.io/library/test_ros2:v0.1
```

Figure 2.4: Dockerfile build messages

After building the image, we can create the container using the docker run command. as we have done previously:

```
docker run -it --name test_ros_dev test_ros2:v0.1
```

After creating the container, you can use the docker exec command to access more shells.

You now have an idea of how to build a ROS 2 Jazzy image by writing our Dockerfile, so let's walk through the Dockerfile we mentioned above.

The Dockerfile starts from a ROS 2 Jazzy base image. The FROM instruction in the Dockerfile is used to mention the base image we are using. After that, we update and upgrade the packages of the base image. This operation uses the RUN instruction in the Dockerfile. Using the RUN instruction, we can install packages in the base image. The update & upgrade operation itself makes the base image a custom image because the new image has the latest packages; now, we are using RUN instruction to install a new Ubuntu package called python3-pip into the custom image. Finally, the CMD instruction specifies the command we must execute when we start the container.

This command can be overridden by providing the command at the end of the docker run command. There is a similar command called ENTRYPOINT in the Dockerfile, which does the same function, but the command cannot be overridden in docker run.

Let us look at some more complex Dockerfiles for ROS 2-based development. You can find basic Dockerfiles that will be good for starting ROS 2 development. If you switch to Chapter02 | ros2_jazzy_docker/docker_basics, you will find Dockerfile.basic. The default user in the ROS 2 Jazzy base image is the root user. This Dockerfile can create a new user, which restricts the permissions and is safer than the root user. The root user has full permission to do anything in Docker. Sticking to a normal user while developing and using the sudo command to get root access will be better.

To build this file and use it, you can use the same Docker commands that you used for the first Dockerfile example.

So far, we have seen Docker containers that interact with shell commands. What about using GUI applications inside the Docker container? Yes, that is possible as well. In the next section, we can see how to run ROS 2 tools with GUI enabled.

Enabling GUI in a ROS 2 Jazzy container

In this section, we will look at how to enable GUI support in Docker. After enabling GUI support, we can work on the GUI and command-line tools of ROS 2 Jazzy. So, let's get started.

Go to Chapter02 | ros2_jazzy_docker/docker_gui; inside this, you can find a similar Dockerfile to Dockerfile.basic. The name of the Dockerfile is Dockerfile.master_ros2. These two files are almost identical, but the difference is in the docker run command. You can see the shell script along with Dockerfile.master_ros2 for building images, creating, starting, stopping, and removing the Docker containers. This will make the process easier than remembering all the Docker commands. Also, all the scripts will take command-line arguments in which we can mention the Dockerfile, container name, and so on to build the Docker image and run the container.

Building the Docker image

We have a script called build_image.sh, which accepts several arguments such as Docker image name, username, and so on, and uses the docker build command to build the Dockerfile.

We will discuss the usage of the script inside the folder first. Before running the script, create a folder in your home folder called master_ros2_ws/src to keep your ROS 2 packages. You can use the following command to do this:

```
mkdir -p ~/master_ros2_ws/src
```

After creating this folder, you can start building the Docker image using the following command. Make sure you are executing inside the docker_gui folder:

```
./build_image.sh ros2_gui:v0.1 master_ros2_ws robot
```

In this script, the first argument is the *custom Docker image name with version*, the second argument is the *name of the ROS 2 workspace*, which will be discussed in the upcoming section, and the third is the *username* we want to create inside Docker.

After building the image, you can create a container using the following script:

```
./create_container.sh ros2_gui:v0.1 master_ros2_ws ros2_dev
```

When executing this script, we must provide the *image name* we have created, the *ROS 2 workspace name* in the host machine, and the *name of the container*. The script will check if you have an NVIDIA graphics card and its driver installed on your Ubuntu OS. If installed, it will use graphics acceleration from an NVIDIA card. We are only using the docker run command inside this script but with multiple arguments for graphics acceleration, mounting volume, and ROS 2 workspace in our host OS. Creating a container like this provides the environment for running a GUI app from the terminal, and the GUI will pop up.

You will get a shell after creating a container. You can run the following command to check whether the GUI is enabled or not in the container:

```
robot@robot-pc:~/master_ros2_ws$ rviz2
```

This will start RViz2, which is one of the popular ROS 2 GUI tools available. You can see RViz2 like this on the screen:

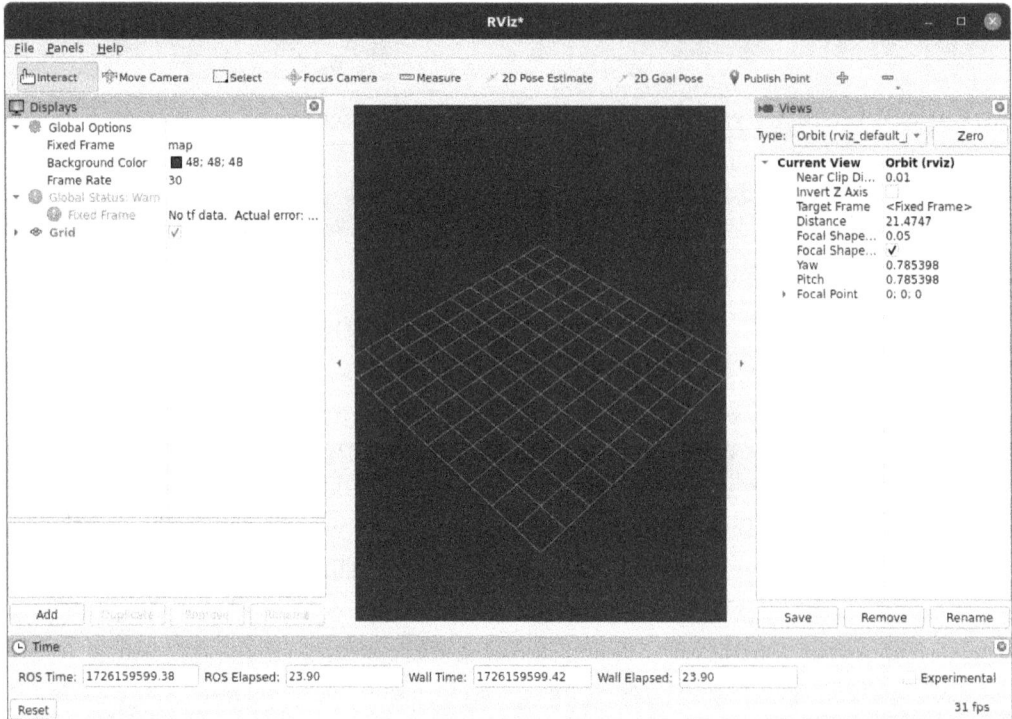

Figure 2.5: Rviz from Docker

Congratulations! We are done creating a Docker container with GUI enabled. The rest of the script helps to start, stop, and remove containers. So, let's see how it is used.

Start a new terminal of the running container. The argument you must provide is the container name, which is ros2_dev:

```
./start_container.sh ros2_dev
```

After starting the new terminal from the container, you will notice that it is in the path of the ROS 2 workspace we created on the host machine:

```
robot@robot-pc:~/master_ros2_ws$
```

This `master_ros2_ws` folder is not inside the Docker container but is mounted from the local machine. If you remember, we created a ROS 2 workspace on the local machine, right? That folder is what we can access inside the Docker. We can do this by volume mounting the host OS folder during Docker container creation using the `docker run` command.

This is an excellent way of working with different ROS 2 distributions on the same workspace using Docker abstraction. The source code is in the host OS, but we can mount the ROS 2 workspace inside the container and build our source code with different ROS 2 distributions, such as ROS 2 Jazzy, Iron, and Humble.

We can even use an IDE such as VS Code to do remote development using a Docker container. So, in short, Docker provides an opportunity for robotics developers to quickly create ROS 2 applications and test them in any of the ROS distributions.

To stop the running container `ros2_dev`, we can use `stop_container.sh` inside the `docker_gui` folder. Run this script and provide the container name as an argument to stop any running container:

```
./stop_container.sh ros2_dev
```

We can run `remove_container.sh` with the container name as the argument for removing the container:

```
./remove_container.sh ros2_dev
```

After creating the new terminal from the Docker container, you can source the following shell script, which is already present in the ROS 2 jazzy base image. This script has a command to source the ROS 2 environment:

```
source /ros_entrypoint.sh
```

We have gone through some important topics of Docker that we will be using for the rest of the chapter. You can also refer to [29] [39] for more information on the ROS 2 Docker setup.

So far, we have seen how to work with a single-container application. Next, we will see how to work with multi-container applications, meaning ROS 2 nodes will work in separate containers, and these two nodes running on these different containers will communicate.

Docker Compose with ROS 2 Jazzy

Docker Compose [*30*] is another useful feature in Docker for robotics applications. We have worked with individual Docker containers using Docker command-line tools. What about working with multiple containers? For example, in a robotics application, we have a front-end application that is working on a JavaScript framework, a ros 2 navigation application, and a deep learning application to interact with this navigation application. In this situation, it will be better to keep all three kinds of applications in different Docker images and start communicating with each other separately from different containers. In this kind of scenario, docker-compose is a better option, as it helps to create and manage multiple containers with a single command. We can also configure the Docker network settings so that all these containers can communicate using ROS 2 DDS. The docker-compose part of the command-line tool is more like a plugin. This has already been installed in our Docker setup script.

We can write a docker-compose configuration file that contains the configuration of these multiple containers, including the Docker image, container name, and other configurations mentioned in the docker run command. Once these configuration files are written, we can start these containers with a single command.

You can find a set of Docker Compose configurations in the Chapter02 | ros2_jazzy_docker | docker_compose folder. The default name of each docker-compose configuration file is docker-compose.yml. You can find a basic docker compose file in this folder, and this is how it will look:

```yaml
version: '3.8'
services:
  talker:
    image: osrf/ros:jazzy-desktop-full
    command: ros2 run demo_nodes_cpp talker

  listener:
    image: osrf/ros:jazzy-desktop-full
    command: ros2 run demo_nodes_cpp listener
    depends_on:
      - talker
```

If you check this configuration file, you can find the version of Docker Compose at the beginning of the file. After that, you can see the services section, which defines the containers starting as part of this compose file. In this example, talker and listener are the two containers starting with the services section. If you check this container, it uses ros-jazzy-desktop-full as the image and runs publisher and listener nodes in ROS 2 for testing. The depends_on tag says that the listener service depends on the talker. docker-compose will start the talker service first before the listener starts.

To start the docker-compose file, you can use the following command. Make sure you are inside the docker-compose code folder:

```
docker compose up
```

It will start and run all the services defined in the .yml file. By allowing you to define services, networks, and volumes in a single YAML configuration file, it simplifies the process of managing multi-container Docker applications.

You will find the output of this command as follows:

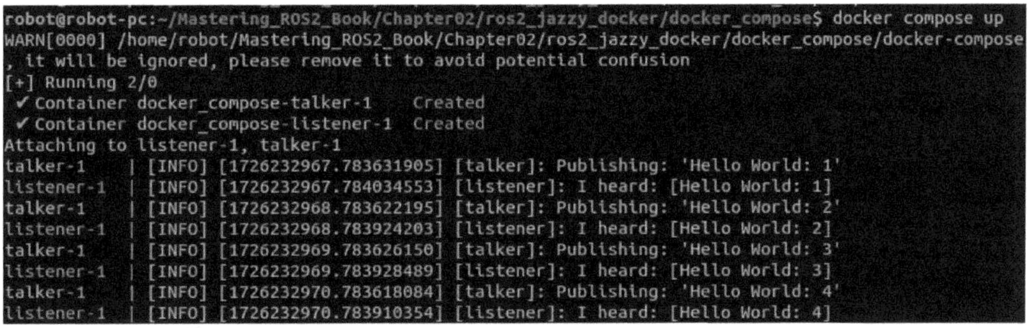

```
robot@robot-pc:~/Mastering_ROS2_Book/Chapter02/ros2_jazzy_docker/docker_compose$ docker compose up
WARN[0000] /home/robot/Mastering_ROS2_Book/Chapter02/ros2_jazzy_docker/docker_compose/docker-compose
, it will be ignored, please remove it to avoid potential confusion
[+] Running 2/0
 ✔ Container docker_compose-talker-1    Created
 ✔ Container docker_compose-listener-1  Created
Attaching to listener-1, talker-1
talker-1    | [INFO] [1726232967.783631905] [talker]: Publishing: 'Hello World: 1'
listener-1  | [INFO] [1726232967.784034553] [listener]: I heard: [Hello World: 1]
talker-1    | [INFO] [1726232968.783622195] [talker]: Publishing: 'Hello World: 2'
listener-1  | [INFO] [1726232968.783924203] [listener]: I heard: [Hello World: 2]
talker-1    | [INFO] [1726232969.783626150] [talker]: Publishing: 'Hello World: 3'
listener-1  | [INFO] [1726232969.783928489] [listener]: I heard: [Hello World: 3]
talker-1    | [INFO] [1726232970.783618084] [talker]: Publishing: 'Hello World: 4'
listener-1  | [INFO] [1726232970.783910354] [listener]: I heard: [Hello World: 4]
```

Figure 2.6: Docker Compose output

You can see both the talker and listener service talking to each other from different containers.

If you want to stop the service, you can use:

```
docker compose down
```

Make sure your terminal is in the docker_compose folder.

You can also find a detailed docker-compose file from the same folder called docker-compose1. yml. This file shows more arguments that can be used in the configuration file. You can rename this file to docker-compose.yml and execute the docker compose up/down command.

Installing ROS 2 Jazzy in robots

We have seen how to set up ROS 2 Jazzy in development machines, and now we can see how to set it up in robots.

In robots, we mostly use a **single-board computer (SBC)** or a custom-developed board with a computer module. If you examine the available popular SBCs and compute modules, you'll find both the x86_64 and ARM64 architectures. You can install Ubuntu on these platforms and work with Docker. Two popular boards used in robots are Raspberry Pi and NVIDIA Jetson series boards.

You can find the latest Raspberry Pi boards and modules at [*31*]. The latest Jetson series boards and modules can be found at [*32*].

You can install Ubuntu 24.04 LTS 64-bit in the latest Raspberry Pi, and this is the tier 1 OS for ROS 2 Jazzy, meaning you can install ROS 2 from the binaries directly using the ROS 2 install script in the Chapter 2 code GitHub folder for this chapter. The ARM 32-bit OS is tier 3 for ROS 2 Jazzy; we must install ROS 2 by building source code. The default OS that comes with Raspberry Pi is called Raspberry Pi OS, which is a Debian-based OS that only has tier 3 support. However, you can set up Docker on Raspberry Pi OS using the Docker setup script and work on ROS 2 Jazzy in Ubuntu 24.04 (tier 1 OS) from Docker.

Here is a reference to installing Ubuntu 24.04 LTS on a Raspberry Pi board: [*33*].

You can also use Docker to set up ROS 2 Jazzy in Raspberry Pi using the following commands, as we have already seen:

```
docker pull ros:jazzy-ros-core
docker run -it --rm ros:jazzy-ros-core
```

The Jetson series boards have Ubuntu by default, which is customized with NVIDIA drivers and the Jetpack SDK [*34*]. NVIDIA maintains its Debian packages for ROS 2. You can install their ROS 2 Jazzy on the host OS, or you can use Docker to use ROS 2 Jazzy. NVIDIA also provides jetson-containers [*35*] to build Docker images with other libraries. There are AI libraries, ROS, vision, and so on here, and you can choose any combination along with a script provided by NVIDIA. This is extremely useful for robotics applications.

Here is an example of using jetson-containers with multiple libraries of robotics and AI:

```
jetson-containers build --name=my_container pytorch transformers
ros:jazzy-desktop
```

Working with Docker in the robot computer will be the better approach because it helps with the easier deployment of robot software without worrying about dependencies. It also helps to update the robot software easily by pulling a new image.

We have seen different methods of installing ROS 2 Jazzy in development machines and robot computers. The next section is about learning different concepts and tools in ROS 2.

Mastering ROS 2 tools and concepts

In this section, we will explore important concepts in ROS 2 using a hands-on approach. We must understand all these concepts before we start programming using ROS 2 Jazzy. We will see different ROS 2 tools along with understanding ROS 2 concepts. We will explain each concept using an example.

Before jumping into the concepts, we must understand why we use ROS 2 for robot programming. ROS 2 is a software framework that provides a set of libraries, tools, and capabilities for building your robotics applications. So, what is the fundamental feature of ROS 2 bringing to robot programming? It is inter-process communication, meaning the communication between the different processes in the OS. As you know, a robot can have multiple sensors, actuators, and computers. The robot sensor data has to be acquired and then processed to generate control signals to control the actuators. Generally, these operations may not be included in a single process running on the computer. The main reason is that if any operation fails, it can crash the entire process. We write multiple processes to accomplish this operation. That is where ROS 2 brings the power of inter-process communication; it can provide you with different APIs in your C++/Python and help these programs exchange data in different fashions. The data may be sent continuously to the other program, like a request-and-response interaction. This is a core feature that ROS 2 gives to robotics developers. All other features are built on top of this core feature. So, let us dive into the ROS 2 concepts.

First, we can see how to run a program in ROS 2. We are not writing a new program and running it; instead, we are trying to run an existing program, which is available in ROS 2 when you install it.

How to run ROS 2 nodes/apps in your robot

As we already know, using ROS 2, we can create our own robotics nodes/apps for performing specific tasks in the robot. We are going to see how exactly we can run these nodes next:

1. ROS 2 provides a command-line tool called ros2. This tool helps us perform multiple operations in the ROS 2 framework. Let's start with your ROS 2 installed machine; it can be your host OS or Docker container.

Take a terminal first, and make sure you source the ROS 2 environment. For demonstration, we are using a Docker container that was already created with the GUI in the past session. Execute this script from the docker_gui folder:

```
./start_container.sh ros2_dev
```

2. Source the ROS 2 environment using the following command:

```
source /ros_entrypoint.sh
```

3. Execute the ros2 command in your terminal:

```
$ ros2
```

If your ROS 2 environment is correctly set, you will see this output in the terminal:

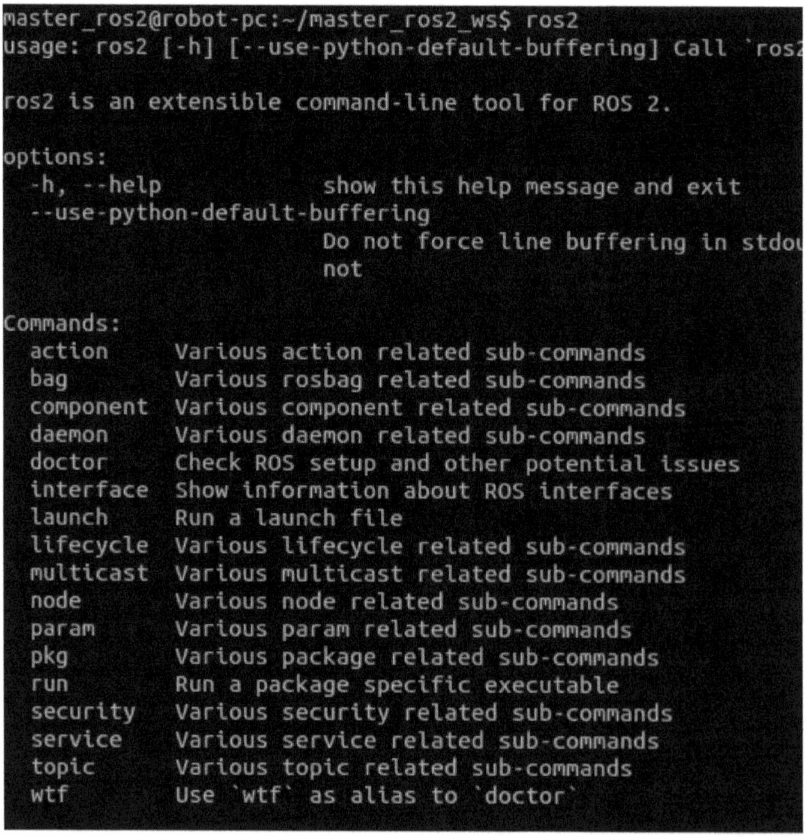

```
master_ros2@robot-pc:~/master_ros2_ws$ ros2
usage: ros2 [-h] [--use-python-default-buffering] Call 'ros2

ros2 is an extensible command-line tool for ROS 2.

options:
  -h, --help              show this help message and exit
  --use-python-default-buffering
                          Do not force line buffering in stdou
                          not

Commands:
  action     Various action related sub-commands
  bag        Various rosbag related sub-commands
  component  Various component related sub-commands
  daemon     Various daemon related sub-commands
  doctor     Check ROS setup and other potential issues
  interface  Show information about ROS interfaces
  launch     Run a launch file
  lifecycle  Various lifecycle related sub-commands
  multicast  Various multicast related sub-commands
  node       Various node related sub-commands
  param      Various param related sub-commands
  pkg        Various package related sub-commands
  run        Run a package specific executable
  security   Various security related sub-commands
  service    Various service related sub-commands
  topic      Various topic related sub-commands
  wtf        Use `wtf` as alias to `doctor`
```

Figure 2.7: ros2 command-line output

The ros2 command is the main command in ROS 2, which comes with sub-commands, as shown in *Figure 2.7*. You can find sub-commands such as run, which helps to run a specific ROS 2 node. From the above list, you can identify the use of each sub-command. You can find the usage of each sub-command by simply entering it into the terminal. For example, if you enter ros2 run, you will see the sub-arguments we must pass through this terminal. The ros2 command is the main command of the ROS 2 CLI.

4. To run a specific program/executable of ROS 2, use the following command:

```
ros2 run ros_pkg_name executable_name
```

Eg:

```
ros2 run demo_nodes_cpp talker
```

In this example, demo_nodes_cpp is a ROS 2 package, and talker is the name of the C++ program executable inside this package. demo_nodes_cpp is installed along with ROS 2 Jazzy.

You may wonder what a ROS 2 package is. So, let us see what a ROS 2 package is and continue with the ros2 run command.

What is a ROS 2 package?

A **ROS 2 package** is a software organization within the ROS 2 framework. It contains the necessary code and files to implement specific functionalities or features in a robotic application. Typically, a ROS 2 package comprises nodes (programs that execute computations), libraries, configuration files, launch files, and other resources such as message and service definitions.

Everything in ROS 2 is modeled inside a package. A package is simply a folder that we can create using the ros2 pkg command, and it will have files such as package.xml, CMakeLists.txt, and so on to keep the identity of the package. The information, such as the package's name, dependencies of the package, and so on, will be included in these files.

When we install ROS 2, we will get its core packages by default. We will also get tons of ROS 2 packages from the community. These packages are easily redistributed via Git or can be added to ROS 2 official repos, and you can install their binaries.

A useful feature of ROS 2 is that it is easy to reuse the packages built by other developers in your robot. Each package is created for specific applications. For example, the demo_nodes_cpp package in ROS 2 contains ROS 2 C++ examples.

We will see more details of the structure of a ROS 2 package in the upcoming sections.

So, returning to the ros2 run command, you can see the first argument we mention is the package name and then the executable name. If you are writing a C++ program using ROS 2, it should be compiled, and we will get an executable. In this example, that executable is what we are mentioning in this command. These demo examples have already been installed with ROS 2. If you create a ROS 2 package with C++ programs, we can compile those programs and build the executable. In the next chapter, we will learn how to make a package and put C++ code inside the package.

When you run this example command, you can see the executable start running:

```
[INFO] [1726326377.958376860] [talker]: Publishing: 'Hello World: 1'
[INFO] [1726326378.958355664] [talker]: Publishing: 'Hello World: 2'
[INFO] [1726326379.958358086] [talker]: Publishing: 'Hello World: 3'
```

Once the executable starts running, a ROS 2 node will be created.

What is a ROS node?

When you start a ROS 2 executable, it will run and become a process. This process is called a **ROS 2 node**. So, when we write a program in C++/Python using ROS 2 APIs and compile/build and run the executable, we will get a ROS 2 node. A ROS 2 node is a single process that performs some sort of computation, such as collecting sensor data, processing that data, or other operations in the robot PC or the operator PC. Nodes in ROS 2 can publish and subscribe to diverse data types with the help of underlying DDS middleware. A robotic application will have a set of ROS 2 nodes for different purposes. Each node can be launched using ros2 run; other techniques, such as ros2 launch file, allow you to launch multiple nodes in one command.

To inspect the complete details of a ROS 2 node, we can use the ros2 node command. This command gives us information about the specific node we are mentioning and a list of nodes running in the OS.

If you run the ros2 node list command in a new terminal, it will list the running nodes. In this example, the output of the command is /talker.

/talker is not our executable name; instead, the node name is what we give inside the code itself. It is not visible to us now. In the next chapter, we will demonstrate the same. You can give any name to your node, and no two nodes will have the same name. Their names should be unique!

The following command will list out details of these nodes, which include the *Subscribers, Publisher, Services*, and *Actions*:

```
ros2 node info /talker
```

Here is how we will see the output of the same:

```
Subscribers:
Publishers:
   /chatter: std_msgs/msg/String
Service Servers:
Service Clients:
Action Servers:
Action Clients:
```

In this output, there are no Subscribers, Service Servers, Clients, or Action Servers, but you can find a Publisher name, /chatter. We do not know much about ROS 2 Publisher, Subscribers, Services, and Actions yet. These terms refer to communication patterns between the different nodes. Understanding these terms will be better before returning to this point.

What is a ROS topic?

We have seen the Publisher and Subscriber terms in the above command output. A publisher in a node can send a type of data, and the subscriber can also receive a type of data. The nodes publish and subscribe to several types of data through **ROS topics**. ROS topics are a medium of communication between different nodes. It is called a *named data bus* in which nodes can exchange various kinds of data. We can create any number of topics in our ROS node and send various kinds of data, such as integer, float, array, image, and so on. We can also subscribe to various kinds of data inside a ROS node. ROS topics are one communication type we use in ROS nodes. Communication with ROS topics is asynchronous, meaning the publisher can send continuous data without waiting for the receiving node. The publisher can't even know much about who is receiving the data. We can say it is an N-to-M communication mechanism.

In the above example, the topic for publishing data is /chatter(std_msgs/msg/String). Along with the topic name, you can see the data type it is publishing: a string. In the next section, we will learn more about the different ROS data types.

We can now start a subscriber node called listener, which is subscribed to the same /chatter topic. Here is the command to run the listener node:

```
ros2 run demo_nodes_cpp listener
```

Make sure you have opened a new terminal for running this command. Also, do not confuse the executable name and node name here. The node name is defined inside the code and the executable is just a binary file. In this example, node name and executable are same, but they will not be the same in all cases.

You will get the following output with the listener node:

```
[INFO] [1726333039.114079927] [listener]: I heard: [Hello World: 1]
[INFO] [1726333040.113948341] [listener]: I heard: [Hello World: 2]
[INFO] [1726333041.113945517] [listener]: I heard: [Hello World: 3]
```

After running the `talker` and `listener` nodes, you can run the following command:

```
ros2 node list
```

And the output will be:

```
/listener
/talker
```

This output shows that, currently, two nodes are running in our system. If we try the `ros2 node info /listener` command, it will show the topic the `/listener` node is subscribed to:

```
Subscribers:
  /chatter: std_msgs/msg/String
Publishers:
```

If we want to see how the nodes are communicating, we can use a ROS 2 GUI tool called rqt. Open a new terminal and type rqt, and you will see an empty window. Go to **Plugins | Introspection | Node Graph**. You can see the output like this:

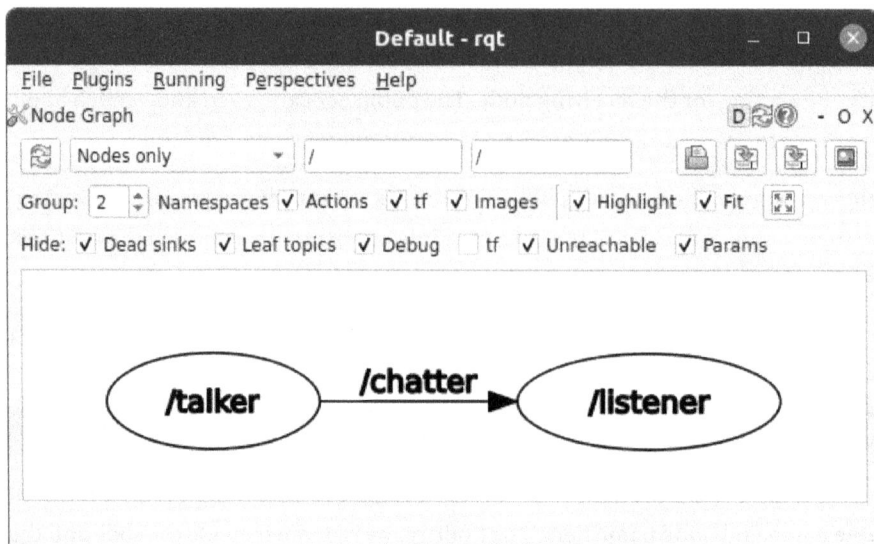

Figure 2.8: rqt node graph

The arrow indicates that the talker is publishing a topic named /chatter, and the /listener is subscribing to this topic. This visualization is called a **node graph** or **ROS computation graph**. After visualizing the graph, you can close the window or press *Ctrl* + *C* to close it via the terminal.

The concept of ROS computation graphs is important to understand, so let us see more on this topic.

What is a ROS computation graph?

The **ROS computation graph** refers to a peer-to-peer network of ROS processes that process data together. It shows how the various system components, such as nodes, topics, services, and actions, interrelate and interchange data. The computation graph is also the least visible layer of the architecture in a ROS system. It reveals how information flows and how various parts of the software running on the robot interact.

Visualizing the computation graph will help us understand how the nodes communicate and find any problems in the communication.

Coming back to ROS 2 topics, assuming that the talker and listener are running on two terminals, take a third terminal and check the following command, which is mainly for checking the ROS 2 topics:

```
ros2 topic list
```

This command will list the topics that are currently published/subscribed to.

Here is what the output looks like:

```
/chatter
```

There is only one active topic now, which is /chatter.

Another useful command is:

```
ros2 topic echo /chatter
```

This command will subscribe to the topic /chatter and print out the data. The echo command prints messages from the specified topic. The echo can be shown as a command.

You can see the following kind of output from this:

```
data: 'Hello World: 1'
---
data: 'Hello World: 2'
--
```

We can try some commonly used sub-commands with the ros2 topic command.

The following command will print the information about the given topic. It will show how many publishers and subscribers there are for this topic, as well as the data type of this topic:

```
ros2 topic info /chatter
The output will look likeType: std_msgs/msg/String
Publisher count: 1
Subscription count: 2
```

We can even create a topic and publish data through this command. Here is an example of the usage:

```
ros2 topic pub /chatter std_msgs/msg/String "data: 'Hello, ROS 2'" -r 1
```

This command mentions the topic name, message type, and Hello, ROS 2!, the string data to publish.

If you are running the talker node, it is already publishing the /chatter topic with string data. If you are publishing another string data type on the same topic, both data strings can be seen in the /chatter topic, and you can see both publishing if you are subscribing to this topic. If you check the terminal messages of the listener node, you will be able to find messages like this:

```
[INFO] [1726339920.694865075] [listener]: I heard: [Hello, ROS 2]
[INFO] [1726339920.853698114] [listener]: I heard: [Hello World: 1]
[INFO] [1726339921.694919145] [listener]: I heard: [Hello, ROS 2]
[INFO] [1726339921.853678698] [listener]: I heard: [Hello World: 2]
```

We can publish different message types on the very same topic. The subscriber will only show the message type to which it is subscribed.

For example, the following commands allow you to publish a string and integer message type to the /chatter topic:

```
ros2 topic pub /chatter std_msgs/msg/String "data: 'Hello, ROS 2'" -r 1

ros2 topic pub /chatter std_msgs/msg/Int32 "data: '2'" -r 1
```

After running both commands in two terminals, run the listener node using the following command:

```
ros2 run demo_nodes_cpp listener
```

You can find that only the string data is subscribed. If you create a subscriber node for Int32, it will subscribe only to the published integer data. The ros2 topic echo topic will not work because of multiple message types. Mixing different message types on the same topic is discouraged and can cause runtime errors.

You can read more about the usage of ros2 topic at [36].

Next, we can discuss **ROS messages**, that are used in ROS topics.

What is a ROS message?

In ROS 2, messages are the data structures used for communication between nodes. Messages are sent over topics (for publish/subscribe communication), through services (for request/response), or in actions (for long-running tasks). These are also ROS interfaces. A message in ROS 2 defines the type and structure of the transmitted data. These messages are defined in the .msg files, where each message combines different fields that represent specific data types (integers, strings, arrays, etc.). ROS 2 provides a set of packages dedicated to predefined message types such as std_msgs, sensor_msgs, and geometry_msgs. The std_msgs message types contain data types such as string, integer, etc. The sensor_msgs message types have a data type for images and point clouds, whereas geometry_msgs contains messages for storing poses, velocity, etc.

ROS 2 messages will have multiple fields inside them. It may not be a single string, but it can be a combination of multiple data types. The ros2 interface command is used to get the list of fields inside the ROS 2 message.

Here is an example of listing the fields inside std_msgs/msg/String:

```
ros2 interface show std_msgs/msg/String.
```

Here is the output:

```
string data
```

So, to fill the std_msgs/msg/String message with string data, you have to fill the data field inside the message.

You can find out more about ROS 2 messages from [37].

Now we can explore the concept of ROS services and actions with some examples.

What is a ROS service and how does Turtlesim work?

In ROS 2, a **service** is a communication model based on a call-and-response model. It involves bidirectional communication: a client sends a request to a server, and the server processes that request and sends back a response. This concept is different from ROS topics, which are unidirectional and follow a publish-subscribe model. While the underlying pattern of services is synchronous, service calls in ROS 2 can be implemented asynchronously at the node level, allowing the client to continue processing while waiting for a response.

Let's look at an example service use case. If we want to turn something *on/off* in the robot, you can write a service for this, and when the client calls this service, it will execute the turn operation *on/off*. There are many use cases for ROS services in robots. The following figure illustrates a ROS 2 service server and client. In this diagram, two service clients interact with a ROS service server.

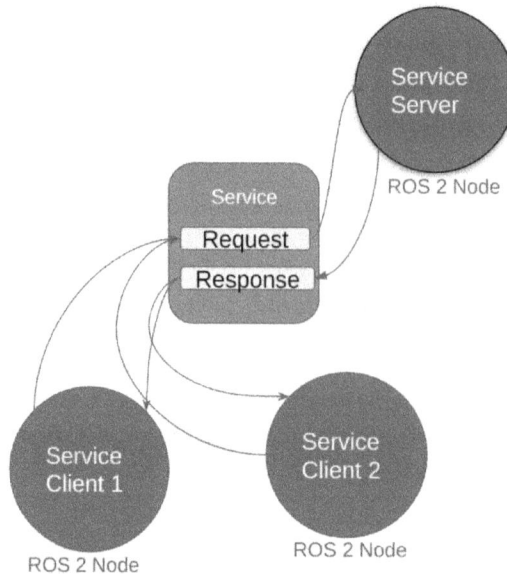

Figure 2.9: ROS 2 service server and client

Working with examples can help us learn more about the ROS 2 service. To get hands-on with the ROS 2 service, we can use **Turtlesim**, a pre-installed 2D simulator in ROS 2 packages. Turtlesim is a ROS 2 node with topics, services, parameters, and actions. We can use this node to learn about all the ROS 2 concepts.

You can use the following node to start turtlesim:

```
ros2 run turtlesim turtlesim_node
```

You will see the following window if the command works correctly:

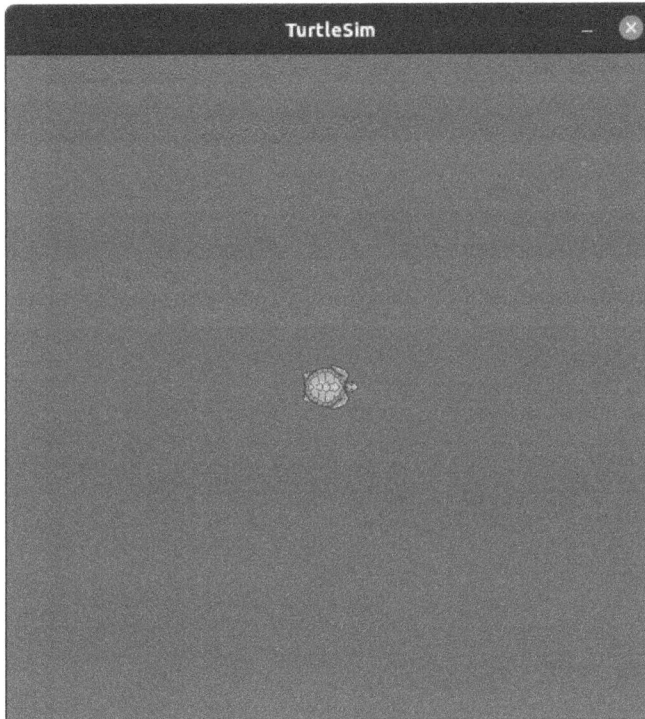

Figure 2.10: Turtlesim 2D simulator

Turtlesim in ROS 2 is a graphical 2D simulator packaged with the ROS 2 desktop installation. It is mainly used for learning and experimentation with ROS 2 concepts. These tools help to understand how the ROS 2 communication concepts work.

Turtlesim is a ROS 2 node with a GUI. In this simulator, you can see a turtle at the center. The turtle is a robot; we can send velocity commands to move it. We can interact with this simulator using ROS 2 topics, services, parameters, and actions. The turtle is equipped with a pen, which can be enabled/disabled using a ROS service. The turtle will draw on the surface when it moves in the 2D plane. The color of the pen is configurable, too. It has a color sensor that will publish the color it detects from the plane, and values will be published to a topic. The drawing made by the turtle can be cleared using ROS 2 services. We can even reset the entire turtlesim simulator by calling the service.

Let us learn how a ROS 2 service works in ROS 2. Like ROS 2 topic command-line tools, there are command-line tools to analyze ROS 2 services.

We can start listing the nodes first using the following command:

```
ros2 node list
```

And you will get the node as:

```
/turtlesim
```

If you run:

```
ros2 node info /turtlesim
```

you will get the complete details of the /turtlesim node. The output is given below:

```
/turtlesim
  Subscribers:
    /turtle1/cmd_vel: geometry_msgs/msg/Twist
  Publishers:
    /turtle1/color_sensor: turtlesim/msg/Color
    /turtle1/pose: turtlesim/msg/Pose
  Service Servers:
    /clear: std_srvs/srv/Empty
    /kill: turtlesim/srv/Kill
    /reset: std_srvs/srv/Empty
    /spawn: turtlesim/srv/Spawn
    /turtle1/set_pen: turtlesim/srv/SetPen
    /turtle1/teleport_absolute: turtlesim/srv/TeleportAbsolute
    /turtle1/teleport_relative: turtlesim/srv/TeleportRelative
  Service Clients:
  Action Servers:
    /turtle1/rotate_absolute: turtlesim/action/RotateAbsolute
  Action Clients:
```

If you check the output in the Service Server section, you can find a set of services such as /clear, /kill, /reset, /spawn, etc. This says that Turtlesim already has these services, and you can call these services from a service client. You can also find the service data type along with the service name. The service data type will have two entries. One is for the *request*, and one is for the *response*. There can be multiple fields in the request and response. If you want to see what is inside the service type, you can use the following command.

For example, if you want to understand what fields are inside the /spawn service, you can use the following command:

```
ros2 interface show turtlesim/srv/Spawn
```

You will get the following output:

```
float32 x
float32 y
float32 theta
string name # Optional.  A unique name will be created and returned if
this is empty
---
string name
```

The /spawn service creates a new turtle in the turtlesim. If you call the spawn service with the position of the new turtle and name, it will create a new turtle and return the name as a response if the service call is successful. The first part of the service definition is the request and the second is the response. These two parts are divided by - - - lines.

Now, let us call this service from the command line itself.

Here is the syntax for calling a service. The ros2 service call with *service name*, *type*, and necessary data in the fields is the way to call a service from the command line. This command works as a ros 2 service client:

```
ros2 service call <service_name> <service_type> <arguments>
```

Here is the example command to create a new turtle in the turtlesim. If you call the /spawn service of turtlesim with x, y, and theta values of the new turtle, it will create a new turtle in the corresponding pose. The origin is the top-left corner of the turtlesim, with the horizontal axis being X and the vertical axis being Y:

```
ros2 service call /spawn turtlesim/srv/Spawn "{x: 2, y: 2, theta: 0.2,
name: 'turtle5'}"
```

After executing the command, you can see the following message if the service call is okay:

```
waiting for service to become available...
requester: making request: turtlesim.srv.Spawn_Request(x=2.0, y=2.0,
theta=0.2, name='turtle5')
response:
turtlesim.srv.Spawn_Response(name='turtle5')
```

After this message in the terminal, you can find a new turtle just below the turtle at the center, as shown:

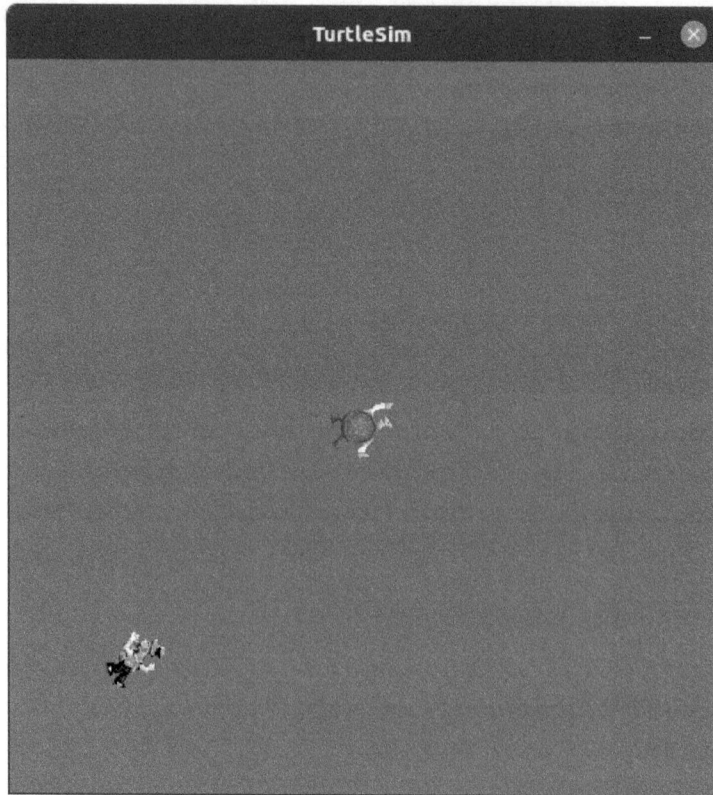

Figure 2.11: Turtlesim with spawned turtle

You can list the services that nodes provide using the following command:

```
ros2 service list -t
```

The -t says to show the *service type* along with the name of the service.

You will most likely get the following output:

```
/clear [std_srvs/srv/Empty]
/kill [turtlesim/srv/Kill]
/reset [std_srvs/srv/Empty]
/spawn [turtlesim/srv/Spawn]
```

Here are a few other service call examples you can try with turtlesim.

The following command will reset the entire turtlesim. When resetting the turtlesim, all spawned turtles will be cleared, all the drawings will also be reset, and the turtle position will reset to the center:

```
ros2 service call /reset std_srvs/srv/Empty {}
```

The following command will clear the drawing made by the turtle:

```
ros2 service call /clear std_srvs/srv/Empty {}
```

If we want to tele-operate the turtle using a keyboard, there is a node for the same. The following command will start the node, and you can move the robot using the keyboard arrow keys:

```
ros2 run turtlesim turtle_teleop_key
```

This node simply publishes linear and angular velocity to /turtle1/cmd_vel, and the message type is geometry_msgs/msg/Twist. This topic is subscribing to the *turtlesim* and moving the robot based on the velocity commands. So, in this case, /teleop_turtle is the publisher node and turtlesim is the subscriber node.

Here is one source you can refer to read more about the ROS 2 service: [*38*].

In this section, we explored how to work with ROS 2 services using Turtlesim and ROS 2 command-line tools, demonstrating the synchronous communication between nodes and various service operations such as spawning, resetting, and controlling the turtle.

Summary

This chapter provided a practical guide to setting up and working with ROS 2, focusing on installing ROS 2 Jazzy on various platforms such as Ubuntu, Windows, and macOS, and using virtualization tools such as Docker and VirtualBox. It introduced ROS 2 basics, including key concepts such as nodes, topics, packages, and messages, while using tools such as Turtlesim to demonstrate inter-process communication. The chapter also covered using ROS 2 client libraries for application development in multiple programming languages and emphasized setting up a development environment, building robot software, and understanding ROS 2 concepts through hands-on examples.

In the next chapter, we will continue with ROS 2 actions and ROS 2 package creation, and start with ROS 2 programming.

References

- [1] https://ubuntu.com/download/desktop
- [2] https://ubuntuhandbook.org/index.php/2024/04/install-ubuntu-24-04-desktop/
- [3] https://mac.getutm.app/
- [4] https://www.virtualbox.org/wiki/Downloads
- [5] https://www.vmware.com/products/desktop-hypervisor
- [6] https://itslinuxguide.com/install-ubuntu-virtualbox/
- [7] https://youtu.be/SgfrHKg81Qc
- [8] https://mac.getutm.app/
- [9] https://www.linuxbuzz.com/how-to-install-ubuntu-on-wsl/
- [10] https://www.docker.com/
- [11] https://hub.docker.com/
- [12] https://raspberrytips.com/install-ubuntu-desktop-raspberry-pi/
- [13] https://ubuntu.com/download/nvidia-jetson
- [14] https://docs.ros.org/en/jazzy/Installation.html
- [15] https://gnupg.org/
- [16] https://launchpad.net/ubuntu/+ppas
- [17] https://ubuntu.com/desktop/wsl
- [18] https://docs.ros.org/en/jazzy/Installation/Windows-Install-Binary.html
- [19] https://mac.getutm.app/
- [20] https://docs.ros.org/en/jazzy/Installation/Alternatives/macOS-Development-Setup.html
- [21] https://youtu.be/qjfBP4UYx9c?si
- [22] https://ubuntuasahi.org/
- [23] https://www.docker.com/
- [24] https://docs.docker.com/engine/install/ubuntu/
- [25] https://docs.nvidia.com/datacenter/cloud-native/container-toolkit/latest/index.html
- [26] https://hub.docker.com/
- [27] https://hub.docker.com/r/osrf/ros/tags

- [28] https://docs.docker.com/get-started/docker_cheatsheet.pdf
- [29] https://roboticseabass.com/2023/07/09/updated-guide-docker-and-ros2/
- [30] https://docs.docker.com/reference/cli/docker/compose/
- [31] https://www.raspberrypi.com/products/
- [32] https://developer.nvidia.com/buy-jetson
- [33] https://ubuntu.com/download/raspberry-pi
- [34] https://developer.nvidia.com/embedded/jetpack
- [35] https://github.com/dusty-nv/jetson-containers
- [36] https://roboticsbackend.com/ros2-topic-cmd-line-tool-debug-ros2-topics-from-the-terminal/
- [37] https://ros2-tutorial.readthedocs.io/en/latest/messages.html
- [38] https://docs.ros.org/en/jazzy/Tutorials/Beginner-CLI-Tools/Understanding-ROS2-Services/Understanding-ROS2-Services.html
- [39] https://github.com/2b-t/docker-for-robotics
-

Join our community on Discord

Join our community's Discord space for discussions with the authors and other readers: https://packt.link/embeddedsystems

3

Implementing ROS 2 Concepts

In the last chapter, we discussed various ROS 2 concepts that we need to know before starting to program with ROS 2.

In this chapter, we will continue with a few topics we left out in *Chapter 2*. After discussing these concepts, we will start implementing them using `rclcpp`, the ROS 2 client library for C++.

This chapter will help you build a strong foundation for implementing different ROS 2 concepts. We will see the detailed implementation of ROS 2 concepts using C++ that can be used in various robot use cases. It is very important to understand all these basic ROS 2 concepts before diving into the more advanced concepts of ROS 2.

Here are the important topics we will discuss in this chapter:

- What is a ROS 2 action?
- What is a ROS 2 parameter?
- What is a ROS 2 launch file?
- How do we build a ROS 2 package?
- Introduction to ROS 2 client libraries
- Diving into ROS 2 nodes
- Implementing ROS 2 topics in C++
- Implementing ROS 2 parameters in C++
- Implementing ROS 2 services in C++
- Implementing ROS 2 actions in C++
- Configuring DDS/Zenoh and domain IDs

Technical requirements

To follow along with this chapter, you will need to have a computer/embedded board (e.g., Raspberry Pi, Jetson boards, etc.) with any OS with Ubuntu 24.04 LTS in WSL2, a VM, Docker, or a real machine itself. The reference materials for this chapter can be found in the `Chapter03` folder of the following GitHub repository: `https://github.com/PacktPublishing/Mastering-ROS-2-for-Robotics-Programming/tree/main/Chapter03`.

What is a ROS 2 action?

Let's start with **ROS 2 actions**. We have seen what a ROS 2 service is. It is a request/reply kind of communication; it is suitable for short tasks like enabling/disabling some components in the robot. If the task execution of the service takes time, the client must wait for a reply. There is no option to cancel the service if it is taking longer than expected. Also, there is no feedback from the server node on whether to cancel the request or not. That is where ROS actions come in.

A ROS action is well suited for long-running tasks, such as navigation of the robot from A to B, moving an arm from the current position to the goal position, etc. In these kinds of tasks, the task can take time, and getting feedback on the status of the task will be useful. A ROS action involves two key participants: the **action client**, which sends a goal and can request feedback or cancel it, and the **action server**, which receives the goal, processes it, and returns the result, possibly with intermediate feedback. The following image illustrates how a ROS action works.

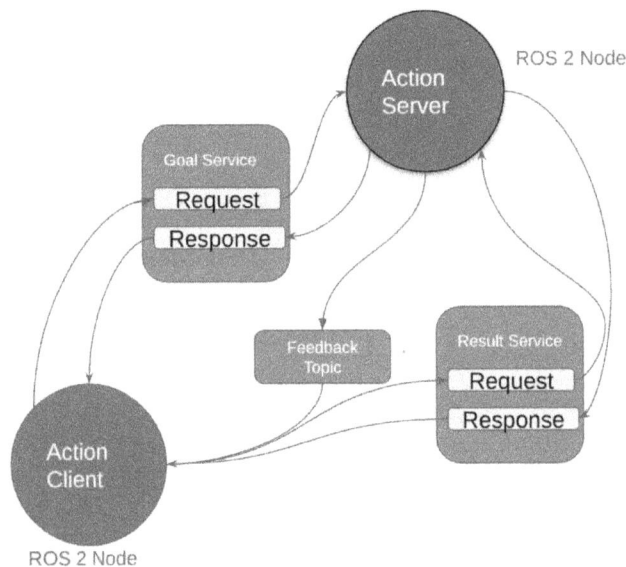

Figure 3.1: ROS 2 action

Like a ROS service, we can interact with a ROS 2 action with the ros2 action command. To list the action with its action types, you can use:

```
ros2 action list -t
```

If you are running the turtlesim node, you can find the following action with the action type:

```
/turtle1/rotate_absolute [turtlesim/action/RotateAbsolute]
```

If you want to see the action field, you can use:

```
ros2 interface show turtlesim/action/RotateAbsolute
```

You will get the following output:

```
# The desired heading in radians
float32 theta
---
# The angular displacement in radians to the starting position
float32 delta
---
# The remaining rotation in radians
float32 remaining
```

The above action definition has three main fields: the first one is the goal request field (theta), the second one is the result (delta), and the third one is the feedback (remaining). The action definition is for rotating the turtle at a certain angle. Once we send the goal angle, the client will start getting feedback about the remaining angle. This is stored in the remaining variable, and after completing the rotation, the result will be stored in the delta variable, which is the angular displacement in radians from the starting position.

Like the ROS 2 service, you can use the ros2 action command to send the goal values. The goal value is 1.57 in radians. The send_goal command is used to send the action goal:

```
ros2 action send_goal --feedback /turtle1/rotate_absolute turtlesim/
action/RotateAbsolute "{theta: 1.5708}"
```

Once you execute the command, you will see the turtle rotating *90 degrees* in the anticlockwise direction, and after that, you will see a message like this in the terminal:

```
Feedback:
    remaining: 0.018799901008605957
Result:
    delta: -3.1040000915527344
Goal finished with status: SUCCEEDED
```

Another command you can try is ros2 action info, which shows the information of this ROS 2 action, like which node is the action server and which node is the action client:

```
ros2 action info /turtle1/rotate_absolute
```

We can refer to the page linked here to find out more about ROS 2 actions [1].

So far, we have briefly covered the ROS topic, service, and action concepts. Now, we can discuss another useful concept: the ROS parameter.

What is a ROS parameter?

A ROS node can be configured using **parameters**. It can store parameters such as integers, floats, Booleans, strings, and lists. The node can read these parameters and control the program flow. These parameter values can be set/get through the ros2 param command-line tool. Commonly, in robotic applications, we use a YAML file to hold this parameter. The main reason is that there will be multiple parameters per node, and there can be multiple nodes inside a robotic application. Keeping parameters inside a YAML file will give great flexibility in saving and loading during the startup of the node. The ROS launch files help to load multiple nodes along with all these parameter files. ROS 2 parameters are stored in the nodes themselves, and whenever there is a change in the parameter, it can be handled inside the node using a callback if required. We will see more about the launch file in the next section.

Here is the ROS 2 command-line tool to list set/get parameters.

Here is how we list the parameters of the running nodes:

```
ros2 param list
```

Here are the main parameters of the `/turtlesim` node:

```
/turtlesim:
    background_b
    background_g
    background_r
    holonomic
    . . . . . . . . . . . . . . . .
```

You can see the r, g, b color values as parameters, which refer to the background color of the turtlesim. We can change these values through the command line and the color of the background color will change instantly.

Here is the syntax and an example of setting the parameter value:

```
ros2 param set <node_name> <parameter_name> <value>
ros2 param set /turtlesim background_r 150
```

After setting the red element of the background to *150*, you can see that the background color changes from blue to violet.

Also, if you want to get the value of some parameter, you can use `ros2 param get`.

Here is the syntax of the ros2 param get command:

```
ros2 param get <node_name> <parameter_name>
```

In this example, we are retrieving the same parameter we have already set, and we will get the same value we have set as the output:

```
ros2 param get /turtlesim background_r
```

Here is what the output looks like:

```
Integer value is: 150
```

We can even initialize the ROS 2 parameters during the initialization of the node by passing them as a command-line argument. You can use `--ros-args -p` to mention the parameters as command-line arguments. Here is an example usage:

```
ros2 run turtlesim turtlesim_node --ros-args -p background_r:=255 -p
background_g:=255 -p background_b:=255
```

You can learn more about ROS parameters using the following link [2].

Now, let us look at the ROS launch file in the following section.

What is a ROS 2 launch file?

ROS 2 launch files are powerful tools for launching multiple nodes, configuring parameters, re-mapping topic names, and controlling the execution of nodes in a complex robotic system. Launch files are extremely useful if your application has multiple nodes. It is not easy to run each node using the ros2 run command, but launch files provide a way to run nodes with all their settings, and you can run these launch files with a single command.

The ros2 launch command is used to launch a launch file. Launch files are kept inside the ros 2 package. In ROS 2, the launch file can be written using Python, XML, and YAML. The Python launch file gives more flexibility compared to other options, especially in complex robotics applications. If you are writing the Python launch file, the extension will be * . py, and usually a naming convention like * . launch . py is followed.

The syntax of the ros2 launch command is given below:

```
ros2 launch pkg_name launch_file_name.py
```

Here is an example of running a launch file. This launch file is already inside the demo_nodes_cpp package:

```
ros2 launch demo_nodes_cpp talker_listener_launch.py
```

This launch file will start the talker and listener, and you will see the following message:

```
[INFO] [launch]: Default logging verbosity is set to INFO
[INFO] [talker-1]: process started with pid [1505]
[INFO] [listener-2]: process started with pid [1506]
[talker-1] [INFO] [1726427687.713985453] [talker]: Publishing: 'Hello
World: 1'
[listener-2] [INFO] [1726427687.714343316] [listener]: I heard: [Hello
World: 1]
[talker-1] [INFO] [1726427688.712840861] [talker]: Publishing: 'Hello
World: 2'
[listener-2] [INFO] [1726427688.713186962] [listener]: I heard: [Hello
World: 2]
```

Here is what this launch file looks like:

```python
"""Launch a talker and a listener."""
from launch import LaunchDescription
import launch_ros.actions
def generate_launch_description():
    return LaunchDescription([
        launch_ros.actions.Node(
            package='demo_nodes_cpp',
            executable='talker',
            output='screen'),
        launch_ros.actions.Node(
            package='demo_nodes_cpp',
            executable='listener',
            output='screen'),
    ])
```

In this launch file, you can find a set of Python modules that are used inside the launch file. You can also find a single function called generate_launch_description(). This function is standard in ROS 2 launch files, and whenever we run a launch file, it will call this function and should return a LaunchDescription object. The LaunchDescription class is a container object for the launch file, which has information about what nodes, parameters, etc. have to be launched. We can also see the Node() class, which helps to run a node with its configuration. Node objects are put inside the LaunchDescription and returned by the generate_launch_description(), which runs the nodes inside it.

We will discuss more details about the ROS 2 launch file in the next chapter. Here is the link to read more about ROS 2 launch files [3].

After discussing the most important ROS 2 concepts, let's get hands-on with ROS 2 demo packages.

Building a ROS 2 package

Packages are basic software units in ROS 2. They are organized in a ROS 2 workspace, where we can build the packages and run the nodes. Creating a ROS 2 workspace is very easy; we can create any number of ROS workspaces in our OS. The main purpose of creating a ROS workspace is to organize a set of packages. For example, if we are working on a navigation project, we can keep all the navigation-related packages inside this workspace. This is a good practice to get into to organize the robot packages.

There are two types of workspaces in ROS 2. First is the **base workspace,** which refers to the ROS 2 installation itself. We are adding the source /opt/ros/<distro>/setup.bash command in the ~/.bashrc file to source the base workspace. If the base workspace is not sourced, the core ROS packages and tools will not be visible in the terminal. The next type of workspace is an **overlay workspace**. These are *user*-created workspaces. Once created, you can build the workspace and overlay it on the base workspace by sourcing its setup.bash file in the install folder. We can create multiple workspaces in ROS 2 and overlay them.

Let's see the instruction to create an overlay workspace in ROS 2.

Creating a ROS 2 workspace

The ROS 2 workspace is simply a folder that contains the src subfolder. Here is a command to create a ROS 2 workspace called master_ros2_ws in the home folder. The command also creates a src folder inside the master_ros2_ws:

```
mkdir -p ~/master_ros2_ws/src
```

After creating both folders, switch to the src folder. Here is where we can create new packages or copy the existing packages:

```
cd ~/master_ros2_ws/src
```

Once you are done with the packages, switch to the ROS 2 workspace folder:

```
cd ~/master_ros2_ws
```

Now we can build the workspace. We can build the workspace even without any packages in the workspace.

Building a workspace

Before building the workspace, it is best to use the following command to install the dependencies of these packages:

```
rosdep install -i --from-path src --rosdistro jazzy -y
```

The rosdep command finds the dependencies of the packages inside the src folder and checks whether the packages have already been installed on the OS. If not installed, they will be automatically installed. This is a handy command for managing dependency issues in ROS 2.

After installing the dependencies, you can finally build a workspace.

You can use the following command to build the packages inside the workspace:

```
colcon build
```

The colcon command is the build tool commonly used in ROS 2 to build the packages inside the ROS 2 workspace. We have to be in the ROS 2 workspace folder before building the packages. We can either build all packages or selectively build the packages in the workspace. The colcon build command will build all the packages inside the ROS 2 workspace. The `colcon build --packages-select <package_name>` command will selectively build the packages in the workspace. The `colcon build --symlink-install` is another command to build the workspace. The `symlink-install` part creates symbolic links (symlinks) in the `install/` directory instead of copying files. This is a good option when you are using ROS 2 Python nodes. If we modify the Python node, we don't have to rebuild the package because there is no copying to the install folder, but the actual node is already linked in the install directory.

Once you execute this command, you can see messages confirming that these packages have been built. The building of packages involves building the source code, like C++. After successfully building, you can find three main folders along with the `src` folder, which are `build`, `logs`, and `install`. The `install` folder is where the installed executable, scripts, and configuration files are stored, and the build folder is where the intermediate build files are stored. The `logs` folder contains log messages of ROS 2 nodes. You can read more about the `colcon` command using the following link [4].

After successfully building the workspace, we can add an overlay to the workspace using the following command:

```
source ~/master_ros2_ws/install/setup.bash
```

After this overlay, we can run the nodes and launch files inside these packages.

We will learn more about ROS workspaces in the next chapter. You can read more about ROS workspaces with this link [5].

We have discussed most of the important concepts in ROS 2. Now, let us see how we can implement these concepts in our ROS 2 code.

Introduction to ROS 2 client libraries

The ROS 2 concepts we have seen in this chapter can be implemented in our nodes. We can create any number of topics, services, actions, and parameters in our ROS nodes. So, how can we implement these concepts in our program? The answer is **ROS 2 client libraries**. ROS 2 comes with a set of libraries called client libraries. These libraries provide APIs that allow users to implement all the concepts in ROS 2. There are two popular client libraries that ROS 2 officially supports. Those are `rclcpp` and `rclpy`. The `rclcpp` library is the client library for C++, and `rclpy` is the client library for Python. As developers, we only need to learn the APIs provided by these libraries to implement ROS 2 nodes.

We can choose the client library for our application. If you are working with faster and more efficient code, you can go with the C++ client library, and if you require faster development time, you can go with Python. One important thing to note is that ROS 2 nodes written in different client libraries can communicate and share messages with each other.

All client libraries in ROS 2 are built on a common layer called the **ROS Client Library** (rcl) [6]. This layer implements logic and behavior of ROS concepts that are not specific to any language. This makes the client library development easier for any language.

There are multiple client libraries in ROS 2, other than the two previously mentioned official libraries. A list is given below. These libraries are community-maintained:

- **Rust**: `rclrs` is the client library for writing ROS 2 nodes in Rust.
- **Node.js**: `rclnodejs` is a Node.js client for ROS 2.
- **JVM and Android**: `rcljava` is the ROS 2 Java client, and `ros2_java_android` is the Android bindings for ROS 2.
- `rclc`: This is a client library for C programming.
- **C#/.NET**: `rcldotnet` is a C#/.NET client library for ROS 2.

We can also write a client library for a programming language. Here is the API of `rcl` to implement language-specific client libraries [7].

You can refer to the following link if you want to read more about ROS 2 client libraries [8].

We have covered the basics of ROS 2 client libraries. Now, let's explore more concepts relating to the ROS 2 node before implementing ROS 2 nodes using C++.

Diving into ROS 2 nodes

In *Chapter 2*, we discussed what a **ROS 2** node is. When we run a ROS 2 program/executable, it can start a single or multiple nodes. In ROS 2, a node is a fundamental component of a robotic system that performs a specific task, such as sensor data processing, actuation, or communication. While a node is often associated with a process, ROS 2 allows multiple nodes to exist within a single process, offering greater flexibility and efficiency.

According to the ROS 2 documentation, *"A node is a participant in the ROS 2 graph, which uses a client library to communicate with other nodes. Nodes can communicate with other nodes within the same process, in a different process, or on a different machine. Nodes are typically the unit of computation in a ROS graph; each node should do one logical thing."*

Depending on the robotics application in ROS 2, multiple nodes can work and communicate together to accomplish a robotics application. Nodes in ROS 2 use topics, services, and actions to communicate with each other. We can run nodes in the same machine or multiple machines, and it can communicate over a network. This allows developers to build complex robotics applications that are scalable and modular.

Different types of ROS 2 nodes

ROS 2 comes with different types of nodes. Here is a comparison of different types of nodes, their advantages, and their disadvantages.

Standard (non-composable) nodes

Definition: A non-composable node in ROS 2 runs as an independent process with its own memory space. An executor manages how a node processes callbacks, using single- or multithreaded models. The executors are responsible for coordinating the execution of callbacks (like subscribe callbacks/functions) in ROS 2 nodes. There are single-threaded executors and multithreaded executors. A single-threaded executor executes the callbacks of a node in a single thread, whereas a multithreaded executor executes in parallel using multiple threads, which allows greater concurrency.

The executor in ROS 2 acts as a scheduler, deciding when the callback has to run. When multiple nodes are loaded into the container, the executor helps manage the callbacks of all nodes within that container. Depending on the choice of executor type, the nodes' callbacks execute either sequentially or in parallel (multiple threads).

You can run multiple nodes in one process by manually creating them and sharing an executor. This offers isolation and simplicity, but with higher resource overhead. They can be individually launched from the command line or launch files. Non-composable nodes are isolated processes, so in terms of CPU usage, more memory will be consumed, and there will be potential latency in communication between nodes. There are advantages to this method; for example, if one node crashes, it will not affect the other nodes. This makes the system more robust in some situations.

Usage: It can be used where the nodes need to be less dependent on one another, meaning a crash of one node will not directly make the other node crash.

Example: An example of a non-composable node is a standalone sensor driver node like LIDAR, camera, etc., which reads sensor data and publishes it. The other nodes can subscribe to these topics for processing. The driver node can independently run without depending on other nodes.

Composable/component nodes

Definition: In composable nodes, we can load multiple nodes into a container and execute all nodes in the same process along with other nodes. A container in ROS 2 is essentially a process that can host multiple composable nodes. It works like a node manager. The container uses ROS 2 (usually multithreaded) to manage all loaded components. Composable nodes allow multiple nodes to share computational resources and memory, thereby reducing communication latency through zero-copy communication and improving overall efficiency. They provide a more modular and resource-efficient design. These nodes can be dynamically loaded and unloaded into a container at runtime.

Usage: Composable nodes are a good choice if many nodes need to communicate frequently, like in a robot navigation system. This will help minimize the communication overhead.

Example: Here is one example of composable nodes. Node 1 reads from a LIDAR sensor and publishes LIDAR data, Node 2 creates a map using LIDAR data, and Node 3 navigates the robot using the map created. We can execute all nodes in a multithreaded executor to make the application faster. The single-threaded executor will be appropriate for applications where there is little processing in each node's callback.

Lifecycle nodes (managed nodes)

Definition: The lifecycle node is a newly added feature in ROS 2 that provides a managed state machine inside the node. This will help the node transition from specific states such as `unconfigured`, `inactive`, `active`, and `finalized`. This feature gives more control over the node's initialization, execution, and cleanup process.

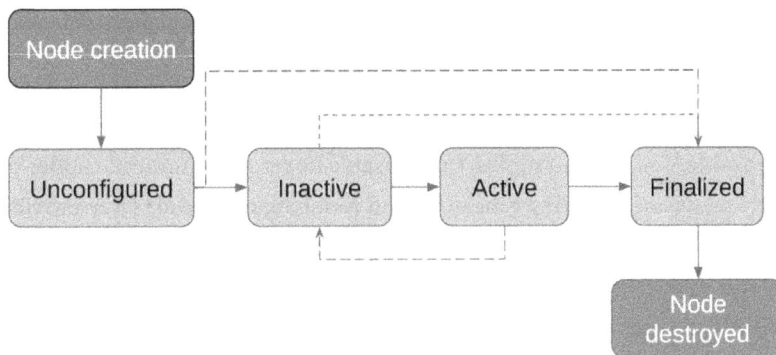

Figure 3.2: Lifecycle node

As you can see in *Figure 3.2*, the lifecycle node transitions from four states. Compared to standard nodes, which directly go from inactive to active, the state of the lifecycle node can be controlled. Here is an overview of the lifecycle node states:

- **Unconfigured**: This is the initial state of the lifecycle node when it is created. The node started but has not yet performed its functionality. In this state, the node can't communicate with other nodes and has no communication with subscribers or services. The node is idle.

- **Inactive**: After transitioning from the unconfigure state, the node moves to the Inactive state. In this state, the node has been configured but it is not performing a task like publishing and subscribing.

- **Active**: If we switch the state from Inactive to Active, the node can fully operate, including publishing, subscribing, services, action, etc. In this state, the node will work like a standard node.

- **Finalized**: This is the final state of the node. After reaching this state, the node can't transition to any other state. After this state, the node will shut down.

You can read more about lifecycle nodes at the following link [9].

Usage: Lifecycle nodes are ideal when controlled startup, shutdown, and runtime configuration are needed. This is best suited for industrial robots or autonomous vehicles.

Example: A robotic arm control node needs to be initialized, actively controlled, and safely shut down.

We have seen various types of nodes in ROS 2. Here are key takeaways from this section:

- **Non-composable nodes**: These are useful for isolated tasks but take more resources and have latency in communication.

- **Composable/component nodes**: Composable nodes allow multiple nodes to run within a single process, improving efficiency and reducing overhead. They provide a modular approach to deploying ROS 2 applications by enabling dynamic loading of nodes at runtime. This makes them especially suitable for resource-constrained environments, such as embedded systems.

- **Lifecycle nodes**: Lifecycle nodes introduce a state machine that defines how a node transitions between different stages of operation. This allows developers to control when a node initializes, starts doing work, stops, or shuts down—useful in complex systems.

In the next section, we will see how ROS 2 nodes communicate with each other.

How do ROS 2 nodes communicate?

We know DDS is the core of ROS 2, which provides features like discovery, data distribution, and **quality of service (QoS)**. Here is how nodes communicate in ROS 2:

- **Discovery mechanism**: DDS offers automatic discovery for ROS 2 nodes using its discovery protocol. Once we start the ROS 2 node, it will broadcast its presence on the network. If a node begins publishing a topic and another subscribes to the same topic with the same message type, DDS will connect the nodes automatically and they will start communicating with each other. Once the node is shut down, the node sends an update to DDS about it as well.

- **QoS**: The QoS policies in ROS 2 allow developers to control communication parameters like reliability, latency, durability, etc. These policies help the ROS 2 node to handle different network conditions and ensure reliable data transmission.

- **Transport mechanism**: DDS uses UDP, TCP, and shared memory based on the QoS policies set by the developer.

In ROS 2 node communication, understanding the various QoS policies is important to configure each node for different applications. The coming section will discuss various QoS policies and their importance.

Diving into QoS in ROS 2 nodes

In this section, we will look at different QoS policies we can use to configure a ROS 2 node. We will discuss each policy, the values we can configure, and example use cases. Here is a table that shows a comparison of each policy.

QoS Policy	Description	Possible Values	Example Use Cases
Reliability	This policy controls the guarantees of message delivery between nodes.	**Reliable:** This value ensures every message is delivered. **Best-Effort:** This value sends messages without ensuring delivery.	**Reliable:** Use for important messages like the robot velocity command. **Best-Effort:** Use for high-frequency sensor data like camera or LIDAR drivers.
Durability	This policy determines whether the past message is available for late subscribers.	**Volatile:** The message will be discarded after sending the message. **Transient Local:** This option will store and deliver past messages and new subscribers.	**Volatile:** Useful for real-time sensor driver nodes where old data is invalid. **Transient Local:** Option is useful for sharing parameters of map data.
History	This policy decides how much data should be stored for late subscribers.	**Keep Last:** This option only stores recent messages. **Keep All:** This option will store all messages until processed or the memory is exhausted.	**Keep Last:** This is for real-time streaming, where the latest data matters. **Keep All:** This will be ideal for critical control and data logging.

QoS Policy	Description	Possible Values	Example Use Cases
Depth	This policy sets the maximum number of messages in the queue before overwriting older ones.	The value is an integer.	**Low depth (e.g., 5 –10):** Suited for low-latency applications. **High depth:** Suited for bursty communication, meaning a short period of intense activity followed by long periods of silence.
Deadline	This policy ensures messages are delivered or received within a certain time frame. The node will receive a callback if it is violated.	The possible values are in milliseconds (e.g., `100ms`).	Sensor data must arrive within a specific time interval.
Liveliness	This policy controls how the nodes declare whether they are still alive despite not communicating.	**Automatic:** The DDS (middleware) automatically manages liveliness. **Manual:** The node must send a liveliness signal explicitly.	**Automatic:** Most nodes use this method. **Manual:** Critical nodes like controllers use the manual method.
Lifespan	This policy defines the duration for which a message is valid. After this duration, the message will be discarded and not delivered.	Duration (e.g. 3s, 10s)	Use for sensitive data where outdated information must be ignored.

QoS Policy	Description	Possible Values	Example Use Cases
Ownership	This policy determines whether the publisher has exclusive ownership of a message on a topic.	**Shared ownership:** This enables multiple publishers to write about a topic. **Exclusive ownership:** Only one publisher can send a message on the topic.	**Shared ownership:** Suited for distributed systems with multiple publishers on the same topic. **Exclusive ownership:** Suited for critical topics with only one publisher.

Table 3.1: QoS policies in ROS 2

We can refer to this table to configure the nodes we are going to develop in the upcoming sections.

You can read more about QoS in ROS 2 at the following link [*10*].

Now, we will start implementing ROS 2 nodes. We will see how to implement ROS 2 topics, parameters, services, and actions.

Implementing ROS 2 topics in C++

This section will show how to implement a publisher and subscriber using C++ with `rclcpp` APIs. We will see how to implement a publisher node using custom ROS 2 message interfaces and standard ROS 2 messages. The publisher's objective is to publish string data using the standard string msg-type and a string with an integer using a custom message interface. The subscriber node will subscribe to both of these topics.

Figure 3.3 shows how communication happens between the publisher and subscriber nodes. The names of the topics the publisher publishes are `/custom_topic` and `/std_string_topic`. The `/custom_topic` publishes custom ROS 2 messages, whereas `std_string_topic` uses standard string ROS 2 messages.

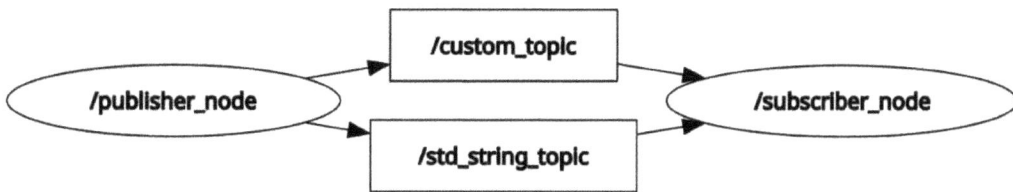

Figure 3.3: ROS 2 publisher and subscriber

In *Figure 3.3*, you can see publisher_node on the left and subscriber_node on the right. In between, we can see the topics these nodes are publishing and subscribing to.

Now, let's start implementing the custom ROS 2 message interface, as well as the publisher and subscriber nodes, in C++.

First, we have to create the custom interface; then we can use it for publishing and subscribing.

Creating a custom interface ROS 2 package

The first step is to create a ROS 2 package. Take a terminal and switch to the src folder of our current ROS 2 workspace that we have created.

Creating a ROS 2 package for a custom interface

Here is the command we can use to do this:

```
cd ~/master_ros2_ws/src
ros2 pkg create master_ros2_interface --build-type ament_cmake
```

ros2 pkg is the command used to work with the ROS 2 package. You can use this command to create a new ROS 2 package. It also helps to list the installed ROS 2 packages on the computer.

Using the ros2 pkg create subcommand, you can first give the package's name and then mention its build type. We can use the ament_cmake build type if we are using CMake as the build tool and ament_python build for a Python package. If we want to create a custom interface package, we must use the ament_cmake build type because the custom messages must be converted into corresponding C++ or Python code for our application.

Defining the custom message

Create an msg folder inside this package and add a custom message file called CustomMsg.msg:

```
cd ~/master_ros2_ws/src/master_ros2_interface
mkdir msg
```

You can use a text editor and enter these two data fields:

```
string data
int32 number
```

Note that we can add any data here, including standard message types from ROS 2 and even custom ROS 2 messages. After that, you can save the file as CustomMsg.msg in the master_ros2_ interface/msg folder. The custom ROS 2 message for publish and subscribe can be defined in the .msg file, which can be organized into an msg folder. This custom ROS 2 message contains string and integer data.

Editing CMakeLists.txt to add message generation

After adding the .msg file, we have to edit CMakeLists.txt to convert the .msg file into C++/ Python files.

You can find this line in CMakeLists.txt:

```
find_package(ament_cmake REQUIRED)
```

Just after this line, add the following lines to generate the message:

```
find_package(rosidl_default_generators REQUIRED)
rosidl_generate_interfaces(${PROJECT_NAME}
  "msg/CustomMsg.msg"
)
```

The ROS **Interface Definition Language** (IDL) default generator creates C++ and Python code for messages, services, and actions. This package automates the conversion of .msg, .srv, and .action to a usable ROS interface. **IDL** is the data types and structures used by DDS, which is the core of ROS 2.

Editing package.xml to add dependencies.

package.xml contains the metadata about the package. It has the package name, version, description, dependencies, licensing, and authorship. The colcon build tool will check package. xml and include the dependencies for building the package.

To build the custom ROS 2 message, you must add the following dependencies to build the messages:

```
<build_depend>rosidl_default_generators</build_depend>
<exec_depend>rosidl_default_runtime</exec_depend>
<member_of_group>rosidl_interface_packages</member_of_group>
```

After updating package.xml, we can build the package.

Building the interface package

We can build the interface package using the following command:

```
cd ~/master_ros2_ws/
colcon build --packages-select master_ros2_interface
```

If everything goes well, you will get the following message:

```
Summary: 0 packages finished [0.20s]
```

This means that the interface package is built properly.

Now we can create the main package, which has publisher and subscriber code.

Creating the main ROS 2 package

Let's start building the main ROS 2 package. We will see how to create publishers and subscribers.

Creating the package

Here is the command to create a new package:

```
cd ~/master_ros2_ws/src
ros2 pkg create master_ros2_pkg --build-type ament_cmake --dependencies
rclcpp std_msgs master_ros2_interface
```

The name of the package we have created is master_ros2_pkg. The build-type value is ament_
cmake. We can also explicitly mention the package dependencies using --dependencies along
with the creation of the package.

Creating the src directory for a C++ node

The src folder inside a ROS 2 package is where we commonly keep our C++ source code. The
following command creates a src folder inside the master_ros2_pkg:

```
cd ~/master_ros2_ws/src
mkdir -p ~/master_ros2_pkg/src
```

We can start with a publisher node in C++. You can find the publisher source code in Chapter03
| master_ros2_pkg | src | publisher_node.cpp.

You can copy this code directly from the repository into the src folder of your ROS 2 package.
Let's discuss how this code works.

What does a publisher node do?

The publisher's objective is to publish two topics. The first topic, /std_string_topic, uses a standard ROS string message (std_msgs::msg::String), and the next topic, /custom_topic, publishes a custom ROS message type (master_ros2_interface::msg::CustomMsg) that we have already created. These two topics will be published every second.

Let's dive into the publisher code now.

Node header files

The publisher node requires the main header file, which is rclcpp/rclcpp.hpp. This is the header file of the rclcpp client library. If we include this header file, we will get access to APIs for creating topics, services, actions, parameters, etc. This is the main header file to include in every C++ ROS 2 node for accessing ROS2 C++ APIs:

```
#include "rclcpp/rclcpp.hpp"
#include "std_msgs/msg/string.hpp"
#include "master_ros2_interface/msg/custom_msg.hpp"
```

In order to get access to the standard string message and custom message, we have to include these header files.

Node class definition

In the publisher code, we are going to create a non-composable node. To create an independent C++ node, we have to create a class that is inherited from rclcpp::Node. The following code snippet shows the inheritance:

```
class PublisherNode : public rclcpp::Node {
public:
    PublisherNode() : Node("publisher_node") {
```

Node("publisher_node") calls the base class constructor to initialize the node with the name "publisher_node".

You can get the complete reference of rclcpp::Node from the following link [11].

Setting QoS policies

We can define the QoS policies to the publisher in this ROS 2 node. We can specify QoS policies using the rclcpp::QoS class. In this publisher, we have configured three main policies:

```
auto qos_profile = rclcpp::QoS(rclcpp::KeepLast(10)).reliable().transient_
local();
```

We have set the History QoS as KeepLast(10), meaning it will keep the last 10 messages. We set the Reliability QoS as reliable, meaning messages are guaranteed to be delivered. The third setting is for the Durability QoS. We have set the value as transient_local, meaning it will keep the last published message so new publishers can immediately receive it.

You can get the complete QoS policies setting from the following link [12].

Creating publishers

The node creates two publishers, one for each type of message:

```
publisher_ = this->create_publisher<std_msgs::msg::String>("std_string_
topic", qos_profile);
custom_publisher_ = this->create_publisher<master_ros2_
interface::msg::CustomMsg>("custom_topic", qos_profile);
```

The create_publisher function creates a publisher for a specific message type. The first publisher publishes the std_msgs::msg:String message on the "std_string_topic" topic. The second publisher publishes master_ros2_interface::msg::CustomMsg on the "custom_topic" topic.

We can include the qos_profile object for each publisher to apply the QoS profile for each ROS 2 topic.

You can refer to rclcpp::Node class [12] for more information on this API.

Timers for periodic publishing

We have declared the two publishers; now, we have to publish the data using a publisher.

create_wall_timer() creates a timer that triggers at fixed intervals. In our case, it is 1 second:

```
timer_ = this->create_wall_timer(
    std::chrono::seconds(1), std::bind(&PublisherNode::publish_messages,
this));
```

When the timer times out, it will call a `publish_messages` function inside the `PublisherNode` class. This function publishes the data for `std_string_topic` and `custom_topic` topics.

Publishing messages

`publish_messages` publishes data to both of these topics:

```
void publish_messages() {
    auto string_msg = std_msgs::msg::String();
    string_msg.data = "Hello, world!";
    RCLCPP_INFO(this->get_logger(), "Publishing: '%s'", string_msg.data.c_
str());
    publisher_->publish(string_msg);
```

In the above snippet, we are creating an instance of `std_msgs::msg::String`, and then setting the data field inside the message to `"Hello World"`. After updating the string message inside the data field, we use the `publish()` function inside the publisher we have created for the standard string message. This will publish the given data:

```
    auto custom_msg = master_ros2_interface::msg::CustomMsg();
    custom_msg.data = "Custom Hello";
    custom_msg.number = 42;
    RCLCPP_INFO(this->get_logger(), "Publishing custom message: data='%s',
number=%d", custom_msg.data.c_str(), custom_msg.number);
    custom_publisher_->publish(custom_msg);
```

In the second publisher, we are doing the same process, but instead of a standard string, we are creating the instance of `master_ros2_interface::msg::CustomMsg`, and setting the data field of string member inside the custom message to `"Custom Hello"` and an integer value, 42. After setting both the values, we publish this topic.

Main function

In the `main()` function, we can see that `rclcpp::init(argc, argv)` will initialize the resources needed by the middleware and the client library. This is a mandatory function to be called to start a ROS 2 C++ node. The next function is `rclcpp::spin(std::make_shared<PublisherNode>())`, which will start the node and wait for the timer to call the publish function we have defined. The `spin()` function basically executes the callback functions in ROS 2 and, finally, the `rclcpp::shutdown()` function shuts down the ROS 2 node and cleans up its resources.

Now we can start discussing subscriber code.

What does the subscriber node do?

The subscriber's objective is to subscribe to two topics. The first topic, /std_string_topic, uses a standard ROS string message (std_msgs::msg::String), and the next topic, /custom_topic, uses a custom ROS message type (master_ros2_interface::msg::CustomMsg). Let's dive into the subscriber code now.

If you check both publisher and subscriber code, you will find the same header file and Node class with different node names. The QoS setting is also the same. So, what is different in subscriber code? The main difference is that instead of publishing, we are using subscribe APIs to subscribe to topics.

You can find the subscriber source code in Chapter03 | master_ros2_pkg | src | subscriber_node. cpp.

Subscribe to topics

The following code snippet shows how to create a subscriber object for a specific topic and message with the defined qos_profile. The first line is for subscribing std_string_topic:

```
subscription_ = this->create_subscription<std_msgs::msg::String>(
    "std_string_topic", qos_profile,
    std::bind(&SubscriberNode::string_callback, this,
std::placeholders::_1)
);
```

The second line is for subscribing to the custom message we have created. Once a message is received, the subscribers will call a callback or a function:

```
custom_subscription_ = this->create_subscription<master_ros2_
interface::msg::CustomMsg>(
    "custom_topic", qos_profile,
    std::bind(&SubscriberNode::custom_msg_callback, this,
std::placeholders::_1)
);
```

When the subscriber receives a message, the first subscriber calls the string_callback(const std_msgs::msg::String::SharedPtr msg) callback, and the second calls the custom_msg_callback(const master_ros2_interface::msg::CustomMsg::SharedPtr msg) callback.

Callback functions

These are the functions that handle the message once they are received by the subscriber. We can manipulate the received data according to our logic. In our current code, we are simply printing the received messages.

This is the first callback, and it is receiving `std_msgs::msg::String`:

```
void string_callback(const std_msgs::msg::String::SharedPtr msg) {
    RCLCPP_INFO(this->get_logger(), "Received: '%s'", msg->data.c_str());
}
```

The second callback, which will print the received data from the custom message we have created, looks as follows:

```
void custom_msg_callback(const master_ros2_
interface::msg::CustomMsg::SharedPtr msg) {
    RCLCPP_INFO(this->get_logger(), "Received custom message: data='%s',
number=%d", msg->data.c_str(), msg->number);
}
```

If you check the `main()` function of the code, it is also the same as the publisher code; the only difference is the change in the node class name.

As of now, we have walked through the publisher and subscriber code. Now, we will continue with the modifications we need to make to compile and build the source code to create executables.

Editing CMakeLists.txt to build the node

After adding publisher and subscriber source code, we have to edit CMakeLists.txt in the package. We have to add lines to CMakeLists.txt for building and installing the executables of the publisher and subscriber. Here is how we do that.

After the `find_package()`, you can add the following lines to create executables of the two sets of source code we have created. These lines will be compiling, linking, and installing the executables. Once it is installed, we can run these executables using the `ros2 run` command:

```
# Add executable for publisher node
add_executable(publisher_node src/publisher_node.cpp)
ament_target_dependencies(publisher_node rclcpp std_msgs master_ros2_
interface)
```

```
# Add executable for subscriber node
add_executable(subscriber_node src/subscriber_node.cpp)
ament_target_dependencies(subscriber_node rclcpp std_msgs master_ros2_
interface)
install(TARGETS
  publisher_node
  subscriber_node
  DESTINATION lib/${PROJECT_NAME}
)
```

After changing CMakeLists.txt, next is editing the package.xml file.

Edit package.xml

Editing package.xml is needed if we are using new dependencies other than those we gave during package creation. In our case, we are not using new dependencies, so we don't have to edit the package.xml.

Building the package

We are done with creating packages that contain publisher and subscriber code. Now, let's build the package and run the executable.

To build all the packages in the workspace, we can use the following command:

```
colcon build
```

You can selectively build this package using the following command:

```
colcon build --packages-select master_ros2_pkg
```

If you are done with building packages, you will get the following output if everything is successful:

```
Starting >>> master_ros2_interface
Finished <<< master_ros2_interface [0.94s]
Starting >>> master_ros2_pkg
Finished <<< master_ros2_pkg [1.09s]
Summary: 2 packages finished [2.23s]
```

Congratulations! You are done with building the packages. Now it's time to run the nodes.

Running the nodes

To run the executables, you have to first source the `master ros2_ws` we created. You can either add the following line to the `.bashrc` file or execute the command in all the terminals you create.

To run the publisher and subscriber, two terminals are required.

We can run the publisher node in the first terminal:

```
source ~/master_ros2_ws/install/setup.bash
ros2 run master_ros2_pkg publisher_node
```

We can run the subscriber node in the second terminal:

```
source ~/master_ros2_ws/install/setup.bash
ros2 run master_ros2_pkg subscriber_node
```

If everything works well, you will get the following output in the terminals. You can see that the publisher and subscriber are communicating with each other.

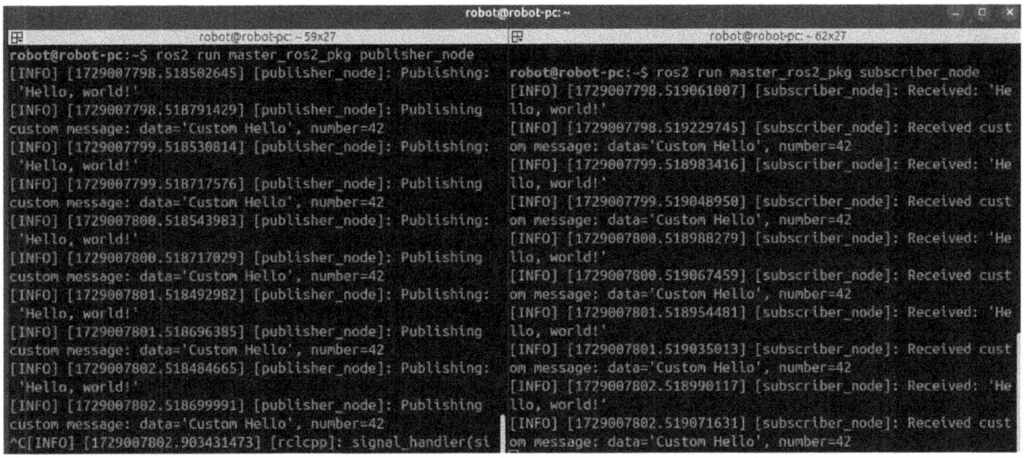

Figure 3.4: Output of publisher (left) and subscriber (right)

In the next section, we will see how to work with ROS 2 parameters.

Implementing ROS 2 parameters in C++

We are going to implement ROS 2 parameters in the publisher code we have already worked with. Here is the objective of the updated code.

The new node we are going to create will have two parameters: a *string* and an *integer*. The value will be published using the custom message topic we have already created. So, if we set these parameters outside the node during the runtime, those values will be taken for publishing. After publishing the new value, the parameter will be set to default values. You can find the source code in `Chapter03 | master_ros2_pkg | src | publisher_node_params.cpp`.

Let's check out this code and see how we can declare the parameters in a C++ node.

Declaring ROS 2 parameters

This is how we declare new parameters in a C++ node. The `declare_parameters` function is used to declare a new parameter. Here is an example usage of this function:

```
this->declare_parameter<std::string>("custom_string", "Hello World");
  this->declare_parameter<int>("custom_number", 42);
```

Inside the node class, you can find the declaration of string and integer parameters. The parameters' names are `custom_string` and `custom_number`.

When we declare a new parameter, we can add a default value for that parameter. In this case, the default string value is `"Hello World"` and the integer value is 42.

Reading values of ROS 2 parameters

After declaring the parameters, we access the values of these parameters inside the `publish_message` function. Using the `get_parameter` function, we can read the value of the parameter to a variable.

In the following snippet, we can see how we read and store the value of ROS 2 parameters:

```
std::string custom_string_param;
int custom_number_param;

this->get_parameter("custom_string", custom_string_param);
this->get_parameter("custom_number", custom_number_param);
```

After reading the values from the parameters, we assign these two data to the custom message we have created. After putting the data in the custom ROS message, we publish this message to the custom ROS topic.

Note that we can also use a callback function to receive the changes in the ROS 2 parameter. So, whenever the parameter changes from outside, this callback function will be called. Inside the callback function, we can do the rest of the processing if needed. Here is a reference that explains how to do this [19].

Setting ROS 2 parameters

After publishing the topic, we set the default values back to the parameters using the set_ parameter() function:

```
this->set_parameter(rclcpp::Parameter("custom_string", "Hello String"));
this->set_parameter(rclcpp::Parameter("custom_number", 42));
```

After creating the source code, we can edit CMakeLists.txt to build the source code.

Editing CMakeLists.txt

Adding to CMakeLists.txt follows the same procedure we have used for publisher and subscriber nodes. We have added lines for compiling and building the code and the target executable inside the install () function:

```
add_executable(publisher_node_params src/publisher_node_params.cpp)
ament_target_dependencies(publisher_node_params rclcpp std_msgs master_
ros2_interface)
```

After editing CMakeLists.txt, you can carry out colcon build, and if everything builds correctly, you can execute the node.

Starting a ROS 2 node with parameters

In this section, we will see how to run publisher_node_params and how to set the ROS 2 parameter in the command line.

Here is the command to run the publisher node with parameters:

```
ros2 run master_ros2_pkg publisher_node_params
```

After running this node, you can see it start to print a message in the terminal.

Now, start the `subscriber_node` that we have already created. The `publisher_node_params` and `publisher_node` are the same with the same topics and ROS message type; the only difference is the inclusion of ROS 2 parameters.

Here is the command to start the subscriber:

```
ros2 run master_ros2_pkg subscriber_node
```

Now, take a new terminal and set the parameters using the `ros2 param` command:

```
ros2 param set publisher_node_params custom_string "Test"
ros2 param set publisher_node_params custom_number 20
```

Now, you can see the values we have set as ROS 2 parameters are printed in the terminal, and the exact value is published in the ROS 2 topic.

So, when we set the parameters, the values that the ROS 2 node publishes change. After publishing the new values, in the next iteration, the default values mentioned in the code get assigned for publishing.

You can see the changed value in subscribers as well.

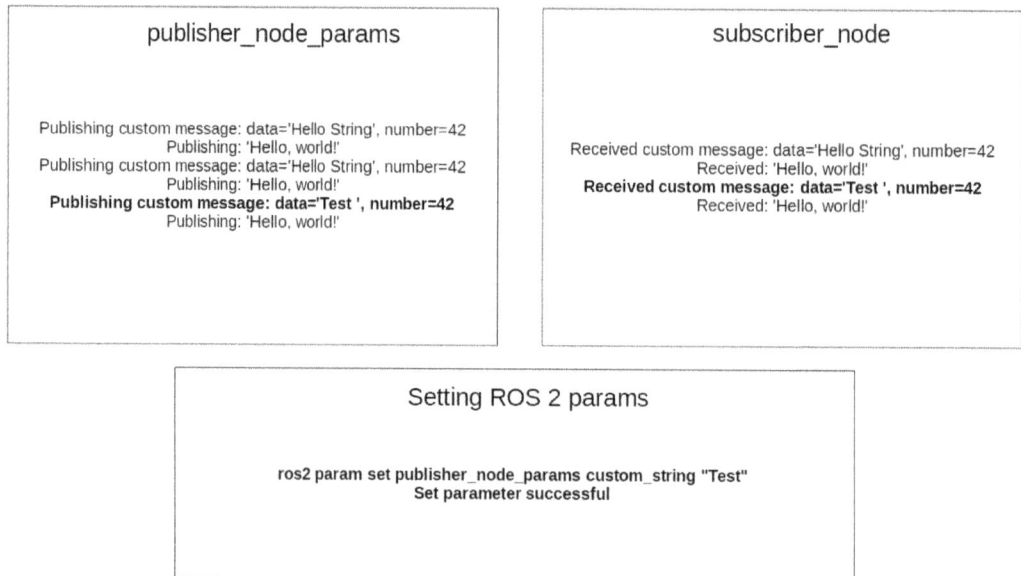

```
            publisher_node_params                                    subscriber_node


  Publishing custom message: data='Hello String', number=42
             Publishing: 'Hello, world!'                    Received custom message: data='Hello String', number=42
  Publishing custom message: data='Hello String', number=42             Received: 'Hello, world!'
             Publishing: 'Hello, world!'                   Received custom message: data='Test ', number=42
  Publishing custom message: data='Test ', number=42                   Received: 'Hello, world!'
             Publishing: 'Hello, world!'
```

```
                              Setting ROS 2 params


           ros2 param set publisher_node_params custom_string "Test"
                           Set parameter successful
```

Figure 3.5: Output of the publisher (left), subscriber (right), and set parameters (bottom)

In *Figure 3.5*, on the left side, you can see the publisher_node_params messages; on the right side, you can find messages of subscriber_node, and at the bottom, you can find the setting of the ROS 2 parameter. We have set the custom_string parameter to Test. Once we set the parameter, you can see the publisher and subscriber messages change. The change of message is shown as bold in *Figure 3.5*.

In the next section, we will see the implementation of the ROS 2 service.

Implementing ROS 2 services in C++

In this section, we will implement a ROS 2 service server and client using C++. The service server listens to a service called concat_strings with a custom service type of master_ros2_interface::srv::ConcatStrings. If it gets a request from the service client, the server will concatenate both strings it got and reply to the client.

You can find the server and client code in Chapter03 | master_ros2_pkg | src | simple_server. cpp and simple_client.cpp.

Adding a custom service interface

The first thing to do before writing server and client code is to write a custom service type.

Here is the custom service type we have defined:

```
string str1
string str2
---
string concatenated_str
```

We have to save this definition as master_ros2_interface/srv/ConcatStrings.srv. The first two strings are for the request field, and the third is for the reply field. The request and reply are separated by ---.

Editing CMakeLists.txt

After saving the srv definition, we have to edit the CMakeLists.txt to convert the srv file definition into C++/Python modules:

```
rosidl_generate_interfaces(${PROJECT_NAME}
  "msg/CustomMsg.msg"
  "srv/ConcatStrings.srv"
)
```

We are done with adding a custom service interface. Now, it's time to write the server and client.

ROS 2 service server

In `simple_server.cpp`, you can find the header file for the custom service type. It is mandatory to include this header to access the service type in the server and client code:

```
#include "master_ros2_interface/srv/concat_strings.hpp"
```

Now, we can define a ROS 2 service using the `create_service` function. In this function, we can include the type of the service, the name of the service, and its callback:

```
service_ = this->create_service<master_ros2_
interface::srv::ConcatStrings>(
            "concat_strings", std::bind(&StringConcatService::handle_
service, this, std::placeholders::_1, std::placeholders::_2));
```

When the service server gets a request, it will call a callback called `handle_service`. This callback will receive those two strings, concatenate both strings, and send the response as a concatenated string that will be received by the client:

```
    void handle_service(
        const std::shared_ptr<master_ros2_
interface::srv::ConcatStrings::Request> request,            std::shared_
ptr<master_ros2_interface::srv::ConcatStrings::Response> response)
    {
        response->concatenated_str = request->str1 + request->str2;
    }
```

Now we will see what is happening to the service client.

ROS 2 service client

In the service client, like the service server, we have the `create_client` function to create a service client. We can mention the service type and the name of the service to which the client has to communicate:

```
client_ = this->create_client<master_ros2_
interface::srv::ConcatStrings>("concat_strings");
```

After creating a client, we can send a request to the server using the send_request (const std::string &str1, const std::string &str2) function. This function allows us to pass two strings, and the string will be sent to the server using the async_send_request function:

```
void send_request(const std::string &str1, const std::string &str2)
{
    auto request = std::make_shared<master_ros2_
interface::srv::ConcatStrings::Request>();
    request->str1 = str1;
    request->str2 = str2;
    auto future_result = client_->async_send_request(request);
    if (rclcpp::spin_until_future_complete(this->get_node_base_
interface(), future_result) ==
        rclcpp::FutureReturnCode::SUCCESS)
    {
        RCLCPP_INFO(this->get_logger(), "Result: concatenated_
str='%s'", future_result.get()->concatenated_str.c_str());
```

If the client is successful, it will get the response from the server, which is the concatenated string.

After writing the server and client, we can build the nodes by editing CMakeLists.txt.

Building server and client nodes

In order to build the server and client, we can edit the CMakeLists.txt by adding the following lines:

```
add_executable(simple_server src/simple_server.cpp)
ament_target_dependencies(simple_server rclcpp master_ros2_interface)

add_executable(simple_client src/simple_client.cpp)
ament_target_dependencies(simple_client rclcpp master_ros2_interface)
```

We can also add the executables in the install () function to install the generated executables.

After editing CMakeLists.txt, we can carry out colcon build to build all packages.

Running nodes

After building, we can run the server and client for testing.

You can run the server node in terminal 1:

```
ros2 run master_ros2_pkg simple_server
```

You can run the client node in terminal 2:

```
ros2 run master_ros2_pkg simple_client
```

If everything works fine, you will get the following output in the terminal:

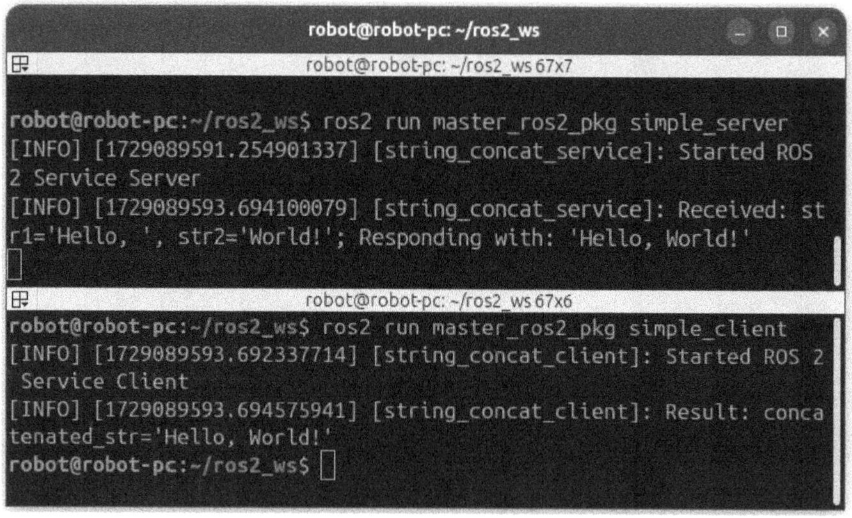

Figure 3.6: Output of service server and client

In the next section, we will discuss implementing a ROS 2 action.

Implementing a ROS 2 action in C++

In this section, we will implement an action server and action client in ROS 2 C++ APIs. The custom action type we will create is master_ros2_interface/action/MyCustomAction.action, and the action name is "my_custom_action". The action client will send a value as the goal value, and the action server will count from 0 to that value with a 1-second delay. The action server will also send the client feedback on the current count. If the count is complete, it will send the final count.

You can find the action server and action client in Chapter03 | master_ros2_pkg | src | action_server.cpp and action_client.cpp.

Creating a custom action interface for the ROS 2 action and server

Let's create a custom action type inside the master_ros2_interface/action folder. The name of the action file is MyCustomAction.action. The .action file is used to define an action type in ROS 2. Here is the definition of the MyCustomAction.action file:

```
# Goal
int32 goal_value
---
# Result
int32 result_value
---
# Feedback
float32 progress
```

The action files have three sections: the first is for the goal value, the second is for the result, and the third is for the feedback. We have to separate each data field with "---."

After creating our action file, we just need to edit CMakeLists.txt and package.xml.

Editing CMakeLists.txt and package.xml

In CMakeLists.txt, update rosidl_generate_interfaces() by adding the action file:

```
rosidl_generate_interfaces(${PROJECT_NAME}
  "msg/CustomMsg.msg"
  "srv/ConcatStrings.srv"
  "action/MyCustomAction.action"
)
```

In package.xml, we have to add action_msgs to build the custom action type:

```
<depend>action_msgs</depend>
```

Writing a ROS 2 action server

After creating the custom action, we can start writing the action server.

To access the custom action in the action server code, we have to include the header file that will be generated by the master_ros2_interface package:

```
#include "master_ros2_interface/action/my_custom_action.hpp"
```

Here is the declaration of the action server. The `rclcpp_action::create_server()` is used to declare a new action. We have to mention the action type and the name of the action in the function. Along with these, we need to add three callbacks as well. One is for handling the goal, one is for handling/executing the goal, and one is for handling the cancellation of the goal:

```cpp
action_server_ = rclcpp_action::create_server<MyCustomAction>(
    this,
    "my_custom_action",
    std::bind(&ActionServer::handle_goal, this, std::placeholders::_1,
std::placeholders::_2),
    std::bind(&ActionServer::handle_cancel, this,
std::placeholders::_1),
    std::bind(&ActionServer::handle_accepted, this,
std::placeholders::_1)
  );
```

When the action server receives a goal, it first calls the `handle_goal` function, receives the goal value, and returns whether we have to accept the execution. If the execution is accepted, the `handle_accepted` callback is called, and the execution function called `execute(const std::shared_ptr<GoalHandle> goal_handle)` starts. This is the main function of the action server that processes the goal. If the client cancels the goal, it calls the `handle_cancel` function.

The `execute(const std::shared_ptr<GoalHandle> goal_handle)` function is given below. The function gets the goal value and starts a feedback loop. After the loop, the result values are published:

```cpp
void execute(const std::shared_ptr<GoalHandle> goal_handle) {
const auto goal = goal_handle->get_goal();
 auto result = std::make_shared<MyCustomAction::Result>();
 auto feedback = std::make_shared<MyCustomAction::Feedback>();
   for (int i = 1; i <= goal->goal_value; ++i) {
      feedback->progress = i ;
      goal_handle->publish_feedback(feedback);
      rclcpp::sleep_for(std::chrono::milliseconds(500));
   }
    result->result_value = goal->goal_value;
   goal_handle->succeed(result);
   RCLCPP_INFO(this->get_logger(), "Goal succeeded");
 }
```

The rest of the code is the same as the nodes that we have already seen before. Now we will see what is in the action client code.

Writing the ROS 2 action client

In the action client, we use the `rclcpp_action::create_client` function, and inside this function, we have to mention the type of the action and the name of the action. After creating the client object, we call the `send_goal()` function:

```
client_ = rclcpp_action::create_client<MyCustomAction>(this, "my_custom_
action");
send_goal();
```

In the `send_goal()` function, we create a goal message and set the goal value to send to the server as 10:

```
auto goal_msg = MyCustomAction::Goal();
goal_msg.goal_value = 10;
```

We also assign callbacks for feedback and the results when the client receives feedback and the result from the server:

```
auto send_goal_options = rclcpp_
action::Client<MyCustomAction>::SendGoalOptions();
send_goal_options.feedback_callback = [this](GoalHandle::SharedPtr, const
std::shared_ptr<const MyCustomAction::Feedback> feedback) {
    RCLCPP_INFO(this->get_logger(), "Feedback: %.2f", feedback-
>progress);
    };
    send_goal_options.result_callback = [this](const
GoalHandle::WrappedResult &result) {
    RCLCPP_INFO(this->get_logger(), "Result: %d", result.result->result_
value);
    };
```

After assigning the callback, we use the `async_send_goal` function to send the goal message we have assigned:

```
client_->async_send_goal(goal_msg, send_goal_options);
```

After calling this function, the client will send the goal immediately to the server.

Building nodes

To build the nodes, we must add the same lines we did for the previous nodes in `CMakeList.txt`. After editing `CMakeLists.txt`, you can build using the `colcon build` command.

Running nodes

After building the nodes, we can run the nodes using the following command.

You can run the action server in terminal 1:

```
ros2 run master_ros2_pkg action_server
```

After running the action server, you can run the action client in terminal 2:

```
ros2 run master_ros2_pkg action_client
```

In *Figure 3.7*, you can see the goal received message in the server and see that the client gets feedback from the server and the result.

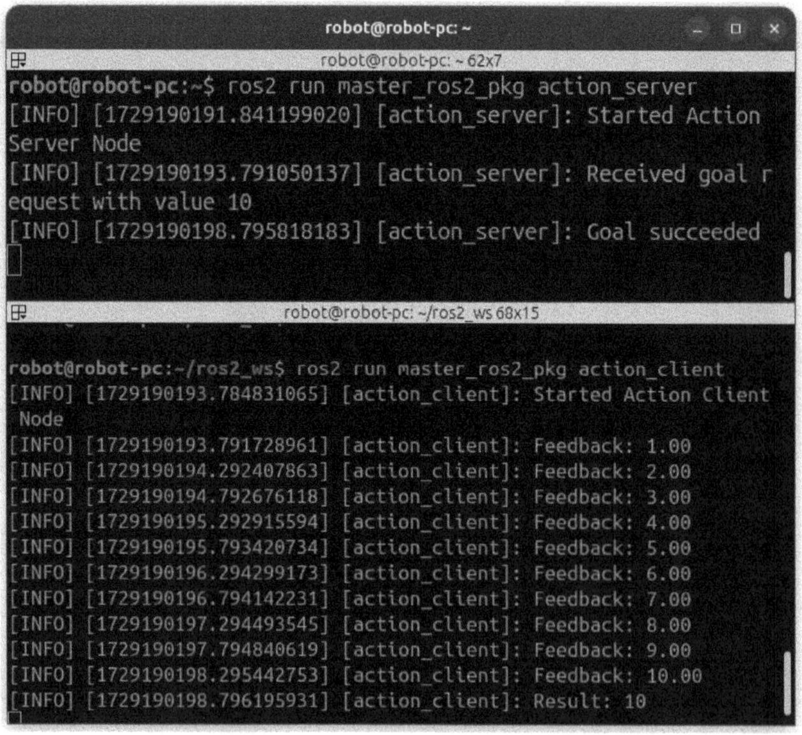

Figure 3.7: Output of action server and client

In the next section, we will see how we can launch these nodes from the launch files.

Writing launch files for nodes

In this section, we will see the launch files for launching these nodes together. In the Chapter03 | master_ros2_pkg | launch folder, you can find the following launch files to start nodes together. We've already discussed how to write a basic launch file, so we will not discuss the concept in detail:

- pub_sub.launch.py: This launch file will start the publisher and subscriber.
- pub_params_sub.launch.py: This launch file will start the publisher_node_params node and a normal subscriber.
- server_client.launch.py: This will start the service server and client.
- action_server_client.launch.py: This will start the action server and client.

> Implementing ROS 2 composable nodes
>
> In this chapter, we have focused mainly on non-composable nodes. Here is the reference if you want to implement composable nodes [13]. Here is the reference for different types of executors available in ROS 2 [14].

Before concluding this chapter, you must understand a few tips on configuring different DDS for communication and configuring ROS_DOMAIN_ID.

Configuring ROS 2 DDS/Zenoh and ROS_DOMAIN_ID

Let's start by configuring DDS for your ROS 2 installation. So, you may ask why we need to change DDS rather than using the default one. The answer is each DDS is different. Some DDS implementations work best for some applications. So, to get better results, it is better to change the DDS.

Let's explore how to change the DDS of your ROS 2 installation.

Configuring ROS 2 DDS

Setting a new DDS is straightforward. First, select the DDS you want to use in a robot, and then install the DDS implementation packages if they are not already installed.

We will look at the installations of different DDSs here:

- **Install Fast DDS**: You can use the following command to install Fast DDS:

```
sudo apt install -y ros-jazzy-rmw-fastrtps-cpp
```

After installing Fast DDS, you can export the `RMW_IMPLEMENTATION` variable to `rmw_fastrtps_cpp`. You can do this by adding the following line to the end of the `.bashrc` file. We have to re-source the terminal or take a new terminal to see the updated DDS settings. After setting this, Fast DDS will be used as the new DDS:

```
echo "export RMW_IMPLEMENTATION=rmw_fastrtps_cpp" >> ~/.bashrc
```

The same procedure is used to install Cyclone DDS.

- **Install Cyclone DDS**: Let's see how we can install and configure Cyclone DDS.

  We can use the following command to install Cyclone DDS on our machine:

  ```
  sudo apt install -y ros-jazzy-rmw-cyclonedds-cpp
  ```

  After installing Cyclone DDS, set it as the new DDS using the following command:

  ```
  echo "export RMW_IMPLEMENTATION= rmw_cyclonedds_cpp" >> ~/.bashrc
  ```

- **Installing Zenoh**: We can also set non-DDS frameworks like Zenoh as middleware. You can install Zenoh from the apt package manager or build it manually using the source code. Here is the command to install Zenoh from the apt package manager.

  ```
  sudo apt install ros-jazzy-rmw-zenoh-cpp.
  ```

  Here is the GitHub repository to build it from the source code [15]. After building the middleware, you can export the variable:

  ```
  echo "export RMW_IMPLEMENTATION= rmw_zenoh_cpp" >> ~/.bashrc
  ```

You can read more about DDS configuration at this link [16]. Here are some detailed references to configuring Fast DDS [17] and Cyclone DDS [18] specifically.

Setting ROS_DOMAIN_ID

`ROS_DOMAIN_ID` in ROS 2 is a unique identifier that isolates a group of nodes that can communicate with each other. For example, if there are multiple robots in the same network, we can use this identifier to isolate the communication for each robot. Nodes running on the same domain ID can find each other, but they are isolated and cannot communicate with another domain ID. The default value of `ROS_DOMAIN_ID` is 0. It is an integer, and you can set values from 0 to 232, which can vary based on the underlying DDS and the OS.

Setting a domain ID is very easy, like configuring DDS, which we did earlier.

For example, this is how we set the ID to 10:

```
echo "export ROS_DOMAIN_ID=10" >> ~/.bashrc
```

In this section, we have learned how to set up and configure different DDS in ROS 2 and set up ROS_DOMAIN_ID to isolate nodes in the robot network. Configuring DDS in robots may be required because of different working environments.

The following section will show how to configure Docker, Docker Compose, and Dev Container for ROS 2 Jazzy development.

Setting up ROS 2 Jazzy development in Docker

The scripts and Dockerfiles from Chapter03/docker_dev can be used to build and run the ROS 2 packages in Chapter03 using Docker.

Here is the command to build the ROS 2 Jazzy custom image.

```
./build_image.sh ros2_dev:v0.1 master_ros2_ws robot
```

Here, ros2_dev:v0.1 is the name of the custom image, master_ros2_ws is our ROS 2 workspace where we can put our Chapter03 ROS 2 packages, and the robot is the user's name inside the container.

After building the ROS 2 custom image, we can create the container using the following command.

```
./create_container.sh ros2_dev:v0.1 master_ros2_ws ros2_dev
```

We need to provide the image name, the ROS 2 workspace name, and the container name we need to make.

After creating the container, you can see that the master_ros2_ws is mounted inside the container. We can build the ROS 2 workspace inside the container and run the nodes.

If we want to open more terminals for the same container, you can use the following command:

```
./start_container.sh ros2_dev
```

This will attach a new terminal if the container is already running or start it if it has stopped. You need to provide the container name as the argument for this script.

After attaching a new terminal, make sure you have source the ros_entry_point script using the following command:

```
source /ros_entrypoint.sh
```

The following section provides instructions for building, creating, and running containers using Docker Compose.

Setting up ROS 2 Development in Docker Compose

This section shows how to build and start containers for `Chapter03` packages using Docker Compose.

Switch to `Chapter03 | docker_compose_dev` folder and execute the following command to start building the Docker image and starting the container:

Use the following command if you are using a non-NVIDIA graphics card on your PC.

```
docker compose -f docker-compose-gui.yml build
docker compose -f docker-compose-gui.yml up
```

If you do have an NVIDIA graphics card and the driver is properly installed, use the following command to start the container.

```
docker compose -f docker-compose-nvidia.yml build
docker compose -f docker-compose-nvidia.yml up
```

Once you start this command, the image will be built first, and the container will start. You have to use another terminal to attach to the container. You don't have to close this terminal; if you cancel the command by pressing *Ctrl + C*, it will stop the running container.

Using the following command, you can create a new terminal from the running container.

```
./start_container.sh ros2_dev
```

Now source the ROS 2 environment using the following command and you can build the ROS 2 workspace which is mounted inside the container.

```
source /ros_entrypoint.sh
```

After starting the container, if you want to stop or remove it, you can execute the command from a new host terminal. Make sure you are executing inside the `docker_compose_dev` folder.

```
docker compose -f docker-compose-gui.yml down
```

or

```
docker compose -f docker-compose-nvidia.yml down
```

Next, let's see how to set up VS Code Dev Container for ROS 2 development.

ROS 2 Development using VS Code Dev Container

If you want to set up a Dev Container [20] in VS Code, make sure you have created the ROS 2 workspace named master_ros2_ws and open the Chapter03 folder using VS Code. This folder has a .devcontainer folder, which has the devcontainer.json file, and the instructions for using the docker-compose file we have used in the above section for the container. When you open the folder, it will prompt you to install the Dev Container extension and **Reopen in Container**. If you select this option, it will build the container, set the environment, mount the ROS 2 workspace as a volume, and connect the editor to it. We can also see the mounted volume, which is the master_ros2_ws folder in VS Code itself.

Summary

This chapter covered implementing key ROS 2 concepts using the rclcpp library for C++. It introduced ROS 2 actions, comparing them to services, highlighting that actions are more suited for long-running tasks with feedback and cancellation capabilities.

The chapter also discussed parameters and how they can be used to configure nodes using YAML files for flexibility. Additionally, it covered the creation of ROS 2 launch files to manage multiple nodes efficiently, and how to build a ROS 2 workspace. The rclcpp client library (C++) was introduced, allowing users to implement nodes.

The chapter also discussed different types of ROS 2 node (non-composable, composable, and lifecycle nodes). It explained how nodes communicate using DDS, offering various QoS configurations to ensure reliability and efficiency. The chapter also touched on building custom interfaces and messages, managing ROS parameters, and setting up DDS/Zenoh and ROS domain ID configurations for better node communication.

In the next chapter, we will see how to build 3D robot models in ROS 2 using URDF.

References

- [1] https://docs.ros.org/en/jazzy/Tutorials/Beginner-CLI-Tools/Understanding-ROS2-Actions/Understanding-ROS2-Actions.html

- [2] https://docs.ros.org/en/jazzy/Tutorials/Beginner-CLI-Tools/Understanding-ROS2-Parameters/Understanding-ROS2-Parameters.html

- [3] https://docs.ros.org/en/jazzy/Tutorials/Intermediate/Launch/Creating-Launch-Files.html

- [4] https://docs.ros.org/en/jazzy/Tutorials/Beginner-Client-Libraries/Colcon-Tutorial.html

- [5] https://docs.ros.org/en/jazzy/Tutorials/Beginner-Client-Libraries/Creating-A-Workspace/Creating-A-Workspace.html

- [6] https://github.com/ros2/rcl

- [7] https://docs.ros.org/en/jazzy/p/rcl/

- [8] https://docs.ros.org/en/jazzy/Concepts/Basic/About-Client-Libraries.html

- [9] https://design.ros2.org/articles/node_lifecycle.html

- [10] https://docs.ros.org/en/jazzy/Concepts/Intermediate/About-Quality-of-Service-Settings.html

- [11] https://docs.ros.org/en/jazzy/p/rclcpp/generated/index.html

- [12] https://docs.ros.org/en/ros2_packages/jazzy/api/rclcpp/generated/classrclcpp_1_1QoS.html

- [13] https://docs.ros.org/en/jazzy/Tutorials/Intermediate/Composition.html

- [14] https://docs.ros.org/en/jazzy/Concepts/Intermediate/About-Executors.html#executors

- [15] https://github.com/ros2/rmw_zenoh

- [16] https://docs.ros.org/en/jazzy/Installation/DDS-Implementations.html

- [17] https://fast-dds.docs.eprosima.com/en/latest/fastdds/ros2/ros2_configure.html

- [18] https://husarion.com/tutorials/other-tutorials/husarnet-cyclone-dds/

- [19] https://docs.ros.org/en/jazzy/Tutorials/Intermediate/Monitoring-For-Parameter-Changes-CPP.html

- [20] https://code.visualstudio.com/docs/devcontainers/containers

4

Working with Robot 3D Modeling in ROS 2

In the last chapter, we discussed implementing different ROS 2 concepts, such as topics, services, actions, and parameters, using C++ and the `rclcpp` client library. This chapter will show how we can apply these communication concepts to robot modeling, simulation, and control.

In this chapter, we focus more on robot modeling in ROS 2 using the **Universal Robot Description Format (URDF)**, which can model the kinematics and dynamics of the robot. This 3D model can be used for visualization, simulation, motion planning, sensor and actuator integration, and real robot control. URDF is a useful feature in ROS 2 to keep the robot representation simple and modular.

We will start by discussing the importance of robot modeling and see the basics of URDF/Xacro modeling. After discussing the basics of URDF/Xacro, we will see how to convert a 3D CAD model of a robot to URDF. After building the URDF model, we will visualize it in RViz. Finally, we will discuss the best practices for creating a URDF/Xacro model. In this chapter, we will discuss the following important topics:

- Introduction to robot modeling in ROS 2
- Introduction to URDF and Xacro
- Exporting 3D CAD models to URDF
- Visualizing URDF models of existing robots
- Best practices of URDF/Xacro modeling

Technical requirements

To follow along with this chapter, you should install Ubuntu 24.04 LTS with a ROS 2 Jazzy desktop. It can be in a VM, Docker, WSL 2, or a real machine. The reference materials for this chapter can be found in the `Chapter04` folder of the following GitHub repository: `https://github.com/PacktPublishing/Mastering-ROS-2-for-Robotics-Programming/tree/main/Chapter04`.

Introduction to robot modeling in ROS 2

Let's start by understanding robot modeling and its relevance in building robot software.

What is robot modeling?

Robot modeling is the process of developing a mathematical and conceptual representation of a robot's structure, kinematics, dynamics, and functionality. The process mainly concerns the robot's physical and mechanical characteristics, such as how the robot looks, how many links and joints are present, and the shape and size of each link. It also defines dynamic parameters like mass and inertia and additional information like sensors/actuators present in the robot.

Here are important types of modeling within robot modeling:

- **Kinematic modeling**: A robot is a combination of links and joints. Links are the rigid body part of the robotic system, and joints are the interconnection of multiple links. The links and joints are mainly responsible for the robot's motion. Robot kinematics is the study of a robot's motion without considering the forces or torques that cause the motion. Kinematic modeling is an important part of robot modeling. In the robot model, you can find accurate information regarding the position of each link and joint, types of joints, limits of joints, and shape of joints.

- **Dynamics modeling**: In this modeling, we consider the forces/torque acting on the robot links and joints. Dynamic modeling is very important because these parameters help to simulate the robot model before prototyping the actual robot. Tuning these parameters in simulation will help to build better hardware components.

- **Geometric modeling**: In this modeling, we define the shape, size, and physical structure of the robot's links or parts. This is essential for visualizing the robot and detecting collisions with its environment. The robot's geometry helps it plan its path better and avoid obstacles.

- **Control modeling**: In control modeling, we develop a control system that allows the robot to perform certain tasks, such as following a path or picking up objects. This modeling helps create better motion control and feedback loops in the robot.

- **Sensor and actuator modeling**: The sensor and actuator models help to simulate both virtually in a robot simulator. These models help to iterate different sensors on the robot before buying them for the real robot. The same applies to actuators. Modeling different actuator profiles in a simulation helps us understand which actuator has to be chosen for the real robot.

- **Environmental modeling**: This involves modeling the physical surroundings, allowing the robot to interact and navigate. Accurate environmental modeling is important for testing the robot for multiple use cases.

Here is an example of a 3D CAD model of a two-wheeled robot in Fusion 360 [1]. These types of CAD tools allow us to model the robot's geometry, kinematics, and dynamics.

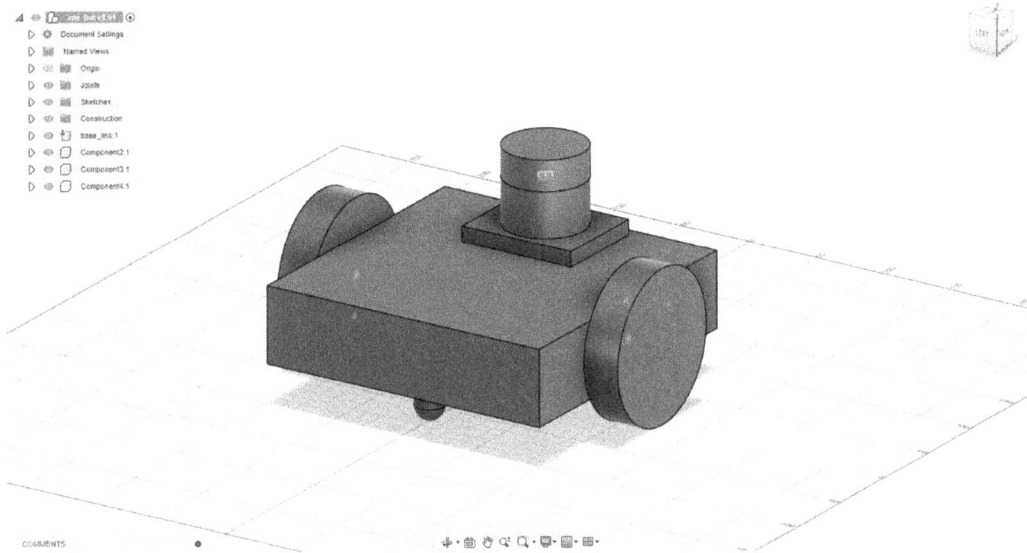

Figure 4.1: 3D CAD model of a two-wheeled robot in Fusion 360

In the upcoming sections, we will understand the importance of robot modeling and learn more about CAD tools and compare them in the context of robot modeling.

Why is robot modeling important?

We have seen the different types of modeling involved in robot modeling. You may already understand the importance of robot modeling, but let's summarize the main points here:

- **Visualization and development**: A 2D or 3D CAD model of the robot helps the developers visualize it and its movement during robot application development. Visualization is not a simulation; it is for visualizing the motion of each joint of the robot and checking whether the robot is in a collision. Visualizing the model allows us to evaluate the kinematics and the robot's response to each motion command.

- **Robot simulation**: Once we have an accurate robot model, we can perform a robot simulation. The robot simulation helps the developer identify design flaws and optimize them. Using simulators, developers can reiterate the design without spending any money. The reiterated design will allow the developer to construct and choose more accurate hardware components, resulting in successful robotic products. Even though the simulators are not an accurate replica of the actual robot, they can still give a good idea of the working of your actual robot.

- **Controls**: With an accurate robot model, we can even tune control algorithms to ensure smoother movement in the actual robot.

- **Planning and navigation**: With the help of a simulator, we can use robot models to test different robotic applications, such as pick-and-place and autonomous navigation.

Now, let's have a look at some of the popular CAD modeling tools used for robot modeling.

Robot modeling tools

3D CAD tools are mainly used to model the kinematics and dynamics of the robot. CAD tools like **SolidWorks** [2], Autodesk **Fusion 360** [3], and **CATIA** [4] are widely used in modeling robots. These tools provide the option to model the links and joints of the robot and can assign dynamic properties, like mass, inertia, etc., to the robot's links. Tools like SolidWorks and Fusion 360 offer options to simulate the joints and help to do structural analysis.

Figure 4.2: Popular 3D CAD tools for robotics

Here is a comparison of the features of popular CAD tools used in robot modeling:

Feature	Autodesk Fusion 360	SolidWorks	CATIA
Major focus	Quick and easy 3D CAD designing, simulation, and collaboration.	Advanced 3D CAD designing for engineering and manufacturing.	High-end engineering and complex assembly and design. Good with surface modeling.
Simulation	Perform basic **Finite Element Analysis (FEA)** and basic motion studies.	Advanced FEA, motion studies, thermal and kinematic analysis.	High-level FEA, motion, structural, and kinematics analysis.
Assembly modeling	Handles simple to moderate assemblies.	Ideal for complex assemblies and dependencies.	Best in class for large and complex assemblies.
Collaboration	It has excellent cloud collaboration version control.	Limited cloud option, mainly using local file management.	It is integrated with **Product Lifecycle Management (PLM)** tools.
User interface	Easy to use, clean, cloud-connected UI, and intuitive.	It features a rich UI and has a powerful and steeper learning curve.	The UI is complex, customizable, and has an industrial interface.
Parametric modeling	User-friendly and strong parametric tools.	Industry-leading parametric modeling.	Extremely robust, suited for complex, high-precision assemblies.
File export for robotics	Supports STL, OBJ, step, and third-party plugins for ROS URDF export.	Supports STL, OBJ, step, and third-party plugins for ROS URDF export.	Supports STL, OBJ, step, and third-party plugins for ROS URDF export.
Rendering	It has basic visualization with cloud rendering.	Good-quality rendering with Photoview 360 or add-ons.	It has advanced rendering and visualization features.

Feature	Autodesk Fusion 360	SolidWorks	CATIA
Cost	It must have a subscription-based policy (free and affordable for students and startups).	High-cost licensing for the full suite.	Very expensive and designed for enterprise usage.
Platform compatibility	Cloud-based, works with Windows and macOS.	Primarily works with Windows and some cloud-based features.	Primarily work with Windows.
Learning curve	Moderately easy for beginners.	Steeper for beginners, but powerful once mastered.	Steeper for beginners, but powerful once mastered.

Table 4.1: Comparison of popular CAD tools for robotics

In the preceding table, you can see that Autodesk Fusion 360 is good for beginners, but if you plan to create a complex system assembly, it is better to go with SolidWorks or CATIA.

Now, we can discuss the next step after the robot's 3D CAD modeling. After developing the CAD model, we need to export it to other formats for further simulation, visualization, and control of the physical robot. So next, we will see how to export CAD models into formats compatible with robot simulators like Gazebo, MuJoCo, Webots, NVIDIA Isaac Sim, and CoppeliaSim, and robotics frameworks such as ROS 2 for robot control.

In this chapter, we will focus on exporting the CAD model to a ROS 2-compatible robot model so that we can use it for simulation and ROS 2-based hardware control. Before starting to discuss the export operation, it is good to understand the robot model format in ROS 2 for visualization, simulation, and control: URDF/Xacro.

Introduction to URDF and Xacro

In ROS 2, we use the **URDF/Xacro** format to represent the robot model. URDF is an XML format, and inside URDF, there are tags to describe the robot's structure, kinematics, appearances, collision, and basic dynamics parameters. It can also hold simulation tags, which can be used for robot simulators like Gazebo.

Writing URDF can sometimes be lengthy and complex. It doesn't offer any programmability. We need to add hardcoded values for joints and links. That's where Xacro comes in. **Xacro** (or **XML Macros**) is a tool in ROS 2 to simplify complex URDF files. As the name suggests, it enables us to use macros/functions inside URDF.

Along with macros, we can use variables and conditional statements with XML, making it easier to build, reuse, and modify large robot models. Using Xacro, we can create reusable templates and parameters to make URDF development easier. After creating the URDF model using Xacro, we will use the Xacro tool in ROS 2 to parse the file and convert it to regular URDF. The developer does not need to worry about conversion; the Xacro tool will take care of it. Writing URDF with Xacro is preferred because it offers developers more flexibility and programmability.

The main limitation of URDF/Xacro modeling is that we can only represent tree structures, so parallel robots can't be modeled inside URDF. Also, we assume robots are rigid bodies connected by rigid links connected by joints. Flexible elements are not supported.

We can create URDF/Xacro manually or with the help of export plugins from CAD tools. To create a model or edit existing models manually, it is good to understand the basic components of URDF. The following section describes the basic components of URDF.

Components of URDF/Xacro

As already discussed, URDF has pre-defined XML tags to build the robot model. Here are the main components or tags in URDF/Xacro:

- `<robot> </robot>`
- `<link> </link>`
- `<joint> </joint>`
- `<transmission> </transmission>`
- `<ros2_control> </ros2_control>`
- `<sensor> </sensor>`
- `<gazebo> </gazebo>`

We will mainly discuss tags such as `<robot>`, `<link>`, and `<joint>` in this chapter. We will discuss the rest of the tags in *Chapter 5*, which discusses the simulation of the robot, as the remaining tags are mainly used in simulation.

<robot> tag

The <robot> tag is the root element in URDF, which contains the complete definition of the robot model, consisting of several rigid components, also referred to as **links**, which are connected through **joints**. Joints can be either fixed, unactuated, or controlled by actuators. Additionally, sensors can be added to URDF, which is particularly useful for simulation. The <robot> tag has an attribute called name, a unique identifier for the robot model.

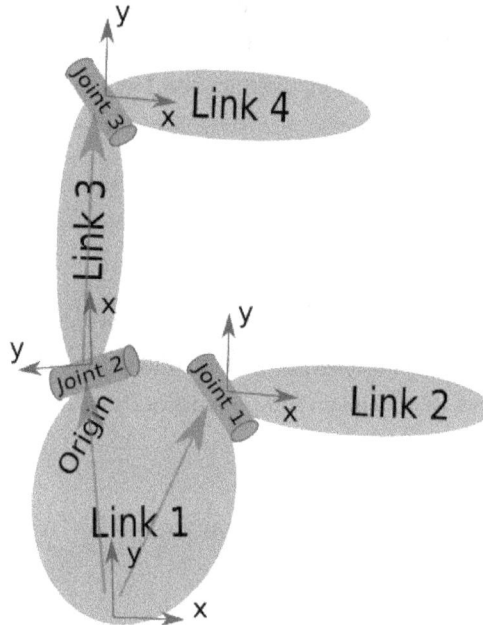

Figure 4.3: Structure of the <robot> tag (source: https://wiki.ros.org/urdf)

In *Figure 4.3*, you can see how the links and joints are interconnected inside the robot tag. Here is an example of the <robot> tag in a URDF file. In this template, master_robot is the name of the robot definition. Inside the robot tag, we are defining all other tags:

```
<robot name="master_robot">
  <link> ... </link>
  <link> ... </link>

  <joint>  .... </joint>
  <joint>  .... </joint>

  <transmission> </transmission>
```

```
    <sensor> </sensor>
    <gazebo> ....   </gazebo>

  </robot>
```

We can see more details about each tag we used inside the <robot> tag. Here is a reference link for the <robot> tag [5].

Now, let's look at the <link> tag.

<link> tag

This tag represents a part of the robot called a link. The link can be a wheel, an arm, or a sensor. The link component has subcomponents like geometry, visual properties, collision properties, and physical characteristics. *Figure 4.4* shows various components in a <link> tag.

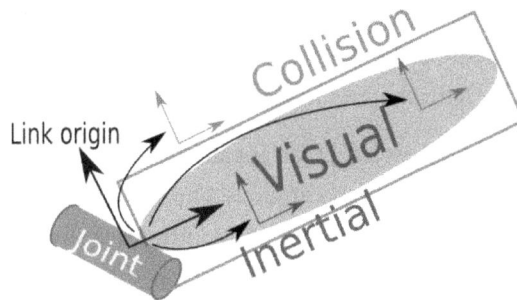

Figure 4.4: <link> tag (source: https://wiki.ros.org/urdf)

Here is an example of the definition of a link in URDF:

```
<link name="base_link">
<!-- Visual tag -->
  <visual>
   <origin xyz="0 0 0" rpy="0 0 0 1"/>
    <geometry>
      <box size="0.5 0.5 0.1"/>
    </geometry>
    <material name="blue"/>
  </visual>

<!-- Collision tag -->
    <collision>
```

```
    <origin xyz="0 0 0" rpy="0 0 0 1"/>
     <geometry>
       <box size="0.5 0.5 0.1"/>
     </geometry>
   </collision>

 <!-- Inertial tag -->
 <inertial>
     <mass value="2.0"/>
     <origin xyz="0 0 0.1" rpy="0 0 0" />
     <inertia ixx="0.1" iyy="0.1" izz="0.1" ixy="0.0" ixz="0.0" iyz="0.0"/>
   </inertial>
 </link>
```

In this example, you can see that the definition of a link starts with the `<link name="base_link">` tag. The `base_link` is the name of the link we are going to define. The `</link>` tag is used to end a link definition. Inside the definition of a link, you can find visual, collision, and inertial tags:

- `<visual>` tag: This describes the link's appearance, including geometry, materials, and, importantly, where the geometry's origin is. The visual of a link can be a primitive shape like a box or even a mesh file. URDF supports primitive shapes like boxes, spheres, and cylinders. We can easily create simple robots using these shapes.

- `<collision>` tag: This tag defines the collision geometry of the link. This is like a visual tag; the only difference is that collision geometry is for detecting whether the robot's link is in a collision. It is not for visualization purposes like visual tags. The collision geometry overlays on top of the visual model. The collision meshes or models are simpler compared to visual meshes. This can make collision checking fast and efficient.

- `<inertial>` tag: This tag defines the mass properties of a link in a robot, the center of mass, and the inertia matrix. These parameters are important for physics simulation and control calculations in robotics.

Check out [6] for a detailed reference to the `<link>` tag.

Now let's see what the `<joint>` tag is.

<joint> tag

In URDF, the <joint> tag defines the interconnection of two links in a robot, allowing them to move relative to each other. Each <joint> tag can specify the name of the joint, the type of joint, the axis of movement, the origin of the joint, and properties like joint limits, damping, etc. *Figure 4.5* shows the different parameters of a joint tag.

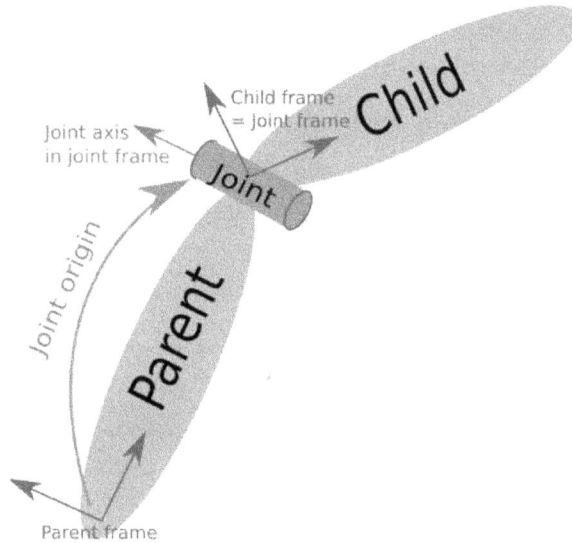

Figure 4.5: <joint> tag (source: https://wiki.ros.org/urdf)

Here is an example code snippet of the <joint> tag in URDF:

```
<joint name="base_link_joint" type="revolute">
    <parent link="base_link" />
    <child link="elbow_link" />
    <origin xyz="0 0 1" rpy="0 0 0" />
    <axis xyz="0 0 1" />
    <limit effort="5.0" velocity="1.5" lower="0.0" upper="1.57" />
    <dynamics damping="0.1" friction="0.01" />
</joint>

<link name="elbow_link">
..............
</link>
```

In this example, you can see that the name of the joint is base_link_joint, and we define the <parent> link and the <child> link. The <parent> link acts as a reference for the joint movement. The <child> link is a link that moves relative to the <parent> link. In this example, the parent link is base_link, as seen in the link section, and the child link is elbow_link. The elbow_link is an imaginary link just for an explanation of the joint. In the <joint> tag, we can see the origin of the joint; the axis of rotation; the limits of the joint on position, velocity, and torque/effort; and parameters like damping and friction. Another important parameter inside <joint> is the type of joint. There are multiple types of joints available:

- **Fixed:** This type of joint creates a rigid connection between two links. It is preferred when no relative motion between parent and child links is required.
- **Revolute:** This kind of joint is like a hinge joint, allowing rotation through a certain axis within a minimum and maximum angle. These joints are applied in robotic arms and similar structures that require limited rotational movement.
- **Continuous:** This type of joint is like a revolute joint, but the rotation axis is not limited. It is used in the wheels of a robot or any joint with continuous rotation.
- **Prismatic:** This joint allows linear motion in a single axis, with a limit on the range. It helps create sliding mechanics like a piston or links that extend.
- **Floating:** This allows six degrees of freedom (translation and rotation around the X, Y, and Z axes). It is typically used to represent the robot's free movement in space, such as base_link.
- **Planar:** This type of joint can move in the X and Y axes and rotate around the Z axis. It is good for mobile robots or structures where parts need to slide and rotate in a 2D plane.

Check out [7] for a complete reference on the <joint> tag in URDF.

After discussing the basic tags in URDF, let's do some basic modeling, first with URDF and then with Xacro.

Building our first URDF model

Let's start modeling a basic robot using URDF. You can find the URDF code in `Chapter04 | simple_rrbot.urdf`. This is a **2-DOF** (short for **two degrees of freedom**) robotic arm called *rrbot*. As we have already seen in the above sections, the URDF code is primarily the combination of `<link>` and `<joint>` tags. ROS 2 provides tools to visualize, parse, and interact with URDF/Xacro-based models.

The best practice to manage URDF/Xacro files in ROS 2 is to create a separate ROS 2 package named `<robot_name>_description`. This package will be used only to keep URDF/Xacro files, mesh files we used for URDF, configuration files, and launch files. For example, URDF/Xacro models of **universal robots** (**URs**) are kept in `ur_description` [8]. You can find more examples on the ROS package index website [9].

We can also keep the URDF file without a package for learning purposes if it is a single file without many dependencies. For example, `simple_rrbot.urdf` is a URDF file that is not in a package but we can still visualize and analyze it.

Here are some important things to keep in mind when creating a URDF file manually:

- **Time-consuming:** Creating a URDF file manually takes time. We have to manually identify the link and joint origin, link geometry, collision, and inertia. This process will take longer and may have to be repeated if the links or joints are modified.

- **Finding links and joint values:** It is better to have the 2D sketch of the robot ready before starting to model the robot in URDF. The links and joints in URDF are modeled relative to the parent link. It is recommended to have a look at the official ROS 2 URDF tutorial to understand this process correctly [10]. This tutorial will ensure you have a proper idea of how to model `<link>` and `<joint>` in URDF. Discussing this goes beyond the scope of this chapter.

- **Trial and error:** Creating a URDF file may involve a lot of trial and error. We may need to do it to correct the axis of rotation, place the joint origin, etc.

- **Using the VSCode IDE:** VSCode IDE helps streamline URDF modeling. It has a ROS extension, which has the option to preview the URDF file in the IDE itself [11]. This will increase the speed of URDF development.

After going through the basics of URDF from the official tutorial, let's go through ROS 2 URDF tools to analyze and visualize the `simple_rrbot.urdf` file.

Verifying URDF files

The check_urdf command in the ros-jazzy-desktop-full installation can parse a URDF file, show the kinematic chain of the robot, or show an error message if there is any.

Open a terminal inside the Chapter04 folder and run this command:

```
check_urdf simple_rrbot.urdf
```

If the command is successful, you will get the following output in the terminal:

```
robot name is: rrbot
---------- Successfully Parsed XML --------------
root Link: world has 1 child(ren)
    child(1):  single_rrbot_link1
        child(1):  single_rrbot_link2
            child(1):  single_rrbot_link3
```

The output means that the URDF file has parsed successfully and shows the root links as world. We can see the respective child links as well.

Visualizing URDF links and joints

If we want to visualize the tree structure of the URDF file, we can use the following command. This is also installed along with the ros-jazzy-desktop-full installation:

```
urdf_to_graphiz simple_rrbot.urdf
```

If it is successful, it will create a PDF file showing the tree structure of links, joints, and the translation and rotation between each joint.

Using the following command, you can visualize the PDF:

```
evince rrbot.pdf
```

The output looks as shown in *Figure 4.6*.

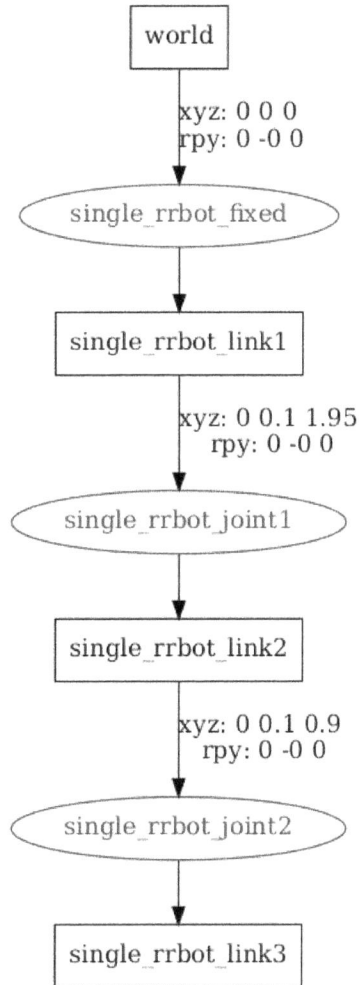

Figure 4.6: URDF tree structure of the rrbot robot

In the output diagram, we can see the tree structure of the robot's joints. The name of the joints and the translation and rotation of each joint relative to the previous joint are also shown.

After visualizing the robot links and joints, let's see how to visualize the robot in 3D with the help of the ROS 2 RViz tool. As you know, RViz helps the developer to visualize the robot model in 3D.

There is already an official tutorial and package available in ROS 2 to get started with URDF modeling. We will see how to install this package and how we can use it to visualize our models as well.

Visualizing URDF in RViz

To visualize the URDF file in RViz, we have to run a set of ROS 2 nodes. Usually, we must write a launch file for it or reuse an existing one.

Let's install the `urdf-tutorial` package, which gives us sample URDF files as well as a launch file to visualize any URDF files. The following command will install the *urdf-tutorial* package on your system:

```
sudo apt install -y ros-jazzy-urdf-tutorial
```

You can also find the source code of this package at [12].

After installing this package, we can start visualizing `simple_rrbot.urdf` using the following command; make sure you are inside the `Chapter04` folder before executing the command:

```
ros2 launch urdf_tutorial display.launch.py model:=$PWD/simple_rrbot.urdf
```

You will get the RViz window shown in *Figure 4.7* with the robot model loaded into it. To see the model in RViz, make sure **Fixed Frame** in RViz is set to `world`. You can also find a GUI with a slider called **Joint State Publisher**. Using the slider, you can move the robot's joint.

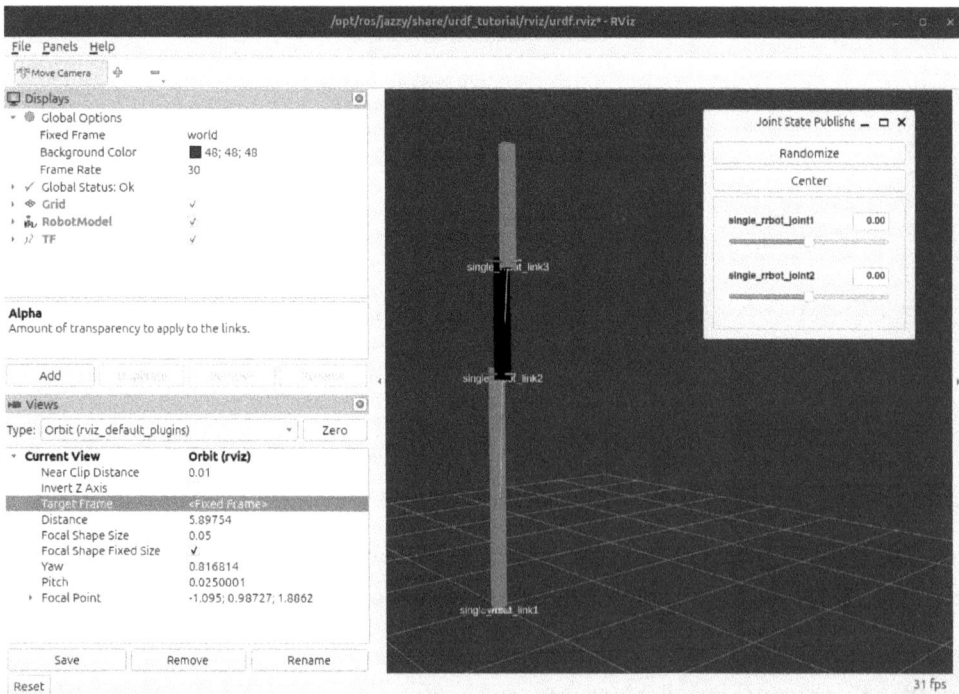

Figure 4.7: URDF visualization in RViz

You can see the robot model in the 3D viewport of RViz. The root frame of the URDF is the world. If we change **Fixed Frame** to **world**, the model will show the origin with regard to the world frame. In RViz, we can add different visualizations by adding display types. In *Figure 4.7*, you can see a display type called **RobotModel**, which loads the URDF model to the 3D viewport. The model you see in RViz is not a simulation but a visualization; it has joints and links that you can move based on the joint type, and it doesn't apply the dynamics parameters of the robot model, like mass, inertia, etc.

Now, let's have a look at how a URDF file is visualized using the launch file we have used.

Parsing a URDF file

Once we start `display.launch.py` with a command-line argument called `model`, which contains the path of the URDF file, the launch file will start several nodes to parse the URDF file, publish the joint states, and publish the **Transform** (**TF**) of each joint. We will discuss TF further in the next chapter.

Figure 4.8 shows how a URDF file is read and visualized in RViz.

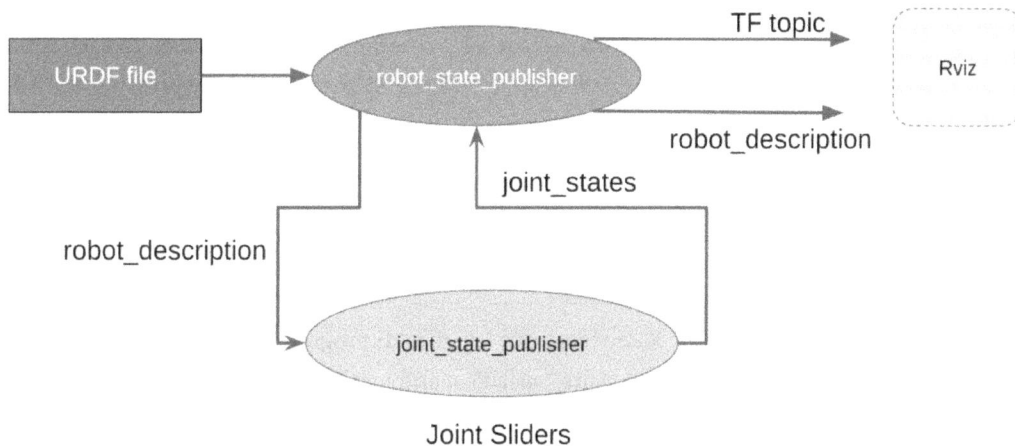

Figure 4.8: Parsing and visualizing URDF in RViz

When we launch the `display.launch.py` file, it will start with two main nodes, which are already installed on ROS 2. Here is an explanation of the nodes that are started along with the launch file:

- `robot_state_publisher`: This is an important node inside the `robot_state_publisher` package in ROS 2. The role of this node is to read the URDF file, parse the tags, and publish the URDF content in a topic called `/robot_description` with a ROS message type of `std_msgs/msg/String`. It also publishes TF [13], which is the relationship between joints and links in the kinematic structure of the robot. In ROS 2, we use the tf2 library to broadcast this information. The `robot_state_publisher` uses this library to send this information to a topic called `/tf`, which has a ROS 2 message type called `tf2_msgs/msg/TFMessage`. It also subscribes to a topic called `joint_state`, which has a ROS message type of `sensor_msgs/msg/JointState`. The `joint_state` topic has updated the values of robot model joints. It only contains the actuated joints, not the fixed joints. The TF topic values will be updated based on the new joint values, and you can view the change in RViz.

- `joint_state_publisher`: This node subscribes to the `/robot_description` topic and publishes the `/joint_state` topic. The `/joint_state` topic updates when we move the slider in the GUI, and the `robot_state_publisher` topic updates the TF topic based on the new values. In *Figure 4.7*, you can see a 3D coordinate frame attached to each robot joint, which is what the TF is. We need to add the TF display type by pressing the **Add** button in RViz to visualize the TF message.

The next section will discuss creating a new ROS 2 package to keep the robot model description in Xacro format. We will also write a launch file to visualize it.

Working with the Xacro model

As we have already discussed, the Xacro format in URDF adds programming capabilities to URDF, such as using macros/functions, constants, variables, and math equations, which makes URDF development easier and more efficient. We can see an example of Xacro's implementation of rrbot in the `Chapter04 | rrbot_description` package. You can use this package as a template for creating your robot description packages.

Here is the folder structure of this package:

```
rrbot_description
├── CMakeLists.txt
├── launch
│   └── rrbot.launch.py
├── package.xml
├── rviz
│   └── view_robot.rviz
└── urdf
    ├── rrbot_description.urdf.xacro
    ├── rrbot.materials.xacro
    └── rrbot.urdf.xacro
```

Figure 4.9: rrbot_description package structure

Let's look at the use of each file in this package:

- `rrbot.launch.py`: This will start `robot_state_publisher`, `joint_state_publisher`, and RViz and visualize the rrbot model in RViz.

- `rrbot.urdf.xacro`: Xacro files have the extension `.xacro`. We can write Xacro files for each section of the robot model and include them in the main Xacro file. This will increase the modularity of the robot model. The `rrbot.urdf.xacro` is the main Xacro file, and you can find macro/function definitions inside the `rrbot_description.urdf.xacro` and `rrbot.materials.xacro` files. These two files are included in this main Xacro file.

To visualize the Xacro model, you can copy the `rrbot_description` package to a ROS 2 workspace and do the building of the workspace. After that, you can use the launch file to visualize the model:

```
ros2 launch rrbot_description rrbot.launch.py
```

Let's walk through the main Xacro file, which is `rrbot.urdf.xacro`.

In normal URDF, we use the `<robot>` tag with the name, but in Xacro, we have to mention an XML namespace in the robot tag for Xacro functions. It will allow the developer to create a Xacro definition inside the URDF file:

```
<robot xmlns:xacro="http://www.ros.org/wiki/xacro" name="simple_rrbot">
```

Now we can see how we can include another Xacro file definition inside a Xacro file:

```
<xacro:include filename="$(find rrbot_description)/urdf/rrbot_
description.urdf.xacro" />
```

The above definition includes the main Xacro definition of the robot model. This Xacro file has a macro called `rrbot`. If we call the macro, we will get the definition of the joints and links mentioned inside this macro. Like the rrbot macro, we import material Xacro files in this file. This is one flexibility that Xacro offers to developers. If the robot model is big, we can write macro definitions and keep them in separate Xacro files. This will increase the modularity and efficiency of the robot model development.

Defining and calling a macro in a Xacro file

As we know, `rrbot_description.urdf.xacro` contains the macro called `rrbot`. Here is the template for defining a macro/function in a Xacro file:

```
<xacro:macro name="rrbot" params="parent prefix *origin">
. . .
. . .
</xacro>
```

The definition of macros will always be inside a `<robot>` tag. If you define multiple macros for your robot model in separate files, ensure they are all inside the `<robot>` tag. If you check the macro definition, you can see parameters, which are the parent link of the robot, which, in our case, is its world. The prefix, which is optional, and the `*origin` tag allow the user to pass the origin values while calling this macro. We can have different origin values whenever we call this macro.

Now, let's see how we can call this macro inside the `rrbot.urdf.xacro` file. Here is how we can call macro and pass parameters. You can find this call on `rrbot.urdf.xacro`:

```
<xacro:rrbot parent="world" prefix="$(arg prefix)">
    <origin xyz="0 0 0" rpy="0 0 0" />
</xacro:rrbot>
```

We are passing arguments to this macro, such as parent links, prefixes, and the origin of the robot base. We can call the macro to replicate the robot model multiple times; there is no need to rewrite the section again and again like in URDF.

Constants and variables in Xacro

In `rrbot_description.urdf.xacro`, you can find the use of constants.

In the following snippet, we are defining the mass and width of a link, you can see that `xacro:property` is used to define a constant. Here, the mass is assigned to 1 and the width is assigned to 0.1.

```
<xacro:property name="mass" value="1" />
<xacro:property name="width" value="0.1" />
```

> **Note**
>
> ROS 2 utilizes SI units for measurements and coordinate conventions. Here, mass is in kg and width is in meter.

To access the constant values, we can use `"${mass}"` and `"${width}"`. Here is a code snippet showing how the `<visual>` tag uses constants to set the origin and geometry of the link:

```
<visual>
    <origin xyz="0 0 ${height1/2}" rpy="0 0 0"/>
    <geometry>
        <box size="${width} ${width} ${height1}"/>
```

This is a very useful feature in Xacro; we don't have to put hardcoded values inside URDF, but we can use constants. We can change only those constant values and adjust different parameters quickly.

Math equations in Xacro

In Xacro, we can use math equations, as shown below. The `<inertia>` tag shows that the constants we define are used in the equation to compute the inertial matrix:

```
    <inertia ixx="${mass / 12.0 * (width*width + height1*height1)}"
ixy="0.0" ixz="0.0"
        iyy="${mass / 12.0 * (height1*height1 + width*width)}" iyz="0.0"
        izz="${mass / 12.0 * (width*width + width*width)}"/>
    </inertial>
```

The math equations in Xacro avoid manual computation by the developer, but instead, they can be computed from the Xacro itself.

Converting Xacro to URDF

ROS 2 has a xacro-to-urdf converter tool, which is inside the xacro package. We can use the following command to convert the Xacro to URDF:

```
xacro <input_file.xacro> -o <output_file.urdf>
```

or

```
ros2 run xacro xacro <input_file.xacro> -o <output_file.urdf>
```

Here is an example command to convert rrbot Xacro to a URDF file. Make sure you are inside the urdf folder of rrbot_description before executing this command:

```
xacro rrbot.urdf.xacro -o rrbot.urdf
```

or

```
ros2 run xacro xacro rrbot.urdf.xacro -o rrbot.urdf
```

After running this command, you will see that rrbot.urdf was created.

We discussed this conversion because it is using the launch file we are going to discuss in the next section.

Writing the ROS 2 launch file for visualizing a URDF/Xacro file

The nodes that started visualizing and interacting with URDF/Xacro are robot_state_publisher, joint_state_publisher, and the rviz2 node. We can use the xacro command to convert the Xacro file to URDF and pass it to the robot_state_publisher node. The xacro command will also work if you directly pass the *.URDF files without any Xacro elements. Go to Chapter04 | rrbot_description/launch/rrbot.launch.py for the launch file for the rrbot visualization.

So far, we have seen how to model robots manually using URDF. The following section will give you an idea of how we can model a robot using a CAD tool and export it to URDF.

Exporting a 3D CAD robot model to URDF

Creating a URDF/Xacro file manually is a time-consuming task. If the model is not complex, we can use manual URDF modeling. But in cases of building a complex robot model, we may have to consider converting the 3D CAD model into URDF directly. So, is this possible? Yes, it is possible for a few CAD tools. We can convert the designed model directly to a ROS 2 package with the help of plugins. Very few plugins are official; they are mostly third-party plugins.

Here are some plugins and tools that are available to export CAD models in different software to URDF/Xacro format. The reference link has the instructions to set the plugin:

- **SolidWorks to URDF Exporter**: This is a third-party open source plugin available for SolidWorks to convert its assembly format, *SLDASM,* to *URDF*. When we export the model, the plugin can auto-generate the robot description package and generate URDF inside it. ROS 1 package generation is currently supported, but we can use that URDF file and move it into our ROS 2 description package. We can expect that the ROS 2 update will be supported soon. Here is where the URDF exporter plugin for SolidWorks can be found [*14*].

- **Fusion 360 to URDF**: This third-party open source Python script is available to change the Fusion 360 model to URDF. We must ensure the CAD model is compatible with the export script. The instructions are given in the related GitHub repository. Like the SolidWorks plugin, it will create a robot description package. Both ROS 1 and ROS 2 Python scripts are available. If the ROS 2 script is not working for you, try the ROS 1 script and copy the URDF file into your ROS 2 description package. Here is a link to the add-in script for exporting Fusion 360 to URDF for ROS 2 [*15*].

- **OnShape to URDF**: This is a third-party open source tool available based on *OnShape APIs* to get the OnShape assemblies and build a URDF model with the dynamic parameters. Here is a plugin to convert an OnShape model to URDF using the OnShape API [*16*].

- **Blender to URDF**: There are multiple third-party tools available for converting Blender models to URDF. One of the popular tools or add-ins available is Phobos. The Phobos project is a CLI tool and add-in for Blender for converting a model into a URDF model. Here is where you can find this project [*17*].

- **Export URDF**: This project is a URDF converter library for CAD programs like Fusion 360, OnShape, and SolidWorks [*18*].

Refer to [*19*] for details about more URDF export plugins.

The generated URDF/Xacro files can again be optimized. You can add more macros to Xacro by manually editing each file if needed. In some models, there may be some tuning required, especially in inertia values during simulation. Also, editing is required to add a ROS 2 controller like a differential drive and sensors like LiDAR to a robot.

In the next section, we will see how to install Autodesk Fusion 360, model a two-wheeled robot, and export the model to a ROS 2 URDF description package.

Installing Autodesk Fusion 360

Modeling a robot in Autodesk Fusion 360 to export to a ROS 2 URDF model has the following prerequisites.

The first prerequisite is to install Fusion 360 if it is not already installed on your machine. We can install Fusion 360, which is primarily supported in Windows, but there is an experimental project that can also help with Fusion 360 in Linux. Experimental projects may not be fully stable. Here is a link to install Fusion 360 on Windows [26]. Fusion 360 is free for students, educators, hobbyists, and some startup companies. The installation is straightforward in Windows. The main hardware requirement while working with Fusion 360 is a good GPU, preferably from NVIDIA. If you want to try the experimental Fusion 360 setup in Ubuntu, you can refer to the following project [27]. After setting up Fusion 360, you may have to sign up for an account that will help you to upload and share the CAD model over the cloud.

After installing Fusion 360, the next prerequisite is to install the Fusion 360 to URDF plugin/add-in to convert the designed model to URDF.

Installing the Fusion 360 to URDF plugin

Installing the Fusion 360 to URDF plugin is straightforward. Download the following GitHub repository [28], which has the plugin as a ZIP file. Unzip the file and extract it to some location first. After extracting the file, open Fusion 360 and press *Shift + S* to show the **Scripts and Add-Ins** window in Fusion 360. Inside this window, locate the option called MyScripts, and to add a new plugin, press the green + icon, which is shown as the first step in *Figure 4.10*

When we click this icon, a file dialog will pop up and we can browse the path to the folder called Fusion_URDF_Exporter_ROS2, as shown in *Figure 4.10*. This is the folder that has the plugin.

Click on the selected folder, and if everything works, you will see Fusion_URDF_Exporter_ROS2, as shown in the second step in *Figure 4.10*:

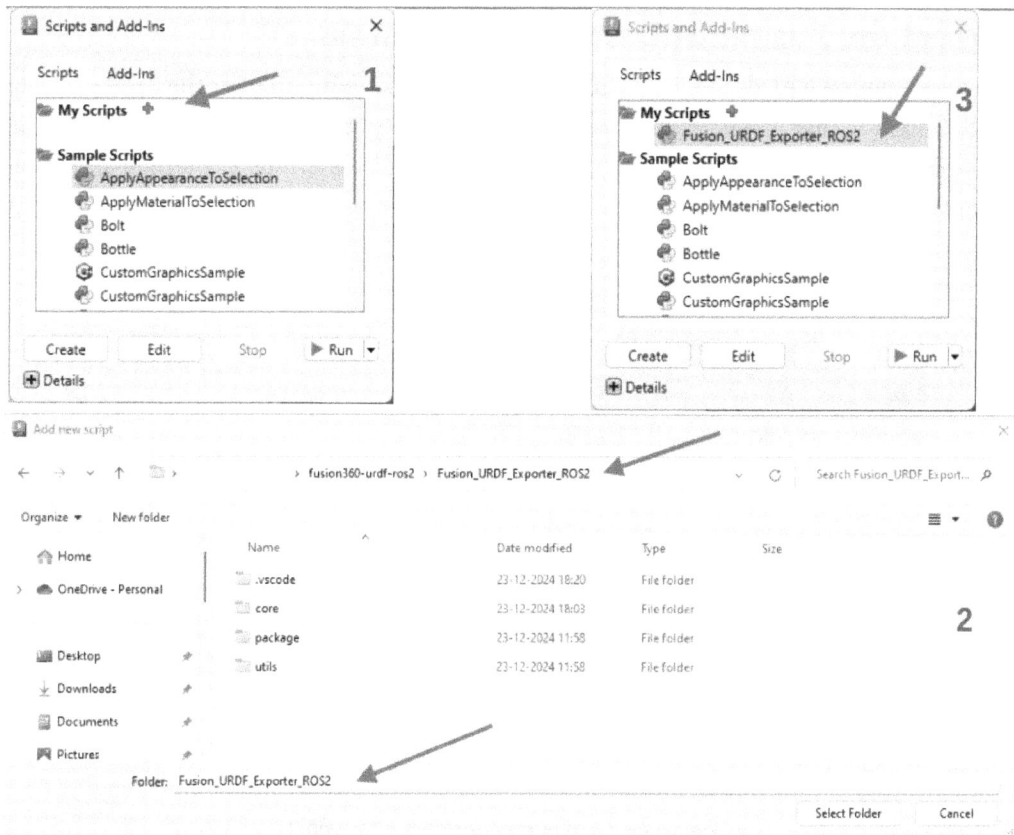

Figure 4.10: Fusion 360 Scripts and Add-Ins window

Once we set up the Fusion URDF Export ROS 2 plugin, we can start modeling the robot. In the next section, we will examine the design practices we must follow before modeling a robot in Fusion 360 to make it compatible with the Fusion URDF Export ROS 2 plugin.

Important design practices for the URDF Export plugin

Here's a list of things you must consider before you start modeling the robot to make it work with the script.

Correct the Fusion 360 coordinate system

When designing the robot model, we must follow the right-hand rule for the cartesian coordinate system so that it will properly export with the correct orientation in ROS 2 URDF. This section describes the coordinate system used in the project. *Figure 4.11* shows the right-hand-rule demonstration with the robot.

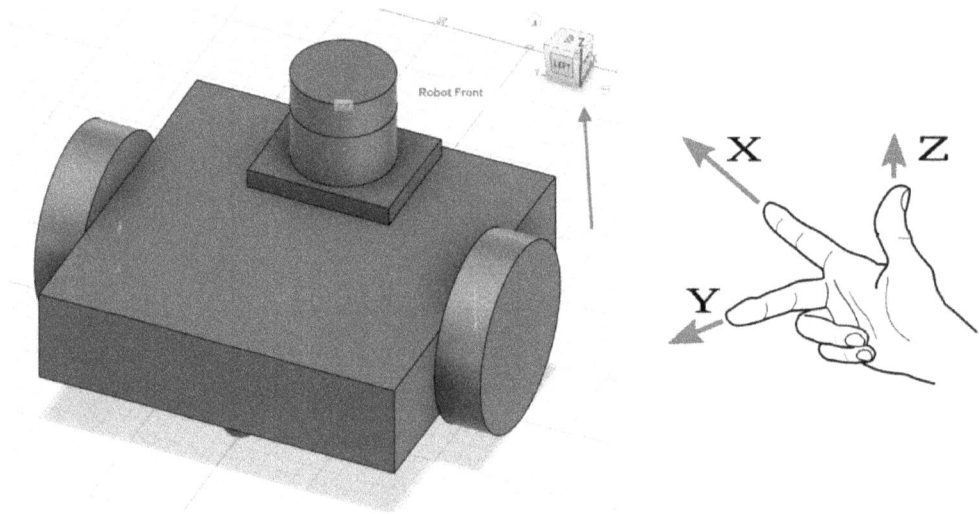

Figure 4.11: Right-hand-rule demonstration

In the figure:

- **Index finger (X axis)**: Represents the positive direction of the X axis; the robot model should always point to the +X direction in Fusion 360. This axis corresponds with the length of the robot.

- **Thumb (Z axis)**: Represents the positive direction of the Z axis. This axis corresponds with the height of the robot.

- **Middle finger (Y axis)**: Represents the positive direction of the Y axis. This axis corresponds with the robot's width.

We need to follow this coordinate system to visualize and spawn the robot model correctly in RViz and Gazebo in ROS 2.

Defining links of the robot

We must ensure that each robot link is defined as a separate **component**. The root link of the robot must be named base_link.

Defining joints of the robot

When defining joints, parent links must be set as Component2, not as Component1.

Defining a component of the robot

Components should contain only *bodies*. Nested components are not supported. Avoid components that have other components inside them. *Figure 4.12* shows the components and their bodies in the rosbot robot.

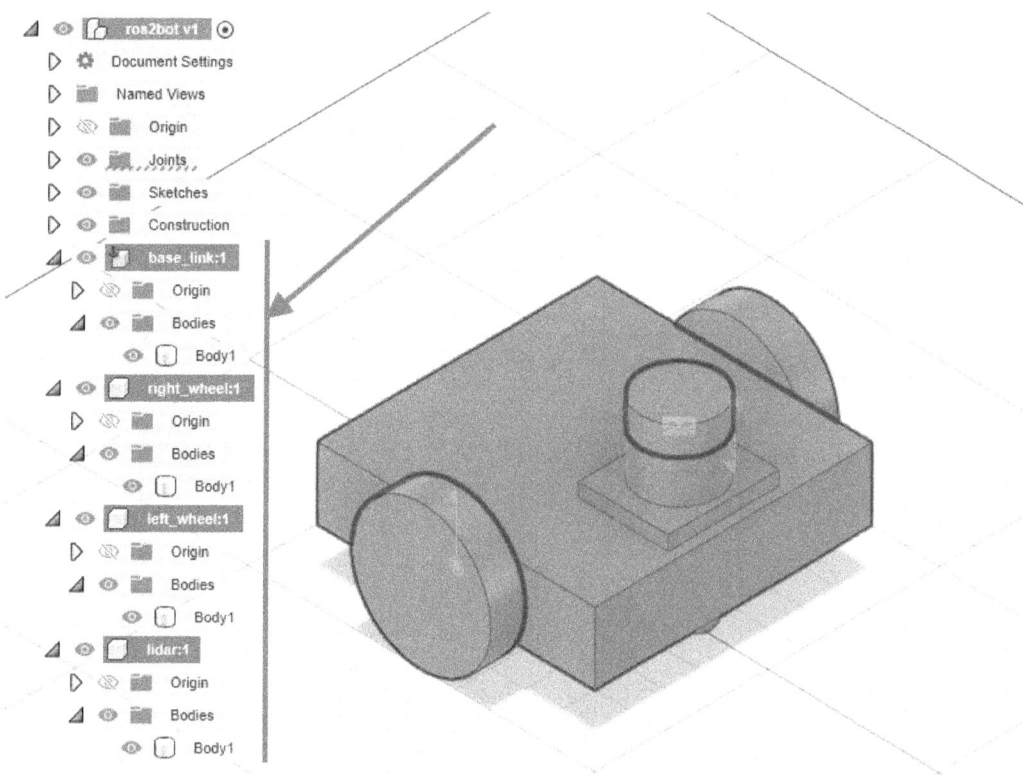

Figure 4.12: Components and bodies of the rosbot robot

Here are some limitations of the Fusion 360 to URDF plugin:

- Supported joint types: Rigid, Slider, and Revolute.
- Avoid using Fusion 360's inbuilt joint editor for positioning joints in complex kinematic loops.
- Misalignments can occur during initial joint positioning in Fusion. Manual adjustments can cause cascading issues with visual and collision properties.
- Turn off **Capture design history** before exporting. Use distinct names for components and save individual components in separate folders to prevent issues.

Now, let's start modeling our first robot, named rosbot, which is shown in *Figure 4.11*.

Modeling a robot in Fusion 360

Here is a set of instructions for modeling a sample robot called rosbot using Autodesk Fusion 360.

Setting the design plane for export

We must follow the right-hand rule to set the plane before starting the modeling. If we do this, the exported URDF model will face the *+X axis*. *Figure 4.13* shows the top view of the Fusion 360 viewport.

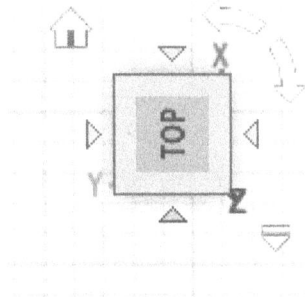

Figure 4.13: Setting the design plane of Fusion 360 for robot modeling

This is the axis we need when we visualize robots in ROS 2.

Sketching the robot base

After selecting the plane, we can start sketching the robot's base. We have to draw a 2D sketch of the plane first and extrude it to create the box, which acts as the robot base.

Select **Menu | SOLID | Create Sketch**. After pressing this option, it will ask which plane we have to draw the sketch. It will show different planes, and choosing the exact plane we want may be confusing. We can use the *Shift + Mouse Center button* to rotate the 3D view and select the same plane we saw in the first step.

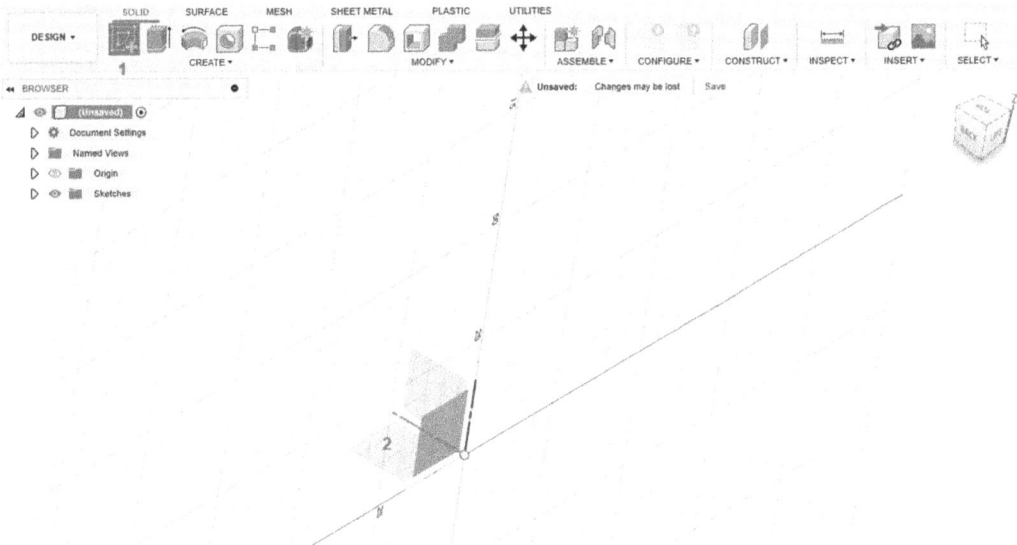

Figure 4.14: Choosing plane for drawing sketch

After selecting the plane, orbit the 3D scene to make the **+X axis** always the front.

Now, you can select the **2-point rectangle** from **SKETCH**, as shown in *Figure 4.15*. From the **Sketch palette** window on the right side, choose the **center rectangle** option, as shown below. This option can draw a rectangle from a center point.

Press the *Tab* key to switch between the square dimensions and enter the dimensions. You can give 200 mm as the width and length for base_link.

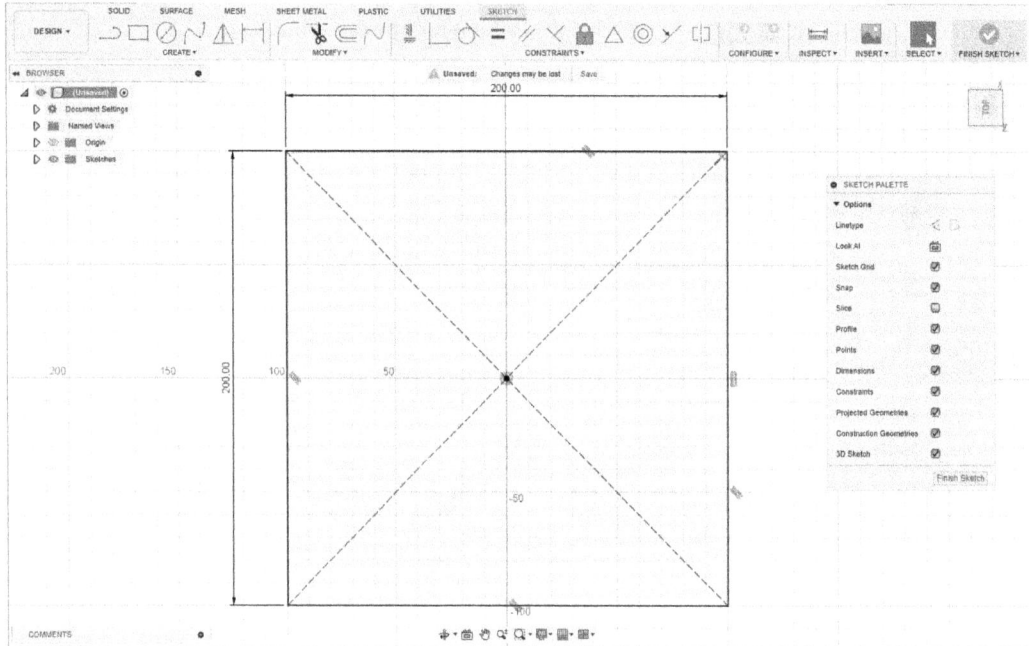

Figure 4.15: Drawing a rectangular sketch

After drawing the correct dimensions, you can click the **FINISH SKETCH** button at the top right to complete the sketch. After completing the sketch, you can click on the top to select the sketch's top area.

Now press the *Q* key (**Menu Solid | Modify | Press Pull**) to extrude the sketch surface to make a box. Once you press the *Q* button, you will see an arrow key that will extrude the sketch to some height. You can give a value of 50 mm as the height.

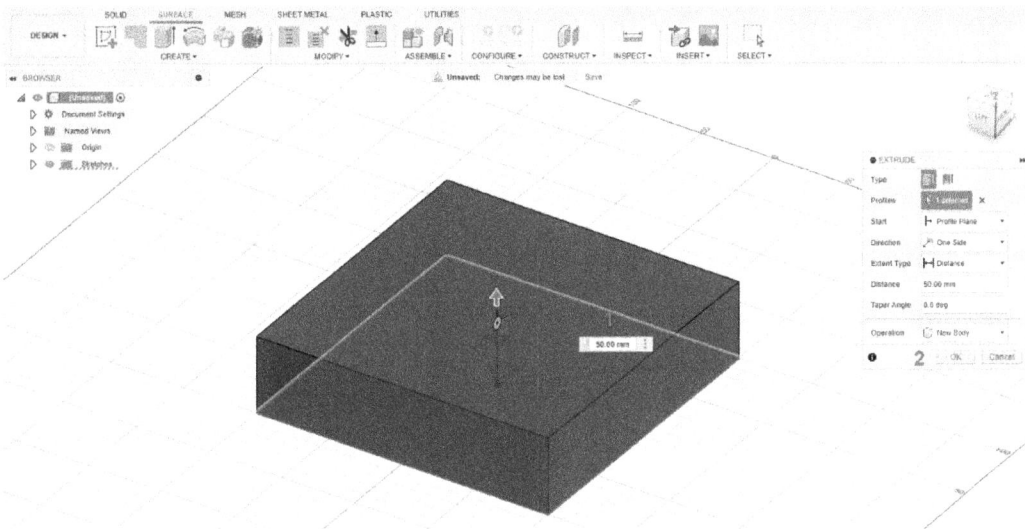

Figure 4.16: Extruding the base plane

After setting the height to 50 mm, select the Operation option from the Extrude window on the right side. We must choose **New Body**. After selecting this option, we can press **Ok**. The above steps are shown in *Figure 4.16*.

Adding wheels to the robot base

We can add wheels after making the robot's main chassis/base_link. The chassis must have two active and two passive caster wheels. *Figure 4.17* shows the Z-X plane, which shows the side of the chassis on which we have to add wheels.

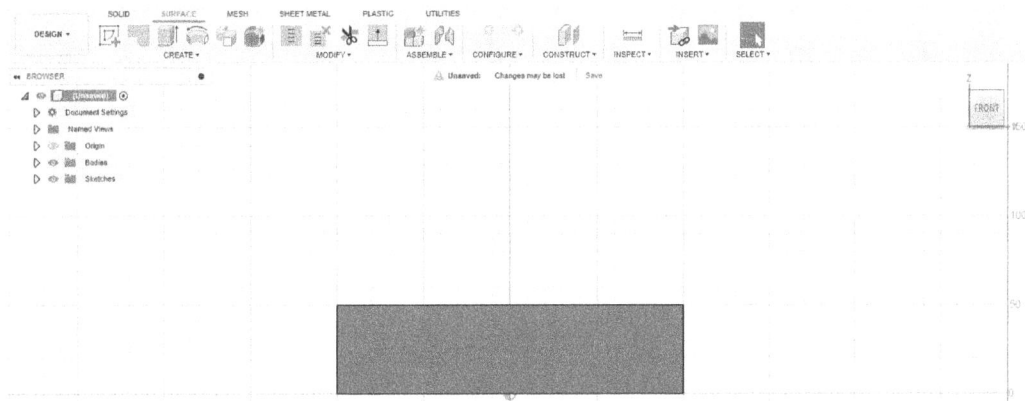

Figure 4.17: Side view of the chassis

We can start a sketch and extrude it like we did for the chassis to create wheels. In *Figure 4.18*, we can see that you have chosen the Sketch option and chose a circle with a center-diameter circle. Then, select the center of the chassis, as shown in *Figure 4.18*. Give a diameter of 100 mm and press **Finish**.

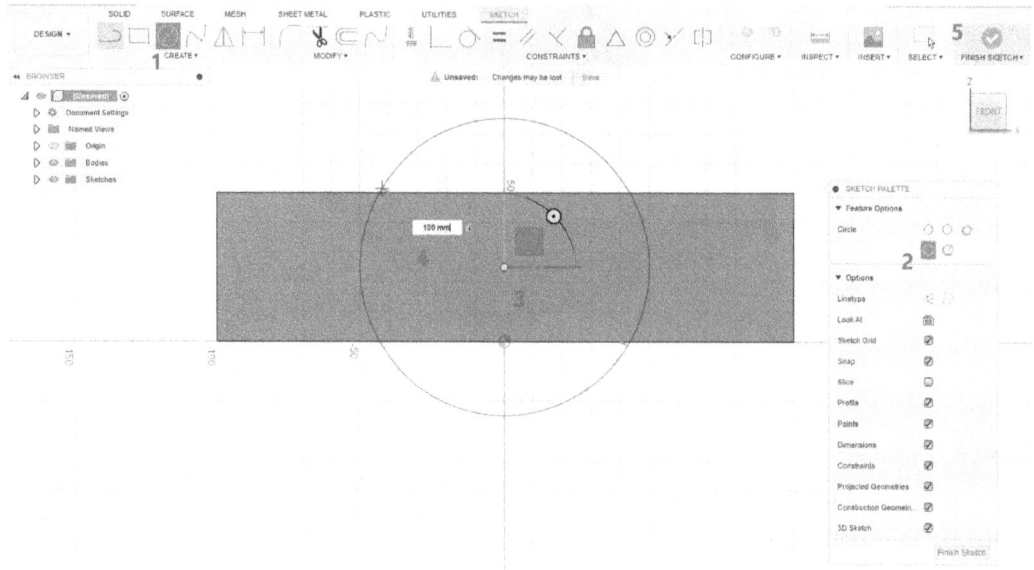

Figure 4.18: Sketching the wheels

Now, you can click on the wheel sketch. You may have to press the *Shift* key to select each wheel segment. Now, press *Q* to extrude it and make the distance 25 mm, the thickness of the wheel. The important thing to note is that we have to make the wheel a new body in the operation option in extrude. This makes a new wheel a new body.

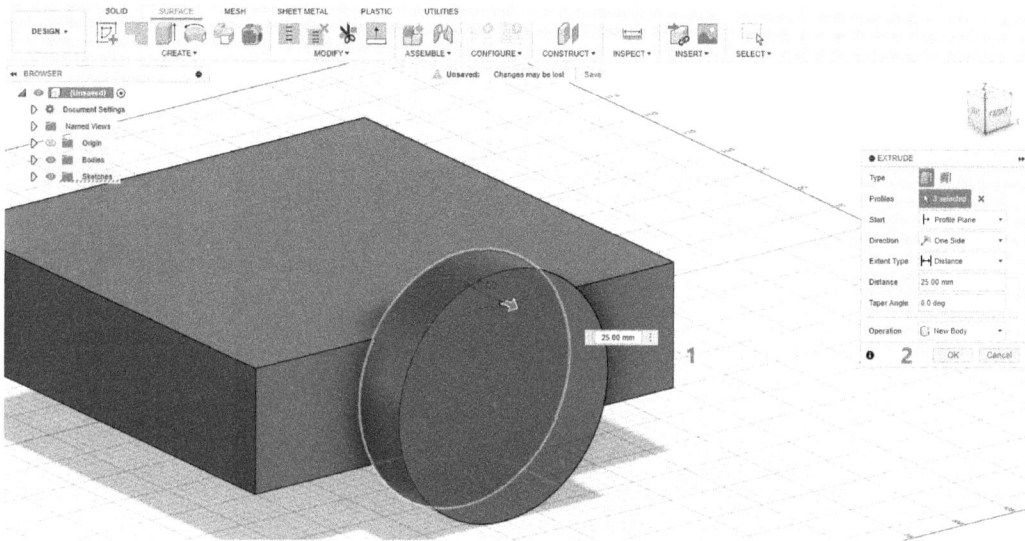

Figure 4.19: Extruding the wheels

The steps are shown in *Figure 4.19*. We can use the same process to create the next wheel.

Moving the robot to ground level

After creating two wheels and the base_link, we have three independent bodies. The next step is to move the entire robot above the design plane. You can compute the distance by measuring it and moving the robot using the **Move** button. Make sure you have selected all three bodies before you move. To lift the robot from the design floor, you can roughly put 25 mm as the Z value in the Move window. You can find the robot's position in *Figure 4.20*.

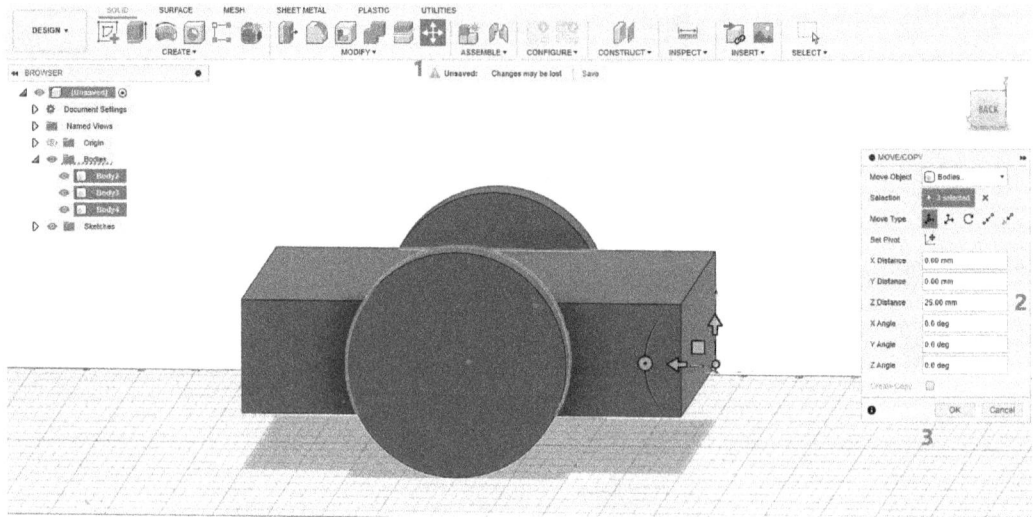

Figure 4.20: Lifting the robot to ground level

The next step is to create caster wheels for the robot. The caster wheels provide support for the robot.

Adding caster wheels to the base of the robot

After lifting the robot, the next step is to add caster wheels. We have to add caster wheels on the front and back of the robot, as shown in *Figure 4.21*. As already discussed, casters are passive wheels that help the robot balance and distribute weight. To add two casters, we must create two small cylinders on the bottom side of the chassis. You can put the center of the circle 25 mm from both sides and have a diameter of 24 mm. To create a cylinder, we can extrude a circle sketch. The length of the extrude can be 24 mm, a few millimeters less than the robot's height from the ground.

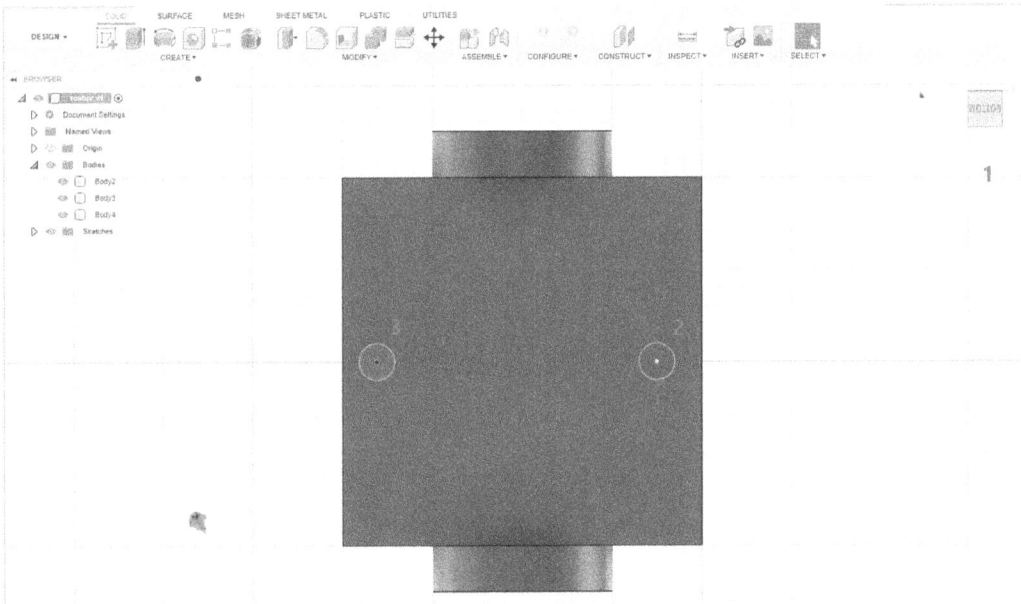

Figure 4.21: Sketching the caster wheel

Figure 4.22 shows how we extrude the caster wheel. Make sure the **Operation** is a **Joint**, NOT a **New body**. The caster is a part of the chassis.

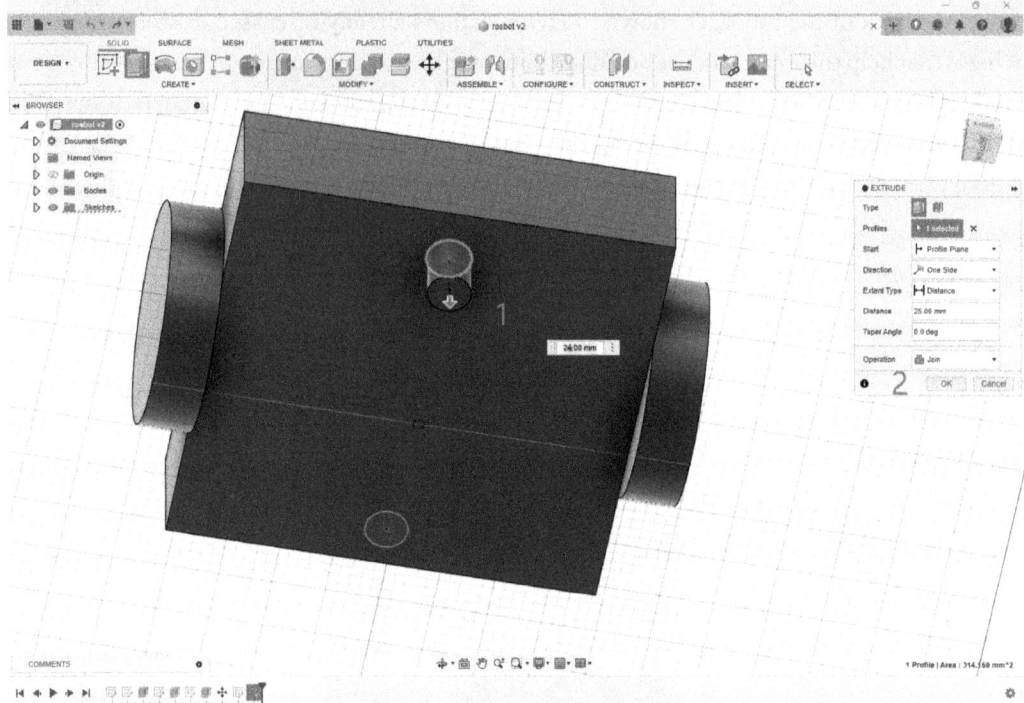

Figure 4.22: Extruding the caster wheel

After creating the cylinder on both sides, we can make the bottom face of the cylinder spherical. Select the face of the cylinder, press *F* or go to **Menu Surface | Modify | Fillet**, and using the mouse, create a spherical face from the flat surface.

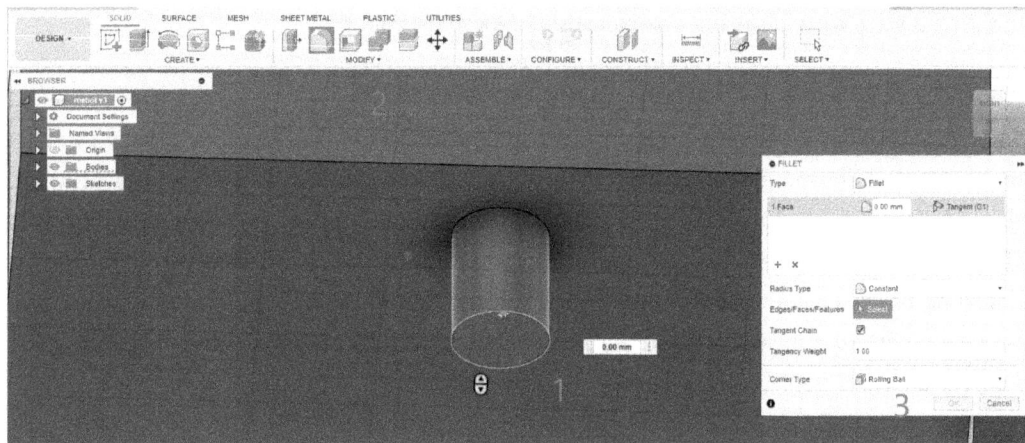

Figure 4.23: Shaping the caster wheel

We can do the same operation for both of the caster wheels, and the final output will look like *Figure 4.24*.

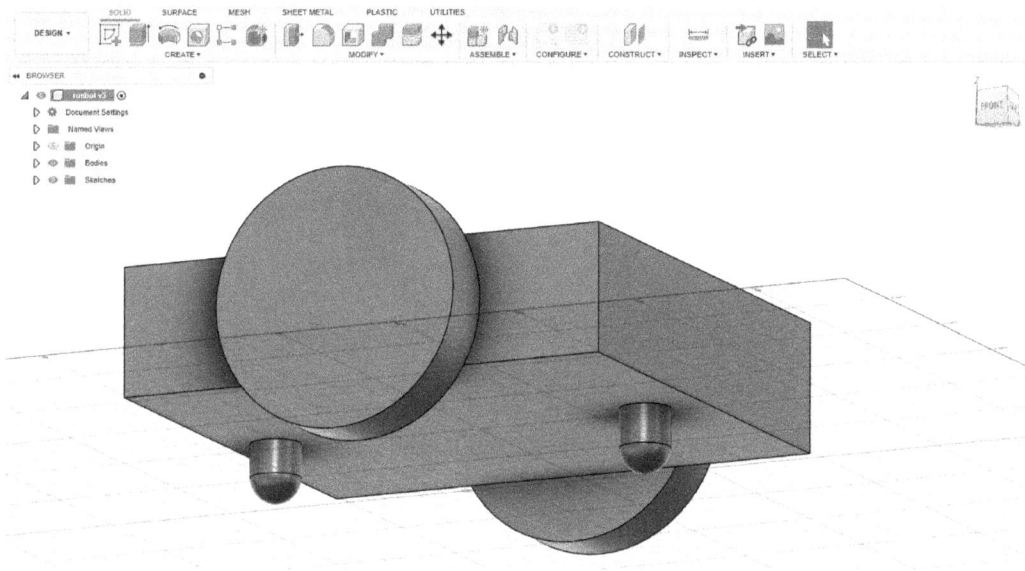

Figure 4.24: Final caster wheel design

In the next step, we will see how we can add LIDAR to the robot.

Adding a LiDAR base and lidar to the robot

Once the caster design is completed, we can add lidar to the front of the robot. First, we have to build a fixed platform. After adding the base, we can create a cylinder shape to replicate lidar, as shown below. You can draw a centered rectangle sketch of 70 mm (length) x 60 mm (width) with an extrude height of 45 mm (height). The center of the box can be placed 50 mm from the front of the robot. The box height can vary based on the obstacle profile in the environment. You can vary the height of the box based on the object's height. A typical lidar platform is shown in *Figure 4.25*.

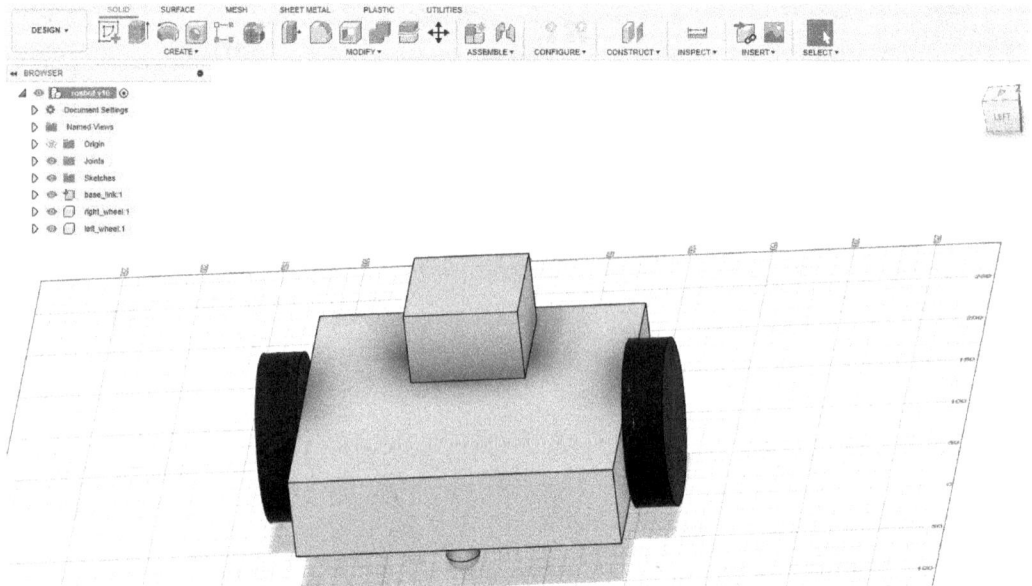

Figure 4.25: Creating a LIDAR support box

After creating the box, we can make a circle (29.5 mm radius) on the top and create a cylinder by extruding the circle by 20 mm. Make sure you are creating a new body when you extrude the object. The lidar in the robot is shown in *Figure 4.26*.

After creating all the bodies, you can rename them to meaningful names as shown in *Figure 4.26*.

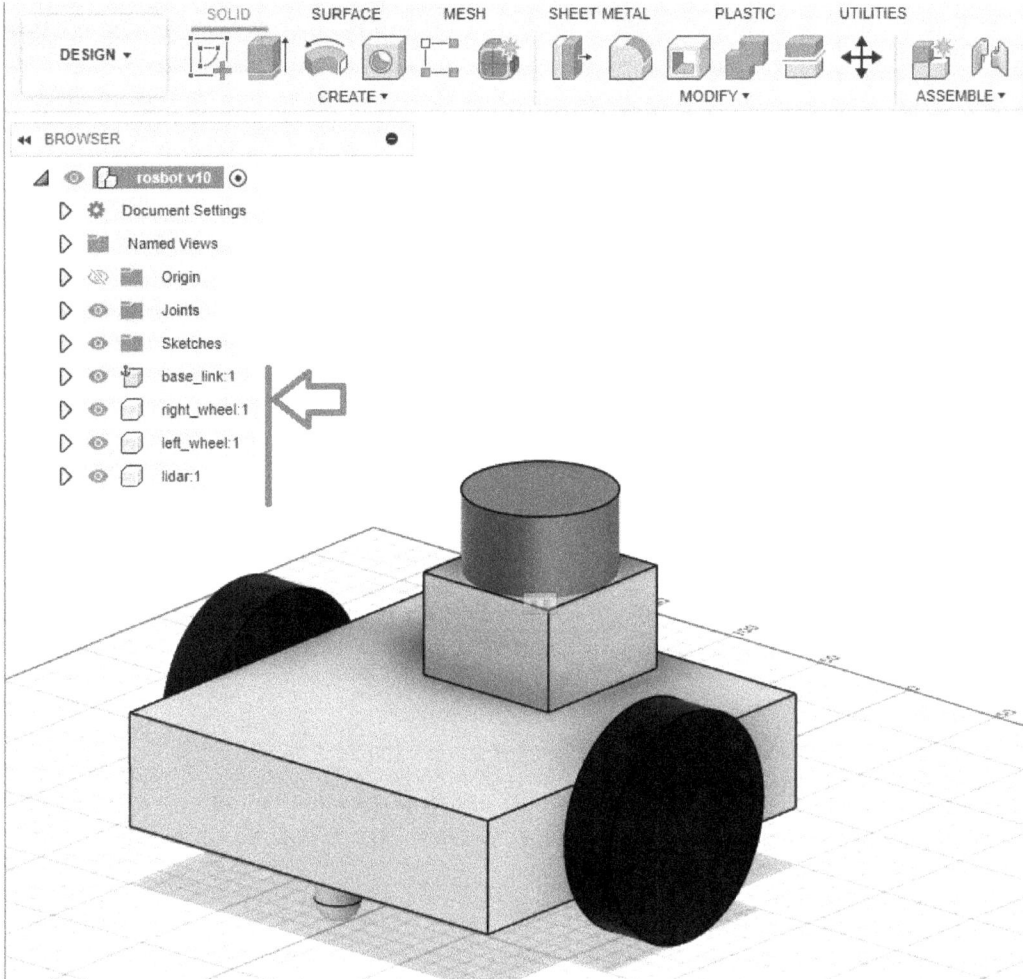

Figure 4.26: Naming robot bodies

The chassis has to be named base_link; this is mandatory. You can give the left and right wheels the same name, and you can also add a name to the lidar structure.

Adding a material type and color

After creating the model, we can go to each body, right-click on it, and choose **Physical materials**. This allows us to assign material properties to each link, as shown in *Figure 4.27*.

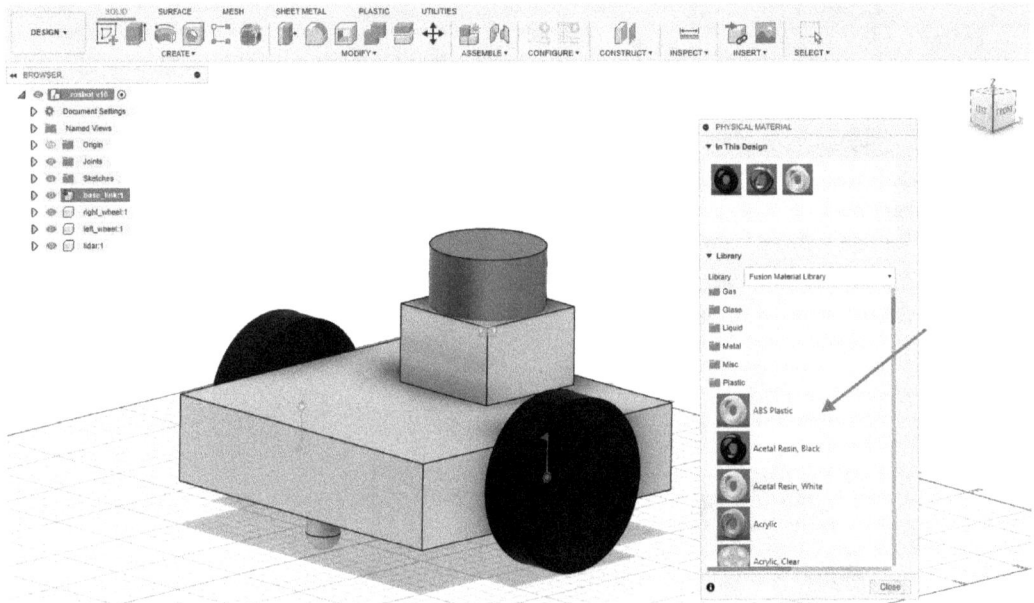

Figure 4.27: Adding materials to robot bodies

Search for ABS Plastic for the base link. Just click and drag the material to the link to apply the material. Choose the material Rubber black for the wheels and laminate blue for lidar.

Converting bodies to components

After adding the material's properties, we must convert the individual bodies to components. The conversion from bodies to components is easy.

Here is how we can do it. Click on the **Bodies** option and choose the **Components from Bodies** option, as shown in *Figure 4.28*. A body is a single shape within a component, which can hold multiple bodies. To export to URDF, we need to make individual robot components.

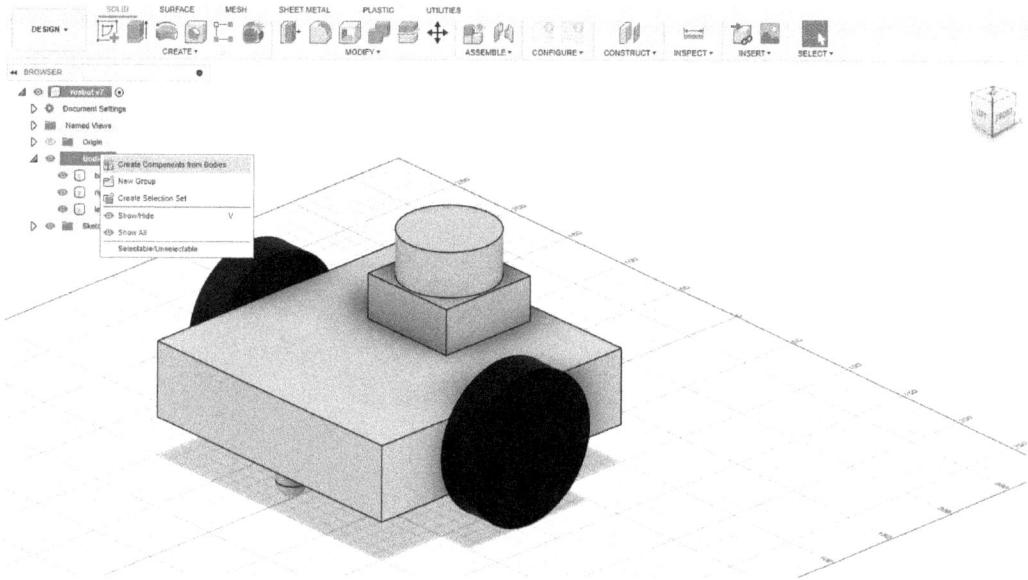

Figure 4.28: Adding materials to robot bodies

After converting bodies to individual components, we can assign joints to the robot.

Adding joints to the robot

After assigning the materials, we must assign the joints for connecting wheels to base_link and attach the lidar link. This is the most crucial step in modeling. Without assigning joints, the robot cannot move. Here are the steps to assign a joint in Fusion 360.

First, we can check how to create a joint between the wheels and the base_link. First, we must hide the base_link component and press **J** (**Menu Solid** | **Assemble** | **Joint**) to create a new joint. After invoking the joint option, we must provide the components (link) in the joint. We can create a revolute joint between base_link and the two wheels. To create a joint, we need two components: the first component should be the wheel, and the second will be the base_link, as shown in *Figure 4.29*.

We have to hide the base_link first and click on the center of the wheel, as shown in *Figure 4.29*, which is attached to the base_link.

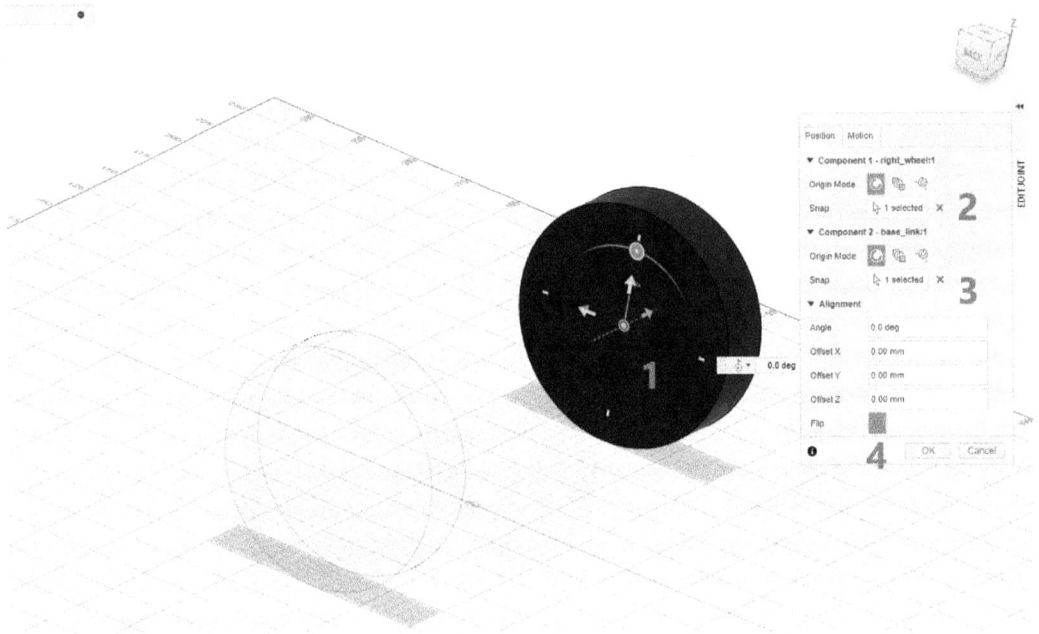

Figure 4.29: Adding materials to robot bodies

After clicking on the center of the wheel, we can see a coordinate frame on the wheel. Next, we can hide the wheels and attach the frame in the base_link, as shown in *Figure 4.30*.

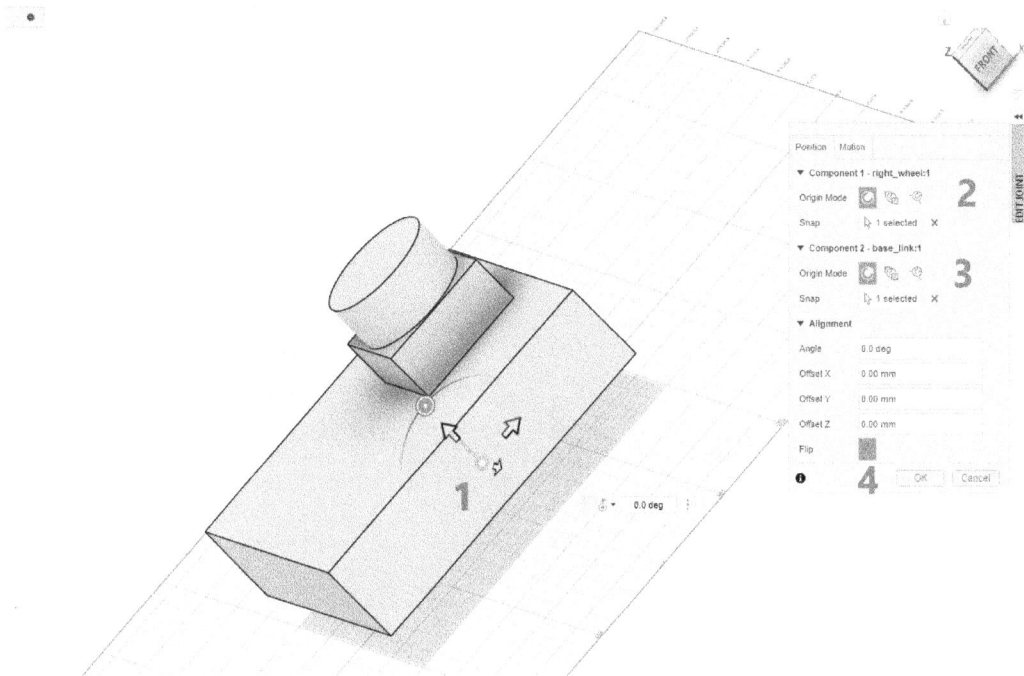

Figure 4.30: Assigning joints in the wheel

Once it is done, you can press the **Motion** tab in the **Edit Joint** option to select the type of joint. We need the revolute joint for the wheels, so select it, and you can preview the motion of the joint, as shown in *Figure 4.31*. After setting one joint, you can also do the same for the next wheel.

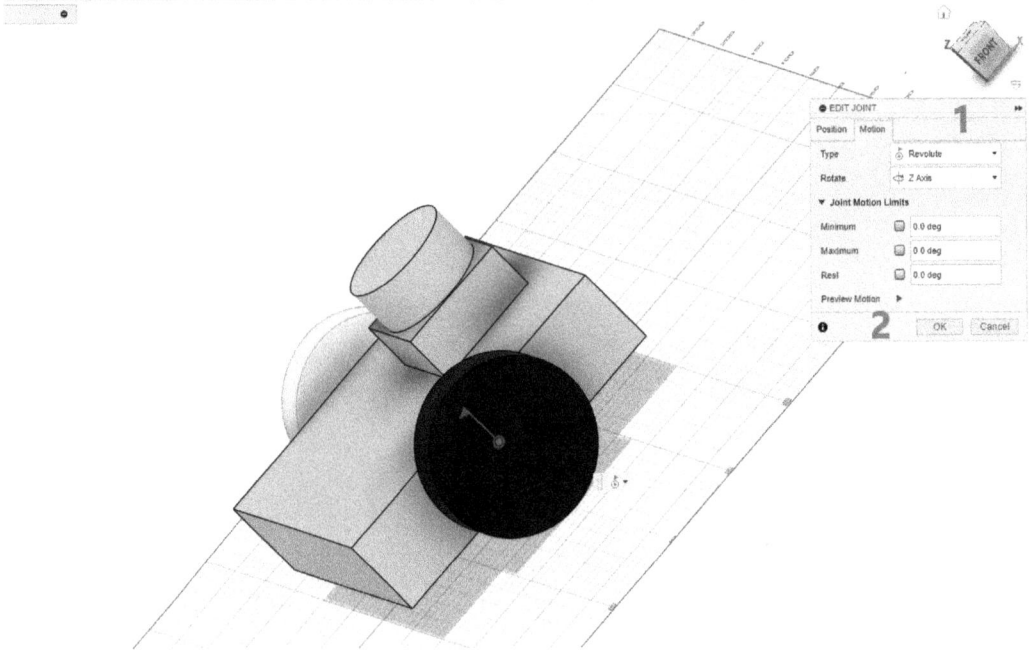

Figure 4.31: Testing the joints of the wheel

We have to create a rigid link between the lidar component and base_link for the lidar link. In the Browser section of Fusion 360, go to Joints and rename each joint as right_wheel_joint, left_wheel_joint, and lidar_joint.

Congratulations! You have completed the robot's modeling phase. The final model is shown in *Figure 4.32*. Now, we can export the model to URDF.

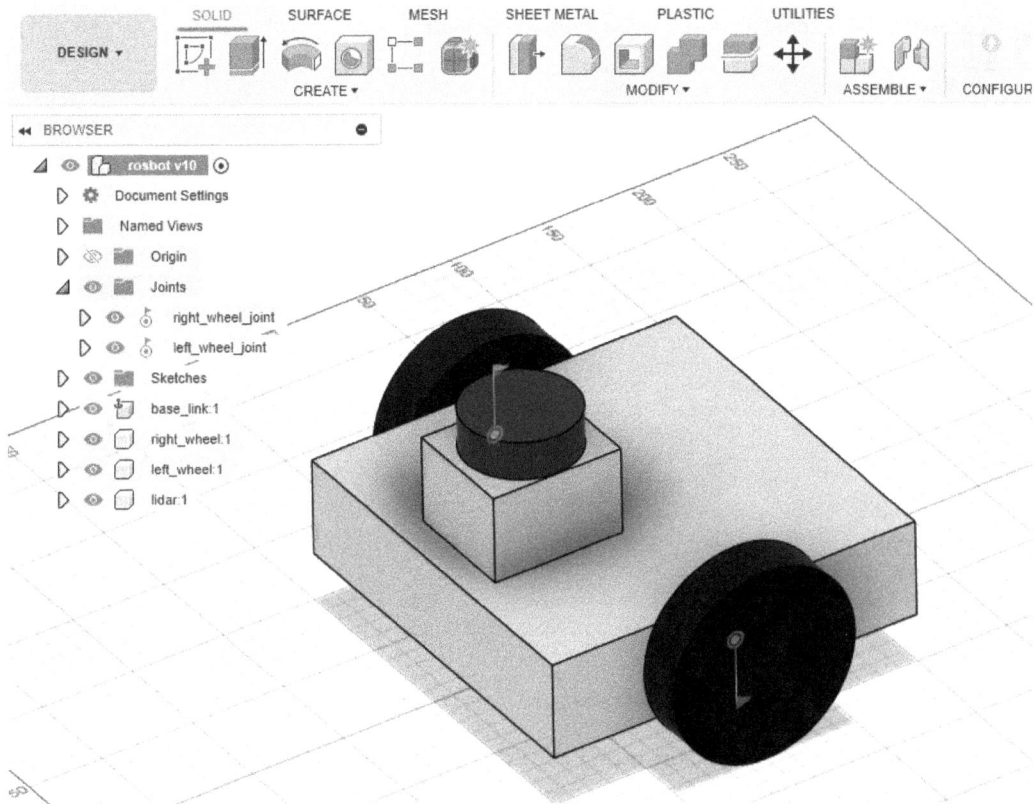

Figure 4.32: Final robot model

Converting a Fusion 360 model to URDF for ROS 2

After completing the CAD model in Fusion 360, press *Shift + S* to open the script box and select the Fusion_URDF_Exporter_ROS2 script from My Scripts.

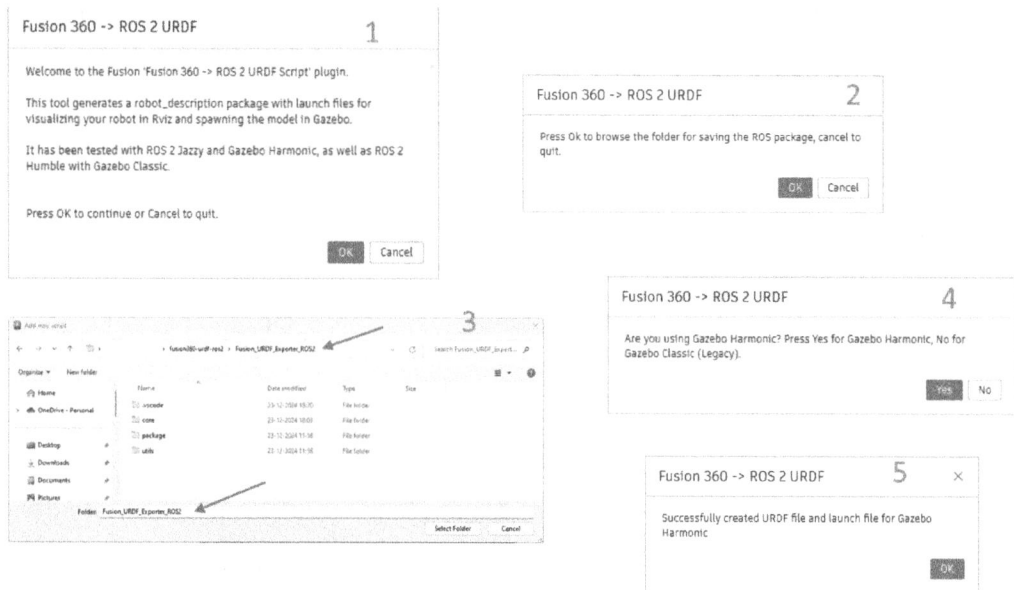

Figure 4.33: Converting the model to a ROS 2 package

Figure 4.33 shows the steps in converting the Fusion 360 model to a URDF package. Let's see each step in detail:

1. We will see a welcome screen with basic information about the script, which will ask the user whether to proceed with the conversion.

2. After pressing the OK button, the program will ask for the folder where the ROS 2 package must be created.

3. When we press the OK button, the browse dialog will appear, and we can select a folder.

4. After selecting the folder, we need to select the Gazebo version we want. There are two options currently available (Gazebo Harmonic or Classic). Based on the input, the launch file will be created.

5. Once we select the Gazebo version, the final message will indicate whether the conversion was successful. After this conversion, the ROS 2 description package will be created.

After converting the robot model to ROS 2 packages, we can see how to visualize the URDF model.

Building a ROS 2 description package

After creating the ROS 2 package for your robot, you can copy it to your ROS 2 workspace. If you work in Windows 11, you can work on ROS 2 using WSL or a virtual machine. Otherwise, you can reboot and select Ubuntu 22.04 for ROS 2 Humble/Ubuntu 24.04 for ROS 2 Jazzy.

For example, if you use the `rosbot` model from the demos folder and convert it to the ROS 2 package, you will get a package named `rosbot_description`. The package has also been put in the demos folder for your reference. Copy it to your ROS 2 workspace.

For example, let's say `master_ros2_ws` is the name of the workspace, and you copied the package to the `src` folder of the workspace.

Switch to the ROS 2 workspace folder and build the new packages using the following command.

```
cd ~/master_ros2_ws
colcon build
```

After building the package, run `source` on the workspace:

```
source install/setup.bash
```

After running `source` on the workspace, we can visualize and simulate the robot.

Visualizing the robot in RViz

Here is the command to visualize the robot in RViz:

```
ros2 launch rosbot_description display.launch.py
```

This will show RViz along with the `joint_state_publisher_gui` node, as shown in *Figure 4.34*.

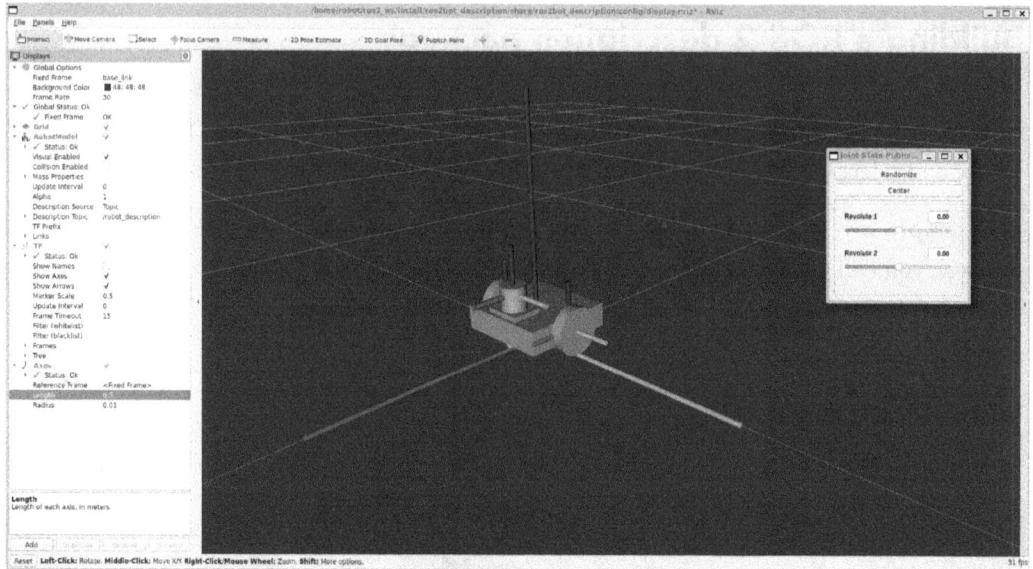

Figure 4.34: Visualizing rosbot in RViz

In the next section, we will see the visualization of the URDF models of some existing robots. These models can be used as a reference when creating our own URDF models.

Visualizing URDF models of existing robots

To visualize some of the existing robot URDF models, you can download the ROS 2 description packages that are publicly available, such as on GitHub, or install binaries of robot models from the apt package manager.

Here are some of the models you can install and visualize in RViz:

- **Universal Robot** [20]
- **TurtleBot 4** [21]
- **Leo Rover** [22]

Here is a command to install those description packages using the apt package manager:

```
sudo apt install -y ros-jazzy-ur-description ros-jazzy-turtlebot4-
description  ros-jazzy-leo-description
```

After installing the packages, let's see how to visualize a UR robot in the following section.

Visualizing the Universal Robot model

We can change the type of robot and visualize multiple types of robots. Here are the options available (ur3, ur3e, ur5, ur5e, ur10, ur10e, ur16e, ur20, and ur30). We will use ur30 as an example:

```
ros2 launch ur_description view_ur.launch.py ur_type:=ur30
```

Figure 4.10 shows the visualization of the UR30 robot model.

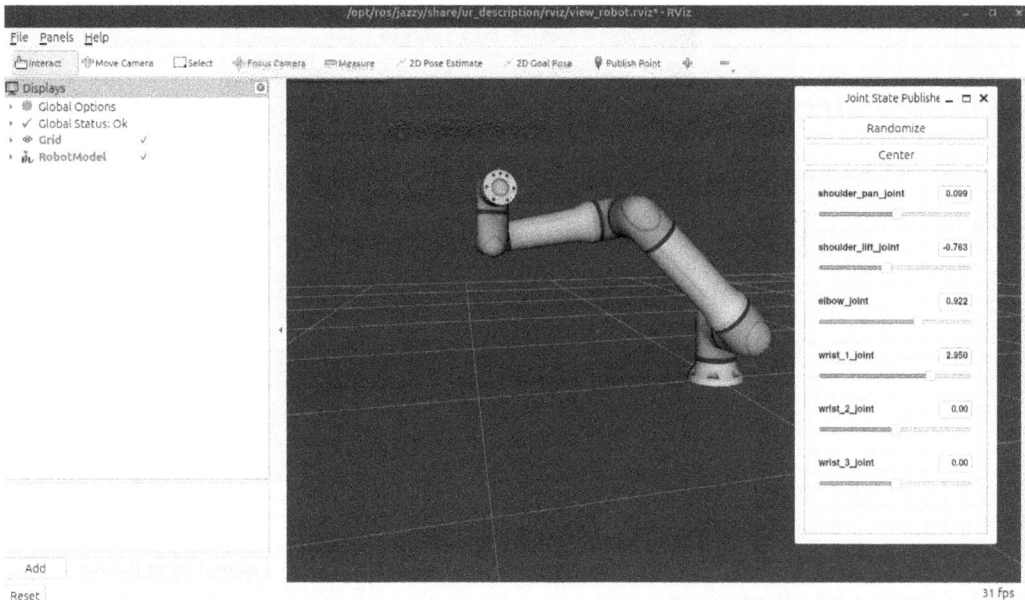

Figure 4.35: UR robot visualization in RViz

To visualize other description packages, we need to switch to those installed paths and visualize using the display.launch.py launch file inside urdf_tutorials.

Visualizing the TurtleBot 4 model

To visualize the **TurtleBot 4** model, you must switch to the turtlebot4_description package to visualize the URDF file.

First, we must switch to the urdf folder of the turtlebot4_description package.

Here is the command to switch to the folder.

```
cd /opt/ros/jazzy/share/turtlebot4_description/urdf/standard/
```

Execute the following command to visualize `turtlebot4` in RViz:

```
ros2 launch urdf_tutorial display.launch.py model:=$PWD/turtlebot4.urdf.
xacro
```

Figure 4.11 shows the visualization of the turtlebot4 robot model:

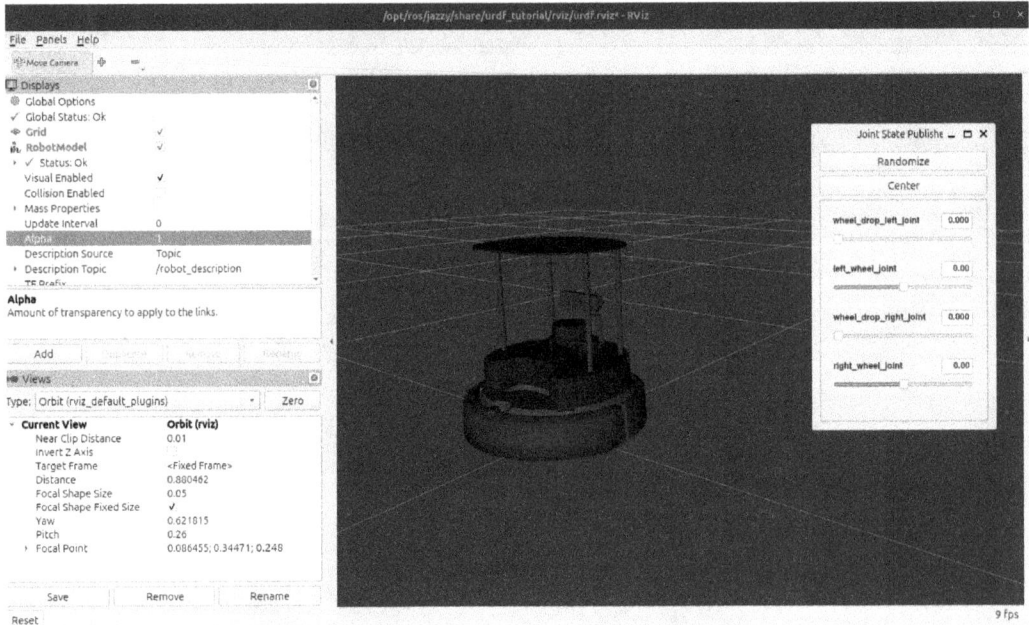

Figure 4.36: TurtleBot 4 visualization in RViz

Visualizing the Leo Rover model

To visualize **Leo Rover** model, you have to switch to the `leo_description` package to visualize the URDF file.

First, we must switch to the `urdf` folder of the `leo_description` package.

Here is the command to switch to the folder:

```
cd /opt/ros/jazzy/share/leo_description/urdf/
```

Execute the following command to visualize the Leo Rover in RViz:

```
ros2 launch urdf_tutorial display.launch.py model:=$PWD/leo.urdf.xacro
```

Figure 4.12 shows the visualization of the Leo Rover robot model.

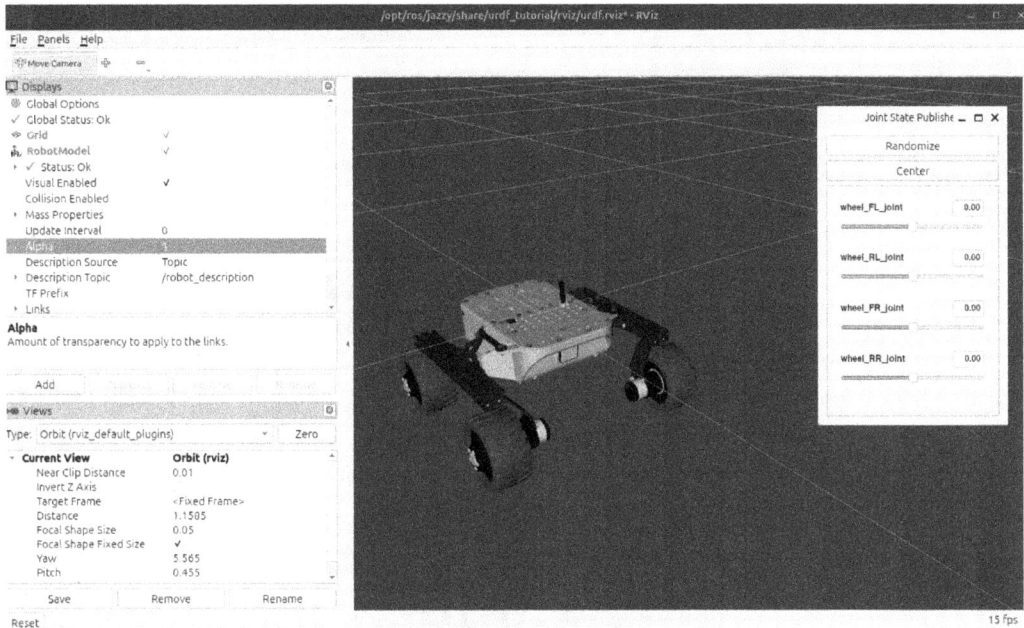

Figure 4.37: Leo Rover visualization in RViz

We have completed the visualization of multiple robots in RViz; now let's see what the best practices are for creating robot models using URDF/Xacro.

Official ROS 2 URDF tutorials

In this section, we will discuss the official ROS 2 tutorials for URDF modeling. The urdf_tutorial tutorial package is provided to help with understanding URDF modeling from scratch. You can find the source code of the urdf_tutorial package in Chapter04 | urdf_tutorial or on GitHub [23].

The official tutorials can be found at this link [24].

In order to visualize the robot, you can either install urdf_tutorial from the apt package manager or copy the source code to the ROS 2 workspace and build.

After setting this package, open a terminal and switch the path to Chapter04 | urdf_tutorial/ urdf.

You can see the development of the r2d2 robot from the basics to the Xacro model. This tutorial will give you a walkthrough of URDF modeling from scratch.

The following command visualizes the final Xacro model of R2D2:

```
ros2 launch urdf_tutorial display.launch.py model:=$PWD/08-macroed.urdf.
xacro
```

Here is the visualization of the r2d2 robot in RViz:

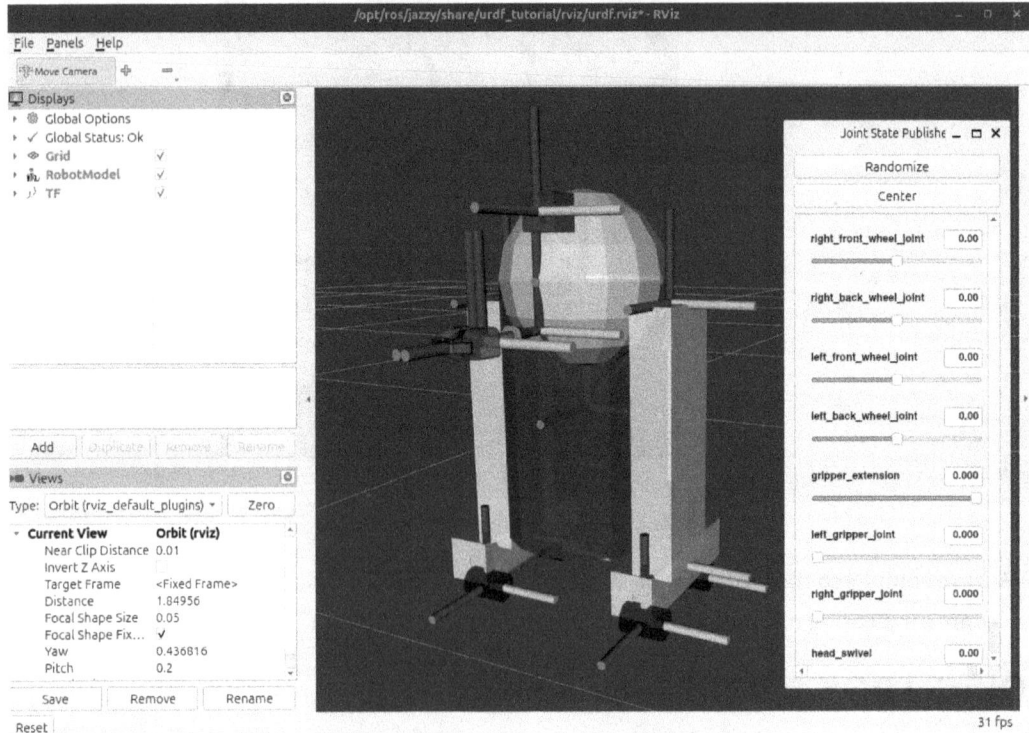

Figure 4.38: R2D2 robot visualization in RViz

The following section will show how to configure Docker, Docker Compose, and Dev Container for ROS 2 URDF development.

Setting up ROS 2 Jazzy URDF development in Docker

The scripts and Dockerfiles from Chapter04/docker_urdf can be used to build and run the ROS 2 packages in Chapter04 using Docker.

Here is the command to build the ROS 2 Jazzy custom image.

```
./build_image.sh ros2_urdf:v0.1 master_ros2_ws robot
```

Here, ros2_urdf:v0.1 is the name of the custom image, master_ros2_ws is our ROS 2 workspace where we can put our Chapter04 ROS 2 packages, and the robot is the user's name inside the container.

After building the ROS 2 custom image, we can create the container using the following command.

```
./create_container.sh ros2_urdf:v0.1 master_ros2_ws ros2_urdf
```

We need to provide the image name, the ROS 2 workspace name, and the container name we want to create.

After creating the container, you can see that the master_ros2_ws is mounted inside the container. We can build the ROS 2 workspace inside the container and run the nodes.

If we want to open more terminals for the same container, you can use the following command:

```
./start_container.sh ros2_urdf
```

This will attach a new terminal if the container is already running or start it if it has stopped. You need to provide the container name as the argument for this script.

After attaching a new terminal, make sure you have sourced the ros_entry_point script using the following command:

```
source /ros_entrypoint.sh
```

The following section provides instructions for building, creating, and running containers using Docker Compose.

Setting up ROS 2 URDF Development in Docker Compose

Let's build and start containers for Chapter04 packages using Docker Compose.

Switch to Chapter04 | docker_compose_urdf folder and execute the following command to start building the Docker image and starting the container:

- Use the following command if you are using a non-NVIDIA graphics card on your PC.

```
docker compose -f docker-compose-gui.yml build
docker compose -f docker-compose-gui.yml up
```

- If you do have an NVIDIA graphics card and the driver is properly installed, use the following command to start the container.

```
docker compose -f docker-compose-nvidia.yml build
docker compose -f docker-compose-nvidia.yml up
```

Once you start this command, the image will be built first, and the container will start. You have to use another terminal to attach to the container. You don't have to close this terminal; if you cancel the command by pressing *Ctrl + C*, it will stop the running container.

Using the following command, you can create a new terminal from the running container.

```
./start_container.sh ros2_urdf
```

Now source the ROS 2 environment using the following command and you can build the ROS 2 workspace which is mounted inside the container.

```
source /ros_entrypoint.sh
```

After starting the container, if you want to stop or remove it, you can execute the command from a new host terminal. Make sure you are executing inside the docker_compose_urdf folder.

```
docker compose -f docker-compose-gui.yml down
```

or

```
docker compose -f docker-compose-nvidia.yml down
```

Now, let's set up VS Code Dev Container for ROS 2 URDF development.

ROS 2 URDF development using VS Code Dev Container

If you want to set up a Dev Container in VS Code for ROS 2 URDF development, make sure you have created the ROS 2 workspace named master_ros2_ws and open the Chapter04 folder using VS Code. This folder has a .devcontainer folder, which has the devcontainer.json file, and the instructions for using the docker-compose file we have used in the above section for the container. When you open the folder, it will prompt you to install the Dev Container extension and **Reopen in Container**. If you select this option, it will build the container, set the environment, mount the ROS 2 workspace as a volume, and connect the editor to it. We can also see the mounted volume, which is the master_ros2_ws folder in VS Code itself.

Finally, we will discuss some of the best practices that we can follow during URDF/Xacro modeling.

Best practices of URDF/Xacro modeling

Here are some best practices and tips for developing a robot model using URDF/Xacro:

- **Use Xacro for modeling**: As you know, Xacro provides more flexibility than URDF. It increases modularity and also enables code reuse. So, Xacro is the best choice for starting robot modeling in ROS 2.

- **Follow REP (ROS Enhancement Proposals) conventions**: Use REP [25] to name the links and joints in URDF.

- **Follow the modular design of models**: Split the robot model into macros, which can be kept inside separate Xacro files and organized inside a package properly.

- **Use the proper naming convention**: Using proper naming for joints and links avoids complexity in the URDF modeling.

- **Use TF prefixing**: It is important to use **prefixes** in Xacro in case you want to use multiple sensors at the same time or multiple robots. For example, in this macro definition, `<xacro:macro name="sensor_macro" params="prefix">`, we can add as many sensors as we want by providing a different **prefix**.

- **Organize models in a package**: Create a robot description package and organize all Xacro, URDF, and launch files within the package.

- **Minimize hardcoding values**: We can use *Xacro constants* to minimize the hardcoding of values in the model.

- **Add meaningful comments**: Add comments in URDF; it will help with understanding the model, especially if it is complex.

- **Keep testing**: We can keep testing and fine-tuning the model parameters as much as possible, which will improve the model's overall accuracy.

- **Optimize for performance**: We can use mesh files like STL, DAE, and OBJ inside URDF as the geometry of visual and collision of a link. Adding more complex meshes will increase the computation and the overall performance will be reduced. Make sure meshes are down-sampled properly before using the URDF model. We can also use simple shapes like spheres and boxes for visual and collision links, which can minimize the overall computation for visualizing and simulating the URDF model. Simplifying the collision meshes is more important than visual meshes.

- **Use the proper texture and colors**: We can use the proper texture for mesh files and shapes to distinguish the parts and make the model visually appealing.

- **Create a flexible design for future-proofing**: Create a modular and flexible design so that sensors and actuators can be added to the robot model in the future.

- **Implement documentation and version control**: It is a best practice to maintain version control and add documentation to understand the model design.

We have seen some of the best practices and tips for developing a better robot model. In the next chapter, we will look at simulating robots.

Summary

This chapter covered creating 3D robot models in ROS 2, using URDF and Xacro to define a robot's structure, kinematics, dynamics, and control. It began by introducing different modeling types (kinematic, dynamic, geometric, control, and sensor-actuator) that are essential for accurate robot visualization and simulation. Key elements like `<link>` and `<joint>` tags were explained, enabling the representation of a robot's physical and functional aspects. The chapter also outlined exporting CAD models to URDF for ROS compatibility, utilizing ROS 2 tools to verify and visualize models, and applying best practices like modular design and minimal hardcoding to create efficient, adaptable robot models.

In the next chapter, we will discuss how to simulate the robot we have modeled in this chapter using the Gazebo simulator and ROS 2. We will also explore different URDF tags that we use mainly for simulating the robot in Gazebo.

References

- [1] https://www.autodesk.com/in/products/fusion-360/
- [2] https://www.solidworks.com/
- [3] https://www.autodesk.com/in/campaigns/education/fusion-360-education
- [4] https://www.3ds.com/products/catia
- [5] https://wiki.ros.org/urdf/XML/robot
- [6] https://wiki.ros.org/urdf/XML/link
- [7] https://wiki.ros.org/urdf/XML/joint
- [8] https://index.ros.org/p/ur_description/
- [9] https://index.ros.org/packages/
- [10] https://docs.ros.org/en/jazzy/Tutorials/Intermediate/URDF/Building-a-Visual-Robot-Model-with-URDF-from-Scratch.html
- [11] https://marketplace.visualstudio.com/items?itemName=ms-iot.vscode-ros

- [12] https://github.com/ros/urdf_tutorial/tree/ros2

- [13] https://docs.ros.org/en/jazzy/Tutorials/Intermediate/Tf2/Tf2-Main.html

- [14] https://github.com/ros/solidworks_urdf_exporter

- [15] https://github.com/runtimerobotics/fusion2urdf-ros2

- [16] https://github.com/Rhoban/onshape-to-robot

- [17] https://github.com/dfki-ric/phobos

- [18] https://github.com/david-dorf/ExportURDF/tree/main

- [19] https://docs.ros.org/en/jazzy/Tutorials/Intermediate/URDF/Exporting-an-URDF-File.html

- [20] https://www.universal-robots.com/

- [21] https://clearpathrobotics.com/turtlebot-4/

- [22] https://www.leorover.tech/

- [23] https://github.com/ros/urdf_tutorial/tree/ros2

- [24] https://docs.ros.org/en/jazzy/Tutorials/Intermediate/URDF/URDF-Main.html

- [25] https://ros.org/reps/rep-0000.html

- [26] https://www.autodesk.com/in/education/edu-software/fusion

- [27] https://github.com/cryinkfly/Autodesk-Fusion-360-for-Linux

- [28] https://github.com/runtimerobotics/fusion360-urdf-ros2

Join our community on Discord

Join our community's Discord space for discussions with the authors and other readers: https://packt.link/embeddedsystems

5

Simulating Robots in a Realistic Environment

Building a new robot from scratch takes time and can be expensive. After getting the robot's requirements, we will first design it and create a 3D model of the robot. In the previous chapter, we saw how to build the kinematic and dynamic model of the robot using URDF. This chapter will discuss how to simulate the robot using Gazebo and ROS 2 to iterate on the robot model created and identify any issues in the designed model. The simulation is crucial in robot development because it allows for easy verification of the design without incurring any hardware costs. The simulation can't replicate the actual robot hardware properties completely, but it can give an overall idea of how the system works.

In this chapter, we will see how to simulate a robot in Gazebo Sim using the ROS URDF model. We will use Gazebo Sim plugins and the ROS 2 controller to simulate and control the robot. After simulating different robots in Gazebo Sim, we will explore other simulators, such as Webots and Isaac Sim, which can be used in conjunction with ROS 2.

The simulation of robots is useful not only for validating robot designs but also for developing ROS 2-based robotics applications. We can use the simulation to test robot navigation, robotic arm manipulation, and perception applications. We will discuss these topics in the upcoming chapters.

After completing this chapter, you will understand how to simulate a robot from scratch in Gazebo and ROS 2.

In this chapter, we are going to cover the following main topics:

- Introduction to Gazebo Sim
- Simulating a robot using Gazebo Sim
- Simulating a robot using ROS 2 and Gazebo Sim
- Introduction to the Webots simulator
- Introduction to Isaac Sim

Technical requirements

To follow this chapter, you should install Ubuntu 24.04 LTS with **ROS 2 Jazzy** desktop-full installation. It can be installed on a **virtual machine (VM)**, **Docker**, **Windows Subsystem for Linux (WSL)** 2, or on a physical machine. This chapter uses terms like **Gazebo project**, **Gazebo Classic**, and **Gazebo Sim**. Before the introduction of the new Gazebo Sim, we used the term *Gazebo* to refer to the Gazebo project, which encompasses both Gazebo Classic and Gazebo Sim. After the introduction, the term *Gazebo* was intended for use with Gazebo Sim only. The reference materials for this chapter can be found in the Chapter05 folder of the following GitHub repository: https://github.com/PacktPublishing/Mastering-ROS-2-for-Robotics-Programming/tree/main/Chapter05.

Introduction to Gazebo Sim

We have already discussed the importance of robotic simulation in robot development. When considering robot simulators, we have multiple options available. Some of the popular choices are Gazebo [1], **Webots** [2], **Isaac Sim** [3], **Coppelia Sim** [4], **PyBullet** [5], **MujoCo** [6], **Unity** [7], and **Player/Stage** [8].

Why do we focus on Gazebo Sim in this chapter? The main reasons are that it is quite popular, has a strong community, is compatible with most PC configurations, features an excellent ROS 2 interface, and offers good tutorials. It has decent physics and rendering features, but not superior to other simulators. Moreover, it is free and open source.

Let's dive into Gazebo and explore how to create engaging simulations using it.

The Gazebo project provides a free and open-source robot simulator, development libraries, and cloud services to simplify simulation. There are two main versions of the Gazebo simulator: Gazebo Classic [9] and Gazebo Sim [10]. Gazebo Classic is the legacy version, whereas Gazebo Sim is the latest version.

The Gazebo simulators (Classic and Gazebo Sim) feature high-fidelity physics, rendering, and sensor models, all supported by a plugin-based interface. The plugin-based architecture enables switching between different physics and rendering engines.

Gazebo simulators feature a graphical user interface that simplifies simulation and plugins that enhance the simulation's capabilities. Developers can write custom plugins for their robots. The Gazebo simulators also feature an asynchronous message-passing interface and support services such as ROS.

Gazebo simulators are independent simulators that allow us to create robot models using the **Simulation Description Format (SDF)** [11] and plugins to simulate the model's characteristics. Developers can develop simulations independently or using the ROS interface. Gazebo Classic includes Gazebo ROS plugins that enable communication between ROS and Gazebo. In Gazebo Sim, the ROS bridge [12] helps developers connect with ROS 2. Using this ROS 2 interface, developers can receive sensor data from Gazebo Sim into ROS 2 topics and interact with the robot through these topics. We will see more details on the ROS 2 interface in the upcoming sections.

Figure 5.1 shows the user interface of Gazebo Classic and Gazebo Sim. We will explore the features of Gazebo Classic and Gazebo Sim in the upcoming sections.

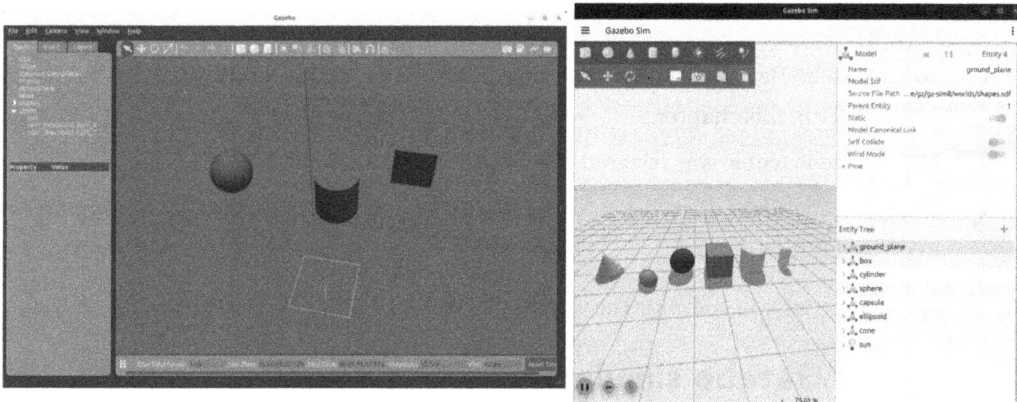

Figure 5.1: Gazebo Classic (left) and Gazebo Sim (right)

Let's go through the major development milestones of the Gazebo project. We can learn how this project evolved from its inception and how it is going now.

Major milestones of the Gazebo Project

Here are the major milestones of the Gazebo project:

- **2002**: Gazebo Classic started at the University of Southern California.

- **2007–2011**: Willow Garage supported and accelerated the Gazebo project. Major developments in the Gazebo Classic version occurred during this time, particularly the integration of ROS 1 and Gazebo.

- **2012**: From 2012, Open Robotics (formerly **Open-Source Robotics Foundation (OSRF)**) developed and maintained the Gazebo Classic project.

- **2017**: The Gazebo project forked into two versions: Gazebo Classic and the new Ignition Gazebo. Gazebo Classic is the legacy version, and it has a monolithic architecture; however, Ignition has transitioned to a modern software architecture, which features modular, loosely coupled libraries.

- **2019**: The first version of Ignition Gazebo was released (Ignition Acropolis). In the same year, they released Ignition Blueprint and Ignition Citadel.

- **2020**: Gazebo Classic 11 was released, the last version of Gazebo Classic.

- **2022**: Ignition Gazebo was renamed to Gazebo Sim. In the same year, they released Gazebo Garden.

- **2023**: Gazebo Harmonic LTS was released. We are using **Gazebo Harmonic** along with ROS 2 Jazzy in this chapter.

- **2024**: Gazebo Iconic was released. This version also works with ROS 2 Jazzy.

- **2025**: Gazebo Classic reaches **End of Life (EOL)** – no more Gazebo Classic support for ROS 1 and ROS 2.

In the next section, we will compare the essential features of Gazebo Classic and Gazebo Sim.

Features of Gazebo simulators

Table 5.1 shows the comparison between the features of Gazebo Classic and Gazebo Sim. This comparison highlights the evolving capabilities and performance improvements in the newer Gazebo Sim platform. Understanding the differences between the two versions can help users select the most suitable version based on their specific simulation requirements.

Feature	Gazebo Classic	Gazebo Sim
Development Status	This is mature and stable, but it will depreciate in 2025. No more major updates.	Actively developing with a lot of modern features.
Architecture	Monolithic and tightly integrated components.	Modular architecture with separate libraries for physics, rendering, and transport.
Physics Engines	Support ODE, Bullet, DART, and Simbody.	Multiple engine support like DART, Bullet, ODE, and TPE, with better customization.
Rendering	Uses OGRE for rendering with limited modern effects.	Rendering with OGRE 2, Vulkan support, and realistic lighting.
Networking	Has a built-in messaging system that is outdated.	Uses a combination of Google Protobuf + ZeroMQ for efficient messaging.
Graphical User Interface (GUI)	Less customizable, traditional GUI.	Modern and customizable GUI built with Qt.
ROS Integration	Has strong ROS 1/ROS 2 support.	Mainly focus on ROS 2 integration.
Ease of Extensibility	Limited modularity and difficult to extend.	Highly modular, easy to extend and integrate.
Community and Ecosystem	Large and mature community with tutorials.	Growing community and development support from Open Robotics.
Performance	Suitable for individual robot simulations but can struggle in large-scale simulations.	Optimized for large-scale and distributed simulation.
Future Support	No long-term development. Will depreciate in 2025.	Actively maintained and will be the future of robotics simulation.
Use Cases	Works better for legacy projects.	New projects that require modern features and scalability.

Table 5.1: Comparison between Gazebo Classic vs Gazebo Sim

Table 5.1 illustrates that Gazebo Sim is a futuristic robotics simulation, focusing on scalability, modularity, extensibility, and improved integration with ROS 2. On the other hand, Gazebo Classic can be used to maintain the legacy system. We may not receive any significant updates for Gazebo Classic after 2025, so it would be better to focus on Gazebo Sim and ROS 2 for future simulation development. If you have already worked on Gazebo Classic, migrating to a new simulator may not be that difficult.

In this chapter, we will focus on **Gazebo Sim**, specifically **Gazebo Harmonic**, and work on integrating **ROS 2 Jazzy**.

In the next section, we will briefly see Gazebo Sim's architecture and understand its core components.

The architecture of Gazebo Sim

Let's have a look at how Gazebo Sim works. *Figure 5.2* shows the architecture of Gazebo Sim. We will discuss each component of the simulator. This will help us create better and more optimized simulations for your robots.

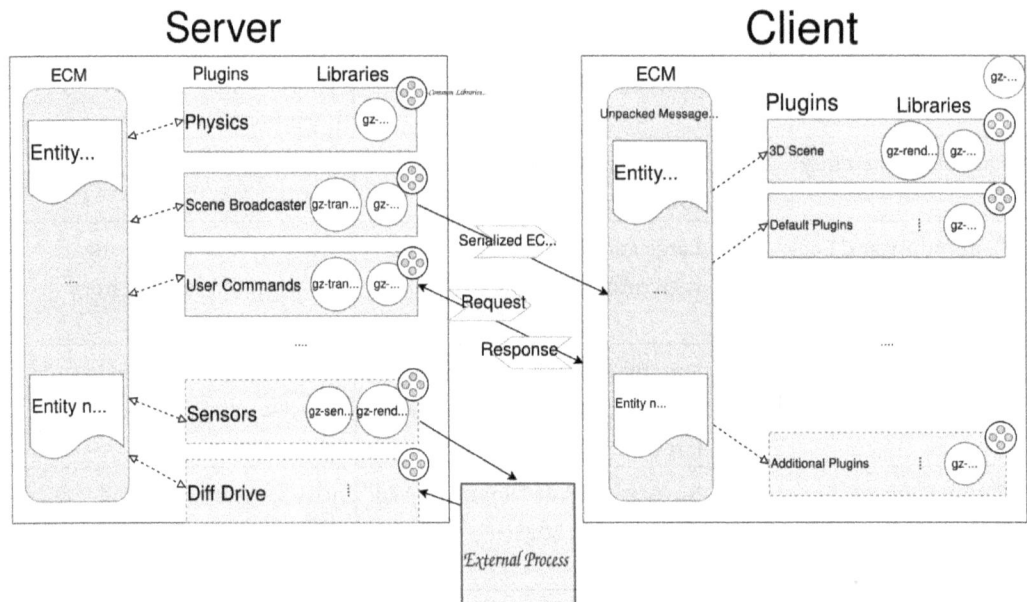

Figure 5.2: Architecture of Gazebo Sim (source: https://gazebosim.org/docs/latest/architecture/)

The Gazebo Sim architecture is designed to be modular and scalable. This architecture helps the developers create complex robotic simulations.

The architecture consists of two main components: a server and a client. The server acts as the backend, performing core simulation processes such as physics calculations, sensor data generation, and scene updates. In contrast, the client mainly handles visualization of the simulation, interaction with the user, and other extensions. The architecture is designed for flexibility and extensibility through plugins and external integration.

Communication between the server and the client is achieved through serialized messages, ensuring simulation synchronization.

Gazebo Sim server/backend

The server acts as the backend, processing physics, sensor data, and user commands.

Here is a brief overview of the server's sub-components:

- **Entity Component Manager (ECM)**: This module manages the entities of the simulation, including simulation objects, robots, and their environment. It also manages the entity's state and life cycle using a modular **Entity Component System (ECS)** framework.
- **Plugins**: The plugins on the server extend the server's functionalities. Multiple plugins on the server have different functions. Here are some examples:
  - **Physics Plugin**: As the name suggests, this manages the physics calculations using the physics engines we saw in the feature list. Physics calculations involve detecting collisions, calculating force and motion, detecting contacts, and custom dynamics such as fluid dynamics and soft bodies. This is a critical component of the server.
  - **Scene Broadcaster Plugin**: This plugin transmits updates on the simulation scene to connected clients. This includes model states, poses, sensor data, and other environmental data over the network. This helps the visualization tool and client sync with the simulation in real time. This is particularly important when we utilize sensors in the simulation.

- **User Commands Plugin:** This plugin handles user interaction with the simulation. It processes user commands from the client or external systems, which can modify entity parameters, change simulation parameters, and control robot movements. Examples of user commands include pausing, resuming, and resetting the simulation, as well as adding, removing, and changing properties of entities. Additionally, these commands encompass high-level robot movement, processing serialized requests from clients, and sending back proper responses.
- **Sensor Plugins:** These plugins can simulate sensor data, such as camera and LiDAR data.
- **Diff Drive Plugin:** This plugin can control a differential drive robot's kinematics.

- **Libraries (gz-*):** Gazebo Sim has multiple modular libraries inside plugins for rendering, transport, and physics. Here is the reference for all libraries in Gazebo Sim: [13]. The prefix gz indicates a library belonging to the Gazebo project. For example, the gz-physics library provides an abstract physics interface for simulation. The prefix was ign in the previous Gazebo before the rename.

- **External Processes:** These external modules interact with the server using APIs or other protocols or utilize the gz-transport library. This serves as a bridge between simulation and external tools, such as controllers, real-world hardware, or AI systems.

We have discussed the essential components of the Gazebo Server, so now let's see how the Gazebo client works.

Gazebo client

The client can communicate with the server/backend and visualize and control the simulation. The client can be a GUI, as we saw in *Figure 5.1*, or it can be an external application. Here are the major components of the client:

- **ECM:** The client also features an ECM for managing and unpacking data about entities received from the server.
- **Plugins:** The client has plugins for visualization and interaction with the user. There are example plugins such as the 3D Scene plugin, which helps to visualize the simulation in a GUI, and some default plugins provide the functionality for user interaction.
- **Additional Plugins:** These plugins extend the client's capabilities. Examples of these plugins are custom visualization or analysis tools.
- **Libraries (gz-*):** Like the server, the client uses Gazebo libraries for its operation.

- **Unpacked Messages:** These are messages from the server. The client unpacks it and updates the simulation state for visualization or interaction.

The server and client communicate using serialized messages, specifically **Entity Component (EC)** data. The server sends data to the client, whereas the client requests information from the server and updates the visualization and entity properties based on the server data.

You can refer to the following link to learn more about Gazebo Sim architecture: [*14*].

We have explored significant components of Gazebo Sim's architecture; now, let's discuss how to install Gazebo Sim and integrate it with ROS 2 Jazzy.

Installing and configuring Gazebo Sim

Let's discuss how to install **Gazebo Harmonic** for **ROS 2 Jazzy** in **Ubuntu 24.04 LTS**.

As you have seen from the milestones of the Gazebo project, the stable version of Gazebo, which is included with ROS 2 Jazzy, is **Gazebo Harmonic**. It is also the default Gazebo Sim version that ships with ROS 2 Jazzy. ROS 2 Jazzy will also support **Gazebo Iconic** and **Gazebo Jetty**.

This chapter will use **Gazebo Harmonic**, which is the default version in ROS 2 Jazzy. The simulation we built in Harmonic will also be mostly compatible with future versions.

Installing Gazebo is straightforward; you just have to install a single ROS 2 package. This package will automatically install the dependent packages and fully set up Gazebo Harmonic.

The following command will install Gazebo Sim and the ROS 2 Jazzy interface packages in Ubuntu 24.04 LTS. These interface packages provide tools to connect/bridge Gazebo Sim to ROS 2. By connecting them, both can publish and subscribe to data with each other. We can use this for building ROS 2-based robotic simulation applications:

```
sudo apt-get install ros-${ROS_DISTRO}-ros-gz
```

The ROS_DISTRO environment variable in Ubuntu, set while installing and configuring ROS 2, specifies the name of the current ROS 2 version.

A detailed Gazebo Sim installation reference is available at the following link: [*15*].

After installing Gazebo Sim packages using the above command, we can start the Gazebo Sim GUI client.

> **Installing Gazebo in Docker**
>
> If you are working with Docker, you can find the Docker files and scripts in the Chapter05/docker_gazebo folder.

Once installed, you can take a terminal and execute the following command to launch the Gazebo Sim GUI:

```
gz sim
```

If you have configured the graphics driver in Ubuntu 24.04 LTS, you should be able to see the GUI of Gazebo Sim. If you work with a VM, such as **VMware** or **VirtualBox**, you may encounter issues with the graphics driver.

If you are encountering any issues with graphic acceleration, there are a couple of workarounds.

Here is the first solution. This solution sets software rendering instead of hardware rendering. This is a workaround solution for basic simulation, but we do not recommend it for complex simulations:

```
echo 'export LIBGL_ALWAYS_SOFTWARE=1' >> ~/.bashrc
source ~/.bashrc
```

After these commands, you can start the gz sim command to verify that the simulator is showing up, or open a new terminal to test it.

If the first solution doesn't work, you can try a second solution. Gazebo Sim is built using the Qt framework. Setting a different X11 client-side library for the **Qt** application can work in most cases:

```
echo 'export QT_QPA_PLATFORM=xcb' >> ~/.bashrc
source ~/.bashrc
```

After running the above commands in the terminal, try gz sim to check whether the simulator appears.

If neither solution works, there are some troubleshooting tips at the following link: [*16*].

You can also find some solutions to fix graphics acceleration issues in the Docker container at this link: [*32*].

If everything works fine, you can view the Gazebo Sim GUI, as shown in *Figure 5.3*. It may initially display a startup window for selecting an existing simulation; you can proceed with an *empty* world.

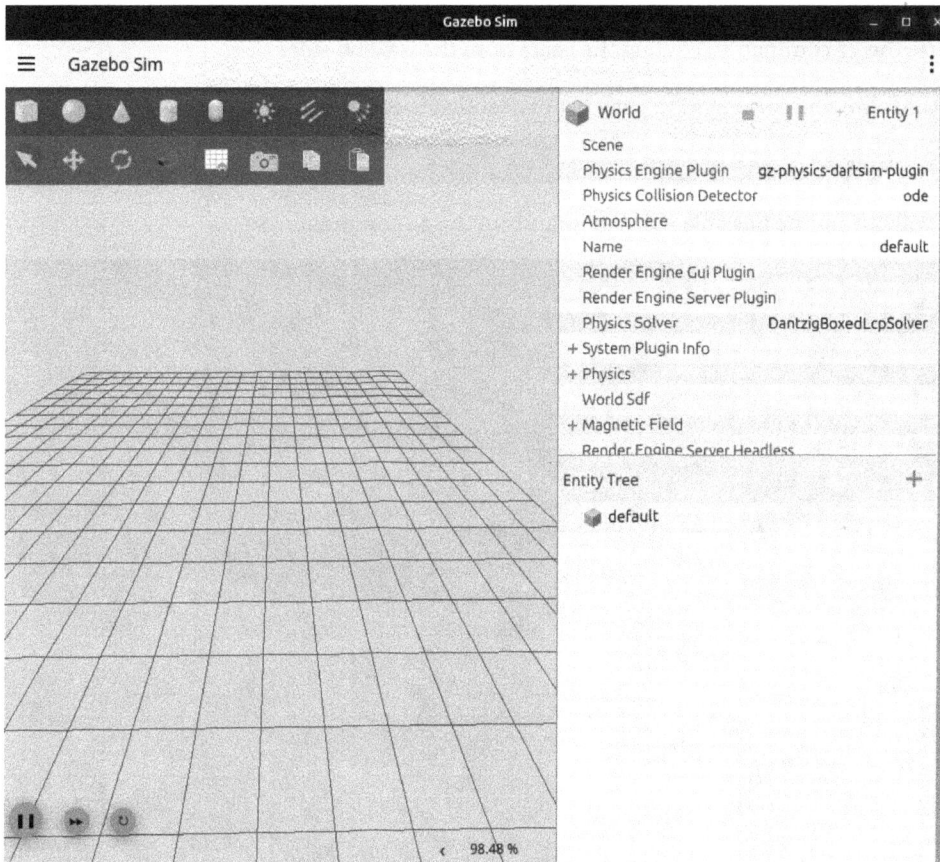

Figure 5.3: Gazebo Sim GUI

As we discussed earlier, we can work on the Gazebo simulation independently. The gz sim command starts Gazebo independently without using any ROS 2 launch file. The gz command is the primary command-line tool in Gazebo for interacting with Gazebo topics, services, and so on, similar to the ros2 command. Using this command, we can interact with the Gazebo server.

Gazebo Sim also features a message-passing interface, including topics, services, and parameters, similar to ROS 2. Both concepts are the same, but the communication protocols differ.

Let's look at some gz sub-commands that can help you interact with Gazebo independently. These commands are beneficial, especially when interfacing the simulation with ROS 2. For example, if communication between Gazebo and ROS 2, or between ROS 2 and Gazebo, is not working, we can use the gz command to debug the issue from the Gazebo side.

Run the following command to get a list of useful sub-commands in Gazebo Sim:

```
gz help
```

This will output the possible sub-commands in the gz command:

```
robot@robot-pc:~$ gz help
The 'gz' command provides a command line interface to the Gazebo Tools.

  gz <command> [options]

List of available commands:

  help:          Print this help text.
  fuel:          Manage simulation resources.
  gui:           Launch graphical interfaces.
  log:           Record or playback topics.
  model:         Print information about models.
  msg:           Print information about messages.
  param:         List, get or set parameters.
  plugin:        Print information about plugins.
  sdf:           Utilities for SDF files.
  service:       Print information about services.
  sim:           Run and manage the Gazebo Simulator.
  topic:         Print information about topics.

Options:

  --force-version <VERSION>  Use a specific library version.
  --versions                 Show the available versions.
  --commands                 Show the available commands.
Use 'gz help <command>' to print help for a command.
```

Figure 5.4: The gz command help

You can use gz topic and gz service to interact with the Gazebo Sim topic and service, respectively. Like ROS 2, we can list the topic and service, publish a topic, and call a service from the command line. You can also use gz topic -h and gz service -h to get help from the sub-commands.

In the next section, we will see how to start a robot simulation using **Gazebo Sim**.

Simulating a robot using Gazebo Sim

Here is an example of a Gazebo simulation that does not use ROS 2 components. You can find the SDF file in Chapter05/moving_robot.sdf. The SDF file format is very similar to URDF. Both are used to represent the 3D robot model. SDF is the format for simulation in Gazebo. To interface ROS 2 and Gazebo, we usually convert the URDF/Xacro files to SDF format and start the simulation.

The example sdf file represents a differential drive robot. To start the simulation, you can open a terminal, switch the path to the sdf file path, and execute the following command:

```
gz sim moving_robot.sdf
```

We can mention the sdf file and the gz sim command to start the simulation. After seeing the Gazebo Sim window, press the **Play** button in the bottom-left corner to start the simulation. *Figure 5.5* shows the simulation output of the above command.

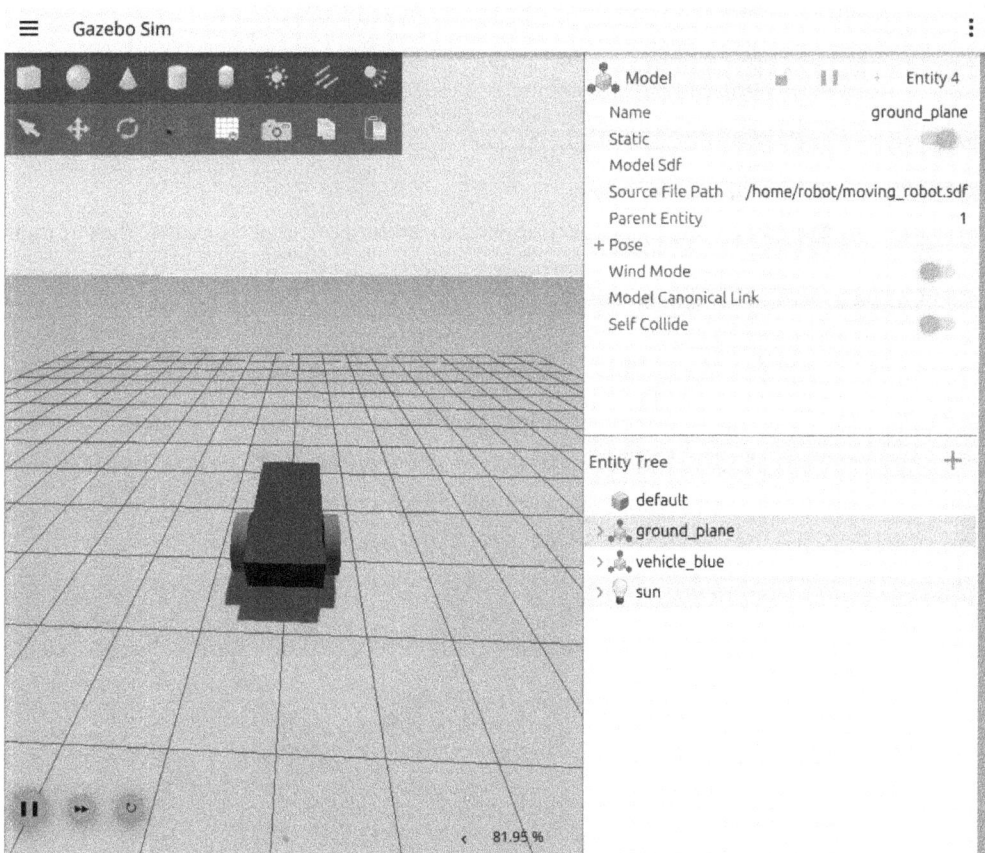

Figure 5.5: Gazebo Sim with differential drive robot simulation

Gazebo GUI

The GUI we are seeing while launching Gazebo Sim is the client. It is the easiest way for us to interact with the simulation. Let's have a quick walkthrough of the Gazebo GUI. In *Figure 5.5*, we can see the complete Gazebo window. The 3D viewport is where you see the robot and all the models/entities. You can interact with the viewport using the mouse and find translation and rotation tools from the toolbar at the top. We can move the object and spawn primitive objects, such as cubes and cylinders. On the right side, you will find two sections: the top section displays the properties of the world and its entities. It can show the plugins we have loaded and the properties of the model. Just under the model properties, we can see an entity tree. This will show the list of entities in the simulation. It can include models, lights, and other elements.

In the bottom-left corner of the 3D viewport, you can find the button to *start*, *pause*, and *reset* the simulation. In the top-left corner, you can see the different options to save/load the current simulation as an sdf file and save/load the current Gazebo client configuration.

After simulating the robot, we can use the following command to move the robot. The command is publishing to a Gazebo topic called /cmd_vel:

```
gz topic -t "/cmd_vel" -m gz.msgs.Twist -p "linear: {x: 0.6}, angular: {z: 0.06}"
```

The -t argument mentions the topic name, the -m argument mentions the Gazebo message type, and the -p argument mentions the topic content. In the topic content, we have provided linear and angular velocity. After executing this command, the robot will start moving in a circular path. To stop the robot, you can publish the linear and angular velocity as 0, like this:

```
gz topic -t "/cmd_vel" -m gz.msgs.Twist -p "linear: {x: 0.0}, angular: {z: 0.0}"
```

After this command, the robot will immediately stop.

Let's see the various Gazebo plugins used inside moving_robot.sdf and discuss how the simulation works.

How does Gazebo simulation work?

When we run the gz sim command with an sdf file, the server and client initialize, and the server parses the tags inside the sdf file. The main tags in sdf files are <world>, <model>, <light>, <plugin>, <link>, and <joint>. The <world> tag is a root tag, similar to the <robot> tag in URDF. It contains plugins and models for the simulation. In this case, we have a model definition of two-wheeled robots, including their links and joints, as well as plugins for the Gazebo simulation and lighting parameters. After parsing the SDF, the plugins and models are loaded into the server. The simulation updates are sent from the server to the client; in this case, the GUI is the client.

As we saw in Gazebo architecture, we need to load multiple plugins onto the server to start the simulation. If we perform a walkthrough of moving robot.sdf, we can see the following plugins included in this simulation, which we discussed in the architecture:

- **gz-sim-physics-system**: This plugin defines the physics parameters for this simulation. You can see that we have set the physics engine as DART and also configured its parameters.

- **gz-sim-user-commands-system**: This is the user command system plugin. This enables users to interact with the simulation.

- **gz-sim-scene-broadcaster-system**: This is the scene broadcaster plugin. It will send the simulation updates to the clients.

- **gz-sim-diff-drive-system**: This is the differential drive plugin. We have included this plugin in the simulation because we are working on a differential drive robot. In the plugin definition, we can see the topic as /cmd_vel, which means that if we publish a gz.msgs. Twist message in Gazebo, it will convert that into wheel velocity and send the velocity commands to the two-wheeled joints. This is how the robot moved when we published the Twist message in the last section. Along with moving the robot, it can also compute odometry values in another topic.

- **gz-sim-triggered-publisher-system**: This is a plugin that subscribes to a topic and triggers another topic. In this simulation, when the user presses a keyboard key, it will trigger a command velocity topic and move the robot.

After running the simulation, you can try the gz topic -l and gz service -l commands to list the commands and services the simulation provides.

Now, we have a fundamental understanding of how to work with Gazebo simulators. The following section will discuss how to interface ROS 2 and Gazebo.

Simulating a robot using ROS 2 and Gazebo

Interfacing Gazebo Sim and ROS 2 involves controlling the simulated robot from ROS 2 using ROS topics, services, actions, and parameters, and subscribing to various types of robot sensor data from Gazebo as ROS 2 topics.

In this section, we will discuss how to simulate the URDF robot model that we designed in *Chapter 4*. The name of the robot we designed was *rrbot*, which is a robotic arm. We will discuss how to simulate and control this movement in Gazebo Sim. After discussing the *rrbot* simulation, we will see how to simulate wheeled robots in Gazebo Sim.

Integration of ROS 2 and Gazebo Sim

When you install Gazebo by installing the ros-${ROS_DISTRO}-ros-gz package, it will install a series of ROS 2 packages that integrate ROS 2 and Gazebo Sim. The ros-gz package is a meta package, meaning it doesn't have any specific files, but it can install a set of dependent packages for ROS 2-Gazebo integration. Here is a list of packages that are installed along with it. It is essential to understand these packages before we work with ROS 2 and Gazebo Sim.

ros_gz is the meta package we installed earlier to get the Gazebo Sim simulator. Along with the Gazebo Sim simulator, it will install a set of packages that help to interface ROS 2 and Gazebo. Here is the complete list of packages for ROS 2 and Gazebo interfacing: [32]. The important list of packages is as follows:

- ros_gz_bridge: This is an important package that interfaces ROS 2 and Gazebo. It features a bridge node that enables bidirectional transport between Gazebo messages and ROS. We can include the topic names of Gazebo and ROS 2, along with their message types, in a configuration file, and the communication can begin based on the direction of transport we choose. Here are the types of messages we can bridge between ROS 2 and Gazebo: [17].
- ros_gz_sim: This package has launch files and an executable for using Gazebo Sim with ROS. The launch files start the Gazebo simulation from ROS 2 by simply passing the SDF or URDF file.
- ros_gz_image: This package is specifically for transporting images from Gazebo to ROS 2. The image topics can also be bridged using the standard ROS 2 bridge, but the image bridge is more optimized and can publish a compressed stream of images.
- ros_gz_sim_demos: This package includes multiple demos of Gazebo robot control, sensor integration, and more. It will help the developer learn about integration.

- `ros_gz_point_cloud`: This package includes a plugin for publishing point clouds from Gazebo Sim to ROS.

> **Important note**
>
> When we install ROS packages using the apt package manager, we can see a hyphen (-) for connecting each word in the package name. However, after installing the packages, we will use an underscore (_) for connecting the names. The package name typically uses a hyphen, whereas ROS packages conventionally use an underscore.

We will use these packages and nodes to integrate Gazebo into ROS 2. So, why do we need a Gazebo integration to ROS 2? Here are the main reasons:

- **The ROS 2 launch file**: It can better orchestrate simulation components and robotic applications by launching everything in a single command.
- **The ros_gz bridge**: Using the ros_gz bridge, we can access the Gazebo topics, services, and parameters in ROS 2, which can be easily used for further processing and visualization. We can also utilize these topics to interface with ROS's high-level capabilities, such as Nav2 (autonomous navigation) and MoveIt 2 (robot manipulation).
- **Simulate ROS URDF**: Using the ROS-Gazebo interface, we can spawn a model in Gazebo from a ROS 2 URDF file at runtime.

Now let's start Gazebo Sim from the ROS 2 launch file.

Starting Gazebo from ROS 2

We are going to launch some launch files inside the `ros_gz_sim` package. It has two main launch files named `gz_server.launch.py` and `gz_sim.launch.py`. The first launch file will start only the Gazebo server, whereas the second launch file can start the Gazebo server and GUI client.

We can use `gz_sim.launch.py` to start the `moving_robot.sdf` file. Here is the command; you can switch to the sdf file path and execute the following command:

```
ros2 launch ros_gz_sim gz_sim.launch.py gz_args:=moving_robot.sdf
```

This will spawn the same differential-drive robot demonstrated earlier using the `gz sim` command. We can use this launch file inside a custom launch file and pass the model's name along with other nodes.

Spawning a URDF model to Gazebo Sim

This section will show you how to spawn the URDF model we created in the previous chapter into the Gazebo simulation. You need to take a few steps before simulating a URDF model in a simulated environment. Here are the steps.

1. **Update URDF tags for simulation**: To do simulation, you must update the collision and inertial tags of links. You must also define parameters such as damping, effort, and limits accurately for the joints. Besides the basic tags, you must include `<gazebo>` tags in URDF Gazebo-specific parameters such as material, friction, and Gazebo-ROS2 plugins in the URDF. Finally, if we use ROS 2 controllers for simulation, we must define the `<ros2_control>` tags for each joint. We will see more about the ROS 2 controller in *Chapter 6*. These are the main changes you have to make before doing a simulation.

2. **Create a world file for simulation**: You need to create a world file, which is an SDF file, and include the other models/entities in the environment from either the package path or the fuel repository. The **Fuel** repository [*18*] is an online application that allows you to view, download, and get the SDF snippet to load the model in our simulation. The downloaded models from Fuel are placed in a path specified by the `GZ_SIM_SYSTEM_PLUGIN_PATH` environmental variable. By default, the path of the models will be in the `$HOME/.gz/` folder.

3. **Create the configuration files**: In the Gazebo simulation with ROS 2 controls, there are two important configuration files we need to create. One is for the ROS Gazebo bridge. This file lists topics from Gazebo and ROS that we have to bridge. The other file loads the list of ROS 2 controllers when the simulation is launched.

4. **Create the simulation launch file**: This is the final step for the simulation. We need to create a launch file to start Gazebo Sim, pass the world file, spawn the URDF model in Gazebo, and initiate the `ros-gz` bridge node and ROS 2 controllers.

Let's dive into the Gazebo simulation package for *rrbot*. Here, we are not creating a new package or adding stuff. Instead, we can directly check the package from `Chapter05/rrbot_gazebo`.

We can do a walkthrough and check whether we have followed the simulation steps we have seen before.

Updating URDF tags for simulation

In the rrbot_gazebo | urdf folder, you can find three files. The rrbot.xacro file is the main URDF/ Xacro file. Inside this main file, you will see the following line:

```
<xacro:include filename="$(find rrbot_description)/urdf/rrbot.urdf.
xacro"/>
```

The above line includes the URDF/Xacro file from the description package we created in *Chapter 4*. This Xacro file has all the necessary tags for simulation, such as <inertia>, <collision>, etc.

The following line includes a Gazebo-specific Xacro file. This file is already located in the same folder as we mentioned above. This Xacro file primarily contains the <gazebo> tag, which is used in Gazebo simulations. Using this tag, we can include Gazebo-specific parameters and plugins, such as sensor plugins (e.g., depth cameras and LiDAR). It also contains materials and other simulation-specific parameters:

```
<xacro:include filename="$(find rrbot_gazebo)/urdf/rrbot.gazebo.xacro"/>
```

The following line adds the ROS 2 control-specific tags. This will interface the robot joints to a ROS 2 controller. We can then send the joint commands to a controller, which will control the robot joints:

```
<xacro:include filename="$(find rrbot_gazebo)/urdf/rrbot.ros2_control.
xacro"/>
```

For the simulation purpose, we will be using the rrbot.xacro file, located inside the rrbot_ gazebo package, as it includes all the necessary components. However, ensure that you have the rrbot_description package in your ROS 2 workspace.

You can review other Xacro files to see how we defined them. We are now done updating URDF/ Xacro. Let's move on to the world file.

Creating the world file for simulation

Go to the rrbot_gazebo | worlds folder and find empty.world. This is the world file we will be using for this simulation. If you open this file, you will see the definitions of all the models and entities in the robot environment.

Creating the configuration files

The two configuration files we need are inside the rrbot_gazebo | config folder. The first configuration is for the ros-gz bridge. ros_gz_bridge.yaml is the configuration file. We can map the ROS 2 topic and Gazebo with the message type in this configuration. Here is the complete reference of topic types we can map with Gazebo and ROS. This also has some examples of how to try the ros-gz bridge independently: [19].

The following configuration is for the ROS 2 controller. You will find rrbot_controllers.yaml as the configuration file and can view the definitions for arm_controller and joint_state_broadcaster. The arm_controller is a joint trajectory controller [20] in ROS 2, which can send a trajectory to a list of joints. Meanwhile, joint_state_broadcaster publishes the joint state value on a topic. In this case, we have joint1 and joint2 as the main joints.

Creating a simulation launch file

After completing the above steps, we can check that the simulation launch file is working. In the rrbot_gazebo | launch folder, you can find rrbot_gazebo.launch.py. This launches robot_state_publisher, which parses the URDF file of rrbot and publishes the URDF model /robot_description as a topic. We will start the Gazebo simulator with the world file and spawn the URDF model in Gazebo. It will load all the plugins inside the world and the URDF model. After starting the Gazebo simulation with the world file, we will start the ros-gz bridge and the configuration file. After starting the bridge, we will start the arm controller and joint state broadcaster. The ROS 2 controller configuration file is already loading inside the ros2 control plugin inside rrbot.gazebo.xacro. The ROS 2 controller manager is also loading.

Launching the simulation in Gazebo

Before starting the simulation, we have to install some dependencies. These are the main dependencies for launching a simulation in Gazebo Sim with ROS 2 controllers:

```
sudo apt install -y ros-${ROS_DISTRO}-ros2-control ros-${ROS_DISTRO}-gz-
ros2-control ros-${ROS_DISTRO}-gz-ros2-control-demos ros-${ROS_DISTRO}-
ros2-controllers ros-${ROS_DISTRO}-rqt-joint-trajectory-controller
```

You can run the above command in the terminal to install all the dependencies. After installing the above dependencies, you can copy the rrbot_gazebo and rrbot_description packages to your ROS 2 workspace and build the ROS 2 workspace using the colcon build command.

After building the ROS 2 workspace, you can launch the rrbot simulation using the following command:

```
ros2 launch rrbot_gazebo rrbot_gazebo.launch.py
```

If everything is successful, you will find the rrbot simulation spawned in Gazebo along with other models in the environment and you will see the *rrbot* model in Rviz. Ensure you check the terminal messages, and make sure that the arm controller and joint state broadcaster are loaded successfully. You can see the *rrbot* simulation with a depth camera and lidar sensor visualization in *Figure 5.6*.

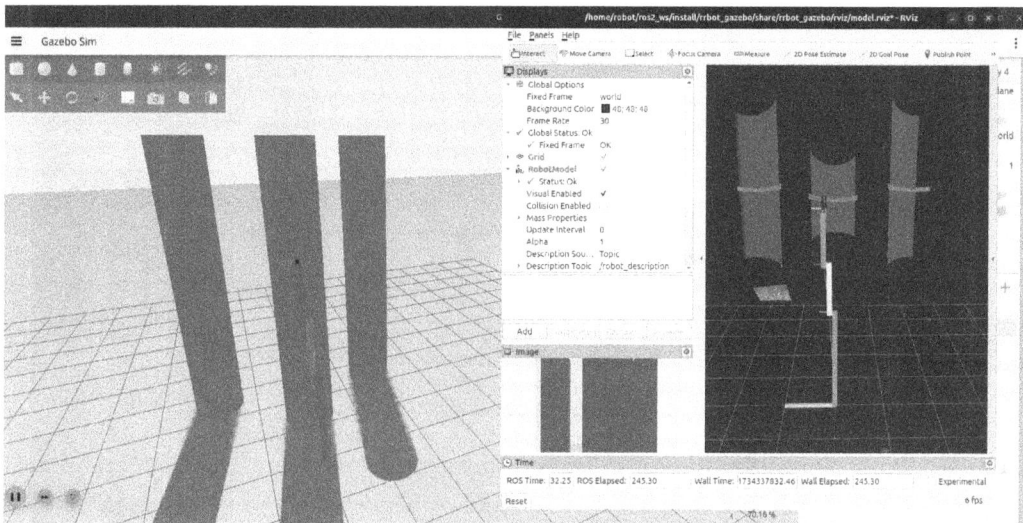

Figure 5.6: Gazebo Sim with the rrbot model

Moving the robotic arm

Here is how we can move the robot joint. As we already know, we have configured the robot joints to be controlled by a trajectory controller. To move these joints, we can publish a topic that the controller subscribes to, and then the joints will start moving.

You can publish the topic manually or through the GUI. You can use the rqt plugin called rqt_joint_trajectory_controller to publish to the controller. It is already installed on the system and it will start along with the launch file.

In the `rqt` plugin, you will see two drop-down lists. Select the running controller from that list and press the turn-on button. It will now display two sliders, allowing you to move the joints by adjusting these sliders. When you move the slider, it publishes the joint values to the controller, and the controller moves the robot.

Figure 5.7: Moving rrbot using the rqt plugin

The *rrbot* project is one of the basic projects you can refer to when creating a robotic arm simulation. This template will help you interface the simulation into a framework such as MoveIt [21], which is used for motion planning.

Now we will see a few more example simulations of robots, especially mobile robots.

Simulation of differential drive robots

You can also see a simulation of a differential drive robot in Chapter 05/diffbot_gazebo. In this package, we have simulated the same robot we saw in *Figure 5.5*. The only difference is that we have created a URDF for the same robot instead of an SDF file. Additionally, you can control the simulated robot in two ways. One method uses the differential drive Gazebo plugin we saw earlier, and the other uses ROS 2 differential controllers [22]. You can find two launch files to start the robot using either the differential drive Gazebo plugin or the ROS 2 controller.

Here is the launch file to run a simulation with the Gazebo differential drive plugin:

```
ros2 launch diffbot_gazebo diffbot_gz.launch.py
```

In this approach, we are not using any ROS 2 controller for joint states and controlling the wheel joints. Instead, everything is controlled by the Gazebo simulation's built-in plugins. You can see the `rqt steering` plugin starting along with the launch file, and you can control it using its slider. So, why do we need ROS 2 controllers if this approach works? Gazebo plugins are a good choice if you are only doing a simulation. If you plan to perform hardware interfacing after the simulation, it may be better to use ROS 2 controllers. The same controller can be run on the real hardware with ROS 2 control, while that is not the case with Gazebo plugins.

Here is the launch file to simulate with Gazebo and the ROS 2 controller. There is no difference in the method; the only difference is in the backend controls:

```
ros2 launch diffbot_gazebo diffbot_gz_ros2_control.launch.py
```

Similar to *rrbot*, we have integrated Gazebo sensor plugins, such as a depth camera, laser scanner, and IMU, into the robot for your reference.

Figure 5.8 shows the Gazebo, Rviz, and `rqt steering` plugins for moving the robot. The vertical slider moves the robot forward and back, and the horizontal slider turns the robot left and right.

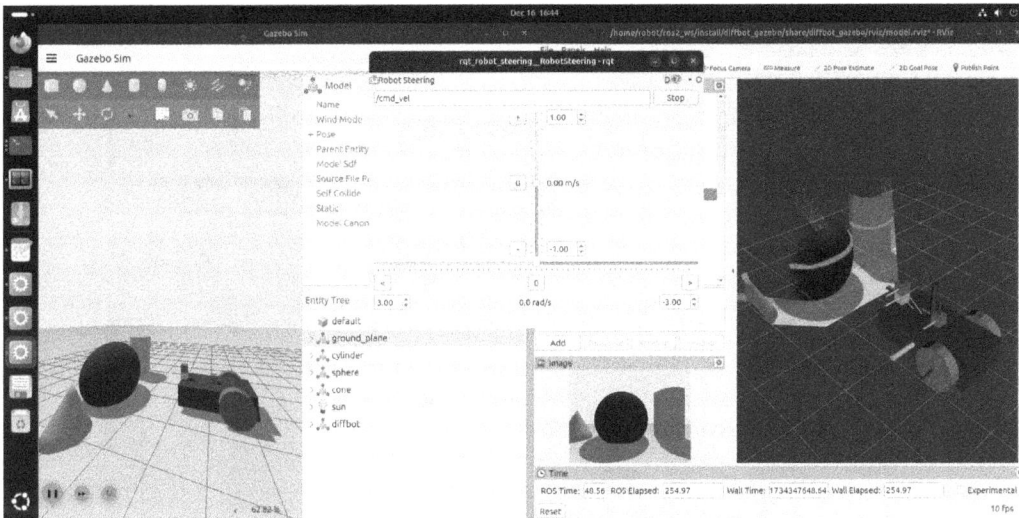

Figure 5.8: Moving the robot using the rqt plugin

In Rviz, you can find visualizations of the point cloud, RGB images from the depth camera, lidar scan, and IMU data visualization.

In the next section, we can see how to simulate the *rosbot* URDF model we generated in *Chapter 4* using **Fusion 360** with the **URDF** plugin.

Modifying the Fusion 360-generated URDF package for simulation

In *Chapter 4*, we modeled a differential drive robot using Fusion 360 and converted it to a ROS 2 URDF package. The generated package can be found in `Chapter 04/rosbot_description`. If you build this generated package in `master_ros2_ws`, you will see a `gazebo.launch.py` file in `rosbot_description | launch`. If you launch this file, you will see the spawned model in Gazebo Sim. You can use the following command to spawn the model in Gazebo Sim:

```
ros2 launch rosbot_description gazebo.launch.py
```

Figure 5.9 shows the spawned model of the rosbot model in Gazebo Sim. The robot shown in the image is not functional. To make it move and add sensors, we have to add Gazebo Sim plugins or ROS 2 controllers.

In this section, we will see how to modify this package to simulate the robot, which involves adding Gazebo plugins to control the robot and getting the laser scan data. We can later use the modified model for performing navigation.

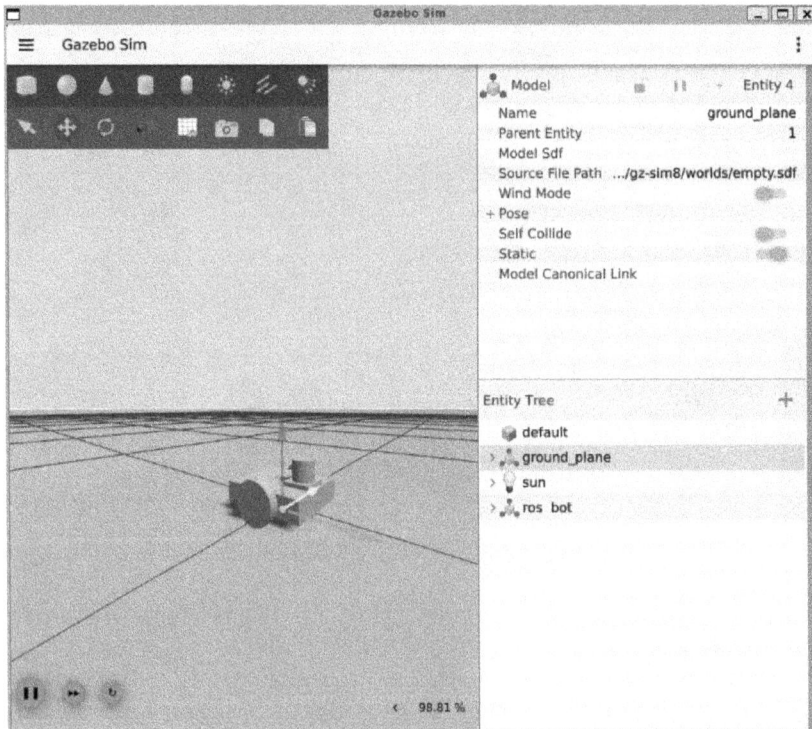

Figure 5.9: Simulating the rosbot model in Gazebo Sim

If you are using Gazebo Sim, you can visualize the center of mass, collision, and inertia by finding the robot's name in the **Entity Tree** section and right-clicking on it. You can use an option called **View**, which allows you to view all these parameters. *Figure 5.10* shows the visualization of these parameters. It is important to view and verify that these parameters are correct; otherwise, the robot model may not work as expected. If the inertia values are wrong, it can affect the robot's motion.

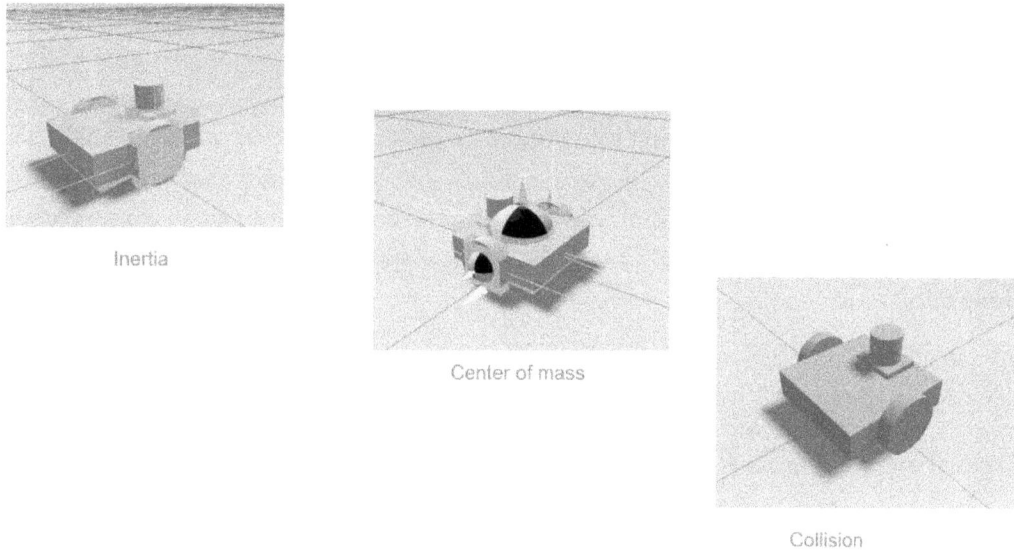

Figure 5.10: Visualizing inertia, center of mass, and collision of rosbot

You can find the fully modified URDF package in Chapter05/rosbot_description.

Here are the important steps to consider while modifying a generated ROS 2 URDF package to a functioning package.

Correction of the Xacro file

After generating the ROS 2 URDF model, we may encounter URDF model errors due to modeling errors in Fusion 360 or bugs in the ROS 2 conversion plugin. Although the URDF is autogenerated, it is essential to have a basic understanding of URDF. If the generated model has an issue, we may have to correct it.

The first step in correcting the URDF model is to visualize it in Rviz and test the robot's joints using joint_state_publisher_gui. We can visualize the URDF model using the following command:

```
ros2 launch rosbot_description display.launch.py
```

The expected behavior of the rosbot wheel joints is that the wheels rotate in a clockwise direction, with the positive value of the joints displayed in the GUI. If you are not getting it, we must edit the generated Xacro file. In the case of the generated rosbot URDF, the direction of rotation was wrong. Therefore, we need to adjust the axis of rotation of the wheels. You can find the new Xacro file at `Chapter05/rosbot_description/urdf/rosbot.xacro`. One of the changes we have to make is the axis of rotation of the right wheel.

The next modification we have to make is to add Gazebo Sim plugins.

Adding Gazebo Sim plugins/ROS 2 controllers

To make the robot move and collect sensor data, we need to add the Gazebo Sim plugins and controllers. The `Chapter05/rosbot_description/urdf/rosbot.gazebo` file has been modified to add the required plugins, such as differential drive and lidar. We have to configure these plugins with accurate parameters. `rosbot.gazebo` is an example; we can use it to configure a differential drive with a laser.

We can add more plugins to this file such as IMU and a depth camera. This file is dedicated to simulated related tags.

Updating Gazebo-ROS 2 bridge topics

After updating the plugins, if you run the Gazebo Sim simulation using the launch file, you will find the Gazebo topics using the following command:

```
gz topic -l
```

These topics are mostly publishing and subscribing by the plugins we have added to the `rosbot.gazebo` file. To bridge the Gazebo topics to ROS 2, we can add the bridge topics in a YAML file. The modified YAML file can be found in `Chapter05/rosbot_description/config/ros_gz_bridge_gazebo.yaml`. You can see the complete mapping of ROS 2 and Gazebo topics here.

You can copy the modified version of `rosbot_description` to `master_ros2_ws`, start the Gazebo launch file, and see the Gazebo simulation and visualization of the rosbot.

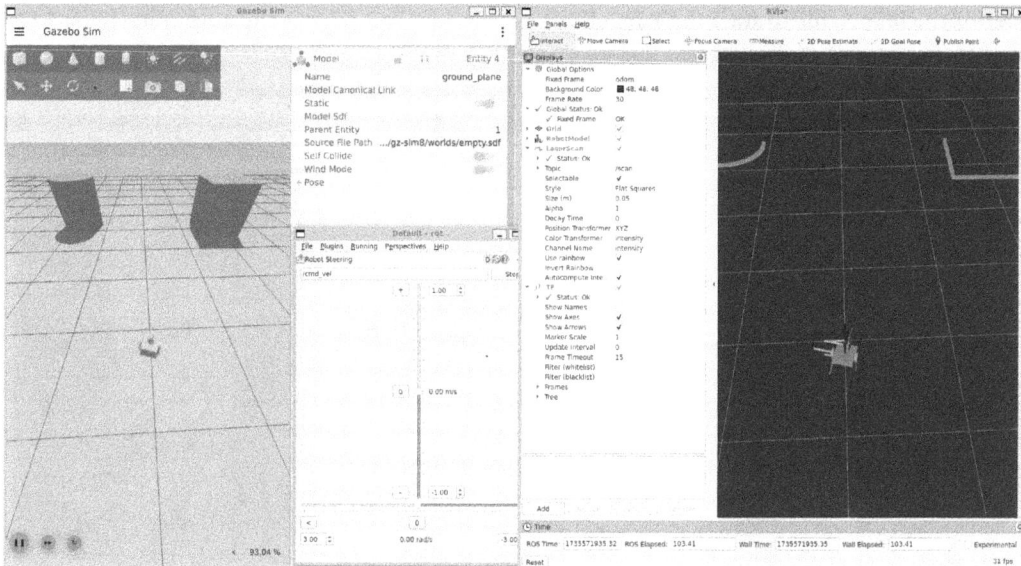

Figure 5.11: Simulation and visualization of the rosbot in Gazebo Sim (left) and Rviz (right)

We need to add the obstacle around the robot manually, and you can also see the laser scan around the robot in RViz, as shown in *Figure 5.11*.

Gazebo simulation of existing robots

We can also install and try out some existing robot simulations in ROS 2 Jazzy. Here is the Gazebo simulation of Leo Rover and TurtleBot 4. We can install the simulation packages using the following command:

```
sudo apt install ros-${ROS_DISTRO}-leo-simulator ros-${ROS_DISTRO}-turtlebot4-simulator
```

After installing the package, you can start the simulator using the following launch files.

Here is the launch file to start Leo Rover. You can see the output in *Figure 5.12*. You can open Rviz and visualize the robot topics:

```
ros2 launch leo_gz_bringup leo_gz.launch.py
```

Here is the launch file to start the TurtleBot 4 simulation. You can see the output in *Figure 5.12*:

```
ros2 launch turtlebot4_gz_bringup turtlebot4_gz.launch.py
```

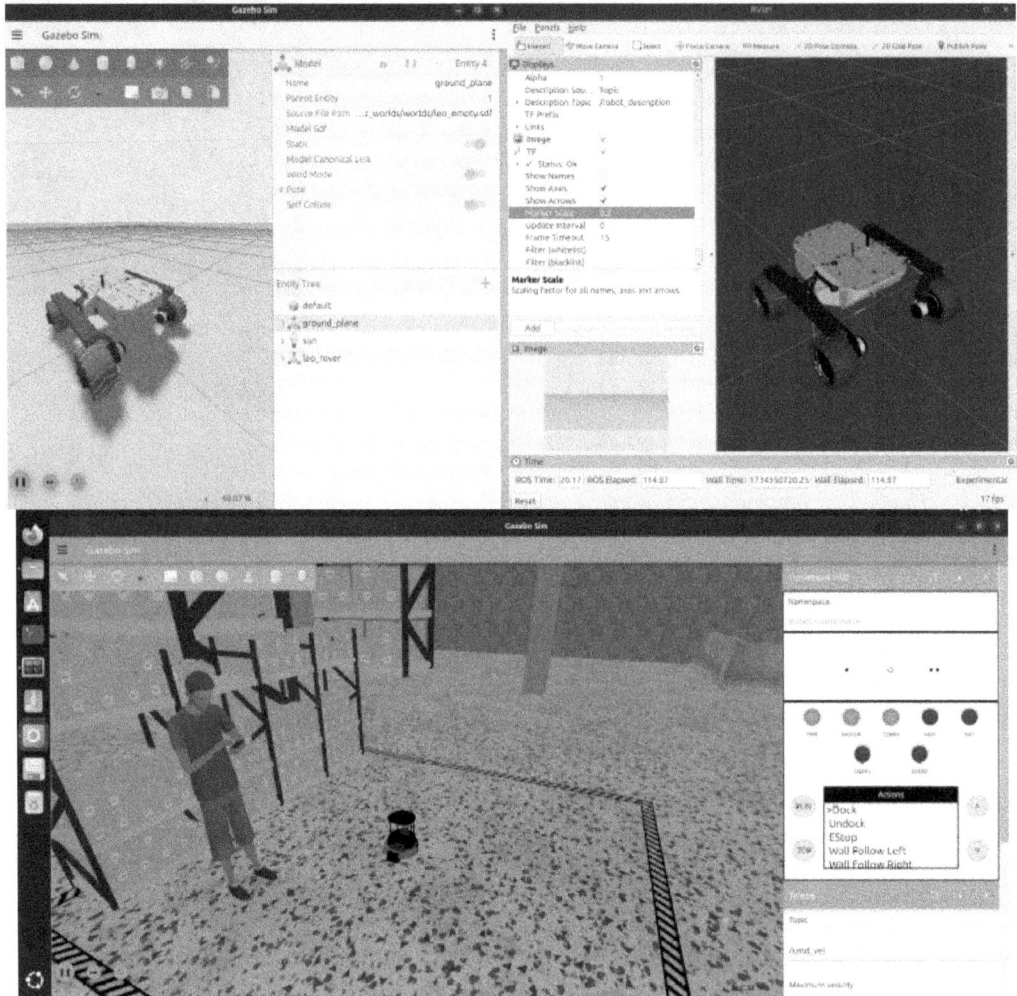

Figure 5.12: Leo Rover simulation (top) and TurtleBot 4 simulation (bottom)

You can find a few more references to the Gazebo-ROS 2 simulation project at [23] and [24].

Simulation using Docker

We can set up the Gazebo simulation in Docker, just as we did with ROS 2 in *Chapter 2*. We may have to add the new dependencies in the Dockerfile to build the simulation Docker image. The latest Dockerfile and build scripts are included in the Chapter05 | docker_gazebo folder.

Before building a Docker image, make sure you have created a ROS 2 workspace folder on your machine. Here is the command to create the ROS 2 workspace:

```
mkdir -p ~/master_ros2_ws/src
```

Copy `rrbot_description`, `rrbot_gazebo`, `urdf_tutorial`, and `diffbot_gazebo` into the `src` folder inside the ROS 2 workspace. After completing this step, we can begin building the image and start the container. The reason is that the container will mount this ROS 2 workspace folder, allowing us to build packages inside the container.

Now, switch to the `Chapter05/docker_gazebo` folder and execute the following command to start building the Docker image:

```
./build_image.sh ros2_sim:v0.1 master_ros2_ws robot
```

The name of the image is `ros2_sim:v0.1`, the ROS 2 workspace path name in the user home folder is `master_ros2_ws`, and the username of the container is `robot`.

After building the image, you can create the container using the following command:

```
./create_container.sh ros2_sim:v0.1 master_ros2_ws ros2_dev
```

This script will create a new container called *ros2_dev* from the build image and mount *master_ros2_ws*. You will get the terminal from the container, and you can now build the ROS 2 workspace we have created from inside Docker:

```
cd ~/master_ros2_ws/
colcon build
source install/setup.bash
```

Now we can start executing the simulation launch files:

```
ros2 launch rrbot_gazebo rrbot_gazebo.launch.py
```

You can start the existing container or create a new terminal from the running container using the following command:

```
./start_container.sh ros2_dev
source /ros_entrypoint.sh
source install/setup.bash
```

Simulation using Docker Compose

In this section, we can see how to build and start containers for simulation using Docker Compose.

Switch to the Chapter05/docker_compose_gazebo folder and execute the following command to start building the Docker image and start the container:

- Use the following command if you are using a non-NVIDIA graphics card on your PC:

```
docker compose -f docker-compose-gui.yml build
docker compose -f docker-compose-gui.yml up
```

- If you do have an NVIDIA graphics card and the driver is properly installed, use the following command to start the container:

```
docker compose -f docker-compose-nvidia.yml build
docker compose -f docker-compose-nvidia.yml up
```

Once you start this command, the image will be built first and the container will start, and you will have to use another terminal to attach to the container. You don't have to close this terminal; if you cancel the command by pressing *Ctrl + C*, it will stop the running container.

You can create a new terminal from the running container using the following command:

```
./start_container.sh ros2_dev
```

Now source the ROS 2 environment:

```
source /ros_entrypoint.sh
```

Build the ROS 2 workspace:

```
colcon build
```

Source the ROS 2 workspace:

```
source install/setup.bash
```

Now, we can launch the simulation launch file:

```
ros2 launch rrbot_gazebo rrbot_gazebo.launch.py
```

After starting the container, if you want to stop the container and remove it, you can execute the command from a new host terminal. Make sure you are executing from inside the docker_compose_gazebo folder:

```
docker compose -f docker-compose-gui.yml down
```

or

```
docker compose -f docker-compose-nvidia.yml down
```

In the next section, we will see how to set up VS Code Dev Containers for running simulations.

Simulation using VS Code Dev Containers

If you are interested in setting up a development container in VS Code, make sure you have created the ROS 2 workspace named master_ros2_ws and then open the Chapter05 folder using VS Code. This folder has a .devcontainer folder. This has the devcontainer.json file, which has the instructions to use the Docker Compose file we used in the above section for the container. When you open the folder, it will prompt you to install the Dev Containers extension and reopen it in the container. If you select this option, it will build the container, set the environment, mount the ROS 2 workspace as a volume, and connect the editor to it. We can also see the mounted volume, which is the master_ros2_ws folder in VS Code itself.

Here is the source you can use to learn more about Docker in ROS 2: [33].

Note that you can use the above instructions for building and running the packages from *Chapters 2* and *3* as well.

In the next section, we will discuss other simulators that work along with ROS 2.

Introduction to the Webots simulator

One of the simulators that works with ROS 2 is Webots from Cyberbotics [25]. It is a powerful open-source robotic simulator for designing, modeling, and testing the robotic system in a realistic 3D environment. Webots has multiple sensor models and actuator support, which make it suitable for education, research, and industrial applications. A decent specification required to run this simulator is a processor with more than 2 GHz, 8 GB RAM, and a graphics card such as NVIDIA or equivalent.

Key features of Webots

Here are some of the unique features of this simulator:

- **Integrated Development Environment (IDE) Support**: This simulator comes with an IDE, which is uncommon in other simulators. The IDE, which includes a code editor, tools, and a scene editor, makes development more straightforward and quicker.

- **Realistic Physics**: This uses **Open Dynamics Engine** (**ODE**), which can simulate robots accurately by considering collision detection, dynamics, and so on.

- **Cross-Platform and Multi-Language Support**: The simulator works on Windows, macOS, and Linux, enabling developers to work on their preferred OS. Webots offers support for multiple programming languages, including Python, C++, Java, and MATLAB, making this simulator more attractive.

- **ROS Compatibility**: It offers ROS 1/ROS 2 support, and developers can integrate and test their ROS-based applications in Webots.

- **Open-Source and Extensible**: It is open-source, so developers can contribute and extend their capabilities.

Let's see how to set up this simulator in Ubuntu 24.04 LTS and integrate **ROS 2 Jazzy**.

Installing Webots and the ROS 2 interface

Installing **Webots** is easy if you are using an Ubuntu desktop environment. You can install it directly from the *Ubuntu software package manager*. Just search for *Webots* and then install it. If not, you can go to the website [*25*] and download the .deb file:

1. Go to the downloaded location, open a terminal, and install using the following command:

```
sudo apt install ./downloaded_file_name.deb
```

2. Ensure you have used the exact name of the Debian file in the command. After installing **Webots**, you can install the Webots ROS 2 interface using the following command:

```
sudo apt-get install ros-${ROS_DISTRO}-webots-ros2
```

3. After installing the package, you have to set a variable called WEBOTS_HOME to get the Webots installation path. If you installed it from binaries, it will be installed in the following path:

```
echo "export WEBOTS_HOME=/usr/local/webots" >> ~/.bashrc
source ~/.bashrc
```

4. After setting this variable in the terminal, you can start a demo simulation using ROS 2 with the following command:

```
ros2 launch webots_ros2_universal_robot multirobot_launch.py
```

If everything works fine, you will see the simulation in *Figure 5.13*.

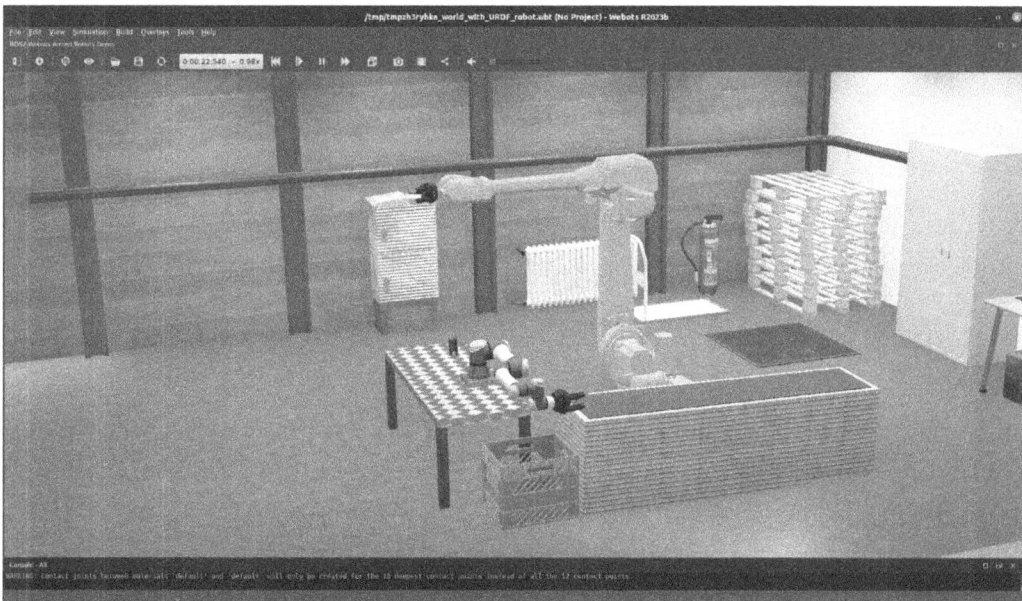

Figure 5.13: Webots with the ROS 2 interface

This demo shows the UR robot taking the coke can from the conveyor and placing it on the table, and the ABB robot picks up the can and places it into another position.

Note that you can get graphics issues in **VMware** and **VirtualBox**. You can check the list of bugs here to fix them: [*26*]. Make sure you have a good graphics card and driver installed.

In the next section, we will discuss the **NVIDIA Isaac Sim simulator**.

Introduction to Isaac Sim

Gazebo Sim and Webots may work on most PCs with average specifications. If you have these specs, you can use these simulators, but If you have a PC with high-end specifications such as *32 to 64 GB of RAM, NVIDIA RTX 40XX series* graphics card with >=8 GB VRAM, and a high-end CPU, you can try out the **NVIDIA Isaac Sim simulator** [*27*]. NVIDIA Isaac Sim is an open-source application on NVIDIA Omniverse for developing, simulating, and testing AI-driven robots in realistic virtual environments [*34*]. The main difference NVIDIA brings is that it has a photo-realistic, physics-accurate, and scalable simulation of robots. It is also integrated with NVIDIA GPU-accelerated technologies, which allows real-time rendering and physics-based simulation. Isaac Sim is used to collect datasets and train robot models.

It features good ROS 2 integration, allowing you to simulate complex scenarios that leverage the high-end capabilities of ROS 2. You can see the installation instructions in the next section.

Installing NVIDIA Isaac Sim in Ubuntu 24.04 LTS with ROS 2 Jazzy

Installing Isaac Sim is straightforward. There is an installer available for downloading it from the NVIDIA website [*28*], which automates the installation of Isaac Sim modules. Isaac Sim is available in Windows and Linux.

The installation instructions for a workstation are mentioned in the following link: [*29*].

Figure 5.14 shows an example simulation Isaac Sim GUI after installation.

Figure 5.14: Isaac Sim GUI

There are multiple examples already available in Isaac Sim. Here is the reference to start with Isaac Sim tutorials: [*30*].

Summary

We discussed three simulators in this chapter and learned how to create a simulation from a ROS URDF robot model.

This chapter delved into the significance of robotic simulation in robot development processes, which enables the validation and refinement of robot designs in a virtual environment. It highlighted the integration of ROS 2 and Gazebo Sim for creating advanced simulations using URDF models, leveraging plugins for physics, visualization, and control.

The architectural advantages of Gazebo Sim, such as modularity, extensibility, and seamless ROS 2 compatibility, were contrasted with Gazebo Classic, emphasizing the former's suitability for scalable and modern robotics projects. After discussing the features, we saw how to implement multiple robot simulations in Gazebo. We also saw how to run the simulation using Docker.

Additionally, the chapter introduced Webots, with its built-in IDE and multi-language support, and NVIDIA Isaac Sim, offering photorealistic rendering and high-fidelity physics for complex simulations. These tools enable developers to prototype, test, and optimize robotic systems for navigation, manipulation, and sensor integration.

In the upcoming chapters, we will apply the simulation to various applications, such as navigation and manipulation.

References

- [1] https://github.com/gazebosim
- [2] https://cyberbotics.com/
- [3] https://developer.nvidia.com/isaac/sim
- [4] https://www.coppeliarobotics.com/
- [5] https://pybullet.org/wordpress/
- [6] https://mujoco.org/
- [7] https://unity.com/products/unity-engine
- [8] https://playerstage.sourceforge.net/
- [9] https://classic.gazebosim.org/
- [10] https://gazebosim.org/home
- [11] http://sdformat.org/
- [12] https://github.com/gazebosim/ros_gz
- [13] https://gazebosim.org/libs/sim/
- [14] https://gazebosim.org/docs/latest/architecture/
- [15] https://gazebosim.org/docs/harmonic/ros_installation/
- [16] https://gazebosim.org/docs/latest/troubleshooting/
- [17] https://github.com/gazebosim/ros_gz/tree/ros2/ros_gz_bridge
- [18] https://app.gazebosim.org/fuel/models
- [19] https://github.com/gazebosim/ros_gz/tree/ros2/ros_gz_bridge
- [20] https://control.ros.org/jazzy/doc/ros2_controllers/joint_trajectory_controller/doc/userdoc.html
- [21] https://moveit.ai/
- [22] https://control.ros.org/jazzy/doc/ros2_controllers/diff_drive_controller/doc/userdoc.html

- [23] https://github.com/blackcoffeerobotics/bcr_bot

- [24] https://github.com/linorobot/linorobot2

- [25] https://cyberbotics.com/

- [26] https://cyberbotics.com/doc/guide/general-bugs

- [27] https://developer.nvidia.com/isaac/sim

- [28] https://docs.omniverse.nvidia.com/isaacsim/latest/installation/index.html

- [29] https://docs.omniverse.nvidia.com/isaacsim/latest/installation/install_workstation.html

- [30] https://docs.omniverse.nvidia.com/isaacsim/latest/introductory_tutorials/tutorial_intro_interface.html

- [31] https://index.ros.org/r/ros_gz/

- [32] https://github.com/2b-t/docker-for-robotics/blob/main/doc/Gui.md

- [33] https://github.com/2b-t/docker-for-robotics/tree/main/templates/ros2

- [34] https://github.com/isaac-sim

Part 2

ROS 2 Applications: Navigation, Manipulation, and Control

This part explores advanced ROS 2 applications, focusing on robot control, navigation, manipulation, and perception. You will learn to use `ros2_control`, Behavior Trees, and the Nav2 and MoveIt 2 stacks and integrate computer vision to build intelligent robotic behaviors.

This part includes the following chapters:

- *Chapter 6, Controlling Robots Using the ros2_control Package*
- *Chapter 7, Implementing ROS 2 Applications Using BehaviorTree.CPP*
- *Chapter 8, ROS 2 Navigation Stack: Nav2*
- *Chapter 9, Robot Manipulation Using MoveIt 2*
- *Chapter 10, Working with ROS 2 and Perception Stack*

6

Controlling Robots Using the ros2_control Package

The lowest layer of a robotic software architecture consists of controllers that connect high-level commands to the robot's actuators, such as its wheels or joints. In this chapter, we will introduce the **ros2_control** package, a framework designed to simplify the integration of hardware with control algorithms in robotics applications. We will discuss the use of the Controller Manager and the framework's structure. Then, we will demonstrate how to integrate specific controllers with a robot, consisting of two joints, simulated using Gazebo. Finally, we will show how to create custom controllers by implementing them as plugins.

Here's a list of the main topics that will be covered in the chapter:

- Understanding the ros2_control framework
- The ros2_control framework architecture
- Interfacing with simulated controllers using Gazebo
- Interacting with the ros2_control framework using the CLI
- Implementing a new controller

Technical requirements

To follow this chapter, you should have one of the following setups on your computer:

- A standard computer running Ubuntu 24.04 LTS operating system
- A Docker container installed as discussed in *Chapter 2* on your Linux host machine or a ROS 2 Jazzy desktop full installation

The reference code for this chapter can be found in the `Chapter06` folder of the following GitHub repository: `https://github.com/PacktPublishing/Mastering-ROS-2-for-Robotics-Programming/tree/main/Chapter06`.

Understanding the ros2_control framework

In a typical robotic application, once the desired motion—such as actuator position or wheel speed—is determined, the command must be sent to the robot's hardware or its simulation. ROS 2 provides the `ros2_control` framework, a collection of packages for low-level robot control. Evolved from `ros_control` in **ROS 1.x**, `ros2_control` separates hardware-specific code from control logic, enabling controller reuse across different hardware with minimal changes. It offers user-friendly interfaces for interacting with sensors and actuators and tools for efficient component management. This framework simplifies hardware integration and control algorithm development, reducing the complexity of robot control system maintenance. Another important advance of the `ros2_control` framework is the possibility of defining a chain of controllers. In this way, controllers can be composed properly by linking their input and output.

Let's discuss in detail the main packages comprising the `ros2_control` framework:

- `ros2_control`: This is the central package, providing the main interfaces and components necessary for robot control. Some elements of this package are as follows:

    - **Hardware interfaces**: These define how to interact with different robot hardware components, such as sensors and actuators. They abstract the hardware specifics, making the control logic hardware-agnostic.

    - **Controller interfaces**: These are standard interfaces for creating different types of controllers that perform specific tasks, such as position, velocity, or effort control.

    - **Controller Manager**: A crucial component that manages the lifecycle of controllers. It loads, unloads, starts, and stops controllers dynamically, ensuring efficient resource management.

- ros2_controllers: This is a collection of widely used controllers that can be easily integrated into robot applications. Some controllers are as follows:

  - forward_command_controller: A simple controller that forwards commands directly to the hardware. It's often used for basic control tasks where complex processing is unnecessary.

  - joint_trajectory_controller: Manages the execution of trajectories for joints. It interpolates between points in a trajectory and sends the appropriate commands to the joints to follow the desired path.

  - diff_drive_controller: Specifically designed for differential drive robots. It converts velocity commands into appropriate wheel commands, handling the kinematics of such robots.

- realtime_tools: This is a general toolkit aimed at providing support for real-time applications. It includes components that help ensure real-time safety and performance, such as the following:

  - RealtimeBuffer: Thread-safe buffers that allow for safe data exchange between real-time and non-real-time parts of the system

  - RealtimePublisher: Specialized ROS publishers designed to work within real-time constraints, ensuring timely and deterministic message publishing

- control_msgs: This defines common message types used in the ros2_control ecosystem. These messages facilitate communication between different parts of the control framework, ensuring standardized data exchange. The most common messages are as follows:

  - JointControllerState: Messages that convey the state of joint controllers, including current position, velocity, and effort

  - FollowJointTrajectoryAction: Messages used for sending and managing joint trajectory commands

These modules interact to let the hardware devices communicate with the controllers, as described in the software architecture discussed in the next section.

Understanding the ros2_control framework architecture

Considering the packages described in the previous section, the overall ros2_control framework architecture is depicted in *Figure 6.1* and the main elements are detailed in the following list:

- **Controller Manager**: In the ros2_control framework, the Controller Manager serves as the primary user entry point, connecting controllers to hardware-abstraction layers via ROS services. Implemented as a node without an internal executor, it relies on an external executor that manages callbacks, timing, and control loops for the ROS node. The Controller Manager's responsibilities include managing controllers—loading, activating, deactivating, and unloading them—and interfacing with hardware components through the Resource Manager. It matches required and provided interfaces and reports conflicts, ensuring a smooth operation within the ROS control ecosystem.

- **Resource Manager**: The Resource Manager coordinates access to hardware resources such as actuators (or their simulated version). It loads hardware components using pluginlib, manages their lifecycle, and handles their state and command interfaces.

- **Controllers**: Controllers in the ros2_control framework follow control theory principles, comparing reference values with measured outputs and calculating system inputs based on the error. Derived from ControllerInterface and exported as plugins via pluginlib, controllers such as forward_command_controller in ros2_controllers manage their lifecycle through the LifecycleNode class. In control-loop execution, the update() method accesses the latest hardware state and enables controllers to write to command interfaces.

- **Hardware components**: Hardware components in the ros2_control framework communicate with physical hardware and are exported as plugins via pluginlib. Managed by the Resource Manager, they fall into three categories:

  - **System**: For complex multi-DOF robotic hardware, supporting both reading and writing capabilities (e.g., industrial robots).

  - **Sensor**: For sensing hardware, providing read-only capabilities (e.g., encoders, force/torque sensors).

  - **Actuator**: For simple 1-DOF (only one joint) hardware such as motors and valves, supporting reading and writing, but reading is optional (e.g., DC motor with Arduino).

These components are modular and can be used in complex systems with independent communication channels.

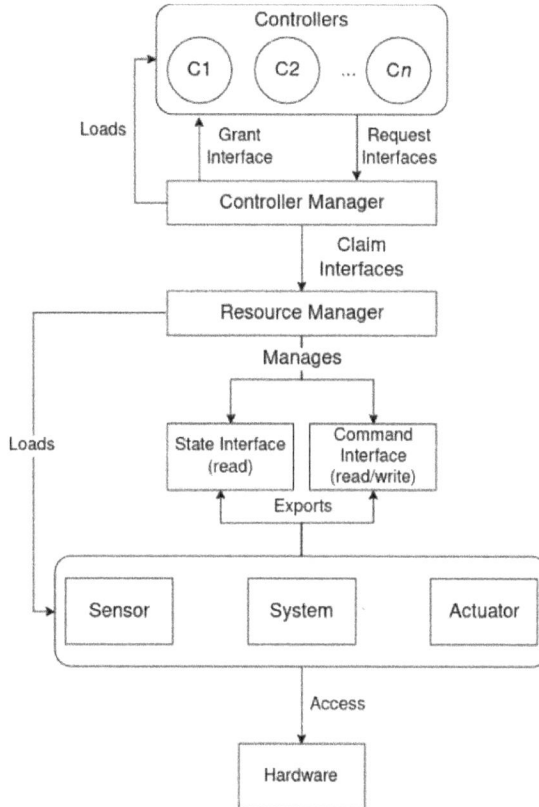

Figure 6.1: The ros2_control framework architecture

In this chapter, we will go through the different elements implemented in the ros2_control framework. This framework consists of different resources that are continuously updated. For this reason, in the next section, we will list some important references.

The ros2_control framework documentation

In the following, the main references of the ros2_control framework are listed:

- ROS2 documentation [1]: The official ROS2 documentation provides an overview of ros2_control, including its architecture and main components.

- The ros2_control GitHub repository [2]: The main repository for ros2_control on GitHub is a great place to explore source code, issues, and discussions. The repository also includes example configurations and explanations of the system's structure.

- ROS 2 hardware interface documentation [3]: This documentation explains the hardware abstraction layer and how `ros2_control` connects with various hardware interfaces.
- Controller Manager documentation [4]: Detailed information on the `Controller Manager` node, its role, and its services can be found within the ROS 2 documentation.
- The `ros2_control_demos` package [5]: This package contains example setups demonstrating how to use `ros2_control`. It's helpful for seeing practical implementations.

These resources should give you a strong starting point for exploring `ros2_control` and understanding its parts and functions in ROS 2. Let me know if you need more specific information. However, we need a way to simulate the presence of a controller connected to the simulated robot models. For this reason, in the next section, we will learn how to include controllers in our robot simulation models.

Interfacing with simulated controllers using Gazebo

A crucial aspect of robot simulations is accurately replicating real-world conditions, including modeling control interfaces. The `ros2_control` framework enables simulating robot controllers to interact with simulated hardware. This section covers integrating `ros2_control` with Gazebo, starting with creating a robot model containing `ros2_control` plugins to move the robot's joints. To do this, the following steps must be taken.

Step 1 – Creating the ROS 2 package

The first step to include controllers in a simulated robot is to obtain the simulation model. We already discussed the 3D simulation models of robots and showed how to create them and import them in simulation software such as Gazebo in *Chapters 4* and *5* of this book. Let's create a package containing the necessary files to simulate a robot with two joints: a revolute one and a prismatic one. Move into the source folder of your ROS 2 workspace and use the following command:

```
ros2 pkg create two_joints_robot --build-type ament_cmake
```

You can download this package from the `/two_joints_robot` folder of the book repository.

However, inside this package directory, let's create the following directories:

- A `urdf` folder to contain the robot model file
- A `launch` folder containing the files used to start the simulation
- A `config` folder for the configuration file of the controllers.

We are now ready to develop the robot model file.

Step 2 – Creating a robot model

We already discussed the xacro formalisms to develop new robot models. For this reason, and to improve the chapter's readability, we avoid reporting the whole content of the file here. However, the full content of the robot model file can be found in the package in the urdf subfolder in the urdf/two_joints_robot.xacro file. This file model contains the following elements:

- Three links:

  - base_link, defined as a base plate

  - link1 and link2, represented by cylinders

- Two joints:

  - A revolute joint (called base_joint), connecting link1 with base_link

  - A prismatic joint (called link1_link2), connecting link2 with link1

The model can be visualized in Rviz2 after implementing a proper launch file, in which the xacro file is loaded, and then joint_state_publisher_gui and robot_state_publisher are started, along with Rviz2. In Rviz2, the model description can be added to see the robot in the scene, as shown in *Figure 6.2*:

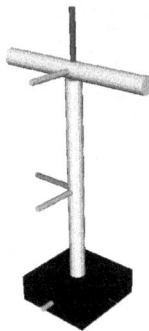

Figure 6.2: The two-joint robot implemented in the xacro file

Step 3 – Adding controllers to the robot

Now, let's add controllers to the robot using ros2_control plugins:

1. If the ros2_control framework is not yet installed in your system, you can install it using the following command:

```
sudo apt install ros-jazzy-ros2-control ros-jazzy-ros2-controllers
```

2. At the start, we'll use pre-built controllers from the ros2_control package. Later, we'll implement a custom controller as a plugin enabled by the Controller Manager. To use controllers in the simulated robot, modify the robot model file to include the `<ros2_control>` tag for accessing and controlling robot interfaces. We should include the following:

   - A specific `<plugin>` for our robot
   - A `<joint>` tag including the robot controllers: commands and states

3. In the same section, the GazeboSimSystem plugin is used to define that the hardware we are contacting is a simulated system:

```
<ros2_control name="2DofControl" type="system">
    <hardware>
        <plugin>gz_ros2_control/GazeboSimSystem</plugin>
    </hardware>
```

4. For each joint we want to control using the ros2_control package, we must define which kind of command interface is available. Basic interfaces are in position and velocity. For both joints, we defined position and velocity as the command interface:

```
<joint name="base_joint">
    <command_interface name="position" />
    <command_interface name="velocity" />
```

5. Similarly, we must specify state_interface. This is the output of the actuator, which can be streamed via the /joint_state topic. In this case, we specify that the state of the actuator is composed of position, velocity, and effort. In addition, we can set an initial value for the motor as a parameter of state_interface in position:

```
<state_interface name="position">
    <param name="initial_value">0.0</param>
</state_interface>
<state_interface name="velocity"/>
</joint>
```

6. A similar configuration is added for the second joint of the robot:

```
<joint name="link1_link2">
    <command_interface name="position" />
    <command_interface name="velocity" />
    <state_interface name="position" />
    <state_interface name="velocity"/>
</joint>
</ros2_control>
```

7. Finally, to add the controllers, we must include the ros2_control plugin. In this case, we need to import the gz_ros2_control-system plugin:

```
<gazebo>
    <plugin filename="gz_ros2_control-system" name="gz_ros2_
control::GazeboSimROS2ControlPlugin">
```

8. This plugin needs a .yaml parameter file in which the controllers are configured. In this example, we placed the configuration file into the config folder and installed it by modifying CMakeList.txt (we will discuss this in *step 5*). To find this file in the computer files system, we can use the $(find PKG_NAME) command:

```
<parameters>$(find two_joints_robot)/config/controller.
yaml</parameters>
        </plugin>
</gazebo>
```

Step 4 – Creating launch and configuration files

In the previous step, we saw how a .yaml file is needed to inform the ros2_control framework about the controller configuration. In this example, we place the configuration file into the config folder of the two_joints_robots package:

1. Of course, before we can use this file, we have to install it. For now, just check its content. This is a typical ROS 2 parameter file of the .yaml type:

```
controller_manager:
  ros__parameters:
update_rate: 100  # Hz
```

2. To add a new controller, specify its name and type. The name is arbitrary for later refer-
    ence, while the type must be chosen from available low-level controllers in your system.
    For instance, you might name the first controller position_control and set its type to
    ForwardCommandController from the forward_command_controller package. This con-
    troller forwards input from the ROS2 topic to the robot joint. The control interface will be
    detailed later. We define two such controllers to enable both position and velocity control:

    ```
    position_control:
            type: forward_command_controller/ForwardCommandController
    Velocity_control:
            type: forward_command_controller/ForwardCommandController
    ```

3. A third controller added to the list is joint_state_broadcaster. This controller publishes
    the /joint_state topic with the information about the motor configuration:

    ```
    joint_state_broadcaster:
            type: joint_state_broadcaster/JointStateBroadcaster
    ```

4. The controllers defined previously are configured here, where the joints that represent
    the target of the control action are specified:

    ```
    position_control:
        ros__parameters:
    ```

5. We specify that both joints are controllable using the position_control controller. Also,
    the state interface of this control (which kind of data can be used from the joint state) is
    reported here:

    ```
    joints:
            - base_joint
            - link1_link2
    interface_name: position
    state_interfaces:
            - position
            - velocity
    ```

6. A similar configuration is made for the velocity, `velocity_control`. The difference here is that the `interface_name` value is `velocity`:

```
velocity_control:
  ros__parameters:
joints:
      - base_joint
      - link1_link2
interface_name: velocity
state_interfaces:
      - position
      - velocity
```

7. After defining the configuration files, add a launch file to your package to start the simulation and spawn the robot. In the example package, the launch file is called `launch/start_simu.launch.py`. This is similar to the launch file discussed in *Chapter 5*. However, you need to add nodes to configure the controllers. For each controller, initialize the ones to be used to actuate the robot using the `ros2 control` command with specific parameters. This is done using the `ExecuteProcess` function in the launch file to run a command-line command. In this case, the command is the following:

```
ros2 control load_controller --set-state active joint_state_
broadcaster
```

8. The code in the launch file instead will be the following:

```
load_joint_state_broadcaster = ExecuteProcess(
        cmd=['ros2', 'control', 'load_controller', '--set-state',
    'active', 'joint_state_broadcaster'])
```

9. We repeat the same instructions for the `position` and `velocity` controllers. However, we should choose the command interface to use, since we cannot control the robot both in `position` and `velocity` at the same time. For this reason, we choose to activate only the `position` controller, while setting the `velocity` one to `inactive`:

```
load_position_controller = ExecuteProcess(
        cmd=['ros2', 'control', 'load_controller', '--set-state',
    'active', 'position_control'])
load_velocity_controller = ExecuteProcess(
        cmd=['ros2', 'control', 'load_controller', '--set-state',
    'inactive','velocity_control'])
```

10. Of course, with the previous code block, we are defining nodes to launch. We have to insert them in the launch description object created from the launch file. Here is an example:

```
ld = LaunchDescription()
ld.add_action( load_position_controller )
return ld
```

Just one last step is missing before testing our ros2_control in the Gazebo simulation: the installation of configuration and launchS files, as discussed in the following step.

Step 5 – Installing the necessary files

The last step before launching the simulation with the ros2_control integration is to install the necessary files such as the robot model, the launch files, and the .yaml configuration. These files must be placed into the install folder of the workspace in order to be fully accessible as a shared resource of the ROS 2 system. To do this, edit the CMakeList.txt file of the two_joints_robot package, as shown in the following:

```
install(DIRECTORY launch urdf config DESTINATION share/${PROJECT_NAME})
```

Now, you can compile the workspace using the colcon build command, after moving in your ROS 2 workspace with the terminal:

```
colcon build --symlink-install
```

After successfully compiling the workspace, you can start the simulation and interact with the ros2_control framework using command-line tools, as discussed in the next section.

Interacting with the ros2_control framework using the CLI

It is now time to start the simulation to interact with the controllers. Let's start by installing the dependencies:

```
sudo apt-get install ros-jazzy-xacro ros-jazzy-ros-gz-sim ros-jazzy-gz-
ros2-control-demos
```

Assuming you already initialized and sourced the workspace, run the following commands:

1. To start the simulation, use the following command:

```
ros2 launch two_joints_robot start_simu.launch.py
```

With this command, along with the simulation, we launch the controllers of the robot.

2. For example, if you want to move a joint, you can directly publish the position command using the ros2 topic pub command:

```
ros2 topic pub /position_control/commands std_msgs/msg/
Float64MultiArray "{data: [3, 0]}"
```

3. In this way, you request to move the first joint of the robot to 3 radians, while bringing the second joint to 0 radians. The result of this motion can be seen in *Figure 6.3*.

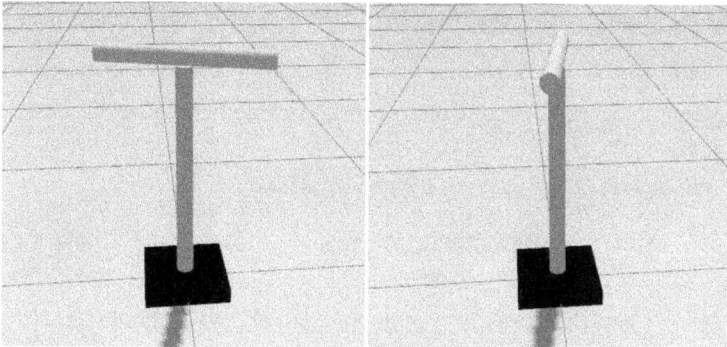

Figure 6.3: Robot configuration – initial (left) and final after accomplishing the requested motion (right)

4. Along with the controllers, the Controller Manager node has started as well. The Controller Manager node provides commands accessible via the command line to retrieve the state of the controllers and change their status. For example, using the list_controllers command, you can retrieve the list of current active controllers:

```
ros2 control list_controllers
joint_state_broadcaster[joint_state_broadcaster/
JointStateBroadcaster] active
position_control [forward_command_controller/
ForwardCommandController] active
velocity_control [forward_command_controller/
ForwardCommandController] inactive
```

As you can see from the command output, the controllers specified in the launch file are listed and, as requested, velocity_control is inactive.

5. You can switch controllers if you want to control the velocity of the actuator instead of the position. Activate velocity_control and deactivate position_control with the following:

```
ros2 control switch_controllers --activate velocity_control
--deactivate position_control
```

6. You can now check the status of the controllers with the ros2 control command. Other useful commands are available in the ros2 control commands list, and you can easily print them, with a small description, by typing the following command (of course, you can use the *Tab* key to see all the available commands):

```
ros2 control
```

Up to now, we just used the controllers already defined in the ros2_control package. Sometimes, this is not enough, and custom controllers must be implemented, as discussed in the next section.

Implementing a new controller

The ros2_control framework supports various controllers beyond the basic forward_command_controller, such as diff_drive_controller for mobile robots. For custom needs, you can create specialized controllers that directly implement control laws and interact with hardware without using ROS 2 communication. These controllers are dynamic libraries loaded by the Controller Manager via pluginlib, allowing modular and on-demand loading. For instance, we'll create a controller that generates sinusoidal motion for the robot's joints, using ROS 2 topics for signal specifications. This setup is useful for testing motor performance and involves specific creation steps.

Step 1 – Creating the ros2 package

The first step is to set up the ros2 package continuing our controller. Let's create it with the following command to include all the dependencies:

```
ros2 pkg create sine_ctrl --dependencies rclcpp std_msgs controller_
interface pluginlib
```

The source code of the controller can be placed in the source directory of the package. Let's create a source called sine_controller.cpp. We are now ready to write the source code of the controller.

Step 2 – Writing the source code of the controller

The source code of a ROS 2 controller of the `ros2_control` package has a fixed structure with a well-defined pipeline. The controller is developed as a plugin that inherits from the `ControllerInterface` class and, as such, must implement several abstract methods defined in its base class. The entry point of the controller is the object constructor. The following are the steps needed to implement a new controller:

1. Create a constructor to initialize member variables, although initialization can also occur in the on_init method.

2. Implement the on_init method to perform initial setup, initialize variables, reserve memory, and declare node parameters.

3. Implement the on_configure method to prepare the controller by reading parameters and completing any necessary setup before starting.

4. Define the required interfaces using `command_interface_configuration` and `state_interface_configuration`.

5. Implement the on_activate method. This checks and sorts interfaces, and assigns initial values. This method is called every time the controller has been activated.

6. Implement the on_deactivate method. This method is called when the controller is deactivated.

7. Implement the update method. This is the main loop of the controller, which runs with the controller frequency to update the input of the hardware interface.

8. Export the controller class. Add the `PLUGINLIB_EXPORT_CLASS` macro at the end of your file after the namespace.

The source code implementing the described steps is shown in the following code blocks:

1. At the start, we include the header files to use the ROS 2 function, access the controller interface, and handle the `Float32MultiArray` data. Finally, we define a variable specifying the number of joints for the robot:

```
#include "rclcpp/rclcpp.hpp"
#include "controller_interface/controller_interface.hpp"
#include "controller_interface/helpers.hpp"
#include "std_msgs/msg/float32_multi_array.hpp"
#define J_SIZE 2
```

2. The controller must be implemented inside a namespace. Inside the namespace, we must define the controller class that inherits from the base class:

    ```
    namespace sine_controller {
      class SineController : public controller_
    interface::ControllerInterface {
    ```

3. Among the different variables, we have to provide the joint state interface with access to the current state of an actuator (position, velocity, and effort). The ros2_control framework implements this with LoanedStateInterface, which provides temporary, controlled access to state data for real-time operations, ensuring safe and synchronized interactions within a controller. It helps manage access to state data without causing conflicts or inconsistencies in the system.

    ```
    rclcpp::Duration dt_;
    template<typename T>
    ```

4. To use LoanedStateInterface, we define a type alias for a 2D vector of std::reference_wrapper<T>. The joint_state_interfaces_ variable uses this type to manage references to hardware_interface::LoanedStateInterface objects:

    ```
    using InterfaceReferences = std::vector<std::vector<std::reference_
    wrapper<T>>>;
    InterfaceReferences<hardware_interface::LoanedStateInterface> joint_
    state_interfaces_;
    ```

5. Finally, a vector of string vectors is declared to define the interface name. We have to consider a new name for each joint and interface, such as joint_name/position, joint_name/velocity, joint_name_2/position, and so on:

    ```
    std::vector<std::vector<std::string>> state_interface_names_;
    ```

6. Other class variables are used to handle the control data generated into the controller:

    ```
    float initial_joint_position_[J_SIZE];
    float desired_joint_positions_[J_SIZE];
    float amplitude_[J_SIZE];
    float frequency_[J_SIZE];
    double t_;
    ```

7. As already stated, the sinusoidal specifications are set via ROS 2 topics, using a vector of four elements: amplitude joint 1, frequency joint 1, amplitude joint 2, and frequency joint 2:

```
rclcpp::Subscription<std_msgs::msg::Float32MultiArray>::SharedPtr
sine_param_sub_;
 public:
SineController() : controller_interface::ControllerInterface(), dt_
(0, 0)  {}
```

8. The callback uses the received data to fill in amplitude and frequency defined as class members. First, we check that the format of the data is correct. We need four numbers to set the parameters correctly:

```
void sine_param_cb(const std_msgs::msg::Float32MultiArray::SharedPtr
msg)  {
      if( msg->data.size() != 4 ) {
          RCLCPP_ERROR(this->get_node()->get_logger(), "Wrong number
of sine parameters");
return;
      }
      amplitude_[0] = msg->data[0];
      amplitude_[1] = msg->data[2];
      frequency_[0] = msg->data[1];
      frequency_[1] = msg->data[3];
  }
```

9. We are now ready to define the state and the command interfaces. These functions are called automatically by the Controller Manager:

```
controller_interface::InterfaceConfiguration state_interface_
configuration() const     {
```

10. Here, we can hardcode the name of the state interfaces. The syntax is `joint_name/interface`. Since in the configuration of the joints we share the position and the velocity as joint states and we have two joints, we will add four elements to the `state_interfaces_config_names` vector:

```
std::vector<std::string> tate_interfaces_config_names;
state_interfaces_config_names.push_back("base_joint/position");
state_interfaces_config_names.push_back("link1_link2/position");
state_interfaces_config_names.push_back("link1_link2/velocity");
```

In this section of code, we hardcoded the names of the joints. A more industrial-ready solution would be loading the names from a YAML param file.

11. To effectively set the interfaces, we have to return the interface list. In this case, we specify them using the `INDIVIDUAL` property; we specify a detailed list of required interfaces, formatted as `<joint_name>/<interface_type>`:

```
return {
controller_interface::interface_configuration_type::INDIVIDUAL,
state_interfaces_config_names};}
```

12. The same thing is done with the command interfaces. Of course, in this case, we just specify the position since we want to control the position of the joints:

```
controller_interface::InterfaceConfiguration command_interface_
configuration() const {
     std::vector<std::string> command_interfaces_config_names;
command_interfaces_config_names.push_back("base_joint/position");
command_interfaces_config_names.push_back("link1_link2/position");
```

13. Also, in this case, we return the list of the `INDIVIDUAL` interfaces participating in the motor control:

```
     return {
controller_interface::interface_configuration_type::INDIVIDUAL,
command_interfaces_config_names};}
```

14. In the `on_configure` function, we can do all the operations needed before starting the controllers. Here, we initialize the subscriber of the sinusoidal parameters:

```
controller_interface::CallbackReturn on_configure(const rclcpp_
lifecycle::State & ){
```

```
_sine_param_sub =   get_node()->create_subscription<std_
msgs::msg::Float32MultiArray>("/sine_param", 10,
std::bind(&SineController::sine_param_cb, this,
std::placeholders::_1));
```

15. As for the _dt variable, it is the step time of the update function. The get_update_rate() function is used to retrieve the rate of the controller from the ROS 2 parameter server. As seen, we specified the parameters in the .yaml file to configure the controllers:

```
dt_ = rclcpp::Duration(std::chrono::duration<double, std::milli>(1e3
/ get_update_rate()));
amplitude_[0] = amplitude_[1] = frequency_[0] =    frequency_[1] =
0.0;
```

16. Then, we resize the command to the interface vectors. The state interface is the only one that needs four elements (two elements, velocity and position, for each joint):

```
command_interfaces_.reserve(J_SIZE); state_interfaces_.reserve(2*J_
SIZE);
        joint_state_interfaces_.resize(J_SIZE);
        state_interface_names_.resize(J_SIZE);
```

17. We also initialize a list of the interfaces, as we will use it later:

```
std::vector<std::string> joint_name = {"base_joint", "link1_link2"};
        for(int i = 0; i < J_SIZE; i++) {
            state_interface_names_[i].resize(2);
            state_interface_names_[i][0] = joint_name[i] + "/position";
            state_interface_names_[i][1] = joint_name[i] + "/velocity";
        }
```

18. This function must return the eventual SUCCESS or FAILURE state of the initialization. Imagine that you need to read some parameters in this function. If the parameters don't exist or are not correctly specified, you could get FAILURE in return; however, it's SUCCESS in our case:

```
return controller_interface::CallbackReturn::SUCCESS;
}
```

19. Another function to implement is the on_activate function. This function is called when the controller passes from an inactive to active state:

```
controller_interface::CallbackReturn on_activate(const rclcpp_
lifecycle::State &) {
        for(int i = 0; i < J_SIZE; i++)
```

20. We call the get_ordered_interfaces function from the controller_interface name-space, which is used to retrieve and organize a list of interfaces, specifically, state_interfaces:

```
        controller_interface::get_ordered_interfaces( state_
interfaces_, state_interface_names_[i], std::string(""),joint_state_
interfaces_[i]);
```

21. Then, we retrieve the joint position to save the initial value of the motor control:

```
        initial_joint_position_[0] = joint_state_interfaces_[0][0].
get().get_value();
        initial_joint_position_[1] = joint_state_interfaces_[1][0].
get().get_value();
        RCLCPP_INFO(get_node()->get_logger(), "Activate successful");
```

22. The local time variable, used to calculate the sinusoidal signal, is reset every time the controller is activated. Finally, we set the SUCCESS state as the return value of the function:

```
        t_ = 0.0;
        return controller_interface::CallbackReturn::SUCCESS;
}
```

We don't do any operation in the on_init and deactivate functions:

```
controller_interface::CallbackReturn on_init() {
        return controller_interface::CallbackReturn::SUCCESS;
}
controller_interface::CallbackReturn on_deactivate(const rclcpp_
lifecycle::State & ) {
        return controller_interface::CallbackReturn::SUCCESS;
}
```

23. Finally, we can write the update function. Here, we must calculate the desired values of the joints that follow the sinusoidal profile:

```
controller_interface::return_type update(const rclcpp::Time & ,
const rclcpp::Duration & ) {
```

24. We increment the local time variable that is used to proceed with the sinusoidal signal. Then, for each joint, we calculate the desired position with the classical sinusoidal formula – x(t) = Amplitude*sin(2*pi*Frequency*time):

```
        t_ += _dt.seconds();
        for (int i = 0; i < J_SIZE; i++) {
                desired_joint_positions_ [i] =
initial_joint_position_[i] + (amplitude _ [i] * std::sin(2 * M_PI *
frequency_[i] * t_));
```

25. Finally, we can set the desired position value using the command interface:

```
command_interfaces_[i].set_value(desired_joint_positions_[i]);
        }
        return controller_interface::return_type::OK;
}};}
```

26. We are now ready to install the plugin. At this stage, we use the PLUGINLIB_EXPORT_CLASS macro. This macro is defined in the pluginlib/class_list_macros.hpp header file. For this reason, we need to include this header file in our source code. To successfully export the controller, we must specify the class containing the controller implementation as the first parameter, such as <controller_name_namespace>::<ControllerName>, and the base class of the controller as the second parameter, which is controller_interface::ControllerInterface:

```
#include "pluginlib/class_list_macros.hpp"
PLUGINLIB_EXPORT_CLASS(sine_controller::SineController, controller_
interface::ControllerInterface)
```

Step 3 – Compiling the controller plugin

Before integrating the controller into our robot, we must properly install the controller into the ROS 2 system:

1. First, we define a .xml file called sine_controller.xml describing the plugin class. This file is called from the CMakeLists.txt file, as described later. Note that the class name is fundamental to specify the right controller:

    ```
    <library path="sine_controller">
    <class name="sine_controller/SineController" type="sine_
    controller::SineController" base_class_type="controller_
    interface::ControllerInterface">
    <description>
                    ..
            </description>
    </class>
    </library>
    ```

2. Now, we can edit the CMakeLists.txt file. Here, we add a library called sine_controller, which was written in the previous step:

    ```
    add_library(sine_controller SHARED src/sine_controller.cpp)
    ```

3. We can export the plugin of the controller by exploiting the .xml file written earlier:

    ```
    pluginlib_export_plugin_description_file(controller_interface sine_
    controller.xml)
    ```

4. Remember to add the dependencies to the sine_controller library and install the generated objects:

    ```
    ament_target_dependencies(sine_controller
    rclcpp controller_interface pluginlib
    )
    install( TARGETS sine_controller
        LIBRARY DESTINATION lib
    )
    ```

Before configuring the controller, use the colcon build command to compile the workspace and source it. We are now ready to add the controller to the robot.

Step 4 – Configuring the controller

Now, the controller is ready to be inserted into the simulated robot model:

1. Let's move into the package where the robot model is implemented (in our case, the two_joints_robot package). Here, let's add the dependency to the CMakeLists.txt file:

    ```
    find_package(sine_ctrl REQUIRED)
    ```

    Next, we need to modify the controller.yaml file adding the sinusoidal controller.

2. First, define the controller type:

    ```
    sine_controller:
    type: sine_controller/SineController
    ```

3. Then, configure the controller:

    ```
    sine_controller:
     ros__parameters:
       update_rate: 100
       joints:
         - base_joint
         - link1_link2
    ```

4. Finally, request the loading of the controller from the start_simu launch file:

    ```
    load_velocity_controller = ExecuteProcess(
    cmd=['ros2', 'control', 'load_controller', '--set-state',
    'inactive', 'sine_controller'])
    ```

Step 5 – Starting the controller

We already saw how to start and activate the controller. Compile and source the workspac and then start the simulation using the following command:

```
ros2 launch two_joints_robot start_simu.launch.py
```

You can check whether the controller is present in the controller list with this command:

```
ros2 control list_controllers
velocity_control [forward_command_controller/ForwardCommandController]
inactive
joint_state_broadcaster[joint_state_broadcaster/JointStateBroadcaster]
active
```

```
position_control [forward_command_controller/ForwardCommandController]
active
sine_controller [sine_controller/SineController] inactive
```

As you can see, position_control is active, while sine_controller and velocity_control are inactive. Let's now shut down the position controller by turning on the sine_controller. The switch_controllers method of the ros2 control command allows you to do both steps at the same time:

```
ros2 control switch_controllers --activate sine_controller  --deactivate
position_control
```

Now, the controller is active, but the robot on Gazebo is not moving. This is because we have to set the sinusoidal parameters. We can do this with the following command:

```
ros2 topic pub /sine_param std_msgs/msg/Float32MultiArray "{data: [1.3,
0.1, 0.02, 0.1]}"
```

Looking at the Gazebo scene, you can see that both the joints are moving, demonstrating the effectiveness of the controller. This motion is depicted in *Figure 6.4*.

Figure 6.4: The motion of the robot actuated using sine_controller

Of course, the motion depicted in *Figure 6.4* is never-ending and cyclical. To stop the robot's motion, sine_controller must be deactivated.

ros2_control on real robots

In this chapter, we explored how to use standard controllers on simulated robots and how to design new ones. However, many modern robots rely on the ros2_control framework. This framework enables the native integration of controllers to operate actuators and control the robot base. A notable example is the **Take It And Go (TIAGo)** platform developed by the Spanish robotics company *PAL Robotics*. TIAGo is a mobile manipulator robot that combines a mobile base with one or two arms and a pan-and-tilt head. It is widely used in industrial and research tasks.

TIAGo leverages the `ros2_control` framework to manage its hardware interfaces for mobility, manipulation, and sensors. The specific controllers used depend on the robot's configuration (e.g., base, arm, or sensors) and its intended use. The following are the common types of controllers typically employed by TIAGo:

- **Base controllers** (`diff_drive_controller`): Manages the differential drive base providing velocity control for the wheels, enabling the robot to move and rotate in 2D space.

- **Arm controllers**:

  - `position_controllers/JointPositionController`: Controls the arm's joints individually or as a group for static positions or trajectories

  - `effort_controllers/JointEffortController`: Provides low-level effort control for specific joints, often used in research or advanced tasks

  - `joint_trajectory_controller`: Enables trajectory-based control of the arm, facilitating smooth motion between waypoints in Cartesian or joint space

- **Gripper controller** (`gripper_controller` or `position_controllers` for gripper joints): Tiago is endowed with a gripper to perform object manipulation. This controller is used to control the opening and closing of the gripper fingers for grasping tasks.

- **Head controllers** (`position_controllers/JointPositionController`): Manages the pan and tilt movements of the robot's head.

- **Torso controllers** (`position_controllers/JointPositionController`): Adjusts the height of the torso to provide flexibility for tasks requiring varying workspace levels.

TIAGo uses additional controllers to manage its sensors, such as the IMU and the force-torque sensor, which can be installed between the robot arm and the gripper. This demonstrates how TIAGo effectively integrates multiple controllers to handle the diverse components of its platform. It combines a mobile base and various actuators that need to be controlled simultaneously, making it an excellent example of managing heterogeneous systems.

Summary

In this chapter, we discussed a fundamental problem of all robotic systems: how to control the motors of the robot. The main solution offered by ROS 2 is provided from the `ros2_control` framework, a collection of packages allowing developers to directly contact the robot hardware. ROS 2 already comes with a series of controllers: both basic controllers that directly forward a desired command to a hardware interface, and something more complex, such as the differential drive controller (`diff_drive_controller`) that transforms the input data to desired commands for the joints.

Another possibility offered by the ros2_control framework is the possibility of implementing a custom controller to perform specific actions. This topic was discussed with the implementation of a controller moving the joints of a simulated robot in Gazebo.

In this chapter, we discussed the possibility of controlling a robot from a low-level point of view; in the next chapter, we will see how to schedule and handle the execution of the high-level action of an autonomous agent using the behavior tree formalism, using the BehaviorTree.cpp library integrated with ROS 2.

References

- [1] https://control.ros.org/humble/index.html
- [2] https://github.com/ros-controls/ros2_control
- [3] https://control.ros.org/humble/doc/ros2_control/hardware_interface/doc/ hardware_interface_types_userdoc.html
- [4] https://control.ros.org/rolling/doc/ros2_control/controller_manager/doc/ userdoc.html
- [5] https://github.com/ros-controls/ros2_control_demos
- [6] https://pal-robotics.com/es/robot/tiago/
- [7] https://pal-robotics.com/

Join our community on Discord

Join our community's Discord space for discussions with the authors and other readers: https:// packt.link/embeddedsystems

7

Implementing ROS 2 Applications Using BehaviorTree.CPP

Implementing robot autonomy is a complex task. Beyond executing individual tasks such as navigation, manipulation, and sensing (e.g., image processing and mapping), coordinating these tasks presents an additional challenge. For example, programming a warehouse robot to retrieve and deliver items requires carefully sequencing actions and making decisions based on the outcome of previous tasks. Traditionally, this is done using **finite state machines (FSMs)**, but a newer approach in robotics is the use of **behavior trees (BTs)**. An interesting scientific paper introducing BTs in the robotics environment can also be found at this link [1].

In this chapter, we will introduce the basic concepts of BTs and explain how to implement them using the BehaviorTree.CPP **library**, a flexible C++ tool that integrates easily with ROS 2 to handle robotic program flow based on the BT framework. We will see how to create both basic and complex structures and how to use ROS 2 functions in the BT nodes. We will also see how to use Groot, a graphical tool to create the BT by dragging, dropping, and connecting the nodes of the tree.

Here's a list of the main topics that will be covered in the chapter:

- Understanding BTs
- Introducing the BehaviorTree.CPP library
- Implementing your first BT

- Integrating ROS 2 and `BehaviorTree.CPP`
- Integrating BTs with ROS 2 actions

Technical requirements

To follow this chapter, you should have one of the following setups on your computer:

- A standard computer running the Ubuntu 24.04 LTS operating system
- A Linux machine with a ROS 2 Jazzy version installed or with a running Docker container configured, as discussed in *Chapter 2*

The reference code for this chapter can be found in the `Chapter07` folder of the following book code repository: `https://github.com/PacktPublishing/Mastering-ROS-2-for-Robotics-Programming/tree/main/Chapter07`.

Understanding BTs

BTs are a modular and hierarchical framework designed to manage complex behaviors. Originally developed in the gaming industry to control the actions of **non-player characters (NPCs)**, BTs have gained popularity in robotics due to their flexibility, reusability, and ability to handle dynamic and unpredictable environments. By providing a structured approach to organizing and executing behaviors, BTs are particularly well-suited for complex robotic systems.

In contrast, **FSMs** offer another common method for managing robotic behaviors. An FSM models a system's behavior using a set of states and transitions, with the robot residing in one specific state at any given time and transitioning to another state when certain conditions or events occur. FSMs are straightforward and intuitive, making them ideal for modeling simple and well-defined tasks. However, as tasks become more complex, FSMs become increasingly challenging to manage due to the rapid growth in the number of states and transitions required to address all possible scenarios. This "state explosion problem" makes FSMs less practical for handling intricate or dynamic systems.

To illustrate the complexity of modeling even simple tasks with FSMs, *Figure 7.1* depicts a state machine for a pick-and-place task using a mobile robot equipped with an arm. In this example, the robot must move toward an object, grasp it, and deliver it to a designated location. While this task may seem straightforward, various conditions must be considered. For instance, what happens if the robot's battery depletes before the task is completed? In the FSM shown, only a failure to reach the destination is addressed. Questions arise, such as where to resume the task later or whether the task is truly sequential.

Could it be restructured to include additional actions, such as searching for the object if it is not found? Addressing these scenarios would require adding new conditions and transitions, complicating the implementation and making the source code harder to write, maintain, and read.

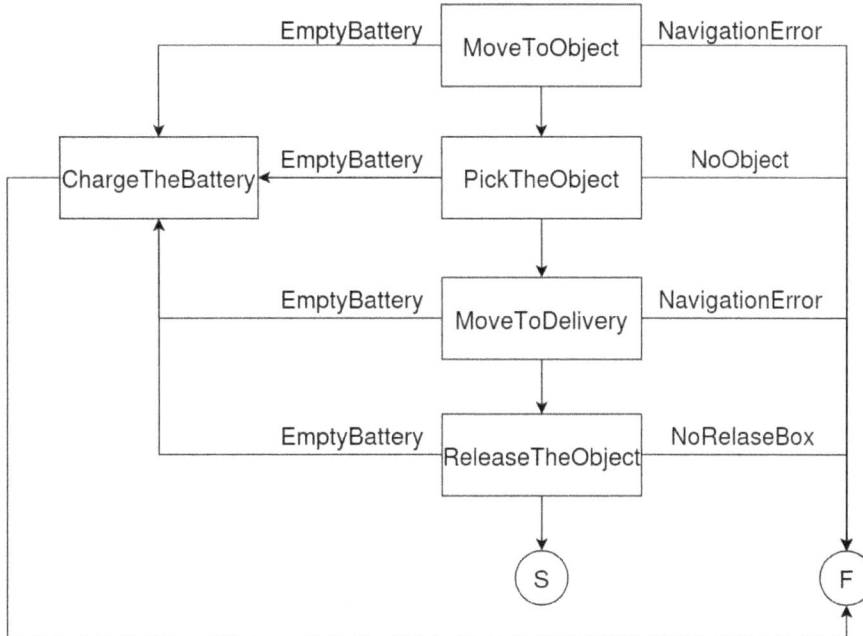

Figure 7.1: Example of an FSM for a pick-and-place task

In the rest of this chapter, we will explore how this task can be formulated more effectively using the BT framework, which simplifies handling such complexities,

unlike traditional FSMs, which can become cumbersome with increasing complexity. Unlike FSMs, which rely on predefined transitions between states, BTs use nodes (selectors, sequences, etc.) to evaluate conditions in real time, enabling a more scalable and adaptable approach to decision-making. BTs provide clearer execution flow and better modularity, making them ideal for complex robotic tasks.

Let's begin by introducing the basic theoretical concepts of the BT framework. In the following subsection, we will cover the BT key concepts and elements.

Basic concepts of BTs

BTs are composed of nodes connected with arcs. Their type of execution model resembles directed trees, where nodes are structured in a hierarchical manner, typically referred to as **parent** and **child nodes**. At the top is the **root node**, which uniquely has no parent, serving as the starting point of the execution. From here, the execution process traverses the tree from top to bottom and left to right. The root node initiates the behavior by sending a signal known as a **tick** to its child nodes, prompting them to execute their designated actions or evaluations. We will introduce the kinds of nodes that can compose the tree. However, let's start with how the nodes are executed into a tree.

The first concept that we must know about BTs is the tick. In BT, a tick is a fundamental concept that represents a single update cycle or execution step for the tree. The tick is responsible for performing the following operations:

- **Execution trigger**: A tick initiates the process of evaluating the BT. Each tick updates the state of the tree and processes the nodes to determine their status and actions.

- **State update**: During a tick, the tree's nodes are assessed based on their current state and the conditions defined within them. The tree transitions through its nodes, updating their states according to the logic specified.

- **Decision-making**: As the tick progresses, it evaluates the nodes to make decisions about which actions to take. This involves checking conditions, executing tasks, and managing transitions between nodes based on their behavior.

- **Iteration**: The tree is generally ticked repeatedly at a regular interval, allowing it to continually assess and respond to changing conditions in the environment or system. This repetition ensures that the tree remains responsive and adaptive.

The tick frequency of a BT is crucial for system responsiveness. A higher frequency ensures quick updates, which is important for recognizing dangerous or unexpected situations, but it also increases computational load. Balancing responsiveness with efficiency requires matching the tick frequency to the system's performance capabilities. Testing different frequencies, typically between 10 to 100 Hz, helps find the optimal balance for smooth tasks without overwhelming the system.

Two additional fundamental elements of a BT are the blackboard and the ports:

- The **blackboard** is a shared memory that various nodes in the tree can read from or write to. It serves as a global storage space where information is stored for use by the BT's nodes during execution. The blackboard is used to maintain state, share information across different parts of the tree, and facilitate communication between nodes. It acts as a central repository for storing variables or state information that different parts of the tree might need to access or modify.

- **Ports** are interfaces through which nodes in the BT communicate with each other or with the blackboard. They serve as connection points for input and output data, allowing the nodes to pass information or receive data from the blackboard:

  - **Input ports**: These are used by a node to receive data necessary for its execution

  - **Output ports**: These are used by a node to send data back to the blackboard or to other nodes

The final core concept in working with BTs is understanding **nodes**. In a BT, nodes serve as the fundamental building blocks, typically implemented in C++ or Python, and can be combined to create complex behaviors. Each node has a specific function, representing actions, conditions, or control flow, which contribute to the robot's decision-making process. Understanding the differences among node types is crucial for building complex trees. The following subsection will discuss the various node types.

BT nodes

The types of nodes can be broadly categorized into different types, each serving a particular role within the tree. A typical set of nodes is reported in the following:

- **Root node**: This is the starting point of the BT. It does not perform any action itself but serves as the entry point from which the tree is executed. It connects the tree to the agent's update loop and initiates the evaluation of child nodes.

- **Control flow nodes**: These dictate the execution order of their child nodes. They are critical for managing the logic and flow of the tree. The most common control flow nodes are as follows:

  - **Sequence**: This executes its child nodes in order. It returns success only if all child nodes succeed. If any child fails, the sequence stops and returns failure. It's used for tasks that require multiple steps to be completed in a specific order.

- **Selector (fallback)**: A selector node evaluates its child nodes sequentially from left to right, succeeding when one succeeds. If all fail, the selector fails. It's used to choose the first successful action or behavior in decision-making.

- **Parallel**: This runs multiple child nodes simultaneously and waits for them to complete. The result depends on the configuration (e.g., succeed if most children succeed or fail). It's used when multiple actions need to occur concurrently, such as moving and scanning for enemies at the same time.

- **Decorator nodes**: These modify the behavior of a single child node. They can change the outcome of the child or impose conditions on its execution:

  - **Inverter**: This flips the result of its child node. If the child succeeds, the inverter returns failure, and vice versa. It's used to create opposite conditions or to negate the result of a condition.

  - **ForceSuccess**: This forces the result of an action to success, even though the action node returns a failure.

  - **Repeat**: This continually re-executes its child node a set number of times or indefinitely.

- **Leaf nodes**: These are the endpoints of a BT and do not have children. They perform specific actions or check conditions. They represent a specific task or operation that the robot can perform. Typically, leaf nodes have a return type that represents the result of the action implemented into the node. If the action succeeded, it returns SUCCESS, or FAILURE otherwise. If the action is still executing, it returns RUNNING.

Depending on the specific library used to implement the BT, the list of available nodes can vary. In this book, we consider the implementation provided by the BehaviorTree.CPP library, introduced in the next section.

Introducing the BehaviorTree.CPP library

BehaviorTree.CPP is a modular C++ library for creating and running BTs in robotics, originally developed by Davide Faconti at Eurecat Centre Tecnològic of Catalonia. It's designed for easy customization, allowing users to define custom nodes. As will be discussed in *Chapter 8*, this library is used in the ROS 2 **navigation stack (Nav2)** for tasks such as *path planning* and *obstacle avoidance*. Its extensibility makes it adaptable to various applications.

The following list outlines key elements of the BehaviorTree.CPP library:

- **Type-safe ports and blackboards**: The library uses **type-safe ports** for data communication between nodes, ensuring that data passed through the tree is consistent and reduces runtime errors. In addition, the library provides a blackboard mechanism, a shared memory space where nodes can store and retrieve information. The blackboard supports type-safe access to stored data, improving the reliability of the tree.

- **Asynchronous execution**: Nodes in BehaviorTree.CPP can run asynchronously, which is essential for applications such as robotics, where non-blocking operations are critical. This feature allows for more responsive and concurrent behaviors, such as parallel processing of sensor data while making decisions.

- **Action and condition nodes**: The library includes predefined nodes such as action and condition nodes, which are the building blocks of BTs. These nodes can be customized or extended based on specific requirements.

- **Control nodes**: BehaviorTree.CPP supports various control nodes such as sequences, selectors, and decorators (such as Inverter and Repeater), allowing complex decision-making processes to be constructed easily.

- **Integration with ROS**: BehaviorTree.CPP is designed to integrate seamlessly with ROS 2, making it a popular choice for robotics applications.

- **XML-based tree definition**: BTs in BehaviorTree.CPP can be defined using XML, which allows for a clear and structured representation of the tree. This feature also makes it easier to modify and maintain BTs without changing the underlying C++ code.

BehaviorTree.CPP also supports **Groot**, a graphical interface that makes designing, debugging, and monitoring BTs more accessible. Groot allows users to define trees using a drag-and-drop interface, bridging the gap between coding and visual management. In this chapter, we will use Groot to design nested BT structures and add new nodes later implemented as ROS 2 programs. BehaviorTree.CPP has evolved from version 3.x to 4.x, with version 4 offering a simplified API, improved performance, enhanced integration with Groot, additional built-in node types, streamlined custom node registration, and better support for asynchronous execution. These updates make version 4 more efficient and user-friendly while maintaining some backward compatibility.

Now that we have introduced the basic concepts of the BT framework and the library used to implement BTs that can be integrated with ROS 2, let's implement our first tree.

Implementing your first BT

The first step to create and execute a BT is to create a ROS 2 package to store all the necessary files to load and run the tree. Even if in this first example we will not use any ROS 2 API, its executor and package structure simplify the developer work.

The first step is to install the library. It can be installed directly from the APT repository:

```
sudo apt-get install ros-jazzy-behaviortree-cpp
```

Now, moving into the src directory of the ROS 2 workspace, let's create the first_bts package:

```
ros2 pkg create first_bts --dependencies rclcpp std_msgs behaviortree_cpp
```

Now that the library is installed and the package storing the tree and the source code has been created, let's see the necessary steps needed to create our first BT.

Step 1 – Defining the tree model

The first step is to define the model of the tree to execute, and we are going to directly write the .xml file representing the tree model. The goal of this tree is to run in sequence two nodes that have an input port called msg containing a message to print in the terminal. The tree structure is very easy: a root node with one child, and a Sequence node connected with two action nodes. Let's create a folder called trees in the package and create a file called sequence.xml. The content is reported in the following:

1. The file starts with the root tag, specifying the version of the library. In this case, version 4 is used:

    ```
    <root BTCPP_format="4">
    ```

2. The BehaviorTree tag allows us to specify the nodes of the tree. It accepts as an argument the name of the tree, representing its name:

    ```
    <BehaviorTree ID="sequence">
    ```

3. The Sequence node is then included and must contain all the nodes that must be executed:

    ```
    <Sequence>
    ```

4. To define a new action node, its name must be defined and can be specified as a tag. In this example, we define two nodes of the same type, HelloNode, called HelloNode1 and HelloNode2. Both nodes have an input port called msg. The value of this port is hardcoded and can be used in the execution of the node:

```
<HelloNode1 msg="Hello from Node1"/>
<HelloNode2 msg="Hello from Node2"/>
</Sequence>
</BehaviorTree>
```

5. Finally, the tree model terminates by closing the root tag:

```
</root>
```

Step 2 – Creating the tree executor

To execute the tree, we must create a C++ source code that configures, loads, and ticks it. To do this, we must use the following steps:

1. **Include the headers**: Along with the typical headers used in ROS 2, we need to add the ones related to the BehaviorTree.CPP library – the behavior_tree.h and bt_factory.h headers:

```
#include "rclcpp/rclcpp.hpp"
#include "std_msgs/msg/string.hpp"
#include "behaviortree_cpp/bt_factory.h"
#include "behaviortree_cpp/behavior_tree.h"
```

2. **Define the BT nodes**: For each node defined in the tree, we must create a C++ class representing the body of the action to execute. In this example, we have two nodes of the same type. For this reason, we must just define one class. Note that this class's name is arbitrary and not associated with the .xml file defining the tree. We will see later the association between the class object and the tree of the node. This node is a StatefulActionNode; this means that the action node can return a state that could be SUCCESS, RUNNING, or FAILURE:

```
class HelloNode : public BT::StatefulActionNode {
  public:
```

The constructor receives two parameters. One is the name of the action, and the other is the node configuration. Using the `conf` variable, we can access the BT blackboard once initialized, as we will see in the next example. In this example, the constructor is empty:

```
HelloNode(const std::string & action_name, const BT::NodeConfig &
conf) : BT::StatefulActionNode(action_name, conf) {}
```

3. **Implement the BT methods:**

   1. To define a BT node, we must implement some methods. The `onStart` method is called the first time a node is ticked. Here, we can put initialization stuff that must be executed every time the tree tick returns on this node:

      ```
      BT::NodeStatus onStart() {
      ```

   2. Using the `getInput` method of the `BehaviorTree.CPP` library, we retrieve the value assigned to the input port:

      ```
      getInput<std::string>("msg", hello_msg _ );
      ```

   3. Finally, to continue the execution of the tree, we return the `RUNNING` status:

      ```
      return BT::NodeStatus::RUNNING;
      ```

   4. The next step is to implement the `onRunning` method. This is the actual body of the action. Here, we just print on the screen the value contained in the port. To proceed with the execution of the other nodes of the sequence, the function returns a `SUCCESS` value:

      ```
      BT::NodeStatus onRunning() {
      std::cout << _hello_msg << std::endl;
            return BT::NodeStatus::SUCCESS;
      void onHalted() { return; }
      ```

   5. The `providedPorts` method is used to configure the ports of a node:

      ```
            static BT::PortsList providedPorts() {
            return {
      ```

In this example, we have only one port, called `msg`, which contains a `string` data type:

```
      BT::InputPort<std::string>("msg")
```

4. **Define the tree executor:**

    1. A ROS 2 node that executes the tree must be defined. As already discussed, to run the tree, we need to tick it. Let's see the definition of the `BTExecutor` class:

       ```
       class BTExecutor : public rclcpp::Node {
       public:
       ```

    2. In the constructor, we call the `init_tree()` function, which initializes the tree starting from the `.xml` file and starts a timer. The callback of the timer ticks the tree. The time runs at 2 Hz. This means that the tree is ticked at 2 Hz:

       ```
       BTExecutor() : Node("bt_executor") {
       init_btree();
       timer_ = this->create_wall_timer( 0.5s,
       std::bind(&BTExecutor::tick_function, this));
       ```

    3. The `init_tree` method initializes the tree. To create the tree, we use the `BehaviorTreeFactory` object, which is used to register node types and create BTs from definitions (e.g., XML files):

       ```
       void init_btree() {
       ```

    4. For each node of the tree definition (the XML), we must specify the representative class (in our case, `HelloNode`) and a name. The name must be the same as the one included in the tree definition. In this way, each node of the `.xml` file has a physical implementation in this C++ source file:

       ```
       factory_.registerNodeType<HelloNode>("HelloNode1");
           factory_.registerNodeType<HelloNode>("HelloNode2");
       ```

    5. To load the tree, we must point to the `.xml` file. To avoid absolute paths, we share the file path from a convenient launch file, using the ROS 2 parameter:

       ```
       this->declare_parameter<std::string>("tree_xml_file", "");
       std::string tree_file;
       this->get_parameter("tree_xml_file", tree_file);
       ```

    6. Finally, after obtaining the `.xml` file path, we can create the tree starting from it:

       ```
       tree _ = factory_.createTreeFromFile(tree_file);
       ```

7. `tick_function` ticks the tree at the frequency specified in the timer creation:

```
void tick_function() {
    tree _.tickOnce();
}
```

5. **Define the main function**: The main function just creates the ROS 2 node and spins it:

```
int main(int argc, char * argv[]) {
rclcpp::init(argc, argv);
auto node = std::make_shared<BTExecutor>();
rclcpp::spin(node);rclcpp::shutdown();
return 0;
}
```

Step 3 — Compiling and installing the necessary files

To compile and install the executable files and the other necessary resources, such as the XML model tree and the launch files, we must edit the `CMakeLists.txt` file of the package:

1. In particular, let's add the executable files with its dependencies:

```
add_executable( sequence_tree src/sequence.cpp )
ament_target_dependencies(sequence_tree rclcpp std_msgs
behaviortree_cpp)
```

2. Then, install the executable:

```
install(TARGETS sequence_tree RUNTIME DESTINATION lib/${PROJECT_
NAME})
```

3. Finally, install the directory containing the XML model of the tree and the launch file we are going to create in the next and last step:

```
install(DIRECTORY launch trees DESTINATION share/${PROJECT_NAME})
```

We are now ready to create the launch file to start the tree executor.

Step 4 – Creating a convenient launch file

Follow these steps to create a convenient launch file:

1. Create a launch directory in the first_bts package folder.

2. In this folder, create a launch file called sequence_tree.launch.py.

3. In the sequence_tree.launch.py file, the first operation is to retrieve the path of the XML model file defining the tree. We must refer to the share directory of the first_bts package, attaching to it the path to the sequence.xml file:

   ```
   tree_path = PathJoinSubstitution ([get_package_share_
   directory('first_bts'), 'trees', 'sequence.xml'])
   ```

4. Finally, we create the node to launch:

   ```
   bt_node = Node(package='first_bts',
   executable='sequence_tree',
   name='sequence_tree',
   output='screen',
   ```

5. As a parameter to the node, we must pass the path assigned to the tree_xml_file parameter:

   ```
   parameters=[{'tree_xml_file': tree_path}],)
   ```

6. We can finally compile the workspace, source it, and launch the ROS 2 node using the following commands, after moving into the ROS 2 workspace using the terminal:

   ```
   colcon build –symlink-install
   source install/setup.bash
   ros2 launch first_bts sequence_tree.launch.py
   ```

   As you can see from the terminal, the output will be like the one shown in the following:

   ```
   [sequence_tree-1] Hello from Node1
   [sequence_tree-1] Hello from Node2
   ```

   This means that the two nodes are executed in sequence as specified by the tree structure. You can see how, by changing the content on the node ports in the XML file, the content of the print message will change.

Now that we have seen the first example of a BT, let's try to implement something more complicated and integrated with ROS 2 API.

Integrating ROS 2 and BTs

In this second example, we will create a more complex BT, using the blackboard to share a ROS 2 node variable, to use ROS 2 publishers, and the input port of a node to get information about which message to publish. We will create two nodes: a CheckNumber node, which generates a random number and tests whether it is lower than a given value. If it is lower, the node returns SUCCESS, or FAILURE otherwise. This is repeated three times, considering a higher value for the number checking. The generated number is then sent to the PublishResult node, which uses the ROS 2 node object to publish the generated value. To create such a testing structure, we will use the fallback control node while, to create the tree, we will use Groot 2, as discussed in the next section. Apart from the implementation discussed in this chapter, some wrappers for ROS 2 nodes shaped as BT nodes can be found at this link [2]. This wrapper can be used to speed up the implementation of the already wrapped nodes; however, the library is sporadically maintained and might not be suitable for specific use cases.

Creating a tree using Groot 2

To use Groot 2, we first must install it in our system. We can do it by downloading Groot from the official web page: https://www.behaviortree.dev/groot/. It is downloaded as a .run file that can be executed to start an installation wizard. Assuming that the downloaded version is 1.6.1, you can install it with the following command:

```
./Groot2-v1.6.1-linux-installer.run
```

Notice that the name of the executable in the preceding command could change based on the downloaded version. However, after starting the installation wizard, you can follow the steps to finally install it and select the installation folder. In the selected installation folder, create a directory called Groot2. Assuming that Groot has been installed in the home folder, you can run it with the following command:

```
~/Groot2/bin/groot2
```

At this point, the main window of Groot is opened. From here, you can select different options – from opening already developed trees (for example, you can try to visualize the sequence.xml model tree file) to creating a new tree from scratch. Let's create a new tree model. Click on **Create Empty File** to open a new blank page where we can drag and drop new nodes. The Groot 2 interface is intuitive and allows you to save the generated tree model with a desired filename and create projects with multiple trees inside.

Now, we can start to add the nodes that will be implemented in the C++ source code after the creation of the tree model. To do this, we must use the **Models** panel placed at the bottom left of the interface. In this panel, you can select an already present model (such as **Fallback** or **Sequence** or similar) or decide to add a new one. To add a new model, click on the + icon to open the **Node Model Editor** panel, as shown in *Figure 7.2*.

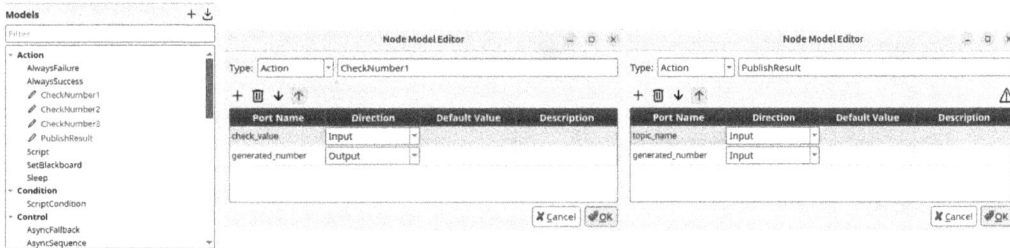

Figure 7.2: The Models and Node Model Editor panels in Groot 2

In the **Node Model Editor** panel, we can select the name of the action to be added and the eventual ports. We need to select two ports for the check_value and generated_number fields: an **Input** port, which represents the value to check, and an **Output** port, which shows the eventually generated number. We can also choose to add a default value for the ports. After completing the creation of the node, by clicking on the **OK** button, it will appear with a different color in the available node models. As you can see from the final shape of the tree (*Figure 7.2*), you should repeat the creation of this node three times (CheckNumber1, CheckNumber2, and CheckNumber3) to create different nodes working on the same input-output data types. Finally, you can create the last node type of the tree, the PublishResult node, consisting of two input ports: the topic_name port on which the generated number is to be published, and the generated_number port containing the value of the generated number.

Now, you have all the tools to create the tree. The final structure is shown in *Figure 7.3*.

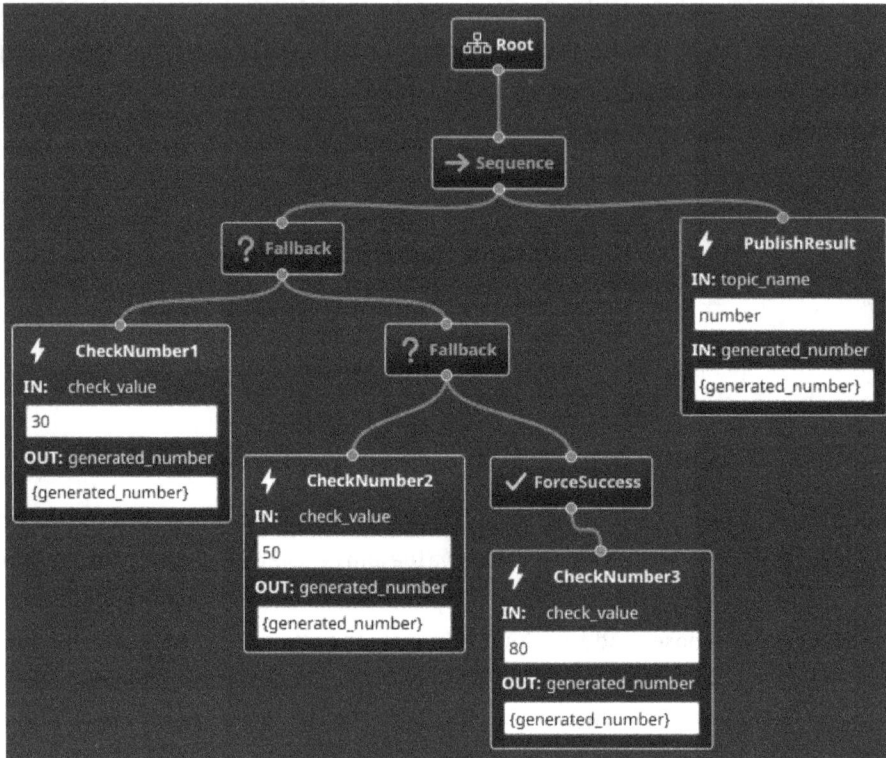

Figure 7.3: The number_checker.xml tree edited using Groot 2

As you can see, creating complex tree structures is quite easy using Groot. Let's analyze the defined tree:

- After the root node, a Sequence node regulates the sequential execution of the two node blocks: the one checking the value of the generated number and the one that publishes the final result.

- In the left part of the tree branch, we need to test whether the generated number is lower than the one provided in the input port. The concept is that, in sequence, it will be more difficult to pass the first two checks than the last one.

- In any case, we want to continue the execution of the tree, executing the right branch even if the third CheckNumber3 fails. For this reason, we use a ForceSuccess decorator node. In this way, if CheckNumber3 returns failure, the fallback node receives success.

- How can we get the generated number to publish it on the ROS 2 topic? We can use the BT blackboard. To do this, the nodes generating the number save the output on a BT port using the label {generated_number}. This value is filled in the C++ source code. The PublishResult node reads this data from the same label. This is how we force data sharing among the nodes of the tree.

You can now save the generated tree as an .xml file. Let's put it into the trees subfolder of the first_bts package, calling it number_checker.xml. Let's discuss now how to implement the executor of this tree.

Using the BT blackboard

In this section, we will analyze the implementation of the BT nodes. Since the structure is like the one already discussed in the previous example, here, we will just explore the main differences between the two implementations. However, the complete source code can be found in the book's code repository: https://github.com/PacktPublishing/Mastering-ROS-2/tree/main/Chapter07/first_bts.

First, let's consider the BTExecutor class. We must declare the BT blackboard as a private member of this class:

```
BT::Blackboard::Ptr _blackboard;
```

As you can see, it is represented by a pointer. In the constructor's body, we must initialize it:

```
_blackboard = BT::Blackboard::create();
```

At this point, in the initialization function, we must assign the ROS 2 node variable to a key of the blackboard. In this case, we set the key as node. This key must be used to retrieve the saved variable. To retrieve the node object, we use the shared_from_this function, which is used to obtain a std::shared_ptr that shares ownership of the current object (this):

```
void init_btree() {
_blackboard->set<rclcpp::Node::SharedPtr>("node", this->shared_from_
this());
```

An additional difference with respect to the first example is that, here, we pass the _blackboard variable in the node creation. In this way, we link the tree with the model with the defined blackboard:

```
_tree = _factory.createTreeFromFile(tree_file, _blackboard);
```

In this example, the init_btree function is called directly in the tick function. This is because to obtain the ROS 2 node object (that we save into the blackboard), we must wait for the constructor to terminate its execution. For this reason, we use a flag variable (first) to understand whether this is the first execution of the function (and so, initialize the tree before ticking it):

```cpp
        void tick_function() {
if( first) {
init_btree();
first = false;
```

We must implement two classes, the NumberChecker and PublishResult classes. In providedPorts of the NumberChecker class, we set an input port (check_value) and an output port (generated_number) with the relative data types:

```cpp
static BT::PortsList providedPorts() {
return {
BT::InputPort<int>("check_value"),
BT::OutputPort<int>("generated_number")};
```

The value saved in the input port representing the threshold value is retrieved with the getInput function. Since the code cannot work correctly without a proper parameter, we can check whether it has been correctly set from the specification of the tree. This prevents the situation in which a wrong type is inserted (e.g., a string or a float):

```cpp
if(!getInput<int>("check_value", num_threshold_)) {
        throw BT::RuntimeError("missing required input [goal]");
}
```

In the onRunning method, we generate a random number between 1 and 100 (random_number). If this number is lower than the control value, we assign a value to the output port and return a SUCCESS state, or FAILURE otherwise. In this latter case, a -1 value is assigned to the output port:

```cpp
if( random_number < _num_threshold) {
setOutput("generated_number", random_number);
return BT::NodeStatus::SUCCESS;
}
else {
setOutput("generated_number", -1);
return BT::NodeStatus::FAILURE;
```

Finally, `PublishResult` must be implemented. As a class member, we declare the object to store the ROS 2 node variable, along with the publisher:

```
rclcpp::Node::SharedPtr _node;
rclcpp::Publisher<std_msgs::msg::Int32>::SharedPtr _pub;
```

In its constructor, we use the `conf` input variable to access the BT blackboard and save the shared content of the `node` key stored in the blackboard:

```
PublishResult(const std::string & action_name, const BT::NodeConfig &
conf) :
BT::StatefulActionNode(action_name, conf) {
node _ = conf.blackboard->get<rclcpp::Node::SharedPtr>("node");}
```

In the `onStart` method, we retrieve the input port value, defining the name of the topic on which to publish the generated value:

```
BT::NodeStatus onStart() {
std::string topic_name;
getInput<std::string>("topic_name", topic_name);
```

Then, the publisher is initialized:

```
pub_ = node_->create_publisher<std_msgs::msg::Int32>(topic_name, 1);
```

When executing the `onRunning` method, the `generated_number` port, which is an input for the `PublishResult` node, contains the value to publish. So, we can retrieve its value using the `getInput` function and publish it:

```
getInput<int>("generated_number", value );
std_msgs::msg::Int32 v;
v.data = value;
pub_->publish( v );
```

As described in the previous example, the launch file and the `CMakeLists.txt` file must be edited to launch and compile the executor nodes. An example of the execution of the implemented tree is shown in the following:

```
[number_checker-1] Generated number: 48 - Threshold: 30 - Failure!
[number_checker-1] Generated number: 58 - Threshold: 50 - Failure!
[number_checker-1] Generated number: 47 - Threshold: 80 - Success!
```

As you can see from the previous output published on the Linux terminal, the tree nodes are executed in a sort of sequence, since the first two CheckNumber nodes fail in their execution.

We have seen with this example how to create a more complex BT using Groot 2 and ROS 2 API functions. However, in both examples seen so far, the actions programmed in the tree are trivial: just print or perform conditional statements. In the next section of this chapter, we will discuss how to implement BTs to execute more complex tasks.

Integrating BTs with ROS 2 actions

The execution of a BT should never be blocked. If certain nodes within the tree perform checks during their tick to modify the robot's actions and react to unexpected situations, the tree's flow must remain uninterrupted. So, how can we allow complex task execution, such as commanding the robot to reach a given location or perform a manipulation task? The general way to do this is to implement the core functions with long-term executions as a ROS 2 server. The client is implemented in the tree nodes. Based on the result of the ROS 2 action, the node in which the client is implemented can return RUNNING (the action is not completed), SUCCESS (the action returns a successful state), or FAILURE (the action returns a failure state). Let's discuss this case in the following example.

The steps to implement a similar tree are the same as already seen in the previous examples. The source code discussed here is included in the ROS 2 package called bt_action_node. However, to create this package from scratch, you can use the following command:

```
ros2 pkg create rclcpp rclcpp_action rosidl_default_generators
behaviortree_cpp
```

In this package, we must implement a dummy server since we must execute the client of the ROS 2 action. In this example, the server has the goal to receive two coordinates (x and y), and a timeout to reach these coordinates from the 0, 0 starting point. The server generates a random velocity used to integrate the position. If, by using the generated velocity, the fake robot reaches the coordinates within the time, it returns success, or failure otherwise. We will not report the code of the server here, since it is quite trivial. However, you can check the full source code in the reach_location_server.cpp file.

The action is implemented in the header contained in the bt_action_server package.

Before contacting the server, the client should wait until the server is available. We can exploit the Sequence node to map this check in the BT formulation. The overall tree is depicted in *Figure 7.4*. We can use the Sequence decorator node to first check whether the server is running or not (the WaitForServer node) and then call the action (in the CallAction node).

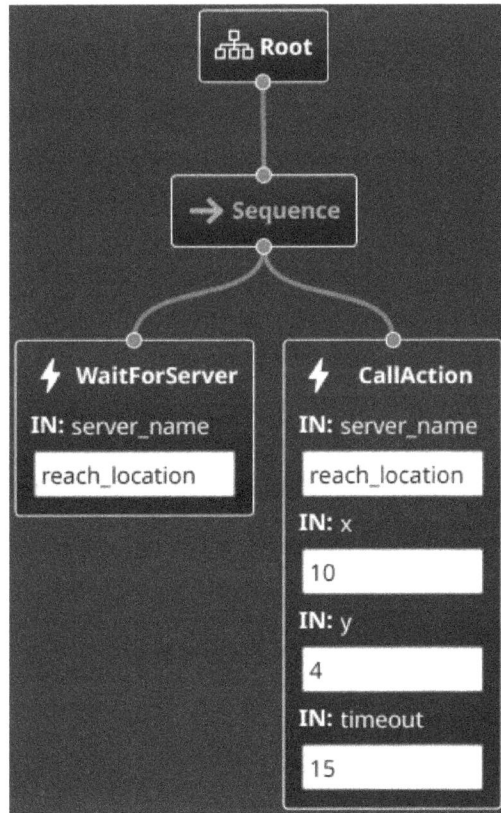

Figure 7.4: BT to implement the ROS 2 action client

Let's discuss the implementation of the two BT nodes. At the start, the needed header files must be included. Along with the BT header files, the .hpp files to implement the ROS 2 client and the message to correctly invoke the server must also be included. In addition, we need to define an alias called Action to simplify the usage of the ReachLocation data type:

```
#include <bt_action_server/action/reach_location.hpp>
#include <rclcpp_action/rclcpp_action.hpp>
using Action = bt_action_server::action::ReachLocation;
```

To represent the outcome of the action, we define an enumeration type that includes possible results – success, failure, and cancellation:

```
enum class ActionResult : uint8_t {
        ActionFailed,
        ActionCancelled,
        ActionSucceded
};
```

To implement the first behavior node, the WaitForServer behavior, we must define a proper class. Among the different members of this class, let's declare a ROS 2 client object:

```
rclcpp_action::Client<Action>::SharedPtr _client;
```

In the constructor of the WaitForServer class, we must initialize a ROS 2 node object. This can be done by retrieving its value from the BT blackboard:

```
WaitForServer(const std::string & action_name, const BT::NodeConfig &
conf) : BT::StatefulActionNode(action_name, conf) {
node _ = conf.blackboard->get<rclcpp::Node::SharedPtr>("node");
```

In the onStart method, we instantiate the server. The name of the server is taken as input in the node port. As you can see from *Figure 7.4*, the name is reach_location:

```
BT::NodeStatus onStart() {
std::string server_name;
getInput<std::string>("server_name", server_name );
_client = rclcpp_action::create_client<Action>(_node, server_name);
```

Finally, in the onRunning method, we return FAILURE if the action_server_is_ready() function is false, or SUCCESS otherwise:

```
BT::NodeStatus onRunning() {
if (!_client->action_server_is_ready())
return BT::NodeStatus::FAILURE;
return BT::NodeStatus::SUCCESS;
```

The second BT node to implement executes the action call, and it is called `CallAction`. In the representative class of the behavior, we must create a new ROS object node to handle everything related to the server. So, let's define the following class attributes – a new ROS 2 node and the `client` object:

```
rclcpp::Node::SharedPtr _node2;
rclcpp_action::Client<Action>::SharedPtr _client;
```

In the constructor the node variable is initialized.

```
node2_ = rclcpp::Node::make_shared("action_client_node");
```

At this point, in the onRunning method, we must call the server, if it has not been called yet. For this reason, we consider a Boolean flag, `_server_called`, which switches to true after the server is called:

```
if ( !_server_called ) {
    _server_called = true;
```

The goal of the action is filled with the data received from the input ports. The server is called after the goal object is filled:

```
auto goal = Action::Goal();
goal.x = _x;
goal.y = _y;
goal.timeout = _timeout;
auto send_goal_future = _client->async_send_goal(goal);
```

We can now spin the ROS 2 node initialized in the constructor to check whether the goal has been correctly sent:

```
if(rclcpp::spin_until_future_complete(node2_, send_goal_future)!=
rclcpp::FutureReturnCode::SUCCESS)
return BT::NodeStatus::FAILURE;
```

We can now spin the ROS 2 node initialized in the constructor to later check the status of the action.

At each tick of the tree, we must wait for the server to complete its execution using the goal_handle variable. If this variable has a null value, the server has not accepted the goal. For this reason, we return a FAILURE state:

```
auto goal_handle = send_goal_future.get();
if (!goal_handle)
                return BT::NodeStatus::FAILURE;
```

At the same time, we define a callback function that is invoked when the server completes its execution:

```
_client->async_get_result(goal_handle, std::bind(&CallAction::result_
callback, this, std::placeholders::_1));
```

As you may know, to allow the callback of a node to receive new data, the spin function must be called. Of course, if we call spin now, we lock the execution of the BT node. For this reason, we will use the spin_some function:

```
rclcpp::spin_some( _node2 );
```

In the result_callback function, we check the server's termination status and update the _action_result variable to indicate whether the server execution was successful or failed. The variable is set to 2 if the action succeeded, and to 1 or 0 if it terminates in an aborted or failed state. The same variable is used in the running function of the CallAction node to return the SUCCESS, FAILURE, or RUNNING status. Since the action_result_ variable has been initialized with -1, until it doesn't change its value, the BT node running function returns the RUNNING status since it is still waiting for the execution of the action:

```
if(action_result ==  ActionResult::ActionSucceded )
return BT::NodeStatus::SUCCESS;
else if( action_result_ == ActionResult::ActionFailed)      return
BT::NodeStatus::FAILURE;
else if( action_result_ == ActionResult::ActionCancelled)
return BT::NodeStatus::FAILURE;
```

To run the tree correctly, you must clone the bt_action_server package from the GitHub repository of the book: https://github.com/PacktPublishing/Mastering-ROS-2. Then, after compiling and sourcing the workspace, you must run the following commands:

```
ros2 run bt_action_server reach_location_server
ros2 launch bt_action_server bt_action.launch.py
```

As a result, on the terminal, you can see the flow of the nodes. First, the success of the WaitForServer node, then the wait for the action accomplishment, and finally, the success when the server terminates correctly:

```
[bt_action-1] [Node WaitForServer]: Success
[bt_action-1] [Node CallAction]: Waiting server execution
[bt_action-1] [Node CallAction]: Waiting server execution
[bt_action-1] [Node CallAction]: Success
```

You can try to change the value associated with the input ports of the node to check how the result of the action changes. This additionally shows how flexible the BT framework is. If the behavior nodes are properly designed, you can use the node ports to adapt the execution of the program to the robot environment, without modifying the source code directly.

Summary

In this chapter, we introduced the BT framework, a modern method for implementing robot autonomy. A BT offers a straightforward and efficient way to define and manage the actions and control nodes that guide a robot's behavior. We covered the fundamental elements of the BT framework and the key concepts behind it.

We also introduced BehaviorTree.CPP, a popular C++ library that seamlessly integrates with ROS 2. BehaviorTree.CPP includes support for Groot, a graphical interface for creating and visualizing BTs. To illustrate the framework, we presented three examples of varying complexity, from defining the tree using XML models to integrating ROS 2 actions for executing long-term tasks.

Additionally, we highlighted how BehaviorTree.CPP is utilized by the ROS 2 navigation stack (nav2), which will be explored further in the next chapter. The upcoming chapter will delve into how to enable robots with navigation capabilities.

References

- [1] https://arxiv.org/abs/2005.05842
- [2] https://github.com/BehaviorTree/BehaviorTree.ROS2

8

ROS 2 Navigation Stack: Nav2

This chapter will discuss one of the popular robotics capabilities in ROS 2: autonomous navigation and mapping. This capability is one of the main reasons ROS has become popular. Many robots use this capability to navigate in different environments. Autonomous/self-driving robots can map the environment and navigate autonomously from point A to point B. The Nav2 project is a popular ROS 2-based project that provides ready-made packages and nodes for any mobile robot to implement autonomous navigation quickly without re-implementing the wheel.

We will start the chapter with an introduction to Nav2, a brief overview of its architecture, and the installation of Nav2 in ROS 2 Jazzy. After that, we will see how to set up and configure mapping and navigation using SLAM Toolbox and Nav2 for our robot. After configuring the robot, we will see how to create a behavior-tree-based application in Nav2. Finally, we will look at a case study using Nav2 to deploy a mobile robot in hospitals.

After completing this chapter, you will have practical experience configuring and tuning the Nav2 for our robot.

In this chapter, we're going to cover the following main topics:

- Getting started with Nav2
- Configuring Nav2 and Slam Toolbox for your robot
- Mapping and navigation using Nav2 and Slam Toolbox
- Case study: Using Nav2 for healthcare robots
- Developing a BT (behavior tree) application using Nav2

Technical requirements

To follow this chapter, you should install Ubuntu 24.04 LTS with the ROS 2 Jazzy desktop. This can be done in a VM, Docker, WSL 2, or on a physical machine. The reference materials and code for this chapter can be found in the `Chapter08` folder of the following GitHub repository: `https://github.com/PacktPublishing/Mastering-ROS-2-for-Robotics-Programming/tree/main/Chapter08`.

Getting started with Nav2

In this section, we will go through the basic concepts of the Nav2 project, which include the definition, history, architecture, and features of the project. Let's first look at the Nav2 project in detail.

What is the Nav2 project?

The **Nav2** project [1] offers autonomous navigation capabilities for mobile robots based on ROS 2. This project aims to enable navigation for nearly any mobile robot in complex environments. Developers using ROS 2 can readily integrate Nav2 capabilities into their robotics applications.

The Nav2 project offers modules for planning, control, localization, perception, visualization, and more to develop a stable and reliable autonomous system. It includes a collection of pre-built ROS 2 nodes and plugins that developers can use to configure the modules above. Nav2 can accept a list of waypoints as input and dynamically plan the path to these points. It can also avoid obstacles and ultimately compute the velocities of the robot's motors.

Nav2 is integrated with the **behavior tree** (**BT**) library [2], which assists developers in creating intelligent navigation motions by facilitating communication with the individual modules in Nav2.

The Nav2 project is the successor of the ROS Navigation stack [3] in ROS 1. The ROS Navigation stack was intended for research applications, but Nav2 can be used for both research and commercial products. More than 100 companies worldwide use Nav2, including NVIDIA, Toyota, and Bosch, which leverage it for autonomous navigation in their robotics platforms.

N A V 2

Figure 8.1: Nav2 Logo

Figure 8.1 shows the logo of the Nav2 project. The following section outlines the major milestones in the Nav2 project.

Milestones of the Nav2 project

The Nav2 project is developed and maintained by **Open Navigation LLP** [*4*], under the leadership of Steve Macenski [*5*]. He has played a key role in the development of several important ROS 2 projects, including Nav2 and SLAM Toolbox, and has contributed to components like **rclcpp**.

As we have already discussed, Nav2 began as a successor to the ROS Navigation stack, which was available in ROS 1. Here are the key milestones of this project [*31*]:

- **2018**: The Nav2 project was initiated to develop a modular, scalable, and flexible navigation stack for ROS 2, starting with early distributions like Bouncy and Crystal.
- **2019**: Basic features were implemented as Nav2 matured alongside ROS 2 Dashing. It gained traction among ROS 2 developers.
- **2020**: Lifecycle management and behavior trees were added to support ROS 2 Eloquent and Foxy.
- **2021**: New planners and costmap improvements were compatible with ROS 2 Foxy and Galactic.
- **2022**: Stability, obstacle handling, and multi-robot features improved with ROS 2 Galactic and Humble.
- **2023**: Simulation, SLAM, and hybrid planning were enhanced in sync with ROS 2 Humble and Iron.
- **2024**: Tools and plugin support expanded to align with ROS 2 Iron and Jazzy releases.
- **2025**: AI integration and cloud-based fleet coordination are advancing with support for ROS 2 Jazzy and the upcoming K-Turtle.

We have gone through the Nav2 milestones. Now let's explore various features of Nav2.

Features of Nav2

Here are the important features of the Nav2 project:

- **Modular and flexible design**: Nav2 is built to be modular, enabling developers to customize and replace each component as necessary. It employs behavior trees, which facilitate flexible navigation tasks.

- **Navigation core components**: Nav2 consists of the following core components for navigation:

  - *Localization*: It integrates with **AMCL (Adaptive Monte Carlo Localization)** to estimate the robot pose with respect to the map.

  - *Path planning*: It has global and local planners. The global planner plans a path from the current position to the goal position, whereas the local planner is a segment of the global planner where the robot tries to move. The common global planners are **A*** and **Dijkstra's algorithm**, and the common local planners are **DWB (Dynamic-Window Approach)** or **TEB (Timed Elastic Band)**.

  - *BT framework*: The BT framework is integrated into Nav2, assisting in orchestrating task execution, including navigating to a goal, recovering from failure, and executing custom motion behaviors.

  - *Controller server*: This will execute the path computed by the local planner and move the robot.

  - *Recoveries*: The recovery behaviors are a set of predefined motions or routines executing when the Nav2 fails to move the robot. Simple motion can be spinning, and routines can clear obstacles on the costmap.

  - *Lifecycle management*: The Nav2 nodes are built on the lifecycle nodes of ROS 2, which can enhance startup and shutdown processes.

- **Dynamic obstacle avoidance**: Nav2 can dynamically avoid obstacles during navigation. It has plugins for the obstacle layer and a costmap for dynamic environments.

- **Multi-robot support**: Nav2 supports multi-robot navigation, allowing multiple robots to operate simultaneously in the same environment.

- **SLAM integration**: The Slam Toolbox is a separate project that performs mapping and localization. It is not a part of Nav2, but it works well with Nav2 for generating maps in real time.

- **Customizable**: Nav2 can be customized to adapt to different types of robots and environments. The BT customization allows developers to extend the application logic as well.

- **Multi-map and map-less navigation**: Nav2 supports switching the map dynamically for multi-floor and multi-environment scenarios.

- **Integration with sensors**: Nav2 supports a variety of sensors like LIDAR, depth cameras, and ultrasonic sensors for mapping, localization, and obstacle detection.

- **3D Visualization and control**: Nav2 provides a set of Rviz panels to visualize and modify various navigation parameters for the robot during its navigation.

- **Advanced Nav2 capabilities**: Nav2 offers advanced features in navigation, including auto-docking, charging, collision monitoring, assisted teleoperation, and waypoint execution. These features are continuously evolving.

- **Simulation support**: Nav2 can be easily used with robotics simulators like Gazebo Classic or Gazebo Sim. We can test the Nav2-based application using a simulator before testing it on the robot hardware.

- **Extensive documentation and tutorials**: Nav2 comes with extensive documentation and tutorials, allowing developers to get started quickly with Nav2.

Now that we have seen the important features of Nav2, we can discuss the architecture of Nav2 and how it works.

Nav2 architecture

Figure 8.2 illustrates the Nav2 architecture. Let's explore this architecture and, after understanding the important nodes in Nav2, we can see how it functions in a robot.

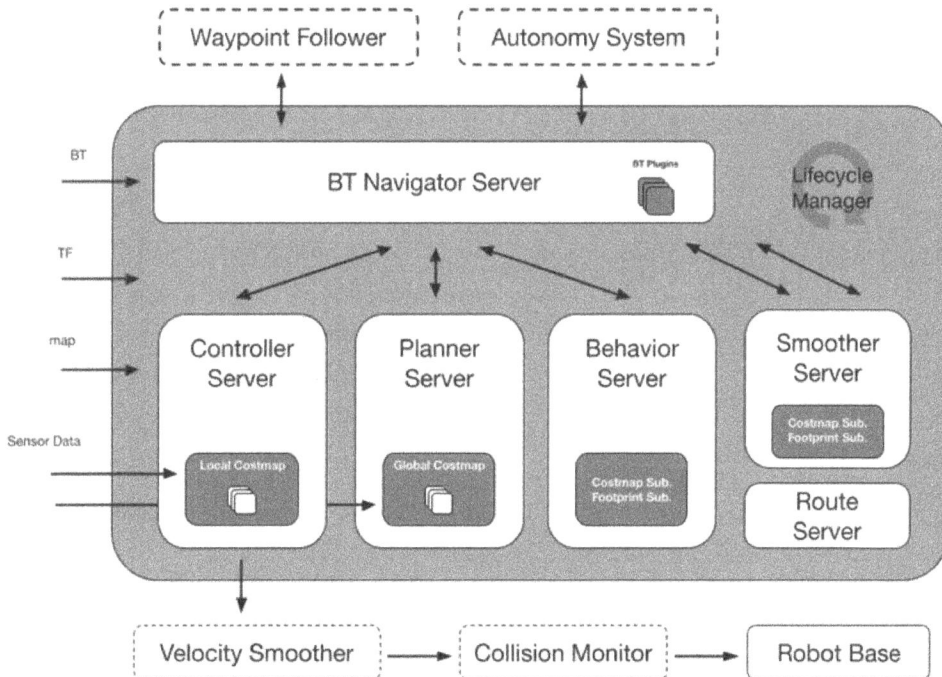

Figure 8.2: Nav2 architecture (source: https://docs.nav2.org/index.html)

Nav2 is a collection of nodes and plugins designed to perform navigation tasks. All nodes are based on ROS 2 lifecycle nodes, and each node functions as an action server. The Nav2 Lifecycle Manager oversees the state of each server within Nav2. It can start the nodes in a specified order and establish a bond connection with the server to ensure they remain operational. If any node fails or crashes, it can transition other nodes to a down state to prevent critical failure. Nav2 utilizes a wrapper around the ROS 2 Lifecycle Manager, simplifying the management process.

Each node in Nav2 is highly configurable with ROS 2 parameters. The following section will explore how to configure these parameters and their references.

Here are the different components in the Nav2 architecture.

Lifecycle Manager

The Nav2 nodes are implemented as ROS 2 lifecycle nodes. The **Lifecycle Manager** module includes methods for transitioning the states of the Nav2 nodes in a deterministic manner. Users can configure the Lifecycle Manager with a set of Nav2 nodes, enabling it to activate or change the state of each node individually. It can also deactivate all Nav2 nodes if any are unresponsive or have crashed. Additionally, it establishes a bond connection with each node, ensuring that all nodes remain operational and running.

The complete list of parameters for configuring the Lifecycle Manager is available in [6].

BT Navigator Server

The **BT Navigator Server** serves as the core of Nav2. This node orchestrates various Nav2 nodes using a behavior tree. The developer may load a specific behavior tree file into this node or choose the default option. The BT XML file specifies how to process the incoming goal pose. This node operates as an action server, capable of receiving navigation goals from clients such as waypoint followers or external autonomy systems that can interact with this server to set goals. It facilitates communication and coordination between the planner, controller, and smoother servers to enable seamless robot navigation. Furthermore, this node can load a custom BT plugin to implement tailored navigation behavior.

The complete parameters of BT Navigator are documented in [7], and the complete behavior tree plugins are listed in [8].

Planner Server

This action server node is responsible for global path planning. It can compute an optimal path from the robot's current position to the goal while avoiding obstacles on the map. The **Planner Server** uses a global costmap to calculate an obstacle-free path. The costmap is a grid-based map wherein each cell contains a numerical value ("cost") that indicates how difficult and risky it is for the robot to navigate through that location. There are two types of costmap: the global costmap and the local costmap.

The global costmap covers the entire known area of the robot's map. This costmap is used for finding an optimal route to a destination using a static map. The local costmap focuses on the area immediately around the robot, which is used for real-time obstacle avoidance and short-term decision-making. The robot map created by SLAM is the input to the global and local costmaps. These two costmaps add separate layers on the top of the actual map. There are different layers we can add to the global costmap, like the obstacle layer and inflation layer, which can make an additional layer in the actual map to avoid obstacles in advance. The Planner Server can load different global planner plugins based on the configuration.

The complete Planner Server parameters are listed in [9].

Controller Server

The **Controller Server** is mainly responsible for the local planning of robot navigation. The local planner tries to follow a segment of the global plan created by the Planner Server. The Controller Server has a representation of the local costmap. The local planner can compute a feasible path in the local costmap and generate velocity control commands for the robot to follow.

The Controller Server can also load plugins that function as local planners. There are progress checker and goal checker plugins within the Controller Server that monitor navigation progress and verify whether the specified goal has been reached.

The complete list of parameters that we can use to configure the Controller Server is available in [10].

Behavior Server

The **Behavior Server** can host different behavior plugins that handle behaviors like recoveries after a navigation failure. Whenever navigation fails due to sensor failure or any other factor, the Behavior Server can trigger the set of behavior plugins to invoke it. Some available behaviors are spinning, waiting, assisted teleop, etc.

Behaviors such as spinning can assist if the robot is trapped in a corner and unable to find a way out. After performing a spin, it might discover a route to escape from the corner. In the event of total failure, we can initiate a recovery procedure to alert an operator via email, SMS, Slack, etc.

The complete Behavior Server parameter configuration is given at this link [11].

Smoother Server

As the name suggests, this server assists in refining and smoothing the generated planner path to enhance its quality and eliminate abrupt rotations. While smoothing the path, it also considers obstacles and high-cost areas, as it can access the robot's costmap and footprint. The Smoother Server typically receives a path from the Planner Server and returns an improved version.

The complete parameters for the Smoother Server can be found in [12].

Route Server

Traditional path planning may not be efficient in large and complicated environments. The Route Server is a node that can complement the Nav2 Planner Server. Instead of working on an occupancy grid, it creates a pre-generated navigation graph to plan routes. This can significantly reduce the planning computation load and make navigation more efficient, especially in complex environments or large spaces.

Velocity Smoother and Collision Monitor

The velocity command sent from the Nav2 controller server can be fed to a velocity smoother node to smooth velocity, acceleration, and other parameters. This can reduce wear and tear on the robot motors and help avoid jerky movements. The local planner can generate jerky movements that can be fixed by Velocity Smoother nodes.

The Velocity Smoother node can also be configured using parameters, and the reference is at the following link [13].

The Collision Monitor is another node that adds a layer of safety to robot navigation. The planners can even detect dynamic collisions. However, in some instances, particularly with fast-moving robots, entities may move at high speed. If the planner fails to identify the obstacle, the Collision Monitor can sense it using incoming sensor data, bypassing the costmap and trajectory planners. This node can avert a potential collision.

The complete configuration of the Collision Monitor can be found at the following link [14].

Waypoint Follower

The primary input required from the user for Nav2 is the list of waypoints it needs to navigate. The Waypoint Follower node in Nav2 can execute the waypoints using the NavigateToPose [15] action provided by the *BT Navigation Server*. It will take a set of ordered waypoints from the user and execute them sequentially. Additionally, it can perform custom behaviors such as waiting at a waypoint, taking a picture, or executing tasks via its waypoint task executor plugin.

The complete list of parameters for configuring the Waypoint Follower node is available in [16].

We have discussed the key components of the Nav2 architecture; now, let us explore how it functions.

How does Nav2 work?

This section describes how Nav2 works if the robot has to move from point A to point B in a known environment. *Figure 8.3* illustrates the robot configuration necessary for integration with Nav2.

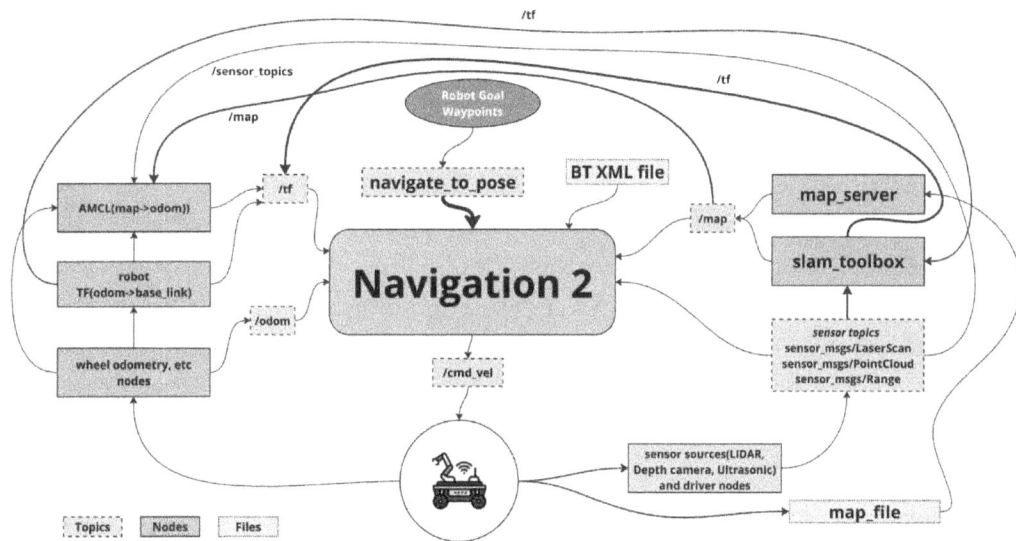

Figure 8.3: Workings of Nav2

In the Nav2 architecture, we have noticed some input to Nav2, correct? *Figure 8.3* depicts the primary input into Nav2 from the robot and the main output relayed to the robot from Nav2.

We can identify the important topics that we need to supply to Nav2, which include `tf` (transformation), `/odom`, `/map`, and sensor topics such as `/scan` with `sensor_msgs/LaserScan`, or topics that publish `sensor_msgs/PointCloud` or `sensor_msgs/Range`. The `tf` frames we must establish before initiating navigation with Nav2 are `map->odom->base_footprint->base_link->(tf of robot links)`. The robot's controller or driver nodes running on the robot can publish the `/odom` topic and transform it from `odom->base_link`.

If you use Gazebo Sim or another simulator, ensure it also publishes the `odom->base_link` transformation. The remaining transformation, `map->odom`, is provided by the AMCL node in Nav2. The AMCL node localizes the robot on the map. It can publish the current pose estimates via `tf` and has a particle cloud that indicates the probability of the robot's pose estimates. A particle cloud that is spread out indicates a less accurate pose.

The `/map` topic can be published by the Nav2 **Map Server** from a saved file, or we can use Slam Toolbox to generate the dynamic map.

Let's now discuss how Nav2 works when providing a single target position: Point B. Ensure that the robot correctly supplies all other Nav2 input topics:

1. **Initial position to localization**: When we start Nav2 and all the nodes shown in *Figure 8.3*, we may see the robot map on Rviz, the robot simulation in Gazebo, or the real robot starting up once Nav2 is initiated. The first thing we may need to do is not set the goal position; however, before that, we must ensure proper localization so that the robot can accurately locate itself on the map. Only if the localization is correct will navigation function properly. AMCL localization is one way of localizing the robot on the map. When we start Nav2, the user may need to provide an initial map position to AMCL for it to begin. Once it has a proper initial pose, it can localize the map using sensor data such as LiDAR. Once localization is complete, you will find all the global and local costmaps appear, ready for goal acquisition.

2. **Goal setup**: Using the Waypoint Follower node, we can provide a single or multiple goal positions to Nav2. Nav2 includes waypoint follower panels, which simplify the process of feeding waypoints from Rviz.

3. **Global planning**: When Nav2 receives the goal position, the Planner Server calculates a path from the current robot location (Point A) to Point B, utilizing a global costmap. This global plan is typically static, meaning it does not account for dynamic obstacles like moving people or vehicles, so it may become outdated in dynamic environments.

Moreover, the global path is often coarse and somewhat jerky, as it's meant to provide a high-level route rather than fine-grained motion. Local planning is then used to refine this path and handle real-time changes.

4. **Local planning**: After generating the global plan using the Planner Server, Nav2 uses the control server to generate the local plan. The local planner uses real-time sensor data (e.g., from LiDAR or cameras) along with the local costmap to avoid dynamic obstacles and adjust the robot's movement accordingly. The local planner ensures the robot follows the global path smoothly and safely, dynamically re-planning short segments to prevent collisions and navigate around unforeseen obstacles. This ensures the robot can move smoothly along the path by avoiding obstacles on the local map.

5. **Execution**: The Controller Server sends velocity commands to the robot's controller board, which then transmits the wheel commands to the actuators (e.g., wheels or motors) to follow the planned path.

6. **Obstacle detection**: If any unexpected obstacles are detected, the local planner recalculates a new path around them, computing the robot's movement in real time. The Collision Monitor also helps the robots avoid immediate collisions.

7. **Arrival**: The task is considered complete once the robot reaches the goal position (Point B). We can also provide goal tolerance if needed.

We have gone through the fundamental concepts of how Nav2 works. The next section will demonstrate how to install Nav2 and set it up for our robot.

Installing Nav2 on ROS 2 Jazzy

Installing Nav2 on ROS 2 Jazzy is straightforward.

The following command will install all Nav2 packages on ROS 2 Jazzy:

```
sudo apt install ros-${ROS_DISTRO}-navigation2
```

The navigation2 package is a meta-package that installs the necessary dependent packages for navigation.

Along with the main package, we may need an additional package called nav2-bringup:

```
sudo apt install ros-${ROS_DISTRO}-nav2-bringup
```

This package includes a set of ROS 2 launch files that facilitate the launching of the Nav2 nodes and provide the necessary configuration. These launch files enable developers to set up Nav2 for their robot quickly.

After installing Nav2 on ROS 2 Jazzy, we can set up a demo simulation with its Nav2 configuration package to test its features.

Nav2 demo using TurtleBot3

We will install the simulation and navigation package for the **TurtleBot 3** demo here.

Here's the command to install the simulation and navigation packages:

```
sudo apt install ros-${ROS_DISTRO}-nav2-minimal-tb*
```

After installing the package, we can execute the following command to initiate the simulation in Gazebo Sim:

```
ros2 launch nav2_bringup tb3_simulation_launch.py headless:=False
```

The headless argument is set to False to visualize the simulation in Gazebo Sim; if it is True, it will simulate without a Sim window.

After executing the command above, we will have the Gazebo Sim, Nav2 nodes running, and the Rviz window, as shown in *Figure 8.4*.

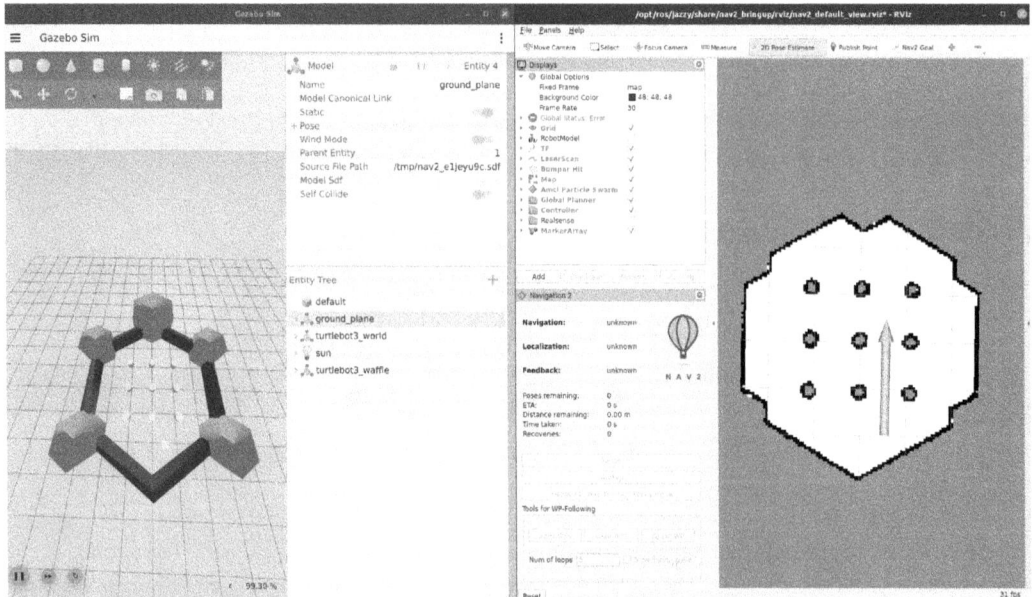

Figure 8.4: Nav2 demo using TurtleBot 3

When we initiate navigation, the robot might not be able to localize the map. An initial position is required to start localization. We can set the initial pose using Rviz. After clicking the **2D Pose Estimate** button, you can select the robot's position on the map. You may need to rotate the map orientation to align it with the Gazebo world. Once the robot's initial pose is established, the navigation nodes will begin, and you can view the global costmap and local costmap on the main map. You can check the status of navigation and localization in the **Navigation 2** toolbar in Rviz to make sure everything is initialized correctly.

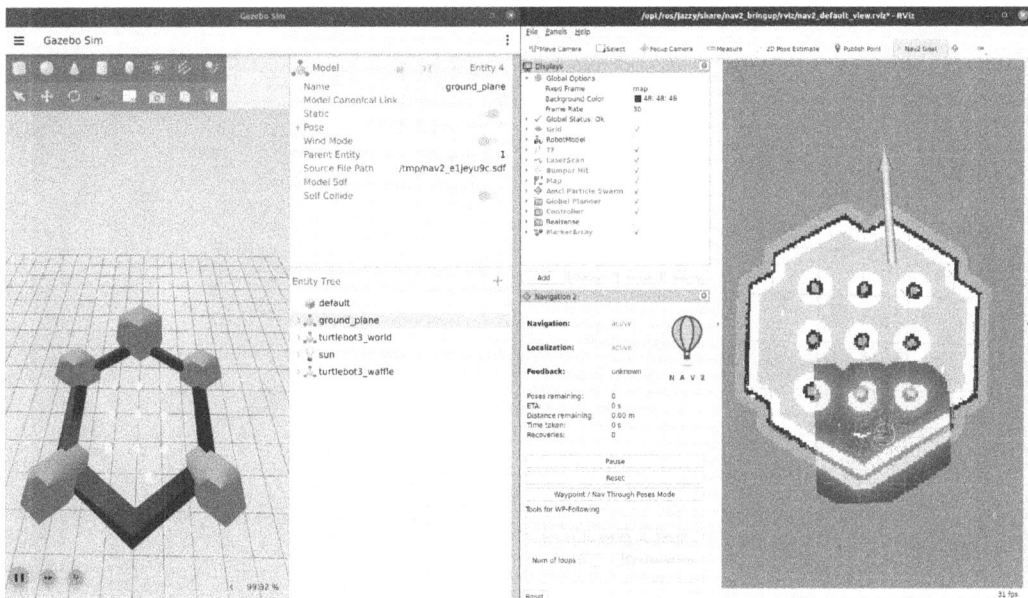

Figure 8.5: Nav2 demo navigation

Once Nav2 is initialized, you can find an additional layer on the top of the static map, which appears as *light blue*, which is called the global costmap. The global costmap inflates the obstacle in the static map to make navigation safer. The global planner in Nav2 uses a global costmap for computing the high-level path from start to goal. The global costmap will not update frequently with dynamic obstacle data.

The local costmap focuses on the area immediately around the robot, which appears mostly as a *violet color*, and updates using real-time sensor data. It can capture dynamic obstacles like people or moving objects. The local costmap is used by the local planner to make safe, short-term motion decisions.

We can now set individual goals or waypoints in Rviz using the **Nav2 Goal** button. Click the **Nav2 Goal** button and click on a point on the map to provide a goal position. *Figure 8.5* illustrates a sample goal position given for navigation.

The **Navigation2** widget displayed in Rviz features a button labeled **Waypoint**. After clicking the **Waypoint** button, we can set multiple waypoints on the map using the **Nav2 Goal** button. Once the waypoints are created, click **Start Nav Through Pose** to begin the waypoint navigation.

Figure 8.6 shows single waypoint vs multi-waypoint navigation in the map.

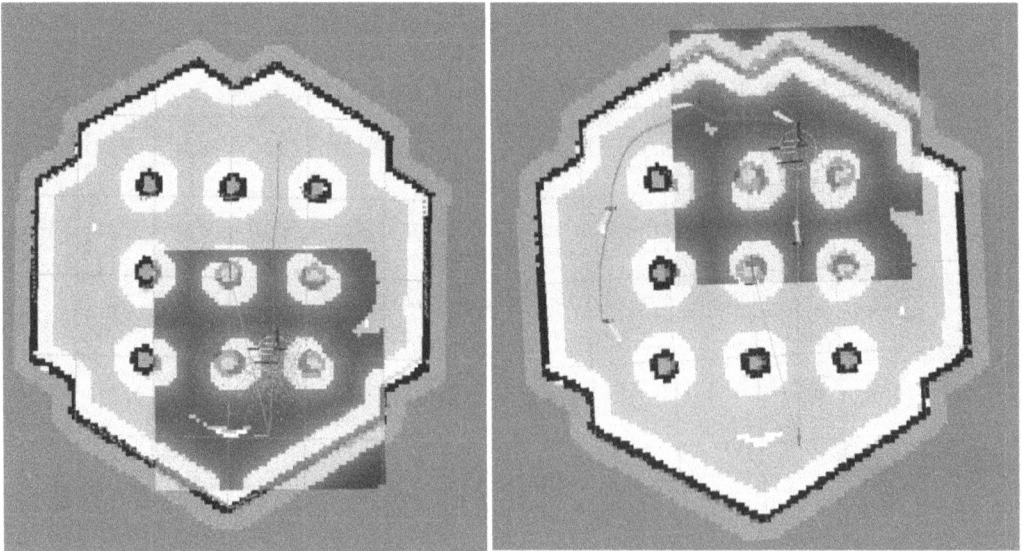

Figure 8.6: Single waypoint (left) vs multi waypoint (right) navigation demo

You can set up Nav2 on an Ubuntu 24.04 desktop version or test it in a Docker container. When working with real robots, using Docker will simplify deployment significantly. In the next section, we'll explore setting up Nav2 in Docker.

Setting up Nav2 in Docker

You can find the Dockerfile and shell script to create a custom image for running Nav2-based simulation and application in Chapter08/docker_nav2.

Here is the command to build the Nav2 image:

```
./build_image.sh ros2_nav:v0.1 master_ros2_ws robot
```

Here, `ros2_nav:v0.1` is the name of the custom image, `master_ros2_ws` is our ROS 2 workspace where we can put our custom robot simulation and navigation packages, and the `robot` is the user's name inside the container.

After building the Nav2 image, we can create the container using the following command:

```
./create_container.sh ros2_nav:v0.1 master_ros2_ws ros2_nav
```

We need to provide the image name, the ROS 2 workspace name, and the container name we need to make.

After creating the container, you can start running the navigation and mapping commands. The following demo simulation launch file can be used to test the container:

```
ros2 launch nav2_bringup tb3_simulation_launch.py headless:=False
```

If you want to open more terminals for the same container, you can use the following command:

```
./start_container.sh ros2_nav
```

This will attach a new terminal if the container is already running, or start the container if it has stopped. You need to provide the container name as the argument for this script.

After attaching a new terminal, make sure you have sourced the `ros_entry_point` script using the following command:

```
source /ros_entrypoint.sh
```

We can test all the packages in this chapter using this Docker image. You can create a new package by placing it in the ROS 2 workspace and building it.

Here are the instructions to build, create, and run a container using Docker Compose.

Setting up Nav2 in Docker Compose

In this section, we will see how to build and start containers for simulation using Docker Compose.

Switch to the `Chapter08/docker_compose_nav2` folder and execute the following commands to start building the Docker image and start the container.

- Use the following command if you are using a non-NVIDIA graphics card on your PC:

```
docker compose -f docker-compose-gui.yml build
docker compose -f docker-compose-gui.yml up
```

- If you do have an NVIDIA graphics card and the driver is properly installed, use the following command to start the container:

```
docker compose -f docker-compose-nvidia.yml build
docker compose -f docker-compose-nvidia.yml up
```

Once you start this command, the image will be built first, the container will start, and you will have to use another terminal to attach to the container. You don't have to close this terminal; if you cancel the command by pressing *Ctrl + C*, it will stop the running container.

You can create a new terminal from the running container using the following command:

```
./start_container.sh ros2_nav
```

Now source the ROS 2 environment:

```
source /ros_entrypoint.sh
```

Build the ROS 2 workspace:

```
colcon build
```

Source the ROS 2 workspace:

```
source install/setup.bash
```

Now, we can launch the simulation launch file:

```
ros2 launch nav2_bringup tb3_simulation_launch.py headless:=False
```

After starting the container, if you want to stop the container and remove it, you can execute the command from a new host terminal. Make sure you are executing inside the docker_compose_nav2 folder:

- If you are using a non-NVIDIA graphics card:

```
docker compose -f docker-compose-gui.yml down
```

- If you are using an NVIDIA graphics card:

```
docker compose -f docker-compose-nvidia.yml down
```

In the next section, we will see how to set up VS Code Dev Containers for running a simulation.

Nav2 using VS Code Dev Containers

If you are interested in setting up a dev container in VS Code, make sure you have created the ROS 2 workspace named `master_ros2_ws` and open the `Chapter08` folder using VS Code. This folder has a `.devcontainer` folder, which has the `devcontainer.json` file, which has the instructions to use the Docker Compose file we used in the above section for the container. When you open the folder, it will prompt you to install the Dev Containers extension and **Reopen in Container**. If you select this option, it will build the container, set the environment, mount the ROS 2 workspace as a volume, and connect the editor to it. We can also see the mounted volume, which is the `master_ros2_ws` folder in VS Code itself.

We have seen how to set up the Nav2 demo on Docker, Docker Compose, and Dev Containers. In the next section, we will explore how to use the Slam Toolbox to create a map of the robot's environment.

Mapping using Slam Toolbox

In this section, we will explore what the `slam_toolbox` project is and how to use it with Nav2.

What is Slam Toolbox?

Slam Toolbox [17] is a ROS 2 project that includes nodes for implementing 2D SLAM [18] in mobile robots. **SLAM (Simultaneous Localization and Mapping)** is a set of algorithms in robotics used to localize and map the robot environment using different sensors like cameras or lasers to *see* the surroundings. The generated map can be stored and can later be used for navigation. Examples of 2D SLAM are FastSLAM, Hector SLAM, and Cartographer.

With 2D SLAM, we can create a 2D map of the robot's environment, which can later be used for navigation.

Steve Macenski, who also leads the Nav2 project, created the Slam Toolbox project. Samsung Research and the open-source community are currently maintaining the project.

Here are the main features of Slam Toolbox:

- **2D mapping**: It has 2D SLAM, built for creating and saving a map. It also has features to refine, remap, and continue mapping a saved pose graph.
- **Life-long mapping**: This is the concept of being able to map a space, entirely or partially, and over time, you can refine and update the map as you continue to interact with the space.

- **Synchronous and asynchronous mapping**: It supports synchronous mapping, suitable for real-time navigation, whereas asynchronous mapping is ideal for offline mapping and large environments.

- **Rviz plugin**: It has the Rviz plugin for interacting with the mapping.

Figure 8.7 illustrates the topics subscribed to and published by the slam_toolbox node and its various components.

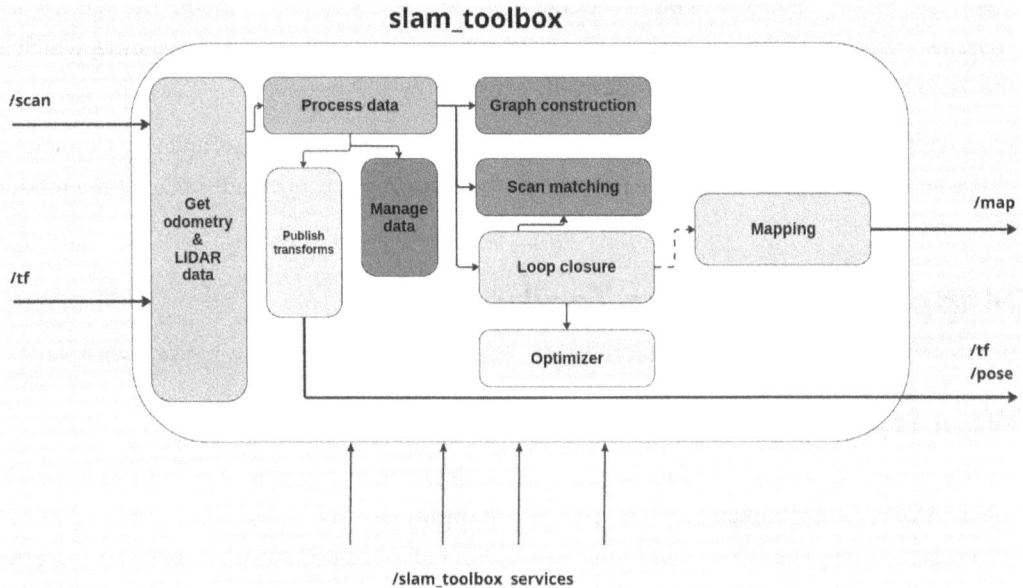

Figure 8.7: Block diagram of slam_toolbox node

The node subscribes to the laser scan topic /scan and the robot's TF /tf (odom->base_link). Once the node has subscribed to these topics, it processes the data for graph construction. This includes filtering the data, reducing noise, and preparing for scan matching. After processing the data, the node constructs a graph of the environment. In the graph, each node represents a robot pose, while each edge represents the spatial relationship between poses. The processed data is then used for scan matching, which aligns the current LiDAR scans with previous ones to estimate the robot's relative position. This process is crucial for localization and mitigating map drift. Loop closure [32] detects when the robot revisits a previously mapped area, adding constraints to the graph that correct drift over time. The optimizer refines the entire graph and produces a consistent map, which minimizes errors in the graph's pose estimation and ensures map alignment. The mapping section generates and publishes the final optimized graph.

The node publishes map data and the robot's pose to the map frame.

The `slam_toolbox` node also exposes many services like save map, serialize map, and deserialize map.

The Slam Toolbox for ROS 2 provides different modes of operation. Commonly used modes of operations are:

- **Online Synchronous (sync)**: In this mode, SLAM runs in sync with incoming sensor data. Each scan is processed and updates the map before the next arrives. This method is CPU-efficient because it does not do the queuing of the sensor messages. This method is used where real-time responsiveness is crucial. It is suited more for a low-speed robot.

- **Online Asynchronous (async)**: In this mode, sensor data is queued and processed in a separate thread asynchronously. This is useful if the scan rate is slower than the scan arrival. This will be useful where SLAM needs time to process. It takes more CPU because of queuing and multi-threading. It is suited to high-speed robots with high data rates.

We will see how to use both in the upcoming section on configuring Slam Toolbox.

We have explored important features of Slam Toolbox; now we will see how to install ROS 2 Jazzy.

Installing Slam Toolbox in ROS 2 Jazzy

To install Slam Toolbox in ROS 2 Jazzy, we can use the following command:

```
sudo apt install ros-${ROS_DISTRO}-slam-toolbox
```

SLAM Toolbox is already included in the Dockerfile if you use the provided Docker container.

After installing `slam-toolbox`, let's see a mapping demo using TurtleBot 3 simulation.

Mapping demo using Slam Toolbox

To test the mapping process, we can utilize the same launch file within the nav2_bringup package we previously tested for Nav2.

Here is the demo launch file we can use to start mapping:

```
ros2 launch nav2_bringup tb3_simulation_launch.py headless:=False
slam:=True
```

As you can see, we are using the same demo launch file to test navigation, but here, we set `slam` to `True` to enable mapping.

Here's how the mapping process works. The launch file starts the TurtleBot 3 simulation in Gazebo and initiates the `slam_toolbox` and Nav2 nodes. We can see a section of the map that was created and visualize it in Rviz. To complete the mapping process, we have to teleoperate the robot around the environment. As the robot moves, Slam Toolbox can start generating and updating the map.

In Rviz, you can see a map being created while you move the robot. You can move the TurtleBot3 robot using the following command:

```
ros2 run teleop_twist_keyboard teleop_twist_keyboard
```

We can use keyboard buttons to drive the robot. We can also use the `rqt` and **Robot Steering** plugin to drive the robot. If we use Gazebo Sim, we can teleoperate the robot from the GUI panel itself. In addition to the robot's manual driving and mapping, we can also perform mapping with Nav2. In the `tb3_simulation_launch.py` launch file that we used above, we are running `slam_toolbox` alongside Nav2. We can command the robot to reach a goal position on the incomplete map, and the robot can move to that position while simultaneously building a map.

You can click on the **Nav2 Goal** button in Rviz and provide the goal position, and it will build the map like we do using keyboard teleoperation. You can use the automatic mapping technique until the map is fully finished. This configuration is also used for exploration algorithms capable of automatically moving around an unknown environment and building a map without providing the manual goal position.

After navigating the robot through the environment several times, you can view the entire map, as shown in *Figure 8.8*.

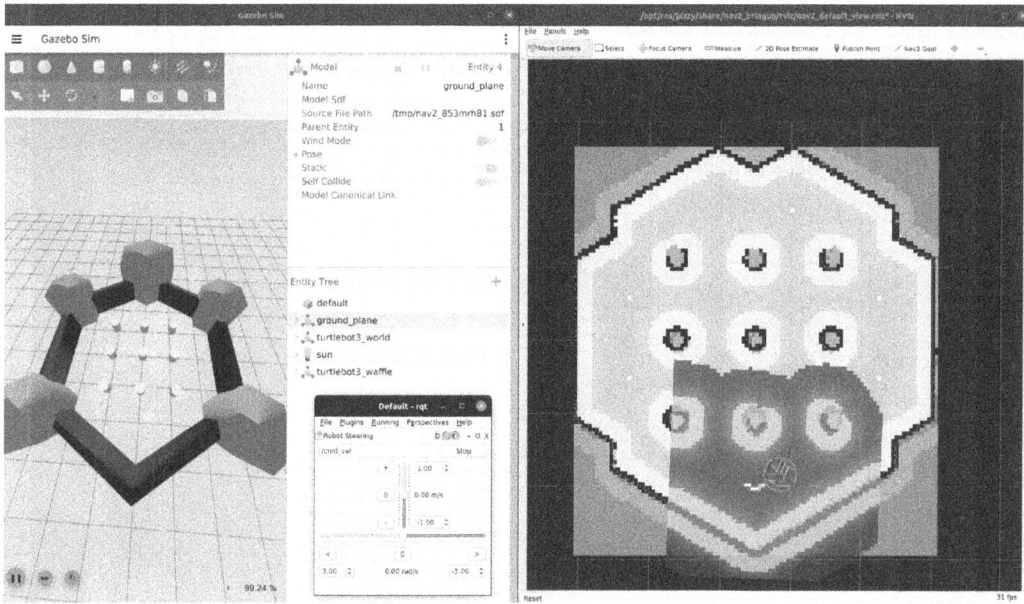

Figure 8.8: Manual mapping using Slam-toolbox

After completing the map, we can save the map using another command:

```
ros2 run nav2_map_server map_saver_cli -f ~/map
```

The map_saver_cli node can save the map with the name provided as an argument. The name is map.pgm, and the map configuration file is map.yaml.

The map can also be saved from Rviz. Slam Toolbox provides an Rviz panel with the option to save, serialize, or deserialize the map. To load the panel, go to **Panel** | **Add New Panel** | **slam_toolbox** | **SlamToolboxPlugin.** We will get the following panel in Rviz.

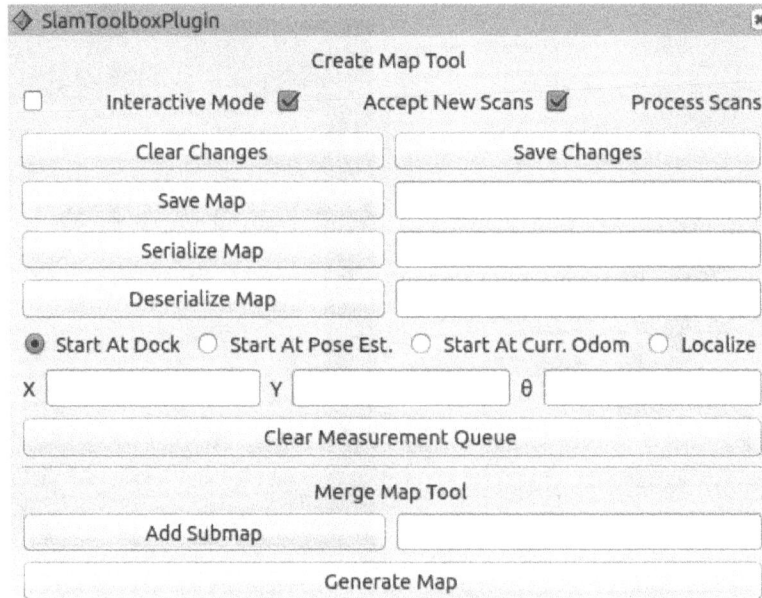

Figure 8.9: Slam Toolbox Rviz panel

The map's name can be mentioned in the box beside the **Save Map** button. After mentioning the name, you can click the **Save Map** button. The map will be saved in the path where we start the mapping launch file.

You can find the different parameters of the SLAM Toolbox in the README of the project [*19*].

In the next section, we will explore how to create a navigation package for the new simulated robot we developed in *Chapter 5*.

Configuring Nav2 and Slam Toolbox for your robot

This section shows how to create a ROS 2 package to implement autonomous navigation for our robot using Nav2. The package mainly contains launch and parameter files for starting and configuring Nav2 nodes. It can be found in the Chapter08/rosbot_nav2_bringup folder.

The rosbot navigation package contains the following files:

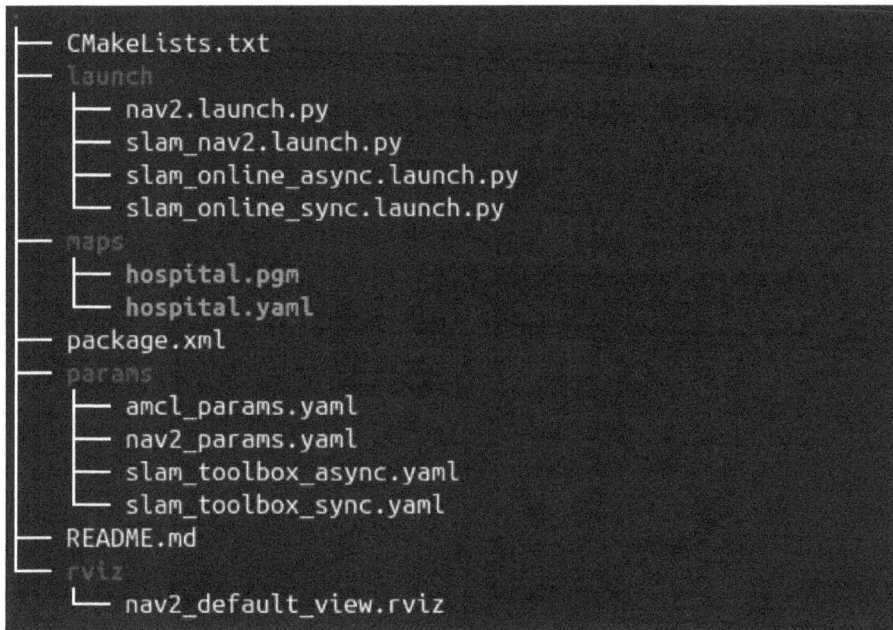

```
├── CMakeLists.txt
├── launch
│   ├── nav2.launch.py
│   ├── slam_nav2.launch.py
│   ├── slam_online_async.launch.py
│   └── slam_online_sync.launch.py
├── maps
│   ├── hospital.pgm
│   └── hospital.yaml
├── package.xml
├── params
│   ├── amcl_params.yaml
│   ├── nav2_params.yaml
│   ├── slam_toolbox_async.yaml
│   └── slam_toolbox_sync.yaml
├── README.md
└── rviz
    └── nav2_default_view.rviz
```

Figure 8.10: rosbot navigation 2 package structure

You can find a set of launch files in the launch folder: nav2.launch.py, which starts the Nav2 nodes, slam_online_async.launch.py and slam_online_sync.launch.py for mapping, and slam_nav2.launch.py for mapping in conjunction with navigation. In the maps folder, we can see a saved map of a *hospital* environment. Following the launch files, the next important part of the package is the params folder. It contains parameters for the AMCL node, Nav2 nodes, and Slam Toolbox. Configuring the Nav2 stack involves setting these parameters. We have observed the list of parameters for each module in Nav2. What we are doing in this package is simply configuring those parameters for our robot and initiating all nodes using the launch file.

At first glance, the process seems simple: getting the robot up and running with the Nav2 stack, but the real challenge lies in tuning the parameters. With over 500 parameters for all these nodes, fine-tuning them to enhance navigation is quite difficult.

In this chapter, we will not discuss the individual parameters of Nav2. However, we will provide a general overview of how to set up a Nav2 package with default parameters and a reference for each parameter.

We will use `rosbot_description`, which we have generated and modified by converting the Fusion 360 model to URDF for interfacing with Nav2.

So, let's start interfacing the `rosbot` simulation with Nav2.

Robot prerequisites for Nav2

Here are the prerequisites for the robot in simulation or for the actual robot to interface with Nav2:

- **Publishing TF of the robot**: We must ensure the robot publishes the TF frame from `odom->base_footprint-> base_link(robot_link)`. When we activate the navigation and localization nodes, the AMCL node will also publish the transformation from the `map->odom`. In short, we must confirm that when we start navigation, we see the TF from `map-> odom-> base_footprint-> base_link-> (robot_link)`. If Nav2 is not functioning correctly, the first check you should perform is to visualize the TF tree in `rqt`. If the TF tree is broken, we need to address that.

- **Setting ROS 2 topics**: Here are the important checks we must do in ROS 2 topics before interfacing with Nav2:

    - We must ensure that the sensor topics are published, including the `/scan` topic for the laser and the `/odom` topic for the wheel encoder.

    - We also need to confirm that the Gazebo Sim differential drive plugins or ROS 2 controllers are configured properly.

    - We need to verify that the robot driver nodes are functioning correctly on the actual hardware.

    - Another important topic to check is the robot's command velocity, which drives the robot.

- We need to make sure that the command velocity topic, by default /cmd_vel, aligns with the robot driver or the Gazebo Sim differential drive plugin topic. The robot can only move if the topics align; otherwise, it will plan a path but will not be able to move. Therefore, if the robot is not moving, we need to verify that the command velocity topic is published and subscribed to correctly.

- Additionally, we must ensure that the map topic is being published. If the map is not published, Nav2 will not function. We must ensure map_server is configured correctly and the map file is provided appropriately for navigation. If we are using slam_toolbox and Nav2, we must ensure that slam_toolbox nodes are publishing the map data correctly.

We can start interfacing Nav2 with our custom rosbot robot if these modifications are done.

Let's start discussing the Nav2 launch files in the next section.

ROS 2 navigation and mapping launch files

In this section, we will discuss writing the Nav2 launch file for navigation and the Slam Toolbox launch file for mapping. We will see the important nodes and configurations we use inside these launch files.

Launching navigation

Once the robot prerequisites are met, we can create a launch file to start the Nav2 node, AMCL, and map server. Nav2 has already been given a package called nav2_bringup, with launch files to start navigation. It will make the entire process easier. In our example, the rosbot_nav2_bringup/ launch/nav2.launch.py file includes bringup_launch.py and passes the arguments to this launch file. The nav2.launch.py file will start the AMCL and map_server nodes, and the nav2_bringup/ launch/bringup_launch.py file will start nodes such as nav2 life cycle manager, controller_ server, smoother_server, planner_server, behavior_server, velocity_smoother, collision_ monitor, bt_navigator, waypoint_follower, and docking_server. Along with loading all the nodes, this launch file also loads parameter files like rosbot_nav2_bringup/params/nav2_params. yaml and amcl_params.yaml, which have a configuration of all the nodes for navigation.

Launching mapping

In this section, we can see how to run the Slam Toolbox in async and sync mode, which we have seen in the description of Slam Toolbox.

The `rosbot_nav2_bringup /launch/slam_online_async.launch.py` launch file runs the nodes to run Slam Toolbox in *async* mode by loading the parameter file called `rosbot_nav2_bringup/params/slam_toolbox_async.yaml`, whereas `rosbot_nav2_bringup/launch/slam_online_sync.launch.py` starts Slam Toolbox in *sync* mode by loading the parameter file called `rosbot_nav2_bringup/params/slam_toolbox_async.yaml`.

Launching navigation and mapping

If we want to run `Nav2` and `slam_toolbox`, we can use `rosbot_nav2_bringup /launch/slam_nav2.launch.py`. This launch file starts all `Nav2` and `slam_ toolbox` nodes except AMCL. The Slam Toolbox node itself carries out the localization.

We can use these launch files as templates and can use them for any other robot. The main changes we may have to make for a new robot are in the Nav2 parameter file, which will be discussed in the next section.

ROS 2 navigation parameter files

Our robot navigation configuration file is at `rosbot_nav2_bringup/params/nav2_params.yaml`. By checking this file, we can find the parameter configuration for each node we have started. This configuration contains more than 500 parameters, making it difficult to learn about each one. The basic adjustments you may need to make pertain to any changes in the topic's name, the name of the TF frames, etc.; we might need to change those. We can leave the other parameters as they are.

The list of parameters for each node is provided in [20], where you can find information on all the parameters. The detailed tuning guide is available in [21].

In the next section, we will explore how to launch the navigation and mapping of the rosbot robot.

Launching rosbot simulation and navigation

You can keep the `rosbot_description` and `rosbot_nav2_bringup` in your ROS 2 workspace. If you use Docker, copy to the `master_ros2_ws/src` folder and build the workspace.

The following `launch` commands will start the navigation with the available map:

- This command will start the `rosbot` simulation in Gazebo Sim:

```
ros2 launch rosbot_description gazebo.launch.py
```

- We can start the navigation launch using the following command:

```
ros2 launch rosbot_nav2_bringup nav2.launch.py
```

After starting the navigation, you can give the initial pose for AMCL and start putting waypoints using the Rviz **2D Nav goal** button, and you can see the robot is moving, as shown in *Figure 8.11*.

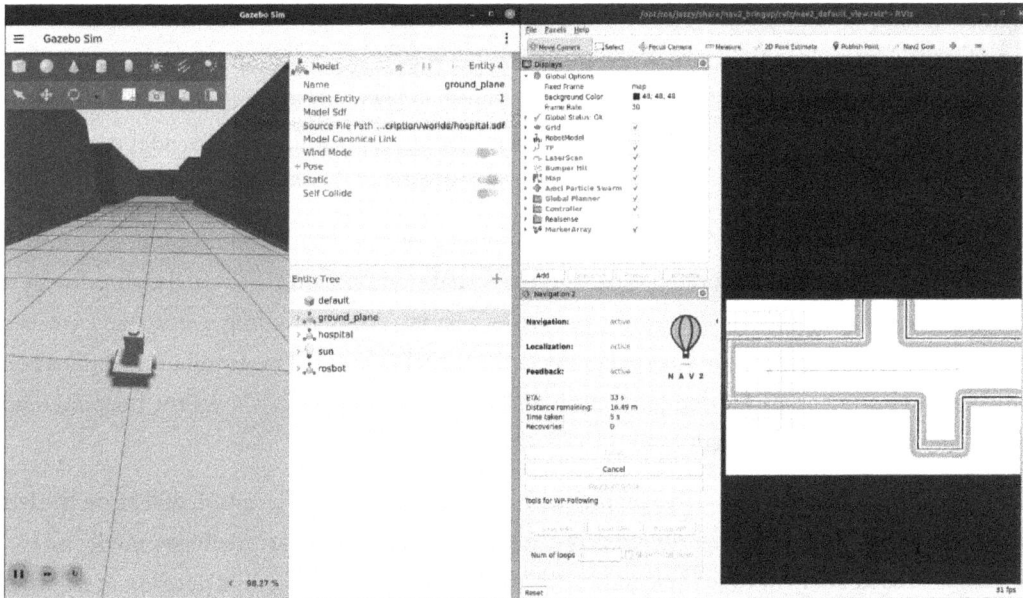

Figure 8.11: rosbot Gazebo simulation with Nav2 in Rviz

To manually start mapping, launch the following file:

```
ros2 launch rosbot_nav2_bringup   slam_online_async.launch.py
```

This will activate the `rqt` steering plugin, allowing you to drive the robot manually and create the map.

The following launch file can be used to map the world using Slam Toolbox and Nav2:

```
ros2 launch rosbot_nav2_bringup slam_nav2.launch.py
```

As we did for TurtleBot 3, we can start providing waypoints, and the robot will traverse an unknown area to complete the map.

After successfully setting up the rosbot navigation package, let's examine a case study of Nav2 utilizing mobile robots in hospitals to deliver medicine to patients during COVID-19.

Case study: Nav2-based robots during COVID-19

During COVID-19, some hospitals deployed robots to deliver items like medicines to patients to avoid transmitting the virus [30]. While most of these robots were tele-operated, we would like to implement a robot in the rest of this chapter that delivers medication to patients in an automated manner. In this section, we will look at a Nav2-based application that provides medication to patients in the room.

The simulation world we saw in the last section was a section inside the hospital. As you will understand, this is a very simplified version of the actual environment. The actual environment is much more complex and has more tasks to do, like opening doors, avoiding pedestrians, etc. We need much more robust techniques to deploy in the actual scenario. This simulation application and the environment are for demonstration purposes only. *Figure 8.12* shows the hospital map, with different sections marked.

You can find Room 1, Room 2, and a medicine shop. The robot's initial position will be on the left side of the map. Whenever the robot receives instructions from the user to deliver medicine to a room, such as Room 1, the robot first goes to the medicine shop from its initial position. It will wait for a moment to collect the medicine from there. The robot then moves to Room 1 to deliver the medicine to the patient. After the delivery, it will return to its initial position and dock for charging.

The robot will follow the next instruction once it returns to the initial position.

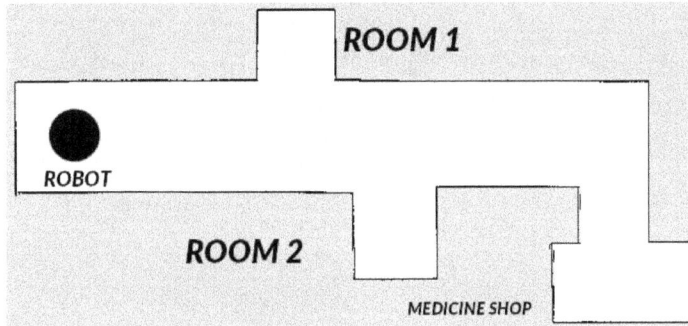

Figure 8.12: Markings of the hospital map

The following section will look at a simple Nav2-based C++ application to achieve this task.

Developing Nav2-based applications using ROS 2 and C++

This section will discuss the ROS 2 C++ application designed to deliver medicine to a specific room.

Figure 8.13 shows how our application communicates with Nav2.

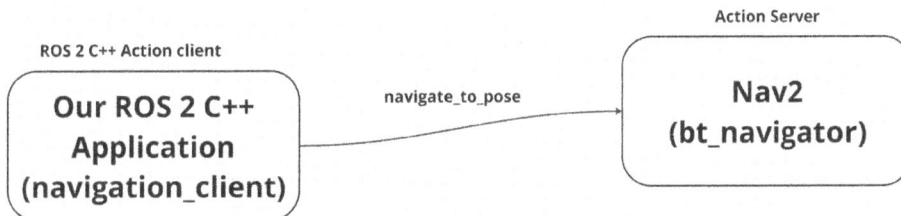

Figure 8.13: Communication between navigation application and Nav2

The application we are developing is a Nav2 action client. We know Nav2 has a BT Navigator Server node, which serves as an action server with an action name called /navigate_to_pose and an action type of nav2_msgs/action/NavigateToPose [22], as well as /navigate_through_poses with an action type of nav2_msgs/action/NavigateThroughPoses [23]. When we call the action /navigate_to_pose with a goal position on the map, the BT Navigator can begin planning the path and move the robot to that location. The request will fail if the pose is invalid or obstructed.

The action /navigate_through_poses allows the robot to move through several waypoints. These actions can also be called from the Rviz Navigation2 panels. We have already experimented with these options in the previous sections.

In our robot application, we use the /navigate_to_pose action, which allows us to send one point at a time.

You can find the application package in Chapter08/nav2_client. Inside this package, you will find nav2_client/include/navigation_client.hpp and nav2_client/src/navigation_client.cpp. This includes defining a NavigationClient class with the action client to send the goal position.

In the header file, you can find the following action client declaration:

```
using NavigateToPose = nav2_msgs::action::NavigateToPose;
rclcpp_action::Client<NavigateToPose>::SharedPtr action_client_;
```

In this code, we can see we are using the same action type we saw earlier. Along with declaring the action client, we can see the goal response, feedback, and results declaration.

In the navigation_client.cpp file, predefined poses are hardcoded in the constructor. These poses correspond to each section of the map, including those for rooms 1 and 2, the medical shop, and the robot's initial pose.

The navigate2Pose() function takes the pose as an argument and executes the action. This is one of the key functions of this class:

```
bool NavigationClient::navigate2Pose(double x, double y, double z, double
orientation_w)
```

The function's arguments are x, y, z, and orientation_w in quaternion. In our case, the z value will be zero because we are moving a plane.

The deliverMedicine() function is another important function that can take order_number, and, based on order_number/room_no, it can call the hard-coded positions in a specific order:

```
bool NavigationClient::deliverMedicine(int order_number)
```

For example, if order_number is 1, it will first navigate the robot to the medical_shop location using the navigate2Pose() function and then load it with the room 1 position and then to the initial position. The same logic applies to order_number 2.

The nav2_client/src/main.cpp is the main application code. It will include the navigation class we created and pass the order number from the user to function inside the class. Once it passes the order_no, the deliverMedicine() function will be executed, and after completion of the order, the user can enter the next order.

In the next section, we will see how to build and run the application.

Running the Nav2 C++ application

You can copy the nav2_client package to master_ros2_ws and build the ROS2 workspace. After building the ROS 2 workspace, execute the following command to start the application:

- The following command will start the simulation of rosbot in Gazebo Sim:

```
ros2 launch rosbot_description gazebo.launch.py
```

- We can start the navigation launch using the following command:

```
ros2 launch rosbot_nav2_bringup nav2.launch.py
```

After the navigation launch, you can provide the initial pose of the robot using the **2D Pose Estimate** button in Rviz and start the following command in another terminal to start the application:

```
ros2 run nav2_client navigation_client
```

The application will ask the user to input the order number like this:

```
[navigation_client]: Navigation client initialized
Enter order number (1 for Room1, 2 for Room2, q to quit):
```

After inputting the order number, the robot plans the path and the remaining distance to the goal in the terminal, as shown in *Figure 8.14*.

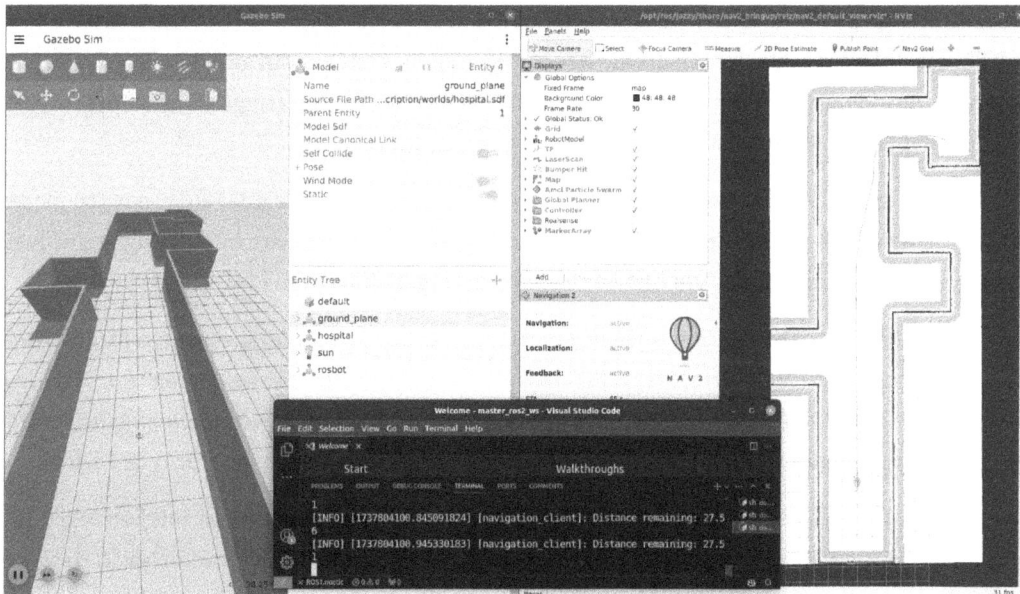

Figure 8.14: Nav2 application for medical robot

We have utilized basic conditional logic to implement the navigation in this application, but what about creating a complex navigation system? In such cases, simple conditional logic may not be reliable or scalable. Imagine that, instead of two rooms, the hospital has 100 rooms. What if there are specific rules for navigating the floor? Additionally, what if we need to include tasks like people detection? This is when we need to consider incorporating state machines or behavior trees into our application.

The following section will explore incorporating a behavior tree into the Nav2 application code.

Developing Nav2-based applications using BT and C++

In this section, we will see how to use BT to make complex applications using Nav2.

There are two main areas where we can use BT along with Nav2:

- BT Navigator Server in Nav2
- In a Nav2 action client

Let's explore each use case in detail here.

BT Navigator Server in Nav2

We have seen that the core part of Nav2 is the BT Navigator Server. A BT file is one of the main inputs to the BT Navigator Server. The BT Navigator Server can be completely configured with our BT file. The BT file decides what to do once it receives a goal pose or set of goal positions. The BT file has different nodes which decide how navigation has to perform and how to provide the recovery. Based on the nodes in the BT file, the Navigator Server can trigger each node, such as the Planner Server, Controller Server, and Behavior Server.

We can configure this node and the input BT node by setting this node's default_nav_to_pose_bt_xml and default_nav_through_poses_bt_xml parameters. If we are not setting any values, it can take some default files. We can find all the existing BT files from [24].

Nav2 provides a set of navigation-specific nodes that can be included in the behavior trees. Here is an introduction to all the Nav2-specific behavior trees [25]. Here is the reference on existing behavior tree nodes in Nav2 [26]. You can find multiple *action plugins, condition plugins, control plugins*, and *decorator plugins* for Nav2 from the list that can be used to construct our BT file.

We can create a custom BT file for the navigator node to change the navigation behavior. We can also write new BT nodes as Nav2 plugins to implement different functions in Nav2. Here is a reference to implement new BT node plugins in Nav2 [27].

Here is the complete reference of BT and Nav2 [*28*].

In the next section, we will see how we can implement BT in a Nav2 client.

BT in the Nav2 action client

In this approach, we use BT outside Nav2 as a Nav2 action client, which uses an action called /navigate_to_pose.

This approach is the same as before for the medical robot; the only difference is that, instead of just a condition statement, we have used a BT-based application. The BT-based Nav2 action client example package is available in Chapter 08/nav2_bt_client. The BT file is placed in nav2_bt_client/bt_xml/nav_tree.xml. *Figure 8.15* shows the visualization of nav_tree.xml in the Groot 2 editor.

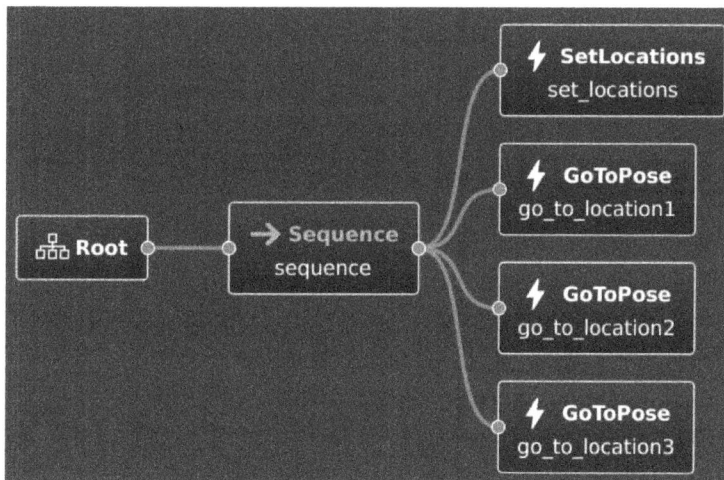

Figure 8.15: BT in nav2_bt_client package

There are two main BT action nodes implemented within this package: SetLocations and GotoPose. The SetLocations node reads predefined map locations from the file nav2_bt_client/config/map_locations.yaml and outputs a list of locations, including the name of each location and the corresponding map locations. The GotoPose node can receive inputs such as the location's name and the location pose. This GotoPose BT node has the Nav2 action client implementation, and it will call the /navigate_to_pose action with the appropriate location. So basically, the above BT application will read the location from the YAML file and move the Nav2-based robot to three map locations.

The nav2_bt_client/src/navigation_behaviors.cpp has the implementation of custom BT nodes, and nav2_bt_client/src/nav2_bt_node.cpp is the ROS 2 node, which initializes the BT and executes it.

Running a BT-based Nav2 action client

Running the node is similar to the action client we have executed for the medical robot. The only difference is that we have to set up a Groot 2 editor to visualize the flow of the BT.

Download the installer script from the following link to set up Groot2 [29]. After downloading the installer, you can execute the following command, and a GUI-based installer will pop up:

```
./Groot2-v1.6.1-linux-installer.run
```

You can click **Next** and install Groot in the home folder. Ensure the groot2 executable is available in /home/<user_name>/Groot2/bin/groot2. You can set up Groot 2 in Docker as well. Copy the installer to the mounted volume and install Groot, or you can also include it in the Dockerfile.

Once we set up Groot 2 correctly, we can copy the nav2_bt_client package to the workspace and build the workspace.

We can execute the following commands to start the BT-based Nav2 action client:

This command will start the simulation of rosbot in Gazebo Sim:

```
ros2 launch rosbot_description gazebo.launch.py
```

We can start the navigation launch using the following command:

```
ros2 launch rosbot_nav2_bringup nav2.launch.py
```

After launching the navigation, you can provide the initial pose of the robot using the **2D Pose Estimate** button in Rviz and start the following command in another terminal to start the BT application:

```
ros2 launch nav2_bt_client start_bt_app.launch.py
```

This launch file starts the Nav2 BT action client node and Groot2 with the nav_tree.xml behavior tree. Once you see the window, you can switch to the real-time mode in Groot 2 to see the status of the BT application. Click on **Real-time mode** and click the **Connect** button to start monitoring the status of the BT application.

Figure 8.16 shows the execution of the BT in the Groot 2 editor.

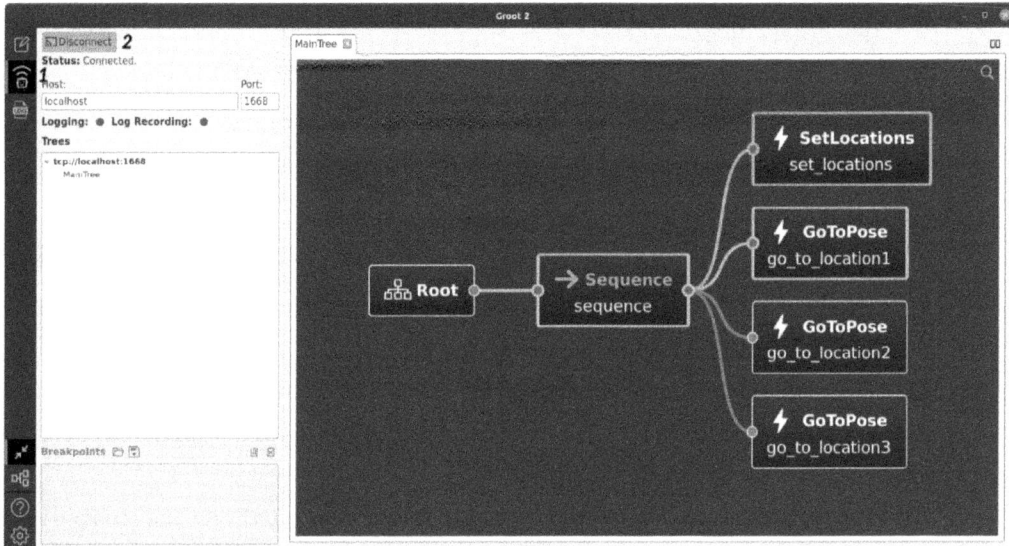

Figure 8.16: Groot2 real-time monitor

As you can see, each action node is executed individually, and the robot moves to each position on the map. We can expand the application by writing more BT nodes and changing the BT tree. Note that, in real robotic applications, the implementation of BT nodes can be very complex. The above example is just for demonstrating the capabilities of a BT in robot navigation.

Summary

This chapter explained how to use the ROS 2 Navigation Stack, called Nav2, for autonomous robot navigation. Nav2 helps robots move from one place to another by planning paths, avoiding obstacles, and controlling movement. The chapter introduced Nav2, its installation on ROS 2 Jazzy, and how to set it up with Slam Toolbox to create maps of the environment. It covered key components like localization, path planning, behavior trees, and lifecycle management, which help in making navigation smooth and efficient. The chapter also included practical steps to configure Nav2 for a robot and demonstrated its use in a hospital scenario for medicine delivery during COVID-19. Additionally, it explained how to develop navigation applications using C++ and behavior trees to automate robot movement. The chapter included guides on installing, configuring, and running Nav2 in simulations and on real robots.

In the next chapter, we will see how to work with a robotic arm using ROS 2 and MoveIt2!

References

- [1] https://nav2.org/

- [2] https://www.behaviortree.dev/

- [3] https://wiki.ros.org/navigation

- [4] https://www.opennav.org/

- [5] https://github.com/stevemacenski

- [6] https://docs.nav2.org/configuration/packages/configuring-lifecycle.html

- [7] https://docs.nav2.org/configuration/packages/configuring-bt-navigator.html

- [8] https://docs.nav2.org/configuration/packages/configuring-bt-xml.html

- [9] https://docs.nav2.org/configuration/packages/configuring-planner-server.html

- [10] https://docs.nav2.org/configuration/packages/configuring-controller-server.html

- [11] https://docs.nav2.org/configuration/packages/configuring-behavior-server.html

- [12] https://docs.nav2.org/configuration/packages/configuring-smoother-server.html

- [13] https://docs.nav2.org/configuration/packages/configuring-velocity-smoother.html

- [14] https://docs.nav2.org/configuration/packages/collision_monitor/configuring-collision-monitor-node.html

- [15] https://docs.nav2.org/configuration/packages/bt-plugins/actions/NavigateToPose.html

- [16] https://docs.nav2.org/configuration/packages/configuring-waypoint-follower.html

- [17] https://github.com/SteveMacenski/slam_toolbox

- [18] https://ouster.com/insights/blog/introduction-to-slam-simultaneous-localization-and-mapping

- [19] https://github.com/SteveMacenski/slam_toolbox/

- [20] https://docs.nav2.org/configuration/index.html

- [21] https://docs.nav2.org/tuning/index.html

- [22] https://docs.ros.org/en/jazzy/p/nav2_msgs/interfaces/action/NavigateToPose.html

- [23] https://docs.ros.org/en/jazzy/p/nav2_msgs/interfaces/action/NavigateThroughPoses.html

- [24] https://github.com/ros-navigation/navigation2/tree/jazzy/nav2_bt_navigator/behavior_trees

- [25] https://docs.nav2.org/behavior_trees/overview/nav2_specific_nodes.html

- [26] https://docs.nav2.org/configuration/packages/configuring-bt-xml.html

- [27] https://docs.nav2.org/plugin_tutorials/docs/writing_new_bt_plugin.html

- [28] https://docs.nav2.org/behavior_trees/index.html

- [29] https://www.behaviortree.dev/groot/

- [30] https://spectrum.ieee.org/how-robots-became-essential-workers-in-the-covid19-response

- [31] https://docs.nav2.org/roadmap/roadmap.html

- [32] https://www.thinkautonomous.ai/blog/loop-closure

Join our community on Discord

Join our community's Discord space for discussions with the authors and other readers: https://packt.link/embeddedsystems

9

Robot Manipulation Using MoveIt 2

In previous chapters, we covered designing and simulating a robotic arm and controlling it using Gazebo. Now, we'll dive into the arm motion planning problem. Manually controlling a robot's joints, especially with position or speed limits, can be tricky, since when we control a robot by joints, each joint movement affects the whole structure, making precise positioning of its end-effector hard. That's why we need an automated way to safely manage the robot's movements. To do this, we'll use **ROS MoveIt 2**, a powerful toolkit in ROS 2 designed to perform robot manipulation tasks. MoveIt 2 simplifies tasks such as motion planning with kinematic models, obstacle detection, and trajectory planning. It offers both a command-line interface and an easy-to-use GUI for adding new robots, plus an RViz2 plugin for planning movements right within the RViz2 environment. Finally, we'll discuss how to plan motions and avoid obstacles using the MoveIt C++ wrapper.

Manipulation is one of the most complex problems of robotics, since it involves different elements, including collision avoidance, trajectory planning, perception, and trajectory execution. Solving this problem also requires good mathematical knowledge to implement the algorithm moving the robot. Using a tool that helps developers to accomplish this task is fundamental to implementing advanced robotic applications.

Here's a list of the main topics that will be covered in the chapter:

- Introduction to MoveIt 2
- Preparing the robot model to use MoveIt 2
- Configuring new robots for MoveIt 2

- Testing MoveIt 2 using RViz2
- Motion planning using the `move_group` ROS 2 wrapper
- Planning with obstacles
- Detecting obstacles using a depth sensor

Technical requirements

To follow this chapter, you need the following requirements:

- A standard computer running the Ubuntu 24.04 LTS operating system
- A Linux machine with a ROS 2 Jazzy installed or with a running Docker container configured as discussed in *Chapter 2*

The reference code for this chapter can be found in the `Chapter09` folder of the following code repository: `https://github.com/PacktPublishing/Mastering-ROS-2-for-Robotics-Programming/tree/main/Chapter09`.

Introduction to MoveIt 2

Before starting programming MoveIt 2, let's discuss its basic components and its architecture. Understanding the architecture of MoveIt 2 is crucial for effectively programming and interfacing a robot with the system. We will briefly review the architecture and key concepts of MoveIt before diving into robot interfacing and programming. You can explore the complete MoveIt 2 architecture on the MoveIt 2 website: `https://moveit.picknik.ai/main/doc/concepts/concepts.html`.

MoveIt 2 system architecture

The `move_group` node is the core of MoveIt 2, integrating robot components and providing actions and services based on user commands. It retrieves robot data (such as kinematics) from *URDF*, *SRDF*, and configuration files. Once set up, users can command MoveIt 2 through *C++*, *Python*, or *RViz2*. The `move_group` node connects functionalities via plugins, sending planned trajectories to the robot's controllers through the `FollowJointTrajectoryAction` interface. It relies on external data, using the `/joint_states` topic for current joint positions and connecting to robot controllers to move motors. It also uses the *ROS 2 Tf* framework to manage frame relationships. MoveIt 2 uses various motion planning algorithms, mainly from the **Open Motion Planning Library (OMPL)**, which includes sample-based planners such as RRT. MoveIt 2 supports mainly sample-based planners, designed for complex environments and large planning spaces, where planning in six dimensions (position and orientation) can be slow with optimal planners.

Sampling-based planners, such as RRT and PRM, quickly find valid paths without focusing on optimality, making them suitable for real-time tasks. In contrast, optimal planners aim for the best path but are slower and require more computing power, making them less ideal for real-time applications. Let's discuss the planning pipeline in the next section.

MoveIt 2 planning pipeline

Once MoveIt starts, it just waits for new planning requests. In this section, we will discuss how the planning process starts and is handled by the MoveIt framework with the following entities:

- **Motion planning request**: Defines start and goal positions and the planning constraints
- **Planning scene**: Represents the robot's environment, including obstacles and constraints
- **Collision detection**: Ensures the planned path avoids collisions
- **Kinematic model**: Helps compute feasible movements for the robot
- **Planner**: Generates a path using algorithms such as RRT, PRM, or similar
- **Trajectory post-processing**: Refines the trajectory for smoothness and feasibility
- **Execution**: Sends commands to the robot's controller to follow the planned path

Let's discuss these steps in detail. A new planning process starts with the planning request. We will use a ROS 2 node with a wrapper for the move_group module. In the planning request, we must specify the start and goal states (positions, orientations, or poses of the robot's end effector or joints), and the eventual planning constraints, such as the allowed tolerance on the final goal of the constraints on the cartesian path.

When a planning request is made, MoveIt 2 creates a planning scene, capturing the robot's environment and current state. This scene includes the robot model and collision objects, allowing MoveIt 2 to perform collision detection and ensure the trajectory avoids obstacles and meets constraints. The system uses the robot's kinematic model to compute forward kinematics (determining a link's position based on joint angles) and inverse kinematics (calculating joint angles to achieve a desired end-effector position).

MoveIt 2 uses a modular architecture to integrate various planning algorithms via the **Open Motion Planning Library (OMPL)**. Once a specific planner is selected, it generates a trajectory from start to goal while meeting constraints. The planning process involves sampling paths, checking constraints and obstacles, and optimizing the path. If a valid path cannot be found or constraints are not met, the planning process may fail.

After the planner produces an initial trajectory, MoveIt 2 can apply additional post-processing steps such as path smoothing to ensure the robot moves smoothly between waypoints, time parameterization to adjust velocities and accelerations to match the robot's capabilities and dynamic constraints (e.g., maximum joint speeds), and interpolation to add intermediate waypoints for finer control. Once the final trajectory is planned, it is passed to the controller for execution. The execution phase involves the following:

- Converting the planned trajectory into motor commands that the robot's actuators can follow
- Using feedback (from joint sensors, cameras, etc.) to make real-time adjustments if necessary
- Ensuring the robot adheres to the planned path and avoids any dynamic obstacles that may have appeared after the planning phase

Finally, during execution, MoveIt 2 monitors the robot's progress, checking that the actual trajectory matches the planned one. If discrepancies or errors are detected (e.g., dynamic obstacles or collisions), the pipeline can trigger a re-planning process or halt the execution.

Now that the basic elements of MoveIt 2 have been introduced, we are ready to put them into practice by integrating it with a simulated robot in Gazebo. First, let's start to prepare a robot model to be controlled with ROS 2.

Preparing the robot model to use MoveIt 2

In this chapter, we will use the **Gazebo** simulator to test MoveIt 2. We'll prepare the **Panda robot model**, developed by *Franka Emika*, which is a versatile arm with 7 degrees of freedom and sensors for force and torque control. The Panda's integration with MoveIt 2 and ROS 2 facilitates advanced motion planning, kinematics, and real-time communication, making it suitable for research and industrial applications.

The robot model is implemented in the panda_robot package, which can be downloaded from the GitHub repository of the book. It consists of a set of xacro files to define the robot structure. To enable communication between MoveIt 2 and the robot model, the following steps must be taken.

Step 1 – Adding robot controllers

As already discussed in *Chapter 6*, to actuate a simulated robot model, the gz_ros2_control plugin must be integrated into the robot model. Let's edit the panda.urdf.xacro and panda_arm. xacro files in the following way:

1. Add the controller plugins in panda.urdf.xacro:

    ```
    <gazebo>
    <plugin filename="gz_ros2_control-system" name="gz_ros2_
    control::GazeboSimROS2ControlPlugin">
    ```

2. This plugin requires as input the controller configuration file. Let's create this file in the config folder of the panda_description package. Later in this section, we will discuss the content of this file:

    ```
    <parameters>$(find panda_description)/config/ros2_controllers.yaml</
    parameters>
    ```

3. Add the ros2_control tag to the panda_arm.xacro file. Within this tag, we must include a name that is arbitrary and a type, which must be "system":

    ```
    <ros2_control name="IgnitionSystem" type="system">
    ```

4. The hardware interface of the simulation of the ros2_control tag is the one to be used in the Gazebo simulation:

    ```
    <hardware>
    <plugin>gz_ros2_control/GazeboSimSystem</plugin>
        </hardware>
    ```

5. In this section, we must specify the command and the state interfaces for each arm. In the current example, the joints are controlled in position, while the position and the velocity are included in the state. The robot model has eight joints (joint1, …, joint8) plus two joints for the gripper. We will report here the configuration only for the first joint:

    ```
    controller_manager:
      ros__parameters:
        update_rate: 100
        arm_controller:
          type: joint_trajectory_controller/JointTrajectoryController
    arm_controller:
    ```

```
    ros__parameters:
      joints:
        - joint1
  ...

      command_interfaces:
        - position
      state_interfaces:
        - position
        - velocity
```

Now we must start the robot simulation with the controllers. To do this, we can use a launch file to start the simulation and the controllers.

Step 2 – Enabling the controllers from the launch file

To start the simulation with the controllers provided, a convenient launch file is needed. The main elements of this file are discussed in the following:

1. Configure the environment to find the meshes of the Panda robot. To do this, the GZ_SIM_ RESOURCE_PATH environment variable must be set to the location where the robot meshes are included. Of course, the files are placed in the install folder of the ROS 2 workspace:

    ```
    workspace_path = os.environ.get('COLCON_PREFIX_PATH') or os.environ.
    get('AMENT_PREFIX_PATH')
        pkg_panda_description = workspace_path + "/panda_description/
    share"
    ```

2. The SetEnvironmentVariable function of the Python launch file is used to export the variable to a desired value:

    ```
            gz_resource_path = SetEnvironmentVariable(
              name='GZ_GAZEBO_RESOURCE_PATH',
              value=[pkg_panda_description]
    ```

3. Configure the controller to start it in an active state using ExecuteProcess in the launch file:

    ```
    load_position_controller = ExecuteProcess(
            cmd=['ros2', 'control', 'load_controller', '--set-state',
    'active', 'arm_controller'], output='screen')
    ```

4. Now everything is ready to start the Gazebo simulation. Let's compile the workspace, source it, and launch the simulator:

```
$ colcon build --symlink-install
$ source install/setup.bash
$ ros2 launch panda_description panda_gazebo.launch.py
```

After Gazebo starts, the simulation scene will appear as shown in *Figure 9.1*. In this example, the initial value of the joints set in the ros2 control tag is the following: [0.0, -0.78, 0.0, -2.35, 0.0, 1.57, 0.78].

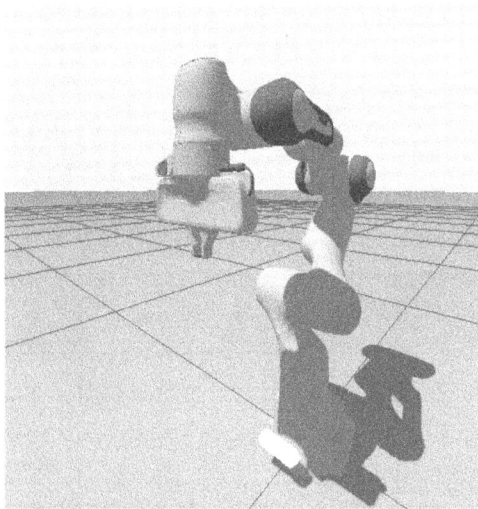

Figure 9.1: The Panda robot created in the simulation scene

Now that the robot is ready to work with MoveIt 2, we must create the proper configuration files. We can do this by using the *MoveIt Setup Assistant*, as discussed in the next section.

Configuring new Robots for MoveIt 2

Before starting the robot configuration, we must properly install MoveIt 2 in our system. In fact, MoveIt 2 is not installed with the full installation of ROS 2. So, to use the MoveIt 2 package, install it using the following:

```
$ sudo apt -get install ros-jazzy-moveit
```

MoveIt 2 is continuously updated, and sometimes the version available in the Ubuntu repository may be older than the latest MoveIt release. If the repository version has any bugs, you may have to wait for the next repository update for them to be resolved. Therefore, it's often better to download and compile the latest MoveIt 2 version directly from the GitHub repository. Use the following commands to do so. First, move into the source directory of the ROS 2 workspace and download MoveIt 2:

```
cd ros2_ws/src
git clone https://github.com/moveit/moveit2.git
```

Then, install the dependencies. The next commands will download new packages in your workspace:

```
for repo in moveit2/moveit2.repos $(f="moveit2/moveit2_$ROS_DISTRO.repos";
test -r $f && echo $f); do vcs import < "$repo"; done
rosdep install -r --from-paths . --ignore-src --rosdistro $ROS_DISTRO -y
```

Finally, compile the workspace:

```
colcon build --event-handlers desktop_notification- status- --cmake-args
-DCMAKE_BUILD_TYPE=Release
```

Notice that the compilation could fully occupy the whole CPU, making your PC stuck. For this reason, we can fix the number of parallel threads started during the compilation using the `--parallel-workers NUMBER` option:

```
colcon build --event-handlers desktop_notification- status- --cmake-args
-DCMAKE_BUILD_TYPE=Release --parallel-workers 1
```

After installing MoveIt 2, we are now ready to configure the Panda robot discussed in the previous section to work with it and implement ROS 2 nodes or configure new robots. To configure new robots, we can use the **MoveIt Setup Assistant** tool. It is a graphical interface designed to configure any robot for MoveIt 2. This tool generates essential files, including the *SRDF*, configuration files, launch files, and scripts, based on the robot's URDF model and our configuration. To launch the MoveIt Setup Assistant, use this command:

```
$ ros2 launch moveit_setup_assistant setup_assistant.launch.py
```

This command opens a window with two options: **Create New MoveIt Configuration Package** and **Edit Existing MoveIt Configuration Package**, as shown in *Figure 9.2*. Since we're creating a new package, select the first option. If you already have a MoveIt package, choose the second option. Next, click on **Create New MoveIt Configuration Package**, and use the browse button to locate and select the URDF file. Navigate to `panda_description/urdf/panda.urdf.xacro`, select it, and then click **Load** to import the *URDF* file.

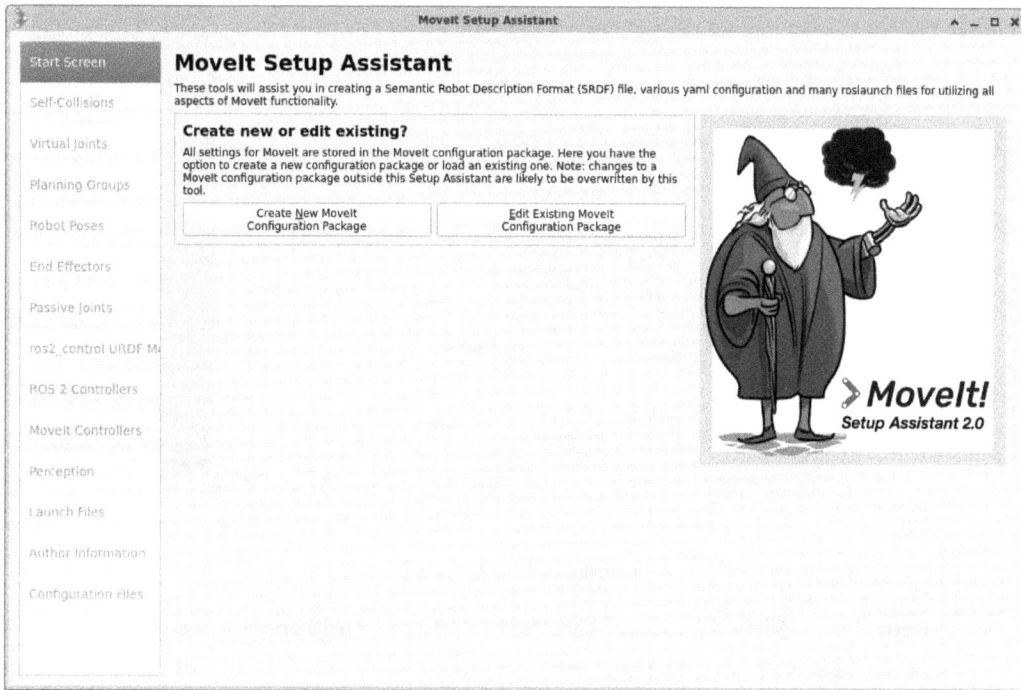

Figure 9.2: Regenerating the Self-Collision matrix

You can now navigate through the panels to configure your robot:

- **Self-Collisions**: MoveIt optimizes collision checking by categorizing robot links as always, never, or sometimes in collision, and disabling pairs prone to collisions. The **Self-Collisions** window lets you adjust sampling density, balancing computation, and collision detection, with a default of 10,000 samples.

Clicking **Regenerate Default Collision Matrix** updates the list of disabled link pairs. This panel is shown in *Figure 9.3*:

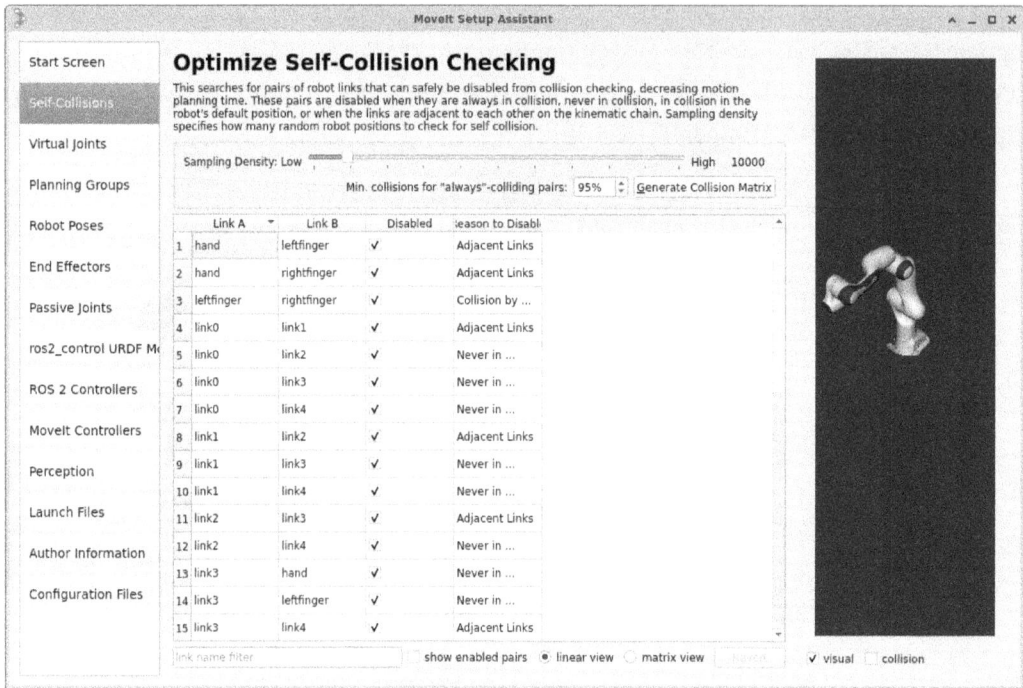

Figure 9.3: MoveIt 2 Setup Assistant

- **Virtual joints**: Virtual joints connect the robot to the world and are necessary when the robot's base position isn't fixed. For static robots that don't move, virtual joints aren't required. However, if a robot arm is mounted on a mobile base, a virtual joint should be defined relative to the odometry frame.

- **Planning groups**: To create a planning group for a robotic arm, navigate to the **Planning Groups** tab and click **Add Group**. Planning groups represent a fundamental element of MoveIt, grouping joints and links of the robot model to define a subset of the robot for which motion planning should be performed. For example, in a robot with multiple arms, each arm might be a separate planning group.

To add a new planning group, in the window that opens (*Figure 9.4*, left), name the group arm and set **Kinematic Solver** to kdl_kinematics_plugin/KDLKinematicsPlugin. Leave the other parameters at their default values. You can add elements to the group by specifying joints, links, or a kinematic chain. For the arm group, add a kinematic chain from base_link to grasping_frame.

Once created, the planning group will appear in the list (*Figure 9.4*, right).

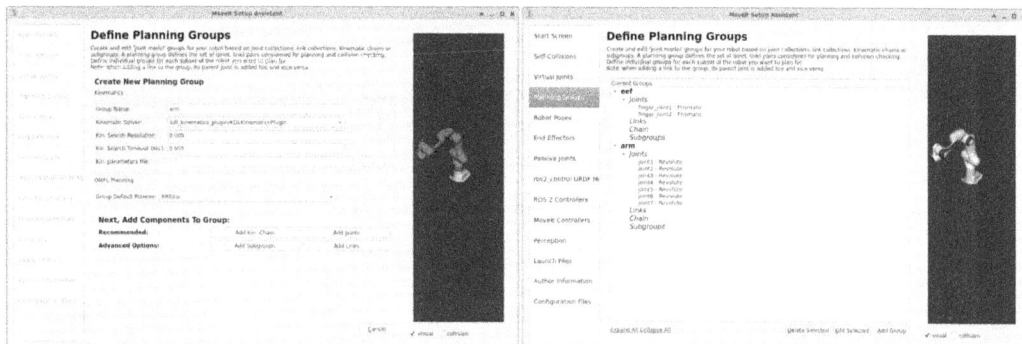

Figure 9.4: MoveIt 2 planning group

- **Robot poses**: Here, you can define fixed poses for the robot, such as home or pick/place positions. These fixed poses, or group states, can be directly used in MoveIt APIs, simplifying tasks such as pick/place and grasping operations by allowing the robot to switch to these positions easily. Notice that inserting such poses could be not trivial since they must be specified by including the joint values.

- **End Effectors**: In this step, name the robot's end effector and assign it to the end-effector group, parent link, and parent group. For our gripper used in pick and place operations, click **Add End Effector**, name it eef, and set the planning group to eef, and the parent link to hand.

- **Passive joints**: In this step, specify the passive joints in the robot. Passive joints are those without actuators and are used to connect different parts of the robot. The Panda robot doesn't have passive joints.

- **ros2_control and ROS 2 Controllers**: This panel guides you to modify the *URDF* of the robot to integrate the robot controllers. However, we already discussed these steps in the previous section, so you can jump these steps.

- **Author Information**: The name and contact information of the developer configuring the robot are added in this tab. In this way, you can distribute your robot configuration package to the ROS 2 community.

- **Perception**: in this tab, we can configure the robot with sensor information to perceive the obstacles of the environment, such as depth sensors or point cloud data. We will discuss how to configure this panel later.

- **Configuration files:** In this final step, you will generate the configuration files needed for MoveIt, as shown in *Figure 9.5*. Click the **Browse** button to choose a folder where the configuration package will be saved. The files will be created in a folder named `panda_moveit_config`. Click **Generate Package** to create a ROS 2 package containing the configuration files that will be placed in the selected folder. Once the process is complete, you can click **Exit Setup Assistant** to close the tool. Of course, it is important to have the package in the ROS 2 workspace, so export it directly to the correct location.

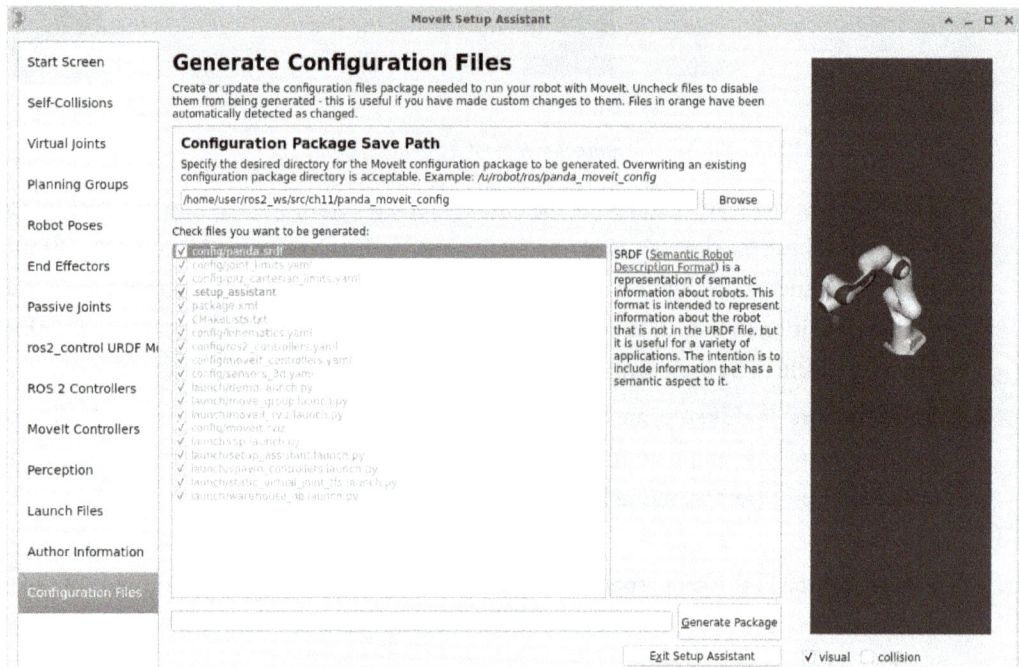

Figure 9.5: Generating a MoveIt configuration package

Now, we have everything needed to run MoveIt to plan and execute robot trajectories. First, we will test the generated file using RViz2 before implementing ROS 2 nodes using MoveIt 2 APIs.

Testing MoveIt 2 using Rviz2

MoveIt 2 provides a plugin for RViz2, which can be used to monitor the robot's state and the environment and allows users to easily make new planning requests and preview the planned motions. After generating the configuration files of the robot to interface it with MoveIt, we can use this plugin to test the robot's motion. First, start the simulation to activate the controllers:

```
ros2 launch panda_description panda_gazebo.launch.py
```

Then, use the demo launch file contained in the `panda_moveit_config` package:

```
ros2 launch panda_moveit_config demo.launch.py
```

Set the simulation time to `true`:

```
ros2 param set /move_group use_sim_time true
```

If everything works fine, we will see the following screen of RViz2 being loaded with the **Motion-Planning** plugin provided by MoveIt 2, as shown in *Figure 9.6*. Here, you have a planning panel (bottom left) that can be used to set up the motion planning problem.

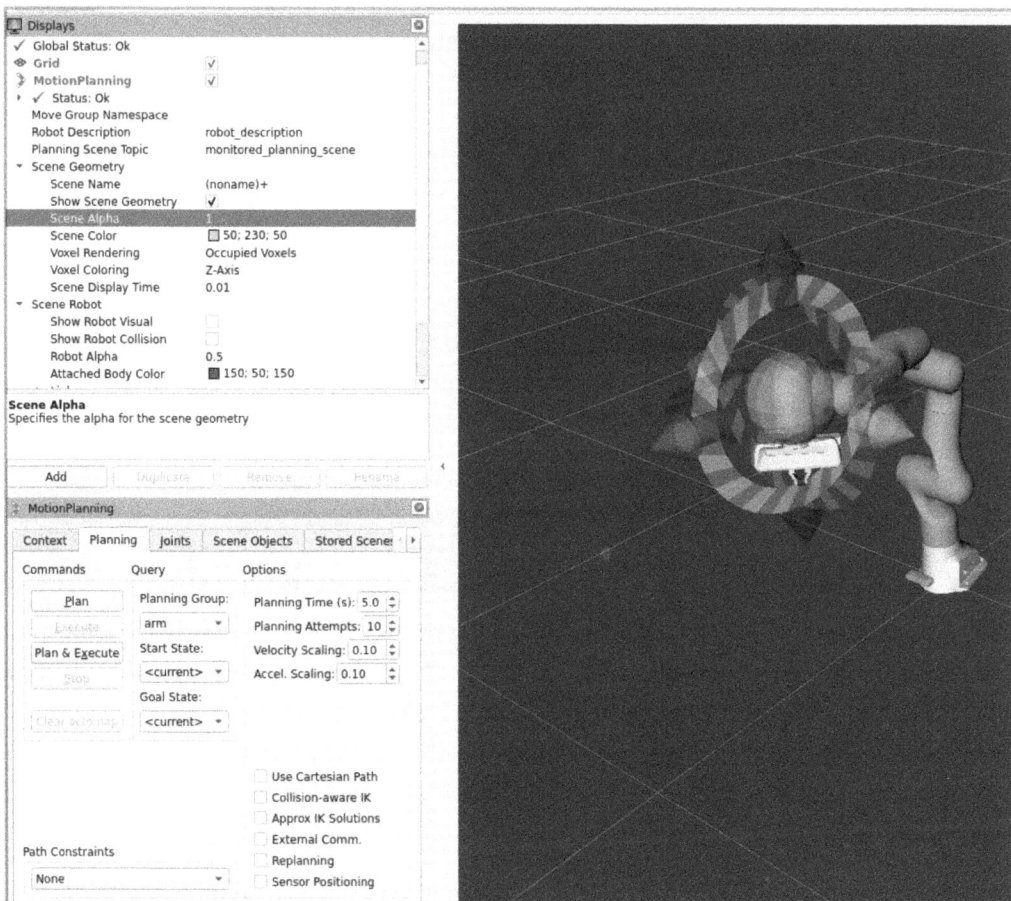

Figure 9.6: Generating a MoveIt configuration package

You can set the robot's start and goal states in the **Query** panel. After setting these states, use the **Plan** button to calculate a path from the start to the goal. If planning is successful, you can execute the path. By default, execution occurs on emulated, fake controllers for visualization in RViz2. To adjust the start and goal positions of the robot's end effector, use the interactive marker attached to the arm gripper. You can translate and rotate this marker. If a valid plan is found, the arm will be highlighted in orange. If the arm does not move or reach the marker's position, it indicates that no **inverse kinematics (IK)** solution exists for that pose. This might be due to insufficient **degrees of freedom (DOF)** or a collision between links.

Moving the robot using RViz2 is useful to quickly test the MoveIt 2 configuration files. However, to implement an autonomous robotic program, we must incorporate MoveIt system calls into ROS 2 nodes, as discussed in the next section.

Motion planning using the move_group ROS 2 wrapper

In this section, we will see how to program the robot's motion using the move_group wrapper implemented in C++. The first step is to create another ROS package that has the MoveIt packages as dependencies. You can get an existing panda_moveit_control package from the code provided with this book, or you can download it from the following repository: https://github.com/PacktPublishing/Mastering-ROS-2/tree/main/Chapter09.

To create the package from scratch instead, use the following command:

```
ros2 pkg create panda_moveit_control --dependencies moveit_ros_planning_
interface rclcpp
```

In the first example, we will use the move group wrapper to execute a motion in the joint space. This means the desired robot configuration is set, specifying the value of each single joint of the robot. This motion has the advantage of being simpler to implement and more computationally efficient because it directly plans in the robot's joint space. However, it has the downside of not providing direct control over the robot's path in Cartesian space, which can result in unexpected or inefficient movements.

To implement joint space motion control, the following steps must be taken.

Step 1 – Implementing the ROS 2 node

Let's add new source code to the src folder of the panda_moveit_control package (joint_space_planning.cpp). The main code blocks contained in this node are explained in the following:

1. Let's start by including the header files. Here, we just include the interface with move_group:

    ```
    #include <moveit/move_group_interface/move_group_interface.h>
    ```

2. In the main function, after initializing the ROS 2 library, a new ROS 2 node is declared:

    ```
    rclcpp::init(argc, argv);
    moveit::planning_interface::MoveGroupInterface::Plan my_plan;
    auto node = rclcpp::Node::make_shared("JointSpacePlanning");
    ```

3. To control the robot, the planning module must be initialized, thanks to the MoveGroupInterface object. Then, we hardcode a set of desired values for the robot joints:

    ```
    moveit::planning_interface::MoveGroupInterface move_group(node,
    "arm");
    std::vector<double> des_joint_pos = {0.0, 0.0, 0.0, -0.35, 0.0,
    1.57, 0.78};
    ```

4. The plan structure is used to store the result of a planning request:

    ```
    moveit::planning_interface::MoveGroupInterface::Plan my_plan;
    ```

5. Then, we will set the target of the joint using the desired one. After it's set, we can also check whether the desired values violate the joint limits:

    ```
    bool within_bounds = move_group.setJointValueTarget( des_joint_pos)
    ```

6. Finally, we call the planner to compute the plan. Note that we are just planning, not asking move_group to move the robot. We can additionally check whether the planning phase has succeeded or not:

    ```
    bool success = (move_group.plan(my_plan) ==
    moveit::core::MoveItErrorCode::SUCCESS);
    ```

7. After generating the plan, if the planning phase was completed successfully, we can move the robot by using the move function. Note that this is a blocking function released only after the robot motion is completed:

    ```
    If (success) move_group.move();
    ```

Step 2 – Creating the launch file

A common way to share the MoveIt configuration file with the ROS 2 node is by using launch files. Let's do it to test the joint space planning program:

1. Create a launch file, called `joint_space_planning.launch.py`, place it into the launch directory of the `panda_moveit_control` node, and add the following content to it. Here, the `moveit_config_utils` module is imported to load the configuration file:

    ```
    from moveit_configs_utils import MoveItConfigsBuilder
    ```

2. The configuration files related to the Panda robot are stored in the `moveit_config` variable:

    ```
    def generate_launch_description():
        moveit_config = MoveItConfigsBuilder("panda").to_moveit_configs()
    ```

3. The definition of the `joint_space_planning` node is completed with some parameters: the ones related to the moveit configuration and `use_sim_time` parameter set to True. This last parameter is fundamental to retrieving the state of the robot using the ROS 2 API:

    ```
    joint_planning_node = Node( package="panda_moveit_control",
    executable="joint_space_planning", output="screen",
    parameters=[ {"use_sim_time": True},
    moveit_config.robot_description,
    moveit_config.robot_description_semantic,
    moveit_config.robot_description_kinematics,])
    ```

Step 3 – Filling the CMakeFile.txt

In this step, we must simply install the source and configuration files, as shown in the following:

```
add_executable( joint_space_planning src/joint_space_planning.cpp )
ament_target_dependencies(joint_space_planning rclcpp std_msgs moveit_ros_
planning_interface)
install(DIRECTORY launch DESTINATION share/${PROJECT_NAME})
install(TARGETS joint_space_planning RUNTIME DESTINATION lib/${PROJECT_
NAME} )
```

Step 4 – Compiling and executing the planning node

A sequence of commands is used to compile and start the simulation and MoveIt 2. Optionally, you can also open Rviz2 to check the robot's state:

1. Let's start by compiling the workspace:

```
$ colcon build --symlink-install
$ source install/setup.bash
```

2. Start the Gazebo simulation:

```
$ ros2 launch panda_description panda_gazebo.launch.py
```

3. Start MoveIt 2:

```
$ ros2 launch panda_moveit_config move_group.launch.py
```

4. Set the use_sim_time variable to true for the move_group node. Without this, the MoveIt planning system will not be able to retrieve the information shared via the ROS 2 system:

```
$ ros2 param set move_group use_sim_time true
```

5. Start the joint space planning node:

```
$ ros2 launch panda_moveit_control joint_space_planning.launch.py
```

After executing this command, the robot is actuated and reaches the configuration specified by the joint commands (as depicted in *Figure 9.7*). Let's now discuss another example in which the motion trajectory is in the Cartesian space.

Cartesian space planning

Cartesian space planning provides precise control over a robot's path, ensuring the end-effector follows a specific trajectory. This results in smoother motion for the robot end effector and easier obstacle avoidance. However, it is more complex and computationally demanding due to the need for inverse kinematics to convert Cartesian paths into joint movements. MoveIt 2's move group wrapper can facilitate this type of motion.

Let's discuss the main elements of the `cartesian_space_planning.cpp` code contained in the `panda_moveit_control` package:

1. In this example, we perform the planning and execution phase in a class function, to additionally show the object-oriented formulation. Let's define the main class. Apart from the class functions, a ROS 2 node pointer object is defined:

```cpp
class CartesianPlanning : public rclcpp::Node {
public:
CartesianPlanning() : Node("cartesian_planning") {}
        void run();
        void plan();
private:
        rclcpp::Node::SharedPtr _node;
```

2. In the `run` and `main` functions, we set all the variables needed to start the planning function. The latter is started as a separate thread:

```cpp
void CartesianPlanning::run() {
    auto node = rclcpp::Node::make_shared("CartesianPlan");
    _node = node;
    std::thread cartesian_plan_t( &CartesianPlanning::plan, this);
    rclcpp::spin(node);
}

int main(int argc, char * argv[]) {
  rclcpp::init(argc, argv);
  CartesianPlanning cp;
  cp.run();
  return 0:}
```

3. The desired path will be a displacement from the current position: 20 cm down, 20 cm on the left, and 20 cm to the top, left, and back. For this reason, the first thing is to retrieve the current pose of the planning frame. We can use the `tf` system to retrieve this information:

```cpp
bool tf_found = false;
geometry_msgs::msg::TransformStamped t;
  auto tf_buffer {std::make_unique<tf2_ros::Buffer>(this->get_
clock())};
```

```
auto tf_listener { std::make_shared<tf2_ros::TransformListener>(*tf_
buffer)};
```

4. The planning interface is initialized and used to retrieve the information about the planning frame (the base frame of the robot) and the end effector frame of the robot that we want to control:

```
moveit::planning_interface::MoveGroupInterface move_group(_node,
"arm");
std::string fromFrameRel = move_group.getPlanningFrame();
std::string toFrameRel = move_group.getEndEffectorLink();
```

5. Then we search for the pose of the end effector frame with respect to the grasping frame. We iterate this process until the tf has been found:

```
t = tf_buffer->lookupTransform(fromFrameRel, toFrameRel,
tf2::TimePointZero);
tf_found = true;
```

6. After retrieving the current pose, we save it into Pose data. Then, we can add slight displacement to define the desired motion:

```
geometry_msgs::msg::Pose target_pose;
std::vector<geometry_msgs::msg::Pose> waypoints;
target_pose.orientation.w = t.transform.rotation.w; target_pose.
orientation.x = t.transform.rotation.x; target_pose.orientation.y =
t.transform.rotation.y;
target_pose.orientation.z = t.transform.rotation.z; target_pose.
position.x = t.transform.translation.x; target_pose.position.y =
t.transform.translation.y;
target_pose.position.z = t.transform.translation.z;
waypoints.push_back(target_pose);
target_pose.position.z -= 0.2;
waypoints.push_back(target_pose);
target_pose.position.y -= 0.2;
waypoints.push_back(target_pose);
target_pose.position.z += 0.2;
target_pose.position.y += 0.2;
target_pose.position.x -= 0.2;
waypoints.push_back(target_pose);
```

7. We can specify the interpolation of the generated Cartesian path. In this case, we chose 1 cm. In addition, we can specify the jump threshold, which limits the maximum distance or jump in joint positions between two consecutive trajectory points. In this example, we are disabling it by setting it to 0. Notice that disabling this parameter on the real system could be dangerous, since it could generate large, unpredictable motions for the redundant joints (redundant joints in robotics mean a robot has more joints than necessary for a task, offering extra flexibility for movement and obstacle avoidance). To plan the trajectory, the `computeCartesianPath` function is used. This function returns a value between 0.0 and 1.0 to indicate the fraction of the path completed based on waypoints, or -1.0 if there's an error:

```
moveit_msgs::msg::RobotTrajectory traj;
const double jump_th= 0.0;
const double step = 0.01;
double fraction = move_group.computeCartesianPath(waypoints, step,
jump_th, traj);
```

8. Finally, we can execute the planned trajectory if the Cartesian path has been planned correctly. In particular, the `computeCartesianPath` trajectory returns three kinds of value:

    *   0.0 to 1.0 or -1: A value of 1.0 means the entire Cartesian path (all waypoints) was successfully planned.
    *   0.0 to 1.0: A value between 0.0 and 1.0 indicates partial success (only a fraction of the waypoints were included in the trajectory).
    *   -1: Finally, a value of -1 indicates a failure to plan any part of the trajectory.

In this example, we execute the planned trajectory at least for 80% of its path. You can look at the Gazebo simulation to see the resultant planned motion of the robot:

```
if( fraction > 0.8 )
move_group.execute(traj);
else
RCLCPP_ERROR(rclcpp::get_logger("moveit_executor"), "Trajectory
calculation failed");
```

After completing the source code of this node, you should edit `CMakeLists.txt` and create a convenient launch file, as already done in the previous example. Finally, to run this node, follow the same commands as shown in the *Step 4 – Compiling and executing the planning node* section. You can now compare the movements done in this example with respect to the joint space motion.

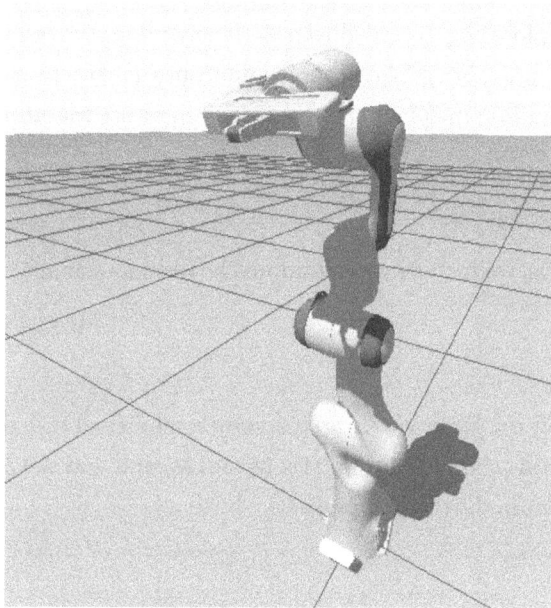

Figure 9.7: Final pose of the joint space planning motion

To start this demo, use the following commands:

```
ros2 launch panda_description panda_gazebo.launch.py
ros2 launch panda_moveit_config move_group.launch.py
ros2 param set move_group use_sim_time true
ros2 launch panda_moveit_control cartesian_space_planning.launch.py
```

Building on the previous example, you can instruct the robot to reach new Cartesian points. However, in this case, MoveIt planned the path in an entirely obstacle-free environment. In the next section, we will discuss how to set up the environment to include obstacles.

Planning with obstacles

In the previous examples, the robot could move freely without considering obstacles, and the motion planner only needed to account for potential self-collisions. However, this is not realistic, as robots typically operate in environments containing objects that might collide with the robot. In this section, we'll explore how to add objects to the planning scene that the robot must avoid or interact with. For instance, in a grasping application, once an object is grasped, it becomes part of the manipulator, requiring the planner to consider it in future trajectories.

Let's discuss the content of the planning_with_obstacles.cpp source file contained in the panda_moveit_control package:

1. In this source file, we include two additional headers to manage collision objects:

    ```
    #include <moveit_msgs/msg/attached_collision_object.hpp>
    #include <moveit_msgs/msg/collision_object.hpp>
    ```

2. Let's now modify the previous example, adding some elements to the CartesianPlanning class. Rename this class PlanningWithObstacles, and add the method that is used to place two objects in the planning scene:

    ```
    void PlanningWithObstacles::setup_world() {
    moveit::planning_interface::PlanningSceneInterface planning_scene_
    interface;
    ```

3. To add an element in the scene, we must define a CollisionObject. It has different proprieties, such as the shape, ID, name, and the position where it falls in the scene:

    ```
    moveit_msgs::msg::CollisionObject obstacle;
    obstacle.header.frame_id = _move_group-
    >getPlanningFrame();
    obstacle.id = "table";
    shape_msgs::msg::SolidPrimitive primitive;
    primitive.type = primitive.BOX;
    primitive.dimensions.resize(3);
    primitive.dimensions[primitive.BOX_X] = 0.1;
    primitive.dimensions[primitive.BOX_Y] = 1.5;
    primitive.dimensions[primitive.BOX_Z] = 0.3;
    ```

```
geometry_msgs::msg::Pose bp;
bp.orientation.w = 1.0;
bp.position.x = 0.48;
bp.position.y = 0.0;
bp.position.z = 0.25;
obstacle.primitives.push_back(primitive);
obstacle.primitive_poses.push_back(bp);
obstacle.operation = obstacle.ADD;
```

4. The planning scene interface is used to put the object into the environment. This object is now recognized as an obstacle for each new trajectory planning task. However, we want to do something more: add an object to the robot end effector of the robot:

    ```
    planning_scene_interface.applyCollisionObject (obstacle);
    ```

5. Let's define a new object that will be grasped by the robot. As in the previous case, we define a new object. However, after defining all its properties (check the full source code in the GitHub book repository), we place the object into the environment. Later, we use the move_group object to attach the object to some frames of the robot:

    ```
    moveit_msgs::msg::CollisionObject grasping_object;
    planning_scene_interface.applyCollisionObject(grasping_object);
    std::vector<std::string> connection_links;
    connection_links.push_back("panda_rightfinger");
    connection_links.push_back("panda_leftfinger");     _move_group-
    >attachObject(grasping_object.id, "hand", connection_links);
    ```

6. Of course, these objects don't react to any physical force, since they are not placed in the simulation but only in the planning scene. For this reason, it is not important where we place them – they can also float into the environment. After calling the setup_world function, we can continue to plan the trajectory, checking that the robot is able to avoid obstacles:

    ```
    std::string fromFrameRel = _move_group->getPlanningFrame().c_str();
    std::string toFrameRel =   _move_group-
    >getEndEffectorLink().c_str();
    setup_world();
    while ( !tf_found ) {
    //Get the Tf
    }
    ```

```
    geometry_msgs::msg::Pose target_pose;
    std::vector<geometry_msgs::msg::Pose> waypoints;
    target_pose.orientation.w = t.transform.rotation.w; target_pose.
orientation.x = t.transform.rotation.x; target_pose.orientation.y =
t.transform.rotation.y;
    target_pose.orientation.z = t.transform.rotation.z; target_pose.
position.x = t.transform.translation.x; target_pose.position.y =
t.transform.translation.y;
    target_pose.position.z = t.transform.translation.z;
    target_pose.position.x += 0.3;
    _move_group->setPoseTarget(target_pose);
    moveit::planning_interface::MoveGroupInterface::Plan my_plan;
    bool success = (_move_group->plan(my_plan) ==
moveit::core::MoveItErrorCode::SUCCESS);
    _move_group->move();
```

7. One last modification applied to this class is that we add the move_group objects to the class member of the PlanningWithObstacles class. This is declared as follows:

```
    moveit::planning_interface::MoveGroupInterface *_move_group;
```

It is initialized in the plan function:

```
    _move_group = new moveit::planning_interface::MoveGroupInterface(_
    node, "arm");
```

In this way, we can use this object in the different functions of our program, both in the plan function and in setup_world. As usual, prepare the package to install the executable and the launch file. Then you can start the node execution, monitoring what is happening from the MoveIt plugin for RViz2. The planning scene during the task execution is shown in *Figure 9.8*, where the robot is overcoming the obstacle, bringing with it the grasped object.

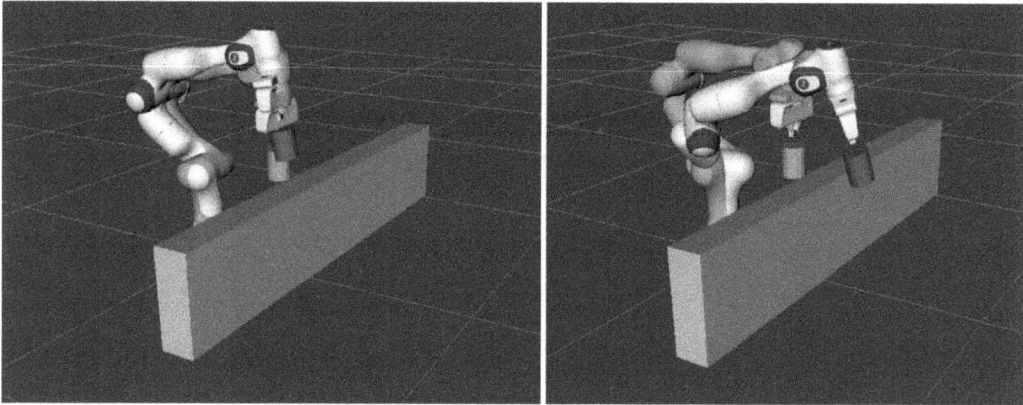

Figure 9.8: Panda robot avoiding obstacles with a grasped object

To start this demo, you must use the following commands. First, open RViz2 to visualize the scene and the robot. Add the `MotionPlanning` plugin using the **Add** button of the RViz2 user interface:

```
rviz2
```

Then, start the simulator and MoveIt using the following commands on different terminals:

```
ros2 launch panda_description panda_gazebo.launch.py
ros2 launch panda_moveit_config move_group.launch.py
ros2 param set move_group use_sim_time true
ros2 launch panda_moveit_control planning_with_obstacles.launch.py
```

We have learned how to add obstacles with known sizes and specific positions. However, in real-world applications, obstacles are usually detected using the robot's sensors, such as cameras or depth sensors. MoveIt 2 allows you to configure sensors that detect obstacles and create an obstacle map, enabling the robot to plan safe paths.

Now, let's explore how to add new sensors to our MoveIt-enabled robot.

Detecting obstacles using a depth sensor

Previously, we manually added obstacles to the virtual environment using the MoveIt 2 wrapper and planning scene. This works well when the robot's workspace is predefined with a 3D mesh. However, in dynamic environments, sensors are needed to detect obstacles in real time. In this section, we'll add a depth sensor to the robot model and configure MoveIt 2 to automatically create a 3D shape of the surroundings.

A depth sensor provides 3D point cloud data of the area around the robot. We'll begin by modifying the panda_arm.xacro file to include this sensor:

1. The sensor exists in the Gazebo simulator and is associated with a particular link – in our case, the first link of the robot. We are going to place the sensor at the base of the robot. The type of the sensor is depth_camera:

```
<gazebo reference="${prefix}${link0_name}">
        <sensor name='d435_depth' type='depth_camera'>
```

2. Some parameters can be added to the sensor, such as the field of view, the resolution, and similar:

```
<camera name='d435'>
...
        </camera>
```

3. To elaborate the data taken from the environment, a specific plugin is used – the libgz-sim-sensors-system.so plugin:

```
<plugin filename="libgz-sim-sensors-system.so"
name="gz::sim::systems::Sensors">
              <render_engine>ogre</render_engine>
        </plugin>
```

4. To also create the whole structure of the sensor, we use the sensor_d435 macro of the realsense2_description package. For this reason, first include the file containing the macro and then instantiate the sensor macro:

```
<xacro:include filename="$(find realsense2_description)/urdf/_d435.
urdf.xacro" />
<xacro:sensor_d435 parent="${prefix}${link0_name}" use_nominal_
extrinsics="$(arg use_nominal_extrinsics)" add_plug="$(arg add_
plug)" use_mesh="$(arg use_mesh)">
<origin xyz="0.1 0.0 0.05" rpy="0 0.0 0" />
</xacro:sensor_d435>
```

5.   As usual, we must use the ROS-Gazebo bridge to share the point cloud data over the ROS 2
     network. For this reason, in the `panda_gazebo_with_obstacles.launch` file, we add two
     additional nodes, one to map the point cloud from Gazebo to ROS 2 and another one to
     create a static TF to link the sensor to the kinematic robotic structure:

```
depth_camera_bridge = Node(package='ros_gz_bridge',
executable='parameter_bridge', name = 'depth_camera_bridge',
output='screen',
arguments =
['/depth_camera' + '@sensor_msgs/msg/Image' +      '[ignition.msgs.
Image',
 '/depth_camera/points' + '@sensor_msgs/msg/PointCloud2' +
 '[ignition.msgs.PointCloudPacked'],)
depth_cam_data2cam_link_tf = Node(package='tf2_ros',
executable='static_transform_publisher', name='cam3Tolink',
output='log', arguments=['0.0', '0.0', '0.0', '0.0', '0.0', '0.0',
 'camera_link', 'panda/link0/d435_depth'])
```

The following figure shows the panel of the MoveIt 2 Setup Assistant to set up the 3D vision.

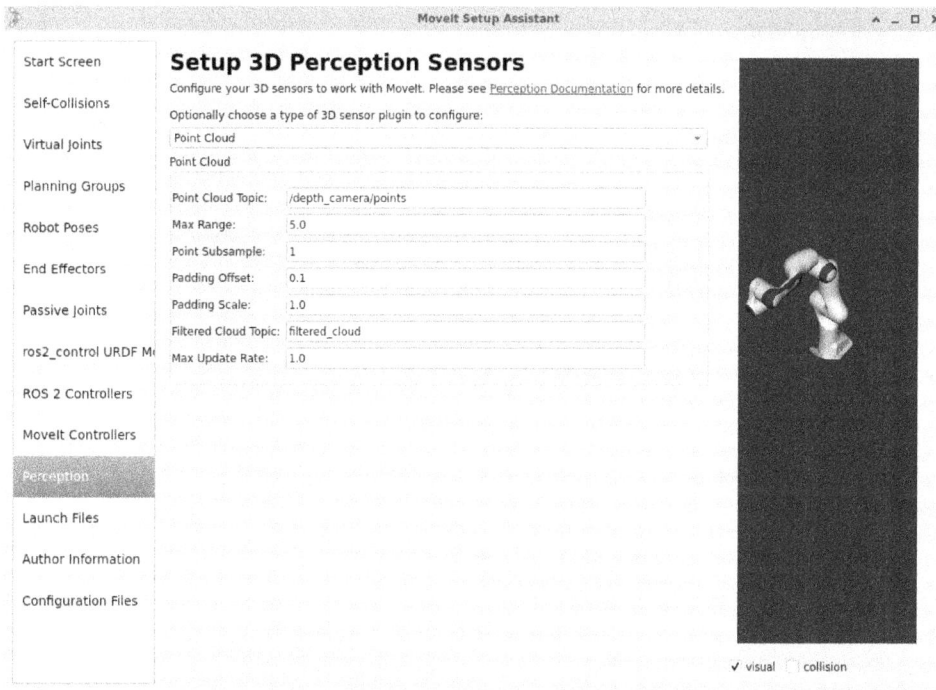

Figure 9.9: Panda robot avoiding obstacles with a grasped object

6. Now, even if the ROS 2 system streams data via topics, we must modify the MoveIt 2 configuration files to directly allow their integration into the planning scene. Launch the MoveIt Setup Assistant again with the following command:

```
$ ros2 launch moveit_setup_assistant setup_assistant.launch
```

7. This time, you must choose just to edit an already configured MoveIt package, selecting the `panda_moveit_config` package. After selecting the package, use the **Load Files** button to retrieve the robot configuration.

8. After the files are loaded, navigate to the **Perception** button and configure it as shown in *Figure 9.9*. Basically, here, you must select the type of data (point cloud), and information about the data to elaborate. For example, in this case, we selected the `/depth_camera/points` topic (that is where the sensor streams the data) and other parameters to better elaborate the points.

9. To save the modifications and update the configuration file, navigate through the **Configuration Files** tab, to export the new version of the MoveIt 2 package (as shown in *Figure 9.5*). Now, everything is ready to detect the obstacles of the environment. Before testing our new perception system, we must add an obstacle to the simulation scene. To do this, a custom model world is placed in the world directory of the `panda_description` package (`planning_world.sdf`).

    1. Here, a rectangular object is placed on the ground as shown in *Figure 9.10*. To load this world when the simulation starts, we can use the `panda_gazebo_with_obstacle.launch.py` file. This file is the same as the `panda_gazebo.launch.py` launch file except for the loading of a custom world file. First, we retrieve the path of the world file:

        ```
        sdf_file_path = os.path.join(FindPackageShare('panda_
        description').find('panda_description'), 'world', 'planning_
        world.sdf' )
        ```

    2. Then, the Gazebo launch file is imported, passing the world path as an argument:

        ```
        ignition_gazebo_node = IncludeLaunchDescription(
            PythonLaunchDescriptionSource(
        PathJoinSubstitution(FindPackageShare('ros_gz_sim'),
        'launch', 'gz_sim.launch.py' ])),
            launch_arguments={'gz_args': f'-r -v 4 {sdf_file_
        path}'}.items())
        ```

10. Now, start the simulation using the `panda_gazebo_with_obstacles.launch.py` file. In RViz2 with the MoveIt plugin, you will see cubes forming around the obstacles (*Figure 9.10*). These cubes represent **OctoMap**, a 3D mapping framework that efficiently models occupied, free, and unknown spaces using an octree structure. OctoMap is widely used in robotics for environment modeling and obstacle avoidance, typically generated from point cloud data, which we will explore further in the next chapter.

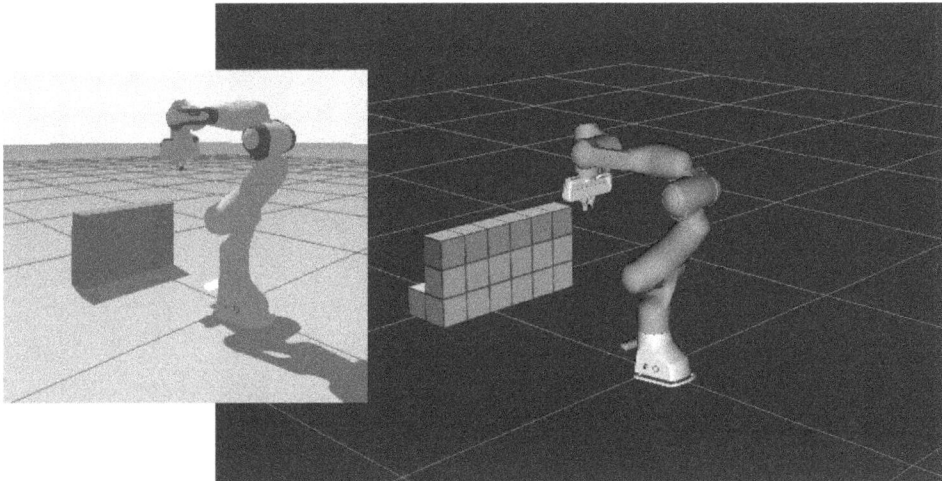

Figure 9.10: OctoMap generated by MoveIt 2 using the point cloud data

Once the simulation and MoveIt 2's move_group are running, you can begin testing how the robot avoids obstacles, such as how it handles virtual objects in the planning scene. Another method for obstacle avoidance in MoveIt involves processing point cloud data to generate collision objects and adding them to the planning scene. This approach can improve planning performance.

Summary

In this chapter, we explored the different capabilities of MoveIt 2, a motion planning framework integrated with ROS 2 that allows developers to implement manipulation operations with industrial arms. MoveIt 2 already supports different models of popular robots, however, new robots can be configured to properly work with it thanks to an intuitive setup assistant that drives the user to create all the necessary configuration files to plan and execute desired motion trajectories.

We started the chapter by discussing the main concepts of MoveIt 2 and then showed how to configure a new simulated robot to properly work with it. Finally, we showed how to create C++ ROS 2 nodes to implement plans and execute obstacle-free motion trajectories, which is the main usage of industrial manipulators.

In the next chapter, we will move on to how to use ROS 2 to implement perception algorithms, implement image elaboration algorithms, and work with 3D point cloud data.

10

Working with ROS 2 and Perception Stack

Robots interact with the environment thanks to their sensors. Without sensors, robots are blind machines unable to react to the world's stimuli and can only perform cyclic motions. However, adding sensors to a robot also means the necessity to implement proper algorithms to process the sensor data. One of the most common sensor types used in robotics is visual sensors, like cameras. In this chapter, we will discuss how to interface standard cameras with our laptops and elaborate images using **Open Computer Vision** (**OpenCV**), a popular open-source library to process video streams. In addition, we will see the main limitations of cameras, that is, the missing information about the depth. For this reason, we will discuss another type of sensor: depth sensors and the processing of their data (point cloud data). Apart from these libraries that offer functionalities to elaborate raw image and spatial data, we will discuss artificial intelligence approaches to solve typical robotics problems associated with computer vision and the usage of the **Graphics Processing Unit** (**GPU**).

As such, we will cover the following main topics in the chapter:

- Integrating robotics and computer vision
- Getting started with depth sensors
- Using NVIDIA ISAAC ROS to speed up image processing

Technical requirements

To follow this chapter, it is best to have a computer with *Ubuntu 24.04 LTS* installed or any other Ubuntu version. Additionally, to fully execute all the examples of this chapter, a standard *USB camera* and an *Intel depth sensor* are required. Finally, in the last part of the book, we will use the *NVIDIA ISAAC ROS* framework, which requires an *NVIDIA CUDA-enabled graphical card* to be installed.

The reference materials for this chapter can be found in the `Chapter10` folder of the following GitHub repository: `https://github.com/PacktPublishing/Mastering-ROS-2-for-Robotics-Programming/tree/main/Chapter10`.

Integrating robotics and computer vision

Robotics and **computer vision** are closely connected fields, as robots rely on computer vision to complete a variety of tasks. The data from computer vision algorithms helps robots with tasks such as:

- **Object recognition**: Identifying and classifying objects, either through semantic classification or 3D shape matching.
- **Obstacle avoidance**: Enabling robots to detect and navigate around obstacles safely.

In simple terms, computer vision allows robots to interpret visual information, recognize objects, and understand their surroundings. Depending on the specific application, different processing techniques or vision sensors may be required. One of the most widely used software libraries for image processing on standard computers is **OpenCV**. OpenCV is an open-source library that offers a wide range of tools and algorithms for computer vision, machine learning, and image processing. It is highly versatile and can be used for tasks such as real-time image processing, object detection, face recognition, and 3D vision. OpenCV has evolved over the years to include many powerful features, including:

- **Image processing**: OpenCV offers various image transformations, such as filtering, resizing, blurring, edge detection, and thresholding.
- **Object detection and recognition**: It provides tools for detecting objects like faces, pedestrians, and patterns using methods like Haar cascades, **Histogram of Oriented Gradients** (**HOG**), and deep-learning-based models.
- **Video processing**: OpenCV can handle video frame processing in real time, making it suitable for applications like surveillance, video editing, and motion analysis.

- **Feature detection**: It includes algorithms like SIFT, SURF, ORB, and FAST for detecting keypoints and features in images, which are useful for tasks like object recognition and image stitching.

One reason standard cameras are popular in many applications is that robots can easily use any USB camera connected to their main computer. These cameras are widely available, affordable, and easy to set up. In contrast, industrial cameras offer more advanced features, such as the ability to adjust settings like frame rate and brightness, but they are more expensive and harder to integrate with ROS 2.

In this chapter, we'll start by integrating a standard USB camera with ROS 2. If you're using a laptop with a built-in camera, you can use that. Otherwise, any USB camera will work for the following example. Notice that, even if you don't have the sensors used in this chapter, you can simulate them using Gazebo and test the examples discussed in this chapter.

Integrating the camera with ROS 2

There are different ways to integrate camera sensors with ROS 2. One is to implement the low-level functions to grab data from a specific sensor using OpenCV libraries. Another way is to use the usb_cam package already present in the ROS 2 package repositories. Let's start with this latter approach:

1. In any case, whatever the chosen approach, the first thing to do is to retrieve the address of the camera device from the operating system. The list of video devices present in the system can be seen with the following command:

    ```
    $ ls /dev | grep video
    ```

    For example, if you have one or more cameras connected to your laptop, the output will be like this:

    ```
    Video0 video1 video2 video3
    ```

2. Among this list, to check which is the correct device, video streaming programs like *VLC* or *cheese* can be used. Let's install the usb_cam package:

    ```
    sudo apt-get install ros-jazzy-usb-cam
    ```

3. To start the camera, we must create a proper launch file. Let's create a package containing the launch file:

```
ros2 pkg create usb_cam_launcher
mkdir usb_cam_launcher/launch
touch usb_cam_launcher/launch/my_usb_cam.launch.py
```

The content of the launch file is described in the following:

1. At the start, the modules are imported:

```
from launch import LaunchDescription
from launch_ros.actions import Node
```

2. We need to start only one node, usb_cam_node_exe initialized with the proper parameters:

```
def generate_launch_description():
    return LaunchDescription([
        Node(
            package='usb_cam',
            executable='usb_cam_node_exe',
            name='usb_cam',
            output='screen',
```

3. As you can see, here we must insert the address of the video device associated with our camera. If we want to start the video device associated with the ID video2, the complete address is /dev/video2:

```
parameters=[
                {'video_device': '/dev/video2'},
                {'image_width': 1280},
                {'image_height': 720},
                {'pixel_format': 'yuyv'},
                {'camera_frame_id': 'usb_camera'}
        ],)])
```

4. To start this launch file, you must modify CMakeLists.txt to install the launch directory. After you have compiled and sourced the workspace, you can start the node with the following command:

```
ros2 launch usb_cam_launcher my_usb_cam.launch.py
```

5. Now you can check the list of topics active in your system with the $ ros2 topic list command. Mainly we are interested in two topics:

- /camera_info: This topic contains information about the intrinsic camera calibration, used to transform image pixels into 2D coordinates. We will learn how to calibrate and use this information later in this chapter.

- /image_raw: The topic containing the image.

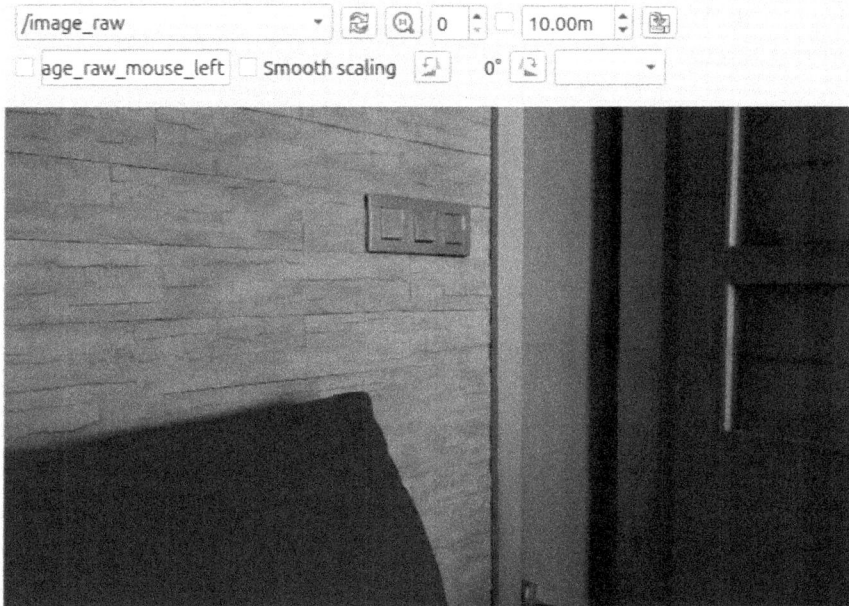

Figure 10.1: rqt_image_view showing the images taken from the USB camera

6. You can use the rqt_image_view program to display the image. If this program is not already installed, you can install it with the following command:

```
sudo apt-get install ros-jazzy-rqt-image-view
```

7. You can now use `rqt_image_view` with the following command. Later, you can see the image by selecting the desired topic on which the image is streamed (see *Figure 10.1*). To start rqt, you can use the following command:

```
ros2 run rqt_image_view rqt_image_view
```

Now that we have a webcam, we can start to elaborate the images using OpenCV libraries, as discussed in the next section.

Getting started with OpenCV – ROS 2 integration

We are now ready to start elaborating images using ROS 2 and OpenCV. On its own, ROS 2 doesn't offer a proper way to perform image processing. As already stated, the main library worldwide used to perform this task is OpenCV. For this reason, ROS 2 offers an interface towards OpenCV that allows ROS 2 topics to be directly converted into the image data structure supported by OpenCV and vice versa. In this way, the main programming pipeline will be:

1. Receiving the image data to elaborate via ROS 2 topics (ROS uses the `sensor_msgs/msg/Image` data type)

2. Convert this to an OpenCV image (the data used is a `cv::Mat`)

3. Process the image

4. Convert the OpenCV image into a ROS 2 message, publishing the eventual result

But what is a `cv::Mat`? In OpenCV, an image is represented as a matrix, where each element corresponds to a pixel in the image. For grayscale images, the matrix has one channel, and each element stores the intensity of the pixel (0-255). For color images, the matrix has three channels (e.g., RGB), with each element containing a vector of three values representing the intensity of red, green, and blue at that pixel. The matrix's dimensions correspond to the image's width and height.

The interface to transform ROS 2 data in OpenCV images and vice versa is implemented in the `cv_bridge` package. Let's use it on a ROS 2 node to perform some basic operations typical of computer vision. For code readability, we report here only part of the whole source code. You can check the full code in the book repository: `https://github.com/PacktPublishing/Mastering-ROS-2.git`.

First, create the ROS 2 package with the correct dependencies:

```
$ ros2 pkg create my_opencv_package --dependencies rclcpp sensor_msgs cv_
bridge
```

Create a source called `image_processing.cpp`. In this code, we will perform the following operations:

- **Conversion from RGB to grayscale**: Reduces a color image to shades of gray by averaging the color channels.

- **Image blur**: Smooths the image to reduce noise using filters like Gaussian blur.

- **Image thresholding**: Converts an image to binary by setting pixel values above a threshold to white and below to black.

- **Contour detection**: Identifies the outlines of objects or shapes within an image.

- **Feature extraction**: Identifies important patterns or points in an image for recognition or matching.

- **ORB**: Detects and describes keypoints in an image for fast feature matching.

- **Corners**: Points where two edges meet, often detected for identifying unique features.

These operations serve different purposes. Techniques like blurring, converting to grayscale, or thresholding are part of image enhancement, which prepares images for further analysis. For instance, blurring helps reduce noise or unnecessary details, making the image easier to process. Similarly, feature extraction methods like ORB or corner detection are used to analyze the camera's environment. These features can outline object shapes, enable object tracking, or support advanced tasks like visual odometry, which calculates the camera's position as it moves.

The content of the `image_processing.cpp` source is reported here:

1. In the header, we need to add both the `cv_bridge` and opencv headers:

```
#include <cv_bridge/cv_bridge.hpp>
#include <opencv2/opencv.hpp>
#include "rclcpp/rclcpp.hpp"
#include "sensor_msgs/msg/image.hpp"
```

2. In the constructor, the input and output of the node are initialized. We subscribe to the topic streamed by the camera sensor, publishing the processed images. In this case, we report only two publishers, but they will be the same for all the other images:

```
class ImageProcessor : public rclcpp::Node {
public:
    ImageProcessor() : Node("image_processor") {
        image_subscription_ = this->create_
subscription<sensor_msgs::msg::Image>("/image_raw",
```

```
10, std::bind(&ImageProcessor::image_callback, this,
std::placeholders::_1));
        contours_imag_pub_ = this->create_publisher<sensor_
msgs::msg::Image>( "contours/image_raw", 1);
        gray_img_pub_ = this->create_publisher<sensor_
msgs::msg::Image>( "gray/image_raw", 1);
    }
private:
```

3. In the image callback, the function toCvCopy is used to store the data received from the callback in the cv_bridge object. This object already contains the cv::Mat element that represents the input image:

```
    void image_callback(const sensor_msgs::msg::Image::SharedPtr
msg) {
cv_bridge::CvImagePtr cv_ptr;
try {
cv_ptr = cv_bridge::toCvCopy(msg, sensor_msgs::image_
encodings::BGR8);
}
catch (cv_bridge::Exception& e) {
    RCLCPP_ERROR(this->get_logger(), "cv_bridge exception: %s",
e.what());
    return;
}
  cv::Mat processed_image = cv_ptr->image.clone();
        cv::Mat contours_image = cv_ptr->image.clone();
        cv::Mat gray_image;
```

4. Let's start by translating the image into a grayscale image and generating its blur version. A mask is used to define the strength of the blur:

```
cv::cvtColor(processed_image, gray_image, cv::COLOR_BGR2GRAY);
        cv::blur(processed_image, blur_image, cv::Size(15, 15));
```

5. This line applies binary thresholding to gray_image, setting pixels above 128 to 255 (*white*) and below to 0 (*black*), storing the result in thresholded_image. The result will be an image with total white or total black:

```
        cv::threshold(gray_image, thresholded_image, 128, 255,
  cv::THRESH_BINARY);
```

6. Then, we extract image contours. Contours are used in computer vision to identify object shapes and boundaries for tasks like detection, segmentation, and measurement:

```
std::vector<std::vector<cv::Point>> contours;
cv::findContours(thresholded_image, contours, cv::RETR_
EXTERNAL, cv::CHAIN_APPROX_SIMPLE);
cv::drawContours(contours_image, contours, -1, cv::Scalar(0,
255, 0), 2);
```

7. Here, we extract ORB features. ORB is used in computer vision to detect and describe keypoints efficiently, making it ideal for fast image matching and object recognition:

```
cv::Ptr<cv::ORB> orb = cv::ORB::create();
std::vector<cv::KeyPoint> keypoints;
cv::Mat descriptors;
orb->detectAndCompute(gray_image, cv::noArray(), keypoints,
descriptors);
cv::drawKeypoints(processed_image, keypoints, keypoints_img,
cv::Scalar(0, 0, 255), cv::DrawMatchesFlags::DRAW_RICH_KEYPOINTS);
```

8. Corners are an image feature used in many computer vision applications because they are distinctive, stable under transformations, and ideal for tasks like image matching and object recognition:

```
cv::Mat dst, dst_norm, dst_norm_scaled;
dst = cv::Mat::zeros(gray_image.size(), CV_32FC1);
const int blockSize = 2;
const int apertureSize = 3;
double k = 0.04;
cv::cornerHarris(gray_image, dst, blockSize, apertureSize,
k);
cv::normalize(dst, dst_norm, 0, 255, cv::NORM_MINMAX,
CV_32FC1, cv::Mat());
cv::convertScaleAbs(dst_norm, dst_norm_scaled);
```

9. To visualize the corners, we can print them over the image:

```
corner_image = processed_image.clone();
for (int i = 0; i < dst_norm.rows; i++) {
    for (int j = 0; j < dst_norm.cols; j++) {
        if ((int)dst_norm.at<float>(i, j) > 200) {
```

```
                                      cv::circle(corner_image, cv::Point(j, i), 5,
          cv::Scalar(0, 0, 255), 2, 8, 0);
                              }
                      }
              }
```

10. We are now ready to generate the output by publishing the images reporting the output of all the operations done so far. Also, in this case, the cv_bridge object is used to translate the image from OpenCV to ROS 2. Here, we must consider the image format. For example, a colored image must be converted considering the bgr8, while the grayscale image should be converted with a mono8 format:

```
          msg_ = cv_bridge::CvImage(std_msgs::msg::Header(), "bgr8",
      contours_image).toImageMsg();
          _contours_imag_pub->publish(*msg_.get());
          msg_ = cv_bridge::CvImage(std_msgs::msg::Header(), "mono8",
      gray_image).toImageMsg();
              }
```

11. As class members, we define the image publishers:

```
      rclcpp::Subscription<sensor_msgs::msg::Image>::SharedPtr image_
      subscription_;
          rclcpp::Publisher<sensor_msgs::msg::Image>::SharedPtr _contours_
      imag_pub;
```

You can now add the source to the CMakeLists.txt compile and source the ROS 2 workspace. Test the OpenCV elaboration node by launching the USB cam and the node described above:

```
$ ros2 launch usb_cam_launcher my_usb_cam.launch.py
$ ros2 run my_opencv_package image_processing
```

A sample output of the node is reported in *Figure 10.2*, where the contours, the ORB features, the blur image, and the threshold ones are depicted:

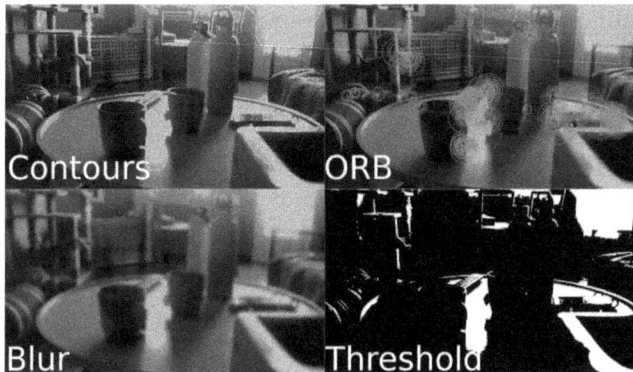

Figure 10.2: Image elaboration result: contours, ORB features, blur, and threshold images

Getting started with camera calibration

In the previous section, we perform basic image elaboration routines that work considering the value of the pixel of the image. In robotics, this is not enough. In fact, we must find a mapping between the pixel of the image and the physical space around the camera sensor. How can we obtain this? Using the intrinsic parameters of the camera. For this reason, we will introduce the differences between the pixel and image spaces:

- **Pixel space:** This refers to the coordinate system defined by the individual pixels of an image. Each pixel has discrete coordinates (x, y) corresponding to its position in the grid of pixels. Pixel space is primarily concerned with the raw pixel values and their arrangement, without considering any geometric relationships to the real world.

- **Image space:** Image space extends beyond pixel coordinates to include a mathematical representation of the image that can relate pixel positions to real-world coordinates. It often considers factors like perspective, camera parameters, and transformations that allow for interpreting the image data in a meaningful way.

To pass between pixel space and image space, we must use the camera calibration. Camera calibration in robotics involves determining the intrinsic and extrinsic parameters of a camera to accurately relate image space to real-world coordinates. This is essential for tasks like navigation, object detection, and mapping, where precise measurements are required. Mainly we have two kinds of calibration. The intrinsic and extrinsic:

- **Intrinsic calibration:** This focuses on the internal parameters of the camera, such as focal length, optical center (principal point), and lens distortion coefficients. Intrinsic calibration corrects for distortions and enables accurate mapping of pixel coordinates to real-world measurements.

- **Extrinsic calibration**: This involves determining the camera's position and orientation in relation to a reference frame or the environment. Extrinsic parameters describe the transformation between the camera coordinate system and the world coordinate system, allowing for the accurate placement of objects detected in the image in their real-world locations.

To perform the calibration of a camera, we need a calibration pattern. Typically, it is a chessboard, like the one shown in *Figure 10.3*. Also, in this case, OpenCV has a procedure to perform the calibration, while ROS 2 has a wrapper for it. Before starting the calibration, we must install the following package:

```
$ sudo apt-get install ros-jazzy-camera-calibration
```

Now, we can start the calibration:

```
$ ros2 run camera_calibration cameracalibrator --size 10x7 --square 0.02
--ros-args -r image:=/image_raw -p camera:=/camera
```

This command contains some parameters depending on the chessboard and the USB camera connected.

- `--size 10x7`: Specifies the checkerboard pattern has 10 internal corners horizontally and 7 vertically.
- `--square 0.02`: Sets the size of each square on the checkerboard to 0.02 meters (2 cm).
- `--ros-args`: Indicates that the following parameters are ROS 2-specific.
- `-r image:=/image_raw`: Remaps the input topic to subscribe to /image_raw for camera images.
- `-p camera:=/camera`: Sets a parameter for the camera namespace or topic to use during calibration.

Figure 10.3: Camera calibration procedure

After that, the calibration starts, and the window shown in *Figure 10.3* is opened. To perform the calibration, you must move the camera, or the chessboard, in different directions and orientations, zooming in and out to improve the quality of the calibration. You can check the quality of the calibration in the top-right panel, which informs you about the single components of the calibration. When the overall quality is acceptable, the calibration button is enabled (**CALIBRATE** in *Figure 10.3*), and you can click on it. In a few seconds, the calibration will be ready, and the **COMMIT** button will be enabled. After clicking this button, the calibration is saved in the ROS 2 system. In fact, the camera calibration is directly saved in a hidden directory of your computer, as you can check on the terminal where the USB camera has started:

```
$ [camera]: writing calibration data to /home/user/.ros/camera_info/
default_cam.yaml
```

After saving the calibration, you can verify that it was saved correctly by restarting the USB camera node and checking the contents of the `/camera_info` topic. This topic includes parameters such as the focal length, optical center, and distortion coefficients. However, these parameters are generally not used directly. Instead, when a ROS 2 node requires these parameters to convert pixel coordinates to spatial coordinates, it subscribes directly to the `/camera_info` topic. However, even though we properly calibrate the camera, there is missing information that is often used in advanced robot applications: the depth information. For this reason, another kind of sensor used in robotics is the depth sensor, as introduced in the next section.

Getting started with depth sensors

Using standard cameras is not possible to obtain information about the distance between the framed objects and the sensor. This makes these sensors unsuitable for many robotics tasks like object grasping, in which it is good to estimate the full pose of the object to manipulate, or obstacle avoidance, in which the distance from the obstacle is fundamental to performing safe navigation. For this scope, a different kind of sensor can be used: the **depth sensor**. Depth sensors are like cameras in terms of size and payload. They are compact devices and can be attached to the robot computer with a USB connector. Unlike cameras, these devices measure the distance to objects in their environment, providing depth information that enhances perception capabilities in robotics. Common types include **LiDAR** or **time-of-flight sensors**. These sensors are well integrated with ROS 2. Depth sensors publish depth in two formats:

- **Disparity matrix**: Exactly like an image, this matrix stores a set of pixel values. Each pixel of the disparity matrix is encoded with the value representing the distance of that pixel from the sensor in meters.

- **Point Cloud**: Generated from the disparity matrix, this data is a collection of points in 3D space representing the external surface of the objects framed by the sensor.

In recent years, **Intel's RealSense** series represented a major development in depth sensing, deploying devices that leverage stereo vision technology combined with infrared filtering to capture high-resolution depth information in real time. Apart from the hardware itself, Intel also provides an SDK to interface a camera with Linux machines and so, with ROS 2.

In this book, we will use the **Intel RealSense D435** (see *Figure 10.4*) to integrate a depth sensor with ROS 2. However, apart from the sensor installation part, you can use any other depth sensor available on the market to test the examples described in the following. In fact, exactly like OpenCV with image processing, we will use a library to manage the data generated from the depth sensors, the point cloud data. This library is called **Point Cloud Library** (**PCL**) and is an open-source library that offers tools for filtering, feature extraction, segmentation, and surface reconstruction for point cloud data.

From a certain point of view, PCL complements OpenCV, which handles 2D image processing, allowing developers to work seamlessly with both 2D and 3D data in robotic applications.

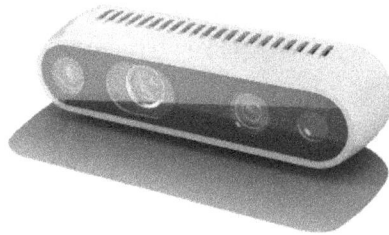

Figure 10.4: RealSense D435 device

Let's start installing the RealSense device before starting to use PCL. To install ROS 2 packages to handle a RealSense device in our system, use the following commands:

```
$ sudo apt-get install ros-jazzy-librealsense2
$ sudo apt-get install ros-jazzy-realsense2-*
```

The last command installs the realsense2_camera ROS 2 package, which includes a useful launch file for easily starting and configuring any supported RealSense devices. For example, after attaching the device to your laptop, use the following command to start streaming sensor data:

```
$ ros2 launch realsense2_camera rs_launch.py
```

The data generated from this sensor is visible in *Figures 10.5* and *10.6*. In *Figure 10.5*, the rqt_image_view ROS 2 node is used to visualize two images published from this sensor. In the left part of the image, there is the disparity matrix, which gives us information about the depth of the scene. In the right part, there is the RGB camera output.

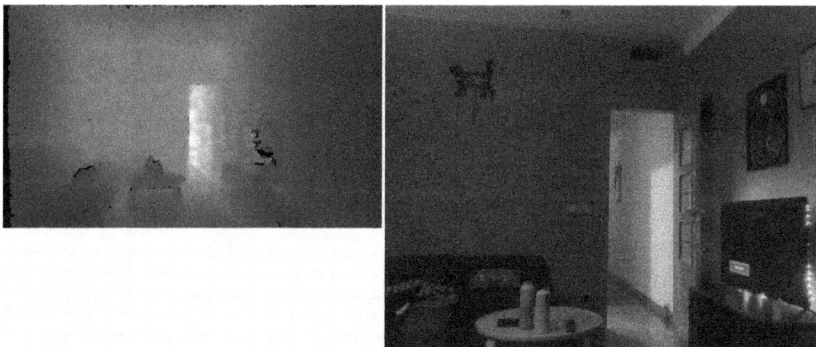

Figure 10.5: RGB image (right) and depth matrix (left) streamed by the Intel RealSense depth sensor

Similarly, the depth sensor publishes the point cloud data. You can visualize such data using Rviz2 after importing the **DepthCloud** plugin (Rviz2 configuration is shown in *Figure 10.6*). In Rviz2, where point cloud data is visualized, you can observe how this data maps the 3D shape of the world using a collection of points. Can you recognize the shape of the hand captured by the RGB camera?

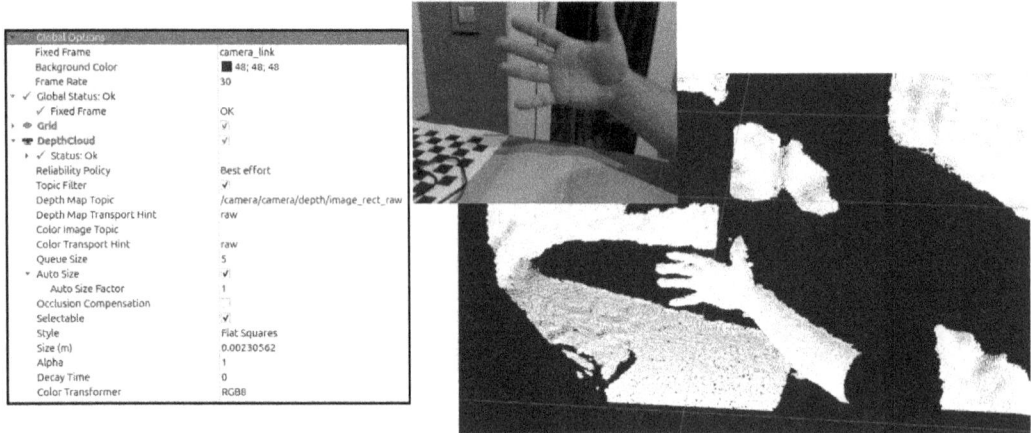

Figure 10.6: Point cloud data shown on Rviz2

Before integrating point cloud data in our ROS 2 node, we must install the proper libraries and interfaces to handle PCL data:

```
$ sudo apt-get install libpcl-dev
$ sudo apt-get install ros-jazzy-pcl-*
```

Let's now start to integrate point cloud data in a ROS 2 node:

```
$ ros2 pkg create --build-type ament_cmake pcl_processing --dependencies
rclcpp sensor_msgs pcl_ros
```

We are now ready to elaborate on our point cloud data. The pipeline process is analogous to the one already considered for OpenCV: the data is received via topics, transformed into a PCL data format, and elaborated using the PCL libraries. Finally, it is published as a ROS 2 message to be used from other software modules.

What is the goal of this code? Crop and subsample a point cloud. In fact, point clouds can generate a huge amount of data and sometimes we don't need all this information. Let's discuss the content of the pcl_processing.cpp file. Also, in this case, we report only the salient parts of the code.

You can download the complete package from the book code repository:

1. Let's start by including the header files. Many of them are part of the PCL headers. In addition, here, we see the data used by ROS 2 to stream point cloud data types, the `sensor_msgs/msg/point_cloud2.hpp`:

    ```
    #include <pcl/filters/passthrough.h>
    #include <pcl/filters/voxel_grid.h>
    #include <pcl/point_cloud.h>
    #include <pcl/point_types.h>
    #include <pcl_conversions/pcl_conversions.h>
    #include <sensor_msgs/msg/point_cloud2.hpp>
    ```

2. In the class of the node, subscribe to the `points` data streamed from the RealSense sensor:

    ```
    class PointCloudProcessor : public rclcpp::Node {
    public:
        PointCloudProcessor(): Node("pointcloud_processor") {
            subscription_ = this->create_subscription<sensor_msgs::msg::PointCloud2>(
                "/camera/camera/depth/color/points", 10,
            std::bind(&PointCloudProcessor::processPointCloud, this,
    std::placeholders::_1));
    ```

3. Additionally, we want to publish the result on other point cloud data, to match the differences between the input and the output:

    ```
            publisher_ = this->create_publisher<sensor_msgs::msg::PointCloud2>("filtered_pointcloud", 10);
        private:
    ```

4. All the work is done directly in the callback of the point cloud data. This also demonstrates the performance of this library, since all these operations are executed at the same framerate of the sensor input:

    ```
        void processPointCloud(const sensor_msgs::msg::PointCloud2::SharedPtr msg) {
    ```

5. First, let's translate the data from the input point cloud ROS 2 side to PCL data:

    ```
            pcl::PointCloud<pcl::PointXYZ>::Ptr cloud(new pcl::PointCloud<pcl::PointXYZ>());
            pcl::fromROSMsg(*msg, *cloud);
    ```

6. The first step is to crop the point cloud. To do this, we create an object called PassThrough, which takes the point cloud data as input. We can crop the data along the three axes: x, y, and z. In this case, we crop along all three axes. For the x-axis, we crop the data between -0.5 and 0.5 meters, meaning we only keep the points that fall within this range along the x direction relative to the sensor:

```
pcl::PassThrough<pcl::PointXYZ> pass_x;
pass_x.setInputCloud(cloud);
pass_x.setFilterFieldName("x");
pass_x.setFilterLimits(-0.5, 0.5);
pcl::PointCloud<pcl::PointXYZ>::Ptr cloud_filtered_x(new
pcl::PointCloud<pcl::PointXYZ>());
```

To perform the crop, apply the filter to the input cloud, saving its result in the cloud_filtered_x object. We perform the same operation for the y-axis. Remember that, for each axis, a new PassThrough object must be declared and properly set. Of course, in the case of the y-axis, the input of the PassThrough object will be the cloud already filtered in the x direction. As for the z-axis, we enlarge the interval, cutting the points upto 1 meter from the sensor:

```
pass_x.filter(*cloud_filtered_x);
pcl::PassThrough<pcl::PointXYZ> pass_y;
pass_y.setInputCloud(cloud_filtered_x);
```

7. After cropping the point cloud, we will down sample the data. For this reason, we apply a pcl/VoxelGrid filter by reducing its resolution. It divides the point cloud space into 3D voxels (cubes) of size 2 cm and keeps only one representative point per voxel, effectively reducing the number of points in the cloud while preserving the overall structure. In this way, we can maintain the shape of the original cloud but at the same time reduce the effort of its future elaboration:

```
pcl::VoxelGrid<pcl::PointXYZ> voxel_grid;
voxel_grid.setInputCloud(cloud_filtered);
voxel_grid.setLeafSize(0.02f, 0.02f, 0.02f);
pcl::PointCloud<pcl::PointXYZ>::Ptr cloud_downsampled(new
pcl::PointCloud<pcl::PointXYZ>());
voxel_grid.filter(*cloud_downsampled);
```

8. Finally, we are ready to convert back the PCL data to a ROS 2 format, publishing it on a topic:

```
sensor_msgs::msg::PointCloud2 output_msg;
pcl::toROSMsg(*cloud_downsampled, output_msg);
output_msg.header = msg->header;
publisher_->publish(output_msg);
```

9. Remember to declare in the class member the subscriber and the publisher of the point cloud data:

```
rclcpp::Subscription<sensor_msgs::msg::PointCloud2>::SharedPtr
subscription_;
    rclcpp::Publisher<sensor_msgs::msg::PointCloud2>::SharedPtr
publisher_;
};
```

10. Our code is now complete. We can add the compilation instructions to the `CMakeLists.txt` file:

```
add_executable(pcl_processing src/pcl_processing.cpp)
ament_target_dependencies(pcl_processing rclcpp sensor_msgs pcl_ros)
target_link_libraries(pcl_processing ${PCL_LIBRARIES})
install(TARGETS pcl_processing DESTINATION lib/${PROJECT_NAME})
```

Finally, compile and source the workspace before executing the PCL processing and the RealSense camera driver. Notice that, in this case, we add a parameter to the `rs_launch.py` file, setting `pointcloud.enable` to true. This allows the RealSense driver to directly stream the point cloud points subscribed by our node:

```
$ ros2 launch realsense2_camera rs_launch.py pointcloud.enable:=true
$ ros2 run pcl_processing pcl_processing
```

Using Rviz2, you can compare the original point cloud with respect to the one generated by the *pcl_processing* node. This comparison is also shown in *Figure 10.7*, where, on the left side, there is the complete cloud, while on the right side, the cropped and down sampled cloud is shown.

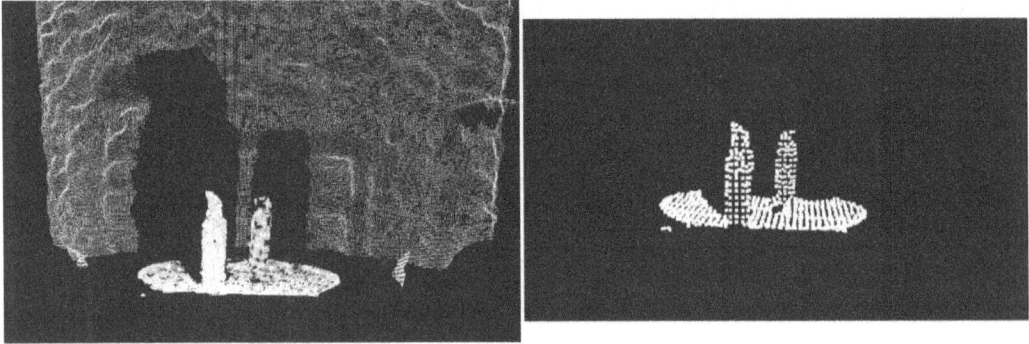

Figure 10.7: Point cloud data elaboration. Left: full point cloud, right: cropped and down sampled point cloud

By comparing the result of this algorithm with the output from OpenCV image processing, you can see the vast range of applications made possible by this information. Robots can gain a comprehensive understanding of their environment, from colors and features to 3D shapes. Developers have long implemented applications based on point cloud data, such as localization, mapping, object detection, and 3D reconstruction. Additionally, depth sensor data can be converted to laser scan messages, providing a low-cost solution for autonomous navigation (as implemented in the pointclud_to_laserscan package [1]). However, processing large datasets like images and point clouds is challenging, which is why developers have increasingly turned to GPUs for faster computation, as discussed in the last section of this chapter.

Using NVIDIA ISAAC ROS to speed up image processing

Processing large amounts of data, such as images or point clouds, can lead to performance issues if algorithms cannot handle the resource demands. To address this, developers have begun leveraging the high computational power of GPUs. This shift has been driven by the popularity of NVIDIA Jetson computers, which are compact devices equipped with powerful GPUs, making them ideal for robotics applications. In this view, NVIDIA directly supports the ROS 2 developers by providing a collection of packages that solve robotics perception problems by directly exploiting the GPU, and directly communicating with the ROS 2 ecosystem. This collection of packages is known as **NVIDIA ISAAC ROS** and covers many problems of robotic perception.

In this section, we will learn how NVIDIA ISAAC is structured and how to install it on our machines, running some of the ROS 2 nodes implemented in this package collection.

ISAAC structure

Before running ISAAC nodes, let's describe how the ISAAC ROS project is structured. ISAAC ROS implements different perception algorithms in the form of the ROS 2 package. Each of them is linked to a code repository. At this link, you can find all the repositories currently maintained [2].

For example, if we are interested in performing marker detection (the first example of this section), we should refer to the main repository page for its documentation [3], and to its package for the tutorial on how to start [4]. In each starting tutorial, you will find all the steps needed to create and properly start the Docker container, download the asset directory (a sort of additional files needed for the package), and start the desired node. We will discuss these steps later in this section.

ROS 2 integration and NITROS

As of now, ISAAC is compatible only with ROS 2 Humble, but support for newer versions like Jazzy is planned. This won't pose a problem for us, as NVIDIA provides all the necessary files to create a Docker container with the appropriate version of ROS 2. Furthermore, our Jazzy ROS setup will communicate seamlessly with the input and output of the NVIDIA packages over our computer network, making the communication process transparent. Therefore, we will establish a separate ROS 2 workspace for running the NVIDIA ISAAC code, while our packages, which utilize the output from ISAAC, will remain in our workspace with the desired ROS 2 version.

Another important feature of ISAAC is the implementation of the so-called **NITROS** (short for **NVIDIA Isaac Toolkit for Robotics Operating System**). NITROS is a framework that provides high-performance communication and interoperability between robotic applications and services. It is designed to enhance the capabilities of ROS 2 by leveraging NVIDIA's hardware and software optimizations, offering efficient data handling and processing for robotics applications. In this way, the computational throughput to copy data from the CPU to the GPU before being processed is minimized.

Now that the general idea of ISAAC ROS has been introduced, we are ready to discuss some initial examples. First, let's start defining the system requirements.

Requirements

NVIDIA ROS requires the CUDA toolkit to be installed on your computer. **CUDA (Compute Unified Device Architecture)** is a parallel computing platform that allows developers to harness the processing power of a GPU. To install CUDA, your computer must have a CUDA-enabled graphics card.

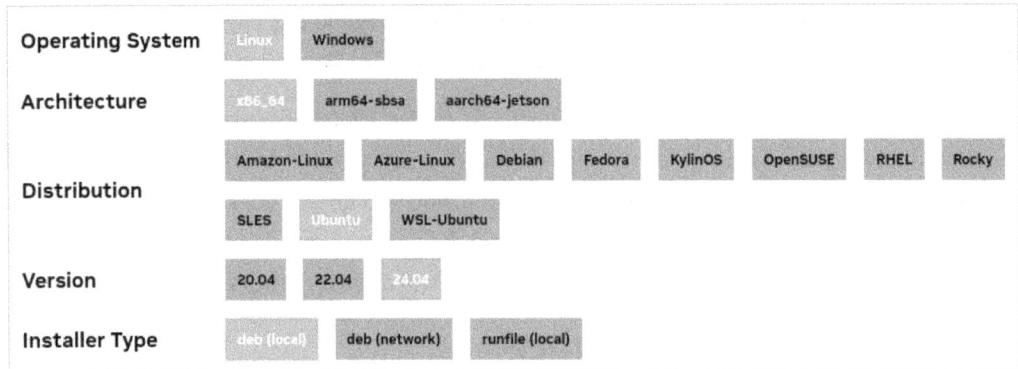

Operating System	Linux	Windows							
Architecture	x86_64	arm64-sbsa	aarch64-jetson						
Distribution	Amazon-Linux	Azure-Linux	Debian	Fedora	KylinOS	OpenSUSE	RHEL	Rocky	
	SLES	Ubuntu	WSL-Ubuntu						
Version	20.04	22.04	24.04						
Installer Type	deb (local)	deb (network)	runfile (local)						

Figure 10.8: Download page of the CUDA toolkit

To install the CUDA toolkit, it's best to follow the steps provided on NVIDIA's official developer page, where you can also download the package for the installation of CUDA [5]. Here, you can select the specs of your system (see *Figure 10.8*). After this selection, you will see a quick guide on how to install the downloaded package. After you've executed all the suggested steps, you can test the installation using the following command:

```
$ nvcc --version
```

Information on the installed CUDA toolkit version should be shown. Now that CUDA is installed, we can start configuring our environment:

1. We need to set up our system to run Docker containers that have access to NVIDIA GPUs. You can do it by following this page [6]. From this page, follow the sections: *Installing with Apt* and *Configuring Docker*.

2. We must create another workspace to store the ISAAC packages.

   For that, we will run the following commands. First, install some programs needed for ISAAC:

```
$ sudo apt-get install git-lfs
```

3. The environment variable ISAAC_ROS_WS will be set to point to the ROS 2 workspace where all the packages needed by ISAAC will be downloaded. For this reason, let's start creating a new folder called isaac_ros-dev and set the value of this variable:

```
$ mkdir -p ~/workspaces/isaac_ros-dev/src
$ echo "export ISAAC_ROS_WS=${HOME}/workspaces/isaac_ros-dev/" >>
~/.bashrc
source ~/.bashrc
```

In the next section, we will explore two common applications of computer vision in robotics: estimating the position and orientation of an object using AprilTag, and identifying the semantic class of an object using YOLO. Both applications will be tested with the ISAAC ROS framework. However, they can also run on a CPU alone, leveraging specific ROS-integrated packages.

Starting the isaac_ros_apriltag node

As already said, ISAAC ROS has already solved several common problems of robotics. Among them, isaac_ros_apriltag provides an implementation of AprilTag, a fiducial marker system that can retrieve the 6D pose of an AR marker. ISAAC has already made available the resources to test these packages using the corresponding bagfiles. Follow these steps to run AprilTag with a bagfile:

1. The first time that we run an ISAAC package, we must download isaac_ros_common in the proper workspace:

```
$ cd ${ISAAC_ROS_WS}/src && \
    git clone -b release-3.1 https://github.com/NVIDIA-ISAAC-ROS/
isaac_ros_common.git isaac_ros_common
```

2. Now it's time to download the asset of the package. For this, the most convenient way is to follow the steps of the *Download Quickstart Assets* section at the link [7].

3. Now, we can start with the AprilTag detector. Download the package from the NVIDIA repository:

```
$ cd ${ISAAC_ROS_WS}/src && git clone -b release-3.1 https://github.
com/NVIDIA-ISAAC-ROS/isaac_ros_apriltag.git isaac_ros_apriltag
```

4. Start the container using the convenient script included in the common resource of ISAAC:

```
$ cd ${ISAAC_ROS_WS}/src/isaac_ros_common && ./scripts/run_dev.sh
```

5. Now you are in the NVIDIA container. The ROS 2 workspace is a shared volume; however, you should leave the code and the configuration file as they are. Install the dependencies of the AprilTag package:

```
$ rosdep install --from-paths ${ISAAC_ROS_WS}/src/isaac_ros_apriltag
--ignore-src -y
```

6. Compile the workspace and source it:

```
$ cd ${ISAAC_ROS_WS}/ &&  colcon build --symlink-install --packages-
up-to isaac_ros_apriltag && source install/setup.bash
```

7. Still inside the Docker container, install the dependencies:

```
$ sudo apt-get install -y ros-humble-isaac-ros-examples
```

8. Use isaac_ros_examples to start the AprilTag detector:

```
$ ros2 launch isaac_ros_examples isaac_ros_examples.launch.py
launch_fragments:=apriltag interface_specs_file:=${ISAAC_ROS_WS}/
isaac_ros_assets/isaac_ros_apriltag/quickstart_interface_specs.json
```

9. Now you should only start the bagfile. Start a new terminal in the same container:

```
$ cd ${ISAAC_ROS_WS}/src/isaac_ros_common && \
./scripts/run_dev.sh
```

10. Start the bagfile:

```
ros2 bag play -l ${ISAAC_ROS_WS}/isaac_ros_assets/isaac_ros_
apriltag/quickstart.bag --remap image:=image_rect camera_
info:=camera_info_rect
```

Now, you can check the result of the detector using rqt_image_view, to display the input marker framed by the camera, and Rviz2 to visualize the pose of the markers in the camera frame, as shown in *Figure 10.9*. Notice that you can start these last two programs from ROS 2 Jazzy Docker or directly from your host computer. Do you now understand how it is possible to integrate ISAAC ROS into your ROS 2 programs?

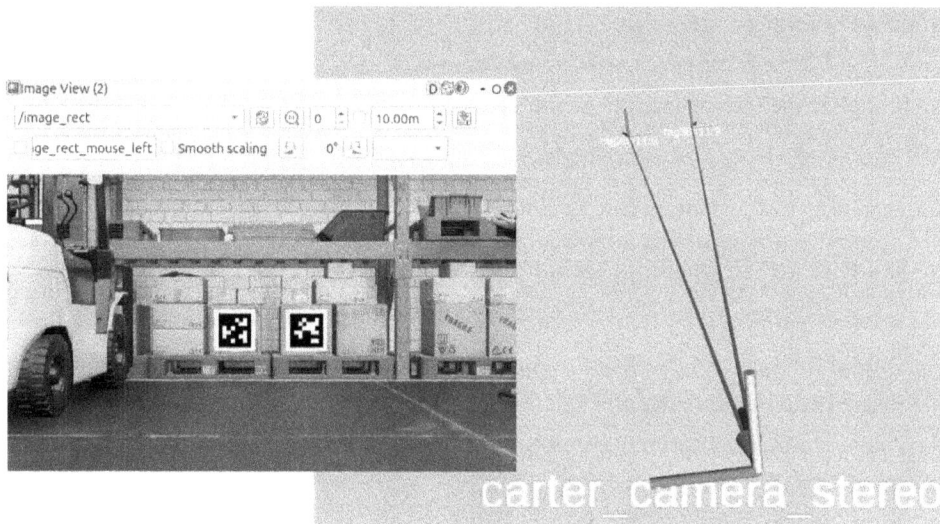

Figure 10.9: Input-output of isaac_ros_apriltg

A key aspect of image processing involves machine learning. Using machine learning techniques for image processing has shown great potential. In the next section, we will discuss a machine learning library integrated into ISAAC, which is used for the semantic classification of objects in images.

Performing object classification using YOLOv8 and NVIDIA ISAAC

A typical problem of advanced robotics is related to object detection and classification using standard cameras. In this way, any robot can directly interact with the world in a smart and efficient way. In recent years, a widespread approach has been the use of the **You Only Look Once (YOLO)** library. This library permits you to detect and classify objects from just one image. The possibility to perform this classification with just one frame, makes YOLO usable in real-world applications. YOLO can run directly on the CPU. However, ISAAC provides an implementation of YOLO (version 8) to run on the GPU. In this way, YOLO runs faster, without impacting the performance of the programs running on the CPU.

In this case, the best way to execute the code is by following the steps on the documentation page of isaac_ros_yolov8 [8].

Of course, you can skip the first instruction – that is, the downloading of the isaac_ros_common package – if you already did so in the AprilTag example. To run YOLO, perform the following steps. Notice that all these actions must be executed in the Docker container:

1. Download Quickstart Assets, as discussed on the documentation page.

2. Start the Docker container:

```
$ cd ${ISAAC_ROS_WS}/src/isaac_ros_common && \
./scripts/run_dev.sh
```

3. Obtain the weight of the YOLO neural network. These weights are used from the neural network implemented in the YOLO library to recognize objects. These weights must be converted from **PyTorch** to **Open Neural Network Exchange (ONNX)** format:

```
$ wget https://github.com/ultralytics/assets/releases/download/
v0.0.0/yolov8s.pt
$ pip3 install ultralytics
$ pip3 install onnx
```

4. To convert the weights, we will use Python functions:

```
$ python3
>> from ultralytics import YOLO
      >> model = YOLO('yolov8s.pt')
      >> model.export(format='onnx')
$ mkdir -p ${ISAAC_ROS_WS}/isaac_ros_assets/models/yolov8
$ cp yolov8s.onnx ${ISAAC_ROS_WS}/isaac_ros_assets/models/yolov8
```

5. Install the YOLO packages:

```
$ sudo apt-get install -y ros-humble-isaac-ros-examples
$ sudo apt-get install -y ros-humble-isaac-ros-yolov8 ros-humble-
isaac-ros-dnn-image-encoder ros-humble-isaac-ros-tensor-rt
```

6. Launch the YOLO node:

```
$ cd /workspaces/isaac_ros-dev && ros2 launch isaac_ros_examples
isaac_ros_examples.launch.py launch_fragments:=yolov8 interface_
specs_file:=${ISAAC_ROS_WS}/isaac_ros_assets/isaac_ros_yolov8/
quickstart_interface_specs.json model_file_path:=${ISAAC_ROS_
WS}/isaac_ros_assets/models/yolov8/yolov8s.onnx engine_file_
path:=${ISAAC_ROS_WS}/isaac_ros_assets/models/yolov8/yolov8s.plan
```

7. Now it's time to stream the data. After being correctly launched, YOLO expects an image or video stream data on the topic /image_rect (note that the word rect in the topic name stands for rectified – a rectified image refers to an image that has been processed to remove distortions or misalignments). You can publish such data using the camera publisher developed in this chapter, simply changing the output topic using the mapping function of the launch file. The result of the elaboration is shown on the /yolov8_processed_image topic, as shown in *Figure 10.10*.

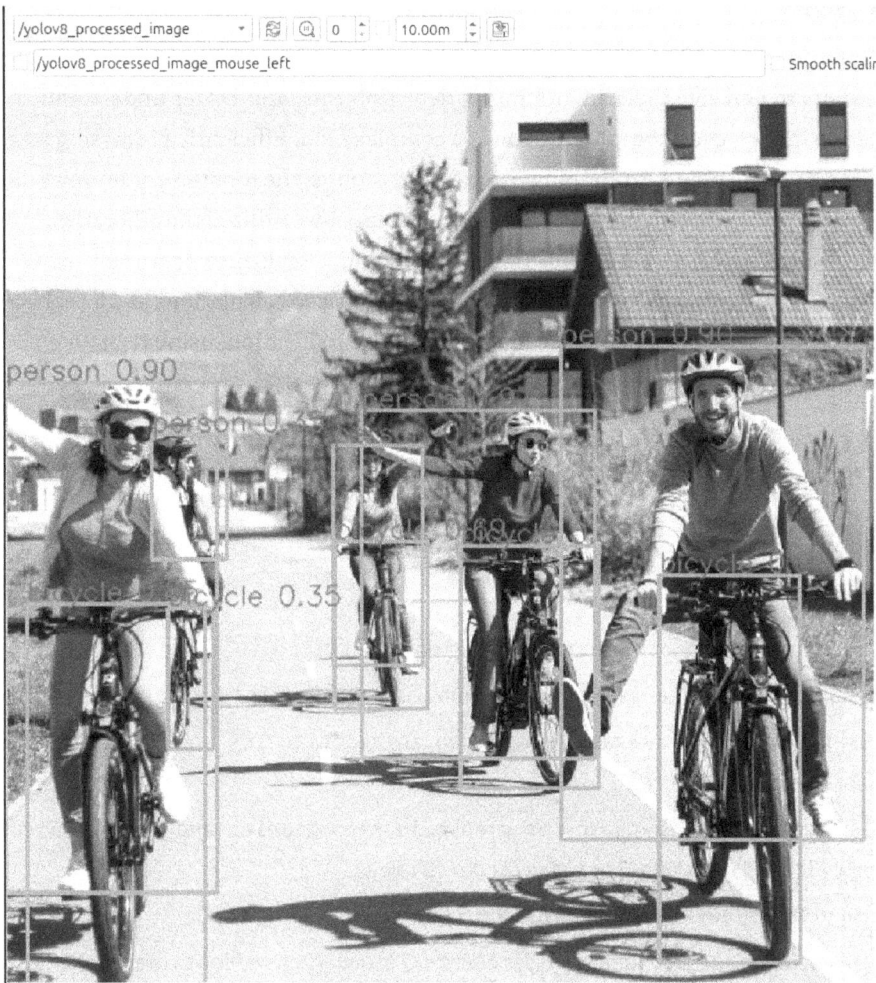

Figure 10.10: Output of YOLOv8 running under the ISAAC framework

NVIDIA Isaac ROS 2 is a powerful framework designed to harness the full potential of GPUs for processing images and other multimedia data. In addition to the pre-built packages it offers, developers can integrate their own algorithms into the Isaac ROS 2 framework. This integration optimizes the communication between the CPU and GPU, leading to faster processing and improved performance for your applications. To better understand how the GPU improves an image processing algorithm, NVIDIA ISAAC ROS provides a benchmark at this reference [9].

Summary

This chapter focuses on integrating computer vision algorithms with robotics. This integration allows robots to perceive their environment, detect objects, and better understand the world they operate in. However, computer vision is a complex field. Efficiently processing images and 3D data can be challenging. To simplify these computations, the robotics community often uses off-the-shelf libraries like OpenCV and PCL. In this chapter, we utilized these libraries, interfacing them with sensors such as a standard USB webcam and a RealSense depth sensor. We also explored ways to accelerate these tasks, first through GPU-based calculations and later by applying machine learning techniques for object detection and classification, using NVIDIA's ROS ISAAC framework and the YOLOv8 library.

This chapter concludes the second part of the book. Moving forward, we will build on what we've learned to explore advanced tools and applications in robotics. The next chapter will dive into the integration of simulated aerial robotics.

References

- [1] https://github.com/ros-perception/pointcloud_to_laserscan
- [2] https://nvidia-isaac-ros.github.io/repositories_and_packages/index.html
- [3] https://nvidia-isaac-ros.github.io/repositories_and_packages/isaac_ros_apriltag/index.html
- [4] https://nvidia-isaac-ros.github.io/repositories_and_packages/isaac_ros_apriltag/isaac_ros_apriltag/index.html
- [5] https://developer.nvidia.com/cuda-downloads
- [6] https://docs.nvidia.com/datacenter/cloud-native/container-toolkit/latest/install-guide.html#installing-with-apt

- [7] https://nvidia-isaac-ros.github.io/repositories_and_packages/isaac_ros_
  apriltag/isaac_ros_apriltag/index.html#quickstart

- [8] https://nvidia-isaac-ros.github.io/repositories_and_packages/isaac_ros_
  object_detection/isaac_ros_yolov8/index.html

- [9] https://developer.nvidia.com/isaac/ros

Join our community on Discord

Join our community's Discord space for discussions with the authors and other readers: https://
packt.link/embeddedsystems

Part 3

Advanced Applications and Machine Learning

This final part dives into advanced robotics topics using ROS 2, including aerial systems, custom mobile robot development, CI/CD pipelines, and integration with AI. You will explore how to interface large language models, apply deep reinforcement learning, and extend ROS 2 with custom executors and simulation plugins.

This part includes the following chapters:

- *Chapter 11, Aerial Robotics and ROS 2*
- *Chapter 12, Designing and Programming a DIY Mobile Robot from Scratch*
- *Chapter 13, Testing, Continuous Integration, and Continuous Deployment with ROS 2*
- *Chapter 14, Interfacing Large Language Models with ROS 2*
- *Chapter 15, ROS 2 and Deep Reinforcement Learning*
- *Chapter 16, Implementing ROS 2 Visualization and Simulation Plugins*

11

Aerial Robotics and ROS 2

So far in this book, we have explored various methods for interacting with and controlling mobile ground robots and manipulators. However, another important class of mobile robots has emerged over the past few decades: aerial robots. These are often referred to by different names, such as drones, multicopters, or, more commonly, **Unmanned Aerial Vehicles (UAVs)**. Like ground-based robots, UAVs can perform service tasks, such as area exploration or inventory management. Because they can fly, UAVs are often faster and more reliable for certain tasks. However, their autonomy introduces additional challenges.

In this chapter, we will first examine the basic structure and equipment of aerial robots. Then, we will demonstrate how to simulate a UAV using Gazebo, integrated with ROS 2, along with the most used control stack for managing these advanced robotic systems: the PX4 control stack.

We will cover the following main topics in the chapter:

- Introducing aerial robotics
- Understanding the hardware and software architecture of unmanned aerial vehicles
- Simulating an aerial robot using Gazebo and the PX4 control stack
- Controlling a UAV using ROS 2

Technical requirements

To follow this chapter, you should have one of the following setups on your computer:

- A standard computer running the Ubuntu 24.04 LTS operating system
- A Linux machine with the ROS 2 Jazzy version installed or with a running Docker container configured as discussed in *Chapter 2*.

The reference code for this chapter can be found in the `Chapter011` folder of the following code repository: `https://github.com/PacktPublishing/Mastering-ROS-2-for-Robotics-Programming/tree/main/Chapter11`.

Introducing aerial robotics

Aerial robotics has been an emerging research field for over two decades, gaining significant momentum since the early 2000s. Today, despite many ongoing challenges, numerous tech companies develop and deploy UAVs to perform a variety of service robotics tasks, such as delivery, agricultural operations, and other specialized applications.

Leading companies in aerial robotics and their objectives

To provide an overview of the activities these companies are involved in, the following section includes a list of key companies and their primary objectives in the field of aerial robotics:

*   **DJI**: DJI [*1*] is the global leader in civilian drones and aerial imaging technology. They offer a wide range of drones for photography, agriculture, inspection, and more.

*   **Autel Robotics**: Autel Robotics [*2*] provides advanced drones for aerial photography, inspection, and public safety applications. They are known for their high-quality cameras and robust flight performance.

*   **Zipline**: Zipline [*3*] specializes in using drones for medical supply deliveries, particularly in remote or hard-to-reach areas, enhancing healthcare logistics.

*   **Delair**: Delair [*4*] offers professional-grade drones and data processing solutions for applications like agriculture, mining, construction, and environmental monitoring.

*   **Flyability**: Flyability [*5*] is a pioneer in designing drones for industrial inspections, particularly in areas that are hard to reach, dangerous, or confined, such as inside industrial plants, power generation facilities, and mines. Their drones are designed to be collision-tolerant, allowing them to operate in complex indoor environments without the risk of damage.

Of course, the above mentioned are only a small portion of the hi-tech companies currently working with aerial robots. Before discussing how to program such systems, let's briefly compare them to the ground robotics problem.

Comparison of ground and aerial systems

Although both aerial and ground robots face challenges such as navigating unstructured environments, avoiding obstacles, and planning paths, UAVs encounter significantly greater difficulties in achieving autonomy. This is mainly due to the complexities of operating in three-dimensional space, as well as the overall complexity of their flight systems. Let's see a brief comparison of ground and aerial systems:

- UAVs must constantly adjust to maintain stable flight in the air. Unlike ground robots that move on a stable surface, UAVs need to control their *altitude*, *pitch*, *roll*, and *yaw* in real time (the *Eulerian angles* defining the attitude of a UAV). These movements must be continuously adjusted based on sensor feedback and environmental conditions, requiring advanced algorithms for flight dynamics control. Small errors in control can lead to instability or crashes, making autonomy particularly challenging.

- While ground robots navigate primarily in two dimensions, UAVs operate in a 3D environment. This adds complexity to navigation and path planning since they must consider obstacles not only around them but also above and below. Autonomous UAVs must integrate multiple sensors (e.g., GPS, LiDAR, cameras) to accurately perceive their environment and plan collision-free trajectories. Path planning in 3D space is computationally intensive, and real-time adjustments are often necessary to avoid dynamic obstacles like birds or other UAVs.

- From a low-level control view perspective, UAVs are highly sensitive to external environmental factors like wind, rain, and air pressure. Autonomous flight systems must constantly compensate for these factors. For example, wind gusts can destabilize a UAV, requiring rapid corrections to maintain course and altitude. The UAV's control system must adapt autonomously to changes in weather conditions without human intervention, which adds complexity to its autonomy software.

- Achieving reliable autonomy in UAVs requires the integration of multiple sensors. Aerial robots rely on a combination of GPS, **IMUs** (short for **inertial measurement units**), barometers, and visual sensors to estimate their position and orientation. However, GPS signals can be lost or degraded in urban areas or indoors, and visual sensors can be affected by poor lighting or dust. UAVs must use sensor fusion algorithms to combine data from multiple sensors to maintain accurate situational awareness. This requires complex software to manage sensor data, detect failures, and switch to backup systems in case of sensor malfunctions.

- UAVs need to make decisions in real time, often in rapidly changing environments. For example, if an obstacle appears suddenly or weather conditions worsen, the UAV's onboard system must quickly decide how to react—whether to adjust its flight path, hover, or return to its base. These decisions must be made autonomously without relying on constant human input. Designing algorithms that can handle such real-time decision-making is a significant challenge, especially when balancing multiple objectives like safety, efficiency, and power consumption.

- In dynamic environments, UAVs must be able to detect and avoid obstacles autonomously. This includes both stationary objects (like buildings or trees) and moving obstacles (like other drones or vehicles). Advanced UAVs use technologies such as LiDAR, optical cameras, and ultrasonic sensors to map their surroundings and detect obstacles. The complexity lies in processing this data in real time, interpreting it, and making split-second decisions on how to navigate around hazards. In confined spaces or environments with complex structures, this becomes particularly challenging, as the margin for error is smaller.

Due to the complexity involved in managing an aerial system, it is essential to use a control stack to ensure stable and secure flight. One of the most widely used control stacks in both hobbyist and industrial applications is the *PX4* control stack. It offers a comprehensive set of algorithms for flight control, such as attitude, position, and velocity control, along with features for navigation, mission planning, and sensor integration. The *PX4* stack communicates directly with ROS 2 and can be used to simulate a multi-copter realistically, which we will explore later in this chapter. However, before introducing the PX4 stack and interfacing a simulated UAV, in the next section, we will first briefly discuss the components of a UAV.

Understanding the hardware and software architecture of a UAV

Aerial robots are composed of different sensors and different shapes. Moreover, the main component of these devices is the autopilot, the central component of a UAV, responsible for initializing and interfacing with onboard sensors. The autopilot, also known as the **Flight Control Unit (FCU)** is a micro-controller board that processes input to control the UAV's actuators, such as its brushless motors. UAVs can have different platform configurations, with the quadrotor being the simplest. Quadrotors typically have four motors arranged in either an *(x)* or *(+)* pattern. In coaxial configurations, two motors and propellers are mounted on each axis, resulting in eight in total. This setup is similar for hexacopters and octocopters. Regardless of the airframe design, control strategies remain the same, as the autopilot translates control signals directly into motor actions.

Another key component of the UAV hardware is the **onboard computer**. While the FCU manages the basic flight operations of the UAV, the onboard computer handles more complex tasks that require high-level computation, such as those involving ROS 2 or other advanced programming frameworks. The onboard computer and the FCU are connected via a wired interface, which ensures safer and more reliable communication with better performance compared to wireless connections. The relationship among the two computation units is schematized in *Figure 11.1*.

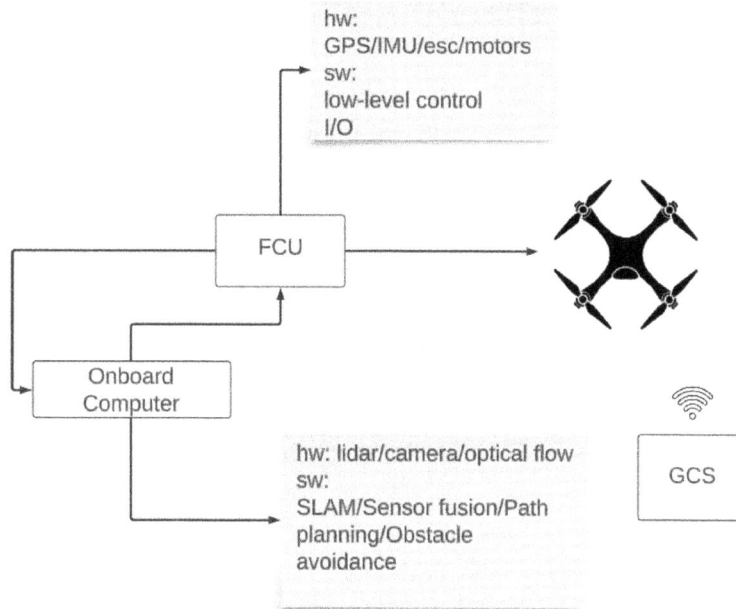

Figure 11.1: UAV hardware/software architecture

Here, the UAV is directly connected with the FCU. Additional hardware and software elements associated with UAVs are:

- **IMU**: The key hardware in the autopilot system is the **inertial measurement units (IMU)**, which helps determine the UAV's attitude, altitude, and flight direction. Actually, an IMU does not directly measure motion, orientation, or forces—instead, it measures linear accelerations and angular velocities. These measurements are integrated over time to estimate the vehicle's motion and orientation and can be used, together with dynamic models, to infer external forces acting on the UAV. The IMU typically consists of an accelerometer, a gyroscope, and often a magnetometer.

- **GPS receiver**: Another essential sensor for UAVs is the **Global Positioning System (GPS)**, which helps estimate the robot's global position in terms of latitude, longitude, and altitude, allowing it to stabilize its location. However, GPS receivers can provide positioning accuracy in the range of 1 to 3 meters. When using **Real-Time Kinematic (RTK)** correction with a base station, this accuracy can be improved to within several centimeters. However, it's important to note that performance can be significantly degraded in cluttered environments, such as urban canyons or areas with dense foliage, where signal reflections and obstructions can introduce substantial errors.

- **I/O**: The FCU handles communication with external software. Not only the onboard computer but also the remote controller and the **Ground Control Station (GCS)**.

- **Low-level control**: The FCU is responsible for the low-level control of the UAV, which includes all the tasks necessary to ensure stable and safe flights. The FCU achieves this by using data from sensors or the onboard computer to make real-time adjustments and maintain flight stability.

As for the onboard calculation unit, it is represented by a small and light computer that runs a Linux operating system. The hardware and software modules used on this laptop are:

- **LIDARs/camera/optical flow sensor**: All the sensors that can provide visual or lidar odometry. Using these sensors, the UAV can overcome its main limitation: lack of stability in indoor environments. In addition, the LIDAR sensor can be used to map the area surrounding the robot and avoid obstacles.

- **Sensor fusion**: Different sensors can be integrated to estimate the current position of the UAV. In this context, SLAM algorithms can be implemented using depth sensors, lidar sensors, IMUs, and similar. This approach allows the UAV to properly navigate environments in which the GPS signal is not working or is weak.

- **Planners**: Using the information of the autopilot and the sensor connected with the onboard computer, a set of planner modules implement the robot autonomy. For example, a 3D obstacle-free path can be generated to drive the motion of the robot in a narrow space.

Another key component of UAV architectures is the GCS software. This is usually a program installed on a ground-based computer that communicates wirelessly with the FCU. The GCS enables developers to monitor and track the UAV's status. In some cases, it also allows them to directly control basic operations, such as takeoff, landing, or navigating to a specific point.

In this chapter, we will cover some of these modules. When it comes to autopilots, we will introduce the Pixhawk, one of the most widely used autopilots for both hobbyist and professional applications, as discussed in the next section.

Pixhawk autopilot and PX4 control stack

The **Pixhawk autopilot** is an open-source hardware platform widely used in both hobbyist and professional UAV applications. It serves as the brain of the UAV, providing the hardware needed to support flight control stacks. Basically, the Pixhawk integrates an IMU sensor and all the communication ports to directly integrate GPS and other similar sensors used to fly. One of the reasons for its popularity is its compatibility with various flight control software systems, such as **ArduPilot** [6] or **PX4** [7], which offer advanced flight modes, autonomous navigation, and customizable options.

This flexibility makes Pixhawk ideal for a wide range of applications, from recreational drones to industrial and research purposes. Additionally, Pixhawk's modular design supports various accessories like GPS, cameras, and communication modules, enhancing the drone's capabilities. The Pixhawk project was started by Lorenz Meier in 2008 as part of his work at ETH Zurich, a leading Swiss university. Pixhawk has since grown into a widely used platform in the UAV industry, and the project is now managed by the Dronecode Foundation, a non-profit organization that promotes open-source software and hardware for drone development. The fact that Pixhawk is open-source means that both the hardware designs and the flight control software are publicly available for anyone to use, modify, or improve. This transparency allows developers, hobbyists, and companies to customize and enhance the system to fit their specific needs.

Different versions of the autopilot are now available on the market, for example, in *Figure 11.2*, the Cube version of Pixhawk is shown, an advanced version of the Pixhawk autopilot, known for its modularity and enhanced performance. Also referred to as the Cube Autopilot, it features a cube-shaped design that houses high-end sensors, processors, and connectors, making it more robust and versatile compared to earlier versions of Pixhawk.

Figure 11.2: Pixhawk autopilot (Cube model)

The Cube's modular design allows it to be easily integrated into different UAV platforms. It connects to a carrier board that expands its functionality by adding ports for GPS, telemetry, power modules, and more. One of its key advantages is its built-in redundancy, with multiple sensors (such as accelerometers, gyroscopes, and magnetometers) to ensure flight stability and safety. This redundancy allows the autopilot to continue functioning even if one sensor fails.

In this chapter, we focus on the PX4 control stack. PX4 is composed of two primary layers:

- **Flight stack**: This layer implements the flight control system.
- **Middleware**: This general-purpose layer supports any type of autonomous robot by managing internal and external communications, as well as hardware integration.

The PX4 control stack is versatile, supporting various airframes that all share the same underlying code. The flight stack itself includes guidance, navigation, and control algorithms designed for autonomous vehicles. It features controllers for different types of airframes, such as fixed-wing, multirotor, and **Vertical Takeoff and Landing** (**VTOL**) aircraft, and also includes estimators for both attitude and position. Even if a physical aerial platform and autopilot are unavailable, it's possible to modify, compile, and run the autopilot's code by connecting it to the Gazebo simulator. In the upcoming section, we will install the PX4 flight stack and explore how to simulate and program autopilot code on a laptop.

The source code of the control stack can be modified to suit specific needs. For most standard applications, the default version of the PX4 control stack is already sufficient. However, understanding its architecture is important for gaining insight into how PX4 integrates with ROS 2. The architecture is shown in *Figure 11.3*.

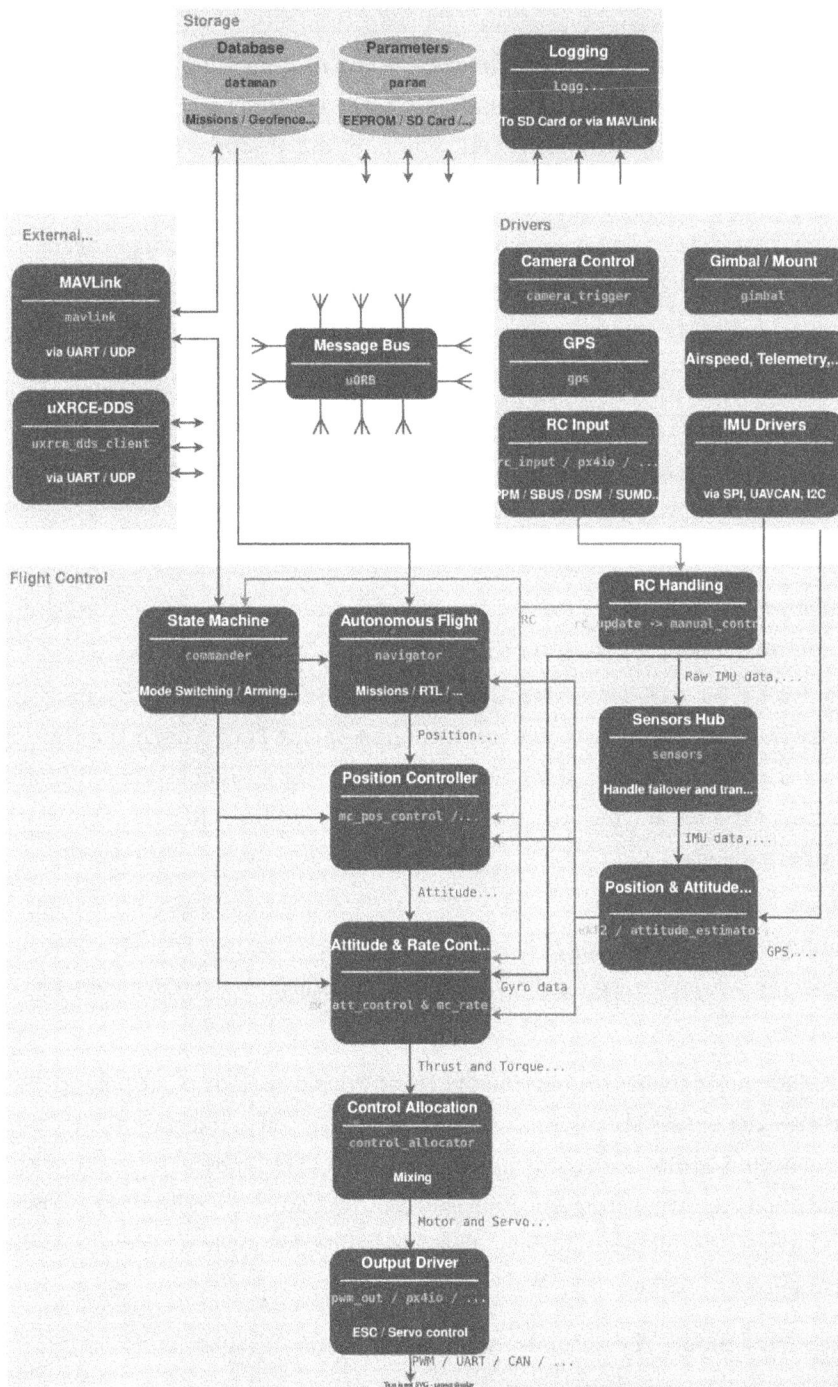

Figure 11.3: PX4 software architecture

The controller's source code is divided into independent modules, with each module representing a specific building block (as shown in *Figure 11.3*). These modules can be found within the firmware's main directory under the source folder. Like ROS 2, PX4 modules communicate using a publish/subscribe message bus called **uORB**. This publish/subscribe system offers the following advantages:

- **Reactivity**: The system operates asynchronously, instantly updating whenever new data is available, with all operations and communication happening in parallel.

- **Thread-safe data access**: System components can safely consume data from any source without threading issues.

The flight stack is made up of guidance, navigation, and control algorithms designed for autonomous drones. It includes controllers for various UAV airframes, including fixed-wing and multirotor configurations, as well as attitude and position estimators. The main modules of the PX4 architecture are:

- **Estimator**: This module processes inputs from one or more sensors, combining them to compute the vehicle's state, such as calculating its attitude from IMU data.

- **Controller**: A controller receives a setpoint and an estimated state (the process variable) and adjusts the process variable to match the setpoint. For example, the position controller takes desired position setpoints as input, uses the current estimated position as the process variable, and outputs attitude and thrust setpoints to guide the vehicle toward the desired location.

- **Mixer**: The mixer translates motion commands (such as turning right) into specific motor commands while ensuring system constraints are respected. These translations depend on factors like motor arrangement relative to the vehicle's center of gravity and rotational inertia.

The use of uORB messages has proven effective for integrating with ROS 2. Unlike earlier versions of ROS, where a custom serial communication layer was needed to translate *uORB* messages into ROS messages, ROS 2 allows direct connection between uORB messages and ROS topics. This direct connection improves communication speed and enhances overall system performance. In addition, PX4 supports different control modes that define the way in which the UAV is operated. The most important ones are:

- **Stabilized mode**: The autopilot stabilizes the aircraft's attitude (pitch, roll, and yaw) while the pilot controls the throttle and direction.

- **Position mode**: Both position and altitude are maintained by the autopilot. The pilot controls the direction and speed.

- **Offboard mode**: External commands are sent to the UAV from a companion computer, enabling real-time control through custom algorithms or scripts.

We will learn how to properly change the control mode to have the requested level of autonomy before discussing the communication between ROS 2 and aerial robots using the PX4 **Software-In-The-Loop** (SITL)

Simulating an aerial robot using Gazebo and the PX4 control stack

Operating UAVs comes with challenges, including instability during flight and the risk of crashes. To mitigate these risks, control algorithms should be tested in reliable simulators before implementation on real hardware. Simulators help developers identify and address issues without risking damage or incurring high operational costs. They also allow for the simulation of various environments and scenarios that may be hard to replicate in real life, ensuring better performance when transitioning to actual UAVs.

A key feature of the PX4 control stack is its ability to operate in **Software-In-The-Loop** (SITL) mode. In this mode, the PX4 flight control software runs on a computer rather than a physical drone, simulating all aspects of flight control, sensor inputs, and external conditions. This allows developers to test and validate algorithms without needing actual hardware, which is essential for identifying bugs, optimizing performance, and experimenting with control strategies in a safe environment. However, SITL has some limitations: it simplifies aerodynamic effects, uses idealized sensor and actuator models, and lacks real-world disturbances like wind, GPS signal variability, or hardware faults. Therefore, while SITL is invaluable for development, real-world testing remains necessary for full validation.

To compile and run the PX4 autopilot code, we must first clone the repository and install the needed dependencies, as discussed in the following:

1. To start the PX4 stack in SITL mode, you first need to download and compile the PX4 firmware. The cloning process may take some time as it downloads additional sub-repositories:

```
$ git clone https://github.com/PX4/PX4-Autopilot.git --recursive
```

This repository contains the control firmware's source code, compilation files, and models for simulating drones in Gazebo. It also includes a script to install the dependencies required for simulation with various simulators.

2. Next, prepare your environment by running the following command, which installs the necessary dependencies and configures the environment:

```
$ bash ./PX4-Autopilot/Tools/setup/ubuntu.sh
```

3. After the script finishes, reload your environment by opening a new terminal or restarting Docker. Then, compile the PX4 software in SITL mode:

```
$ cd PX4-Autopilot/
$ make px4_sitl
```

4. Once compiled, you can start Gazebo with a simulated UAV using the command:

```
$ make px4_sitl gz_x500
```

This command launches a simulation of a drone model called x500, as shown in *Figure 11.4*.

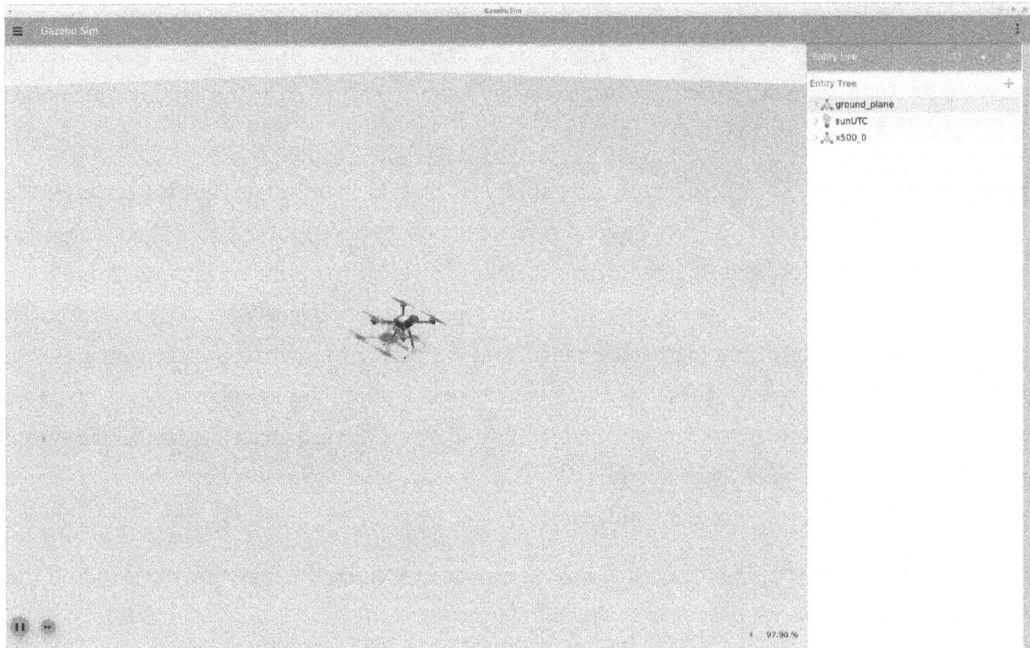

Figure 11.4: UAV simulated in Gazebo using the PX4 SITL

Although we can't directly interact with the UAV without a specific application, the code in the PX4 control stack is currently running and is prepared to handle all requests from external programs. Let's start interacting with the simulated UAV by using a common Ground Control Station program: **QGroundControl**.

QGroundControl is open-source ground control station software designed for operating and managing UAVs. It supports the PX4 control stack and provides various tools for drone control, mission planning, and real-time monitoring. Before using QGroundControl, it needs to be installed. The easiest way to install it on Ubuntu is by using the `.AppImage` file, which includes all necessary dependencies. This method simplifies the installation process by eliminating the need for additional packages or complicated setups. To install **QGroundControl**, download the `AppImage` file from the official download page at the following link: `https://docs.qgroundcontrol.com/master/en/qgc-user-guide/getting_started/download_and_install.html`.

Once downloaded, open a terminal and navigate to the directory containing the `.AppImage` file (assuming it's in the `Downloads` folder), and execute the following commands:

```
$ cd ~/Downloads
$ chmod +x QGroundControl.AppImage
$ ./QGroundControl.AppImage
```

This allows you to run QGroundControl without fully installing it on your system. After launching the application, the main page of the control station will appear. Whether you are using a real drone or a simulated one via Gazebo, the user interface remains consistent, as shown in *Figure 11.5*.

Figure 11.5: Main QGroundControl window

In *Figure 11.5*, the main elements of the GCS are contained. At the top of the window is the **Fly** toolbar. Next to the **Q** icon, there is a text indicator that shows whether the UAV is properly configured and ready to fly. This indicator uses color codes: green for *ready*, yellow for *warnings*, and red for issues that prevent flight. In the **Fly** toolbar, you can also view the current flight mode and change it by clicking on the mode indicator. Additionally, the panel displays the UAV's current attitude, with a horizontal plane for monitoring roll and pitch, and a compass for yaw orientation. Finally, In the left part of the window, a horizontal panel containing some buttons is contained. Using these buttons, we can request some flight tasks, like requesting takeoff/landing or activating a new flight plan.

Try to use QGroundControl to drive the actions of the simulated UAV. It will act exactly like it will in the real system. However, we are not interested in using the GCS to drive the robot, but we want to use ROS 2 nodes. For this reason, let's discuss in the next section how to interface ROS 2 and PX4.

Interfacing ROS 2 and PX4

To properly interface ROS 2 and PX4, we must access the internal *uORB* topics of the UAV controller. In this way, we can read the information generated from autopilot, sending control input or additional information in a transparent way. To implement this, PX4 uses the *uXRCE-DDS* middleware. The communication process is shown in the pipeline depicted in *Figure 11.6*. Put simply, the uXRCE-DDS middleware consists of a client operating on PX4 and an agent running on the companion computer, facilitating bi-directional data exchange via a serial or UDP connection. The agent serves as a proxy for the client, allowing it to publish and subscribe to topics within the global DDS data space.

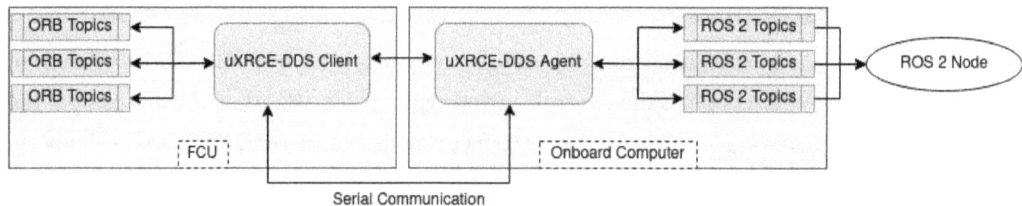

Figure 11.6: ROS 2-PX4 integration

After connecting the client, the uORB messages are streamed toward ROS 2 using the px4_msgs package. Let's install both messages and the uXRCE-DDS library to enable the message exchange between the autopilot code and ROS 2:

1. Install the PX4 messages by cloning and compiling the following package:

    ```
    $ git clone https://github.com/PX4/px4_msgs.git
    ```

2. Compile and install the Micro XRCE-DDS Agent. You can do it by using the following commands to install it; the installation can be done in any system directory, as it is independent of the ROS 2 workspace:

    ```
    git clone https://github.com/eProsima/Micro-XRCE-DDS-Agent.git
    cd Micro-XRCE-DDS-Agent
    mkdir build && cd build && cmake ..
    make
    sudo make install
    sudo ldconfig /usr/local/lib/
    ```

We can now use the commands listed in the next two steps to start the Gazebo simulation and the ROS 2 communication bridge.

3. Start Gazebo using the following command:

```
make px4_sitl gz_x500
```

4. Start the communication bridge:

```
MicroXRCEAgent udp4 -p 8888
```

In this case, the bridge communicates with the PX4 modules using the UDP protocol instantized on port 8888.

You can check that the ROS 2 system correctly communicates with PX4 by checking the active topics. By default, the namespace associated with the topics is `fmu` (Flight Management Unit). We can distinguish two types of topics, the input for the FCU (`/fmu/in/*`) and the output of the FCU (`/fmu/out/*`). Among the different topics, the most interesting ones are:

*   `/fmu/in/offboard_control_mode`: To trigger the offboard control mode. If you don't publish on this topic, the PX4 will not allow you to switch on the offboard control mode to start autonomous navigation.

*   `/fmu/in/vehicle_command`: To request the navigation towards a new setpoint.

*   `/fmu/out/vehicle_local_position`: To read the local position reconstructed from the Px4 based on information like GPS or external position source.

Additionally, the ROS 2-PX4 interface also instantiates a service to request specific commands from the UAV. This service is called `/fmu/vehicle_command` and as an example, it is used to change to UAV control mode.

We will use the topics and the service in the next example of this chapter, where we will control the UAV to perform specific trajectories and basic arm, disarm, and take-off operations.

Controlling a UAV using ROS 2

We are now ready to implement our first ROS 2 application to control a simulated UAV. As previously mentioned, the interface between Gazebo and ROS 2 mimics that of a real autopilot. This means the program presented in this chapter will work the same way with a real robot. The goal of this example is to demonstrate how to perform basic UAV operations. Specifically, we will implement the following functions:

- **Arm**: Start the propellers spinning.
- **Disarm**: Stop the propellers from spinning.
- **Take off**: Lift the UAV to an altitude of 5 meters at its current position.

Additionally, during these operations, the ROS 2 system will monitor the UAV's local position in Cartesian space. After takeoff, the user will be able to specify a target position for the UAV to reach. The UAV will then plan and execute a time-sampled trajectory from its current position to the specified goal. To achieve this, we need to select the **OFFBOARD** control mode. PX4 includes a safety mechanism to prevent accidentally switching to this mode.

Engaging the OFFBOARD mode

To engage **OFFBOARD** mode, we must continuously send a trigger message requesting the desired control mode, as shown in the example below:

1. Start creating a ROS 2 package containing our ROS 2 node. As dependencies, we will specify the px4_msgs to use the data generated by the uXRCE-DDS layer:

```
$ ros2 pkg create px4_ctrl --dependencies rclcpp std_msgs geometry_
msgs px4_msgs
```

2. To implement the ROS 2 node, we will define a header file, the px4_ctrl.h file, where we include the headers and define the class of the node. As for the headers, let's include the interface types to communicate with the autopilot.

```
#include <rclcpp/rclcpp.hpp>
#include <px4_msgs/msg/offboard_control_mode.hpp>
#include <px4_msgs/msg/trajectory_setpoint.hpp>
#include <px4_msgs/msg/vehicle_control_mode.hpp>
#include <px4_msgs/msg/vehicle_local_position.hpp>
#include <px4_msgs/srv/vehicle_command.hpp>
```

3. In the class constructor, link the input and output of the node. First, set up the service for changing the control mode, which uses the px4_msgs::srv::VehicleCommand type. Additionally, we need to publish a trigger to enable offboard control mode. After that, we will publish the desired setpoint that the UAV should reach (we will explain how to properly format these messages later in the example):

```
class Px4Control : public rclcpp::Node {
    public:
        Px4Control()  : Node("px4_ctrl") {
            cmd_client_ = create_client<px4_
msgs::srv::VehicleCommand>("/fmu/vehicle_command");
            traj_cmd_pub_ = create_publisher<px4_
msgs::msg::TrajectorySetpoint>("/fmu/in/trajectory_setpoint", 10);
            offboard_ctrl_mode_publisher_ = create_publisher<px4_
msgs::msg::OffboardControlMode>("fmu/in/offboard_control_mode", 10);
```

4. Alternatively, to receive the estimated position of the UAV in a local frame in Cartesian space, to correctly receive the topic, we have to set the quality of service, as shown below:

```
rclcpp::QoS qos_profile(rclcpp::QoSInitialization::from_rmw(rmw_qos_
profile_default));
qos_profile.reliability(RMW_QOS_POLICY_RELIABILITY_BEST_EFFORT);
qos_profile.durability(RMW_QOS_POLICY_DURABILITY_TRANSIENT_LOCAL);
qos_profile.liveliness(RMW_QOS_POLICY_LIVELINESS_AUTOMATIC);
qos_profile.history(RMW_QOS_POLICY_HISTORY_KEEP_LAST
qos_profile.keep_last(10);
uav_pose_sub_ = this->create_subscription<px4_
msgs::msg::VehicleLocalPosition>("/fmu/out/vehicle_local_
position", qos_profile,  std::bind(&Px4Control::uav_pose_cb, this,
std::placeholders::_1));
```

5. Before completing the constructor, we wait for the service to come online. Without this service, we cannot ask the PX4 to switch on the offboard control mode:

```
while (!cmd_client_->wait_for_service(1s)) {
if (!rclcpp::ok()) {
    RCLCPP_ERROR(this->get_logger(), "Interrupted while waiting
for the service. Exiting.");
    return;
}
```

```
        RCLCPP_INFO(this->get_logger(), "service not available,
waiting again...");
    }
action_done_.store(false);
```

As you can see from the last line of the header file, the action_done_ variable has the shape of boolean data; however, its value is set with the store function. This is an atomic variable that can be used to safely update a shared flag between multiple threads. Atomic variables, like std::atomic<bool>, ensure thread-safe read/write operations without needing a mutex. In this case, action_done_ acts as a flag to indicate whether an action has been completed or not. Since multiple threads may read or modify this flag (e.g., one thread sets it to true when an action is done, while another checks its value), using an atomic variable ensures that no data races or inconsistent reads occur.

In the rest of the class definition, we just define the methods implemented in the .cpp file and some class variables. Let's discuss the content of the source file next.

Exploring the px4_ctrl.cpp file

Here's a breakdown of the px4_ctrl.cpp file:

- The first function to discuss is send_cmd. This is used to fill the fields of the service:

```
void Px4Control::send_cmd(uint16_t command, float param1, float
param2) {
auto request = std::make_shared<px4_
msgs::srv::VehicleCommand::Request>();
VehicleCommand cmd{};
```

  - Based on two parameters, we can select the desired command, namely, arm or disarm, or change the control mode:

```
cmd.param1 = param1;
cmd.param2 = param2;
cmd.command = command;
cmd.target_system = 1;
cmd.target_component = 1;
cmd.source_system = 1;
cmd.source_component = 1;
cmd.from_external = true;
cmd.timestamp = this->get_clock()->now().nanoseconds() /
```

```
    1000;
    request->request = cmd;
```

- When we call the client, we also provide a callback function, which is triggered when the service response is ready:

```
auto result = _cmd_client->async_send_request(request,
std::bind(&Px4Control::srv_callback, this, std::placeholders::_1));
```

- The service callback function is used to wait for the service to return with a value. When it returns, we can consider the requested command executed:

```
void Px4Control::srv_callback(rclcpp::Client<px4_
msgs::srv::VehicleCommand>::SharedFuture future) {
    auto status = future.wait_for(1s);
    if (status == std::future_status::ready) {
        auto reply = future.get()->reply;
        uint8_t service_result_ = reply.result;
        action_done_.store(true);
    }
    else {
        RCLCPP_INFO(this->get_logger(), "Service In-Progress...");
    }
}
```

- The send_cmd function is used in the arm and disarm functions. In the first case, the first parameter is 1 and the second is 0. In the disarm case, both parameters are 0:

```
void Px4Control::arm() {
send_cmd(VehicleCommand::VEHICLE_CMD_COMPONENT_ARM_DISARM,
VehicleCommand::ARMING_ACTION_ARM, 0.0); }
void Px4Control::disarm() {
    send_cmd(VehicleCommand::VEHICLE_CMD_COMPONENT_ARM_DISARM, 0.0,
0.0);}
```

- In the local pose callback, we collect and save the current coordinates of the UAV:

```
void Px4Control::uav_pose_cb(const px4_
msgs::msg::VehicleLocalPosition::SharedPtr msg) {
    curr_x_ = msg->x;
    curr_y_ = msg->y;
```

```
        curr_z_ = msg->z;
    }
```

- To trigger the offboard control mode, we must publish the OffboardControlMode data, specifying the kinds of input data. For example, in this case, we specify that we want to enable the offboard control mode, controlling the desired position. To avoid interruptions, we start this as a thread that runs at 1 Hz:

```
void Px4Control::publish_offboard_ctrl_mode() {
    rclcpp::Rate loop_rate(1);
    while( rclcpp::ok() ) {
        OffboardControlMode data{};
        data.position = true;
        data.velocity = false;
        data.acceleration = false;
        data.attitude = false;
        data.body_rate = false;
    offboard_ctrl_mode_publisher_->publish(data);
        loop_rate.sleep();
    }
}
```

- To allow the user to request a given action, we implement a basic command-line menu. Here, the user can write the desired action: arm, disarm, takeoff, or move:

```
void Px4Control::menu() {
```

- Before asking the user for the desired action, we start the offboard trigger publisher thread:

```
    boost::thread publish_offboard_ctrl_mode_t(
&Px4Control::publish_offboard_ctrl_mode, this );
    string cmd = "";
```

- The action request terminates when the user inserts the exit word:

```
    while (rclcpp::ok() && cmd != "exit") {
action_done_.store(false);
            RCLCPP_INFO(this->get_logger(), "Insert the desired
command");
RCLCPP_INFO(this->get_logger(), "arm - to arm the drone");
RCLCPP_INFO(this->get_logger(), "disarm - to disarm the drone");
```

```
RCLCPP_INFO(this->get_logger(), "takeoff - to take the drone");
RCLCPP_INFO(this->get_logger(), "move - specify a target point to
reach");
RCLCPP_INFO(this->get_logger(), "exit - to exit");

getline( cin, cmd );
```

- After receiving the request, we call the desired function:

```
if( cmd == "arm") {
    arm();
    while( !action_done_.load()) usleep(0.1*1e6);
}
else if ( cmd == "disarm" ) {
    disarm();
    while( !action_done_.load()) usleep(0.1*1e6);
}
```

- For the takeoff command, first, we request to switch on the offboard control mode (param2 = 6):

```
else if ( cmd == "takeoff") {
send_cmd(VehicleCommand::VEHICLE_CMD_DO_SET_MODE, 1, 6);
    sleep(1);
    px4_msgs::msg::TrajectorySetpoint msg{};
```

- Then, we will set the desired position to perform the takeoff. Such a point will be the current location in x and y, and the desired displacement over the z-axis, to actually perform the takeoff. In this case, we request 5 meters:

```
msg.position = {curr_x_, curr_y_, curr_z_-5.0};
msg.yaw = 0.0;
msg.timestamp = this->get_clock()->now().nanoseconds() /
1000
```

- Finally, we publish the desired setpoint. If the robot is armed, and it is in Offboard control mode, it will start to fly:

```
traj_cmd_pub_->publish(msg);
}
```

- As for the move action, we must ask the user for additional information: the destination point. We avoid considering the movements over the yaw angle. So, we just ask for x, y, and z:

```
else if( cmd == "move") {
        float x, y, z;
        std::string input;
        RCLCPP_INFO(this->get_logger(), "Insert the destination
point as x y z:");

        std::getline(std::cin, input);  // Read entire line
        std::istringstream stream(input);
        stream >> x >> y >> z;
```

- Before sending the target position to the UAV, there is an important consideration. The PX4 stack uses a controller to minimize the position error, meaning when we request the UAV to reach a specific position, the PX4 controller moves the UAV to that point automatically. In the code, we use a Point3D structure to store both the current and desired positions. However, the UAV will attempt to reach the target as quickly as possible. If the target is far away, this could result in abrupt and visually unappealing movements, and it might even cause instability. To avoid this, we need to plan a smooth trajectory by generating intermediate waypoints between the starting position and the destination, ensuring smoother and more stable motion. This trajectory is saturated in velocity, requiring a maximum velocity of 0.5 m/s:

```
Point3D start = {curr_x_, curr_y_, curr_z_};
Point3D end = {x, y, z};
double v_max = 0.5;
double time_step = 1.0/10.0;
```

- To plan the trajectory, we use the function planTrajectory:

```
std::vector<Point3D> trajectory = planTrajectory(start,
end, v_max, time_step);
        px4_msgs::msg::TrajectorySetpoint msg{};
        rclcpp::Rate loop_rate(10);
```

- After the trajectory is fully generated, we will stream it point by point with the same frequency as the sample time used in the trajectory calculation:

```
for (const auto& point : trajectory) {
    msg.position = {point.x, point.y, point.z};
    msg.yaw = 0.0;
    msg.timestamp = this->get_clock()->now().
nanoseconds() / 1000;
    traj_cmd_pub_->publish(msg);
    loop_rate.sleep();
    }
  }
 }
}
```

- To support the trajectory calculation, we define a data structure to store the x, y, and z coordinates. In addition, a function to calculate the distance between two points using the Euclidean distance formula is defined:

```
struct Point3D {
    double x, y, z;
};
double calculateDistance(const Point3D& start, const Point3D& end) {

return std::hypot(end.x - start.x, end.y - start.y, end.z -
start.z);
}
```

- The linear interpolation method is used to generate a smooth trajectory between two points, with a maximum velocity and a given time step. This method ensures a straight-line path between the start and end points with a constant speed:

```
std::vector<Point3D> planTrajectory(const Point3D& start, const
Point3D& end, double v_max, double time_step) {
    std::vector<Point3D> waypoints;
double total_distance = calculateDistance(start, end);
    double total_time = total_distance / v_max;
    int num_steps = std::ceil(total_time / time_step);
    double v_x = (end.x - start.x) / (num_steps * time_step);
    double v_y = (end.y - start.y) / (num_steps * time_step);
```

```
        double v_z = (end.z - start.z) / (num_steps * time_step);;
        for (int i = 0; i <= num_steps; ++i) {
            double t = i * time_step;
            Point3D waypoint;
            waypoint.x = start.x + v_x * t;
            waypoint.y = start.y + v_y * t;
            waypoint.z = start.z + v_z * t;
            waypoints.push_back(waypoint);
        }
        return waypoints;
    }
```

- In the main function of the node, the defined ROS 2 class is instantized and the run method is called. In the run method, we start the menu thread and request the node spin:

```
void Px4Control::run() {
    std::thread menu_t( &Px4Control::menu, this);
    rclcpp::spin(shared_from_this());
}
int main(int argc, char *argv[]) {
    rclcpp::init(argc, argv);
    auto node = std::make_shared<Px4Control>();
    node->run();
    rclcpp::shutdown();
return 0;
}
```

We can now compile and start the node after launching the simulation, as discussed in the next section.

Working with the node

To start the ROS 2 developed in the previous section to control the simulated UAV, you need to compile the workspace after modifying the CMakeLists.txt file as shown below:

```
add_executable(px4_ctrl src/px4_ctrl.cpp)
ament_target_dependencies(px4_ctrl rclcpp px4_msgs Boost)
install(TARGETS
  px4_ctrl
  DESTINATION lib/${PROJECT_NAME})
```

Let's try our node action. Start the simulation and the ROS 2 communication layer:

```
$ make px4_sitl gz_x500
$ MicroXRCEAgent udp4 -p 8888
```

Start the px4_ctrl node:

```
$ ros2 run px4_ctrl px4_ctrl
```

Now, you can ask for the desired actions. An example of this interaction is depicted in *Figure 11.7*, where, after the takeoff, the position 3, 8, -10 is requested.

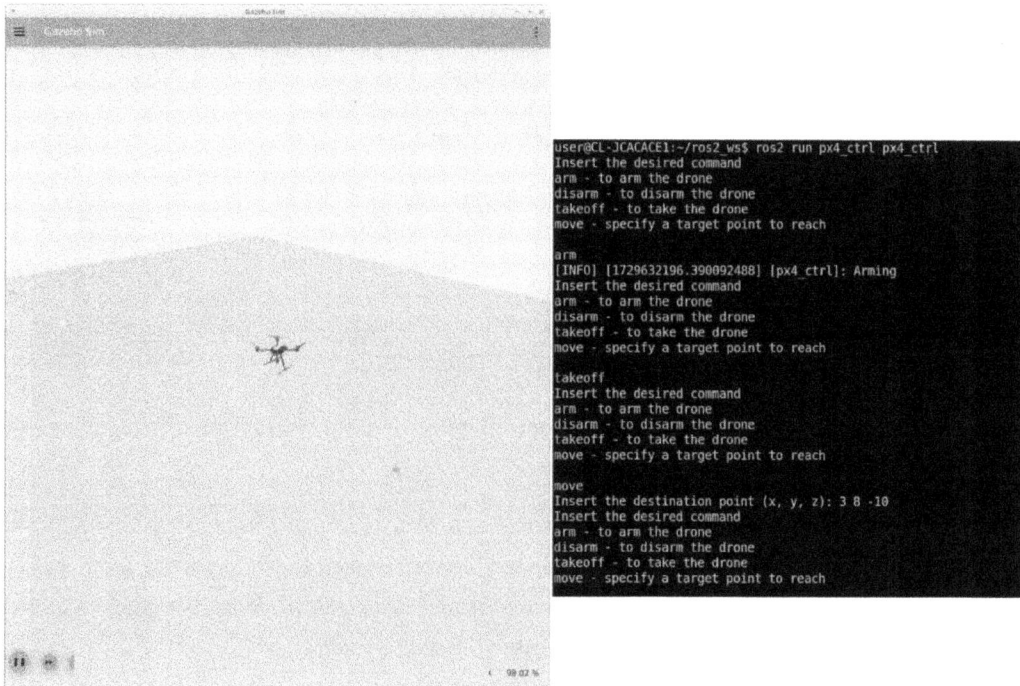

Figure 11.7: px4_ctrl node executed with the Gazebo simulation

However, looking at the coordinates we are sending to the robot, you are probably asking yourself why the altitude is negative. Why –10 meters along the z-axis? The convention adopted by all PX4 systems is called NED or FLU. This means that the axis direction is the following: x-forward, y-left, z-up. Similarly, **NED** stands for **North-East-Down**. This frame is shown in *Figure 11.8*.

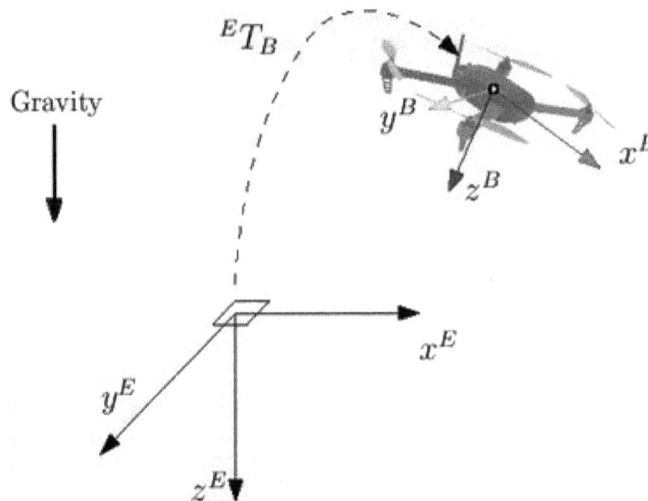

Figure 11.8: PX4 frame convention

This means that you must operate a proper coordinate system transformation to integrate a PX4-based application with other ROS 2 modules.

This section provides a basic example of controlling UAVs. Although the example is conducted in a simulation environment, the PX4 control stack's emulation closely mirrors the behavior of a real aerial system. Furthermore, you can explore all the topics published by Autopilot to gather additional information for integrating them into your ROS 2 nodes.

Summary

In this chapter, we demonstrated how to simulate aerial robots and their hardware. Specifically, we used the **Software-In-The-Loop** (**SITL**) feature of the PX4 control stack, widely used control software for UAVs, to enable simulation in Gazebo. We also showed how to integrate aerial systems in Gazebo with ROS 2, where control inputs and other information from the autopilot are directly linked to the ROS 2 network. Additionally, we implemented a ROS 2 node to control the UAV's position, illustrating how to program basic operations such as starting the propellers and taking off.

In the next chapter, we will explore programming another robotic platform—a mobile robot based on a microcontroller—using ROS 2.

References

- [1] www.dji.com
- [2] www.autelrobotics.com
- [3] www.flyzipline.com
- [4] www.delair.aero
- [5] www.flyability.com
- [6] ardupilot.org
- [7] docs.px4.io

12

Designing and Programming a DIY Mobile Robot from Scratch

In previous chapters, we explored how to install and configure ROS 2 packages to implement autonomous navigation, localization, and mapping for a simulated robot. In this chapter, we will focus on building a simple and affordable differential drive robot and equipping it with navigation capabilities.

To follow along with this chapter, you will need some hardware components. However, the programs and configurations provided here can be slightly adapted to work with any DIY mobile platform. The goal of this chapter is to guide you through configuring the complete navigation pipeline—from low-level motor control to localization and path planning.

We will cover the following topics in this chapter:

- Understanding the DIY mobile robot
- Understanding the electronic connection
- Programming and configuring the DIY robot
- Further improvements

Technical requirements

To follow this chapter, you should have the following hardware components:

- **Raspberry Pi 3 B:** A small single-board computer integrating a standard computer with a series of digital pins that can be used to control electronic components. A microSD used as the main hard drive is still needed.

- **Robot frame:** The main chassis of the robot, composed of two spots for active motors (the differential drive actuation) and a passive wheel.

- **A 2D USB LiDAR:** The sensor used to implement the autonomous navigation of the robot. In this chapter, we will use an *LD20 LiDAR*.

- **Two DC TT motors: Direct current** (DC) motors are cheap and easy to find in different online shops.

- **An L298N controller:** This board is used to control the motors.

- A board that converts (steps down) the higher voltage input signal to a lower 5V power that can be used for powering the Raspberry Pi.

- **A battery pack:** The current source to power the entire system.

The reference materials for this chapter can be found in the `Chapter12` folder of the following GitHub repository: `https://github.com/PacktPublishing/Mastering-ROS-2-for-Robotics-Programming/tree/main/Chapter12`.

Understanding the DIY mobile robot

The objective of this section is to introduce the basic components that are useful for building a tiny mobile robot. Let's start by discussing the hardware of the robot, which must be properly connected to ensure the control of the wheels and the sensors. The main brain of the robot is the onboard computer, the Raspberry Pi. The Raspberry Pi [1] is a widely popular board for prototyping and cost-effective system development. Its appeal lies not only in its affordability, compact size, and versatility but also in its **general-purpose input/output** (GPIO) pins, which enable direct interaction with external devices such as sensors, motors, LEDs, and more.

By leveraging the Raspberry Pi's built-in GPIO pins, there's no need for an additional microcontroller (such as an Arduino) to manage the robot's actuators. Numerous similar robotics platforms have been built using this approach, with many project examples available online, such as PiCar-X [2] – a smart robot car based on Raspberry Pi.

It uses two independently controlled wheels for differential drive motion, or the lidarbot [3], which relies on the same hardware used in this chapter. Depending on your budget, you can choose from various Raspberry Pi models. For example, if you're on a low budget ($10–$20), you can choose the Raspberry Pi Pico ($4–$6) for microcontroller projects or the Raspberry Pi Zero 2 W (~$15) for lightweight IoT and robotics. For a mid-range budget ($35–$70), the Raspberry Pi 3 Model B+ ($40) is great for general projects, while the Raspberry Pi 4 (2GB) ($45) offers better performance for media and automation. If you have a high budget ($80–$150), the Raspberry Pi 4 (8GB) ($100) is ideal for AI and robotics, while the Raspberry Pi 5 (4GB/8GB) ($80–$120) provides high performance for demanding applications.

In this book, we use the Raspberry Pi 3 B. Although this model is relatively old, it is sufficient to equip the robot with navigation capabilities and is cheaper with respect to the newer models. Here are some features of this board:

- The Raspberry Pi features a Broadcom BCM2837 Quad-Core ARM Cortex-A53 processor running at 1.2 GHz and 1 GB of LPDDR2 SDRAM.

- It includes 802.11n Wi-Fi (2.4 GHz) and Bluetooth 4.1 (BLE) for wireless connectivity.

- A 40-pin GPIO header is available for hardware interfacing.

- Ports include four USB 2.0, full-size HDMI output, and a 3.5 mm audio/composite video jack.

- Storage is provided via a microSD card slot for the operating system and data.

- The recommended power supply is a 5V/2.5A input via micro USB.

Let's now discuss how to install and configure the Linux environment and ROS 2 for the companion computer.

Installing Linux on the Raspberry Pi

The Raspberry Pi's hard drive is a microSD card, so selecting a card with high read/write performance is essential to enhance the Pi's computational speed. In this example, we use a 64 GB *SanDisk Extreme Pro microSDXC* card. To set up the Raspberry Pi for the first time, you will need a keyboard and a monitor for the initial configuration, as well as a power supply. The board is powered via a micro-USB cable, so you can use a mobile phone charger or a USB port from a computer. The first step is to install the operating system on the Raspberry Pi's microSD card. Since we are using ROS 2 Jazzy, Ubuntu 24.04 must be installed on the board. To optimize performance and reduce unnecessary overhead, we will use the server version of Ubuntu, which is designed for server environments.

This version does not include a **graphical user interface** (**GUI**), focusing instead on performance and stability for services such as web servers and databases. To install Ubuntu on the Raspberry Pi's microSD card, use the rpi-imager program. Connect the microSD card to another computer running Ubuntu Linux (you'll need a microSD card adapter) and install rpi-imager with the following command:

```
sudo apt-get install rpi-imager
```

After installing rpi-imager, start it with the following command:

```
rpi-imager
```

The main window of the program will now open, as shown in *Figure 12.1*.

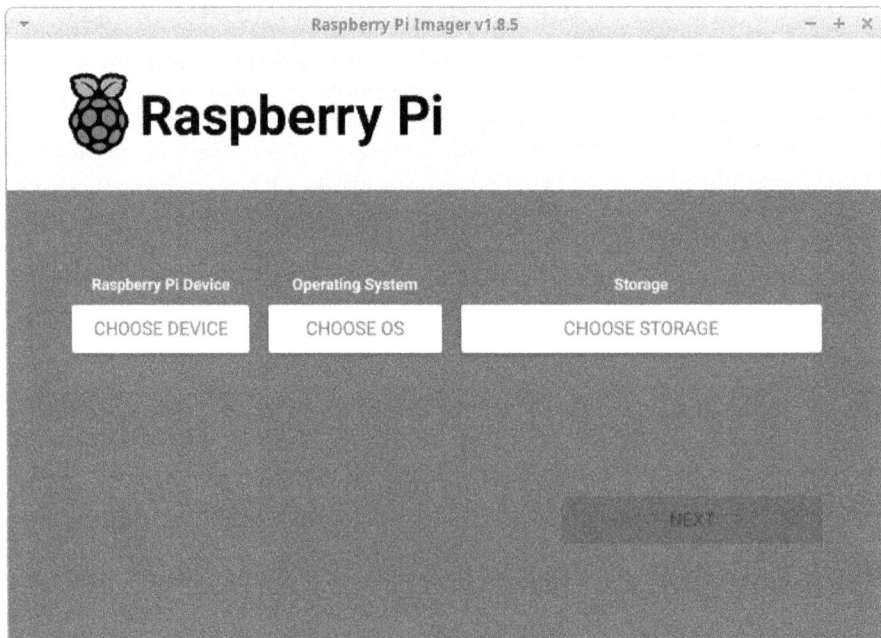

Figure 12.1: The rpi-imager main window

From the main window of rpi-imager, you can choose the target device, that is, the model of the Raspberry Pi you are using, the storage device (the microSD card), and the operating system to install. Here, you can navigate through the following entries:

Other General-Purpose OS -> Ubuntu -> Ubuntu Server 24.04

Before starting the installation process, the program will ask you whether you want to set some advanced options. This step is useful to simplify the usage of the Raspberry Pi after the installation of the system. Here is the setup:

1. First, as shown in *Figure 12.2*, you can set the login data (username and password).

2. Then, add a WiFi network for remote access to the board. By default, your PC's WiFi network (if connected) is already set up. However, you can configure a custom network by following the panel.

3. Finally, in the **SERVICES** tab, you must enable SSH authentication using a username and password.

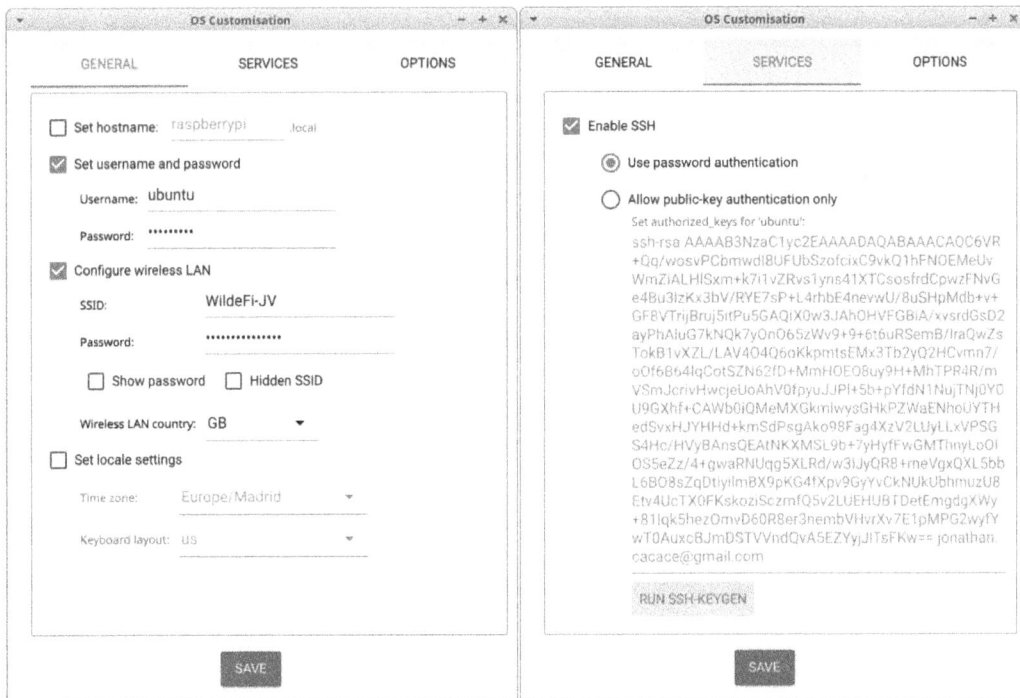

Figure 12.2: The rpi-imager advanced options

After the installation process is completed, insert the SD into the Raspberry Pi, connect the keyboard and the monitor, and finally, start the board with its power supply.

Configuring the Raspberry Pi

Using the keyboard, you can configure the Raspberry Pi to be an external computer controlling our robot. Let's start installing ROS 2 on this device. Also, in this case, we don't need all the packages for the complete installation of ROS 2. For this reason, we can install the base version of ROS 2. The steps for installing ROS are the same as described in *Chapter 2*. You can also find these steps in [2]. Remember that in the last step, you should install the base version of ROS 2 using the following command:

```
sudo apt install ros-jazzy-ros-base
```

You can source the ROS 2 system before creating a new workspace and compiling it. Remember that you can use the .bashrc file to automatically load the workspace at each boot of the system.

Once ROS 2 is installed and configured, you can start using the Raspberry Pi remotely, even when it is mounted on the mobile robot and not directly connected to a monitor and keyboard.

Using the Raspberry Pi remotely

In the final version of our robot, interaction is streamlined through ROS 2, enabling you to visualize its position, view the generated map, or issue position commands. However, there may be instances where you need direct access to the robot's onboard computer for debugging or manually starting specific programs. Since the computer is physically mounted on the robot, using a keyboard and external screen is impractical. To overcome this, we use the **Secure Shell (SSH)** protocol—a secure network protocol that allows remote login and command execution over an unsecured network. SSH ensures encryption, data integrity, and authentication, making it a reliable way to manage servers and devices remotely. To connect to the robot's computer, you need an SSH client, which is available on most Linux and Windows systems. Notice that to establish a connection between your PC and the robot, you need to install two components:

- **Client on your PC**: This is the software that you will use to interact with the robot.
- **Server on the robot**: This is the software running on the robot that allows it to accept commands from the client.

To install the client and the server, respectively, use the following commands:

```
sudo apt-get install openssh-server
Sudo apt-get install openssh-client
```

If you have the robot's IP address (e.g., the Raspberry Pi's IP) and the username of the remote device (in this case, *ubuntu*), you can connect using the following command:

```
ssh -l ubuntu <IP_RASPBERRY>
```

After running this command, you will be prompted to enter the password for the remote device. Since SSH password authentication is enabled, entering the correct password will log you into the robot's computer. However, the simple SSH connection has a problem. If the computer where the connection has been opened loses its connection, all the programs started remotely are interrupted. In addition, you could start the desired programs on the robot before closing the remote connection and wait for it to start operating. For this reason, tmux can be used. tmux is a terminal multiplexer that allows you to manage multiple terminal sessions from a single window, enabling efficient multitasking in a command-line environment. It lets you split your terminal into panes, switch between multiple sessions, and run processes persistently, even after disconnecting from a remote server. You can create a session, detach it to keep processes running in the background, and reattach it later. Basic commands include tmux to start a session and tmux attach to reconnect to an existing session.

You can handle the different panes and sessions using shortcuts. Learning its syntax is not very easy, so we suggest checking a cheat sheet here [4]. However, to start using tmux, you should use the following steps:

1. First, log in to your remote server:

```
ssh user@remote_host
```

2. Install and start tmux:

```
sudo apt install tmux
tmux new -s my_session
```

3. You can work inside tmux to run commands or tasks. Later, you can disconnect from the remote server. If you need to log back in to eventually check the output of your programs, you can use the following command:

```
tmux attach -t my_session
```

tmux is a very interesting tool to handle remote machines without depending on the local connection. Now, the Raspberry Pi is ready to be used as the brain of our robot.

Advanced configuration of the Raspberry Pi

The Raspberry Pi is now ready to be used. However, two additional configuration steps could be useful:

1. First, an additional WiFi can be configured in case you want to connect to another network. To do this, you can use the netplan program. A proper network configuration file is placed in the /etc/netplan directory (called 50-cloud-init.yaml). Here, you must add the new WiFi network and its password to the list of access points.

2. Another useful tip is to increase the swap of the board since the 3b model has only 1 GB of RAM. This can be done using the dphys-swapfile program:

    1. Let's install it with the following command:

        ```
        sudo apt install dphys-swapfile
        ```

    2. Edit the configuration file:

        ```
        sudo nano /etc/dphys-swapfile
        ```

    3. Search the following line and change it with the desired size:

        ```
        CONF_SWAPSIZE=100
        ```

    4. After this, you can save the file and reboot the board to have the new swap area.

    5. You can use the following command to be sure that the changes have been applied:

        ```
        free -h
        ```

We can now move to the rest of the hardware.

Choosing the robot frame

The mobile base platform must have a differential drive actuation. For this reason, any kind of frame considering two wheels placed on the same axes and controlled by two separate motors will be suitable for this task. In our example, we simply rely on a plastic frame with the following data (see *Figure 12.3*):

*   Base length: 22 cm
*   Base width: 16 cm
*   Wheel separation: 14 cm
*   Wheel diameter: 6.5 cm

You can choose any kind of frame based on the shape you prefer. Of course, consider the components that must be placed on it and the presence of two active wheels. Such frames, along with the motors, can be found on webstores such as **AliExpress** [5] by searching for objects such as "smart robot car" or "wheeled robot frame." Typically, these frames come equipped with the motors that will be used for the robot actuation, the passive wheel, and the tools needed to assemble it. A power button is also useful to start and stop the robot without disconnecting the power supply.

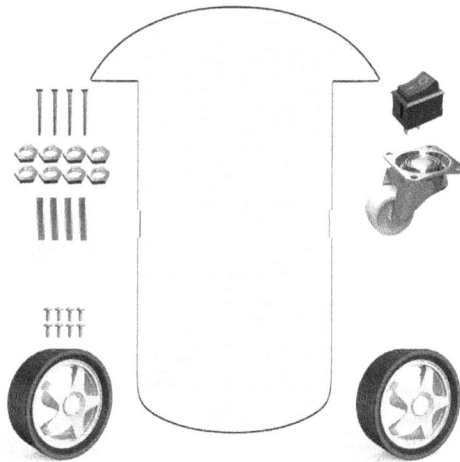

Figure 12.3: Differential drive robot frame

As for the power supply, any kind of source from 9 to 12 volts can be used. Let's now discuss the electronics components and the actuators.

Mobile robot electronics and sensors

As already stated, the Raspberry Pi works as the main brain of the robot, running ROS 2 to handle the system navigation and localization and acting as an interface with the operator. However, there are different devices that are needed to create your mobile robot:

- **DC motors**: The robot uses two TT DC gearbox motors with a 1:48 gear ratio, powered by 3–6V DC, and controlled by an L298N driver for bidirectional rotation. These basic motors lack features such as encoders or feedback, so odometry will be calculated using a LiDAR sensor, as detailed later in the chapter, in the *Odometry calculation* section.

- **LiDAR sensor:** A 2D LiDAR sensor is used to calculate the robot odometry since the motors don't provide the odometry itself and to implement the localization and mapping functions from the ROS 2 navigation stack. We used an *LD20 LiDAR* provided by **youyeetoo** [6]. This is a chip LiDAR with a 360-degree field of view and an update rate of 6 Hz. It can be connected to the onboard computer using the USB port.

- **Motor controller:** The L298N motor controller is a dual H-bridge driver module used to control the speed and direction of two DC motors or one stepper motor. Acting as an interface between the Raspberry Pi and motors, it allows low-power control signals to manage high-power motor operations. Powered by 5V to 35V, it supports **pulse width modulation (PWM)** for speed control and digital signals for direction. The module features input pins (IN1–IN4) for direction, enable pins (ENA, ENB) for PWM speed control, output pins (OUT1–OUT4) for motor connections, and power pins for supplying motor and logic power.

- **One current stepdown:** If your power supply exceeds 5V, a regulator is required to power the Raspberry Pi. In this example, a 12V input source is stepped down to 5V using a DollaTek 2596S regulator. This device includes a USB port for directly powering the Raspberry Pi with a cable.

- **Power supply or battery source:** A 12-volt power supply can be used for configuration and testing. Once the setup is complete, switch to a battery or power bank for portability.

Let's see how to connect the single elements in the next section.

Understanding the electronic connection

To ensure the robot operates correctly, all the components described in the previous section must be properly connected. The most complex part is connecting the Raspberry Pi pinout to the motor controller module, as shown in *Figure 12.4*. In *Figure 12.4*, you can see that the Raspberry Pi Model 3B includes several pins designated for similar purposes. First, both boards need to share a common ground. Connect the ground output of the L298N controller to pin 39 on the Raspberry Pi. Next, each motor requires three pin connections:

- **Raspberry Pi PWM outputs -> ENA and ENB:** These pins are used to enable motor actuation and regulate its velocity. The higher the PWM value, the faster the motor will rotate. In the diagram, we used pins 33 and 32 of the Pi.

- **Raspberry Pi GPIO -> IN1 and IN2:** These pins are used to regulate the rotation direction of the motor. We used pins 19 and 21 of the Raspberry Pi; setting the value of the GPIOs to 1 will disable the motor rotation. Conversely, setting pin 19 to 0 and 21 to 1 enables the rotation in a clockwise direction, or counterclockwise if vice versa.

- **Raspberry Pi GPIO -> IN3 and IN4:** These pins are used to control the rotation direction for the other motor. We used pins 24 and 26.

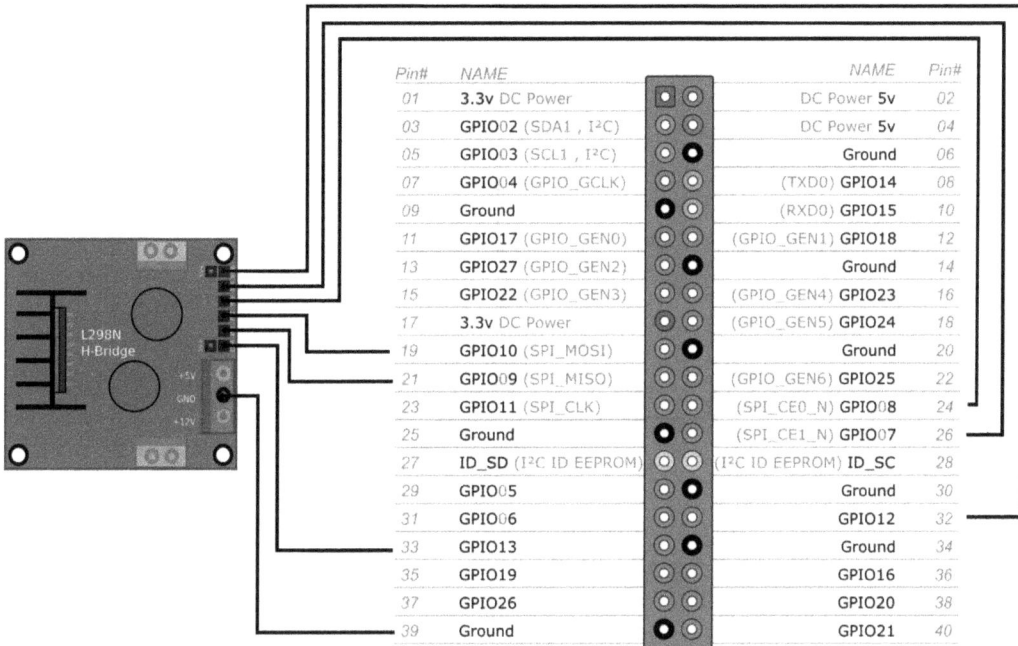

Figure 12.4: Raspberry Pi 3 B and L298N pinout connections

The remaining components can be connected easily. The power pins of L298N should be connected to the motor's +/- input. The connection direction is not critical—if reversed, the wheels will rotate in the opposite direction. This can be corrected by adjusting the GPIO pin configuration in the control code, as explained in the next section, the *Programming and configuring the DIY robot* section. The output of the power supply must be connected with the power input of L298N and the 5V current regulator (in the case that you will use it). Of course, in this case, you must pay attention to connect the positive and negative connections correctly. The Raspberry Pi can be powered directly from the power supply or the regulator.

Finally, the LiDAR sensor can be connected to one of the USB ports available on the Raspberry board. The connection schema is shown in *Figure 12.5*.

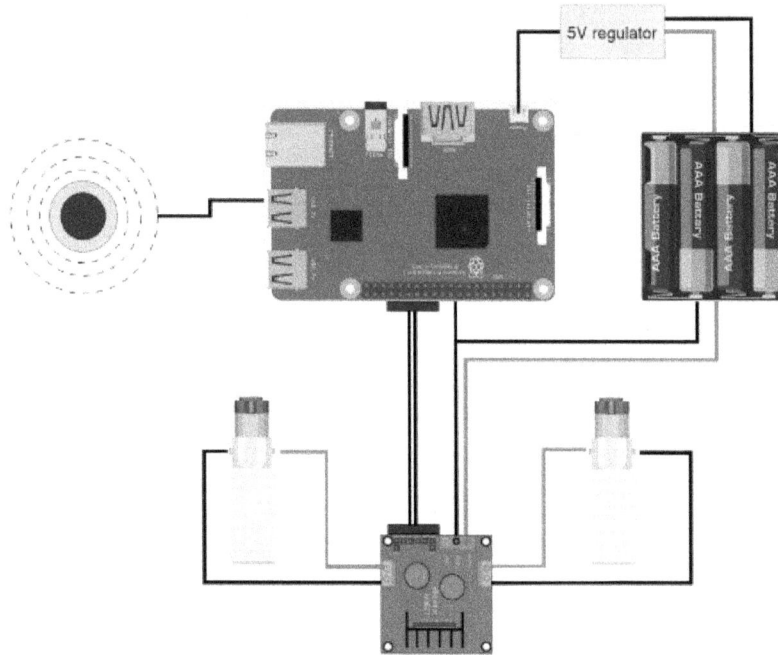

Figure 12.5: Mobile robot electronic connections

Once the components are correctly connected, you can power the system. To make the operation simpler, consider using a power switch to turn the robot on and off without disconnecting the power cables. When powered on, the L298N controller will illuminate a red LED, indicating the system is functioning properly. We can now discuss how to program the robot, move the actuators, and configure the ROS 2 navigation stack.

Programming and configuring the DIY robot

We are now ready to program our robot. The first thing to do to enable our robot to successfully navigate the environment autonomously is to allow access to its motors. We will develop a cpp node in the package `motor_ctrl`. In this node, we will use the `pigpio` library, which allows the control of the Raspberry Pi without the necessity of superuser privileges. From this code, based on the `geometry_msgs::Twist cmd_vel` message, eventually generated from the ROS 2 navigation task, the PWM and digital pins of the board can be controlled. After the interface with the motors, we can move on to the configuration of the other software used to enable the autonomous navigation of the mobile base: the odometry calculation and the ROS 2 navigation stack.

Interfacing the robot's motors

Let's discuss the `motor_ctrl.cpp` source:

- We must include the interface library in the `pigpio` library. We will start the `pigpio` daemon separately, before this node. This interface is used to contact the GPIO daemon:

```
#include <rclcpp/rclcpp.hpp>
#include <pigpiod_if2.h>
#include "geometry_msgs/msg/twist.hpp"
```

- Two PWM values can be set: the maximum PWM determines the motor's top speed, while the minimum PWM must be adjusted based on the robot's weight. Since the motors lack encoders, the minimum value needs to be tested directly on the robot to ensure proper movement:

```
#define PWM_MAX   40000
#define PWM_MIN   8210
```

- In the constructor of the class, the `pigpio` library is initialized. The correct initialization is checked. In this case, `pi_` is a file descriptor that is initialized with a number higher than 0 if the initialization is completed successfully:

```
class MotorControl : public rclcpp::Node {
public:
    MotorControl() : Node("motor_control_node") {
        pi_ = pigpio_start(nullptr, nullptr);
        if (pi_ < 0)
            rclcpp::shutdown();
```

- The PWM output is initialized. In particular, pins 12 and 13, used as PWMs, are set to be output, the range maximum is set (considering the maximum value of PWM defined in the code), and finally, their duty cycle is set to 0 to stop the motors. Notice that good practice is to set the pin numbers (12 and 13 here) as `constexpr` variables within a namespace or static class members for clarity and maintainability. To improve the code readability, in this example, we directly set the pin numbers in the function arguments:

```
set_mode(pi_, 12, PI_OUTPUT);
set_mode(pi_, 13, PI_OUTPUT);
set_PWM_range(pi_, 12, PWM_MAX);
set_PWM_range(pi_, 13, PWM_MAX);
```

```
set_PWM_dutycycle(pi_, 12, 0);
set_PWM_dutycycle(pi_, 13, 0);
```

- Finally, the main loop is started and the subscriber of the cmd_vel topic is initialized:

```
timer_ = create_wall_timer(std::chrono::milliseconds(100),
std::bind(&MotorControl::ctrl_loop, this));
    cmd_vel_subscription_ = create_subscription<geometry_
msgs::msg::Twist>("cmd_vel", 10, std::bind(&MotorControl::cmd_vel_
callback, this, std::placeholders::_1));
```

- In the callback of the velocity command, the velocity data is saved:

```
void cmd_vel_callback(const geometry_
msgs::msg::Twist::SharedPtr msg) {
    cmd_vel_ = *msg;
}
```

- In the main loop, the first operation is to calculate the velocity associated with the single wheels of the platform based on the dimensions of the same—the wheel distances (0.14 cm) and their diameter (0.325 cm):

```
void ctrl_loop() {
    double v_left, v_right;
    calculate_wheel_velocities(cmd_vel_.linear.x, cmd_vel_.
angular.z, 0.325, 0.14, v_left, v_right);
```

- The desired PWM values to actuate the robot must be calculated. Due to the lack of encoders of the motors, this is only an approximation. The pins associated with the left and right motors and their rotation direction are used to enable the correct rotation direction:

```
int pwm_m0 = calculate_pwm(v_left, 7, 10, 12, PWM_MIN);
    int pwm_m1 = calculate_pwm(v_right, 8, 9, 13, PWM_MIN);
    set_PWM_dutycycle(pi_, 12, pwm_m0);
    set_PWM_dutycycle(pi_, 13, pwm_m1);
}
```

- The following functions calculate the PWM value based on a desired velocity and set the motor's direction. The calculate_pwm function maps the absolute velocity to a PWM value within defined limits and determines the motor's direction using set_motor_direction. The latter sets GPIO pins to control forward, backward, or stop states based on the velocity's sign:

```
int calculate_pwm(double velocity, int pin_forward, int pin_
backward, int pwm_pin, int pwm_min) {
    double abs_velocity = std::abs(velocity);
    int pwm_value = static_cast<int>(map_value(abs_velocity,
0.0, 3.07, pwm_min, PWM_MAX));
    set_motor_direction(velocity, pin_forward, pin_backward);
    return pwm_value;
}
void set_motor_direction(double velocity, int pin_forward, int
pin_backward) {
    if (velocity > 0) {
        gpio_write(pi_, pin_forward, 1);
        gpio_write(pi_, pin_backward, 0);
    } else if (velocity < 0) {
        gpio_write(pi_, pin_forward, 0);
        gpio_write(pi_, pin_backward, 1);
    } else {
        gpio_write(pi_, pin_forward, 1);
        gpio_write(pi_, pin_backward, 1);
    }
}
```

Check the CMakeLists.txt file in the book's repository to correctly compile this node. Then, you can execute it using the following command. Remember to start the pigpio daemon the first time:

```
sudo pigpiod
ros2 run motor_ctrl motor_ctrl
```

You can control the robot by sending a `cmd_vel` message using a joypad or the RQT interface, as discussed in previous chapters. By default, other computers on the same network as the Raspberry Pi can communicate directly via topics in ROS 2. If you want to isolate communication, you can use the `ROS_DOMAIN_ID` environment variable, which specifies a unique domain for each application or robot. If communication is not happening automatically, you can use the `ROS_STATIC_PEERS` variable to specify a list of fixed peers for direct communication, bypassing the usual discovery process. For example, if the Raspberry Pi has IP 192.168.1.91 and another computer has IP 192.168.1.43, set `ROS_STATIC_PEERS` to `192.168.1.91` on the Raspberry Pi and to `192.168.1.43` on the other computer. We can put the variable initialization in the `.bashrc` file to automatically load the configuration when the system starts. For example, the list of variables for the ground computer is the following:

```
source ~/dev/ros2_ws/install/setup.bash
export ROS_STATIC_PEERS=192.168.1.91
export ROS_DOMAIN_ID=13
```

In this way, we can start the motor controller program sending the velocity control data from the ground computer using the operating system user interface. After testing that the motors respond correctly to the velocity command, you can continue the configuration of the robot.

Configuring the LiDAR sensor

Now, we can start the sensor. For this, we can use the `ldlidar_sl_ros2` package (`https://github.com/PacktPublishing/Mastering-ROS-2/tree/main/Chapter12/ldlidar_sl_ros2`) to interface the LiDAR sensor. After downloading the package, compile the workspace and launch it:

```
colcon build --symlink-install
ros2 launch ldlidar_sl_ros2 ld20.launch.py
```

In this latter launch file, the only parameter you should adjust is `port_name`. This parameter specifies the USB port where the LiDAR is connected. By default, it is `/dev/ttyUSB0`. You can check the correct port by listing the active ports on your Raspberry Pi:

```
ls /dev | grep tty
```

The output of the previous command may list many entries. Focus on those containing "USB" or "ACM" in their names, such as `/dev/ttyUSB1` or `/dev/ttyACM0`. Once the sensor is started, you can check the LiDAR data published on the `/scan` topic. This data is published in the `base_laser` frame, so to visualize the scan data correctly in RViz2, ensure you set the fixed frame to `base_laser`.

Defining the robot model

Since we are going to use the navigation stack, we need a robot model to describe the connection between the base frame of the robot and the overall shape of the robot. The robot frame and the components are connected as shown in *Figure 12.6*. Of course, the most important connection is between the `lidar_frame` and the `base_footprint`.

Figure 12.6: Mobile platform and its components

As discussed in *Chapter 4*, tools such as Fusion 360 can be used to have a precise 3D model of your robot. However, an easier and faster solution is to represent the components as basic 3D shapes. To visualize the robot model in RViz2, the launch file contained in the `mobile_robot_model` can be used:

```
ros2 launch mobile_robot_model display.launch.py
```

Now you can open RViz2 adding the robot model displayer. The output is shown in *Figure 12.7*.

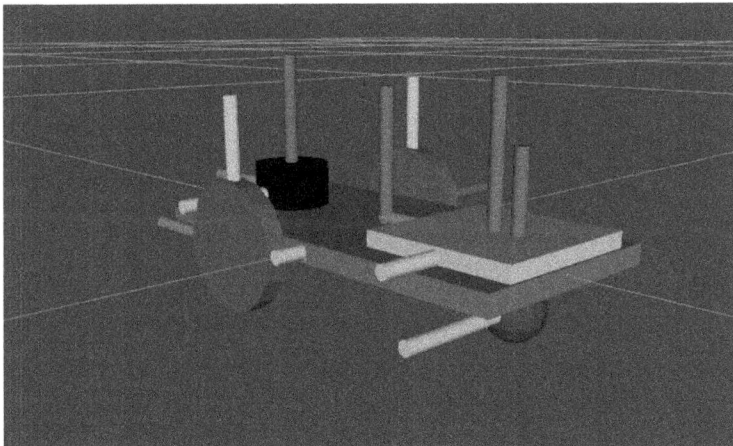

Figure 12.7: Robot model shown in RViz2

This model can be used both in the odometry calculation and in the configuration of the Nav2 stack.

Odometry calculation

As already said, the motors used to build our robot are not equipped with encoder sensors. For this reason, it is not possible to calculate the wheel odometry, which is a rough estimation of the robot's position within a fixed frame. However, we will use odometry for the map generation and localization. We can directly use the scan data from the LiDAR to estimate the position of the robot. This approach is typically referred to as **scan matching**: iterative scans are compared with one another to estimate the linear and angular position of the robot. Among the different packages, rf2o_laser_odometry is particularly efficient and lightweight. You can get it from the book's repository (https://github.com/PacktPublishing/Mastering-ROS-2/tree/main/Chapter12/rf2o_laser_odometry) and compile the workspace. You can use the default launch file contained in the package. From that file, you can set different parameters, including:

- The scan topic name, which is the topic on which the laser scan data is published
- base_frame_id, which is the name of the base link used in the odometry
- odom_frame_id, which is the name of the fixed odometry frame

You can test the odometry calculation by starting the LiDAR sensor, the motor controller, and the rf2o_laser_odometry:

```
ros2 run motor_ctrl motor_ctrl ros2 launch
rf2o_laser_odometry rf2o_laser_odometry.launch.py
ros2 launch ldlidar_sl_ros2 ld20.launch.py
```

You can test how the quality of the odometry changes the fixed frame of Rviz2 to odom while displaying the transforms (TFs). Can you see how the frame of the robot base is moving with respect to the odometry frame? If the robot frame is correctly shown and it moves coherently with the base of the robot, you can move to the next step, the configuration of the navigation stack for mapping and navigation.

Enabling autonomous navigation

We are now ready to enable the autonomous navigation of the robot using the Nav2 stack. For a deep discussion on how to use this framework, we already discussed it in *Chapter 8*. In this section, we can directly use the default launch file of the navigation and mapping packages.

To recap, we need the following launch file:

1. The robot model informs the packages about the TF of the system:

    ```
    ros2 launch mobile_robot_model load_model.launch.py
    ```

2. The LiDAR package streams the scan data:

    ```
    ros2 launch ldlidar_sl_ros2 ld20.launch.py
    ```

3. The odometry calculation package provides a rough estimation of the robot's position without the use of the map:

    ```
    ros2 launch rf2o_laser_odometry rf2o_laser_odometry.launch.py
    ```

4. We can now start the slam toolbox to create the map and, at the same time, adjust the position of the robot inside the map:

    ```
    ros2 launch slam_toolbox online_sync_launch.py
    ```

5. The navigation package generates the cmd_vel data to actuate the robot:

    ```
    ros2 launch nav2_bringup navigation_launch.py
    ```

If everything starts correctly, the mobile base will be displayed on a map that will be updated with the robot's motion (see *Figure 12.8*). Remember that you can directly use RViz2 to request the navigation toward a new point, by selecting a 2D Nav goal from the toolbar and selecting a point on the map.

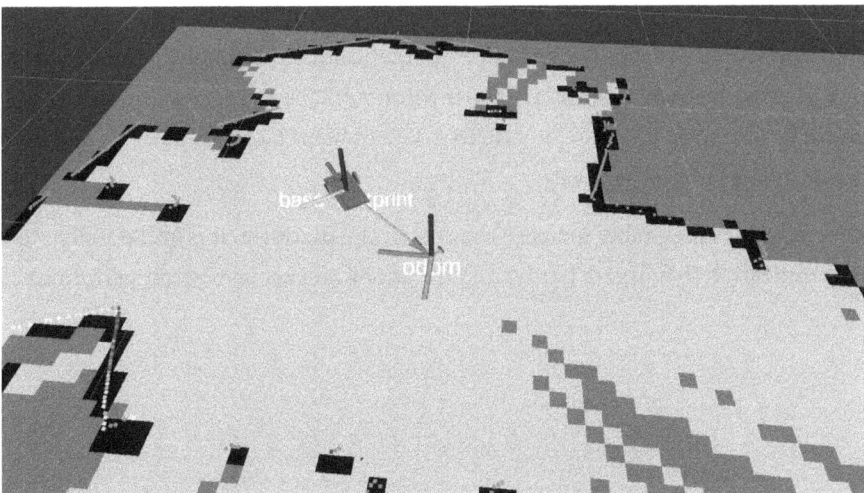

Figure 12.8: Navigation and mapping of the mobile robot

The robot's motion is neither precise nor smooth, as expected. This is primarily because the motors lack encoders, resulting in open-loop control. The PWM signals used to drive the robot's base simply assume a desired velocity without feedback. Consequently, the system cannot account for disturbances such as terrain irregularities or other external noise. For this reason, several improvements can be made to the platform, as discussed in the next section.

Future improvements

The robot presented in this chapter, along with its software, serves as an example of what can be achieved with simple ROS 2 nodes and low-cost hardware. However, there are several improvements that can be made to enhance the robot's performance:

- **Incorporate wheel odometry for improved localization**: A key improvement is using actuators with feedback and precise motion control. To achieve this, DC motors equipped with encoders should be used, allowing the robot to better estimate its position and movement. Additionally, integrating an **inertial measurement unit** (**IMU**) can improve accuracy, as wheel odometry can degrade significantly for differential-drive robots when the wheels experience slippage.

- **Upgrade to a more powerful motherboard**: While the Raspberry Pi 3 B is an affordable and accessible option, its performance is often insufficient for demanding applications. Newer models of the Raspberry Pi, or other compact, GPU-equipped boards such as NVIDIA Jetson devices, can significantly enhance computational capabilities. However, these advanced boards could lack GPIO access. In such cases, microcontrollers paired with ROS 2 packages, such as Micro-ROS [7], can be used to handle GPIO-related tasks.

- **Add additional sensors for enhanced perception**: Expanding the robot's sensor suite can improve its understanding of the environment. Depth sensors and vision-based systems, for instance, can provide valuable data to help the robot perceive and navigate its surroundings more effectively.

While these upgrades inevitably increase the cost of the platform, it is still possible to work on software optimization to mitigate hardware limitations and achieve better performance.

Summary

This chapter explored the process of building and programming a mobile robot platform. A mobile robot consists of hardware components that are properly connected to enable motion and control, along with computational units to process and execute tasks. In this example, we used a popular board—the Raspberry Pi—to control the robot's motors and facilitate intelligent navigation.

The chapter began by detailing how to configure an onboard computer, including the installation of the necessary software to enable remote control of the robot. It then explained the step-by-step process of setting up a mobile platform from scratch. While this chapter focused on a cost-effective mobile platform, additional enhancements were discussed in the final section to illustrate potential improvements to the robot's design and functionality.

In the next chapter, we will cover a fundamental aspect of software development: testing and **continuous integration/continuous deployment** (**CI/CD**). We will explore how to implement these practices using ROS 2.

References

[1] https://www.raspberrypi.com/

[2] https://docs.sunfounder.com/projects/picar-x/en/latest/

[3] https://github.com/TheNoobInventor/lidarbot

[4] https://tmuxcheatsheet.com/

[5] https://www.aliexpress.com/

[6] https://wiki.youyeetoo.com/en/Lidar/LD20

[7] https://micro.ros.org/

Join our community on Discord

Join our community's Discord space for discussions with the authors and other readers: `https://packt.link/embeddedsystems`

13

Testing, Continuous Integration, and Continuous Deployment with ROS 2

During a project, developers often make continuous changes to the same source code to add new features. To prevent introducing bugs or compilation errors, it's essential to have reliable tools that can automatically detect issues early. These tools should run before sharing the updated code with the rest of the team or integrating it into a larger system to avoid disrupting a functioning setup.

This chapter will cover two key practices: code testing, which ensures the code performs as expected, and **Continuous Integration (CI)** and **Continuous Deployment (CD)**, which automate code integration and deployment to check for bugs and streamline the release process. Numerous tools are available for these tasks, and in this chapter, we will use ROS 2 nodes and packages with these tools. For testing, we'll utilize the **Google Test (GTest)** framework, and for CI/CD, we'll leverage a GitHub feature called **GitHub Actions**, which can be accessed directly through the GitHub website.

As such, we will cover the following main topics in the chapter:

- Testing ROS 2 nodes using GTest
- Integrating ROS 2 APIs in the GTest framework
- Implementing CI/CD for ROS 2 packages

Technical requirements

To follow this chapter, you should have one of the following setups on your computer:

- A standard computer running the Ubuntu 24.04 LTS operating system

- A Linux machine with a ROS 2 Jazzy version installed or with a running Docker container configured, as discussed in Chapter 2

- A personal account on GitHub: https://github.com

The reference code for this chapter can be found in the Chapter13 folder of the following book code repository: https://github.com/PacktPublishing/Mastering-ROS-2-for-Robotics-Programming/tree/main/Chapter13.

Testing ROS 2 nodes using GTest

Automated unit testing in ROS 2 offers several key advantages. By running tests after each change, you can make small code updates with confidence that interdependencies across ROS 2 packages won't introduce unexpected issues. This also allows you to refactor code without fear of introducing bugs, as passing tests confirms that functionality remains intact. There are different kinds of testing methods, each devoted to testing a particular aspect of the source code. Among them, **unit testing** is the test type that helps developers ensure that their code works as expected in both basic and corner cases. It involves writing tests for small, self-contained pieces of code, typically functions or methods, to ensure they generate the expected output values. These tests are usually automated and can be run frequently throughout the development process. They can be defined by the developer themself, ensuring that both basic functionalities and critical aspects of a function are tested.

A common library to perform unit testing is GTest, and we can easily integrate GTest in ROS 2 nodes written in C++. As for the unit test, we can additionally classify two different types of tests: black box and white box. Unit testing with GTest in ROS 2 is primarily **white-box testing**. In white-box testing, developers have knowledge of the internal structure and code, allowing them to test specific functions, conditions, and branches within the code. Since unit tests in ROS 2 using GTest focus on individual functions, nodes, and components with a direct understanding of the internal implementation, they fall under this category. On the other hand, **black-box testing** applies to integration, system, or acceptance tests, where the internal workings of the components may not be fully visible to the tester. In black-box testing, the focus is on validating the outputs against expected results based on inputs without considering the internal code structure.

Exploring the GTest features and programming pipeline

GTest provides a rich set of features that make it easy to create robust and efficient tests for C++ applications, including those built on ROS 2. The main elements of the GTest library are the following:

- **XML test reporting**: After the execution of the tests, you can generate XML reports of test results, making it easy to analyze the success or failure of given tests.

- **Test fixtures**: GTest allows you to create test fixtures, which are reusable setup and teardown routines that can be shared across multiple tests. This is useful for initializing complex objects or resources that multiple tests might use.

- **Assertions**: The framework provides a variety of assertions to check conditions in your tests, such as EXPECT_EQ, ASSERT_TRUE, EXPECT_NE, and more. We will discuss these assertions in more detail in the code examples. However, they help you validate that your code behaves as intended.

- **Parameterized tests**: GTest supports parameterized tests, allowing you to run the same test logic with different inputs. This is useful for testing functions with multiple edge cases.

- **Death tests**: You can write tests to verify that your code handles fatal failures correctly, ensuring that your application behaves as expected even under error conditions.

Before implementing our first example of code testing associated with ROS 2, let's briefly discuss the typical GTest programming pipeline:

1. **Set up**: Include the GTest library in your ROS 2 package, and you can define your tests in a separate source file.

2. **Write tests**: Write test cases using the GTest framework, defining specific input and expected output scenarios. Each test case is usually encapsulated in a function that begins with TEST(), followed by the test name.

3. **Run tests**: Compile the test code and run the tests using the provided ROS 2 test tools or directly through GTest, which gives a detailed report of passed and failed tests.

4. **Check results**: Analyze the report files generated from the GTest library to eventually know which tests have been passed or not.

We are now ready to implement our first examples using GTest and ROS 2.

Integrating GTest with ROS 2 for robust testing

First, let's create a ROS 2 package to store our tests. In this first example, we will not use any function from the ROS 2 API, such as services, publishers, or subscribers; we will just use the GTest framework to test the result of a basic function that translates a given angle from radians to degrees, bounding it in the interval –pi, pi (-1.57, 1.57). We can create this package as a normal ROS 2 package:

```
$ ros2 pkg create first_gtest --dependencies rclcpp std_msgs
```

The source code of the package is placed in the src folder of a package, while the test files must be placed in the test folder. Let's create a test folder and a test source file called first_test.cpp:

```
$ cd first_gtest
$ mkdir test && touch first_test.cpp
```

The content of this file is as follows:

1. As already said, we don't need to use ROS 2 API functions, so we will not include a header from it. We will include the gtest.h header (already installed with the desktop version of ROS 2):

    ```
    #include <gtest/gtest.h>
    ```

2. We initialize a constexpr variable and a function. These expressions are evaluated at compile time and can be used to define true constant values in a type-safe way. We define the value of pi and a function to convert a given degree value to radians. This requires the constant pi (approximately 3.1415), which can be obtained using the M_PI symbol from the <cmath> header:

    ```
    constexpr double DEG_TO_RAD = M_PI / 180.0;
    ```

3. We can now define the function to test. This function takes a degree value as input and returns the corresponding radian value. Additionally, it ensures that the output is bounded within the interval [-pi; pi). This notation excludes one of the two boundaries to guarantee a unique representation of the 180 and –180 angles. In practical applications such as robotics, graphics, and physics, this convention is preferred because it eliminates redundancy and ensures a consistent representation of angles.

Restricting a robot's estimated angle in this interval is helpful for different reasons. For example:

- **Avoids ambiguity**: This keeps the angle unique, as values such as 2pi and 0 are equivalent but can otherwise appear different.

- **Simplifies rotational calculations**: Limiting the angle range helps calculate angular differences easily, always choosing the shortest path without multiple rotations.

- **Prevents discontinuities**: As a robot rotates continuously, the angle could grow indefinitely; keeping it in this range avoids instability.

The degreesToRadians function is used to perform the conversion:

```
double degreesToRadians(double degrees) {
    double radians = degrees * DEG_TO_RAD;
    while (radians >= PI) radians -= 2.0 * PI;
    while (radians < -PI) radians += 2.0 * PI;
    return radians;
}
```

4. Until now, we showed a simple C++ code. Let's define the test functions. We can define different tests that prove the robustness of the code. The TEST keyword is used to define a function containing a desired number of tests. The TEST function accepts two input values: the suite and the test names. The suite name specifies a group of related tests. For example, in the AngleConversionTest suite, we want to test the conversion in radians in the desired interval for positive angles (HandlesPositiveAngles):

```
TEST(AngleConversionTest, HandlesPositiveAngles) {
```

5. To check that the function generates the correct value, we use the EXPECT_NEAR macro, which is used to check whether two floating-point values are nearly equal, accounting for small differences due to floating-point precision. In the first line, for example, we check that the conversion of 0 degrees is 0 radians. In this case, we can assume that the result of the conversion is exactly 0.0, while, in other cases, some numbers can be placed in the floating part of the number. With EXPECT_NEAR, we request that the output value and the checked one differ by a maximum of 0.000000001:

```
EXPECT_NEAR(degreesToRadians(0), 0.0, 1e-9);
EXPECT_NEAR(degreesToRadians(180), PI, 1e-9);
EXPECT_NEAR(degreesToRadians(90), PI / 2.0, 1e-9);
```

```
    EXPECT_NEAR(degreesToRadians(360), 0.0, 1e-9);
}
```

6. We can add different other tests:

```
TEST(AngleConversionTest, HandlesNegativeAngles) {
  EXPECT_NEAR(degreesToRadians(-180), -PI, 1e-9);
  EXPECT_NEAR(degreesToRadians(-90), -PI / 2.0, 1e-9);
  EXPECT_NEAR(degreesToRadians(-360), 0.0, 1e-9);
}
TEST(AngleConversionTest, HandlesOverflowAngles) {
  EXPECT_NEAR(degreesToRadians(720), 0.0, 1e-9);
  EXPECT_NEAR(degreesToRadians(540), PI, 1e-9);
  EXPECT_NEAR(degreesToRadians(-540), -PI, 1e-9);
}


TEST(AngleConversionTest, HandlesSmallAngles) {
  EXPECT_NEAR(degreesToRadians(1), DEG_TO_RAD, 1e-9);
  EXPECT_NEAR(degreesToRadians(-1), -DEG_TO_RAD, 1e-9);
}
```

7. In the main function, we initialize the GTest framework and request to start all the tests defined in the test file. The framework automatically detects all the TEST functions defined in the test source file, executing them in a sequential way:

```
int main(int argc, char** argv) {
  testing::InitGoogleTest(&argc, argv);
  return RUN_ALL_TESTS();
}
```

Before running these tests, we need to configure the CMakeLists.txt file to compile them. Tests are not treated as executables in ROS 2, so we cannot define them using the standard executable definition. Instead, we use ament_add_gtest to define the test. We'll place the test in the BUILD_TESTING section of CMakeLists.txt, which is enabled by default in the colcon build system. After adding first_test.cpp to this section, we also specify its dependencies:

```
if(BUILD_TESTING)
  find_package(ament_cmake_gtest REQUIRED)
  ament_add_gtest(first_test test/first_test.cpp)
```

```
    ament_target_dependencies(first_test
      std_msgs
    )
endif()
```

To run the tests, you must follow these steps:

1. Compile the workspace to generate the test executables:

```
$ colcon build --symlink-install
```

2. Run the test. Here, we can optionally specify the package:

```
$ colcon test --ctest-args tests first_gtest
```

3. Check the results:

```
$ colcon test-result --all --verbose
```

The output of the previous command is quite long and difficult to read. However, you should be able to notice the following lines:

```
Failure The difference between degreesToRadians(540) and
3.14159265358979323846 is 6.2831853071795862, which exceeds 1e-
9, where degreesToRadians(540) evaluates to -3.1415926535897931,
3.14159265358979323846 evaluates to 3.1415926535897931, and 1e-9
evaluates to 1.0000000000000001e-09.
```

As you can see from the previous output, the result of the degreesToRadians function on the 540 input and the check value pi=3.1415 differ by 6.2831, which is higher than the allowed threshold of 1e-9. In fact, the output of the function is pi and not –pi. Our function works correctly; the error here is in the test definition. We included this test solely to demonstrate how to detect a failure. However, this example highlights an important point: we must carefully consider the test design and input values. Otherwise, we risk identifying bugs that don't actually exist in our code.

4. Inspect the .xml file. For each test, an .xml report is generated that contains the same information already shown in the terminal with the previous command. The file is placed inside the build folder. In our case, it will be placed in the following location:

ros2_ws/build/first_gtest/test_results/first_gtest/first_test.gtest.xml

We completed our first GTest on a very simple function. Let's discuss another example, in which the ROS 2 API functions are integrated into the GTest framework.

Integrating ROS 2 APIs in the GTest framework

In the previous example, we learned how to run GTest using ROS 2 commands. However, in a real robotic application, that example may not be very practical. Let's take our use of GTest a step further with a new example. In this example, we'll test the output of a ROS 2 node that publishes to a ROS 2 topic. The purpose of the node is to convert an input string (received on a topic) to all lowercase letters. For instance, the string INpUt would be converted to input. To start, we need to create a package and the node we want to test. We'll create the following source files:

- to_lowercase.h to store the definition of the ROS 2 node class and its variables
- to_lowercase.cpp to implement the functions to convert the letters from uppercase to lowercase
- main.cpp to instantiate and spin the ROS 2 node

We will separate the class and function definitions into different source files, allowing us to replace the main function with the one defined in the test file, as we will discuss later in the chapter.

Exploring the content of the source files

Let's start by discussing the header file and then move on to the other two:

- to_lowercase.h:

  - Here, we just include the node headers and define the ToLowercase class:

    ```cpp
    #include <rclcpp/rclcpp.hpp>
    #include <std_msgs/msg/string.hpp>
    #include <algorithm>
    class ToLowercase : public rclcpp::Node {
    public:
    ToLowercase() : Node("lowercase_string_node") {
    ```

  - The node receives the string to convert on the /input topic while publishing the output on the /output topic:

    ```cpp
    _input_sub = this->create_subscription<std_msgs::msg::String>
    ("input", 10, std::bind(&ToLowercase::input_str_cb, this,
    std::placeholders::_1));
    _output_pub = this->create_publisher<std_
    msgs::msg::String>("output", 10);
        }
    ```

```
        void input_str_cb(const std_msgs::msg::String::SharedPtr
msg);
    private:
        rclcpp::Subscription<std_msgs::msg::String>::SharedPtr
_input_sub;
        rclcpp::Publisher<std_msgs::msg::String>::SharedPtr _
output_pub;
    };
```

- `to_lowercase.cpp`:

    - In the source file, we just write the body of the input callback, convert the string, and republish it into a lowercase one:

        ```
        #include "to_lowercase.h"
        void ToLowercase::input_str_cb(const std_
        msgs::msg::String::SharedPtr msg) {
            std::string lowercase_str = msg->data;
        ```

    - To do this, the function `transform` is used. Finally, the resultant string is published:

        ```
            std::transform(lowercase_str.begin(), lowercase_str.
        end(), lowercase_str.begin(), ::tolower);
        auto message = std_msgs::msg::String();
        message.data = lowercase_str;
        _output_pub->publish(message);
        }
        ```

- `main.cpp`: In the `main.cpp` file, we just spin the ROS 2 node implemented with the defined class (`ToLowercase`):

    ```
    #include "to_lowercase.h"
    int main(int argc, char **argv) {
        rclcpp::init(argc, argv);

        auto node = std::make_shared<ToLowercase>();
        rclcpp::spin(node);
        rclcpp::shutdown();
        return 0;
    }
    ```

Before defining a test for this ROS 2 node, let's execute it to check how it works. Add the executable to the CMakeLists.txt file:

```
add_executable(to_lowercase src/to_lowercase.cpp src/main.cpp)
ament_target_dependencies(to_lowercase rclcpp std_msgs)

install(TARGETS
  to_lowercase
  DESTINATION lib/${PROJECT_NAME}
)
```

Finally, compile the workspace, source it, and run the node:

```
$ colcon build --symlink-install
$ source install/setup.bash
$ ros2 run to_lowercase to_lowercase
```

Check the output by reading the output topic:

```
$ ros2 topic echo /output
```

On another terminal, publish the string tOLoWER:

```
$ ros2 topic pub /input std_msgs/msg/String "data: tOLoWER" --once
```

As you can see from the topic output, the code works as expected. But what if we slightly modify the code, changing how the string is converted? While this example is simple, it gives us an idea of the potential of the GTest framework. We can automatically define tests to run after any code change, helping us ensure everything still functions correctly.

Implementing automatic testing using GTest

Let's define a test for this ROS 2 node. Create a directory called test in the to_lowercase package, containing a test file called to_lowercase_test.cpp. Its content is described here:

1. In addition to the ROS 2 headers, we need to include the header file where the ROS 2 node is defined, using a relative path. Since the files are in the same package, this approach will not cause any compilation errors, even on other machines:

    ```
    #include <algorithm>
    #include <gtest/gtest.h>
    #include <rclcpp/rclcpp.hpp>
    ```

```
#include <std_msgs/msg/string.hpp>
#include "../src/to_lowercase.h"
```

2. We are going to define only one test and one test suite, the package_name test, which will be automatically translated with the name of the package, and the UpperToLower suite, to test the effectiveness of the ROS 2 node:

```
TEST(package_name, UpperToLower) {
```

3. First, we must create the ROS 2 node, spinning it with an executor. This will allow the node to work correctly with the callbacks:

```
auto to_lowercase_node = std::make_shared<ToLowercase>();
rclcpp::executors::SingleThreadedExecutor executor;
executor.add_node(to_lowercase_node);
```

4. We must define a callback that receives the output of the publisher on which the result of the string conversion is published. We will use a lambda function in this test. A lambda function is useful for short, one-time operations, often passed as arguments to other functions, without needing a full function definition. We will pass the function two variables—a Boolean one that is set to true when the output of the conversion is received, and a string that stores the output of the conversion:

```
bool ready = false;
std::string value;
auto output_callback = [this, &ready, &value](const std_
msgs::msg::String::SharedPtr msg) {
    value = msg->data;
    ready = true;
};
```

5. We define the publisher and the subscriber next:

```
rclcpp::Subscription<std_msgs::msg::String>::SharedPtr output_sub;
output_sub = to_lowercase_node->create_subscription<std_
msgs::msg::String>("/output", 10, output_callback);
rclcpp::Publisher<std_msgs::msg::String>::SharedPtr string_pub;
string_pub = to_lowercase_node->create_publisher<std_
msgs::msg::String>("/input", 10);
```

6. The string ROS 2 message is initialized and published. In this first test, we use the string TOLOWER:

```
std_msgs::msg::String s;
s.data = "TOLOWER";
string_pub->publish( s );
```

7. After publishing the string, we must only wait for the conversion to be performed and published on the /output topic:

```
rclcpp::Rate rate(5);   // Set rate to 1 Hz (once per second)
while( !ready ) {
   executor.spin_once(std::chrono::milliseconds(100)); // Process
callbacks with a timeout of 100 ms
   rate.sleep();
}
```

8. Now, we can evaluate the test result. If the conversion output is the string tolower, the test is considered passed. We've added a while loop, which could run indefinitely if the string is never published for some reason. However, the GTest framework includes a timeout feature: if the test takes longer than expected, it will be automatically aborted. To check the value of the generated string, we use the ASSERT_EQ keyword, which checks the exact value of the control value:

```
ASSERT_EQ(value, "tolower");
```

9. We can test with another string that could be considered more complex, TO-LOWER-2:

```
ready = false;
s.data = "TO-LOWER-2";
string_pub->publish( s );
while( !ready ) {
   executor.spin_once(std::chrono::milliseconds(100)); // Process
callbacks with a timeout of 100 ms
   rate.sleep();
}
ASSERT_EQ(value, "to-lower-2");
}
```

10. Like the previous test, in the main function, we must just initialize the GTest framework and run the tests. Before running the tests, we must also initialize the ROS 2 system:

```
int main(int argc, char** argv) {
  testing::InitGoogleTest(&argc, argv);
  rclcpp::init(argc, argv);
  return RUN_ALL_TESTS();
}
```

As already done in the previous test, we must modify the CMakeLists.txt to compile the test. The source code must be included in ament_add_gtest. In this case, we must add not only the test file discussed above but also the source file in which the ROS 2 node to test is implemented (to_lowercase.cpp):

```
ament_add_gtest(to_lowercase_test test/to_lowercase_test.cpp src/to_
lowercase.cpp)
ament_target_dependencies(to_lowercase_test rclcpp std_msgs)
```

Now, you can use the commands already seen so far to compile, run, and inspect the results of the test:

```
$ colcon build --symlink-install
$ colcon test --ctest-args tests to_lowercase
$ colcon test-result --all –verbose
```

What you should see is the result of all the tests of your ROS 2 workspace. Regarding the ROS 2 node just developed, the output will be the following:

```
    build/to_lowercase/Testing/20241031-1639/Test.xml: 1 test, 0 errors,
0 failures, 0 skipped
    build/to_lowercase/test_results/to_lowercase/to_lowercase_test.gtest.
xml: 1 test, 0 errors, 0 failures, 0 skipped
```

As you can see from the output, the .xml is generated, reporting a list of tests done with their status (errors, failures, or skipped).

These tests must be executed by the developers every time a new feature is added, and the source code must be shared or integrated into a more complex system. Unit testing is not the only method available for developers to be sure that the new code is ready to be deployed and distributed. In the next section, we will discuss the CI/CD process that automates and manages the entire code testing and deployment pipeline.

Implementing CI/CD for ROS 2 packages

As shown in the previous section, unit testing involves testing individual code components or functions to ensure they work as expected. Here we will introduce a new tool for developers, called **CI/CD**. This is a broader process that automates code integration, testing, and deployment, ensuring that changes are tested and deployed reliably and quickly.

If your code has a compilation error or depends on other system packages, you need an automated tool to prevent deployment and distribution if it fails to compile or causes issues for other packages. This is where a CI/CD tool comes in. Here, we'll use GitHub Actions, a feature provided by GitHub, to implement these testing mechanisms. However, there are many tools available for this purpose, such as the following:

- **Jenkins:** This is the most famous one. It is an open-source automation server and is highly customizable with plugins for various CI/CD workflows.

- **GitHub Actions:** This is integrated directly into GitHub, enabling easy setup of CI/CD pipelines with GitHub repositories.

- **GitLab CI/CD:** This is built into GitLab, offering robust CI/CD capabilities directly within the GitLab environment.

- **CircleCI:** This is a cloud-based CI/CD tool known for its speed and Docker support.

- **Azure DevOps:** This is Microsoft's CI/CD platform, integrated with Azure for easy deployment to cloud services.

- **Bitbucket Pipelines:** This is built into Bitbucket, enabling seamless CI/CD pipelines within Bitbucket repositories.

- **AWS CodePipeline:** This is part of AWS services, enabling CI/CD pipelines within the AWS ecosystem.

The use of **GitHub Actions** is interesting because, to use it, you only need a GitHub account without any premium subscription. But in a few words, what is Github Actions? It is a feature of GitHub that allows you to automate tasks in your development workflow directly in your GitHub repository. It enables you to set up **CI/CD pipelines** and automate actions such as running tests, building and deploying code, or handling project management tasks whenever specific events occur (such as pushes, pull requests, or new issues). GitHub Actions uses *YAML configuration files* (stored in .github/workflows) to define workflows, which specify what triggers the action, the jobs it runs, and the steps within each job. This can range from simple automation to complex workflows and is easily integrated with other services and APIs to create a custom workflow.

Using GitHub Actions for code compilation

To add a new GitHub action to test code compilation, follow these steps:

1. Write your code

2. Create a GitHub repository

3. Write the GitHub action

4. Commit and push your code to the repository

This action should be configured to trigger whenever new changes are pushed to the repository. The trigger depends on the specific action you want to implement, but a key first step is ensuring your code has no compilation errors. Even if your code is compiling correctly in your own workspace, this check is essential. A successful compilation locally doesn't guarantee that others won't have issues. For example, dependencies may be incorrectly linked, missing, or not present in their workspace. The purpose of this action is to confirm that anyone who downloads the repository and follows the provided compilation instructions can compile it without issues.

Let's implement the steps listed above:

1. **Write your code:** Let's create a new ROS 2 package called ros2_ci_cd. This package will contain a simple node publishing a string, just to have a basic ROS 2 C++ node:

```
$ ros2 pkg create ros2_ci_cd --dependencies rclcpp std_msgs
$ cd ros2_ci_cd/src && touch str_pub.cpp
```

1. Let's delve into the content of the source. It is a very basic code. In this code, we start a timer in which a string is published:

```cpp
#include "rclcpp/rclcpp.hpp"
#include "std_msgs/msg/string.hpp"
#include <chrono>
using namespace std::chrono_literals;
class StringPublisher : public rclcpp::Node {
public:
    StringPublisher() : Node("cicd_test") {
        _str_pub = this->create_publisher<std_
msgs::msg::String>("topic", 10);
        _timer = this->create_wall_timer(500ms,
std::bind(&StringPublisher::publish_string, this));
    }
```

```
private:
    void publish_string() {
        std_msgs::msg::String msg;
        msg.data = "CI/CD using ROS 2 and github actions";
        _str_pub->publish(msg);
    }
    rclcpp::Publisher<std_msgs::msg::String>::SharedPtr _str_
pub;
    rclcpp::TimerBase::SharedPtr _timer;
};
int main(int argc, char *argv[]) {
    rclcpp::init(argc, argv);

    auto node = std::make_shared<StringPublisher>();
rclcpp::spin(node);        rclcpp::shutdown();
        return 0;
}
```

2. Then, modify the `CMakeLists.txt` to compile the node. Add the following lines:

```
add_executable(string_publisher src/str_pub.cpp)
ament_target_dependencies(string_publisher rclcpp std_msgs)
install(TARGETS string_publisher
  DESTINATION lib/${PROJECT_NAME})
install(TARGETS
  string_publisher
  DESTINATION lib/${PROJECT_NAME})
```

2. **Create a GitHub repository**: To create a new repository, you should log in to the GitHub page using your account. Then, follow these steps:

    1. *Start a new repository*: On the GitHub home page, click the New button near your repository list, or go to . The creation page is shown in *Figure 13.1* and guides you through the repository creation.

Create a new repository

A repository contains all project files, including the revision history. Already have a project repository elsewhere? Import a repository.

Required fields are marked with an asterisk (*).

Owner *   **Repository name ***

👤 jocacace ▾   /

Great repository names are short and memorable. Need inspiration? How about didactic-spork ?

Description (optional)

⦿ 🖥 **Public**
      Anyone on the internet can see this repository. You choose who can commit.

◯ 🔒 **Private**
      You choose who can see and commit to this repository.

Figure 13.1: GitHub page for repository creation

2. *Name your repository*: Enter a short, clear name for your project in the Repository name field. Optionally, you can add a description explaining the project's purpose.

3. *Choose privacy settings*:

    - **Public**: Anyone can see this repository.

    - **Private**: Only you (and collaborators you invite) can see it.

4. *Create the repository*: Click the **Create repository** button, and your repository will be ready.

5. *Add code*: Once the repository is created, you'll get instructions to add code from your computer or create files directly in GitHub.

3. **Write the GitHub action**: After uploading the code to the repository, it will be shown on the GitHub page. On the same page, there is a menu in which you can handle the repository. In this menu, you can add new actions, as shown in *Figure 13.2*.

☰ 🐙 jocacace / ros2_ci_cd

〈〉 **Code**   ⊙ Issues   ⇡⇣ Pull requests   ⊙ Actions   ⊞ Projects   📖 Wiki   ⓘ Security   〰 Insights   ⚙ Settings

👤 **ros2_ci_cd**   Public

Figure 13.2: GitHub button to add actions

Using the **Actions** button on the GitHub page, you can create a new Actions file by clicking on the **Skip this and set up a workflow yourself** link. This will open an online editor.

Follow these steps to set up the workflow using the newly created action:

1. At the start, we define a name for this action:

    ```
    name: ros2-pipeline-test
    ```

2. We need to define the trigger, which specifies when this action should be executed. For example, we might want the action to run whenever new code is pushed. Additionally, we can specify the branch this applies to—in this case, the action should run only when the master branch is updated:

    ```
    on:
      push:
        branches: [ "master" ]
    ```

3. In the jobs section, we specify the steps to perform. Note that these tests run in a virtual environment that exists only during the action's execution, so we must include all the steps needed to compile the package as if it were on a completely new computer. First, we must select on which operating system this action must be executed. We will select Ubuntu 24.04, which is the one used for ROS 2 Jazzy:

    ```
    jobs:
      build:
        runs-on: ubuntu-24.04
    ```

    1. The first step is to install ROS 2 and configure the workspace.

        ```
        steps:
          - run: |
              # Set up sources
              sudo apt update && sudo apt install -y curl gnupg
        lsb-release
              sudo curl -sSL https://raw.githubusercontent.com/
        ros/rosdistro/master/ros.key | sudo apt-key add -
              sudo sh -c 'echo "deb [arch=$(dpkg --print-
        architecture)] http://packages.ros.org/ros2/ubuntu $(lsb_
        release -cs) main" > /etc/apt/sources.list.d/ros2-latest.
        list'
        ```

2. Install ROS 2 Jazzy packages:

```
sudo apt update
sudo apt install -y ros-jazzy-desktop
```

3. Source ROS 2 environment

```
sudo apt install python3-colcon-common-extensions
- run: |
echo "source /opt/ros/jazzy/setup.bash" >>
~/.bashrc
source ~/.bashrc
mkdir -p ros2_ws/src/ros2_ci_cd
cd ros2_ws
colcon build
source install/setup.bash
```

4. Now that ROS 2 is installed and the workspace configured, we can clone the repository:

```
- uses: actions/checkout@v3
  with:
    path: ros2_ws/src/ros2_ci_cd
- run: |
    source /opt/ros/jazzy/setup.bash
    sudo apt install python3-rosdep
    sudo rosdep init
    rosdep update --include-eol-distros
    cd ros2_ws
    rosdep install --from-paths src -y --ignore-src
```

5. Finally, we can compile the workspace:

```
colcon build
```

6. We can now commit the change, using the top-right button, as shown in *Figure 13.3*.

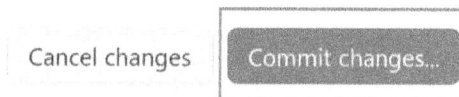

Figure 13.3: GitHub button to commit the change

7. The action is now on the server. Since we are pushed to a new version of the repository (where the action is now present), the same action is triggered. We can monitor its state by clicking on the action and selecting the last commit performed, as shown at the top of *Figure 13.4*. After clicking on the desired commit, you can check the status of the action. We have requested to install ROS 2 and other libraries, which means that the action will require several minutes to be executed.

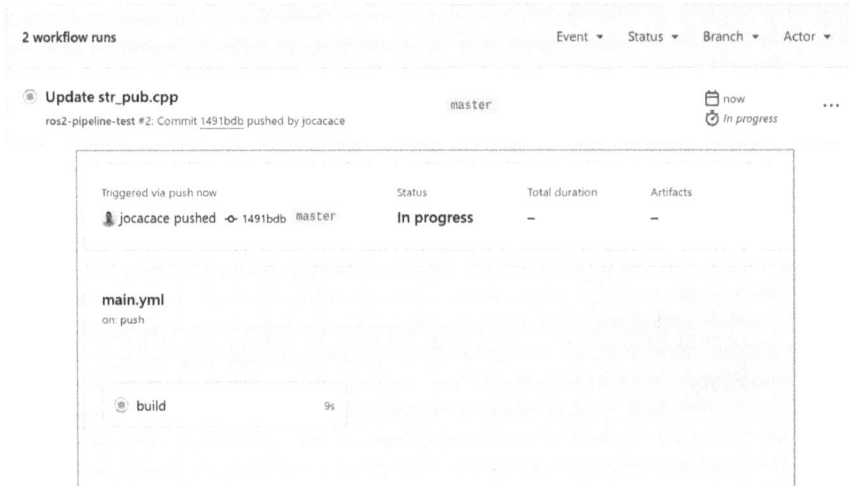

Figure 13.4: Actions related to the commits and their status

8. By clicking on the current status (bottom of *Figure 13.4*), you can follow the currently executed line as included in the main.yml file, as shown in *Figure 13.5*.

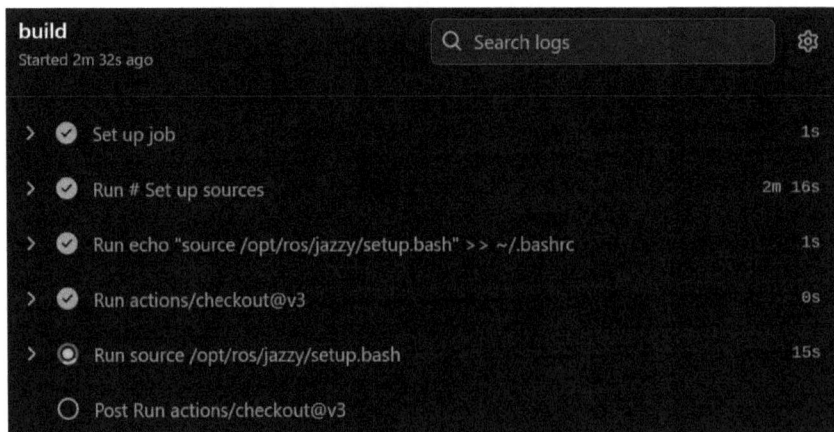

Figure 13.5: Monitoring the action execution

A common way to track the status of the actions is by adding to the repository page a status badge. Let's explore how to do that next.

Adding a status badge

With a status badge, you can easily check that your software integrates well with the rest of the system, without causing issues that might corrupt the installation or deployment. A status badge gives both you and the team a quick indicator of whether the system is functioning correctly by displaying whether actions have completed successfully or failed, preventing the pipeline from completing.

To add a status badge, generate Markdown text and place it in the repository's README.md file. Markdown is a simple formatting language that converts plain text into formatted documents and is commonly used for documentation. The README.md file, typically found in the root of a GitHub repository, provides an overview of the project, instructions, and key details for users. By including a status badge in the README, you can quickly inform your team that your code is free from compilation or integration issues. This badge is a small image in README that shows the status of a GitHub action (e.g., passing or failing) and updates automatically to reflect the current build or test status. We can add the status badge directly generating the Markdown text from GitHub by clicking on the desired action and clicking the three dots on the top-right bar (see *Figure 13.6*). Here, you can click on the *Create status badge* button. This will open a new popup with Markdown text.

Figure 13.6: Button to create a status badge

Create a file called README.md in the root of your ROS 2 package and put the code reported in the **Create status badge** panel. An example of this code is reported here:

```
[![ros2-pipeline-test](https://github.com/jocacace/ros2_ci_cd/actions/workflows/
main.yml/badge.svg)](https://github.com/jocacace/ros2_ci_cd/actions/workflows/
main.yml)
```

This Markdown snippet adds a badge to your GitHub README that shows the status of a CI/CD workflow for a ROS 2 project. The badge links to the specific workflow file (.yml) in your repository, making it easy to check the build status directly from your project's page.

After adding this text to the README file and uploading the repository, the actions will run again, and the badge will update to show the result. You can test this by intentionally creating a compilation error in your code—notice that the badge color changes from green to red, indicating a failure. An example of the two badge states is shown in *Figure 13.7*.

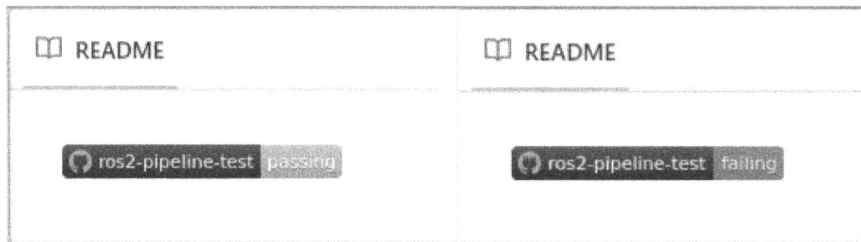

Figure 13.7: Button to create a status badge

Adding the status badge is a good practice also in open-source projects to inform the developers your work can be quickly used without any issues.

Summary

In this chapter, we explored tools for automatically evaluating the status of a ROS 2 package. First, we discussed automatic unit testing, which allows developers to define a set of test cases that continually verify the correct behavior of the code, even as new features are added. Unit testing can also verify the output of a ROS 2 node when it publishes to topics. ROS 2 is already integrated with the GTest framework, a testing library developed by Google. For more advanced testing strategies, developers can refer to the official GTest documentation, which covers topics such as writing test fixtures and using mocks to simulate dependencies.

Beyond unit testing, another essential approach is CI/CD, which helps ensure that code doesn't introduce compilation or integration errors. We used GitHub Actions to easily create automatic checks that run when the code is updated. This provides a quick way to inform developers and the community about the repository's status. Additionally, for more advanced CI/CD workflows—such as publishing Docker images—GitHub Secrets can be used to securely store credentials for services such as Docker Hub.

While using these methods isn't mandatory—especially if you work primarily on your own code—they're invaluable when collaborating with other developers who rely on your code's stability and integration with other modules. Rapidly detecting issues allows you to address bugs or compilation problems promptly.

In the next chapter, we'll discuss another important and emerging area in robotics and artificial intelligence: the use of Large Language Models (LLMs) for planning and executing robotic actions.

14

Interfacing Large Language Models with ROS 2

This chapter will explore the possibilities of using GenAI in robotics by interfacing different **large language models** (**LLMs**) into ROS 2 by building AI agents. LLMs are a subset of GenAI mainly focused on generating text. So why does interfacing LLMs and AI agents with ROS 2 robots matter? Using LLMs and agents, robots can understand user input and generate an intelligent response. Users can use text, images, and voice as input, making the robot capable of answering questions intelligently. Other than interaction, LLM-based AI agents can control a robot by generating corresponding actions for the robot based on user input.

In this chapter, we're going to cover the following main topics:

- LLMs for robotics
- Integrating ROS 2 robots with LLM agents
- Creating ROS 2 AI agents
- Popular ROS 2 AI agent projects

Technical requirements

To follow along in this chapter, you should install Ubuntu 24.04 LTS with ROS 2 Jazzy desktop. It can be in a VM, Docker, WSL 2, or a real machine. Your PC should have a decent NVIDIA RTX GPU with *>8 GB of VRAM*. The reference materials for this chapter can be found in the Chapter14 folder of the following GitHub repository: https://github.com/PacktPublishing/Mastering-ROS-2-for-Robotics-Programming/tree/main/Chapter14.

LLMs for robotics

LLMs are large, deep-learning models trained on vast amounts of data. Their main component is the **transformer model neural network** [1].

A transformer model is a neural network that can learn the context and meaning of a sentence by tracking the relationship in sequential data, such as words, using a mathematical technique called attention. In simple words, transformers can learn and generate human-like text by analyzing patterns from large text data.

Google introduced attention in 2017 as a research paper, *Attention is All You Need* [2], and it is now the foundation model for all the famous LLMs like ChatGPT from OpenAI, Llama from Facebook, and Gemini from Google. These LLMs are great performers in understanding natural language, reasoning, and decision-making. Along with LLMs, there are:

- **Vision language models (VLMs)**, which combine an LLM with a vision encoder, enabling the LLM to understand images and videos that can be used for robot perception.

- **Audio language models (ALMs)**, which are designed to process and generate spoken language. They combine an LLM with speech processing techniques, enabling capabilities like **speech-to-text (STT)**, **text-to-speech (TTS)**, and **spoken language understanding (SLU)**.

In robotics, LLMs can be used as an interface between robots and humans, allowing human-like communication with robots, adaptive learning, autonomous decision-making, and intelligent control of robots.

Here are some important LLM-based use cases that can be applied in robotics:

- **Natural language-based robot control:** We can use LLMs to send robot commands. Users can communicate with the robot using plain language instead of programming or GUIs. For example, the user talks to the cleaning robot to clean the room, and the robot performs the task.

- **Autonomous navigation and manipulation:** LLMs can interpret the high-level instructions for navigation goals and pick and place instructions for the robot. For example, a warehouse robot receives a command like *Fetch a box from shelf five and deliver it to the exit*, which can determine the optimal path for the robot to reach the goal. For the manipulation task example, the user can send instructions in natural language, such as *Pick the red box and place it near the green box*. The LLMs can generate high-level instructions for the robotic arm to perform pick-and-place operations.

- **Robot perception and reasoning**: LLMs with vision can understand the robot environment and clearly describe the objects in the scene. For example, if a user asks the model what the coordinates of a red box are, the model can return them if the box is present in the scene.

- **Error diagnosis and self-repair guidance**: The robot's error logs can be fed to LLMs, which can suggest auto fixes.

- **Simulation and training assistance**: LLMs can help generate training scenarios in robot simulators like Gazebo and Isaac Sim, creating a dynamic environment for robot simulation.

You can find more information about LLM robotics-related research in [3] and [4].

In the next section, we will see how to integrate LLMs directly with ROS 2 by building AI agents.

Integration of ROS 2 robots with LLM agents

The basic idea of an AI agent is to use an LLM as a reasoning engine to determine the appropriate sequence and order of pre-coded actions to take.

By combining an LLM-based agent with ROS 2, we can create multiple robotic applications. For example, it can be used in service robots to interact with the robot and perform meaningful robot actions based on user input. We can also use LLM agents for autonomous navigation and manipulation.

Different software frameworks are available to create an LLM-based agent. We can create an AI agent from scratch, but the development will be much quicker by using a framework. Here are a few popular AI agent frameworks:

- **LangChain** [5]: This is an open-source framework for creating LLM-based AI agents. Developers can create context-aware, reasoning-capable, and tool-integrated AI applications. LangChain has features such as **chains**, which are sequences of LLM calls or tools designed for multi-step processing. It integrates multiple LLMs from OpenAI, Hugging Face, etc. The tools in LangChain are the external services or functions that an AI agent can use to extend capabilities beyond text generation. For example, developers can use external APIs such as ROS 2 inside the agents to communicate with ROS 2-compatible robots. Developers can create custom tools that will trigger after the user's reasoning for the prompt. Using LangChain, we can quickly prototype chatbots interacting with external frameworks such as ROS 2 and Gazebo. LangChain mainly supports Python-based APIs for creating agents. We will discuss LangChain-based ROS 2 agents in the next section.

- **AutoGen** [6]: This is an open-source framework from Microsoft for building multi-agent AI systems that can collaborate and solve complex problems. It can also automate workflows. It helps AI agents communicate with each other and external tools, making it useful for task automation, research applications, and decision-making.

Multiple AI agent frameworks are available besides LangChain and AutoGen. Here is a curated list of the latest agent frameworks and agents: [7].

Choosing the proper framework for creating an AI agent for the robot can sometimes be difficult. We can use both frameworks with ROS 2 in different scenarios. LangChain can be better suited for knowledge retrieval and AI reasoning with ROS 2, whereas AutoGen may be suitable for creating autonomous AI agents to collaborate on robotic tasks. Most of the popular frameworks use Python as the programming language.

The following section shows the block diagram of an AI agent working with a ROS 2 system.

Components of AI agents with ROS 2

Figure 14.1 shows a high-level architecture diagram of a ROS 2 AI agent that integrates LLMs and VLMs using LangChain or a similar framework to interact with the simulation or real robot working in ROS 2.

Here are the core components of an AI agent:

- **Human-robot interface**: This allows the user to interact with the agent. It can be done using voice or text, and we may have to use some speech recognition.

- **The ROS AI agent application**: This central unit is responsible for processing user input using LangChain APIs and communicating with LLMS. It processes user input and triggers appropriate tools based on it. It also receives feedback from the ROS 2 robot through topics, services, parameters, and actions.

- **LangChain/AutoGen**: The agents use APIs from an agent framework such as LangChain and AutoGen to integrate and orchestrate LLMs and multi-model VLMs.

- **Cloud/local models**: LLMs/VLMs can be hosted in the cloud or can be loaded locally. LLMs such as GPT mostly run in the cloud, and open-source models such as Llama can be run in the cloud and locally. The computer should have a good specification if we want to load LLMs/VLMs locally. The specification depends on what model we are loading. For example, for loading Meta LLaMA 2 13B/LLaMA 3 8B, we may need specs such as an 8+ core CPU (Ryzen 7/Intel i7 or better) 32 GB RAM, NVIDIA GPU with 12–24 GB VRAM (e.g., RTX 3080, 3090, 4080, 4090).

We need tools (such as Ollama [8], LM-Studio [9], etc.) to load the LLMs on a local computer. Cloud APIs will be faster than local deployment because they mainly send a request to the cloud, and the cloud infrastructure is good enough to handle and process the request. Cloud inference will be a better choice than local deployment of LLMs for ROS 2 robots running with a small compute footprint. Use the local model only if it can safely run on the compute modules.

- **Custom tools:** These are custom functions that interface the AI agent to an external system such as ROS 2. They are like utilities or plugins that can enhance the AI agent's functionalities. These tools/functions are triggered based on the prompt the user sends to the agent. The tools are Python functions/classes that have external APIs such as *rclpy* (ROS 2 Python client library).

- **ROS 2-based real robot/simulation:** This represents the actual robot or simulated environment running on ROS 2. In the case of a real robot, the ROS 2 driver should be running, and proper topics, services, and actions should be exposed. The agent can communicate with the ROS 2 robot only if the robot driver is up and running. The same applies to simulation. The simulation using Gazebo/Isaac Sim should be properly running along with the agent, and all the ROS 2 topics, services, and actions should be exposed.

- **Feedback, logs, and diagnostics:** This represents real-time feedback from the ROS 2 system. The feedback to the agent can be using ROS 2 topics, services, actions, and parameters. The feedback helps to debug, monitor, and improve performance.

- **Agent response:** This is the final response that the agent shows to the user after triggering the necessary tools. The agent response will give the user an idea of the result operation.

In the next section, we can see how these AI agents work.

How an AI agent works for ROS 2

Here is how the AI agent works. The agent gets the input request from a human via voice/text. Agents use APIs from LangChain/AutoGen to reason with the input. The APIs load the LLMs when the agent is initialized.

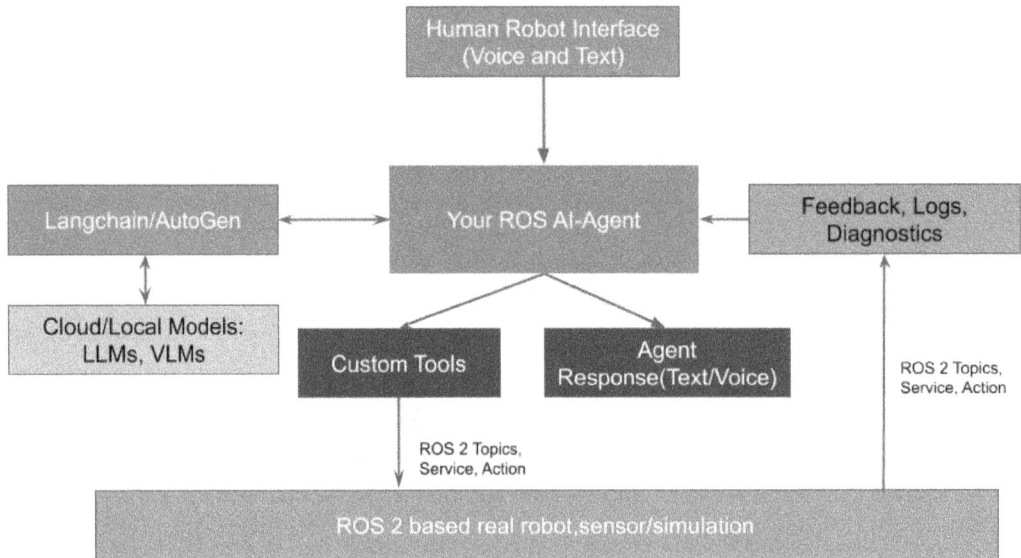

Figure 14.1: Block diagram of AI agent with ROS 2

Based on the reasoning from the LLM, it executes specific actions coded as tools. The tools have ROS 2 APIs, which can publish/subscribe data to a ROS 2-based robot. The feedback from the ROS 2 system is sent back to the AI agent for diagnostics and monitoring. The agent will show a final response after getting the feedback.

Understanding AI agent architecture and working with it helps developers create new agents. In the next section, we will dive into the development of ROS-based AI agents.

Creating ROS 2 AI agents

This section will explore a few ROS 2 AI agent projects from the basics to advanced levels and see how to set them up on a local PC.

In Chapter14/docker_llm, you can find the Dockerfile and scripts to build a new image for the ROS 2 AI agent application.

You can use the following command to build the image:

```
./build_image.sh ros2_llm master_ros2_ws robot
```

In this command, ros2_llm is the Docker image name, master_ros2_ws is the ROS 2 workspace name, and robot is the username of the Docker container.

After building the image, we can create the container using the following command:

```
./create_container.sh ros2_llm master_ros2_ws ros2_ai
```

In this command, we have to provide the image name first, which is ros2_llm, and the second argument is the ROS 2 workspace, which is master_ros2_ws. The third argument is the container name, which is ros2_ai. The container will mount master_ros2_ws from the host machine, so we can build those packages from this container itself.

If we want to attach a new terminal to the container, we can use the following script and command:

```
./start_container.sh ros2_ai
source /ros_entrypoint.sh
```

There are Docker Compose files for this chapter. Switch to the Chapter14 | docker_compose_llm folder and execute the following command to start building the Docker image and start the container:

- Use the following command if you are using a non-NVIDIA graphics card on your PC:

```
docker compose -f docker-compose-gui.yml build
docker compose -f docker-compose-gui.yml up
```

- If you do have an NVIDIA graphics card and the driver is properly installed, use the following command to start the container:

```
docker compose -f docker-compose-nvidia.yml build
docker compose -f docker-compose-nvidia.yml up
```

Once you run this command, the image will be built first, the container will start, and you will have to use another terminal to attach to the container. You don't have to close this terminal; if you cancel the command by pressing *Ctrl + C*, it will stop the running container.

You can create a new terminal from the running container using the following command:

```
./start_container.sh ros2_ai
```

Now source the ROS 2 environment:

```
source /ros_entrypoint.sh
```

After starting the container, if you want to stop the container and remove the container, you can execute the command from a new host terminal. Make sure you are executing from inside the `docker_compose_llm` folder:

```
docker compose -f docker-compose-gui.yml down
```

or

```
docker compose -f docker-compose-nvidia.yml down
```

In the next section, we will see how to set up VS Code Dev Containers for developing and running AI-agents.

ROS 2 AI-agent development using VS Code Dev Containers

If you are interested in setting up a development container in VS Code, make sure you have created the ROS 2 workspace named `master_ros2_ws` and then open the `Chapter14` folder using VS Code. This folder has a `.devcontainer` folder. This has the devcontainer.json file, which has the instructions to use the Docker Compose file we used in the above section for the container. When you open the folder, it will prompt you to install the Dev Containers extension and reopen it in the container. If you select this option, it will build the container, set the environment, mount the ROS 2 workspace as a volume, and connect the editor to it. We can also see the mounted volume, which is the master_ros2_ws folder in VS Code itself.

Let's start building the basic AI agent working with ROS 2.

Building an AI agent for ROS 2

In this section, we will discuss how we can develop our own AI agent for our ROS 2 application. The architecture of the agent will be based on *Figure 14.1*. We use LangChain as the framework for creating AI agents here.

Here is the list of demo AI agents we are going to discuss in this section.

- **Basic ROS 2 agent:** This AI agent performs simple tasks, such as printing the name of the ROS 2 distribution and ROS domain ID. The user can ask about these values in natural language, and it can reply with the values.

- **Basic ROS 2 agent with ROS 2 tools**: This agent can trigger ROS 2 command-line tools using natural language and show their results. For example, the user can ask about ROS 2 topics, services, actions, etc.

- **Agent for turtlesim control**: This agent can move the turtle in turtlesim and get its current position.

- **AI agent for Nav2**: This agent works with Nav2 and TurtleBot 3 simulation. We can ask the robot to navigate to any position on the map and inquire about its current position.

- **AI agent for MoveIt2**: This agent works with MoveIt2 and **universal robot** (UR) simulation, which moves the robot end effector based on the user prompt. It can also retrieve the current gripper position.

The `Chapter14/ros2_basic_agent` package includes the complete source code of the AI agents. This is a simple ROS 2 Python package that has AI agent scripts, launch files, and a config file for OpenAI.

You can find agent scripts at `ros2_basic_agent/ros2_basic_agent/` and launch files at `ros2_basic_agent/launch`. We can copy this package to the ROS workspace, which is `~/master_ros2_ws/src`.

Build the package inside the Docker container using the following command:

```
colcon build --packages-select ros2_basic_agent --symlink-install
```

After building this package, we can launch each agent with the necessary simulator, if any.

For this package, we use cloud-based LLMs, specifically ChatGPT APIs. Cloud-based APIs work with any kind of computer, and the requirements are a steady internet connection and an OpenAI API paid account. If you have a very good local GPU infrastructure, using Ollama and LM-Studio with open-source LLMs such as Llama is another option for the agent. This approach requires no internet connection; the agent can work fully offline.

If we use cloud APIs, we may need to create an API key to access them. The following section shows how to configure OpenAI API keys.

Configuring OpenAI API keys

To connect to cloud-based LLMs, initialize the agent, and connect, we need to generate an API key from the OpenAI website. The ChatGPT account and API access account are different, and the payment is also different. Here is the link to create API keys: [10]. You can create a secret key and copy the key. This is required in our ROS 2 package. Also, make sure you have added 5 to 10 USD to test this package. *Figure 14.2* shows the API key entry once it is successfully created.

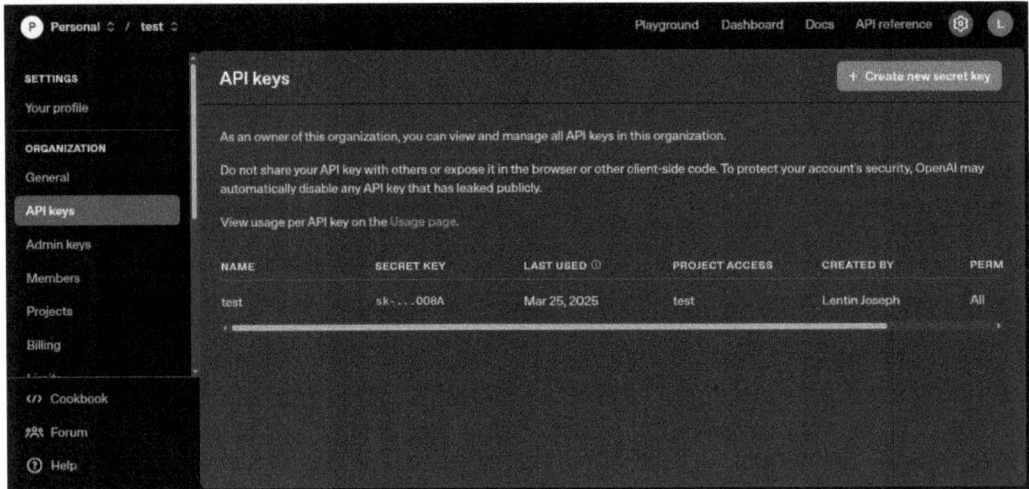

Figure 14.2: OpenAI API web page

Once you copy the keys, navigate to `ros2_basic_agent/config/openai.env` and put it in the `OPENAI_API_KEY` field. Once this is done, you must build the `ros2_basic_agent` package using the following command:

```
colcon build --packages-select ros2_basic_agent --symlink-install
```

Once we have updated the OpenAI API key, we are done with the API key configuration. Now we can discuss the detailed architecture of an ROS 2 AI agent node and how it works.

Architecture of ROS 2 AI agent node

In this section, we will see how the AI agent works inside a ROS 2 node in detail. *Figure 14.3* shows a detailed architecture diagram of the ROS 2 AI agent node based on LangChain. This ROS 2 Python node has ROS 2 APIs and LangChain APIs. The ROS 2 APIs subscribe to a string topic named `/prompt`. This string data will be the input to the agent. The agent uses LangChain APIs and connects to OpenAI for cloud LLMs.

Once the agent understands the context of input, it triggers available tools that are defined and finally comes up with the result.

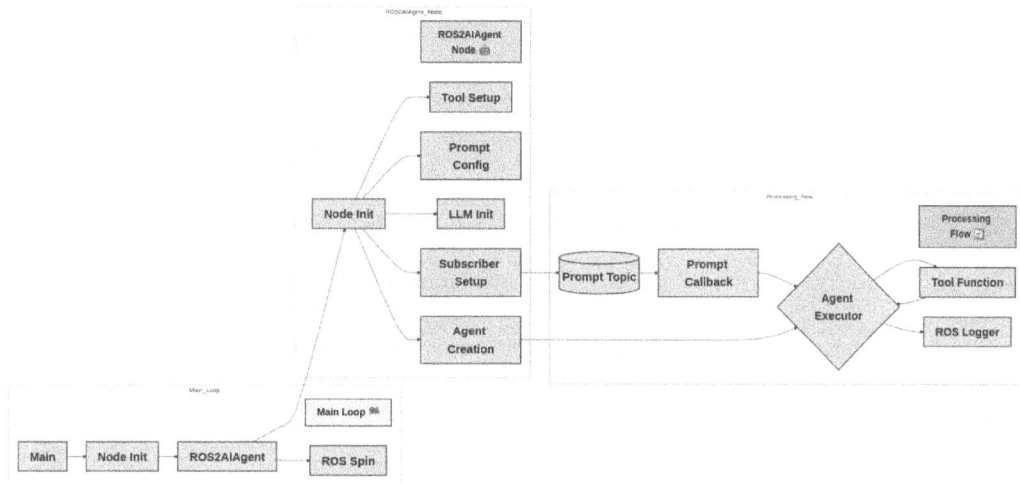

Figure 14.3: Workflow of a basic ROS 2 LangChain AI agent

Here is the code template of a ROS 2 AI agent node. All AI agent APIs are wrapped in a ROS 2 node class:

```
class ROS2AIAgent(Node):
        def init(self):
            # 1. Node initialization
            # 2. Tool setup
            # 3. Prompt configuration
            # 4. LLM initialization
            # 5. Agent creation
            # 6. Subscriber setup
@tool
def tool_function(self) -> str:
    # Tool implementation
    pass

def prompt_callback(self, msg):
    # Message processing
    pass
```

```
def main():
    # Main execution loop
```

Inside the ROS 2 Node class, we initialize the ROS 2 node, LangChain-based custom tools, prompt configuration, and OpenAI LLM. The **prompt configuration** is a description we provide to the AI agent to respond to input prompts. The description defines the agent's behavior, response style, constraint, and output format. The better the description, the better the agent understands the context.

After initializing, the ROS2 node creates the agent and a ROS 2 subscriber named /prompt for receiving input from the user. After receiving the input, it invokes the agent with this input, which triggers the appropriate tools that we have defined. After executing the tools, it will show the result.

Let's start running each agent and see its working.

Running the basic ROS 2 AI agent

Let's start with the first ROS 2 AI agent we include in the ros2_basic_agent package. You can find the basic agent ROS 2 node at ros2_basic_agent/ros2_basic_agent/ ros2_ai_agent_basic. py and the launch file at ros2_basic_agent/launch/ start_ros2_basic_agent.py.

In this agent, the user can ask about the current ROS 2 distribution and ROS domain ID. Based on the queries, the agent can return those values.

Figure 14.4 shows the flow diagram of this agent. It has the same architecture that we have seen in *Figure 14.3*; the only difference you can see is it has two tools, which are get_ros_domain_id and get_distribution:

- get_ros_distro(): Retrieves the current ROS distribution name
- get_domain_id(): Retrieves the current ROS domain ID

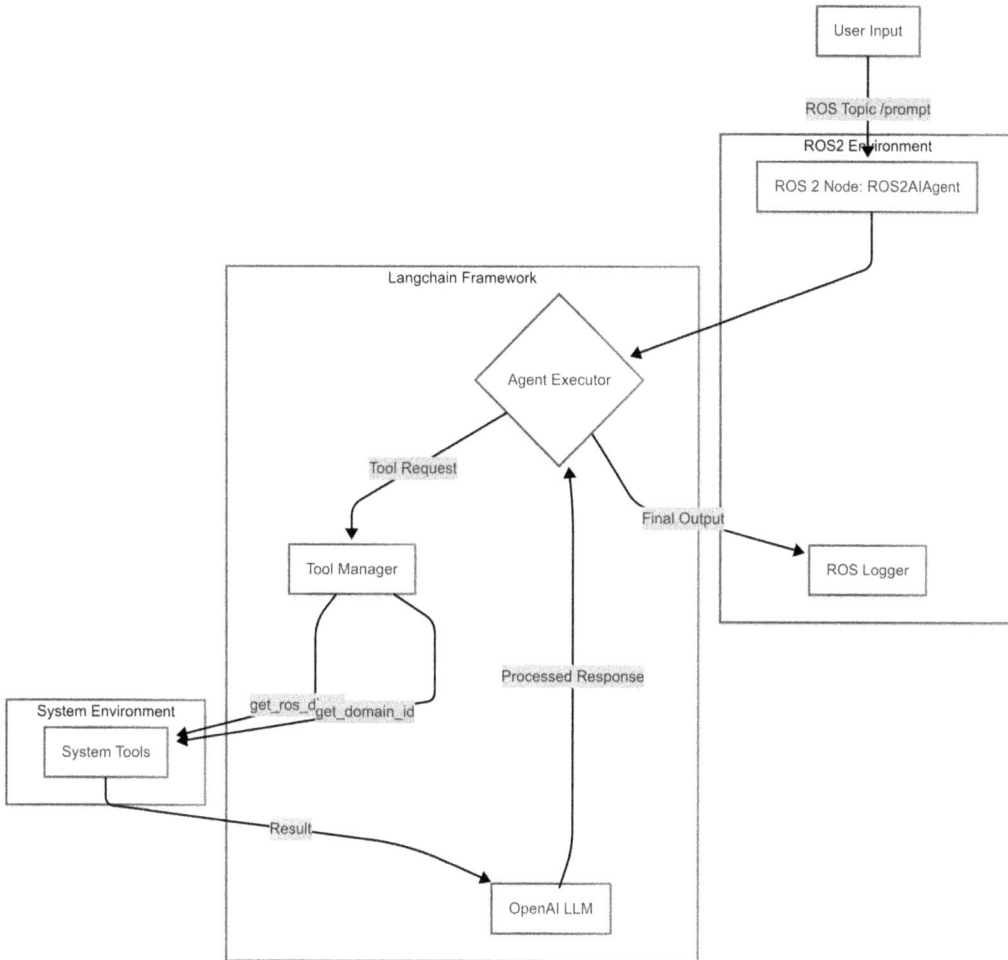

Figure 14.4: Flow diagram of the ROS 2 Langchain AI agent

It is better to work with the agent from a Docker container because all the dependencies are pre-installed. If you have already started the container, follow the commands below to start the basic AI agent:

```
In Terminal 1
```

Switch to the docker_llm folder inside Chapter14. Make sure, you have created the container before starting the launch file. If not, create a container first:

```
./create_container.sh ros2_llm master_ros2_ws ros2_ai
```

If the container is already created, use the following script to start the container or to attach a new terminal:

```
./start_container.sh ros2_ai
```

Once you have the container terminal, execute the following commands to start the launch file:

```
source /ros_entrypoint.sh
source ~/master_ros2_ws/install/setup.bash
```

Here is the launch file to start the agent:

```
ros2 launch ros2_basic_agent start_ros2_basic_agent.py
```

If the agent is running correctly, you might get a message like the following:

```
[ros2_ai_agent_basic-1] [INFO] [1742935925.955416324] [ros2_ai_agent_
basic]: ROS2 AI Agent has been started
```

Note

If you are getting an error from the OpenAI API, make sure you have properly entered the API key and have sufficient credit in the OpenAI account.

Once the agent starts working, we can send a prompt to the agent. Take another new terminal from the container and execute the following command:

```
In Terminal 2
```

We can publish the prompt to the /prompt topic as a string. You only have to publish it once. Once it is published, you can check in the agent terminal and find the response:

```
ros2 topic pub --once /prompt std_msgs/msg/String "{data: 'What ROS
distribution am I using?'}"
```

Here is a typical output that you can see in Terminal 1:

```
[ros2_ai_agent_basic-1] > Entering new AgentExecutor chain...
[ros2_ai_agent_basic-1] [ros2_ai_agent_basic-1] Invoking: get_ros_distro
with {} [ros2_ai_agent_basic-1]
[ros2_ai_agent_basic-1] [ros2_ai_agent_basic-1] Current ROS distribution:
jazzy Current ROS distribution: jazzy
[ros2_ai_agent_basic-1] [ros2_ai_agent_basic-1] > Finished chain. [ros2_
ai_agent_basic-1] [INFO] [1742937262.050775675] [ros2_ai_agent_basic]:
Result: Current ROS distribution: jazzy
```

In the response, it is printed that the current distribution is *jazzy*.

After publishing the first prompt, you can try the following prompt to get the ROS_DOMAIN_ID value:

```
ros2 topic pub --once /prompt std_msgs/msg/String "{data: 'What is my ROS
domain ID?'}"
```

After publishing, you can find the ROS domain ID printed in the agent terminal.

> **Note**
>
> If we prompt a more complex task to this agent, the agent may not be able to deliver it because of the limited number of tools in the agent. To handle more complex prompts, we should add more tools to the agent.

In the next section, we will show the demonstration of the next agent, which has tools that can list ROS 2 topics, services, and actions.

AI agent with ROS 2 tools

In this section, we can see how to run the ROS 2 tools agent and briefly explain its custom tools.

You can find the agent ROS 2 node at `ros2_basic_agent/ros2_basic_agent/ ros2_ai_agent_basic_tools.py` and the launch file at `ros2_basic_agent/launch/start_ros2_tools_agent.py`.

Using the `ros2` command-line tools, we can enquire about topics, services, actions, and parameters. This agent does the same thing, but instead of using commands, we can enquire using natural language.

It has the following custom tools:

- `list_topics()`: Lists all available ROS 2 topics
- `list_nodes()`: Lists all running ROS 2 nodes
- `list_services()`: Lists all available ROS 2 services
- `list_actions()`: Lists all available ROS 2 actions

The difference between the first basic agent and the ROS 2 tool agent is that the former has different prompt configs and different custom tools. The basic architecture of the ROS 2 AI agent remains the same.

Here is the launch file to start the agent:

```
ros2 launch ros2_basic_agent start_ros2_tools_agent.py
```

If the agent starts properly, it will show the following message in the terminal:

```
[ros2_ai_agent_basic_tools-1] [INFO] [1742974052.972036533] [ros2_ai_
agent_basic_tools]: ROS2 AI Agent has been started
```

Now, we can send the prompt to the agent by publishing to the `/prompt` topic. The following prompt asks the agent to list the available ROS 2 topics:

```
ros2 topic pub --once /prompt std_msgs/msg/String "{data: 'Show me all
available topics'}"
```

Figure 14.5 shows the output of the agent once we publish the prompt:

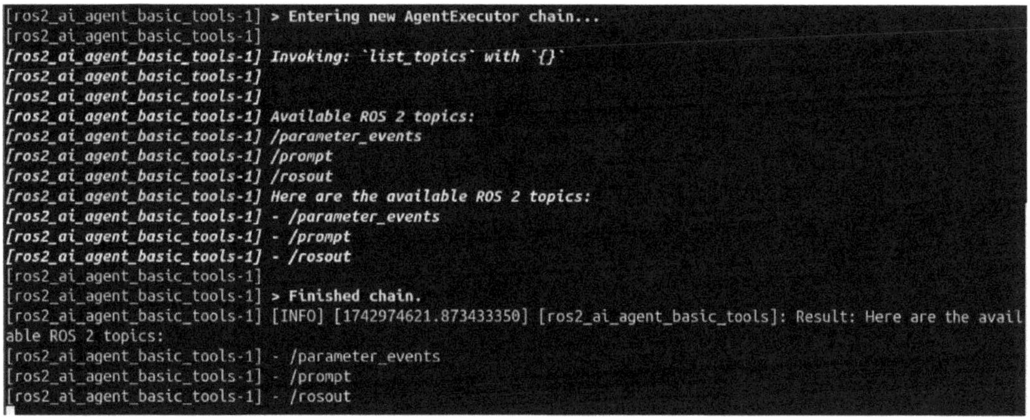

```
[ros2_ai_agent_basic_tools-1] > Entering new AgentExecutor chain...
[ros2_ai_agent_basic_tools-1]
[ros2_ai_agent_basic_tools-1] Invoking: `list_topics` with `{}`
[ros2_ai_agent_basic_tools-1]
[ros2_ai_agent_basic_tools-1]
[ros2_ai_agent_basic_tools-1] Available ROS 2 topics:
[ros2_ai_agent_basic_tools-1] /parameter_events
[ros2_ai_agent_basic_tools-1] /prompt
[ros2_ai_agent_basic_tools-1] /rosout
[ros2_ai_agent_basic_tools-1] Here are the available ROS 2 topics:
[ros2_ai_agent_basic_tools-1] - /parameter_events
[ros2_ai_agent_basic_tools-1] - /prompt
[ros2_ai_agent_basic_tools-1] - /rosout
[ros2_ai_agent_basic_tools-1]
[ros2_ai_agent_basic_tools-1] > Finished chain.
[ros2_ai_agent_basic_tools-1] [INFO] [1742974621.873433350] [ros2_ai_agent_basic_tools]: Result: Here are the avail
able ROS 2 topics:
[ros2_ai_agent_basic_tools-1] - /parameter_events
[ros2_ai_agent_basic_tools-1] - /prompt
[ros2_ai_agent_basic_tools-1] - /rosout
```

Figure 14.5: Output of the ROS 2 tool agent

We can send prompts for services and actions as we did for topics. The example prompt for that is given below.

Here is the prompt for showing the service list:

```
ros2 topic pub --once /prompt std_msgs/msg/String "{data: 'List all
available services'}"
```

Here is the prompt for showing the action list:

```
ros2 topic pub --once /prompt std_msgs/msg/String "{data: 'List all
available actions}"
```

Here is a more complex prompt, asking the agent to list the ROS 2 topics that have a string message type:

```
ros2 topic pub --once /prompt std_msgs/msg/String "{data: 'Which of these
topic messages contain a string field?'}"
```

After interacting with the agent, let's switch to the next agent. The following agent is for interacting with turtlesim.

AI agent for ROS 2 turtlesim

This AI agent can move the turtle in turtlesim. We can prompt it to move or rotate or ask for its current position.

Figure 14.6 shows the node graph of the agent with turtlesim.

Figure 14.6: Workflow of the ROS 2 agent with turtlesim

The agent publishes the cmd_vel and subscribes to the turtle's pose. Based on the prompt from the user, it can trigger the custom tools for publishing cmd_vel for movement and printing the current position.

You can find the agent ROS 2 node at ros2_basic_agent/ros2_basic_agent/ros2_ai_agent_ turtlesim.py. It has the following custom tools:

- move_forward(distance: float): Move the turtle a particular distance.
- rotate(angle: float): Rotate the turtle by a particular angle.
- get_pose(): It should return the current pose of the turtle.

You can find the launch file at ros2_basic_agent/launch/start_turtlesim_agent.py.

Here is the command to start the turtlesim agent with the turtlesim:

```
ros2 launch ros2_basic_agent start_turtlesim_agent.py
```

If the agent starts properly, you can see the turtlesim and the agent started logs from the terminal, as shown in *Figure 14.7*:

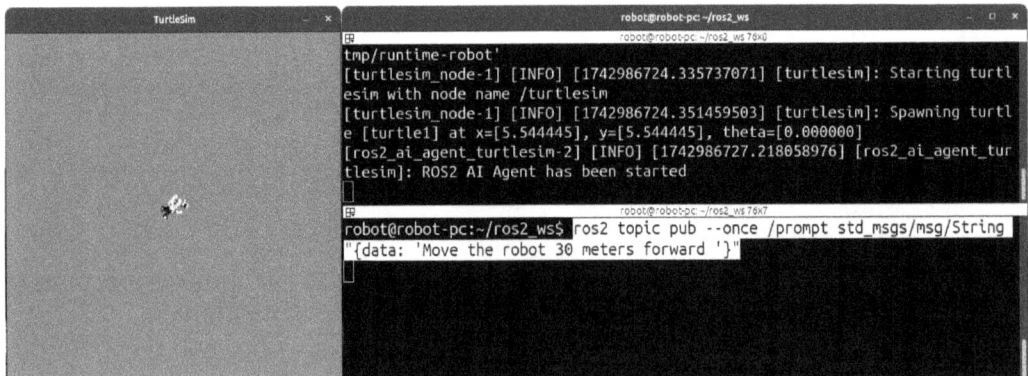

Figure 14.7: Output of the ROS 2 agent for turtlesim

After starting the agent in Terminal 1, publish the prompt as shown in *Figure 14.7*. Here is an example prompt. We can try to move the turtle in the turtlesim:

```
ros2 topic pub --once /prompt std_msgs/msg/String "{data: 'Move the robot
30 meters forward '}"
```

This prompt will move the turtle forward for 30 meters. The value provided to the agent is just a factor. If the value is higher, there is more movement to the turtle.

Figure 14.8 shows the output of the move forward prompt to the turtlesim agent.

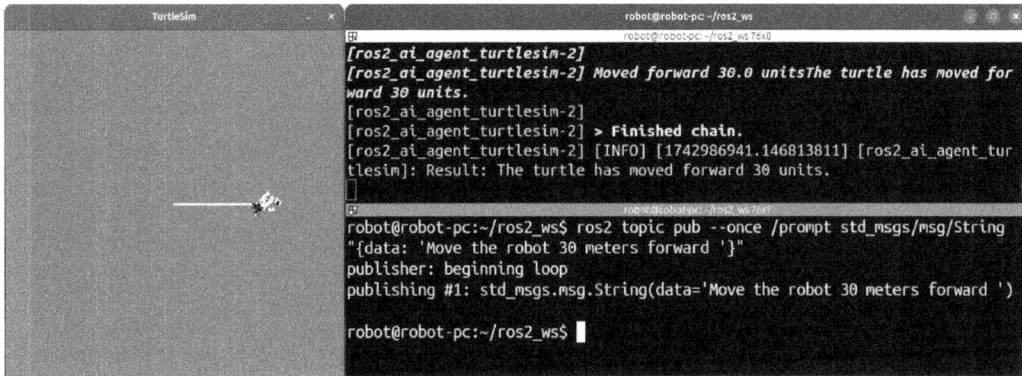

Figure 14.8: Output of the move forward prompt

Similar to move forward, here are example prompts we can try for this agent.

The following prompt can rotate the turtle at a specific angle. In this example, it can rotate 90 degrees:

```
ros2 topic pub --once /prompt std_msgs/msg/String "{data: 'rotate 90
degree '}"
```

The following prompt can retrieve the current position of the turtle in the turtlesim:

```
ros2 topic pub --once /prompt std_msgs/msg/String "{data: 'get current
pose '}"
```

The next agent we will discuss can work with Nav2.

AI agent for Nav2

Using this agent, we can command the robot to move to a position on the map and retrieve its current position.

Figure 14.9 shows the block diagram of the Nav2 AI agent.

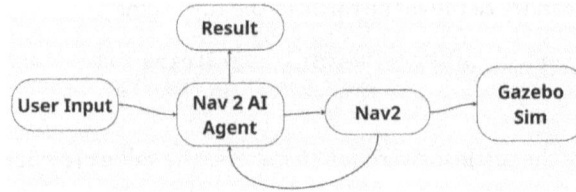

Figure 14.9: Block diagram of the Nav2 AI agent

The agent is connected to Nav2 and sends the target position. Nav2 generates command velocity to reach that position and moves the robot in Gazebo.

You can find the agent ROS 2 node at `ros2_basic_agent/ros2_basic_agent/ros2_ai_agent_turtlebo3_nav2.py` and the launch file at `ros2_basic_agent/launch/start_turtlebot3_nav2_agent.py`. This agent has the following custom-defined tools:

- `move_to_goal(x: float, y: float)`: Navigates the robot to specified x and y coordinates
- `get_current_pose()`: Retrieves the current position and orientation of the robot

These tools use Nav2 simple commander APIs to command Nav2 to set the target position.

Here is the launch file to start the turtlebot3 simulation: `ros2 launch ros2_basic_agent start_turtlebot3_nav2_agent.py`

This will launch the `turtlebot3` simulation in the Gazebo simulator, Nav2, Slam Toolbox, and the Nav2 AI agent. By default, mapping and navigation are enabled. The user can send a prompt to move the robot to a specific distance in x and y, and the robot can navigate to that position.

Here is a sample prompt we can use to move the robot and get the current position:

```
ros2 topic pub --once /prompt std_msgs/msg/String "{data: 'Move the robot
to position x=1.5, y=0.5'}"
```

Once you have given the prompt, the agent will send the target position to Nav2, and the robot will plan a path and navigate to the provided location. The workings of the agent are shown in *Figure 14.10*.

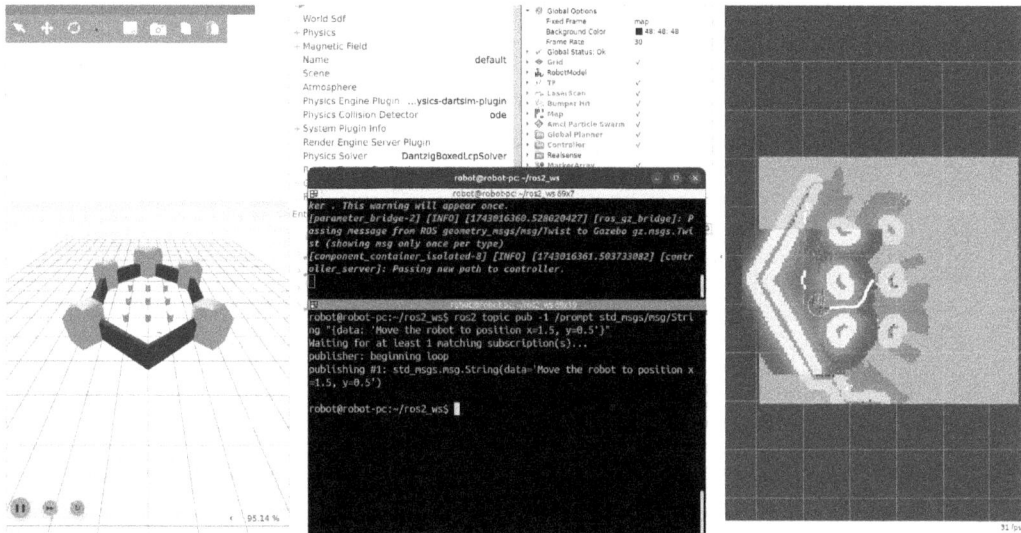

Figure 14.10: Workflow of the Nav2 AI agent

The following prompt will trigger the agent to return the robot's current position:

```
ros2 topic pub --once /prompt std_msgs/msg/String "{data: 'What is the
current position of the robot?'}"
```

Here is the prompt to retrieve the current position and move the robot 1 meter from the current position:

```
ros2 topic pub --once /prompt std_msgs/msg/String "{data: 'Get the current
position and then move the robot 1 meters forward'}"
```

Note

If we prompt a more complex task to this agent, the agent may not be able to deliver it because of the limited number of tools in the agent. For example, if we prompt the agent to move the robot into a particular shape, the agent may fail. To handle more complex prompts, we should add more tools to the agent.

In the next section, we will see how the MoveIt2 agent works.

AI agent for MoveIt2

This agent can work with MoveIt2. Like the Nav2 agent, we can command it to set the robotic arm's target position and retrieve its end effector position.

Figure 14.11 shows the block diagram of the MoveIt2 agent. It is like the Nav2 agent architecture, but the only difference is that Nav2 is replaced with MoveIt2.

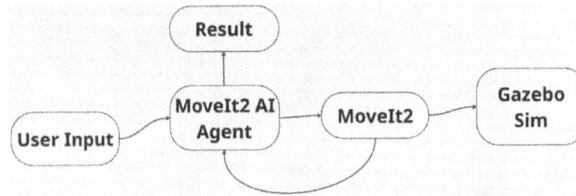

Figure 14.11: Block diagram of the MoveIt2 AI agent

You can find the agent ROS 2 node at ros2_basic_agent/ros2_basic_agent/ros2_ai_agent_ur_moveit2.py and the launch file at ros2_basic_agent/launch/ start_ur_moveit2_agent.py.

This agent has the following custom-defined tools:

- `move_to_pose(self, x: float, y: float, z: float)`: Sets the end effector position of the robotic arm
- `get_current_pose(self)`: Retrieves the current end effector position of the robotic arm

Here is the launch file to start with the universal robot simulation in Gazebo and the MoveIt2 agent: `ros2 launch ros2_basic_agent start_ur_moveit2_agent.py`.

After starting the launch file, we can interact with the agent using the following prompts.

The following prompt will move the robot end effector to a specific position:

```
ros2 topic pub --once /prompt std_msgs/msg/String "data: 'Move the end
effector to position x=-0.392, y=0.358, z=0.623'"
```

Figure 14.12 shows the prompt's output. Once the prompt is published, the AI agent communicates with MoveIt2 to generate a plan and execute it in the commanded position.

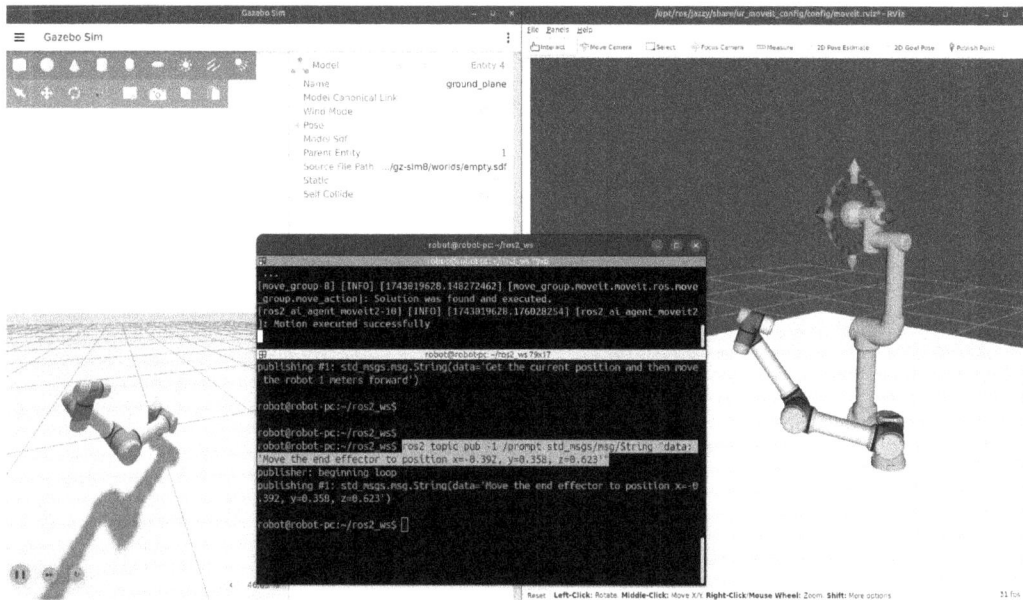

Figure 14.12: Workflow of the MoveIt2 AI agent

Here is the prompt to move the robot to the home position:

```
ros2 topic pub --once /prompt std_msgs/msg/String "data: 'Move the robot
to home position'"
```

Here is the prompt to get the current position of the end effector:

```
ros2 topic pub --once /prompt std_msgs/msg/String "data: 'Get the current
gripper pose'"
```

The following prompt can get the current end effector position, reduce the z value by 0.2, and send it to MoveIt:

```
ros2 topic pub -1 /prompt std_msgs/msg/String "{data: 'Get the current
position of end effector and reduce z value by 0.2'}"
```

> **Note**
>
> If we prompt a more complex task to this agent, the agent may not be able to deliver it because of the limited number of tools. For example, if we prompt the agent to perform a zig-zag movement, the agent may fail. To handle more complex prompts, we should add more tools to the agent.

We have completed the discussion of the custom agents we have created. Now, let's start discussing the existing free ROS 2 agent projects that are available.

Popular ROS 2 AI agent projects

In this section, we will briefly explore some existing ROS 2 AI agent projects.

ROSA

ROSA [*11*] is an AI agent by NASA designed to interact with ROS 1 and ROS 2-based robot systems using natural language queries. It helps robot developers inspect, diagnose, understand, and control robots. It is based on the LangChain framework and has many custom tools.

Figure 14.13 shows the ROSA project banner.

Figure 14.13: ROSA project banner (source: https://github.com/nasa-jpl/rosa)

Developers can create their own ROS 1 and 2-based agents using their APIs. Here are the instructions to configure ROSA with the OpenAI API key: [*15*].

RAI

RAI [*12*] is like ROSA, which was created using LangChain and ROS 2. It has more capabilities than ROSA. It has interfaced with LLMs and VLMs and is vision- and voice-enabled. It has interfaced with Nav2 and MoveIt2, which makes it ideal for controlling any kind of robot.

Figure 14.14 shows the block diagram of the RAI project, which is like the agent we have already created.

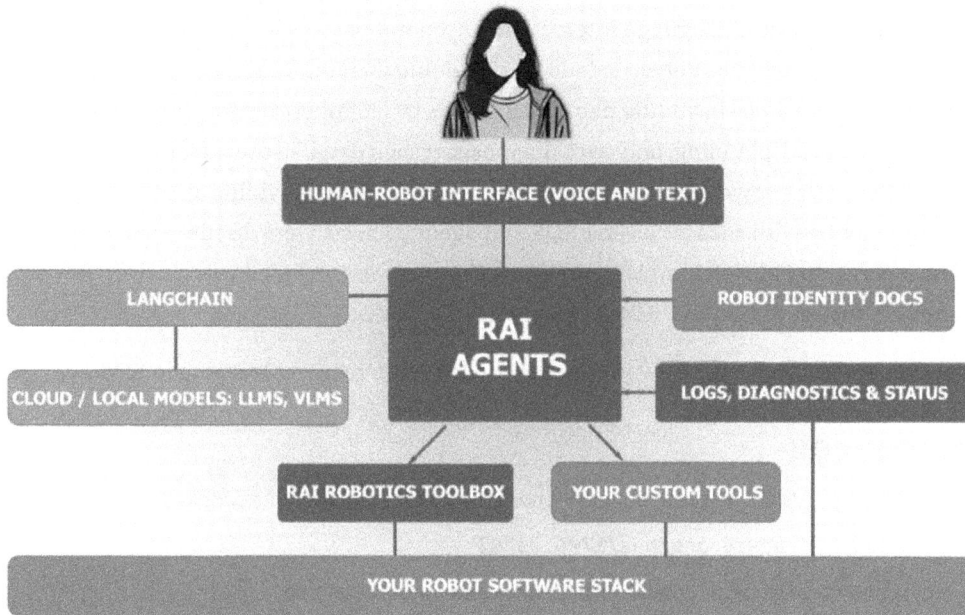

Figure 14.14: Block diagram of RAI

ROS-LLM

ROS-LLM [*13*] is like the above project, focusing on embodied intelligence applications. It is supported in ROS Noetic and ROS 2 Humble. It mainly uses GPT-4 for the LLM and provides communication to the robot using conversational engagement.

ROS 2 NanoLLM

The **ROS 2 NanoLLM** from NVIDIA [*14*] is the interface of NanoLLM to ROS 2. The NanoLLM optimizes LLMs, VLMs, and **Vision Language Action (VLA)** models to run on the NVIDIA Jetson Orin. This project can be directly run on the robot computer without connecting to the cloud.

There are many more agents available as open source. In this section, we have discussed the popular AI agents currently available as open source.

Summary

This chapter explored the integration of LLMs with ROS 2, highlighting their potential to enhance robotics through natural language interaction, autonomous decision-making, and intelligent control. It introduced LLMs, VLMs, and ALMs, explaining their relevance to robotics. The chapter covered key applications, including natural language-based robot control, autonomous navigation, perception, task planning, and error diagnosis. It then detailed the integration of AI agents with ROS 2 using frameworks such as LangChain and AutoGen, providing an architecture for AI agents interacting with robots. Several ROS 2 AI agent projects were discussed, demonstrating turtlesim, Nav2, and MoveIt2 implementations. The chapter concluded with an overview of ROS 2 AI projects such as ROSA, RAI, ROS-LLM, and NVIDIA's ROS2-NanoLLM.

The next chapter will discuss how we can apply deep reinforcement learning in ROS 2.

References

- [1] https://www.datacamp.com/tutorial/how-transformers-work
- [2] https://arxiv.org/abs/1706.03762
- [3] https://github.com/GT-RIPL/Awesome-LLM-Robotics
- [4] https://github.com/thunlp/EmbodiedAIxLLMPapers
- [5] https://github.com/langchain-ai/langchain
- [6] https://github.com/microsoft/autogen
- [7] https://github.com/e2b-dev/awesome-ai-agents
- [8] https://ollama.com/
- [9] https://lmstudio.ai/
- [10] https://platform.openai.com/settings/organization/api-keys
- [11] https://github.com/nasa-jpl/rosa
- [12] https://github.com/RobotecAI/rai/
- [13] https://github.com/Auromix/ROS-LLM
- [14] https://github.com/NVIDIA-AI-IOT/ros2_nanollm
- [15] https://github.com/nasa-jpl/rosa/wiki/Model-Configuration

Join our community on Discord

Join our community's Discord space for discussions with the authors and other readers: `https://packt.link/embeddedsystems`

15

ROS 2 and Deep Reinforcement Learning

In the previous chapter, we discussed LLM and building AI agents. This chapter will discuss the interfacing of reinforcement learning algorithms for robots using ROS 2, specifically deep reinforcement learning. We will discuss how to train, test, and deploy **Deep Reinforcement Learning (DRL)** algorithms and libraries and interface to robots using ROS 2. The primary focus of the chapter will be introducing NVIDIA Isaac Lab, an open-source, unified framework for robot learning that helps developers train, test, and deploy robot learning policies. By combining the NVIDIA Isaac Sim simulator and Isaac Lab, developers can train various robots like robotic arms, wheeled robots, legged robots, and humanoids.

We will discuss the training and testing of robotic arms, legged robots, and humanoid robots using Isaac Sim and Isaac Lab and interfacing to hardware using ROS 2.

In this chapter, we're going to cover the following main topics:

- Dive into deep reinforcement learning
- Setting up Isaac Lab in Ubuntu 24.04
- Training and testing robots using Isaac Lab
- Deploying a trained RL model to a real robot

Technical requirements

To follow this chapter, you should install Ubuntu 24.04 LTS with ROS 2 Jazzy desktop. It can be in Docker, WSL 2, or on a real machine. Your PC will need a decent NVIDIA RTX GPU with *>8GB of VRAM*. The reference materials for this chapter can be found in the Chapter15 folder of the following GitHub repository: https://github.com/PacktPublishing/Mastering-ROS-2-for-Robotics-Programming/tree/main/Chapter15.

Dive into deep reinforcement learning

We humans learn through trial and error to take better actions based on the rewards and punishments we receive. Over time, we optimize our actions by maximizing the rewards and minimizing punishment. This process is called **Reinforcement Learning** (**RL**). This technique is used in various domains like robotics and AI, where agents learn to make decisions by interacting with the environment and receiving feedback.

In this section, we will discuss important concepts in **RL** and **DRL**. This will give you a quick guide before we jump into the application side of things. If you are new to RL, this section will be very useful to you. So, let's begin by discussing RL and DRL.

Basic concepts of reinforcement learning

Reinforcement learning is a type of machine learning in which the agent learns from interacting with the environment. An agent performs actions and receives rewards or penalties. Based on the rewards and penalties, the agent adjusts its behavior to maximize its rewards. *Figure 15.1* shows a block diagram of an RL agent interacting with the environment.

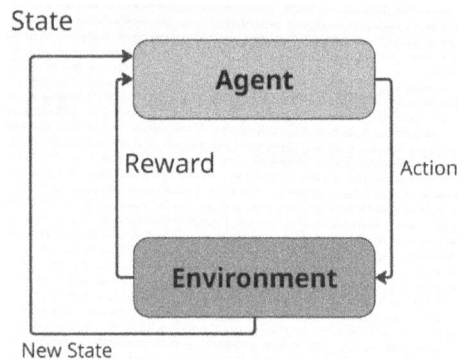

Figure 15.1: Block diagram of RL agent

Here are some important terminologies we have to understand from the RL block diagram:

- **Agent:** This entity can learn and make decisions by interacting with the environment. A policy determines the behavior of the agent. The policy maps from the current observation of the agent to the action output. The policy can function with tunable parameters or a deep neural network [1].

- **Environment:** This is the external world with which the agent interacts.

- **Action (a):** This is the decision made by the agent to influence the environment.

- **State (s):** This is the representation of the environment at a specific time.

- **Reward (r):** This is the value received from the environment after an action. It is used to evaluate the action's success.

The goal of the RL agent is to maximize positive rewards over time by learning the optimal policy. The learned policy will have an accurate mapping from state to actions.

In the next section, we will see the difference between classic and deep reinforcement learning.

Transitioning from classic RL to DRL

Based on the complexity of the agent, the input space and action spaces of the agent may have to use different types of policies. For simple RL applications with limited action space and state, we can use methods like the **Q-learning algorithm** [2]. This algorithm is not a neural network-based model but a simple function suitable for small state and action spaces. These traditional RL policies may fail if the application is complex.

This is where we use DRL. DRL is an advanced form of reinforcement learning that combines traditional RL concepts with deep learning. Classical RL methods rely on tables or simple functions; DRL uses **Deep Neural Networks (DNNs)** to approximate complex functions like value functions, policies, or models of the environment. This makes DRL particularly powerful for tasks with high-dimensional input, such as raw images, LiDAR data, or other rich sensor modalities.

If the RL application needs complex and high-dimensional input spaces like images or sensor data, we may have to use **DQNs (Deep Q-Networks)** [3]. A DQN uses a neural network to approximate the Q-function, which allows the RL agent to scale problems where classical RL algorithms fail. The DQN scales the RL to handle large state spaces like pixels in the images. An RL agent playing video games is an example application of a DQN.

Figure 15.2 shows a block diagram of DRL, which uses a DNN instead of Q-learning in the agent. The state and action space of the DRL agent are complex and high-dimensional. The DNN has parameters (denoted as θ) and defines a policy π (s, a), which tells the agent what action to take in states.

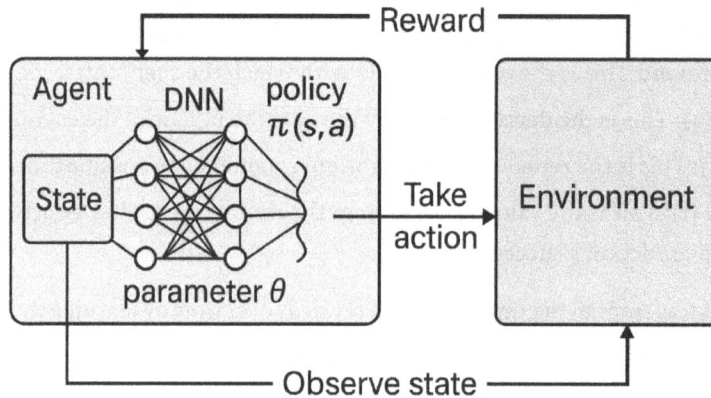

Figure 15.2: Block diagram of DRL agent

In the next section, we will explore the different applications of DRL and a list of popular classic and DRL algorithms.

Application of DRL in robotics

DRL can be extensively applied in robotics. One of the trending areas of robotics is humanoid robots. Many humanoid robot applications can be done using DRL, such as walking, running, jumping, and even backflipping.

Here is a curated list of applications of DRL in robotics:

- **Legged robots**: DRL trains the legged robot to walk, run, climb stairs, and balance on any terrain. Training helps the robot adapt to uneven terrain and recover from failure.

- **Humanoids**: Humanoids are very complex robots with many joints and degrees of freedom, which makes them difficult to control using classic rule-based methods such as finite state machines or PID controllers. They are a special form of a legged robot. Using DRL, they can learn to walk, run, and jump, adapting to new terrains and recovering from failure. They can also manipulate and grasp different objects using vision.

- **Robotic manipulation**: As we saw with humanoids, using independent robotic arms, tasks like pick-and-place, the assembly of parts, and the handling of different tools can be accomplished using DRL. For example, a robotic arm with a gripper grasps a Rubik's cube and learns how to solve it.

- **Autonomous navigation**: Using DRL, we can train mobile robots to perform obstacle avoidance, path planning, and exploration autonomously.

In the next section, we will look at some of the popular DRL algorithms that are used in the above application.

Popular DRL algorithms

In this section, we will look at different classifications of DRL algorithms. We will go through each method and example.

Value-based methods

The algorithms estimate a value from actions or states to help the agent's decision-making process. The agent chooses different actions based on the value assigned to the state or the actions. These values are updated to improve the agent's decision-making.

An example of a value-based method is DQN. It combines Q-learning with a deep neural network. It estimates the Q-values (action-value function) for each state-action pair and chooses the action that maximizes the Q-value.

Policy-based methods

A policy is a mapping from the agent's state to its action. Policy-based methods try to optimize the policy rather than estimate the value function. These methods are gradient-based methods to update the policy.

An example of a policy-based method is **PPO (Proximal Policy Optimization)**. PPO is a policy gradient method that teaches the policy function. It is simple, effective, and stable and works well in environments with both discrete and continuous action spaces.

Actor-critic methods

These methods combine value-based and policy-based approaches. They use two main networks: one is called the actor, which determines the best action to take, and the other is called the critic, which determines how good the selected action is by estimating the value of the state or the state-action pair. In short, the actor uses the feedback from the critic to improve the policy over time, allowing efficient learning.

A couple of examples of these methods are the **DDPG (Deep Deterministic Policy Gradient)** [4] and the **TD3 (Twin Delayed Deep Deterministic Policy Gradient)** [5].

DDPG is an action-critic method intended for continuous action spaces. The actor network suggests an action, and the critic network evaluates the action by computing Q-values.

TD3 is an improvement on the DDPG that reduces the overestimation bias in the value function and stabilizes training. TD3 is more stable and performs better in complex continuous control tasks.

In the next section, we will see how we can set up an RL framework in Ubuntu 24.04 LTS for training, testing, and deployment.

Setting up Isaac Lab and Isaac Sim in Ubuntu 24.04

In this section, we will discuss installing RL frameworks like NVIDIA Isaac Lab and Isaac Sim in Ubuntu 24.04 using Docker. Before setting this up, let's look at the basics of these two frameworks.

What is Isaac Sim and Isaac Lab?

Isaac Sim and **Isaac Lab** are interconnected software developed by NVIDIA for robot simulation and robot learning.

Isaac Sim [6] is a high-fidelity simulator compared to Gazebo, which we saw in an earlier chapter. It is built on the NVIDIA Omniverse platform [7], and it provides photorealistic rendering and precise physics simulations. The simulator supports many robots, such as robotic arms and wheeled, legged, and humanoid robots. It also supports many sensors, like LIDAR, depth cameras, etc.

Figure 15.3 shows the Isaac Sim UI with multiple robots in the simulation.

Figure 15.3: NVIDIA Isaac Sim

The simulator also supports various robotics applications, such as **SLAM** (**Simultaneous Localization and Mapping**), motion planning, and hardware-in-loop testing. It is integrated into ROS 1 and ROS 2, and we can easily integrate it with Nav 2 or MoveIt2, as we have done with Gazebo Sim.

Isaac Lab [8] is a GPU-accelerated, open-source modular framework for robot learning built on top of Isaac Sim. This framework simplifies the development of robot learning applications, such as reinforcement learning and imitation learning, by providing an integrated environment, eliminating the need to implement algorithms from scratch.

Figure 15.4 shows an Isaac Lab training environment in Isaac Sim.

Figure 15.4: Sample NVIDIA Isaac Lab humanoid training environment in Isaac Sim

The framework provides rich APIs and examples to design and test customized robot learning environments and algorithms using Isaac Sim's capabilities. Isaac Lab also includes example robot learning environments for training and testing different learning algorithms. It interfaces standard learning libraries and offers better data collection and training tools. Isaac Lab offers features to train multiple instances of robots in the same environment in parallel with the help of a GPU. This will drastically reduce the training time. Isaac Sim and Isaac Lab provide a foundational simulation environment, APIs, and tools for advanced robotics learning and research.

Figure 15.5 shows the block diagram of Isaac Lab. You can see Isaac Lab is built on top of NVIDIA Isaac Sim.

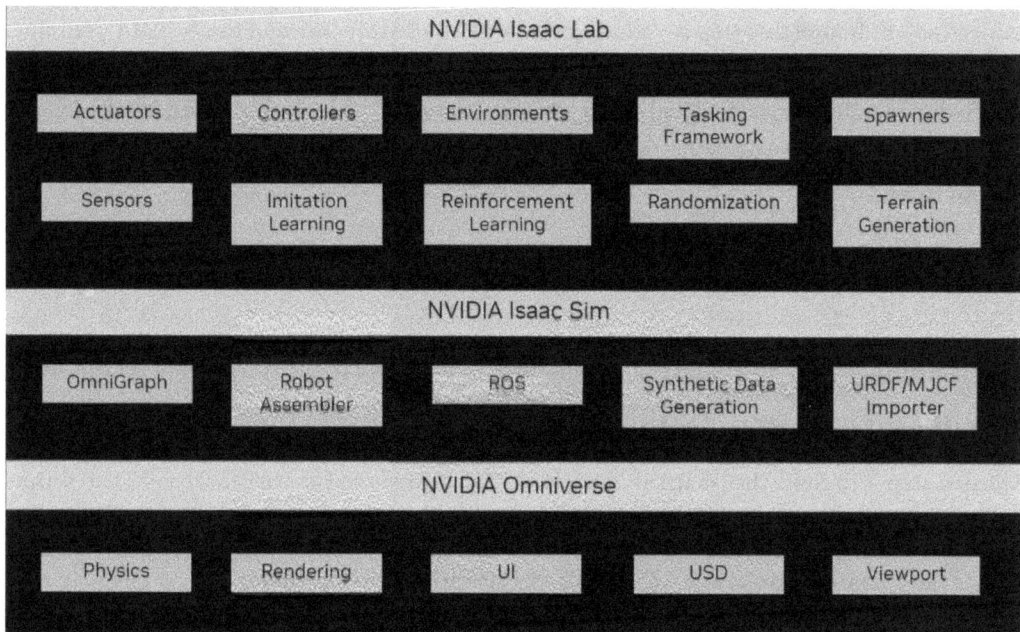

Figure 15.5: Block diagram of Isaac Lab (source: https://isaac-sim.github.io)

Isaac Sim is built on the Omniverse platform. Isaac Lab has many submodules for performing different learning algorithms, such as reinforcement learning and imitation learning. Modules like sensors, actuators, controllers, and the environment help the developer to create the robot's learning environment.

In the next section, we will see how to set up software in Ubuntu 24.04 LTS using Docker.

Installing Isaac Sim and Isaac Lab in Ubuntu 24.04

To set up Isaac Sim and Isaac Lab in Ubuntu 24.04, your PC/laptop should meet the technical requirements mentioned in the chapter. An NVIDIA RTX 40xx with >8 GB VRAM is recommended for good performance. It will also work with 6 GB VRAM. This software will only work if the developer has an RTX NVIDIA graphics card or higher in the system.

After meeting the system specification, make sure you have installed the NVIDIA driver and confirm it is properly working.

Setting up Docker and the NVIDIA Container Toolkit

Once the system specification is checked, the next step is to install Docker with the NVIDIA Container Toolkit. Ignore this step if you have already installed Docker and the NVIDIA Container Toolkit in your system. Otherwise, go to the Chapter15/docker_setup_scripts folder, and you will find an installation script called setup_docker_ubuntu.sh. Run the script and it will automatically install Docker and the NVIDIA Container Toolkit. Make sure there is internet connectivity in your system.

Here is the command to execute the script:

```
./setup_docker_ubuntu.sh
```

After installing Docker and the NVIDIA Container Toolkit, let's set up Isaac Sim and Isaac Lab.

Installing Isaac Sim and Isaac Lab

The first step is to clone the Isaac Lab repository. This repository has the Dockerfiles and scripts to build the Docker image and start/stop the Docker container.

Here is the command to clone the Isaac Lab repository in the home folder:

```
cd $HOME
git clone https://github.com/isaac-sim/IsaacLab.git
```

After cloning the repository, switch to the IsaacLab folder:

```
cd IsaacLab
```

Execute the following command to start building the Isaac Lab image:

```
./docker/container.py start ros2
```

There are two options for creating the image: 'base' and 'ros2'. Since the base doesn't have ros2 installed in the image, we have to use ros2 while building the image and starting the container.

The container.py is the Python script that helps build the image and start the container. This command can take around 5 to 10 minutes to finish based on your internet speed. When you start the script, it will ask whether you want to enable X11 forwarding. As, without this, we will not be able to visualize any GUI applications running inside the container on our host system, we will have to enable this by pressing '1'.". If you can't enter this, you can change the value in the file docker/.container.cfg. Change X11_FORWARDING_ENABLED to 1.

After building the Docker image, the script will start the container. If we execute the command again, the time taken to start the container will be shorter because the Docker image has already been built. When you reboot your PC or laptop, you have to execute the above command once. You only need to do this once after each reboot.

After completing this command, you can access the terminal session of the running container by using the following command:

```
./docker/container.py enter ros2
```

We can use the above command to start any number of terminals. Here is the command to stop the container. It is not required most of the time, but you can use it if you manually stop the container and start it again:

```
./docker/container.py stop ros2
```

You can find the detailed Docker setup instructions for Isaac Lab and Isaac Sim at this link [9].

After setting up Isaac Lab and Sim in Docker, we will see how to train, test, and deploy RL models using these.

Training and testing robots using Isaac Lab

In this section, we will briefly discuss the learning process with Isaac Sim and Isaac Lab.

Isaac Lab architecture

Figure 15.6 shows the architecture of the model's training and deployment and highlights its major building blocks.

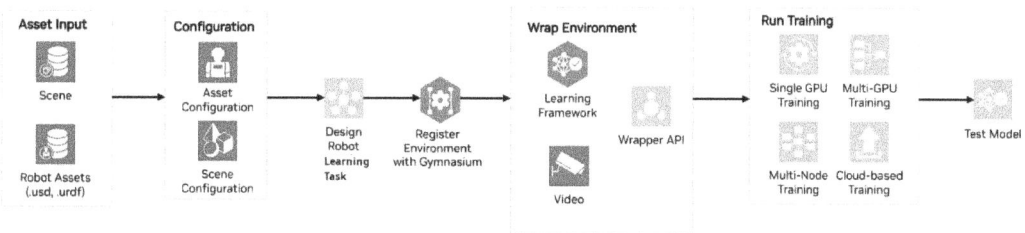

Figure 15.6: Isaac Lab architecture (source: https://isaac-sim.github.io/)

Here are the major components of training and testing using Isaac Lab and Isaac Sim:

- **Asset Input**: Isaac Sim and Isaac Lab use **Universal Scene Description** (USD) [10] as a file format for representing 3D robots and environments. In ROS 2, we used URDF/xacro for the robot model. Isaac Sim offers conversion tools to USD from URDF, MJCF, XML, etc. Importing robot and environment assets into Isaac Lab is the first step in the workflow.

- **Creating Configuration**: After creating the assets as input, we have to create 2 configuration classes in Python:

  - *Asset Configuration*: In this class, we can define all the properties of each asset. A list of examples of asset configuration can be found in the `IsaacLab/source/isaaclab_assets/isaaclab_assets/robots` folder.

  - *Scene Configuration*: After completing the asset configuration, the next step is to put the individual assets together in the scene. The scene configuration is a Python class that initializes all the assets in the scene needed for the learning task and visualization. An example script can be found in `IsaacLab/source/isaaclab_tasks/isaaclab_tasks/manager_based/manipulation/reach/reach_env_cfg.py`.

- **Robot Learning Task Design**: After creating the configuration class, we have to define the robot learning task. We have to define the RL task that the agent is going to do. There are two ways to design the environment for the robot learning task:

  - *Manager-based*: This method uses modular components (managers) to handle various aspects of the environment, such as observation and action. In this method, we have to write different configuration classes for an RL task, such as `Observation Config` (define the agent's observation for the task), `Action Config` (define the agent's action type), `Reward Config` (define the reward function for the task), and `Termination Config` (define the conditions for termination).

  - *Direct*: In this approach, there is a unified class to manage observation, actions, and rewards directly. Examples of learning tasks can be found in the `IsaacLab/source/isaaclab_tasks/isaaclab_tasks` folder.

- **Register with Gymnasium**: After the robot task design, we can register the learning environment with the Gymnasium [11] registry. Gymnasium is a standard library for working with RL with a large collection of reference environments. Once our environment is registered with a unique name, we can access and reuse it with different RL algorithms and experiments.

- **Environment Wrapping**: We may have to reuse the existing environment and change its behavior without modifying the actual environment itself. When interfacing multiple RL libraries, the data type needed by each library differs. To do this, Isaac Lab provides a wrapper API that can modify the behavior. This is an important feature of Isaac Lab because we can create a variation of an environment without touching the actual environment.

- **Run Training**: Now, the final step is running the training. Isaac Lab is integrated with multiple RL libraries, like RSL-RL [12] and SKRL [13]. All these RL integration libraries use GPU-based training. Isaac Lab provides scripts to run training using different libraries. It also facilitates single-GPU and multi-GPU training. We can also configure the training using cloud infrastructure.

- **Run Testing**: After training, we can evaluate the trained model within a simulated environment to benchmark its performance before deploying it to the actual robot.

The complete reference for training and testing using Isaac Lab is mentioned at the link [14].

In the next section, we will work with some sample RL training environments that are available in Isaac Lab.

Training and testing an existing RL environment in Isaac Lab

In this section, we will learn how to train and test an RL task using demo scripts provided by Isaac Lab. Before starting the training, we will check the list of RL environments shipped by Isaac Lab using the following command.

In the Isaac Lab Docker container terminal, we can enter the following command to list out the existing environments:

```
./isaaclab.sh -p scripts/environments/list_envs.py
```

This command will show the registered RL environments that are available in Isaac Lab. You will find different variations of the same environment in the list. We can refer to this list to find the environment we want and do the training and testing. You can find the details of these environments at the following link [15]. If you want to check the robot assets in Isaac Lab, you can go to the IsaacLab/source/isaaclab_assets/isaaclab_assets/ folder and find the robot and sensor folders. We can add robots and sensors to the same folder in the same format. After adding a new asset, make sure you have updated the init.py file to include the new robot or sensor. To check the source code of the available training task, you can check the IsaacLab/source/isaaclab_tasks/ isaaclab_tasks folder. Inside the folder, you can find the task design folders, such as the direct and manager folders. Inside each folder, you can find different categories of robot learning tasks.

Let's start with the training of the sample RL environment.

Training UR-10 using Isaac Lab

In this section, we will see how to train a UR-10 robot to move the end-effector to a different target pose. Basically, this RL task tries to train the RL model to learn the **IK (Inverse Kinematics)** solution for this robot.

We use the **RSL-RL** library to train the robot, so the first step is to install the rsl-rl Python module inside the container. It may not be installed by default.

You can use the following command to install the latest version:

```
./isaaclab.sh -i rsl_rl
```

The isaaclab.sh is the main script provided by Isaac Lab to install modules and run scripts for training and testing the RL environment. By executing the following command, we will get the full command-line arguments of this script:

```
./isaaclab.sh -h
```

After installing the rsl_rl library, we can start using the training script.

Isaac Lab has a demo training script for rsl_rl. We can use the script train.py, which is placed in the script/reinforcement_learning/rsl_rl folder. This script can start training based on the configuration if we mention the environment name as an argument. The following command can be used to train multiple environments using the rsl_rl module:

```
./isaaclab.sh -p scripts/reinforcement_learning/rsl_rl/train.py --task
Isaac-Reach-UR10-v0 --headless
```

In the above command, we use the rsl_rl library in Isaac Lab for training the robot task. The rsl_rl library has the PPO algorithm as the default for RL training. If you check the command, we enabled headless mode in training, meaning the visualization will be disabled, and Isaac Sim will not show the visualization of the training. The headless mode can save on the computation and memory that Isaac Sim consumes. It is better to do training by disabling the visualization of Isaac Sim. If you remove the headless, you can see the training in Isaac Sim. The typical time to complete this training is around 5 to 10 minutes if you have a modern NVIDIA RTX graphics card.

Figure 15.7 shows a screenshot of the terminal during training.

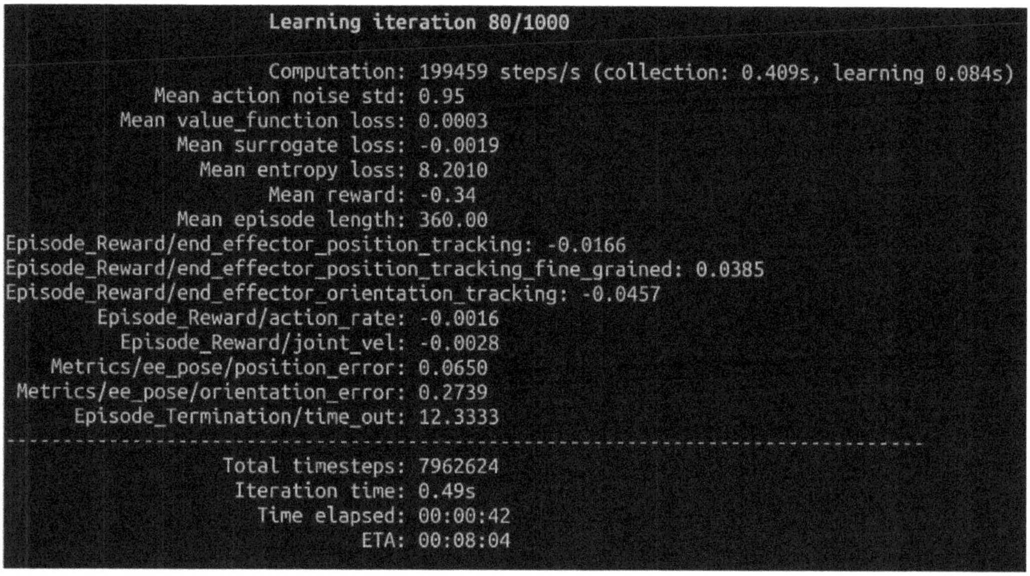

```
                    Learning iteration 80/1000

                    Computation: 199459 steps/s (collection: 0.409s, learning 0.084s)
           Mean action noise std: 0.95
        Mean value_function loss: 0.0003
             Mean surrogate loss: -0.0019
               Mean entropy loss: 8.2010
                     Mean reward: -0.34
             Mean episode length: 360.00
Episode_Reward/end_effector_position_tracking: -0.0166
Episode_Reward/end_effector_position_tracking_fine_grained: 0.0385
Episode_Reward/end_effector_orientation_tracking: -0.0457
         Episode_Reward/action_rate: -0.0016
          Episode_Reward/joint_vel: -0.0028
    Metrics/ee_pose/position_error: 0.0650
 Metrics/ee_pose/orientation_error: 0.2739
      Episode_Termination/time_out: 12.3333
--------------------------------------------------------------------------------
                Total timesteps: 7962624
                 Iteration time: 0.49s
                   Time elapsed: 00:00:42
                            ETA: 00:08:04
```

Figure 15.7: Training of Isaac Lab-based environment

Here are the essential values we have to understand from the training logs:

- **Learning Iteration**: This refers to a cycle in the process of training an agent. It represents an update to the agent's knowledge based on its interaction with the environment. We can configure the maximum value of learning iteration. For some tasks, the agent can learn with a smaller number of iterations, but it depends on many parameters of the learning task.

- **Computation**: This indicates the number of steps processed per second, including data collection and learning phases.

- **Mean Reward**: This is the average reward obtained by the agent in the current iteration. A negative reward means the agent is still learning and has not yet optimized behaviors.

- **ETA**: The estimated time of arrival is the remaining time to complete the whole training based on the current progress.

After completing the training, you can find the trained model in the `/workspace/isaaclab/logs` folder, which is inside the container. Based on the library we have trained on, you can find the folder name as the library name, and inside that folder, you can find sub-folders of the training files. The main files you can find in these folders are the PyTorch models (`.pt`) files. You will see different `.pt` files during different iterations. We can use these models for testing and deployment, which is discussed in the next section.

Testing UR-10 using Isaac Lab

In this section, we will see how to test or validate the trained RL model. The following command can be used to test the UR-10 robot with the pre-trained model:

```
./isaaclab.sh -p scripts/reinforcement_learning/rsl_rl/play.py --task
Isaac-Reach-UR10-v0 --num_envs 32 --use_pretrained_checkpoint
```

The `play.py` script is a demo script from Isaac Lab to load and test the model with Isaac Sim. The num_envs indicates the test will run on 32 parallel environments. The `pretrained_ checkpoint` flag loads the final trained model from the `logs` folder. If we want to load a model specifically, we can use the following command:

```
./isaaclab.sh -p scripts/reinforcement_learning/rsl_rl/play.py --task
Isaac-Reach-UR10-v0 --num_envs 32 --load_run run_folder_name --checkpoint
model.pt
```

In this command, we are specifying the `model.pt`, which is the model to load for testing. Make sure you have copied the right model to the default path of the container before executing this command. You can change the name of the model in the command as well. *Figure 15.8* shows the testing of the UR-10 reaching task. You can find 32 environments of the same arm doing the testing in parallel.

Figure 15.8: Testing UR-10 Isaac Lab environment

In the reaching task, the robot end-effector will move to the random goal position commander from Isaac Lab. The goal position will change once the robot reaches that position.

Next, let's look at another demo of the navigation of a legged robot called ANYmal using Isaac Lab.

Training and testing ANYmal robot navigation

In this section, we will explore the ANYmal robot's navigation being trained and tested. The command to train on the task is given below. The task here is for the ANYmal robot to try to navigate to a random goal position in the environment.

```
./isaaclab.sh -p scripts/reinforcement_learning/rsl_rl/train.py --task
Isaac-Navigation-Flat-Anymal-C-v0 --headless
```

The training time depends on the complexity of the RL environment and the graphics card we are using. For example, to complete the above training on a modern RTX 4060 GPU with 8 GB of VRAM, it will take around 45 min to 1 hr. After training, you can use the following command to test it. We will use pre-trained checkpoints to test the model:

```
./isaaclab.sh -p scripts/reinforcement_learning/rsl_rl/play.py --task
Isaac-Navigation-Flat-Anymal-C-v0 --num_envs 32 --use_pretrained_
checkpoint
```

Figure 15.9 shows the testing visualization of the ANYmal robot in Isaac Sim. There are two green arrows per robot. The arrow in the robot shows its pose, and the arrow outside each robot shows its goal position.

Figure 15.9: Testing AnyMal Isaac Lab environment

When we start testing, 32 robot environments will be spawned in Isaac Sim and start working. Each robot tries to reach the goal position, which will randomly change to a new position once the robot reaches it.

Let's now see another demo of training and testing a humanoid robot using Isaac Lab.

Training and testing of an H1 robot for a locomotion task

In this section, we will see how to train a humanoid robot called an H1 robot from Unitree [16]. The following task will teach the robot to walk on rough terrain by giving a velocity command.

Here is the command to train the humanoid robot:

```
./isaaclab.sh -p scripts/reinforcement_learning/rsl_rl/train.py --task
Isaac-Velocity-Rough-H1-v0 -headless
```

It will take more than 1 hour of training if you are using any RTX 40xx graphics card.

After training, we can start testing the trained model using the following command:

```
./isaaclab.sh -p scripts/reinforcement_learning/rsl_rl/play.py --task
Isaac-Velocity-Rough-H1-v0 --num_envs 32 --use_pretrained_checkpoint
```

Here is the screenshot of Isaac Sim showing the humanoid robot moving in rough terrain:

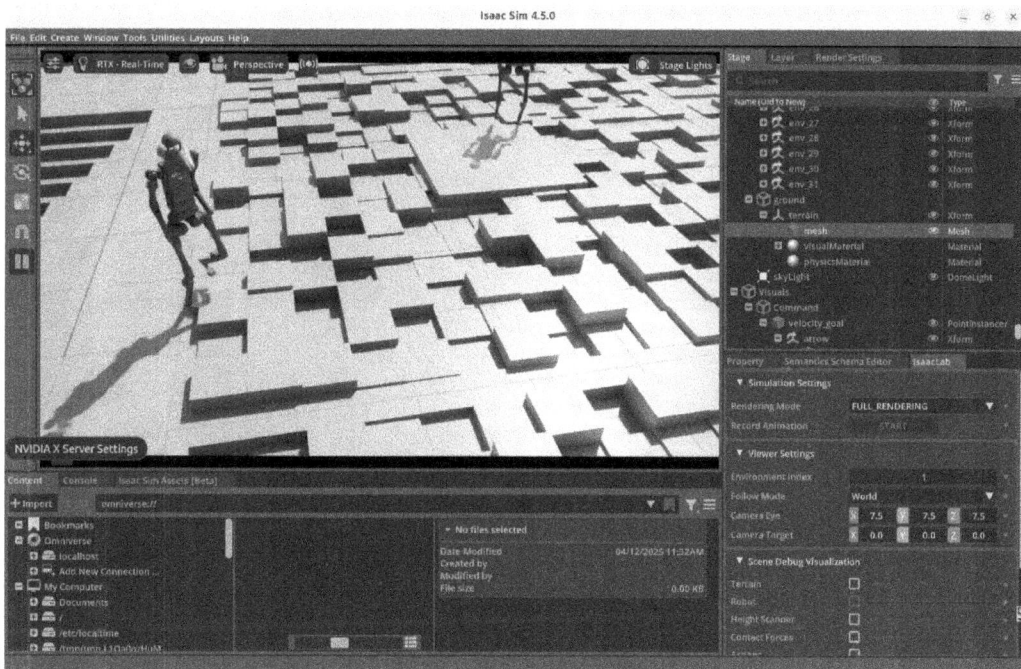

Figure 15.10: Testing H1-robot in Isaac Lab environment

Here is the reference link for training and testing different RL environments in Isaac Lab [17].

Deploying a trained RL model to a real robot

After training and testing the robot in simulation, the final task is to deploy the trained model in the actual robot. There are different ways to do this. One of the sample references from the Isaac Lab website is shown in *Figure 15.11*. The robot should have a powerful computer, like an NVIDIA Jetson board, to interface sensors and run the model on it.

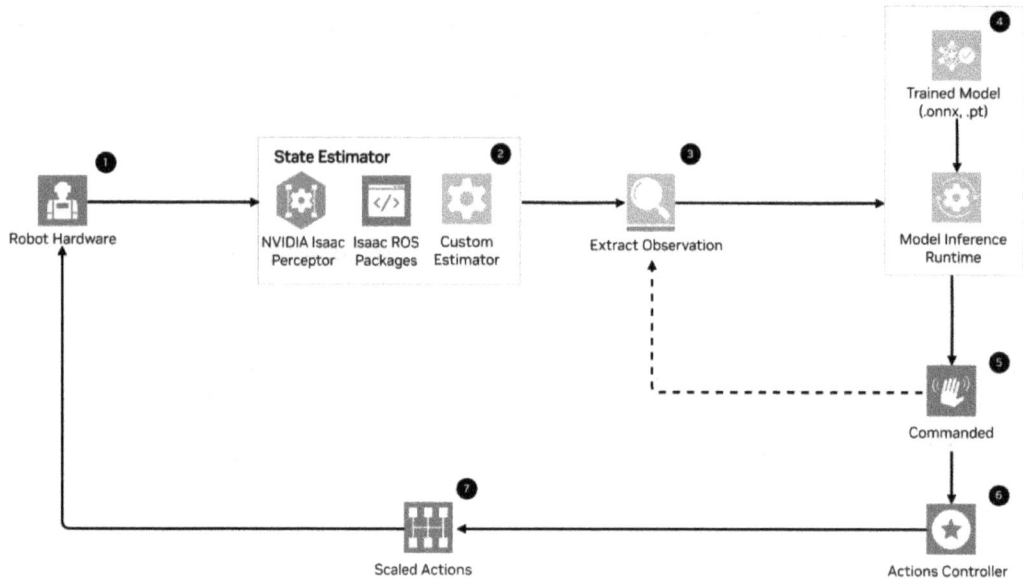

Figure 15.11: Reference diagram of interfacing an RL model to a real robot (source: https:// isaac-sim.github.io/)

The important section of code we have to configure is a state estimator. This is the block delivering the list of observations used for training. Instead of using simulated sensor observations, we are providing real robot observations here. We can use ROS 2 drivers or Isaac ROS packages to get observations from robot sensors. Once the observations are extracted, they will pass into the model inference runtime, which generates the action. The commanded action will be the new set point for the action controller. The action controller output will be scaled, and then it will be used to control the robot to get the next state of the robot. This loop will continue until the task is done.

Note

The sim-to-real transfer is not easy to implement because of the limitation of collecting real-world data. Mostly, a simulation environment is used to gather data and train RL agents. The performance can degrade when we transfer to a real robot with real-world data. Multiple research efforts are happening to reduce the sim-to-real transfer gap. Here is a reference to a research paper showing different approaches to sim-to-real transfer [20].

In the next section, we will see a real example of the hardware interfacing of an RL model trained in Isaac Lab.

Deploying an RL model in the Spot robot from Boston Dynamics

In this section, we will see a sample project that trains, tests, and deploys an RL model in Boston Dynamics' Spot robot. *Figure 15.12* shows the training pipeline using Isaac Lab and Isaac Sim.

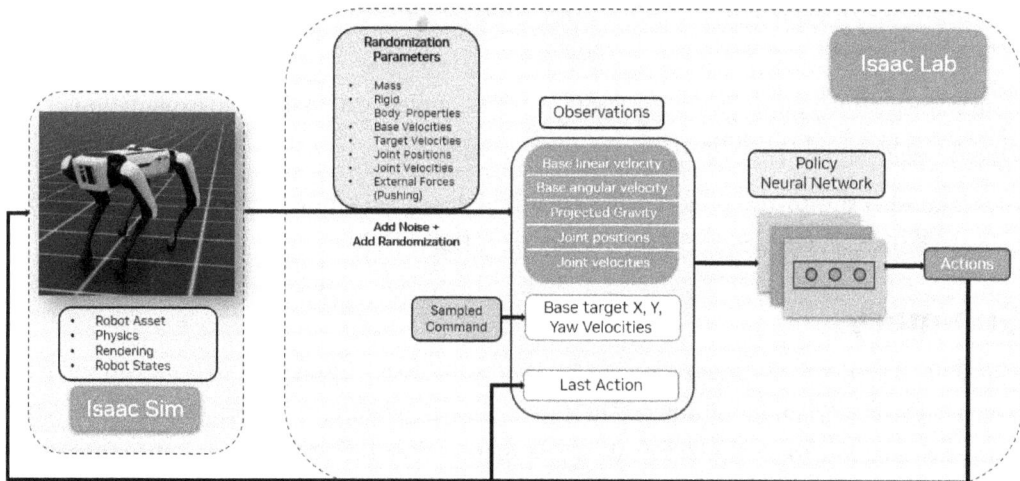

Figure 15.12: Training of Spot robot in simulation for locomotion (source: https://developer. nvidia.com/)

The task they are trying to do is robot locomotion. If we give the velocity command, the robot should move based on it.

After training on the locomotion task in Isaac Sim, *Figure 15.13* shows the testing and deployment of the model on actual hardware.

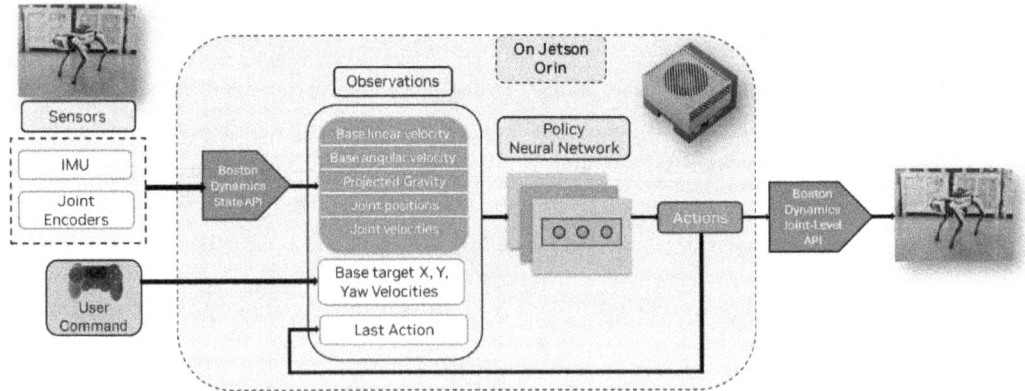

Figure 15.13: Testing of the trained model on actual Spot robot (source: https://developer.nvidia.com/)

They used Jetson Orin as the computer and read the sensor state using their APIs. We can also use ROS 2 or Isaac ROS to get the robot's sensor state. The command to the robot is the velocity command from the user using a joystick. The actions from the RL model are sent to the real robot using Boston Dynamics' joint-level API. We can also use the ROS 2 controller to control the joint values for the robot.

Here is the GitHub repository for the Spot robot's RL project [18]. A detailed explanation of this project can be found at this link [19].

Here is another sim-to-real project using a manipulator called Kinova Gen3. The training is done using Isaac Lab, and sim-to-real deployment using ROS 2 [21].

Summary

This chapter explored the integration of ROS 2 with DRL, focusing on NVIDIA Isaac Lab and Isaac Sim. It began by explaining reinforcement learning basics, where agents learn through interaction with environments to maximize rewards. The chapter then introduced Isaac Lab, a framework built on the Isaac Sim simulator for training robot policies. Key sections covered setting up Isaac Lab in Ubuntu 24.04 using Docker, the architecture of the training process, and practical examples of training different robots like the UR-10 robotic arm, AnyMal quadruped, and H1 humanoid robot. The training process involves configuring assets, designing learning tasks, registering with Gymnasium, and running training using GPU-accelerated algorithms.

Finally, the chapter discussed how to deploy trained models to real robots using ROS 2, with a case study of deploying a locomotion model to Boston Dynamics' Spot robot. Throughout, the text emphasized the workflow from simulation training to real-world deployment of DRL models for robotic applications.

In this next chapter, we will discuss how to implement the ROS 2 visualization plugin for Rviz and the simulation plugins for Gazebo Sim.

References

- [1] https://www.sciencedirect.com/topics/computer-science/deep-neural-network
- [2] https://www.datacamp.com/tutorial/introduction-q-learning-beginner-tutorial
- [3] https://huggingface.co/learn/deep-rl-course/en/unit3/deep-q-network
- [4] https://spinningup.openai.com/en/latest/algorithms/ddpg.html
- [5] https://spinningup.openai.com/en/latest/algorithms/td3.html
- [6] https://developer.nvidia.com/isaac/sim
- [7] https://www.nvidia.com/en-in/omniverse/
- [8] https://isaac-sim.github.io/IsaacLab/main/index.html
- [9] https://isaac-sim.github.io/IsaacLab/main/source/deployment/docker.html
- [10] https://www.nvidia.com/en-in/omniverse/usd/
- [11] https://gymnasium.farama.org/index.html
- [12] https://github.com/leggedrobotics/rsl_rl
- [13] https://skrl.readthedocs.io/en/latest/
- [14] https://isaac-sim.github.io/IsaacLab/main/source/refs/reference_architecture/index.html
- [15] https://isaac-sim.github.io/IsaacLab/main/source/overview/environments.html
- [16] https://shop.unitree.com/products/unitree-h1
- [17] https://isaac-sim.github.io/IsaacLab/main/source/overview/reinforcement-learning/rl_existing_scripts.html
- [18] https://github.com/boston-dynamics/spot-rl-example
- [19] https://developer.nvidia.com/blog/closing-the-sim-to-real-gap-training-spot-quadruped-locomotion-with-nvidia-isaac-lab/
- [20] https://arxiv.org/abs/2009.13303
- [21] https://github.com/louislelay/kinova_isaaclab_sim2real

16

Implementing ROS 2 Visualization and Simulation Plugins

Plugins are essential in modern software development for creating modular, extensible systems. They integrate with host applications to provide extra functionality without modifying core code, relying on the host to load and execute them at runtime. By adhering to standard interfaces, plugins ensure compatibility and flexibility, making them ideal for enhancing tools such as simulators or visualizers. In ROS 2, plugins enable custom data filters, controllers, or visualizations, tailoring systems to specific needs.

Plugins are implemented as shared libraries and can be used in different applications. In this chapter, we will explore three types of plugins: an rqt **plugin** that implements a custom interface for controlling a robot integrated with the RQT framework, an RViz2 **plugin** that creates a custom visualization tool for your data in RViz2, and a **Gazebo plugin** that leverages Gazebo's functionalities for direct integration with simulations.

By the end of this chapter, you will learn how to create new plugins for different scopes enabling the ROS 2 modularity and reusability of your code. This fosters cleaner design, easier integration, and adaptability in robotics applications.

As such, we will cover the following main topics in this chapter:

- Introducing the ROS 2 plugin
- Creating a plugin for rqt

- Developing a Gazebo plugin
- Developing plugins for RViz2

Technical requirements

To follow this chapter, it is better to have a computer with Ubuntu 24.04 LTS installed or any other Ubuntu version.

The reference materials for this chapter can be found in the Chapter16 folder of the following GitHub repository: https://github.com/PacktPublishing/Mastering-ROS-2-for-Robotics-Programming/tree/main/Chapter16.

Introducing the ROS 2 plugin

In this book, we've already created a plugin, though we didn't explicitly call it that. In *Chapter 6*, we developed controllers for the ROS 2 Control package. Unlike typical ROS nodes, these controllers lack a main function and cannot be compiled into executables. Instead, they provide specific functionality for use by other nodes or libraries. This distinction is key to understanding plugins in ROS. So, what is a library? In C++, a library is a collection of precompiled code reused across programs. Libraries can be:

- **Static** (.a): Linked at compile time, making their code part of the executable. This increases file size but eliminates runtime dependencies.
- **Shared** (.so on Linux): Linked at runtime, enabling multiple programs to share the same library. This reduces file size and simplifies updates but requires the library to be available on the system at runtime.

A plugin in C++ is essentially a shared library. Plugins dynamically extend a system's functionality by being loaded at runtime. In ROS 2, plugins are shared libraries managed through frameworks such as pluginlib, which enable modular, scalable components for robotics systems.

Notably, while ROS 2 supports Python for nodes, plugins cannot be written in Python. This limitation arises because Python cannot generate shared libraries directly. Next, let's explore how plugins are managed in ROS 2.

Understanding pluginlib in ROS 2

pluginlib is a C++ tool used in ROS for dynamically loading and unloading plugins within a package. With pluginlib, applications don't need to be explicitly linked to the library containing these classes. Instead, `pluginlib` can load the library and its exported classes at runtime, without the application needing prior knowledge of the library or its headers. This is possible due to interface classes that the implementation inherits from, allowing the application to interact with plugins through polymorphism.

This allows for extending or modifying application behavior without altering the source code of the application itself. To use the `pluginlib` tool in ROS 2, it must be installed using the following command:

```
sudo apt-get install ros-jazzy-pluginlib
```

By using the `pluginlib` tool in ROS 2, we can implement a variety of plugins to be used in your robotic applications. For example, the following plugins can be found:

- **Middleware plugins**: DDS implementations (e.g., Fast RTPS and Cyclone DDS) for flexible communication
- **Robot hardware interface plugins**: `ros2_control` plugins for controlling hardware (e.g., actuators and sensors)
- **Perception and sensor plugins**: Sensor drivers and perception filters for modular sensor integration (e.g., LiDAR and cameras)
- **Navigation plugins**: `Nav2` plugins for custom path planners, costmaps, and recovery behaviors
- **Visualization plugins**: `RViz` plugins for custom data visualization
- **Behavior tree plugins**: Custom actions, conditions, and decorators for decision-making tasks
- **Diagnostics plugins**: Plugins for monitoring and reporting robot health and sensor states
- **Custom node plugins**: Custom nodes for dynamic tasks (e.g., service servers and action servers)
- `rqt` **plugins**: User interface plugins to exchange information with the robot

Glancing at steps for creating, compiling, and loading plugins

Regardless of the type of plugin, the steps to create, compile, and load a given plugin are the same:

1. Create a new package to store the files to generate the library. This package must depend on `pluginlib`.

2. Create a base class that defines the interface your plugin will follow. This class will be used as a contract for the plugin, ensuring that all plugins conform to a specific set of methods.

3. Implement the plugin by inheriting the interface. This implementation will depend on the plugin type that must be implemented.

4. Register the plugin with `pluginlib` and describe it in an XML file. This allows the `pluginlib` tool to load the plugin when required.

5. Build the plugin by compiling the workspace.

After the above steps, we are ready to load the plugin in the application that will use it or in another ROS 2 node. Also, in this case, the loading method will depend on the plugin type. In the example contained in this chapter, we will use `rqt`, RViz, and Gazebo to automatically load the plugin when needed.

In the next section, we will discuss how to implement the above steps to create our first plugin, a plugin for the `rqt` interface.

Creating a plugin for rqt

`rqt` is a Qt-based framework in ROS 2 that provides a set of GUI tools for monitoring, debugging, and visualizing robot systems. It is highly modular, with plugins that support tasks such as plotting data, visualizing topics, configuring parameters, and inspecting logs. But what does Qt-based mean? Qt is a cross-platform software development framework primarily used for creating GUIs It is released under a dual licensing model, which can pose challenges for closed-source and commercial projects due to its high licensing costs. Written in C++, it provides tools for designing intuitive and responsive UIs. We can exploit the `rqt` interface to add new plugins creating custom user interfaces to control our robots, using topics and services to exchange information with robots.

Of course, to develop an rqt plugin, we also need to create the user interface, apart from the source code. We will start from this point, after the creation of the ROS 2 package. Create the package using the following command to include all the needed dependencies:

```
ros2 pkg create cmd_vel --dependencies rclcpp qt_gui_cpp rqt_gui_cpp std_
msgs Qt5Widgets geometry_msgs
```

The goal of this example is to create a custom plugin to control the velocity of a robot using a twist command and a clickable user interface.

Following the next steps, you will able to shape such an interface, like the one shown in *Figure 16.1*.

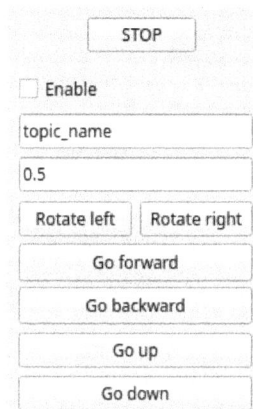

Figure 16.1: The rqt plugin for twist velocity commands

Let's start by discussing how to develop a GUI like the one shown in the previous figure.

Creating a Qt user interface

All the files needed to create the plugin will be included in the package. Let's begin with the user interface. The quickest way to create it is by using **Qt Designer**, a tool included in the **Qt Creator** program. While Qt Creator is primarily an **integrated development environment (IDE)** for programming and debugging Qt applications, it also supports C++ and Python development. Within Qt Creator, Qt Designer provides a visual design interface, allowing you to create layouts and widgets through drag-and-drop functionality without needing to write code. To proceed, let's install Qt Designer using the following command:

```
sudo apt-get install designer-qt6
```

To open the Designer instead, use the following command.

```
designer
```

After executing this command, the Designer user interface is opened. It is easy to use and is organized into the following main components:

- **Widget box**: A panel containing a wide range of widgets (e.g., buttons, labels, sliders, and containers) that can be dragged and dropped into the design area.

- **Design area**: The central workspace where you design your user interface by arranging and customizing widgets. This area represents the application window or dialog you are creating.

- **Property Editor**: A side panel for modifying the properties of selected widgets, such as size, font, color, and alignment. It allows the fine-tuning of widget behavior and appearance.

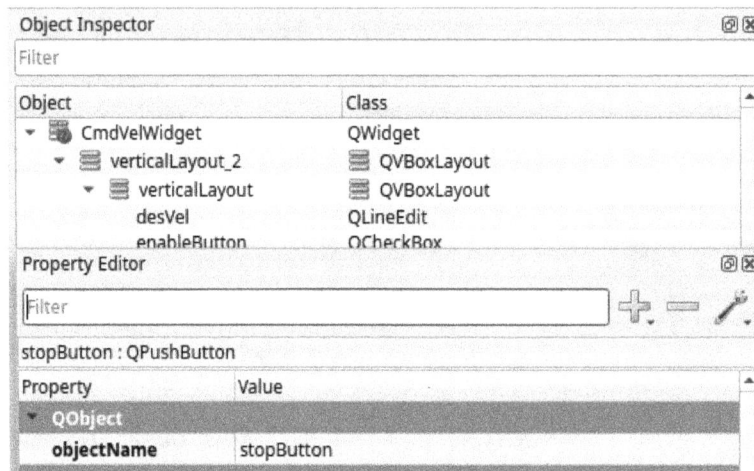

Figure 16.2: Object property for the STOP button

The widgets can be directly dragged and dropped on the design area to create the desired interface. Considering the UI shown in *Figure 16.1*, we mainly used the following elements (also called widgets):

- **QPushButton**: To generate the velocity commands in different directions or publish zero velocities to stop the robot

- **QLineEdit**: To add text such as the topic name or the desired velocity

- **QCheckBox**: To enable or disable data streaming

You can arrange the widgets in any layout you prefer, or you can replicate the design shown in *Figure 16.1*. A crucial step is to assign meaningful names to each widget using the Property Editor. These names will be referenced in the C++ code to interact with the interface, such as detecting when a button is clicked or retrieving the text entered in a line box. For example, *Figure 16.2* shows the Property box for a clickable button called **stopButton**.

After adding all the desired elements of the interface, you can save the source of the user interface in the src directory of the cmd_vel package. The extension of this file will be .ui.

The next step is to create the source code to react to the input received from the user interface, as discussed in the next section.

Implementing the plugin source

The backend of the user interface is implemented as C++ source code. We will define a header file, located in the cmd_vel/include/cmd_vel/ directory, called cmd_vel.h, and source code placed in the cmd_vel/src folder, called cmd_vel.cpp. Let's discuss the content of the header file (check the code repository of the book for the full source code):

- At the start, the header to use the functionalities of the rqt plugin is imported. Using the plugin.h header, we have access to the function allowing the registration of the plugin:

```
#include "geometry_msgs/msg/twist.hpp"
#include <rqt_gui_cpp/plugin.h>
```

- The .ui file is translated into a header file that gives us access to the components of the interface. The name of this file is the same as the one given to the .ui file but with the header file extension (ui_cmd_vel_ui.h). Later, we will discuss how we request the conversion from the .ui file to the .h one:

```
#include "ui_cmd_vel_ui.h"
```

- The plugin code must be included in a namespace. The namespace will be used in the export function. Here, we incorporate the code in the namespace cmd_vel:

```
namespace cmd_vel {
```

- The class that implements the function of the plugin is called CmdVel and is inherited from the rqt_gui_cpp::Plugin class to integrate the rqt framework. In addition, we must add a macro to our class, the Q_OBJECT macro, which is part of the Qt framework. It enables Qt's meta-object features, such as the slots (a sort of callback), dynamic properties, and introspection. Any class that defines custom signals or slots must include this macro:

```cpp
class CmdVel : public rqt_gui_cpp::Plugin {
Q_OBJECT
public:
CmdVel();
```

- The initPlugin function is called when the plugin is initialized. This function must be implemented as part of the rqt framework, such as the shutdown function. Then, we add a series of functions that will be called directly when the user interface is used. For example, the onTextChanged function is called when a new topic name is written into the text box. Some of these functions accept an input value, such as the onEnableButton one:

```cpp
virtual void initPlugin(qt_gui_cpp::PluginContext& context);
        virtual void shutdownPlugin();
void onTextChanged();
void onEnableButton(int state);

...
```

- In the class variable list, we must add an object representing the widget class, generated from the user interface file (.ui), and a pointer to a QWidget, the base class for all GUI objects in Qt that represent the whole plugin window:

```cpp
protected:
        Ui::CmdVelWidget ui_;
        QWidget* widget_;
```

- In addition, we must include the ROS 2 variables, the publisher of the twist command, the twist command, and the ROS 2 node:

```cpp
rclcpp::Node::SharedPtr ros2_node;
rclcpp::Publisher<geometry_msgs::msg::Twist>::SharedPtr cmd_vel_
publisher_;
geometry_msgs::msg::Twist cmd_vel_msg_;
```

Now that the plugin class is prepared, we can implement its behavior in the C++ file, cmd_vel.cpp:

1. In the C++ file, we must include everything that is needed for ROS 2 and Qt to work properly. The rclcpp and the pluginlib headers mainly contain all the functions needed by this code:

    ```
    #include "cmd_vel/cmd_vel.h"
    #include <pluginlib/class_list_macros.hpp>
    #include <rclcpp/rclcpp.hpp>
    #include <sstream>
    ```

2. The class is defined in the same plugin of the header file and extends the Plugin class. The Qt framework allows the initialization of the current working object with a reference name, CmdVel:

    ```
    namespace cmd_vel {
        CmdVel::CmdVel() : rqt_gui_cpp::Plugin(),
            widget_(0),
            enable_streaming_(false) {
            setObjectName("CmdVel");
        }
    ```

3. In the initialization function, we initialize the widget that is the connection point between this code and the elements included in the user interface:

    ```
    void CmdVel::initPlugin(qt_gui_cpp::PluginContext& context) {
    widget_ = new QWidget();
    ui_.setupUi(widget_);
    if (context.serialNumber() > 1)
    widget_->setWindowTitle(widget_->windowTitle() + " (" +
    QString::number(context.serialNumber()) + ")");
    context.addWidget(widget_);
    ```

4. After the initialization of the ROS 2 node that allows us to publish the twist command data, we connect the elements of the user interface with the code. This is a similar approach to callbacks. When an element of the UI is touched correctly, the defined function is called:

    ```
    ros2_node_ = rclcpp::Node::make_shared("custom_cmd_vel_plugin");
    ```

5. For example, we want to change the behavior of the plugin when a new text is written in the topicName box. Of course, the callback of this element must be called only after that enter is pressed on the same box since this means that the user completed writing the desired topic name. For this reason, the onTextChanged function is called when the user presses *Enter* (returnPressed) on the text box:

```
connect(ui_.topicName, &QLineEdit::returnPressed, this,
&CmdVel::onTextChanged);
connect(ui_.desVel, &QLineEdit::returnPressed, this,
&CmdVel::onVelChanged);
```

6. Similarly, the callback of the enable element is called when its state changes. The other callbacks are called when the relative button is clicked:

```
connect(ui_.enableButton, &QCheckBox::stateChanged,
this, &CmdVel::onEnableButton);
connect(ui_.stopButton, &QPushButton::clicked, this,
&CmdVel::onStopButton);
```

7. In the callback of the velocity text box, we retrieve the inserted value, converting it into a double value when this is possible. If the conversion is not possible, the desired velocity quantity remains the same:

```
void CmdVel::onVelChanged() {
    double str2double;
    std::istringstream iss( ui_.desVel->text().toStdString() );
    iss >> str2double;
    if (!(iss.fail() || !iss.eof()) )
        des_vel_ = str2double;
}
```

8. Every time the topic name changes, the publisher of the twist velocity is updated:

```
void CmdVel::onTextChanged() {
    std::string topicNameValue = ui_.topicName->text().
toStdString();
    if( topicNameValue != "" )
        cmd_vel_publisher_ = ros2_node_->create_
publisher<geometry_msgs::msg::Twist>(topicNameValue, 10);
    }
    void CmdVel::onEnableButton(int state) {
```

```
            if( state == Qt::Checked ) {
                enable_streaming_ = true;
            }
            else {
                enable_streaming_ = false;
            }
        }
```

9. Some robot models maintain the command of the last received velocity command, even if it is not published anymore. For this reason, our interface considers a **STOP** button that resets the streaming velocity:

```
        void CmdVel::onStopButton() {
            cmd_vel_msg_ = geometry_msgs::msg::Twist();
            cmd_vel_publisher_->publish( cmd_vel_msg_ );
```

10. Each of the other callbacks changes the current velocity message according to the clicked button.

```
        void CmdVel::onForwardButton() {
            cmd_vel_msg_ = geometry_msgs::msg::Twist();
            cmd_vel_msg_.linear.x = des_vel_;
            if( enable_streaming_ && cmd_vel_publisher_ ) cmd_vel_
    publisher_->publish( cmd_vel_msg_ );
```

11. At the end of the code, we must register the plugin in the `pluginlib` system with the `PLUGINLIB_EXPORT_CLASS` macro. This allows your `CmdVel` class to be dynamically loaded as a plugin by the ROS 2 framework:

```
    PLUGINLIB_EXPORT_CLASS(cmd_vel::CmdVel, rqt_gui_cpp::Plugin)
```

The source code is now complete. We can compile it and configure it.

Adding compilation and configuration files

Each plugin needs an XML configuration file, defining the object that will be loaded when the plugin is requested. Let's discuss the configuration file of the CmdVel plugin. Here, the <library> tag specifies the shared library, cmd_vel. The <class> tag registers the plugin cmd_vel::CmdVel (derived from rqt_gui_cpp::Plugin) with a unique name, cmd_vel/CmdVel. <description> provides a brief summary, while the <qtgui> section customizes the plugin's appearance in the GUI:

```
<library path="cmd_vel">
  <class name="cmd_vel/CmdVel" type="cmd_vel::CmdVel" base_class_
type="rqt_gui_cpp::Plugin">
    <description>
      A GUI plugin to control velocity commands.
    </description>
    <qtgui>
      <group>
        <label>Control</label>
        <icon type="theme">folder</icon>
        <statustip>Plugin</statustip>
      </group>
<label>Vel control</label>
    </qtgui></class></library>
```

After compiling and sourcing the workspace, we can access this plugin in the rqt window by following these steps:

1. Click on **Plugins** in the menu.
2. Navigate to **Control**.
3. Select **Vel Control**.

Finally, we must write the CMakeLists.txt file. The salient part of the file is reported in the following code. It defines a shared library for the cmd_vel plugin. It specifies the source (cmd_vel.cpp), headers (cmd_vel.h), and a Qt UI file (cmd_vel_ui.ui). Qt tools (qt5_wrap_cpp and qt5_wrap_ui) process MOC and UI files.

The library includes directories (such as ${CMAKE_BINARY_DIR}) and links to ROS 2 libraries (rclcpp, qt_gui_cpp, rqt_gui_cpp, and message packages) and Qt5::Widgets. It installs the library, headers, and plugin.xml, and exports the plugin description for pluginlib:

```
add_library(${PROJECT_NAME} SHARED ${cmd_vel_SRCS} ${cmd_vel_MOCS} ${cmd_
vel_UIS_H })
target_include_directories(${PROJECT_NAME} PUBLIC
  "$<BUILD_INTERFACE:${CMAKE_CURRENT_SOURCE_DIR}/include>"
  "$<INSTALL_INTERFACE:include/${PROJECT_NAME}>")
target_link_libraries(${PROJECT_NAME} PUBLIC ${rclcpp_TARGETS} ${qt_gui_
cpp_TARGETS} ${rqt_gui_cpp_TARGETS} ${sensor_msgs_TARGETS} ${geometry_
msgs_TARGETS} Qt5::Widgets)
install( TARGETS ${PROJECT_NAME} EXPORT ${PROJECT_NAME ARCHIVE DESTINATION
lib/${PROJECT_NAME} LIBRARY DESTINATION lib/${PROJECT_NAME} RUNTIME
DESTINATION bin/${PROJECT_NAME})
install(DIRECTORY include/ DESTINATION include ${PROJECT_NAME})
install(FILES plugin.xml
  DESTINATION share/${PROJECT_NAME}
)
```

The plugin.xml file is referenced in the CMakeLists.txt file to correctly reference the loading procedure:

```
pluginlib_export_plugin_description_file(rqt_gui "plugin.xml")
Finally, to convert the .ui file into the header one, we use the following
line:
qt5_wrap_ui(cmd_vel_UIS_H ${cmd_vel_UIS})
To execute the rqt plugin, we must compile the workspace and start the rqt
program:
```

```
colcon build --symlink-install
rqt
```

Now, we can select the plugin and monitor the velocity commands published to the chosen topic. We can test this plugin on a simulated robot. This time, we'll use a simulation plugin that integrates directly with the Gazebo simulator, as discussed in the next section.

Developing a Gazebo plugin

Gazebo plugins are components that extend the functionality of the Gazebo simulator. They allow users to add custom behavior to the simulation, such as controlling sensors, actuators, or environments, and interfacing with other software such as ROS 2. Gazebo plugins can be categorized into two main types: **world plugins**, which modify the simulation environment, allowing you to control how the world behaves or is initialized (e.g., setting up the environment and adding objects), and **model plugins**, which are attached to specific models (e.g., robots or sensors) to control their behavior, such as simulating a robot's motion, controlling actuators, or interfacing with sensors. The plugins can be loaded into Gazebo at runtime via SDF or URDF files. Let's develop a new model plugin that directly controls a differential drive robot by sending control commands on the Gazebo topic for twist velocity. The plugin receives the control data from an external source (such as the plugin developed in the previous section). So, in principle, this plugin emulates the behavior of the Gazebo bridge, but once it receives the desired velocity, it saturates them with a maximum value.

Writing the source code

The Gazebo plugin must be included in a ROS 2 package, so let's start creating it:

```
ros2 pkg create cmd_vel_plugin --dependencies rclcpp std_msgs  geometry_
msg gz-cmake3
```

The dependency from the gz-cmake3 library allows us to link the ROS 2 function with the Gazebo ones. We can now fill in the source code of the Gazebo plugin, pub_cmd_vel.cpp:

1. First, ROS 2 and Gazebo header files are needed. Apart from the ROS ones, the gz header allows the registration and initialization of the new plugin:

   ```
   #include "rclcpp/rclcpp.hpp"
   #include <geometry_msgs/msg/twist.hpp>
   #include <gz/common/Console.hh>
   #include <gz/messages/details/twist.pb.h>
   #include <gz/plugin/Register.hh>
   #include <gz/sim/System.hh>
   #include <gz/transport/Node.hh>

   #include <sdf/sdf.hh>
   ```

2. We can define the plugin class. The `PubCmdVel` class inherits from `gz::sim::System`, the base for all Gazebo plugins, and two specific interfaces: `ISystemConfigure` and `ISystemPostUpdate`. `ISystemConfigure` allows the plugin to handle setup tasks during initialization, such as configuring ROS nodes and subscribers. `ISystemPostUpdate` enables the plugin to execute actions after each simulation update, such as processing data or publishing updates to Gazebo. These interfaces integrate the plugin into Gazebo's lifecycle for configuration and runtime updates:

    ```
    namespace cmd_vel_plugin {
        class PubCmdVel:
        public gz::sim::System,
        public gz::sim::ISystemConfigure,
        public gz::sim::ISystemPostUpdate {
    ```

3. Some system functions that are called automatically with the Gazebo lifecycle can be implemented. The `PostUpdate` function is called directly after an execution cycle of the simulation. In contrast, the `Configure` function is called when the plugin is loaded:

    ```
            public: void PostUpdate(const gz::sim::UpdateInfo &_info,
    const gz::sim::EntityComponentManager &_ecm) override;
    public: void Configure(const gz::sim::Entity &_id,
    const std::shared_ptr<const sdf::Element> &_sdf,
    gz::sim::EntityComponentManager &_ecm, gz::sim::EventManager &_
    eventMgr) final;
    ```

4. Finally, the callback of the topic for the twist velocity, published on the ROS 2 network, is defined:

    ```
    public: void cmd_vel_cb( const geometry_msgs::msg::Twist );
    ```

5. As for class variables, a reference to the ROS 2 node connecting the simulation to the ROS 2 network is defined, along with the ROS 2 subscriber and the Gazebo publisher:

    ```
    private: rclcpp::Node::SharedPtr ros_node_;
    private:
            rclcpp::Subscription<geometry_msgs::msg::Twist>::SharedPtr
    ros_subscriber_;
      gz::transport::Node::Publisher gz_publisher_;
            gz::transport::Node gz_node_;
            gz::msgs::Twist cmd_vel_msg_;
    ```

6. The plugin is registered using the GZ_ADD_PLUGIN function. This line registers the PubCmdVel class as a Gazebo plugin using GZ_ADD_PLUGIN. It specifies that PubCmdVel implements the gz::sim::System base class and the ISystemConfigure and ISystemPostUpdate interfaces. This registration allows Gazebo to recognize and load the plugin, enabling it to participate in the simulation lifecycle for configuration and post-update tasks:

```
GZ_ADD_PLUGIN (
    cmd_vel_plugin::PubCmdVel,
    gz::sim::System,
    cmd_vel_plugin::PubCmdVel::ISystemConfigure,
    cmd_vel_plugin::PubCmdVel::ISystemPostUpdate)
```

7. In the twist message callback, we just saturate the input velocity to a fixed value, 0.2 for linear and 0.5 for angular velocities:

```
void PubCmdVel::cmd_vel_cb( const geometry_msgs::msg::Twist t) {

    _double vx = t.linear.x;
    if( vx > 0.2) vx = 0.2;
    else if (vx < -0.2) vx = -0.2;
    cmd_vel_msg_.mutable_linear()->set_x (vx);
    double vz = t.linear.z;
    if( vz > 0.2) vz = 0.2;
    else if (vz < -0.2) vz = -0.2;
    cmd_vel_msg_.mutable_linear()->set_z (vz);
    double vrot_z = t.angular.z;
    if( vrot_z > 0.5 ) vrot_z = 0.5;
    else if (vrot_z < -0.5) vrot_z = 0.5;
    cmd_vel_msg_.mutable_angular()->setz(vrot_z);
```

8. In the Configure function, the ROS 2 node must be initialized along with the subscriber to the ROS 2 twist message:

```
void PubCmdVel::Configure(const gz::sim::Entity &_
entity, const std::shared_ptr<const sdf::Element> &_sdf,
gz::sim::EntityComponentManager &, gz::sim::EventManager &){
    rclcpp::init(0, nullptr);
    ros_node_ = rclcpp::Node::make_shared("cmd_vel_plugin");
    ros_subscriber_ = ros_node_->create_subscription<geometry_
```

```
msgs::msg::Twist>("/cmd_vel_from_ros", 10,
std::bind(&PubCmdVel::cmd_vel_cb, this, std::placeholders::_1));
```

9. The publisher of the Gazebo `cmd_vel` topic, used from the robot to actuate the differential base, is initialized:

```
gz_publisher_ = gz_node_.Advertise<gz::msgs::Twist>("/cmd_vel");
```

10. In the `PostUpdate` function, we must only apply the velocity commands received as input. We also request to spin the node to enable the input via the callbacks. Once a velocity message is sent, the robot will continue moving, even if no new messages are published. To stop the robot, a velocity message with a value of 0 must be published on the topic:

```
void PubCmdVel::PostUpdate(const gz::sim::UpdateInfo &_info, const
gz::sim::EntityComponentManager &/*_ecm*/) {
    rclcpp::spin_some( ros_node_ );
    gz_publisher_.Publish(cmd_vel_msg_);
}
```

The source code is now complete and can be used. To use it, we must set up the compilation file and add the plugin to a simulation model, as discussed in the next section.

Compiling and executing the Gazebo plugin

The `CMakeLists.txt` of the package must be modified to add compilation options for the plugin. The following lines are used to link the Gazebo functions with the node:

```
gz_find_package(gz-plugin2 REQUIRED COMPONENTS register)
set(GZ_PLUGIN_VER ${gz-plugin2_VERSION_MAJOR})
gz_find_package(gz-sim8 REQUIRED)
set(GZ_SIM_VER ${gz-sim8_VERSION_MAJOR})
```

The shared library is generated starting from the C++ file:

```
add_library(CmdVelPlugin SHARED src/pub_cmd_vel.cpp)
```

Additional libraries are used from the `CmdVelPlugin` one. Finally, ROS 2 dependencies are linked to it:

```
target_link_libraries(CmdVelPlugin
  gz-plugin${GZ_PLUGIN_VER}::gz-plugin${GZ_PLUGIN_VER}
  gz-sim${GZ_SIM_VER}::gz-sim${GZ_SIM_VER}
)
```

```
ament_target_dependencies(CmdVelPlugin rclcpp std_msgs geometry_msgs)
install(DIRECTORY launch urdf DESTINATION share/${PROJECT_NAME})
```

After compiling the plugin, by compiling the workspace, we need to incorporate it into SDF or a .xacro file. In the online version of the package, in the book code repository, a differential drive robot model that already uses this plugin is provided. In particular, `diff_drive.urdf.xacro` contains the following line:

```
<plugin filename="CmdVelPlugin" name="cmd_vel_plugin::PubCmdVel"> </
plugin>
```

Here, we have the following elements:

- `filename="CmdVelPlugin"`: Specifies the name of the shared library file (e.g., `libCmdVelPlugin.so`) that contains the plugin code
- `name="cmd_vel_plugin::PubCmdVel"`: Specifies the fully qualified C++ class name (`cmd_vel_plugin::PubCmdVel`) that implements the plugin

This tells Gazebo to load the `CmdVelPlugin` library and initialize the `PubCmdVel` class as part of the simulation. Now, you can test the plugin by starting the simulation using the following command:

```
ros2 launch cmd_vel_plugin cmd_vel_plugin.launch.py
```

At this point, you can publish desired velocity commands on the topic: `/cmd_vel_from_ros`. As promised above, this is a good chance to use the `rqt` plugin developed in the previous example.

At this point, it is quite clear how plugins can be useful to extend the functionality of software. Another software used in robotics is `RViz2`. In the next section, we will discuss our last example and learn how to create plugins for `RViz2`.

Developing plugins for RViz2

An `RViz2` plugin is a modular extension for `RViz2`, the visualization tool in ROS 2, designed to display and interact with robotic data. Plugins allow users to add custom functionality, such as new display types for specific message formats, custom visualization panels, or tools for user interaction. They are implemented as shared libraries using the `pluginlib` framework, enabling dynamic loading without modifying `RViz2`'s core. By creating `RViz2` plugins, developers can tailor the visualization experience to specific applications, enhancing debugging, monitoring, and control in robotic systems. In this example, we will create a plugin to display a circumference with a given center coordinates and a radius. The final shape of the circumference shown on `RViz2` is displayed in *Figure 16.3*.

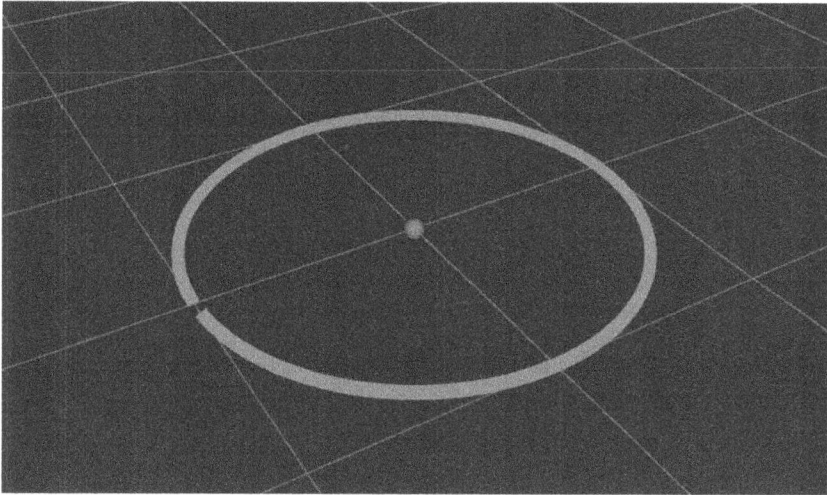

Figure 16.3: Circumference published on RViz2 using a custom plugin

Writing the source code

To develop the plugin, let's start by creating the ROS 2 packages containing the plugin files. First, we need a custom message to receive the data published on RViz2. For simplicity, we avoid discussing how the message is created. However, the type of the message is `circle_msgs::Circle` and the fields of the message are the following:

```
std_msgs/Header header
float32 x
float32 y
float32 radius
```

The package implementing such a message can be found in the GitHub repository of the book. Let's now create the package to implement the plugin:

```
ros2 pkg create circle_display_plugin --dependencies rclcpp pluginlib
rviz_common rviz_rendering circle_msgs
```

Also, in this case, we will exploit the Qt framework to embed the plugin into the RViz2 window. However, differently from the rqt plugin, we will use the elements already available in RViz2 to set up the visualization properties.

Let's start by discussing the header file of the plugin, `circle_display.hpp`:

1. First, the headers to access `RViz2` functionalities must be included. Depending on the shape to visualize, different headers must be included. In this example, we will use the Sphere and the Billboard shapes. For this reason, we will include the relative header files:

    ```
    #include <OgreVector3.h>
    #include <circle_msgs/msg/circle.hpp>
    #include
    #include <rviz_common/display_context.hpp>
    #include <rviz_common/frame_manager_iface.hpp>
    #include <rviz_common/interaction/selection_manager.hpp>
    #include <rviz_common/logging.hpp>
    #include <rviz_common/message_filter_display.hpp>
    #include <rviz_common/properties/parse_color.hpp>
    #include <rviz_rendering/objects/billboard_line.hpp>
    #include <rviz_rendering/objects/grid.hpp>
    #include <rviz_rendering/objects/shape.hpp>
    ```

2. Each object to visualize can be linked with some properties that are set from the `RViz2` interface. For example, from the interface, we can modify the marker color and its width. For this reason, we need to receive a color and width property:

    ```
    #include <rviz_common/properties/property.hpp>
    #include <rviz_common/properties/float_property.hpp>
    #include <rviz_common/properties/color_property.hpp>
    ```

3. In this plugin, the code is encapsulated within a namespace. The plugin's class is inherited from `rviz_common::MessageFilterDisplay` to visualize `circle_msgs::msg::Circle` messages in `RViz2`. It uses Qt functionality via Q_OBJECT and defines two private slots, `updateStyle` and `updateStyleLine`. These slots are functions triggered by inputs from the `RViz2` interface, allowing the display's appearance to be updated dynamically:

    ```
    namespace rviz_circle_plugin {
    class CircleDisplay : public rviz_
    common::MessageFilterDisplay<circle_msgs::msg::Circle{
      Q_OBJECT
      private Q_SLOTS:
      void updateStylePoint();
      void updateStyleLine();
    ```

4. As for the functions, we must provide an implementation for the initialization function. In addition, the processMessage function is called every time a new message is received on the visualization topic:

```
protected:
  void onInitialize() override;
  void processMessage(const circle_msgs::msg::Circle::ConstSharedPtr
msg) override;
    std::unique_ptr<rviz_rendering::Shape> point_shape_;

    std::unique_ptr<rviz_rendering::BillboardLine> circle_line_;
```

5. The properties to customize the visualization are declared:

```
    std::unique_ptr<rviz_common::properties::ColorProperty> color_
property_;
    std::unique_ptr<rviz_common::properties::ColorProperty> line_
color_property_;
    std::unique_ptr<rviz_common::properties::FloatProperty> line_
width_property_;
    std::unique_ptr<rviz_common::properties::FloatProperty> circle_
width_property_;
```

The header file is now complete. We must implement the behavior of the plugin in the source file, circle_display.cpp:

1. Include the header file and define the namespace:

```
#include <circle_display_plugin/circle_display.hpp>
namespace rviz_circle_plugin {
  using rviz_common::properties::StatusProperty;
```

2. In the initialization method, the plugin is initialized with its base class and the required visual elements are created. A sphere (Shape) is used to represent the center point, and a BillboardLine is created to depict the circle's circumference. It also initializes RViz2 properties, such as color and line width, with corresponding update methods (updateStyle and updateStyleLine). These properties allow the dynamic adjustment of the circle's appearance through the RViz2 interface:

```
    void CircleDisplay::onInitialize() {
      MFDClass::onInitialize();
```

```cpp
    point_shape_ = std::make_unique<rviz_rendering::Shape>(rviz_
rendering::Shape::Type::Sphere, scene_manager_, scene_node_);
    circle_line_ = std::make_unique<rviz_
rendering::BillboardLine>(scene_manager_, scene_node_);
      line_color_property_ = std::make_unique<rviz_
common::properties::ColorProperty>(
      "Circle Color", QColor(255, 0, 0), "Color to draw the
circle.", this, SLOT(updateStyleLine()));
    line_width_property_ = std::make_unique<rviz_
common::properties::FloatProperty>(
      "Line Width", 0.1, "Width of the circle line.", this,
SLOT(updateStyleLine()));
    color_property_ = std::make_unique<rviz_
common::properties::ColorProperty>(
        "Point Color", QColor(255, 0, 0), "Color to draw the
point.", this, SLOT(updateStyle()));
    circle_width_property_ = std::make_unique<rviz_
common::properties::FloatProperty>(
        "Center Width", 0.1, "Width to center point.", this,
SLOT(updateStyle()));
    updateStyle();
    updateStyleLine();
```

3. The processMessage method processes incoming circle_msgs::msg::Circle messages. It logs the message, validates the radius, and applies transformations to position the visual elements in the correct 3D space. The center point is set using the message's coordinates, and a series of points approximating the circle's circumference is generated based on its radius and number of segments, adding them to the BillboardLine. But how is this code linked to the input topic? When using MessageFilterDisplay, RViz2 provides a GUI where users can set the topic from which the plugin will subscribe. This is configured dynamically without requiring hardcoding:

```cpp
void CircleDisplay::processMessage(const circle_
msgs::msg::Circle::ConstSharedPtr msg) {
  if( msg->radius <= 0.0 ) return;
  Ogre::Vector3 position;
  Ogre::Quaternion orientation;
  if (!context_->getFrameManager()->getTransform(msg->header,
position, orientation)) {
```

```
      RVIZ_COMMON_LOG_DEBUG_STREAM("Error transforming from frame '"
<< msg->header.frame_id <<
          "' to frame '" << qPrintable(fixed_frame_) << "'");
  }
  scene_node_->setPosition(position);
  scene_node_->setOrientation(orientation);
  Ogre::Vector3 point_pos;
  point_pos.x = msg->x;
  point_pos.y = msg->y;
  point_shape_->setPosition(point_pos);

  // Generate points for the circle
  const size_t num_segments = 100;  // Number of segments to
approximate the circle
  const float radius = msg->radius;
  for (size_t i = 0; i <= num_segments; ++i) {
    float angle = static_cast<float>(i) * Ogre::Math::TWO_PI /
static_cast<float>(num_segments);
    float x = msg->x + radius * std::cos(angle);
    float y = msg->y + radius * std::sin(angle);

    circle_line_->addPoint(Ogre::Vector3(x, y, 0.0f));
  }
}
```

4. The updateStyle method adjusts the color and size of the center point using the configured properties. updateStyleLine modifies the circle's line color and width dynamically.
   These methods are triggered via Qt signals whenever the corresponding RViz2 properties
   are updated, ensuring the visual elements reflect the user's changes in real time:

```
void CircleDisplay::updateStylePoint(){
  Ogre::ColourValue color = rviz_common::properties::qtToOgre(color_
property_->getColor());
  If( point_shape_) {
      point_shape_->setColor(color);
      float size = circle_width_property_->getFloat();
      point_shape_->setScale(Ogre::Vector3(size, size, size));
}
void CircleDisplay::updateStyleLine(){
```

```
    if (circle_line_) {
      Ogre::ColourValue color = rviz_
  common::properties::qtToOgre(line_color_property_->getColor());
      circle_line_->setColor( color.r, color.g, color.b, 1 );
      float line_width = line_width_property_->getFloat();
      circle_line_->setLineWidth(line_width);
```

5. The plugin is registered using `PLUGINLIB_EXPORT_CLASS`, enabling RViz2 to dynamically load and integrate it into the visualization environment. This registration makes `CircleDisplay` available as a custom display type in RViz2:

```
#include <pluginlib/class_list_macros.hpp>
PLUGINLIB_EXPORT_CLASS(rviz_circle_plugin::CircleDisplay, rviz_
common::Display)
```

As usual, the `.xml` file defining the plugin must be created. Here, the namespace and the plugin class must be correctly specified:

```
<library path="circle_display">
  <class type="rviz_circle_plugin::CircleDisplay" base_class_type="rviz_
common::Display">
    <description></description>
  </class>
</library>
```

Adding and configuring the RViz2 plugin

We are now ready to add the plugin. First, compile and source the workspace:

```
colcon build --symlink-install
source install/setup.bash
```

Now, start RViz2:

```
rviz2
```

If the plugin has been correctly compiled, by clicking the **Add** button of the RViz2 interface, we can select the new plugin. As you can see from *Figure 16.4*, it is named as the name of the package implementing the plugin plus the name of the class.

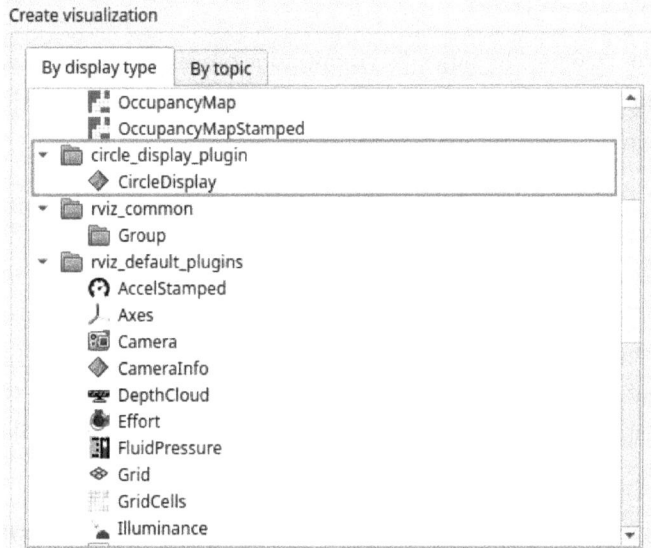

Figure 16.4: Add plugin panel in RViz2 where the custom plugin can be selected

After adding the plugin, it appears in the display panel and can be correctly configured. An example of the use of the plugin can be seen in *Figure 16.5*, where the left part shows the configuration of the plugin, while the right shows rqt publishing the desired circle point. Finally, the center shows the result on RViz2.

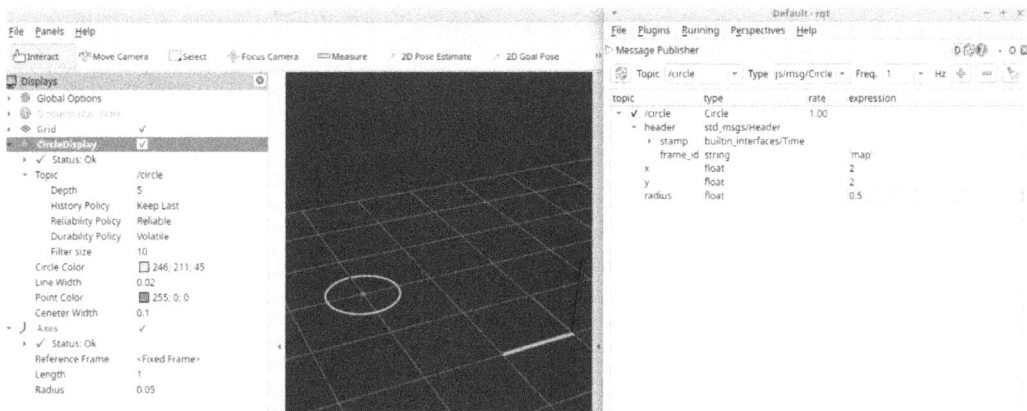

Figure 16.5: CircleDisplay plugin with center coordinates 2, 2, and a 0.5 radius

As you can see from *Figure 16.5*, the topic on which the circle is published has been inserted, and it is /circle. On this topic, the circle_msgs::Circle is published, where the coordinates are x: 2 and y: 2. The radius instead is 0.5. At the same time, it is possible to change the width and the color of the circle and its center.

Implementing custom plugins simplifies the visualization process of robot data without depending on specific ROS 2 node implementations. Additionally, one can customize other aspects of RViz, such as interactive tools for manipulating different objects.

Summary

Plugins are essential for extending the capabilities of ROS 2 and other software. ROS 2 supports various types of plugins, including controller plugins, visualization plugins, and rqt plugins. This chapter focused on visualization and rqt plugins, showcasing how to create a custom user interface for a robot and visualize ROS 2 data. Additionally, an example of a Gazebo plugin was presented, demonstrating how to use Gazebo's features directly in C++ while integrating with the ROS 2 network.

Writing ROS 2 plugins is essential for extending the functionality of robotics systems, as it allows developers to customize and integrate hardware and software components efficiently. Learning to use ROS 2 ensures proficiency in a widely adopted framework, fostering modular development, scalability, and compatibility with cutting-edge robotics tools and technologies. In this chapter, we learned the basic way to develop and integrate plugins in our ROS 2 applications.

This chapter marks the conclusion of the journey through *Mastering ROS 2*. Throughout this book, we have explored and tested key topics in modern robotics, using realistic simulation environments to program mobile, aerial, and industrial robots.

We hope this book serves as a valuable reference for ROS 2 developers, offering guidance on specific topics for everyday projects. Now it's your turn: apply what you've learned by experimenting with the programs and applications from these pages on your robot models, or even on your unique hardware setups.

The authors extend their heartfelt gratitude to you for reading and embracing this work.

Join our community on Discord

Join our community's Discord space for discussions with the authors and other readers: `https://packt.link/embeddedsystems`

‹packt›

packtpub.com

Subscribe to our online digital library for full access to over 7,000 books and videos, as well as industry leading tools to help you plan your personal development and advance your career. For more information, please visit our website.

Why subscribe?

- Spend less time learning and more time coding with practical eBooks and Videos from over 4,000 industry professionals
- Improve your learning with Skill Plans built especially for you
- Get a free eBook or video every month
- Fully searchable for easy access to vital information
- Copy and paste, print, and bookmark content

At www.packtpub.com, you can also read a collection of free technical articles, sign up for a range of free newsletters, and receive exclusive discounts and offers on Packt books and eBooks.

Other Books You May Enjoy

If you enjoyed this book, you may be interested in these other books by Packt:

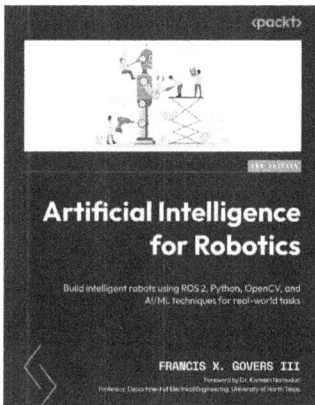

Artificial Intelligence for Robotics - Second Edition

Francis X. Govers III

ISBN: 978-1-80512-959-2

- Get started with robotics and AI essentials
- Understand path planning, decision trees, and search algorithms to enhance your robot
- Explore object recognition using neural networks and supervised learning techniques
- Employ genetic algorithms to enable your robot arm to manipulate objects
- Teach your robot to listen using Natural Language Processing through an expert system
- Program your robot in how to avoid obstacles and retrieve objects with machine learning and computer vision
- Apply simulation techniques to give your robot an artificial personality

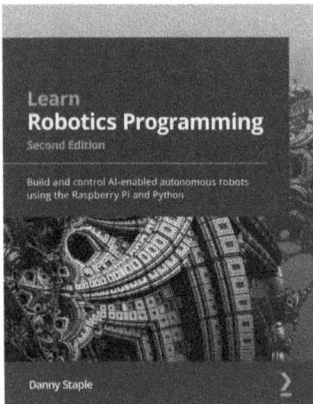

Learn Robotics Programming - Second Edition

Danny Staple

ISBN: 978-1-83921-880-4

- Leverage the features of the Raspberry Pi OS
- Discover how to configure a Raspberry Pi to build an AI-enabled robot
- Interface motors and sensors with a Raspberry Pi
- Code your robot to develop engaging and intelligent robot behavior
- Explore AI behavior such as speech recognition and visual processing
- Find out how you can control AI robots with a mobile phone over Wi-Fi
- Understand how to choose the right parts and assemble your robot

Packt is searching for authors like you

If you're interested in becoming an author for Packt, please visit authors.packt.com and apply today. We have worked with thousands of developers and tech professionals, just like you, to help them share their insight with the global tech community. You can make a general application, apply for a specific hot topic that we are recruiting an author for, or submit your own idea.

Share your thoughts

Now you've finished *Mastering ROS 2 for Robotics Programming, Fourth Edition*, we'd love to hear your thoughts! Scan the QR code below to go straight to the Amazon review page for this book and share your feedback or leave a review on the site that you purchased it from.

https://packt.link/r/1836209010

Your review is important to us and the tech community and will help us make sure we're delivering excellent quality content.

Index

Download a free PDF copy of this book

Thanks for purchasing this book!

Do you like to read on the go but are unable to carry your print books everywhere?

Is your eBook purchase not compatible with the device of your choice?

Don't worry, now with every Packt book you get a DRM-free PDF version of that book at no cost.

Read anywhere, any place, on any device. Search, copy, and paste code from your favorite technical books directly into your application.

The perks don't stop there, you can get exclusive access to discounts, newsletters, and great free content in your inbox daily.

Follow these simple steps to get the benefits:

1. Scan the QR code or visit the link below:

https://packt.link/free-ebook/9781836209010

2. Submit your proof of purchase.
3. That's it! We'll send your free PDF and other benefits to your email directly.